The Declaration of Rights, 1689

The Declaration of Rights, 1689

Lois G. Schwoerer

THE JOHNS HOPKINS UNIVERSITY PRESS

Baltimore and London

This book has been brought to publication
with the generous assistance of the
National Endowment for the Humanities.

The Johns Hopkins University Press, Baltimore, Maryland 21218
The Johns Hopkins Press Ltd., London

Library of Congress Cataloging in Publication Data

Schwoerer, Lois G.
The Declaration of Rights, 1689.

Bibliography: pp. 369–79
Includes index.
1. Great Britain — Politics and government — Revolution
of 1688. 2. Great Britain. Parliament. Declaration of
Rights. 3. Great Britain. Bill of Rights. I. Title.
DA452.S3   342.41'085   81–2942
ISBN 0-8018-2430-3   344.10285   AACR2

Frontispiece

Presentation ceremony. On Ash Wednesday, February 13, 1689, in a
unique ceremony in the Banqueting Hall, the Lords and Commons
presented their claims of rights and then offered the crown of England to
Prince William and Princess Mary of Orange. This print is one of three
undated prints of the presentation ceremony, none of which is
contemporary. (Courtesy of the Print Room, British Museum.)

To John

Contents

PART IV

The Epitome of the Glorious Revolution   265

Appendixes

List of Illustrations

FIGURES

PORTRAITS

Preface

❖

R enewed scholarly and popular interest in the Revolution of 1688–89
and recently recovered source materials[1] invite systematic investigation of documents of the significance of the Declaration of Rights
and the subsequent Bill of Rights. Such a study is the purpose of this book. I
first became interested in the subject several years ago in the course of working on the development of the anti–standing army attitude, an attitude
reflected in article 6 of the declaration, which prohibits the king from maintaining a standing army in time of peace without the consent of Parliament.
In *"No Standing Armies!"* I announced my intentions of undertaking such a
project.[2] It was evident that both the text of the Declaration of Rights and the
political and intellectual context within which it was drafted required examination. Generally speaking, modern historians have focused their attention
on the basic causes of the revolution or on the results and have slighted the
months when the revolutionary crisis and settlement were actually taking
place.

The most serious problem confronting the historian who attempts to
analyze the text of the Declaration of Rights, its political and intellectual context, and the passage of the Bill of Rights — and the probable reason for
neglect of these matters — is the uneven quantity and quality of the surviving
evidence. The papers from these months of the major proponents are virtually absent, some of them possibly having gone to fuel the bonfires that lit up
the London nights that cold winter of 1688–89 to testify approval of a political
step.[3] The accounts of some of the debates in the Convention are thin.[4] The
nature of the readily available evidence, then, makes it necessary to use non-
traditional sources and methods to supplement traditional ones. One
approach that compensated for the uneven quality of written evidence about
political attitudes in 1689 was to construct a group profile (based on questions
normally asked by sociologists) of the members of the two committees in the
House of Commons and the committee in the House of Lords who were
principally responsible for drafting and piloting the Declaration of Rights
through the Convention. That profile yielded valuable information about the
political, religious, and social antecedents and connections of the men which
had only been guessed at before. Another approach was to proceed histori-

cally, focusing on the intention of the authors of the document and the unfolding process of shaping it into final form. I rigorously avoided using noncontemporary evidence to explain the motivation and ideas of the participants: I think that failure to do this is one reason why the Declaration of Rights and the Revolution of 1688–89 have not been accurately understood. A third approach was to examine the text — the language and form — of the Declaration of Rights, and study the legal and constitutional background of each of the thirteen claimed rights. Fourth, I have drawn upon a wide range of sources, both manuscript and printed, some hitherto unknown, others little used, most conventional, some novel. For example, tracts and pamphlets appeared in greater quantity during the months of revolution than has been appreciated: over 300 original pieces or reprints of earlier pamphlets were published during that time. In addition, approximately ten newspapers, which historians have virtually ignored, started up in December 1688, flourished for several months, and disappeared with the resolution of the crisis. These materials illuminated the intellectual context, cast new light on what persons of diverse social and economic background were thinking, and testified to efforts made to shape public opinion. The major visual materials of a political nature — pictures, playing cards, and commemorative medals — served the same purpose. Fifth, the use of the anthropological principle that ceremonies, processions, bonfires, and merrymaking are legitimate parts of the historical record, properly regarded as cultural artifacts capable of being "read" just as the literary record is read, provided insights into the political ideas and intentions of the principals. Finally, inferential judgments and hypotheses, which, if employed with due caution and announcement, are as legitimate for the work of the historian as for that of the scientist, also compensated for the nature of the evidence.

This book has four parts. Part I, in four chapters, introduces the document, provides a group profile of the two rights committees in the House of Commons and individual biographical vignettes of the principals, and examines the political and constitutional origins of each of the claimed rights. Part II, also in four chapters, deals with the immediate political and intellectual context of the Declaration of Rights, in terms of the ideas, the use of the press, and the political maneuvering during the months just prior to the convening of the Convention. Part III, in seven chapters, traces the passage of the Declaration of Rights in both Houses of the Convention, identifying the political, theoretical, and personal considerations that explain it. The roles played by Tories, Whigs, the House of Lords, and Prince William are delineated. The presentation ceremony and the proclamation of the new monarchs on February 13 are analyzed. Part IV discusses in one chapter the process of transforming the Declaration of Rights into the Bill of Rights and surveys the changes made. A final chapter provides a summary and conclusion.

Acknowledgments

The expert assistance and friendly interest of librarians and scholars in the United States, Great Britain, and the United Netherlands have helped to make this book the most intellectually satisfying project I have undertaken. I owe a great debt to the Folger Shakespeare Library, Washington, D.C., which awarded me a Folger–National Endowment Senior Fellowship in 1978–79 and for many years has extended me every courtesy. I am especially grateful to Natia Krivatsky, reference librarian, and, for help in deciphering seventeenth-century orthography, to Letitia Yandell and Giles Dawson. When the Folger closed for renovations in 1979, the Library of Congress provided me a desk and other privileges. Larry Boyer, reference specialist, Law Library, was unusually helpful in locating legal materials. I spent several weeks in 1975 at the Henry E. Huntington Library, San Marino, California, a time memorable for the weather, the unique materials, and the assistance of Jean Preston and Mary Robertson. The staff of the Carl H. Pforsheimer Library, New York, New York, facilitated my brief visit there.

I take pleasure in thanking librarians in England who, over many years, have extended courteous assistance. I am indebted to the staffs of the Print Room and the Numismatic Room of the British Museum, the Manuscript Room and Reading Room of the British Library, the Bodleian Library, the Guildhall Library, and the Public Record Office. I thank especially M. A. Welch, keeper of the manuscripts at Nottingham University Library, and Maurice Bond, clerk of the records, and H. S. Cobb, deputy clerk, House of Lords Record Office. I am particularly grateful to Basil D. Henning, editor of the History of Parliament Trust project for the late seventeenth century, and his colleagues in London for allowing me to use their unpublished biographies. J. F. Ferris of the Trust's staff gave generously of his time and knowledge. Natalie Rothstein of the Albert and Victoria Museum answered questions about court dress, and Hugh Murray Bailey of the Historical Manuscript Commission instructed me in the intricacies of court ceremonials.

Her Majesty the Queen of the Netherlands kindly gave me permission to use the collection at the Koninklijk Huisarchief, where L. van Dorp, director, welcomed me warmly. S. F. M. Plantinga, of the staff of the Algemeen Rijksarchief, also placed me in his debt. For help in translating from the Dutch, I am grateful to Jop Spikerman, University of Leiden, Margaretha Arlman, and Marianne Meijer, University of Maryland. Professor Spikerman enriched the trip I made to the church from whose tower Princess Mary waved farewell to Prince William of Orange as he embarked upon the invasion of England.

I thank those libraries and record offices that answered queries and sent photocopies of material: the Bodleian Library, British Library, Cambridge University Library, Cumberland, Westmorland and Carlisle Record Office, Devon Record Office, Hertford Record Office, and Kansas University Library. I gratefully acknowledge the prompt response of G. van der Meer of the Koninklijk Kabinet, The Hague, to my queries about coins. The National Maritime Museum, the National Meteorological Office, and the New York Public Library, where portions of John Somers's papers are held, also supplied essential material.

Fellow historians and scholars have listened, advised, and encouraged. For particular points I thank David Berkowitz, Esmond S. de Beer, Gary S. DeKrey, Robert Frankle, Christopher Hill, David Hosford, Jay Hughes, James Jacob, Clyve Jones, G. H. Jones, David Lovejoy, Eric McDermott, Peter Opie, J. G. A. Pocock, H. H. Poole, Caroline Robbins, Clayton Roberts, William L. Sasche, Arthur Smith, Henry Snyder, Gerald Straka, and Corinne Weston. For commenting on one or more chapters at various stages, I am grateful to Esther S. Cope, Henry Horwitz, Howard Nenner, Robert Kenny, Joseph Martin, and Irving Wechseler. For allowing me to read in typescript portions of their forthcoming work, I thank Mark Goldie, G. H. Jones, Howard Nenner, and Corinne Weston and Janelle Greenberg. I owe a special debt to Isabel W. Kenrick, who has helped, over many years, to identify and locate materials in English repositories. Barbara Taft, as before, spent hours, without counting them, discussing the seventeenth century and my project and reading the entire manuscript with red pencil at the ready. If errors remain in this book, they are, of course, my own.

Some of the hypotheses in this study were tested in a seminar on the Glorious Revolution which I offered at the Folger Shakespeare Library in the spring of 1976. I thank that lively, wonderful group for an exhilarating intellectual experience, and John Andrews, director of the Folger Institute of Renaissance and Eighteenth-Century Studies, for the invitation to direct the seminar. Portions of this book have drawn upon materials from five of my articles that have appeared in print or are forthcoming. "The Revolution of 1688–89: Glorious, Respectable, and Merry?", read at the Folger Library in February 1976, was published in different form as "Propaganda in the Revolution of 1688/89" in the October 1977 issue of the *American Historical Review*. "A Jornall of the Convention at Westminster begun the 22 of January 1688/9" appeared in the *Bulletin of the Institute of Historical Research* in November 1976. "Press and Parliament in the Revolution of 1689" was printed in *The Historical Journal* in September 1977. A fourth paper, presented at the symposium at the Folger Library in May 1976 appeared in 1980 in *The Three British Revolutions,* edited by J. G. A. Pocock. Finally, a paper delivered at the William Andrews Clark Library in 1978 as part of a series of lectures organized by Stephen Baxter will appear in a book of the collected lectures, to be published by the University of California Press. I am indebted in each case to the appropriate authorities for permission to use material in these articles.

Fellowships and grants have supported the research, writing, and publication of this book. I am deeply grateful to the National Endowment for the Humanities for designating me a Fellow for the calendar year 1975 and for underwriting the Senior Fellowship awarded me by the Folger Shakespeare Library in 1978–79. The Graduate School of Arts and Sciences at the George Washington University granted me stipends for travel to England in 1974 and 1977 as well as funds to aid in the production of the book. I also thank George Washington University for granting me a sabbatical leave during 1978–79, and Peter P. Hill, then chairman of the History Department, and Calvin D. Linton, dean of Columbian College, for approving my request for leave.

Mary Lacey, Douglas Lacey's widow, put at my disposal a photocopy of Roger Morrice's "Entr'ing Book, Being an Historical Register of Occurrences from April, Anno, 1677 to April 1691," and miscellaneous microfilm from Lacey's collection. I thank her sincerely.

The National Portrait Gallery granted permission to reproduce the portraits that appear in this book. The other illustrations are reproduced with the permission of the House of Lords Record Office, the Guildhall Library, and the British Museum.

My husband has not once lost interest in a subject far removed from his own profession. He, too, has counseled and read, insisting that every complexity be clearly expressed.

Virginia M. Williams, assisted at various times by Catherine J. Combs, typed successive versions of the manuscript with her usual competence and unfailing good cheer.

Note on Dating and Style

Dates are given in Old Style, but with the year beginning on January 1. Englishmen in the seventeenth century almost always used this form, whereas on the Continent, New Style dating was employed. The Old Style calendar was ten days behind the New Style. In some cases, to avoid confusion, both dates are given in this book.

Punctuation, capitalization, and spelling have been modernized in almost all instances. The presentation copy of the Declaration of Rights is, however, faithfully rendered in Appendix 1.

The Declaration of Rights, 1689

The Declaration of Rights and
the Bill of Rights: The Historians' View

The Declaration of Rights and the Bill of Rights, its statutory form, encapsulate, as do no other documents, the political aspirations and ideas of the English Revolution of 1688–89. Drafted by the Convention, the revolutionary assembly elected to settle the crisis caused by the policies and flight of King James II and the invasion of Prince William of Orange, the Declaration of Rights "tackt" together all the major resolutions the assembly passed.[1] It asserted what were claimed to be the ancient rights and liberties of the nation, justified the removal of one king and the elevation of another on the grounds of the famous "abdication" and "vacancy" formula, and placed restrictions on the powers of the monarchy. The document was presented to and acknowledged by Prince William and Princess Mary of Orange on February 13, 1689, in a ceremony in the Banqueting Hall of Whitehall Palace immediately before they were proclaimed king and queen of England. These events, which marked the end of the most critical phase of the revolution, resulted in not only a new king on the throne of England but also a new form of kingship. The crown that William accepted in 1689 differed in significant respects from that for which Charles I fought in the 1640s and which Charles II regained in 1660.

That the Glorious Revolution was settled in this way reflected the political realities of the occasion and represented a partial victory for men determined to restrict the powers of the monarchy. Such men hoped for more than they achieved; they achieved more than has been always appreciated. Over the next ten months, the Convention, transformed by its own act into a regular parliament, changed the Declaration of Rights in several particulars, including addition of a clause specifying the religion of future monarchs. On December 16, 1689, the Bill of Rights became law, thereby giving statutory authority to the Declaration of Rights.

The Declaration of Rights resulted from a revolution which, with a minimum of bloodshed, accomplished more of lasting importance than any other revolution in England or Europe in the early modern era. Had the same document resulted from a bloody contest, it is almost certain that today its true nature would be recognized and its contribution acknowledged. The nonviolent feature of the Glorious Revolution has conventionally been taken too much for granted. It is a rare phenomenon in man's history to achieve significant constitutional change without significant violence. In 1689 the virtual absence of bloodshed reflected not only the memory of the earlier Civil War and the aversion of contemporaries to endangering their lives, property, and social status but also the sophistication of the major proponents in political maneuvering, parliamentary tactics, and the use of novel forms of propaganda. Similarly, the absence of economic and social concern and change in the revolution has, I think, contributed to the disparagement of this event; scholars who seek paradigms for revolutions ignore the Glorious Revolution. But political change may be as important as change in other aspects of man's life. In 1689 the Declaration of Rights and the Bill of Rights resolved or laid the foundation for resolving some of the basic constitutional and political issues of seventeenth-century English history. This is an achievement which cannot fairly be diminished because the document failed to address social and economic matters.

The importance of the Declaration of Rights and the Bill of Rights transcends the English Revolution of 1688–89. They are arguably the most important political and constitutional documents of the seventeenth century. There is none to rival them among the many declarations, petitions, manifestoes, and propositions issued by Parliament in the Civil War period or any other part of the century in the attempt to define the relationship between itself and the monarchy. Nor was there a statement of like constitutional and political significance on the Continent, where the major states were moving more or less towards absolute forms of government. The continuing influence of these documents on the constitutional development and political ideas of England and the American colonies in the eighteenth century further underscores the point. An assessment written twenty-five years ago that the Bill of Rights is England's "greatest constitutional document since Magna Carta" remains just.[2]

Both the Declaration of Rights and the Bill of Rights are well known, the latter rather more so than the former, but neither one has been thoroughly studied. Both are mentioned in the more than fifty published histories that cover late-seventeenth-century England. Both have been commented on by many writers of English constitutional and legal history and by authors of all specialized studies of the Glorious Revolution. Both are referred to in histories of eighteenth-century intellectual and political development in England and in studies of the American Revolution and eighteenth-century American history. The chances are excellent that most educated persons in the Anglo-Saxon world, while not able, perhaps, to recite its provisions, would list the Bill of Rights of 1689 along with Magna Charta of 1215, the Petition of Right of 1628, and the Reform Bill of 1832 as the major constitutional and political turning points in early modern English history and as documents that influenced the constitutional and political foundations of the

United States. Yet, in contrast to the scholarly attention lavished on Magna Charta, the Petition of Right, and the Reform Bill, there is no comprehensive study of, and until the past five years or so only perfunctory interest in, either the Declaration of Rights or the Bill of Rights. With but one exception, there has been no attempt to explain the drafting of the Declaration of Rights,[3] and, without exception, no exhaustive effort to account for the passage of the Bill of Rights.[4]

Until recently, the so-called Whig interpretation of the Glorious Revolution and the Declaration of Rights has prevailed. Although prefigured in the writings of early polemicists[5] and eighteenth-century historians and commentators,[6] that interpretation (properly understood as a Court-Whig view) found fullest expression in the nineteenth-century history of Macaulay. In brief, Macaulay explained that a small number of English aristocrats in cooperation with a selfless Dutch prince initiated and managed the Glorious Revolution, whose immediate effect was simply to replace one king with another. In Macaulay's view, the Declaration of Rights simply reaffirmed the ancient liberties of the nation. Macaulay declared that dangers from Ireland, France, the London mob, and the English army compelled the Convention to shorten the lengthy first draft of a claim of right it had prepared.[7] The prince of Orange, who was, Macaulay said, entirely passive in the work of the settlement, willingly accepted the Declaration of Rights as a condition of his being made king. In further comments, marked by inherent contradiction, Macaulay characterized the Declaration of Rights as "revolutionary and irregular"; yet he concluded that it was "equal in authority to any statute" and imposed legal restrictions on the king. Although "revolutionary," the Declaration of Rights did not change the law. Wrote Macaulay, "Not a single flower of the crown was touched. Not a single new right was given to the people. The whole English law, substantive and adjective, was . . . exactly the same after the Revolution as before it." But at the same time, he admitted that some changes were needed to remedy "defects" and ambiguities in the constitution, and these changes the Declaration of Rights supplied. Finally, the document "contained the germ . . . of every good law" passed thereafter, and it laid the foundation for the "popular element" to "become dominant."[8] These broad and contradictory judgments, based on wide knowledge of the available sources but not upon close scrutiny of the document, exerted great influence on subsequent historians. In particular, Macaulay's grand-nephew, George Macaulay Trevelyan, continued the tradition in *The English Revolution, 1688–89*, the classic study of the revolution in the twentieth century, published in 1938 to commemorate the two hundred and fiftieth anniversary of the event.[9] Describing the Declaration of Rights as "an agreed contract . . . between Crown and people," he too asserted that the document was a "condition" to winning the throne, and that it contained no new law.[10] Constitutional historians concurred: Mark Thomson wrote, also in 1938, that apart from determining the succession, the Bill of Rights did "little more than [set] forth . . . certain points of the existing laws; . . . [and] simply secured to Englishmen the rights of which they were already legally possessed."[11]

So the matter rested until 1954, when Lucile Pinkham challenged the Whig view of the Declaration of Rights. Pinkham asserted what had only been hinted at before, namely that the prince's strenuous objections to the claim of rights accounted for the changes made in the first draft.[12] She was the first historian to declare that the crown was not offered conditionally upon William's acceptance of the claim of rights. She maintained that the Declaration of Rights did not impose new restrictions on the monarchy, and that the result of the Glorious Revolution was simply to substitute one king for another. Pinkham was also the first historian to insist upon the need for a thorough investigation of the nature and passage of the Declaration of Rights.

More recently, historians have addressed various aspects of the document. In 1974 Robert J. Frankel presented fresh evidence to show that William's hostility to the claim of rights was a central reason why the Commons shortened the first draft.[13] That same year Henry Horwitz offered new data which reveal that a group of peers opposed to the claim of rights provoked a crisis whose effect was to delay the settlement.[14] On the question whether the Declaration of Rights was a condition that William had to accept to win the throne, scholars are divided, two declaring that it was,[15] and two that it was not.[16] But on the matter of the nature of the Declaration of Rights there is no disagreement. Howard Nenner's judgment may stand for that of all recent scholars who have commented on the Declaration of Rights. Nenner wrote that the Declaration of Rights was a "conservative" document that "quite consciously" omitted anything believed to require new legislation.[17] Such was the view, in essence, of the author of a recent history of the Glorious Revolution.[18] Such also was the conclusion of Lawrence Stone, in "The Results of the English Revolutions of the Seventeenth Century." Stone asserted that "the Declaration of Rights was a mere restatement of tradition, not an assertion of constitutional innovation."[19]

Now, no historian would lightly dispute the conclusions of such distinguished scholars. But this traditional view and the adjustments to it are not the product of exhaustive research or close analysis. Indeed, the traditional view is the product of propaganda from the revolution, of language in the document designed to disarm, and of *ex post facto* interpretations of eighteenth-century Whigs — for example, Edmund Burke [20] — who had their own reasons for insisting upon the conservative character of the Glorious Revolution and the Declaration of Rights. Of the scholars just cited only Howard Nenner focuses on the document itself, and his analysis is restricted to a portion of it. The fact is that the Declaration of Rights, the Bill of Rights, and the immediate political and intellectual context within which they were drafted — namely the months from the spring of 1688 through 1689 — have received only perfunctory attention. The articles that have appeared in the past few years, although they have advanced understanding in some ways, have not offered a comprehensive account, and neither have the recent books on the Glorious Revolution [21] and on the ideas that flourished in late-seventeenth-century England. [22]

This study invites adjustments to some traditional and current views of the Declaration of Rights and the Bill of Rights. It clarifies understanding of the substance, nature, and passage of both, and of the question whether the declaration was a condition to which William had to agree to win the throne. It illuminates the nature, tactics, and strength of Tory and Whig parties at the time of the revolution. It permits a surer answer to the key question of the Revolution of 1688–89: whether it established only a new king on the throne, or also a new kingship.

I
The Text and the Committees

1

The Document

❖

About 10:30 on the morning of February 13, 1689 — a cold and "tempestuous" Ash Wednesday [1] — a number of spiritual and temporal peers and commoners of the Convention assembled in the Banqueting Hall of Whitehall Palace. They had come in grand procession from Westminster, on foot, on horseback, and in carriages, along streets lined with soldiers and great crowds of people. Entering the Banqueting Hall at the north door, the lords stood at the right, the commoners at the left. Then, preceded by the Gentlemen Usher of the Black Rod, the Speakers of both Houses led the peers and commoners across the length of the great hall, lined on both sides by yeomen of the guard. Moving under the magnificent ceiling painted fifty years before by Reubens, the Speakers made at three intervals a deep obeisance as they approached Prince William and Princess Mary of Orange, who were sitting hand-in-hand under a canopy of state at the south end. The marquis of Halifax, Speaker of the House of Lords, addressed the pair, requesting permission to present the declaration both Houses of the Convention had agreed upon. Thereupon, in this close setting, as a later print shows (Frontis) and contemporary accounts confirm, the Declaration of Rights was read by the deputy-clerk of Parliament and the crown of England was offered to William and Mary. [2] Rising to respond for them both, while the princess signified her assent by "her looks and a little curtsy," [3] Prince William accepted the crown and acknowledged the Declaration of Rights in brief remarks. His "acceptance speech" was greeted inside with a great shout, and masses of people outside echoed the cry. Immediately thereafter William and Mary were proclaimed king and queen of England. This ceremony, unique in many of its features, brought the most critical stage of the Revolution of 1688–89 to an end.

What is the Declaration of Rights that the deputy-clerk read that day, almost three hundred years ago? What does it look like? What does it say? Who authored it? What issues does it address? At the outset, a brief statement about these basic things is desirable.

11

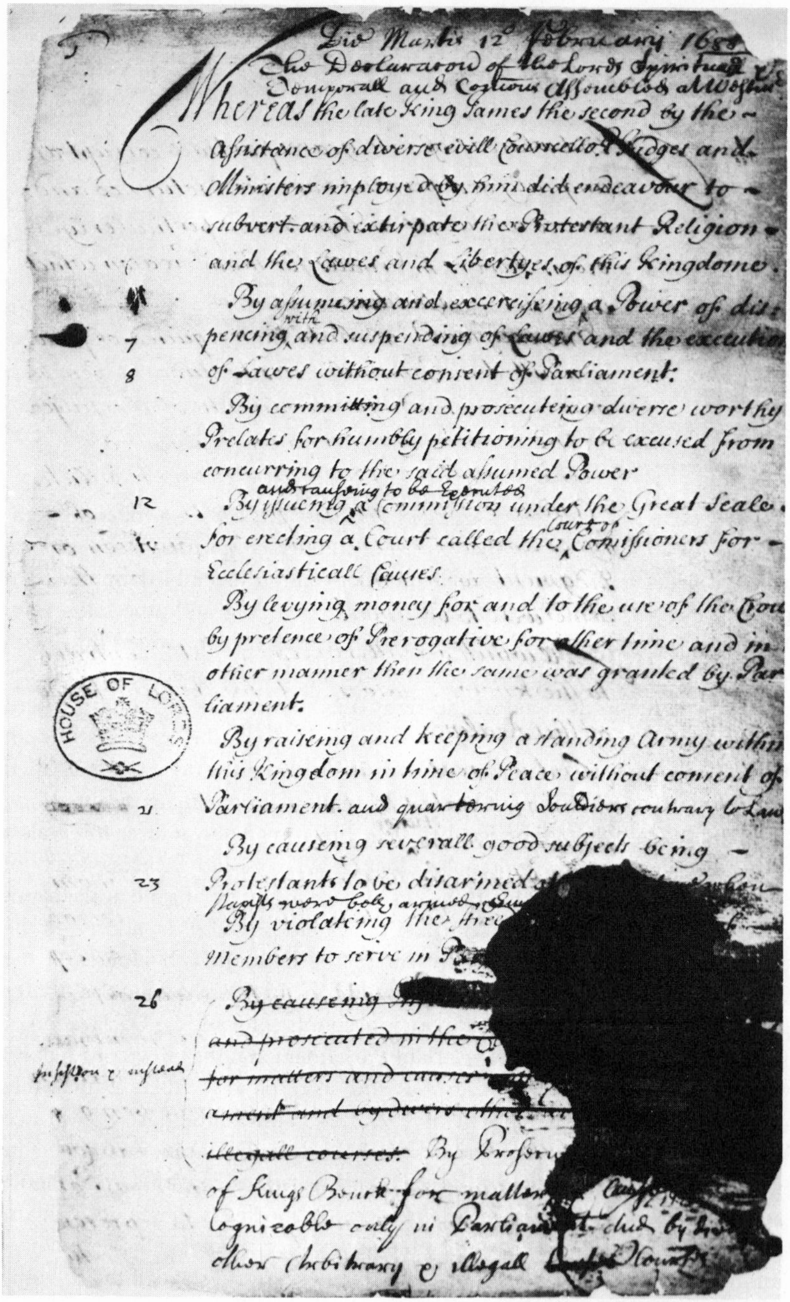

Die Martis 12° Februarii 1688

The Declaration of the Lords Spirituall & Temporall and Commons Assembled at Westm

Whereas the late King James the second by the assistance of diverse evill Councellors Judges and Ministers imployed by him did endeavour to subvert and extirpate the Protestant Religion and the Lawes and Liberties of this Kingdome.

7 By assumeing and excercising a Power of dispencing with and suspending of Lawes and the execution

8 of Lawes without consent of Parliament:

By committing and prosecuteing diverse worthy Prelates for humbly petitioning to be excused from concurring to the said assumed Power

12 By issueing and causing to be executed a Commission under the Great Seale for erecting a Court called the Court of Commissioners for Ecclesiasticall Causes.

By levying money for and to the use of the Crowne by pretence of Prerogative for other time and in other manner then the same was granted by Parliament.

By raiseing and keeping a standing Army within this Kingdom in time of Peace without consent of

21 Parliament. and quartering Souldiers contrary to Law

By causeing severall good subjects being

23 Protestants to be disarmed ... when Papists were both armed ...

By violateing the free...

Members to serve in P...

26 ~~By causeing ...~~

~~and prosecuted in the ...~~

~~for matters and causes ...~~

~~ament and by diverse othe...~~

~~illegall courses.~~ By Prosecu... of Kings Bench for matters & causes cognizable only in Parliament and by diverse other Arbitrary & illegall courses.

Figure 1. Draft of Declaration of Rights, February 8, 1689, with inkblot. Only the third draft of the Declaration of Rights has survived. The House of Lords suggested amendments to this draft, the clerk writing them on the document as shown. The inkblot is contemporary, but no evidence remains to prove, as is sometimes said, that it resulted from an altercation over the claim of rights. (Courtesy of the House of Lords Record Office.)

The copy of the declaration from which the deputy-clerk read was "fairly written in parchment."[4] The scribe either on his own initiative or at the direction of an unidentified person selected an unusually fine piece of parchment sixty-three inches long and fourteen and a half inches wide (two and one half inches wider than normally used for bills) and applied two red lines on either side of the text. He took the time to give the document these marks of importance even though he had only the afternoon and evening of February 12 to prepare it. The "presentation copy" of the Declaration of Rights was (and is) a handsome document. It has, however, lain in obscurity in the House of Lords Record Office for nearly 300 years.[5]

There are no signatures on the Declaration of Rights except that of John Browne, clerk of the Parliament, which was necessary to validate it. The absence of signatures of members of the Convention followed a practice already established. English M.P.'s did not customarily sign the instruments which they presented to the king (or protector, in the case of Oliver Cromwell) during the seventeenth century.[6] In European states, too, declarations and petitions were not signed by the drafters. Of documents comparable to the Declaration of Rights, only the Declaration of Independence of the American colonies was signed by its framers.[7]

Although there was precedent for monarchs to sign parliamentary petitions presented to them, that practice was not followed in 1689. Rumors circulated that whoever won the crown would swear to and/or sign the document,[8] but William did not do so and that Mary would sign was not considered. Since William was prince of Orange when the document was presented to him, his signature, legal opinion held, would have carried no weight in law when he became king. For what he signed before becoming king could not have bound him in law thereafter.[9] Moreover, it was not possible under the circumstances for men in 1689 to win from William, as prince, the formula of assent to their declaration that men in 1628 won from Charles I, as king, for their Petition of Right.[10] Yet, if William had signed the Declaration of Rights or taken an oath to uphold it, that act would certainly have strengthened his moral commitment to it. That he did not do so may, as will be discussed, have been part of a political bargain arranged between him and English political leaders. William, however, did make an "acceptance speech" in response to the reading of the declaration.[11]

The Convention treated the Declaration of Rights as if it were a statute, although in reality it was not. At the initiative of the House of Commons (following disagreement on the point), both Houses ordered that the declaration be engrossed in parchment, enrolled in the rolls of Parliament, the official record of Parliament, and entered in the Court of Chancery "to remain in perpetuity."[12] At the initiative of the Lords, the official version of William's speech was added to the engrossed declaration.[13]

The document that thousands of visitors to Westminster know as the Declaration of Rights — reproduced in Figure 1 — is not the presentation copy, but the report prepared on February 8 at the instruction of the House of Commons by a committee chaired by the then-young John Somers, later to become the lord keeper. The paper on display is interlined and crossed through to indicate the amendments proposed by the House of Lords, and stained by a large ink blot in the lower-right-hand corner. It is the only draft copy of the declaration to have survived. It was brought to the House of Lords by Charles Powlett, marquis of Winchester, late on the afternoon of February 8 following a conference meeting between the two Houses and laid on the table with instructions to be discussed first thing the morning of February 9.[14] The ink blot is almost certainly of contemporary origin, but there is no evidence that it resulted from an ink pot's being thrown in a fit of anger over the terms of the draft, as schoolchildren are sometimes told! [15]

The title of the document read on February 13 is "The Declaration of the Lords Spiritual and Temporal, and Commons, Assembled at Westminster." It announces that both the House of Commons and the House of Lords claim joint responsibility for the declaration. In fact, the House of Commons took the initiative in preparing a statement of rights. The document they sent to the Lords for approval on February 8 was the third draft — a package of all the resolutions the Convention had passed — and a much-watered-down version of the first draft. Not all members of the Commons approved of this procedure. At least one wanted to bypass the Lords and send the statement of rights directly to the prince of Orange, arguing that the peers might weaken or refuse the statement, but others defeated this proposal. In 1689 the House of Lords played an active role only in the last stages of passing the declaration. A group of peers made an attempt to sabotage the statement of rights. But that attempt failing, the Lords appointed a committee of thirteen peers chaired by Thomas Belasyse, Lord Fauconberg, to prepare reasons for the amendments to the Commons' draft, and to defend the proposed changes in conference meetings with the Commons. Several of the Lords' amendments, some of them of genuine significance, prevailed.

The word "declaration" appears in the title of the document. Why was it chosen? The drafting committee had trouble deciding on a title, and the House of Commons twice asked them to supply one.[16] In debates, members had used the words "declaration," "petition," and "address," and it was not until February 11 that the committee settled on the term "declaration." [17] All those words were roughly equivalent. M.P.'s had used them interchangeably throughout the seventeenth century as they debated the nation's grievances.[18] In 1785 the editor of the "Digest" to the first seven volumes of the *Journals of the House of Commons* lumped together references to all these instruments under the heading "Address." [19]

Yet, these words could be distinguished from one another, and a brief statement about the legal and constitutional distinctions will suggest the probable reasons for the title. The word "petition" and the concept it conveyed had had a long and complex history reaching back to the Middle Ages. Then, a "petition" in law was a device by which a subject, whose property, for example, had been seized by the crown, might seek remedy against the king.

English law held it as a maxim that "the king can do no wrong," and, hence, no subject could bring a charge at law against him. But as a petitioner, using a "petition of right" as a legal instrument, the subject might hope for redress because the king was obliged to do "justice in general," to hold himself to the law, even as he obliged his subjects to be regulated by the law. A "petition of right admitted a wrong and remedied it." Used for private and individual matters, a petition of right was an equitable rather than a judicial process.[20]

Between 1603 and 1628 the concept of a parliamentary petition of right emerged. It transformed the earlier process and used it for public and general matters. This development reflected the fact that in the Middle Ages a petition was also a device used in Parliament to ask the king to redress certain grievances. When the king answered such a petition favorably, then the petition was often redrawn as a statute. Thus, the parliamentary petition served as an intermediate step in a legislative process. By the end of the fifteenth century, this legislative procedure no longer operated, but Parliament continued to use petitions as a means of stating their advice and presenting grievances. In the reigns of James I and Charles I a parliamentary petition of right became differentiated from a petition that offered advice to the crown on certain matters. A parliamentary petition of right combined a request for remedy of wrongs that were regarded as proven with a statement of rights that were also regarded as acknowledged. It did not ask the king for mercy, but rather asked that "justice should be done" with respect to the proven grievances and rights therein set forth.

During the early seventeenth century procedures associated with parliamentary petitions of right were regularized. The parliamentary petition of right was to be written, exactly worded, and read twice in the House before being engrossed on parchment. The House of Commons was to take the initiative, but both Houses were to present a parliamentary petition of right. The presentation to the king was a formal occasion. It was expected that the king would answer, and that the petition and the royal reply would be engrossed on parchment and enrolled on the rolls of Parliament. By 1628, the cooperation of the Lords was thought essential, and it was believed that a king could not deny a petition from both Houses.[21] For reasons that scholars have recently elucidated, the Commons in 1628 chose the parliamentary petition of right as the most effective procedure for handling the statement of grievances which became the Petition of Right. Some men in the late seventeenth century, most strikingly William Prynne, who argued the point in a lecture delivered at the Inns of Court in 1661, believed that the Petition of Right was in effect a statute.[22] The theoretical strength of a parliamentary petition of right, whatever the actual fate of the Petition of Right, was not entirely forgotten. For example, in 1673, a member of the House of Commons suggested that a petition be sent to King Charles II asking that he withdraw his Declaration of Indulgence, which suspended the execution of penal laws. The Commons did so, and Charles withdrew the offensive measure.[23]

In 1689 men sought to connect their declaration with earlier parliamentary petitions and addresses. In the document itself they justified what they were doing by saying that they were declaring their rights "as their Ancestors, in like Case, have usually done." In debate they argued, citing Magna Charta and the Petition of Right, that they had a right to make claim of their rights. Moreover, the Declaration of Rights has some of the characteristics of a parliamentary petition of right. For example, the grievances are stated as proven and the rights as acknowledged at law. The two Houses jointly present the document. They enroll it in the Court of Chancery. In several respects, the Declaration of Rights is the last and the greatest of the many instruments setting out the subjects's rights which English parliaments had prepared over the centuries.[24]

A petition, however, implies that there is someone to petition for redress of wrong, and in 1689 that was not the case. There was no king to petition, and from a strictly legal point of view, the Convention was an illegal and revolutionary body. These circumstances, I think, explain why there was confusion over to whom the Convention should address the declaration and over whether they should engross and enroll it. This also explains why the Declaration of Rights could not logically be a parliamentary petition of right, notwithstanding that members evidently intended it to be closely identified with that time-honored device.

The word "declaration" also had a rich history. In common parlance "declaration" was the strongest word of all. Since the fourteenth century it had meant "making clear" or "telling." It also meant "a positive statement or announcement or proclamation in emphatic, solemn or legal terms." [25] In law "declaration" had a technical meaning: it referred to the plaintiff's statement of charges against the defendant which was presented to the court in writing, according to prescribed form, at the opening of a judicial proceeding. A popular legal dictionary defined a declaration as a "shewing in writing the Grief or Complaint of the Demandant or Plaintiff, against the Defendant," and instructed that it be "plain and certain." [26] The first section of the Declaration of Rights has something of the character of a legal declaration; it sets out the charges against King James II and in "plain and certain" terms impeaches him as the "defendant."

The term "declaration" also had a parliamentary and political history. Long before 1689 it appeared in the titles of printed statements issued by English and continental kings and by English parliaments. Printed declarations were a way kings and parliaments communicated with each other in public, in part to explain themselves and enlist the support of the public. European monarchs used declarations in sixteenth-century political, dynastic, and religious contests, and James I in the 1620s and Charles I in 1640 issued declarations to explain and justify their side in disputes with Parliament.[27] Charles II and James II issued declarations too. Their Declarations of Indulgence of 1673, 1687, and 1688 were means to bypass both Parliament and statutory law and to declare liberty of conscience for their

Catholic and dissenting subjects. These declarations did not so much explain or justify — although there is an element of those things in them — as they declared or stated a new policy. The Declaration of Rights shares the character of these royal pronouncements. It "declares" and "asserts" the rights of the nation, and then "resolves" that "William and Mary, Prince and Princess of Orange, be, and be declared, King and Queen of England." Thus, it both announces and creates a new situation. The implication was that the Declaration of Rights carried weight equal to that of a royal pronouncement.

Earlier parliaments had also issued declarations. When the petitioning process failed in the Civil War of 1640, the title in the instruments which the Long Parliament issued changed from "petition" or "protestation" or "remonstrance" to "declaration." [28] These precedents from the Long Parliament were surely known to men in 1689, however much they suppressed reference to them in their general effort to avoid identity with the Civil War. But the Convention of 1660 used the word "declaration" in ways that may have recommended the term to men in 1689. It issued nine "declarations" to deal with aspects of the still unsettled political situation. Since these "declarations" carried authority equal to that of statutes and were issued in roughly comparable circumstances, M.P.'s in 1689 may have thought the title appropriate to their own document.

Outside Parliament, men on the left-hand side of political issues had, throughout the century, also titled their pronouncements "declarations." For example, the first tract in the pamphlet controversy over the Militia Bill/Ordinance controversy in 1642 was *A Declaration of the Great Affaires*. One of the earliest army tracts to appear, in 1647, was *A Declaration; or, Representation of the Army*. Or again, when the duke of Monmouth landed in 1685, he issued *The Declaration of James, Duke of Monmouth*. In each instance these declarations "set forth," explained, or recommended a course of action. Of course, no one in 1689 referred to these radical declarations, although Monmouth's document had some affinities with the Declaration of Rights. The point is that on all sides there was precedent for using the term "declaration" in a political pronouncement.

Still further, in the fall of 1688 the contest between King James II and Prince William of Orange was carried on through printed instruments many of which were called declarations. James regularly issued proclamations, which bore the word "declaration" in their titles, to announce policy and argue his case against William. Some peers of the realm also printed declarations to set out publicly the course of action they recommended the king to follow in the crisis. William had taken the initiative in these exchanges in publishing his *Declaration of His Highness William Henry, Prince of Orange, of the Reasons Inducing Him to Appear in Armes in the Kingdom of England for Preserving of the Protestant Religion and for Restoring the Lawes and Liberties of England, Scotland, and Ireland*. Of all previous declarations the prince's manifesto had the most direct impact on the Declaration of Rights, influencing both its content and passage. Part of a propaganda campaign, this pamphlet provided a "true account of the reasons inducing" William to invade England. Thus, it explained, "made clear," what the prince had decided to do. It also announced William's future policies, stating that he came to rescue the nation's religion, laws, and liberties and to secure Englishmen in "the continual enjoyments of all their just rights," including their "lives and liberties." To accomplish this William promised to call a free parliament, which would deal with the grievances itemized in his *Declaration.* Moreover, a postscript, the *Second Declaration of Reasons,* offered further specific advice. It asserted, "There can be no Redress nor Remedy offered, but in Parliament, by a Declaration of the Rights of the Subjects that have been invaded." In other words, the prince's *Declaration of Reasons* practically instructed the Convention, the surrogate for a free parliament, to prepare a "declaration" of rights. The authors of the Declaration of Rights called upon William's manifesto as model and guide for their own statement of rights. The use of the word "declaration" was a way of establishing a link to the prince's *Declaration,* which had been widely distributed, and thus of making it awkward for William to refuse the Convention's claim because of the embarrassment of publicly disavowing his own well-known manifesto.

The choice of the word "declaration" in the title of the Declaration of Rights could not have been fortuitous. It continued a past practice in political exchanges between king and Parliament which were, of course, known to the authors of the document. It was a provocative term, calling to mind implications that had the effect of giving the Declaration of Rights political force and moral suasion. More, it suggested legal force, for as a legal instrument a declaration had probative value. For lawyers a declaration was something they were accustomed to, a document they regularly drew up with great care to set out the charge of the plaintiff against the defendant, an instrument they were prepared to defend.

The Declaration of Rights was in the line of descent of another tradition in English history. Six times before 1689, Englishmen had removed their kings, each time justifying the step in apologias that defined the authority of the monarchy. These episodes had occurred in (1) 1327, when Edward II was set aside; (2) 1399, when Richard II was deposed; (3) 1460, when Henry VI lost his throne; (4) 1483, when Edward V was deposed and Richard III became king by inheritance and "election"; (5) 1485, when Richard III lost his crown (literally) at the Battle of Bosworth Field to Henry VII; and (6) 1649, when Charles I was condemned by the High Court of Parliament as traitor to the laws of England.[29] In 1689 men in parliamentary debates and pamphlets disclaimed identification with the execution of Charles I, but sought precedent for their acts from early depositions, especially those of Edward II and Richard II. In one debate alone, Richard II was mentioned at least five times.[30] The reference would have been readily understood. William Shakespeare's *Richard II* appeared ten times before 1689, once in 1681 under the title *The Sicilian Usurper,* when it was banned and closed by order of the

Court. Tracts concerning Richard II's deposition appeared in 1641, 1642, and 1689. Sir Robert Howard, better known as poet and dramatist, wrote *The Life and Reign of King Richard the Second,* which appeared in 1681, significantly; and an expanded version titled *Historical Observations upon the Reigns of Edward I, II, III, and Richard II* was licensed without his knowledge, Howard claimed, on January 17, 1689, just five days before the Convention opened.[31] For some men in 1689 one reason for drawing up a statement of the nation's grievances and rights was to explain and justify their setting aside King James II. The Declaration of Rights is like the apologias that men drew up when, earlier in English history, they had deposed their king. And like these earlier apologias the Declaration of Rights defined and sought to limit the authority of the king. But the 1689 declaration differed significantly from all the earlier apologias, for never before in English history had an instrument setting out the rights of the nation been presented to a person before he was king.

The Declaration of Rights comprises all the major resolutions of the Convention. It spelled out King James II's misdeeds (alleged and real), included the famous "abdication" and "vacancy" resolution (shorn of its premises), asserted in thirteen particulars what were said to be ancient rights and liberties of the nation, declared the prince and princess of Orange to be king and queen of England, placed the administration of the government solely in the prince, set forth the succession to the crown, provided new oaths of allegiance, and, in its statutory form, restricted further royal dispensing power, specified the religion of the monarch, and required all future kings to take the Test Act at their accession. It was done this way to assure that the rights of the nation should not be lost in the sense of relief at settling the crisis by offering the crown to William and Mary. It reflected the insistence of men in the Convention who wanted to do what they could to change the kingship by setting out the rights of the nation in a written statement that would be publicly presented to the prince and princess of Orange *before* they were offered the crown of England and were proclaimed king and queen. If others had had their way, there would have been no such statement joined with the offer of the crown. If that had happened, it would be legitimate to call the Glorious Revolution a palace coup, as some scholars have done. But with the presentation of the claim of rights, the very nature of the revolution takes on a different character.

Most people think of the document primarily as a statement of rights. The first section, in a negative way, lists acts which James II and his "evil" advisers allegedly committed in violation of the nation's religion, laws, and liberties (see Appendix 1). As in a parliamentary petition of right, the alleged misdeeds are presented as incontrovertible facts, already proven. Moreover, this section is very like the legal instrument, a declaration, that sets out the case against the accused. The document charges that James had, in thirteen particulars, "endeavoured" to subvert and extirpate Protestantism and the laws and liberties of England:

1. By assuming and exercising a power and dispensing with and suspend-
    ing of laws and the execution of laws without consent of Parliament;
2. By committing and prosecuting divers worthy prelates for humbly peti-
    tioning to be excused from concurring to the said assumed power;
3. By issuing and causing to be executed a commission, under the Great
    Seal, for erecting a court called the Court of Commissioners for Ecclesi-
    astical Causes;
4. By levying money for and to the use of the crown, by pretence of
    prerogative, for other time and in other manner than the same was
    granted by Parliament;
5. By raising and keeping a standing army within this kingdom in time of
    peace without consent of Parliament and quartering soldiers contrary
    to law;
6. By causing several good subjects, being Protestants, to be disarmed at
    the same time when Papists were both armed and employed contrary to
    law;
7. By violating the freedom of election of members to serve in Parliament;
8. By prosecutions in the Court of King's Bench for matters and causes
    cognizable only in Parliament: And by divers other arbitrary and illegal
    courses.

Article 9 begins "And whereas . . .," and the rest of the articles, which cite
alleged violations in legal proceedings, are dependent upon those two words.
The document continues:

9. And whereas, of late years, partial, corrupt, and unqualified persons
    have been returned and served on juries in trials, and particularly,
    divers jurors in trials for high treason, which were not freeholders;
10. And excessive bail has been required of persons committed in criminal
    cases to elude the benefit of the laws made for the liberty of the subjects;
11. And excessive fines have been imposed;
12. And illegal and cruel punishments inflicted;
13. And several grants and promises made of fines and forfeitures before
    any conviction or judgment against the persons upon whom the same
    were to be levied.

The indictment specifically blames James himself, along with his "evil"
advisers, for the nation's grievances. The legal maxim "the king can do no
wrong" had to be set aside if James himself were to be accused. Further, the
indictment declares that James *et al.* had "endeavoured" to subvert the
nation's laws, thereby indicating that a dissolution of the government had *not*
occurred. The word implied that the nation had not been returned to a state
of nature and underlined the politically conservative conclusion of the Convention.

This section ends with the assertion that all of the above acts "utterly and
directly" violated the "known laws and statutes and freedom" of England.

But, in fact, that assertion reflected a partisan interpretation of events, policies, and in some instances (as will be shown) the law itself.

Another section of the declaration "declares" in positive terms thirteen "ancient" rights. A glance at the two sections shows that the thirteen grievances charged against James II have, with two exceptions, been turned around and claimed as the rights of the nation. The exceptions are (1) a portion of the charge in article 5 — "quartering soldiers contrary to law" — which nowhere appears in the declaratory section of the document, and (2) the eighth grievance — "By prosecutions in the Court of King's Bench for matters . . . cognizable only in Parliament" — which also disappears in the list of rights. In fact, however, the issue underlying the eighth grievance inheres in article 9 in the declaratory section — "That the freedom of speech and debates or proceedings in Parliament ought not to be impeached or questioned in any court or place out of Parliament." Moreover, two rights appear in the declaratory section which are not in the indictment: one is the claim of freedom of speech in article 9, and the other is the claim that Parliament ought to meet frequently in article 13. This section reads:

1. That the pretended power of suspending of laws or the execution of laws by regal authority without consent of Parliament is illegal.
2. That the pretended power of dispensing with laws or the execution of laws by regal authority as it has been assumed and exercised of late is illegal.
3. That the commission for erecting the late Court of Commissioners for Ecclesiastical Causes and all other commissions and courts of like nature are illegal and pernicious.
4. That levying of money for or to the use of the crown by pretense of prerogative without grant of Parliament for longer time or in other manner than the same is or shall be granted is illegal.
5. That it is the right of the subjects to petition the king, and all commitments and prosecutions for such petitioning are illegal.
6. That the raising or keeping a standing army within the kingdom in time of peace, unless it be with consent of Parliament, is against law.
7. That the subjects which are Protestants may have arms for their defense suitable to their condition and as allowed by law.
8. That elections of members of Parliament ought to be free.
9. That the freedom of speech and debates or proceedings in Parliament ought not to be impeached or questioned in any court or place out of Parliament.
10. That excessive bail ought not to be required, nor excessive fines imposed, nor cruel and unusual punishments inflicted.
11. That jurors ought to be duly impaneled and returned, and jurors which pass upon men in trials for high treason ought to be freeholders.
12. That all grants and promises of fines and forfeitures of particular persons before conviction are illegal and void.

13. And that for redress of all grievances, and for the amending, strengthening, and preserving of the laws, parliaments ought to be held frequently.

This section ends with the statement that the Lords Spiritual and Temporal and the Commons "claim, demand, and insist upon" all of the above rights as "their undoubted rights and liberties." Thus, the rights of the nation, like the grievances, are, following the form of a parliamentary petition of right, presented as proven, established rights.

Yet there is an interesting distinction among the clauses suggested by the form of the verb which is employed. The declarative form of the verb appears in seven articles — articles 1–6 and 12 — while the conditional form is used in the other six. Thus, the power of suspending laws without the consent of Parliament "is" illegal. The power of dispensing with the laws, as that power has been used of late, "is" illegal. The commission for erecting the Court of Ecclesiastical Causes "is" illegal. The levying of money without grant of Parliament "is" illegal. Still further, the document asserts that the right of the subject to petition the king is legal, and that commitments and prosecutions for such petitioning "are" illegal. The raising and keeping of a standing army within the kingdom in time of peace without the consent of Parliament "is" illegal. And finally, grants and promises of fines before conviction "are" illegal. These seven rights are asserted without ambiguity as "undoubted" rights.

The conditional form of the verb appears in the other articles. Thus, Protestant subjects "may" have arms, suitable to their condition and as allowed by law. Elections to Parliament "ought" to be free. Freedom of speech and debates or proceedings in Parliament "ought" not to be questioned outside of Parliament. Excessive bail "ought" not to be required, nor excessive fines imposed, nor cruel and unusual punishment inflicted. Jurors "ought" to be impaneled and returned, and jurors who sit on trials for high treason "ought" to be freeholders. And finally, Parliaments "ought" to be held frequently. The language is not obligatory, and it conveys some ambivalence about whether the rights are indeed "undoubted," as claimed. These articles really say what "ought" to happen, what is desirable. They imply intention, rather than declare law, notwithstanding that they are included in the section of old, established laws. The langauge of the Bill of the Rights (discussed below), however, strengthens the declaratory section of the document and removes the ambiguities.

The list of rights in the final version of the Declaration of Rights was different from that in the first draft. The first draft contained twenty-eight articles, twenty-three presented by a committee of the House of Commons, five more added by members in debate on February 2. Referred to as the Heads of Grievances (see Appendix 2), this draft embodied a comprehensive program of reform representing the goals of radical Whig members.[32] The draft called, for example, for (1) parliamentary reform: removing the king's power to call and dissolve Parliament at will; (2) reform of law: changing the tenure

of judges from "at the pleasure of the king" to "during good behavior," providing judges a salary out of public revenue and denying them fees, barring a
royal pardon to a parliamentary impeachment, denying the king the power
to suspend and dispense the laws, and dealing with many other details of
judicial reform; (3) reform of the militia laws; and (4) reform of abuses in the
appointment of sheriffs and in the execution of their office. The Heads of
Grievances also called for (5) an "effectual provision" for toleration of Protestants and for reuniting all Protestants. If enacted, these proposed reforms
would have decisively changed the English kingship and the operation of law
and local government.

But on February 4, the House of Commons instructed the committee to
divide the lengthy list into two parts, one part containing articles respecting
allegedly ancient rights, and the other comprising articles that required new
laws. The committee prepared such a draft on February 7.[33] It placed in the
category of declaring ancient rights heads 1-4, 6-10, 19, 21, and 26. It
divided clause 8 into two articles, one concerning free elections to parliament, and the other parliamentary privileges, which were spelled out: "That
the freedom of speech and debates or proceedings in Parliament ought not to
be impeached or questioned in any court or place out of Parliament." It is
noteworthy that the words "freedom of speech" appeared first in this draft.
The words in the original head that sought to preserve the rights and
privileges of Parliament in the intervals of Parliament were moved to the second section. The committee joined heads 9 and 10 into one article that said,
"Parliaments ought to be held frequently, and suffered to sit," the phrase "and
suffered to sit" reflecting clause 10, which read "No interrupting of any session of Parliament, till the affairs that are necessary to be dispatched at that
time are determined." It dropped entirely head 12 — "No pardon to be
pleadable to an impeachment in Parliament." In the category of reforms that
called for new laws, the committee placed heads 5, 8, 9, 11, and 13-28. In
this draft, then, heads 8, 9, 19, 21, and 26 appear in both categories. The
sentences introducing the section of rights that required new laws soften the
apparent inconsistency. They read: "And towards the making a more firm
and perfect settlement of the said religion, laws, and liberties, and for remedy
of several defects and inconveniences, it is proposed and advised . . . that
there be provisions, by new laws." In other words, new laws are needed to
reinforce or remedy defects in ancient rights. Yet, there must have been
doubt in the authors' minds that the rights claimed in the five articles placed
in both categories were indeed "undoubted."

On February 8, the House instructed the committee to drop the section of
reforms that required new laws. The resulting third draft — the package of
the Convention's resolutions — was sent to the House of Lords and amended
there and in conference meetings with the House of Commons. Article 1 was
divided into two articles, one to deal with the royal suspending power, the
other with the dispensing power. The words "and suffered to sit," which had
preserved the principle that parliaments should not be interrupted until the

Table 1. Fate of Clauses in Heads of Grievances

Article No. in H.G.	February 7 Draft			February 8 Draft	Article No. in Final Draft
	In old law	Required new law	Dropped		
1	X			X	1 & 2
2	X			X	3
3	X			X	4
4	X			X	5
5		X			
6	X			X	6
7	X			X	7 (amended)
8	X	X		X(2)	8 & 9 amended
9	X	X		X	13
10	X			X	
11		X			
12			X		
13		X			
14		X			
15		X			
16		X			
17		X			
18		X			
19	X	X		X	10 (amended)
20		X			
21	X	X		X	11
22		X			(implicit in 9)
23		X			
24		X			
25		X			
26	X	X		X	12 (amended)
27		X			
28		X			

business before them had been dispatched, were also dropped. In sum, only eleven clauses from the original twenty-eight Heads of Grievances survived, some in amended form, in the thirteen articles of the Declaration of Rights (thirteen because heads 1 and 8 in the Heads of Grievances each became two articles in the declaration). The eleven heads are 1–4, 6–9, 19, 21, and 26. Head 22 was implicit in article 9 of the Declaration of Rights. Heads 14 and 15 were included in the Bill of Rights. The Declaration of Rights was clearly a casualty of heavy political maneuvering. Table 1 summarizes what happened to the first draft.

The principal authors of the Declaration of Rights were not content simply to preserve their claim of rights. To the statement of rights they linked the Convention's resolutions, one of them significantly amended, and did so in such a way as to convey certain political impressions. The most important resolution the Convention adopted was the famous abdication and vacancy resolution. On January 28, the House of Commons accepted with near unanimity a statement which explained and justified the "vacancy" in the throne and prepared the way for settling the "headship" in the state. In its original form it read: "That King James the Second, having endeavoured to subvert the constitution of this kingdom by breaking the original contract between king and people, and, by the advice of Jesuits and other wicked persons, having violated the fundamental laws, and having withdrawn himself out of the kingdom, has abdicated the government; and that the throne is thereby vacant." In that form the resolution closely reflected the principles of radical Whig members of the House, who had dominated the debate. It emphasized, however opaque the language and contradictory one of the clauses, that James's *acts* had broken the original contract between king and people and violated the nation's fundamental laws, and that they, in effect, amounted to an "abdication" of the government, which rendered the crown "vacant." The original resolution also included a phrase endorsed by Tory M.P.'s — that James had withdrawn himself from the kingdom. That phrase inferred that the throne was vacant but only with respect to James; it was occupied by the legitimate but unnamed successor. The major clauses in the resolution provoked protracted and heated debates in and between both Houses, and it was over a week before the peers accepted the key words "abdicated" and "vacant." As a result, surely, of an arrangement between parliamentary leaders on both sides, other controversial phrases were dropped. "Original contract" and "fundamental laws" were objectionable to Tories, and the reference to the king's withdrawal could not satisfy the Whigs. In the Declaration of Rights, one short sentence refers to the essence of this critically important resolution. Used as the connection between the first and second sections of the document, it reads simply: "And whereas the said late King James the Second having abdicated the government, and the throne being thereby vacant. . . ."

The placement of this sentence directly following the thirteen-point indictment of James II could not have been fortuitous. It intimated that James's *acts* amounted to an abdication and *therefore* to a vacancy in the throne. In the absence of a reference anyplace in the document to the king's withdrawal, it was left open, by inference, that James's misdeeds had broken the original contract between king and people and violated the fundamental laws, as left-wing Whigs had argued in debate and pamphlet.

Another phrase in this resolution also underwent change. The words "by the advice of Jesuits and other wicked persons" disappear. Instead, the paragraph which introduces the Declaration of Rights begins: "Whereas the late King James the Second, by the assistance of divers evil counsellors, judges, and ministers, employed by him." The two phrases carry different intimations. "Jesuits and other wicked persons" calls to mind the detested Edward Petre, James's Jesuit adviser, and Robert Spencer, earl of Sunderland, thought by many to be wicked, and anchors the indictment to James II's reign. But "evil counsellors" was a term often used in earlier declarations critical of the king. It can be found in addresses prepared by Parliament during the Civil Wars. In a more immediate way, it called to mind Charles II's evil counselors and the efforts of the parliamentary opposition to remove them. In like manner, the specification of "wicked persons" as "judges" would have reminded the politically conscious public of the criticism of the judiciary, criticism that was especially virulent during the reign of Charles II. The effect of these adjustments was to suggest, however subtly, that the grievances of the nation were not limited to James's reign.

The handling of the offer of the crown to Prince William and Princess Mary also contains political inferences. With the specification of the succession to the crown to four removes, the offer forms the third section of the document. Preceding it is material that explains the authority by which the Lords Spiritual and Temporal and the Commons, elected from among such persons "as were of right to be sent to Parliament," convened on January 22, 1689. The declaration calls that assembly "a full and free representative." It says that "in the *first* place" (emphasis added) the assembly "(as their ancestors in like case have usually done) for the vindication and asserting their ancient rights and liberties declare" certain rights. Then the second section — using such words as "vindicating," "declaring," "claiming," "demanding," and "insisting upon" — declares thirteen alleged ancient rights. The offer of the crown which follows asks that the prince and princess accept the crown "accordingly." That word means, and was so used in the seventeenth century, "in accordance with the sequence of ideas; agreeably or conformably to what might be expected; in natural sequence, in due course; so." The inferences were that the offer of the crown was conditional upon William's accepting the itemized rights, and that the rights claimed did limit the powers of the crown. A different arrangement of the text would not have conveyed such an impression. For example, the crown could have been offered first, the offer justified by the misdeeds of James II, and then the nation's rights asserted. Such a sequence would not have implied that the crown was conditional upon the prince's accepting the statement of rights nor that the rights limited the authority of the crown. There was nothing inevitable about how the parts of the document should be arranged. It is, therefore, significant that the authors chose to "tack" together the parts in a way that conveyed a political impression.

At the insistence of the House of Commons, the Declaration of Rights spelled out the succession to the crown to four removes. It settled the crown on William and Mary during their joint lives, and then to their surviving children. Should William predecease Mary and they have no issue, the crown was to go to the heirs of the body of the princess; then to her sister, Princess Anne of Denmark, and the heirs of her body; and finally to the heirs of the body of William, should Mary predecease him. The purpose of these limitations was to assure a place in the succession for Anne and her issue before the heirs of William, should Mary predecease him, and to acknowledge William by providing a place for his heirs by another wife in the event of Mary and Anne's predeceasing him without issue.

At the initiative of the House of Lords, the Declaration of Rights included new oaths. All persons required by law to take the former oaths of supremacy and allegiance were to subscribe the new oaths which omitted the words "rightful and lawful" as descriptive of the monarchs. All a person was asked to do was to "promise and swear" to be "faithful and bear true allegiance" to William and Mary, to abjure the idea that princes excommunicated by the Pope may be deposed, and to deny that any foreign person possesses authority within the realm of England. The changes were aimed at easing the consciences of persons who could not regard the prince and princess of Orange as legitimate rulers, but could accept them as *de facto* monarchs.

Either all or parts of the several drafts of the declaration were printed shortly after they were composed, in violation of time-honored orders of the House of Commons that their deliberations were privileged.[34] The first draft of twenty-eight heads reported on February 2 was available as a broadside on either February 4 or 5 under the title *The Publick Grievances of the Nation adjudged necessary by the honorable the House of Commons to be redressed.* Within a few days a portion of the second draft of the declaration was made available. At the bottom of a sheet giving the names of the peers who voted against the abdication and vacancy resolution on February 6 appeared a part of the Declaration of Rights, under the heading: "A form of settling the Crown and Succession agreed on in the House of Commons, and by them communicated to the House of Lords for their concurrence."[35] A contemporary specifically referred to the second draft as being in print, but no copy seems to have survived.[36] The penultimate draft prepared by the House of Commons on February 11 was also printed, under the title *The agreement of the House of Lords, during this session, with the concurrence of the House of Commons, to this present eleventh of February, in the great affairs of these nations.*[37] Despite the title, the Lords amended this draft. Abbreviated versions of the Declaration of Rights appeared in the February 12 issue of two of the new newspapers that had sprung up during the crisis: the *London Intelligence* and the *Orange Gazette.* Finally, on February 15, the House of Lords ordered that the Declaration of Rights and William's answer be "forthwith printed and published."[38] Accordingly, James Partridge, Matthew Gillyflower, and Samuel Heyrick, the officially appointed printers to the House of Lords, printed the declaration with the date February 12 at the top and the title reading *The Declaration of the Lords Spiritual and Temporal, and Commons, Assembled at Westminster, Presented to the King and Queen by the Right Honourable the Marquess of Hallifax, Speaker to the House of Lords. With His Majesties Most Gracious Answer Thereunto.*[39] An unofficial version, without the February 12 date, with William's answer omitted, and with no indication of who printed it, also appeared.[40] And in case a person missed these, the entire document was printed in the body of a pamphlet entitled *An Account of what was done between the time the Prince of Orange came to London, till the Proclaiming him King of England, 1688,* which in turn was reprinted in the *Twelfth and Last Collection of Papers,* printed by Richard Janeway after April 11, 1689.

The Declaration of Rights was given statutory form as the Bill of Rights, which King William III signed into law on December 16, 1689. The Bill of Rights incorporated the Declaration of Rights with three major changes.

First, the bill further secured the crown to a Protestant line. It added that the crown was to be inherited by the next Protestant heir, that persons professing the Popish religion were to be excluded, and that anyone marrying a Catholic was forbidden to hold the crown of England. It also required the heir to the throne to take an oath against transubstantiation, as provided in the Test Act of 1673. Professor J. R. Jones has made the point that these requirements reversed the European principle — *cuius regio eius religio* — that had developed during the Reformation, namely that the religion of the ruler determined that of his subjects.[41] In England the Bill of Rights required the monarch to be of the same religion as most Englishmen: Protestant. The consequence was to exclude the descendants of the Stuarts in the Orleans line and the Palatine line, except for one branch.[42] Theoretically at least, this portion of the Bill of Rights left no doubt where ultimate authority over the monarch resided. Yet the specification of the succession to four removes blunted the implication that Parliament had made the monarchy elective.[43]

Second, the Bill of Rights provided further ruling on the dispensing power. It declared that "from and after this present session of Parliament" there shall be allowed "no dispensation by *non obstante* of or to any statute," except if a dispensation is allowed in the statute, or except in such cases as provided for by subsequent bills passed during the present session of Parliament. It also provided a "grandfather clause," exempting patents or charters granted before October 23, 1688. In point of fact, the Convention Parliament took no further steps to define or limit rather than to forbid the dispensing power, as the language of the Bill of Rights implied that it would do.[44]

Finally, the Bill of Rights supplied a preamble and other connecting material, two features of which are noteworthy. The preamble states that "the Lords Spiritual and Temporal and Commons assembled at Westminster" do "lawfully, fully and freely" represent "all the estates of the people of this realm." What precisely the drafters meant by the last phrase — represent "all the estates of the people of this realm" — is unclear.[45] It not only asserted the legality of the Convention, but it also suggested that the two Houses, without the king, were sufficient to represent the "estates of the people of this realm." It implied that at the moment when the revolutionary settlement was being proclaimed, the sovereign power rested with the Convention. Second, the connecting material linking the assertion of rights and the offer of the crown to the specifications of the succession contained words that reinforce the claim that the rights are "undoubted," as the declaration said. The words describe them as "true, ancient, and indubitable rights and liberties of the people of this kingdom, and so shall be esteemed, allowed, adjudged, deemed, and taken to be." The ambiguities suggested by the form of the verbs in the several clauses are thereby effectively removed, and all the rights are emphatically asserted.

The language of the Declaration of Rights is severe. To the disappointment of some commentators, the document is most unsatisfactory as a statement of political principles.[46] However unsatisfactory the language may be, the document was more than a pragmatic response to the details of a difficult situation. Political and constitutional principles inform the Declaration of Rights. Close attention to the words and organization of the text, to the men who promoted and drafted it, to the political and intellectual context within which it was shaped, and to the political maneuvering that accounts for its passage will reveal that this is so.

2

The Rights Committees
in the House of Commons

The Declaration of Rights was the work of the Convention of 1689, a revolutionary body summoned to settle the crisis. Two committees in the House of Commons served consecutively to draft and manage the passage of the declaration, while one committee in the House of Lords assumed special responsibility for responding to the document sent up by the House of Commons. The full House of Lords and the House of Commons also debated the draft. Yet most of the credit for the Declaration of Rights belongs to the two Commons committees, and this chapter concerns them.[1] A composite profile of their members shows the kind of man the House of Commons trusted to identify the rights of the nation and set out the terms of the settlement, helps explain the content and passage of the document, and clarifies the partisan alignments underlying the declaration.

The functions of the two House committees were distinctly different. The first committee, composed originally of thirty-nine M.P.'s, was appointed on January 29 for the purpose of bringing in "heads of things that were absolutely essential to secure the nation's religion, laws and liberties." Chaired by Sir George Treby, this committee prepared a draft of the "heads" — that is, set out the substance of the document — and presented it to the House on February 2. Two days later, at the instruction of the House, the committee, enlarged to forty members, divided the heads into two categories, one of articles which reaffirmed allegedly old laws, the other of rights which required new legislation, and presented that report on February 7.

The second committee, composed first of twenty-one M.P.'s, was appointed on February 7 for the purpose of amending the motion sent down by the House of Lords to declare Prince William and Princess Mary of Orange king and queen of England. Fortunately for the fate of the Declaration of Rights, all but three of the members — including John Somers, who became the chairman — were also on Treby's committee. Somers took the initiative in asking the full House to direct the committee how to proceed, pointing out that there was at hand an opportunity to connect the statement about rights to the offer of the throne. In response, the House instructed the committee to link together three resolutions: (1) the statement that reasserted the allegedly ancient rights of the nation (leaving out the section of heads that required new laws), (2) the Lords' motion giving the crown to William and Mary, and (3) the new form of oaths which the Lords had also prepared. Enlarged by the appointment of another member on February 12, the committee prepared a package of all the Convention's resolutions. It also prepared and argued in conference meetings the House's response to amendments proposed by the House of Lords, and it presented the final version of the Declaration of Rights. Altogether forty-three men, out of a total of 513 members of the Convention, served on one or both of the committees and had opportunity to contribute directly to the process of formulating and passing the document.[2] (All forty-three men are listed in Appendix 3, along with a summary of pertinent information.)

One of the most striking attributes of the committeemen is their previous parliamentary experience. Seven of the forty-three men had been in the parliaments of the 1640s or 1650s, nineteen in Charles II's Cavalier Parliament, and thirty-two in one or more of the Exclusion Parliaments of 1679, 1680, and 1681.[3] Eighteen had served in James II's only parliament of 1685, three being returned for the first time.[4] Only five of the forty-three members were new men, elected to a parliament for the first time in 1689. Thus, only eight men had *not* been in a parliament during the reign of Charles II. In the entire Convention, there were 183 new men, about forty above the normal number. They may have held the balance of political power in voting in the Commons, as J. H. Plumb has maintained,[5] but few were appointed to these committees.

Many committee members were past leaders in parliamentary, political, and legal circles. There were three former Speakers of the House of Commons: Sir Edward Seymour (Speaker in 1672–73 and again in 1678–79), Sir William Williams (1680–81), and Sir William Gregory (briefly in 1679). Many had served on committees, introduced or helped draft bills, and managed conference meetings. In short, they knew how to work the House to achieve the success of a project. To one degree or another, they had been involved in the major controversies of the past ten to twenty years in opposition to the court.[6] Their views on the issues were well known. For example, the leaders of the anti–standing army efforts in the 1670s were on the committees: Birch, Clarges, Garroway, Lee, Sacheverell, Littleton, and Williams. Some — Treby, Somers, and Gregory — had already explicitly expressed by action or in writing their opinion of the royal dispensing power. Richard Hampden, Howard, and Sacheverell had, in 1680, asserted the subjects' right to petition the king and participated in bitter criticism of Charles's proclamation against petitioning.[7] Nine members of the rights committee had served on earlier committees in 1675 and 1680 to bring in a bill to prevent levying of taxes without Parliament's consent.[8] It is no wonder, then, that Birch felt that the task of identifying the rights of the nation could be accomplished in a day.[9]

The committeemen were mature. Twenty-two of the forty-three were over fifty years old, and one, the oldest, Sir John Maynard, was eighty-seven. Ten were between forty and fifty years of age, ten between thirty and forty. The youngest, Lord Wiltshire, was twenty-eight. The average age was forty-nine.[10] Thus the majority of the committeemen had lived through the civil wars and the Interregnum. The memory of those years must have reinforced a horror of civil war, with its concomitant threats to property and personal life. Such fears were present at the time of the Glorious Revolution and were exploited to promote William's cause and to hasten the resolution of the crisis. They underlay the "swing to the right" which the committee took. And the experience and age of these committee members meant that their views carried weight with the rank-and-file members of the House.

The committees were decidedly Whig.[11] Of the forty-three men, twenty-nine were Whig, fourteen were Tory. On Treby's committee Whig members outnumbered Tories twenty-eight to twelve, while Somers's committee was even more heavily Whig — sixteen to six. This ratio does not reflect the political balance in the full House, which was by no means overwhelmingly Whig.[12] What it does reflect is the superior organization and cohesiveness of the Whigs at this time and the power exercised by the Speaker, Sir Henry Powle, a Whig. Almost certainly, Powle used his position to further Whig interests by acknowledging fellow Whigs who wished to make nominations to the committee. This would help explain how eight Whigs were appointed to Treby's committee before one Tory was named and why the Tory who had initiated the debate that led to the appointment of the committee — Anthony Cary, Lord Falkland — was the sixteenth appointee.[13]

During these weeks of the Convention, the terms "Tory" and "Whig" referred, not to two structured parties with recognized leaders and other trappings of party, but to men who adhered to earlier Tory and Whig alignments and principles and who in 1689 voted for or against "abdication." In the weeks preceding and during the Convention, there was neither acknowledged leadership nor organization of either group. The former Whig party that Anthony Ashley Cooper, first earl of Shaftesbury, had put together in 1679–81 during the Popish Plot and Exclusion Crisis had crumbled before the failure of the Whigs to win exclusion of James, duke of York, from succession to the throne and the success of Charles II's tactics against them in Parliament and court of law. In the absence of a parliament (no parliament was held during James II's reign except for the abortive parliament of 1685), with their leaders dead or in exile, with the Stuart monarchy skillfully exploiting every weapon at hand, the "first Whigs" collapsed.[14] Likewise, the former Tory party organized by Thomas Osborne, earl of Danby, had no strong organization in 1688–89. Described as "auxiliaries" to the crown during the latter years of Charles II's reign,[15] the Tories, while sharing some of the "country" attitudes of the Whigs, firmly adhered to the king, profited from his favor, and participated in implementing repressive policies from 1681 to 1685. Composed largely of Anglican country gentry, the party never achieved the degree of organization or identity the Whigs did. Under James II, the Tories became alienated from the king because of his Catholicizing and centralizing policies and his dismissal of Tory officeholders on the local and national level.

Indeed, for a time during James's reign, it looked as if party divisions might be forgotten in the opposition to the king's policies. Tories and Whigs initiated the steps that led to James's downfall. Anglican Tory clergy were, in the spring of 1688, in the forefront of the preliminaries to the revolution, and they and others tried to effect a rapprochement with Dissenters, whom they had earlier persecuted. In December 1688 (if not several weeks earlier), the general consensus broke, and disagreements over solution and tactics appeared. But there was no time during the weeks prior to the meeting of the Convention to reconstitute party apparatus and leadership such as had existed earlier: (This fact may help explain the election of the unusually large number of new men to the Convention.) Yet, there was not an entire absence of partisan identification. Former Whig stalwarts, among them Treby, Richard Hampden, Sacheverell, and Maynard, and former Tories such as Seymour, Musgrave, and Clarges came forward as leaders. There were only two major questions in the Convention on which to divide: who should be king, and what should be the powers of the kingship. If the work of the Convention is to be properly understood, then the parties and leaders must be judged on the evidence of their views and actions at the time of the Convention and leading up to it, not on evidence of their views and actions later.

Of the twenty-nine Whigs, twenty-two had had close connections with the libertarian political and religious attitudes that characterized the "first" Whigs. In this study they are referred to as "radical" or "worthy" Whigs. The word "radical" is usually regarded as an anachronism when applied to late-seventeenth-century politics, and it is true that a contemporary would not have employed it. As used in this book, the word does not refer to the radical underground of the 1640s and 1650s about which scholars have recently written.[16] In 1689 not one M.P. proposed social and economic reforms that were advocated by the earlier radical underground. Not one was a Leveller. In 1689 not one was an avowed republican. In fact, John Wildman, the former republican, specifically denied that he favored, under the present circumstances, any change in the basic structure of king, Lords and Commons.[17] After the settlement, John Hampden disclaimed his commitment to a republic, and Treby declared that "rather than have a hand in anything of a republic" he "would rather have lost a hand."[18] But these men adhered, as did Shaftesbury and his friends (among whom they may be counted), to the left side of the two central political questions of the century — the nature of the kingship and the relationship of the king and Parliament, and the matter of religious toleration. On these questions they did want "radical" change in the sense that the word had been used since 1651: "touching upon what is essential and fundamental, thorough." [19]

A Whig is counted as radical in this study if, first, he meets two of the following criteria: (1) if he was rated W (for worthy) or H (for honest) by Shaftesbury in a list of members of the House of Commons in 1679 which he marked to indicate a person of whom he approved, on whom he could count, and who shared his views;[20] (2) if he was active in the Exclusion Crisis of 1679–81 on behalf of excluding James, then duke of York, from succession to the throne; (3) if he was involved in the Rye House Plot; or (4) if he was a Dissenter himself or had close ties to Nonconformity. Membership in the Green Ribbon Club enhances his radicalness. Second, in the cases where there are insufficient data to measure a person against these criteria, if other data suggest he is radical, then such a Whig is provisionally so designated.

Thirteen of the Whigs on the rights committees were marked W or H on Shaftesbury's list. [21] At least nineteen of the Whigs had favored Exclusion and worked actively for it in Parliament or by writing tracts.[22] At least four of the Whig committeemen (Boscawen, Wildman, Wharton, and John Hampden) had been suspected of complicity in the Rye House Plot; and at least five (Jephson, Littleton, Treby, Waller, and Wharton) had apparently joined the Green Ribbon Club. [23] Eighteen Whig committeemen were either themselves Dissenters or had sympathetic connections with Nonconformists.[24] Among the latter were Somers, Treby, Pollexfen, and Wharton.[25] Of the men who were themselves Dissenters, Richard Hampden, for years an outstanding spokesman for Dissent, was the most important. He was at the center of a circle of men linked by religious conviction, kinship, and friendship. In that circle was his son John, and Thomas and Paul Foley, whose sister John had married. Richard's son-in-law, Sir William Ellys, said to be the "head of all the Presbyterians" in Lincolnshire,[26] was another member. Moreover, there was Thomas Wharton, with whom Hampden had represented Buckinghamshire in 1681 and whose election in 1685 he had promoted.[27] Philip, Lord Wharton, was also Richard Hampden's close friend. Others in this circle included Boscawen, described by an observer as the "great pillar of the Presbyterians," and Sir Henry Hobart, who was married to the granddaughter of the octogenerian Maynard, also a Dissenter. The Hampden and Hobart families were related through the marriage of Richard's sister Mary to Sir John Hobart.[28]

Nine Whigs on the committees — Colchester, Eyre, Harbord, Hobart, Holt, Pollexfen, Temple, Tipping, and Wiltshire — fail to meet the criteria qualifying them as radical Whigs, though it should be noted that Temple worked hand-in-glove with the radical Whigs in the Convention. Two Whigs, Jephson and Littleton, may be provisionally designated radical.[29] The rest of the Whigs — eighteen of them — qualify as radical in 1689, including Boscawen, the Foley brothers, the Hampdens (father and son), Howard, Sacheverell, Somers, Treby, and Wharton.

The presence of so many powerful radical Whigs assured that the first rights committee would advocate substantial reform and promote the abdication and vacancy resolution. Their presence made it likely that the entire committee would become familiar with the rights and reform tract literature, some of which one among them (Wildman) had written, and another (Somers) collected. The radical Whigs were responsible for the first draft of Heads of Proposals, and it was they who insisted upon connecting the claim of rights to the offer of the throne. It was they whom Morrice had in mind when he wrote that on Treby's committee were men of "ability, integrity, and prospect," who, he was confident, would make it impossible for other men, called "intreaguers," to "delude" the committee.[30]

The "intreaguers" Morrice referred to were the fourteen Tories. Among them were Finch, a former solicitor-general; Sawyer, a former attorney-general; and Sir Christopher Musgrave, one of the "old parliament men," trained as a lawyer, and said to be the "leader of the high Tories and the country gentlemen."[31] The most distinguished Tory was Sir Edward Seymour. A leader of the Tories in the West Country, a man of monumental ego, twice Speaker of the House during the 1670s, and an experienced Parliament man, he was, according to Burnet, the "ablest man of his party."[32] Seymour's circle included his brother-in-law, Sir Joseph Tredenham (together they represented St. Mawe's, Cornwall), his son Henry Seymour (not on the rights committees), and Lord Falkland. The presence of eminent Tory lawyers of stature comparable to those among the Whigs underlines that a strong case in law could be made in support of opposing views. These Tories had legal talent, political skill, and parliamentary experience sufficient to make their views important and to compensate for their minority status.

The nineteen lawyers or men trained in the law dominated both committees.[33] On Treby's committee of thirty-nine (forty), the nineteen lawyers formed a near majority, while on Somers's committee of twenty-one (twenty-two), the thirteen lawyers were a clear majority. Equally as important as their numbers was their previous legal distinction. There were two former solicitors-general, one attorney-general, and three serjeants-at-law.[34] At least six others held or had held the post of recorder in local boroughs.[35] The office of recorder of London, a position of great eminence,[36] was occupied by Treby from 1681 to 1683 and by Holt from 1685 to 1686. Somers refused it in the fall of 1688, and in December 1688 Treby resumed this post. After the revolution these same men were rewarded with the highest legal offices: Giles Eyre and Wogan were made serjeants-at-law, and Eyre and Gregory became justices of King's Bench; Holt was promoted to chief justice of King's Bench; Treby was made chief justice of the Court of Common Pleas, and Somers became solicitor-general and later lord chancellor.

Some of the lawyers, moreover, had taken part in the major legal trials of the era which, in effect, tested the political power and philosophy of the Court and the Whig opposition in the courtroom. They had won renown from this participation. For example, Finch and Sawyer for the prosecution, and Williams, Pollexfen, Maynard, and Treby for the defense, argued the case of Edward Fitzharris in 1681, a case which signaled the opening of Charles II's legal campaign against the Whigs.[37] Or again, in the quo warranto proceedings against London in 1681-82, Finch and Sawyer for the crown confronted Treby and Pollexfen for the City. Pollexfen and Holt were lawyers for the defense of Lord William Russell, the Whig martyr who was executed for treason in 1683. Finally, most of the legal team for the defense and one of the prosecutors in the trial of the Seven Bishops, arguably the most famous legal proceeding of the late seventeenth century and certainly the most important with respect to the Revolution of 1688-89, were on the committees.[38]

These professional links were reinforced by ties of kinship and friendship. Pollexfen and Treby were cousins. Pollexfen was one of Somers's patrons, responsible for the younger man's appointment to the defense team for the Seven Bishops.[39] Holt and Maynard were friends, the former being returned to the Convention by Maynard's safe seat, Bere Alston, Devon.[40] The lawyers shared common background in their education and legal training. At least eleven of them — including Treby, Somers, and Williams — were educated at Oxford,[41] and at least two, at Cambridge.[42] All the Inns of Court were represented; but Gray's Inn and Middle Temple, where both chairmen were trained, claimed the most alumni — six each.[43] The lawyers, then, had known and worked with each other and had built up connections long before serving on these rights committees. This fact must have strengthened their influence as a group.

The lawyers took a prominent part in debate in the Convention and in committee meetings.[44] Some possessed rhetorical talent. Treby enlivened two debates by making a prosopopoeia of James II, that is, imitating the king by gesture and/or voice.[45] Williams injected a humorous note when, having excoriated James II for fleeing to France, he said in an aside, "We never liked anything of France but their wine that indeed we like very well."[46] Not all the lawyers, however, were spellbinders. Somers (and others) loaded their speeches with references to history, statutes, and law cases. One of the younger M.P.'s became so impatient that he complained that "some of the Counsel talk as if they were instructing Juries."[47] Further, lawyers were sensitive to nuances in the meaning of words, rather more so than persons not trained in the law. It is legitimate to assume that those of them who assisted in framing the Declaration of Rights considered carefully what they were saying and what political impression they wished to convey. The debate about the words "abdication" and "vacancy" reveals as much. Such concern invited precision, when that served the purpose, or permitted pretense, when subterfuge was required. Macaulay and others have complained about the debates in the Convention, describing them as wrangling over words, but the words were informed with meaning that the principals well understood. The same is true of the language and organization of the Declaration of Rights.

Lawyers, of course, possessed to a high degree attitudes characteristic of the "legal mind."[48] They reverenced England's ancient constitution, regarding it as prescriptive and precedential in nature and based upon immemorial custom — the principles of common law.[49] Common law, it was believed, revealed itself over time in the decisions of judges and sometimes in statutes. Lawyers tended to argue in historical and legal terms, citing events in the history of England and sometimes other nations, referring to learned commentators such as Bracton, Fortescue, Coke, Selden, Grotius, and Pufendorf, and calling upon old statutes. But reverence for the past and dependence upon history and precedent as argument did not mean unwillingness to change the law and reform the government. In 1673, for example, an M.P. remarked that "laws, when first made, were necessary, and in process of time useless, and may be repealed." In that same debate another M.P. said that "laws may be useful today, and not tomorrow." In 1689 a lawyer — Eyre — argued that precedents for an act cannot always be found; as he demurred, " 'Tis not in every King's reign that he abdicates the government."[50] Lawyers were willing to turn to "necessity" to justify their actions. Further, interest in codifying the laws (although it proved to be abortive) was a feature of legal thinking from Bacon to Sir Matthew Hale. In part it reflected the assumption that old laws could not necessarily apply to the contemporary situation and that a prudent pruning of them was essential.[51] Obviously, statutes not only declared (that is, revealed) the law; they also made new law to deal with new circumstances.[52] The call to decide what powers the king should have and what not — that is, the motion to bring in "heads" that would secure the nation against a repetition of James's policies, the step leading to the Declaration of Rights — itself reflected the recognition that law was flexible, and that it and the constitution could be reformed. Further, the scientific revolution had an impact upon the legal mind in ways that encouraged change. The interest in science promoted an interest in systemization of knowledge, a concern for probability in evidence rather than absolute certainty, an emphasis on judicial impartiality, and a willingness to use civil law and foreign legal systems.[53] Such attitudes have special pertinence to the interest in judicial reform reflected in the Declaration of Rights.

The partisan political allegiance of the lawyers was almost equally divided between Tory and Whig: eight to eleven.[54] Tory lawyers such as Finch, Musgrave, and Sawyer were powerful individuals whose voice on "abdication" found enforcement from the erstwhile Whig, Williams. Their presence helps explain the conservative character of the final version of the Declaration of Rights. The eleven Whig lawyers were men of like political and legal significance. Some among them had had close connections with the "first Whigs." Shaftesbury had rated four (Maynard, Sacheverell, Treby, and Wogan) as "worthy" or "honest." Six, including Somers and Treby, had favored Exclusion, while seven — among them Pollexfen, Somers, and

Treby — were sympathetic to Nonconformity. The point is that previous political and legal experiences guaranteed that the Whig lawyers basically favored restrictions on royal prerogatives.

Tension was predictable between devotion to the ancient constitution, based on immemorial common law, and concern to restrict the monarchy and enlarge and protect the rights of Parliament and subject. As will be seen, this tension produced some ambivalence in the attitude of the lawyers towards the Declaration of Rights. This ambivalence also partly explains the "swing to the right" that the committee took when it sacrificed many of the claims in the first draft of the document. In so doing, the lawyers could say that they were simply restoring the ancient constitution. Yet, at the same time, they willingly placed in the category of "old rights restored" rights which they of course knew were not old, established, "undoubted" law. It was a time-honored device in English political history to describe new law as old law. Scholars seem to have forgotten this in their uncritical acceptance of the language of the Declaration of Rights.

Finally, other legal considerations produced some tension in the minds of the lawyers over drafting a claim of rights. It was the lawyers who advanced the argument that, whatever the claims to the contrary, the claim of rights could not, technically speaking, carry legal weight, for there was no king and the Convention was an irregular body. It was a lawyer who pointed out that William, as king, could not be held to a paper he might sign or swear to as prince. The lawyers, in particular, feared that to claim as rights all the rights in the first draft, many of which were obviously not old rights, was to risk imperiling all rights. These considerations also underlay the "swing to the right" and also competed with the Whiggish political principles to which the majority of the lawyers subscribed.

Many committee members came from parts of England that had favored parliament. For example, eight men came from Bucks, five from Devon, four from Cornwall, and three each from Hereford and Wilts. Bucks, Devon, and Wiltshire were counties strongly in favor of Exclusion; Devon was an area in which Dissent flourished.[55] Seven of the forty-three had the honor to represent their counties; three, the Universities (two from Oxford, one from Cambridge); and thirty-three sat for boroughs.[56]

A contemporary tract unfriendly to William and his friends charged that they had employed every effort to have elected men with some personal grievance against James, men whom the king had "discountenanced, or browbeaten," or declared outlaw.[57] The charge cannot be proved, but it is true that at least twelve committee members had suffered some personal affront during the reigns of Charles II and/or James II. For example, Treby had been dismissed from his post as Recorder of London; Wharton's house was searched for evidence of his complicity in the Rye House Plot; and Williams was prosecuted and heavily fined for licensing, while Speaker of the House of Commons, a tract offensive to Charles II's government.[58]

Fourteen of the forty-three committeemen responsible for drafting the

Declaration of Rights were closely identified in early 1689 with the prince of Orange.[59] For example, William Jephson, William's private secretary, was the fifth man appointed to Treby's committee, being named ahead of far more distinguished members. Among other devoted adherents of the prince in early 1689 were members of the community of English exiles in Holland, including Thomas Tipping, described as "notorious a Whig as any in the country,"[60] who had fled England because of an unsavory breach-of-trust suit, and was exempted from James's general pardon in October 1688. Tipping's family connections reinforced his hatred of the Stuart kings. He was the nephew of Lady Alice Lisle, who was executed, following a trial notable for Judge Jeffreys's excessive brutality, on a charge of complicity in Monmouth's Rebellion. Alice's husband was the regicide John Lisle, who became president of Cromwell's High Court of Justice and was murdered in 1664 by a royalist at Lausanne, where he had sought refuge. Another former exile was William Harbord, formerly secretary to Lord Essex when he was lord-lieutenant in Ireland, said to be "too given to faction,"[61] and reportedly ambitious (to the amusement of the prince's intimates)[62] to be named a secretary of state. These former exiles contributed to William's overestimation of the strength of radicalism in England. Once the prince landed, however, and made contact with prominent men in England, their influence decreased.[63] Their presence on the committees is important because, in view of their background and convictions, these men could be counted on absolutely to support William.

That men close to William were on the committees means that the prince had access to information about the steps in drafting the document and also that members could have known of William's attitude toward the claim of rights. William's friends would have promoted the argument that the prince should not be overloaded with restrictions which he did not favor, and that Englishmen could trust him not to invade their rights. In short, their presence was another consideration that explains the committees' swing to the right.

The rights committeemen in the House of Commons also had connections with the rights committee and other peers in the House of Lords. For example, Holt was one of the legal counsel appointed to advise the upper House. Sir Robert Cotton and William Etterick were Danby's protégés. Wharton's father, Philip, an intimate of Richard Hampden, was on the Lords rights committee. Jephson's closest friend was Lord Lovelace, who organized a petition to both Houses to proclaim William and Mary king and queen immediately. Lovelace was Wildman's father-in-law. There were five sons of peers who after the revolution themselves inherited the title.[64] Such relationships meant that strategically placed men in both Houses had access to current information about what the other House was saying and doing with respect to the abdication and vacancy resolution and the claim of rights. Such information may be another factor that explains the willingness of the Commons' committees to moderate their claim of rights.

All of the committeemen came from the same general privileged classes. Without exception they were landed gentry, wealthy merchants, well-to-do lawyers, servants of the crown, or military leaders. Among them were fourteen knights, seven baronets, and, as just noted, five sons of peers, who after the revolution were raised to the peerage.[65] Whereas the Civil Wars of the 1640s and the governments of the Cromwellian interlude had created situations in which men of humble social origins had taken a direct part in government and in political speculation, no such condition existed in 1688–89. England's traditional ruling groups — the peerage, both spiritual and temporal; the landed gentry, both greater and lesser; and the wealthy urban commercial, moneyed, and professional interests — were restored at the Restoration. If anything, they were more secure now than they had been before the mid-century upheaval. As Professor Plumb has insisted,[66] James II's attempt to reduce the status and interfere with the privileges and position of this ruling elite was one of the most important reasons for the Revolution of 1688–89. Such men regarded the Declaration of Rights, in part, as a way to restore their personal liberties. Moreover, such men abhorred the idea of rebellion and feared the power of the mob.

The men responsible for the Declaration of Rights were in a vortex of frenzied activity during the weeks the Convention met; they dominated all aspects of the proceedings. Of the thirty members selected to serve the Convention in some way, fourteen were on the committees drafting the Declaration of Rights. Of the 293 assignments made to the nine committees appointed between January 22 and February 13, two-thirds, or 180 slots, went to these men.[67] In their own persons they forged a link between the abdication and vacancy resolution and the Declaration of Rights. Over half of the forty-three men who participated in the debate on January 28 which ended in formulating that resolution were appointed the next day to Treby's committee. Twenty-four of twenty-seven persons appointed on February 2 to draw up reasons against the Lords' amendments to the abdication and vacancy resolution also served on the Treby or Somers committee. Obviously the men who were drafting the statement about rights knew concurrently what was being thought and done with respect to the abdication and vacancy resolution. It could not have been otherwise: the same men were shaping the two statements. The assertion that the two measures moved through the Convention quite independently of each other[68] distorts understanding of the drafting process. The overlapping committee assignments help explain the linking of the resolutions into a package that became the Declaration of Rights.

Also on the committee were men who had connections of one kind or another with the press. Treby had defended, in the 1670s, a radical Whig printer, John Starkey, and formed close, friendly ties with him.[69] Somers was on intimate terms with Jacob Tonson, the London bookseller. Somers had written at least three major tracts during the Exclusion Crisis defending certain Whig policies and was a collector of contemporary pamphlets. Wildman was the probable author of at least two tracts printed in the fall of 1688 to support the prince and the rights of the nation. Williams had defended a man for printing a libel on Chief Justice William Scroggs, and had himself published several speeches which he had delivered while Speaker of the House of Commons to retaliate against a charge that he had used extravagant language against the "abhorrers" in 1680.[70] Eyre was possibly the author of a tract printed shortly after the revolution to justify the terms of the settlement.[71] Finally, Hobart is notable for having moved on the first day of the Convention that the votes be printed.[72] Possibly one or all of these men had something to do with the fact that the draft reports of the Declaration of Rights of February 2, 7, and 11 appeared in print in violation of the orders of the House.

There were also on the committees men of considerably less prestige and influence. For example, among Tory backbenchers was Cotton, member from Cambridgeshire, who served only on Treby's committee in the Convention.[73] Another lesser figure was Etterick, a "new" man in the Convention, regarded as being "in the service of" Danby, indeed as Danby's "mouthpiece" in the House of Commons.[74] In view of Danby's prominent role in drafting William's *Declaration of Reasons,*[75] the manifesto which influenced the content and passage of the Declaration of Rights, and of his presence on the rights committee in the House of Lords, the connection he had with the Commons' committees through these two members may be of a significance which the surviving evidence fails to explain.

Among Whig backbenchers was Edmund Waller II (1652-1700).[76] Third son and heir of the distinguished poet, Waller, a "new" M.P., was possibly a Dissenter in 1689 and became a Quaker, although not a firm one, later. A graduate of Oxford, a member of the Middle Temple, and a member of Shaftesbury's Green Ribbon Club until 1681, he had unsuccessfully opposed a Tory candidate in the election of 1685. Yet, James's regulators recommended him as a deputy lieutenant in 1687, and Waller may have been one of the king's Whig collaborators. But when William landed, he joined the prince. Later, in 1697-98, he was a member of the "club" that wrote some of the anti-army tracts and was said to have had a hand in arranging the publication of one of them.[77]

Although these men did not play a prominent role, they must have communicated the work of the committee to their own circles of friends and sources of influence within and without the House. It is reasonable to speculate that they helped to spread knowledge of the issues and the thinking on them and helped thereby to win general concurrence of the House to the Declaration of Rights.

The attributes that make up this composite profile of committee members help illuminate the nature and passage of the Declaration of Rights. A group of politically experienced men, knowledgeable about parliamentary procedures, accustomed to political negotiations, many of them professionally trained in the law, was well equipped to draft a complex constitutional and political statement. Their voices were recognized as authoritative; what they recommended with respect to the Declaration of Rights must have weighed with the House. They knew how to handle objections voiced in the House of Commons and the House of Lords and accept compromise. Furthermore, these men shared a common political tradition and many experiences in Parliament in efforts whose underlying principles would be set out in the Declaration of Rights. They also had in common an intellectual heritage that had been shaped by parliamentarianism and political inquiry reaching back to the Civil War decades and to the Popish Plot–Exclusion Crisis. Although none was an avowed republican, this group had been influenced by republicans and Nonconformity. At the time of the revolution these men were still close to that heritage. Tension developed between their political principles on the one hand, and their respect for law and the ancient constitution on the other. The relative strength of parties, the power of personal ambition, and the attitude of Prince William were other factors important to the drafting process. In the end, the final version of the Declaration of Rights claimed much less than did the first draft, and it won widespread approval. The final text and the manner of presenting the document testify to the parliamentary, political, and legal skill of the principals. Dominated by radical Whigs, the committees drafted a document informed by Whig principles and shaped it to seem to be what in fact it strictly speaking was not: a condition which William had to accept to win the throne and a legal condition on the powers of the kingship.

3
Leaders of the Rights Committees in the House of Commons

O f the forty-three members on the two House of Commons committees, the two chairmen, Treby and Somers, and six others —
Falkland, Richard Hampden, Pollexfen, Temple, Wharton, and
Williams — stand out for the special contributions they made to the drafting
and managing the passage of the Declaration of Rights. Treby and Somers
undoubtedly exercised the major responsibility, but recognition also belongs
to the six members who were chosen to perform certain tasks for the committees, a mark of favor indicating their above-average interest in the proceedings and almost certainly their presence at committee meetings.

Sir George Treby (1643-1700) was well suited to serve as chairman of the
committee that wrote the first two drafts of the Declaration of Rights.[1] Born
in Plympton Erle, Devon, in 1643, he was in 1689 a lawyer of established
reputation, a radical Whig, an experienced parliamentarian, a friend of
Nonconformity, and, as Recorder of London, in a position to provide a
direct link with the City. Treby's connections with the left wing of the Whig
party were close. Educated at Oxford and the Middle Temple and called to
the bar in 1671, he won, over the next few years, a reputation in Devonshire
politics as an opponent of the court. By 1677 he was known to be working
with his cousin, Pollexfen, and Devonshire Dissenters to promote "the good
cause," probably, that is, assisting Dissenters and working for parliamentary
candidates opposed to Charles II. The electors of his hometown returned him
to Parliament in a by-election in 1677 and in every election thereafter, except
that of 1685. Treby received advice about national issues from his constituents and was apparently receptive to their views.[2]

In London, Treby rapidly became identified with critics of the court. He
joined the Green Ribbon Club,[3] served Shaftesbury as liaison between his
followers in London and those in Devonshire,[4] and received a "worthy"
rating from the earl. In November 1677 he defended John Starkey, a radical

Sir George Treby (1643–1700)

A well-known lawyer, earlier a member of the Green Ribbon Club and an associate of the first earl of Shaftesbury, Treby chaired the first rights committee in the House of Commons and piloted the first two drafts of the Declaration of Rights through the House. (Courtesy of the National Portrait Gallery, London.)

Whig printer and possibly a member of the Green Ribbon Club, who was accused of reprinting without a license a "dangerous" book, Nathaniel Bacon's *Historical Discourse of the Uniformity of Government of England,* ascribed to the famous jurist John Selden.[5] Starkey continued to print material offensive to the Stuart government. He also used the press to influence the revolutionary settlement, printing for the third time on January 10, 1689, Bacon's *Historical Discourse*. Starkey and Treby became and remained friends.[6]

In Parliament Treby rose to prominence on the wave of the frenzy over the Popish Plot and the Exclusion Crisis. He chaired the Committee of Secrecy for investigating the Popish Plot and in 1679–80 served as one of the managers of the impeachment of the five Popish lords, among whom was John Belasyse, Baron Belasyse. (It should be noted for its possible significance in 1689, discussed below, that Belasyse was the uncle of Thomas Belasyse, Viscount Fauconberg, the chairman of the committee in the House of Lords in 1689 to which the draft Declaration of Rights was referred.) At the direction of the House of Commons, Treby edited and printed in 1681 the information he had collected,[7] thus bringing himself into direct contact with the publishing world. Observers thought that he was as "likely as any man" to be elected Speaker in 1680, but his poor eyesight, said to hinder his ability to identify members, disqualified him.[8]

Treby's appointment as recorder of London in December 1680 testified further to his growing reputation. This position brought him to the center of the struggle between King Charles II and the opposition in the City. Treby's role in several episodes exposed him to criticism. For example, despite objections from the court, Treby, with a group of extreme Whigs in the City government, in 1680 presented to the king a petition requesting that he immediately call a parliament. Treby managed to escape Charles II's censure, which fell on the London sheriffs.[9] Or again, Edward Fitzharris, who was charged with high treason, accused Treby in print of suborning him to implicate Danby, John Belasyse, and other Popish lords in the murder of Sir Edmund Berry Godfrey. Treby denied the charge in a tract printed in 1681. He insisted that Fitzharris's "confession" exonerated Danby from connection with Godfrey's murder, and accused the court of inspiring Fitzharris's charge of subornation against him to discredit the Whigs. The tract illustrates again Treby's personal awareness of the political uses of the press.[10] Moreover, in the course of his duties as recorder, Treby signed the warrant for the execution of the Whig martyr Lord Russell by the means specified in the treason law — hanging, drawing, and quartering.[11] Although Charles II commuted the sentence to simply beheading, Treby's signing of the warrant still rankled in 1689 with Russell's family and friends in the House of Lords, Bedford (Russell's father) and Devonshire. It cost him appointment as one of the legal counsel to the peers, and it took intervention by Pollexfen — who explained that his cousin was only fulfilling his duties, and had not signed the warrant until reassured by Russell himself — to reconcile Treby and the lords.[12]

Treby used his position as recorder to try, albeit unsuccessfully, to advance the interests of Shaftesbury and the Whigs in the election of Thomas Papillon and John Dubois as sheriff in 1682.[13] He also played an important role in the quo warranto proceedings, unsuccessfully defending the rights of the corporation against the king. In the wake of these proceedings, Treby was dismissed from the post of recorder in 1683.

Treby continued during James II's reign to oppose the court. He appeared before the Ecclesiastical Commission in support of Exeter College's rejection of a fellow appointed to it,[14] and "absolutely refused" in 1686 to argue in Hales's case that the king could dispense with the law.[15] He was one of the counsel for the defense of the Seven Bishops. He resisted importunities in the fall of 1688 that he resume his former position as recorder of London until after James had fled. Reinstated on December 16, Treby used his post to further Prince William's interests in the City. He contrived arguments why the City should *not* congratulate James upon his return to the City after his abortive first flight, and served on the committee that drew up London's address of welcome to William.[16] Deputizing for the ailing mayor of London, Treby headed the procession of city magnates who officially welcomed the prince and made an "excellent" speech which was immediately printed.[17] Further, Treby helped collect a loan for William from the City.[18] Also during these weeks he was called upon to advise whether or not bail should be allowed Robert Brent, the despised agent of James II who was most responsible for regulating the corporations. Treby (and others) recommended bail, as required by law. Brent fled to France. For this advice, Treby was criticized in the Convention on February 6, the day before the second rights committee was appointed.[19]

Treby's personal qualities may have recommended him as chairman. A handsome man, middle-sized, with black hair and a ruddy complexion, Treby was said to be sweet and smiling and to carry himself with "grace and briskness." Although he lived splendidly, he was pious, without hypocrisy, and easy of access.[20] A confident and skilled orator, Treby added vivid moments to the debates by imitating James II through accent or gesture, and he was singled out as speaking "very well" in the February 6 conference meeting between the two Houses, a debate in which several men distinguished for their oratorical abilities took part.[21] His reputed "steady temper," sharp judgment, piety, and "freedom" from "pride," "censure," and "moroseness" were also characteristics desirable in a chairman.[22] But the members of Commons probably chose Treby as chairman of the first rights committee because he was an experienced parliamentarian, an able lawyer, and a man known to favor the prince and the rights and liberties of the nation.

For all his virtues Treby failed to be appointed chairman of the committee that prepared the final version of the Declaration of Rights. Had there been no negative factors in Treby's background, it seems unlikely that the committee would have chosen the less senior and less experienced Somers. The committee may well have decided that it was impolitic to entrust the chairmanship to a person who might provoke hostility for reasons extraneous to the committee's report. In the upper House there were lords who had already expressed anger over Treby's signing Russell's death warrant. Fauconberg, the chairman of the Lords' rights committee, and Danby, a member of the committee, had reason to dislike Treby because of his involvement in the Fitzharris case. In the lower House members had "reflected" on Treby for advising bail for Brent. Furthermore, notwithstanding the moderation of his remarks in the Convention, Treby, as politically informed men knew, was a radical Whig, a former member of the Green Ribbon Club, and closely identified with Shaftesbury. Under the circumstances — when Tories and the upper House would have to be brought along if a settlement and a claim of rights were to be achieved quickly, and when frequent contacts between the two Houses in conference meeting were expected — committee members may have felt it wise to choose a less controversial person.

However it may be explained, John Somers (1651–1716) was designated chairman of the committee that linked the claim of rights to the other resolutions the Convention passed. Like Treby, Somers was a lawyer and, at this time, a radical Whig. Younger than the average committeeman, Somers, at thirty-eight, was just beginning to achieve national recognition as a lawyer and author. Educated at Oxford and the Middle Temple, Somers had made himself master of civil and common law, of history, languages, poetry, contemporary literature, classics, and the works of English and Continental political and legal commentators. His erudition and legal knowledge, displayed in the first major debate of the Convention, must account in part for his appointment to the rights committees and his emergence as chairman of the second committee, for Somers was serving for the first time in Parliament and did not have the personal connections and knowledge of parliamentary affairs that many members of the committees did have. Described as an "ugly man," Somers was said to possess a "remarkably beautiful voice," [23] which may also have charmed the House.

But Somers was not unknown to men on the committee. Earlier he had been associated with advanced Whigs. For example, Somers and Charles Blount, the freethinker and mortalist, both born in Worcestershire, entered the Middle Temple the same year (1669). No evidence has survived of a close connection between the two men, but they shared admiration for Milton.[24] It is possible that a common interest in Milton also drew together Somers, a friend of Nonconformity, and John Toland, the most famous of late-seventeenth-century deists.[25] Another Whig acquaintance, dating from 1672, was Charles Talbot, twelfth earl of Shrewsbury, whose estates Somers's father managed. Shrewsbury introduced Somers to Lord Russell and Algernon Sidney. Somers was said also to be an intimate of Lord Essex. A friendly connection with Shaftesbury rests upon circumstantial evidence,[26] but Somers did know persons close to the earl, such as John Freke and Edward Clarke, and through them was introduced to John Locke, with whom he became close friends after the revolution.[27]

Other left-wing Whigs with whom Somers was intimate prior to 1689 were Sir Francis Winnington (his patron and mentor), a solicitor-general under Charles II, and Sir William Jones, an attorney-general. Both were deeply involved in opposition politics: Winnington sacrificed his office to oppose the king, and he and Jones took a leading part in the attack on Danby in 1679 and in the Exclusion Crisis.

Lord John Somers (1651–1716)

A rising young lawyer elected to Parliament for the first time in 1689, Somers chaired the second rights committee in the House of Commons and initiated steps that led to linking the claim of rights to the offer of the crown. (Courtesy of the National Portrait Gallery, London.)

Somers had also established a reputation prior to the revolution as an author of polemical tracts in opposition to the policies of the Stuart court. Three major pamphlets in which Somers had a hand appeared in 1680 and 1681. The first, *A Brief History of the Succession, Collected out of the Records and the Most Authentical Historians* (1680), addressed the question whether Parliament could settle the succession and answered that history proved that it could. Well-organized, lucidly written, and copiously documented, the tract provoked several replies from firm proponents of the crown, including the well-known Dr. Robert Brady. It was reprinted in 1688–89 in time to influence the deliberations of the Convention, and was also translated into Dutch.[28]

A second pamphlet, *A Just and Modest Vindication of the Proceedings of the Last Two Parliaments* (1681), was thought to have been written by Jones and Somers, with Algernon Sidney perhaps assisting. It displayed Somers's attitude on specific issues that would appear in the Declaration of Rights: (1) that Parliament should be held annually and not prorogued or dissolved until its business was finished, and that the constitution would be imperfect if the king could summon and dismiss Parliament at pleasure;[29] (2) that the king had no power to suspend or dispense with laws; (3) that the right of petitioning should be guaranteed; (4) that a standing army in time of peace was "odious to a free people"; (5) that freedom of debate in Parliament was essential to liberty.[30]

The third tract, *The Security of Englishmen's Lives; or, The Trust, Power, and Duty of the Grand Jurys of England* (1681), responded to court tracts that had excoriated the Middlesex grand jury for its failure to indict Shaftesbury and others for treason. The pamphlet explicated the procedures of English justice, stressing that the "fundamental of government" is the jury system, both grand and petit.[31] Somers insisted that jurors should be of equal social condition with the person under indictment. Jurors, rather than judges, are responsible for the "Reputation, the Fortunes, and the Lives of Englishmen."[32] The "Trust and Power of Grand Juries" are next to those of Parliament.[33] It is essential that jurors be independent of judges if subjects are to be protected, for judges are often corrupted by passion, interest, or the wishes of greater men.[34] This tract, like *A Just and Modest Vindication,* is of special interest because it addressed some issues that appeared in the claim of rights eight years later.

Somers had also built up a reputation as a promising lawyer. When the Whigs were defeated in 1683, he devoted the next few years to the practice of law. In 1683 he was among the lawyers who defended four London sheriffs charged with inciting a riot in the election of sheriffs in 1682. In 1688, at the insistence of Pollexfen, who described him as the "man who would take the most pains, and go deepest into all that depended on precedents and records," Somers assisted in the defense of the Seven Bishops. In that case he argued that the dispensing power was "contrary to law," a view to which he adhered in drafting the Declaration of Rights. His performance advanced his reputation, for within five months he was offered the post of recorder of London, which he declined, but shortly thereafter he accepted the position of recorder of Worcester.[35]

There is no evidence, as is sometimes claimed, that Somers was deeply involved in the conspiracy to bring over the prince, or that he assisted in writing either the "invitation" or the draft of the prince's manifesto, *The Declaration of Reasons.* Somers was elected to the Convention by Worcester. The first draft of the Declaration of Rights reflected views he had set out in earlier tracts. As chairman of the second rights committee, Somers saw to it that the claim of rights should not be lost by insisting that it be linked to the offer of the crown. That contribution alone is enough to secure his importance in the success of the Declaration of Rights, but there is no evidence that he should be credited with authoring the entire document. Treby has much better claim to that honor. But, in truth, both men shared the responsibility for drafting and passing the document with other men on the committee and in the House.

Anthony Cary, fifth Viscount Falkland (1656–94), a Tory, was the person who took the initiative on January 29 in calling for consideration of the rights of the nation before settling the question of who should be king. Little is known about him. A grandson of the second Viscount Falkland, secretary of state to Charles I, and with Sir John Colepeper author of the famous *Answer to the Nineteen Propositions,*[36] Falkland was first elected to Parliament in 1685. There he showed willingness to cooperate with King James, going so far as to sponsor a bill for indemnifying Catholic officers. His confirmation as deputy-lieutenant of Oxfordshire in February 1688 almost certainly reveals that his answers to James's "three questions" were satisfactory to the court.[37] Described as having a "pretty brisk understanding," Falkland also held the post of treasurer of the navy. In 1689, he was returned to the Convention from Great Marlowe, Bucks. His initiative in introducing a proposal of such far-reaching implications in an assembly of distinguished and seasoned men is puzzling. For now, it is enough to notice that his proposal to determine what powers to give to the king and what not was intrinsically radical, far more likely to appeal to Whigs than to Tories. Further, he was on friendly terms with Sir Edward Seymour, his senior and a former Speaker of the House, a powerful leader of the Tories in former parliaments. He had purchased the post of treasurer of the navy from Sir Edward in 1681 and was to become indebted to him for his election to Parliament for Great Bedwin in 1690.[38] Seymour was one of three Tories to vote against the abdication and vacancy resolution. Neither he nor Falkland, who apparently favored Princess Mary, wanted to place William on the throne of England. Their connection and political goals are reasons for the hypothesis (discussed below) that Falkland's motion concealed a partisan parliamentary tactic by Tories aimed at delaying the proceedings of the Convention.

Sir Richard Temple (1634–97), a former Tory who was zealously for the Whigs in 1689, was sharply different from Falkland. An "old parliament man," Sir Richard had, long before 1689, won a reputation for wide knowledge of parliamentary procedure and historical precedent. In the Cavalier Parliament, he served on 314 committees, acted as teller on ten occasions, and made 212 recorded speeches.[39] His appointment to eight of nine committees in the Convention indicates that this respect continued. Sir Richard's parliamentary career, like that of many Restoration M.P.'s, was marked by opportunism, personal selfishness, and concern for the interests of the House of Commons and of one class — the landed gentry.[40] Temple joined the opposition to spite Charles II for not rewarding him adequately at the Restoration, to win personal recognition, and to protect the integrity of the House of Commons against perceived threats from the crown and the House of Lords. For a time, he cut a figure as intrepid critic, arguing so persistently, for example, for enabling machinery in the Triennial Bill of 1664 that he offended moderate men. He supported the impeachment of the earl of Clarendon in 1666, consistently opposed the standing army, and criticized Charles's foreign policy. But in the 1670s, Temple, succumbing to the attractions of lucre and royal favor, accepted the post of commissioner of the customs and a pension from the crown. In these circumstances, he found himself able to argue for Charles's Declaration of Indulgence and against the Test Act, to express disbelief in Titus Oates, and to oppose Danby's impeachment.

In 1683, taking advantage of the court's quo warranto proceedings against borough charters, Temple persuaded the burgesses of Buckingham, who had elected him to every Parliament except in 1656 and 1679, to surrender their charter, and then saw to it that the new charter secured his own position by naming him steward of Buckingham for life and by filling the corporation with his friends. For years Temple had struggled to control local politics by using bribes, treats, and gifts; the promise of timber to build the town hall won him one election and the nickname "Sir Timber Temple." Although he consistently opposed enlarging the electorate, he liked to head the informal poll of freemen and inhabitants (the poll had no legal validity) and spent lavishly to win this sign of popular approval. In 1685, despite intervention by Judge George Jeffreys to prevent his election to James's only parliament, all twelve electors of the borough voted for Temple. In several ways Temple felt the displeasure of the new king. He had supported the Exclusion Bill vigorously enough to be called the "Stoe Monster" by James's supporters,[41] and when early in 1685 he refused to collect the excise without a parliamentary grant, the king dismissed him from his post. In the Parliament of 1685, Temple further irritated the king by opposing his demand for a standing army officered by Catholics. Yet Temple, through incessant importuning, won a pension from James, which the king paid from September 1685 through September 1686. In February 1688, certain of dismissal because of his unsatisfactory answers to James's "three questions," Temple resigned the stewardship of Buckingham. James appointed a Catholic in his place and issued commissions of the peace which advanced Temple's enemies. The king's proposed changes in the corporation were likewise hostile to Temple's interests.

Temple joined the prince of Orange on December 12, 1688, the day after James's flight. Nevertheless, he was suspected of still favoring James, and cries of "no friend of the Prince, no Parliament man" were raised against him in the election in January to the Convention. His opponents unsuccessfully contested his return. In the Convention, Temple acted with the Whigs. From his place at the "uppermost seat"[42] he opposed printing votes, supported the abdication and vacancy resolution, and promoted the Declaration of Rights as a way of achieving substantial change in the government. His notes for his speech on January 29 show the care he exercised in preparing for the debate.[43] Many of the rights he urged as essential appeared in the first draft of the document. Temple's effort to persuade a member of William's Dutch entourage that the Declaration of Rights contained nothing but the recognized rights of the nation testifies further to his special concern.[44] His attitude in 1689 undoubtedly reflected his personal grievances and his assessment of how his personal and class interests might best be served in the crisis. It was consistent with his long-held view that the House of Commons was the most important element in the English government.[45] Temple regained his post at customs after the revolution, prompting a contemporary to compare him to the vicar of Bray and to remark, "Let who will raing, and tho' all hats him [Temple], yet he gets whot he aims at."[46] He remained in the House of Commons as a court-Tory placeman until Whig ministers were successful in removing him in 1694.[47] His papers include a draft of a proviso to the act for restoring corporations which would have exempted from punishment anyone who had surrendered a charter. The draft suggests his continued concern for his own welfare.

Richard Hampden (1631–95), a radical Whig, was perhaps the most beloved member of the rights committees. Son of the famous John Hampden who had led the fight against Charles I's ship money in 1636, Hampden had had much previous experience as a member of Parliament: he served in the Parliament of 1656 and was appointed a member of the House of Lords during the Protectorate. Loyal after the Restoration to the strong Dissenting views of his family, Hampden befriended ministers who had been ejected from their livings as a consequence of the "Clarendon Code." Richard Baxter, the Nonconformist minister, praised him highly, describing him as his "dearly beloved and honored friend," and as the "true heir of his father's sincerity, piety and devotedness to God."[48] In Charles's parliaments[49] he actively supported the interests of Dissenters, arguing for comprehension or indulgence, and, as already noted, was at the center of a circle of prominent Nonconformists. A critic of the king's foreign policy, Hampden promoted the radical proposition that the royal prerogative of making war and peace should be exercised only with the consent of Parliament.[50] In 1677 he supported a bill to disband the standing army. He was in the forefront of the effort to exclude James from the throne, moving the Exclusion Bill of May 1679. Hampden was adamant that a Popish king could not be bound with laws. It was like "binding Samson with withes," he said.[51] Shaftesbury rated him "worthy." Returned to Parliament in 1685, Hampden led the attack on James's standing army and argued for a law to remove the Catholic officers. With his son, John, Richard was among the first of the Presbyterian leaders to declare for William. Meeting in December 1688 with fellow members of Charles II's parliaments summoned by the prince, Hampden was on the committee to draw up the address to William asking him to call a convention and take on the administration of the country until that body convened. He played a prominent role in the Convention. For example, he chaired the committee of the whole on January 28 when the House passed the abdication and vacancy resolution. He skillfully handled that crucial debate in ways that well served Whig interests. Hampden also chaired the committee of the whole on January 29th when the proposal leading to the Declaration of Rights was discussed. Appointed to eight of the nine committees created by the Convention, he performed more tasks (such as reporting from committees and carrying resolutions to the House of Lords) than any other member of the Convention.[52] His intervention at certain points in the passage of the Declaration of Rights was crucial to the survival of the document, and the willingness of the House to follow his lead surely reflected their approbation. Personally devoted to the prince, Hampden declared after the revolution that he served William "as one whom I love."[53] (For his part, William, although he appointed Hampden a privy councillor and in 1690 made him chancellor of the Exchequer, regarded him "with disesteem as to his understanding."[54]) In contrast to Temple, Hampden was a man of rigid integrity who refused a pension when he resigned in 1694, saying that "he had always spoken against giving pensions to others: . . . whilst he had a roll or a can of beer he would not accept sixpence of the money of the nation."[55]

Hampden's apparent gentleness and soft manners were also in contrast to the rough vigor, choleric temper, and intellectual brilliance of Sir William Williams (1634–1700). An experienced parliamentarian, former Speaker of the House, and an able lawyer whose reputation had been made in the defense of Whig martyrs, Williams in 1689 displayed political opportunism, just as he had done earlier in his career. Although his comments in debate suggested otherwise, Williams voted against the abdication and vacancy resolution, thus allying himself with the Tory position.[56] Yet, on the issue of presenting the claim of rights, he forwarded Whig arguments.

Educated at Oxford and Gray's Inn, Williams early gained a reputation as a highly intelligent lawyer and "very acute young gentleman."[57] The city of Chester acknowledged this promise by appointing him recorder in 1667. His entry into national politics was in a by-election in 1673. The local court party favored another candidate and urged Williams to withdraw. Declining the suggestion, Williams fought a hard, ruthless campaign and lost. Disgruntled that the court party had opposed him, Williams thereafter identified with the country opposition. Chester returned him to Parliament in 1675, where he soon became known as an ardent critic of the court. He opposed the grant of supply before redress of grievances, argued against the standing army, and played a major role in the Commons' effort to impeach the king's minister Danby. Although not a member of the Green Ribbon Club, Williams was identified with Shaftesbury, who rated him "worthy" in 1679 and later employed him as his chief legal adviser.[58] At the initiative of Lord Russell, the House of Commons unanimously elected Williams Speaker in the Exclusion Parliament of 1680. A man of "fiery and vicious temper,"[59] he defended the independence of that office so zealously that he refused to make the customary speech of self-abnegation. Following the dissolution of the Oxford Parliament, Williams was engaged as defense counsel for radical Whig defendants (including Algernon Sidney and John Hampden) in the major constitutional actions brought by the court.[60] For this and other reasons, he was very much exposed to attack. In 1684 the court removed Williams from his post as recorder of Chester for having advised in 1681 resistance to the seizure of the municipal charter of Oxford. Also in 1684, at the instigation of Judge Jeffreys, an information was entered against him for having licensed as Speaker of the House in 1680 a tract (Thomas Dangerfield's *Narrative,* impugning the integrity of the Duke of York) which the Court later declared to be a seditious libel. This case was heard in King's Bench in May 1686. With Pollexfen serving as his counsel, Williams rested his defense on the claim that the Court had no jurisdiction over his actions as Speaker of the House of Commons.[61] The proceedings went very poorly for him, and Williams decided to submit himself to the Court. He was fined the enormous sum of £10,000, but thanks to the intervention of the earl of Rochester, James reduced the fine to £8,000. A month later, the earl of Peterborough again brought legal action against him for the same offense. This time, James himself intervened, and Peterborough dropped the charges. Within a year, the king, seeking to take advantage of Williams's legal acumen and of his contacts with Dissenters in the west, restored him to the recordership of Chester and appointed him to the post of solicitor-general. Williams accepted, it was said, because he needed the money to pay his fine.[62] It was in that capacity that he represented the court in the case against the Seven Bishops in June 1688.[63]

His former friends bitterly criticized him as a turncoat. Burnet, for example, characterized him as a "corrupt and vicious man, who had no principles, but followed his own interests." In October 1688 the mob smashed the windows of his rooms in Gray's Inn and "fixt . . . reflecting inscriptions . . . over his door."[64] Williams remained loyal to James until the king failed to call a parliament in the fall of 1688 and to dismiss Jeffreys, whose post he coveted. But on December 16, five days after James's first flight, Williams reverted openly to his former convictions and won an audience with Prince William at Windsor.[65]

Williams represented Beaumaris in the Convention. Although members regarded him with mixed feelings (he was said to "speak very often but not very acceptably to the House"),[66] they appointed him to Treby's committee and added him at the last moment to Somers's committee. Williams did not let fellow M.P.'s forget his former sufferings and evidently excited their sympathy. As will be shown, clause 22 of the Heads of Grievances, calling for the abolition of informations in King's Bench, directly reflected Williams's experience. This clause disappeared in the final draft, but the issue was implicit in article 8 of the list of grievances against James — "By prosecutions in the

Court of King's Bench for matters and causes cognizable only in Parliament" — and in article 9 of the declaratory section of the declaration, which asserted, *inter alia,* that the proceedings in Parliament ought not to be impeached or questioned in any Court or place out of Parliament. The Declaration of Rights served his personal interests well, and it was in terms of his personal interests that Williams, at least in part, championed the claim of rights. Although he cooperated with the Whigs on claiming rights, he voted with the Tories on the abdication and vacancy resolution.

Henry Pollexfen (1632–91), a prominent Whig lawyer, was, like Williams, unable to suffer lesser minds. He had a reputation for being surly and bad-tempered. Pollexfen argued for speed on the part of the Convention and simplicity and brevity in the statement of rights. Acutely conscious of the dangers of delay, sensitive to the illegal status of the Convention and, thus, of any statement of rights it prepared, Pollexfen initially tried to dampen enthusiasm for preparing such a statement.[67] He gave the committee a paper of eight heads presumably to confine its attentions to a limited number of issues. He pointed out that the Convention could not legally hold William as king to something he had agreed to as prince and warned that William might not accept the claim. His concern to hasten the proceedings of the Convention was consistent with the role he had played in December. Then, he had argued that James's flight was a "cession," a forfeiture of royal authority. He urged William to declare himself king and then call a legal parliament. Although not among the prince's intimates, Pollexfen reportedly prepared the circular letters for calling the Convention, reaping the profit therefrom. It is likely that Pollexfen was among members who were responsible for the committee's swing to the right, which resulted in a much-watered-down version of the first draft of the Declaration of Rights.

Although Pollexfen was not among the "worthy" Whigs, his political principles were those of the Whig party. With his cousin Treby and others, he had worked in 1677 in the interests of Noncomformists in Devonshire, where his family had long been established. Roger North, the Tory historian, described him as a "fanatic, and (in the country) frequenter of conventicles."[68] Pollexfen acted for the defense in many of the major cases against Whig political leaders. For example, he was counsel for the city of London in the quo warranto proceedings in 1682, for Lord Russell in 1683, for Sacheverell in 1684, and for Williams in 1686. In 1688 he was among the defense for the Seven Bishops. Yet in 1685, he was one of the prosecutors for the crown at the assizes following Monmouth's Rebellion and presented the evidence for the prosecution against Lady Alice Lisle. This role, for which his Whig friends criticized him, is explained by his being a leader of the circuit.[69] Contemporaries regarded Pollexfen as one of the best lawyers in England, a judgment reflected in the House of Lords's choice of him to advise it in December.[70] Yet, Burnet described him as an "honest and learned but perplexed lawyer."[71] His library, a listing of which survives, attested to wide reading in English and Continental jurisprudence and political theory.[72] It also reveals that he had access to works by Baxter, Harrington, and Machiavelli. Hobbes's *Leviathan* was among his books.

Pollexfen did not serve in Parliament until elected to the convention from Exeter, Devon. His legal reputation undoubtedly preceding him, Pollexfen was appointed to six of nine committees. The fifty-seven-year-old Pollexfen was on intimate terms with the two somewhat younger chairmen of the rights committees. He sought to protect the reputation of his cousin Treby from what he maintained was unjust criticism,[73] and he promoted Somers's career by insisting that Somers be included as a defense counsel for the Seven Bishops. It is possible that he influenced the thinking of both of them; it is noteworthy that at the outset they joined him in expressing reservations about drafting a statement of rights.

The Honorable Thomas Wharton (1648–1715), a radical Whig, must have enlivened the committee meetings with his exuberance of personality, enthusiasm for William, and directness of speech. Said to be "the greatest rake in England," a duelist, and a renowned connoisseur of race horses, Wharton was the son of a strict Calvinist, Philip, fourth Baron Wharton, and was educated privately by an ejected Dissenting minister. His wife, a poetess, was part of Edmund Waller's circle.[74] Wharton had long been connected with the parliamentary opposition. First elected to Parliament in 1673, he was an adherent of Shaftesbury, who rated him "worthy" in 1679. A friend of Lord Russell, he enthusiastically worked for the exclusion of the duke of York, carrying the Exclusion Bill to the House of Lords and moving to indict James for nonattendance at church. He was implicated in the Rye House Plot and suspected of complicity in the Monmouth Rebellion. In the Parliament of 1685, Wharton voted against granting the new king revenue for life on the grounds that the money would be used to maintain and expand a standing army in peacetime.[75]

Wharton was actively involved in the schemes to bring William to England. In early 1687, he was in touch with disaffected Englishmen [76] and perhaps corresponded with the Dutch court.[77] Wharton was part of a circle of Whigs in London which included Jephson; Charles Godfrey, Marlborough's brother-in-law; and Lord Colchester, perhaps Wharton's best friend, who shared his taste for riotous living.[78] One of Wharton's contributions in the spring of 1688 was to travel around the countryside carrying news and keeping up the spirits of the conspirators.[79] Possibly he had a hand in drafting the invitation of June 30.[80] Wharton joined William at Exeter and drew up the address signed by Seymour and others.[81] The arrest of his brother Godwin in October on suspicion of helping William of Orange because he was seen observing the fortifications at Portsmouth must have reinforced Wharton's commitment to the prince.[82] A member of the assembly of M.P.'s from Charles II parliaments that William convened in December, Wharton served on the committee to draft the request that the prince take on the administration of affairs until the Convention convened. He introduced Richard

Hampden, his kinsman, to the prince.[83] Representing Buckinghamshire in the Convention, Wharton was undeviating in his conviction that James should be removed from the throne. In the debate of January 28, 1689, he swept aside theoretical niceties saying, "Whether he [James] may be deposed or deposes himself, he is not our king." And on February 5, 1689, he remarked, "I own driving K. James out; and I would do it again."[84] No political theorist himself, Wharton counted among his friends Andrew Marvell[85] and Henry Neville. He almost certainly wrote "Nicholas Machiavel's Letter to Zanobius Buondelmontius in Vindication of himself and his Writings," which was appended to Neville's printed edition and translation of Machiavelli's complete works in 1675. Under a different title, and with changes to stress the evils of popery and the duty to take up arms against a tyrant, which act should not be regarded as rebellion, the "Letter" was printed in 1689 as a propaganda piece.[86]

Wharton is best known as the author of the song "Lilliburlero." He wrote the words in 1687, and Purcell set them to music. The song was enormously popular. It was said that "all people in city and country were singing it," and Wharton himself boasted that he "had sung a king out of three kindgoms."[87] He combined this liveliness of personality with a shrewd political sense and a decided aversion to Tories.[88] After the settlement, he continued to promote the principles underlying the Declaration of Rights, serving on the committee to translate the document into a statute.

The eight men who had the major part in shaping and passing the Declaration of Rights in the House of Commons were drawn to the project for different reasons. Political principle, partisan considerations, and personal vengeance variously moved them. Four of the eight — the two chairmen and Pollexfen and Williams — were among the most distinguished practicing lawyers of the era. Five had had extensive parliamentary experience. All but two (Falkland and Williams) were in 1689 devoted Whigs. Williams had earlier been closely associated with Whigs and on the matter of the claim of rights continued to be so. Temple, a former Tory, was in 1689 allied with the Whigs. Five were sympathetic to Dissenters; indeed, Richard Hampden was the most important spokesman for Nonconformity of the entire period. Four were radical Whigs: Hampden, Somers, Treby, and Wharton had had connections with Shaftesbury, Exclusion, and Dissent. Temple, while no radical Whig, was determined to achieve a radical reform in the government. It is reasonable to think that these men took the lead in framing the first draft of the Declaration of Rights. Also among the leaders were persons of conservative bent, just as Tories and Whigs were divided on the committees. The final version of the Declaration of Rights reflected this division; the first radical draft was amended to assure that Conservatives (both Whigs and Tories), the House of Lords, and the prince of Orange would agree to it.

4

Rights in the Declaration of Rights

❖

The Declaration of Rights dealt in thirteen articles with twelve inter-related rights.[1] The rights committee in the House of Commons chose the rights from among those set out in the twenty-eight clauses of the Heads of Grievances. All the articles touched on the prerogatives of the king. They dealt with three general questions: (1) royal power with respect to law — the right to suspend and dispense with laws, the right to create an ecclesiastical commission, and several legal procedures; (2) royal military authority with respect to a standing army in time of peace, and the right of the subjects, under certain restrictions, to bear arms; and (3) royal power of taxation. In each of these areas, the Declaration of Rights affirmed the ultimate sovereignty of Parliament. The document addressed the integrity of Parliament in other ways, claiming the rights of free elections, free speech and debates and proceedings, and frequent meetings. Furthermore, it guaranteed the individual certain rights — to petition the king without fear of reprisal; to bear arms (under certain restrictions); to be protected against excessive bail, excessive fines, and cruel and unusual punishments; and to be spared the granting and promising of fines and forfeitures before conviction.

The purpose of this chapter is to discuss briefly the political and constitutional background of each issue. When the declaration is approached from an historical perspective, rather than viewed in terms of its later influence, as is usually done, the significance of what the document did and did not accomplish is clarified. Such an approach also assists in understanding the choice and priority of the issues, the tension among partisan groups during the drafting process, and, most important, the nature of the document — whether it was indeed no more than a reaffirmation of old, indisputable rights, and whether all the grievances charged against King James II were violations of the laws of England.

Article 1

That the pretended power of suspending of laws or the execution of laws by regal authority without consent of Parliament is illegal.

Article 2

That the pretended power of dispensing with laws or the execution of laws by regal authority as it has been assumed and exercised of late is illegal.

The first two articles of the Declaration of Rights addressed the efforts of the late Stuart kings, Charles II and James II, to obtain toleration for their Catholic and Dissenting subjects by exploiting both the crown's legal prerogatives to set aside the law and the king's rightful position as titular head of the Anglican church. Under James II these efforts directly threatened the Anglican church, the Anglican hierarchy in church and university, and the Tory gentry. The priority assigned these articles was meant to appeal to Anglican Tories. But the view that the king had no power to suspend laws or dispense with them had originated in parliamentarian thought at the time of the Civil War and became a principle of the Whig opposition in the early 1680s.

The first clause in the indictment against James II charged him with exercising a power to suspend and dispense with laws without the consent of Parliament. The declaratory section of the document responded by declaring that the royal power to suspend law without the consent of Parliament was illegal, and that the royal power to dispense with laws or the execution of laws, "as it has been assumed and exercised of late," was also illegal. This issue appeared originally in the Heads of Grievances as clause 1, which described the suspending and dispensing powers as "pretended" and condemned both as illegal. The Lords objected to the outlawing of the dispensing power and proposed amendments which would have limited the indictment to James II. Somers's committee proposed, as a compromise, to separate the suspending power from the dispensing power, declaring the former to be illegal and indicting the latter, too, but with qualifying language — "as it has been assumed and exercised of late." The committee deliberately refused words that implied approval of Charles II's use of the dispensing power and, by the phrase "of late," designedly extended the charge to an indefinite time, which, by implication, might include Charles's reign. Following further struggle with the Lords and M.P.'s who wished to preserve the dispensing power, the same men appended a section to the Bill of Rights which prohibited dispensation to law except as allowed for in the statute itself, and except in cases provided for in bills passed by Parliament in the present session. No such bills were passed. The effect of the Bill of Rights was to void the dispensing power as well as the suspending power.[2]

The power to suspend a law was the power to set aside the operation of a statute for a time. It did not mean, technically, the power to repeal it. The power to dispense with a law meant the power to grant permission to an individual or a corporation to disobey a statute. Between them there is a difference in degree, but not in principle.[3] If exploited to the full, these powers could unbalance the government decisively in favor of the king and destroy, in effect, the legislative power of Parliament. Yet there was need to have a special power in the state to set aside the operation of a law in times of emergency or in individual cases of hardship, and such a power was universally an attribute of early kingship. Medieval English kings had exercised such a power over the law from the thirteenth century, in imitation of the Pope, it was said. The power was limited, scholars agree, in vague and imprecise ways, but basically, the king could not suspend or dispense with a law of God or nature, or with common law, nor could he act against the public safety, nor license a public nuisance, nor allow a subject to act against the interest of another. The authority was extended at the Reformation, when English kings took over the power formerly exercised by the Pope over ecclesiastical matters in England. The prerogative aroused no opposition at a time when statutes were often imperfectly drawn and Parliament seldom in session.[4]

Tudor and early Stuart monarchs did not employ the suspending power, but they did regularly dispense with the law, provoking discussion about the limits of their dispensing power in the courts and among political and legal writers. For example, the *Case of Monopolies* in 1602 decided that a king could not issue a *non obstante*[5] that would destroy the intent and spirit of a statute. But the "landmark" *Case of the Sheriffs* in 1487 and Coke's interpretation of it affirmed the power to dispense with statutes.[6] Other commentators, such as Sir Thomas Smith in *De Republica Anglorum* (1565) and Francis Bacon in 1601, granted the monarch the power to dispense with laws.[7] The instrument creating the ecclesiastical commission of 1559 specifically referred to the dispensing power.[8] In the parliament of 1610, when impositions were under discussion, M.P.'s acknowledged the king's power of *non obstante* at the same time that they insisted upon some restrictions on it.[9] Again in 1628, John Glanville, in remarks quoted by one of James II's judges in support of the dispensing power, affirmed the royal dispensing power, but may have intended to restrict it in new ways.[10] Finally, decisions in law cases at the turn of the seventeenth century, most particularly the *Case of Non Obstante* (1605), which held that the king could dispense with any statute seeking to deprive him of a prerogative "inseparably" bound to his person, reinforced the royal dispensing power.

In the Civil War, the dispensing power was not a major issue, and no change in the law occurred. But the emergence at that time of the idea of "mixed monarchy" presaged the demise of the suspending and dispensing power in 1689.[11] Writers seeking to limit the authority of the monarchy — such as Charles Herle, Henry Parker, and Philip Hunton — promoted the notion that power was divided between three "coordinate" estates: king, lords, and commons. This idea was a departure from earlier views of mixed monarchy, which held that the three estates were the lords temporal, lords spiritual, and the commons, with the king as their head, standing apart. This new idea of mixed monarchy contained also the notion that the king's power was community-based — that power flowed from God, to the community, to the king. Although the idea had multiple sources, these parliamentarians drew inspiration from Charles I's *Answer to the Nineteen Propositions* (1642), whose language proved unfortunate from the king's point of view. The *Answer* itself held that England's government was comprised of three estates — king, lords, and commons — representing monarchy, aristocracy, and democracy, and that together these three made law. It also stated that the "experience and wisdom" of Englishmen in the past had "molded" the government into a balanced and mixed form that avoided the inconveniences of any one form. By such a statement Charles invited the inference that he had abandoned the theory of divine right and subscribed to the notion that power flowed from God to the community to the king. Charles used these arguments to charge Parliament with violating the constitution by passing the Militia Ordinance and proposing their *Nineteen Propositions,* and to portray himself as the upholder of law and the constitution. Parliamentarians almost immediately, however, perceived that inherent in the *Answer* were implications that could limit royal power. Those implications were that the king was only one of three estates in the legislative process, that he was essentially subordinate to the other two, and that alone he had no power to set aside the law by suspending or dispensing with it. Charles's *Answer to the Nineteen Propositions* and the parliamentarian responses to it written in the 1640s continued to influence thinking on the nature of the kingship, the relationship among the three estates, and hence the power of monarchy over law. The same points were raised in the 1680s and during the revolution in the fall and winter of 1688–89. At both times, some of the earlier tracts were reprinted.

The king's power to suspend and dispense with law became a political and constitutional issue after the Restoration. The authority was not disallowed in the Restoration Settlement, as were some other prerogatives, and thus, the extent of it remained uncertain.[12] It became the subject of controversy in 1662–63, 1674, and 1685, between the king, who wished to affirm his prerogative, and Parliament, which wished to deny the king sole authority and claim a role for itself. It was tested in law cases, the most important of which were *Thomas* v. *Sorrel* (1675), *Godden* v. *Hales* (1686), and the *Seven Bishops Case* (1688). Moreover, the matter was argued in printed tracts. As a recent study has stressed, the contest was not over whether law could be dispensed, but rather, over who would control it, and to what ends it would be used.[13]

In 1662, Charles sought to bring relief to his Catholic subjects. Rebuffed by Parliament in his effort to soften the Uniformity Bill by adding provisos to it, the king seriously considered suspending the Act of Uniformity. He dropped the idea in the face of his judges' opinion that it would be illegal.

Instead, Charles published a declaration asking Parliament to pass a bill "as may enable us to exercise with a more universal satisfaction that power of dispensing which we conceive to be inherent in us."[14] But Parliament rejected such an idea in a resolution which claimed that laws to assure uniformity in religion "could not be dispensed with, but by act of Parliament."[15] Charles, however, used his power to dispense Catholics from the penal laws, and also dispensed the Navigation Act in 1662, 1665, and 1674 without provoking opposition.[16] Parliament, moreover, tacitly acknowledged the dispensing power in the Irish Cattle Act of 1667 by declaring Irish cattle a public nuisance, because, as already mentioned, the king had no power to license a public nuisance.[17] In 1672 Charles, on the grounds of his suspending power and of his ecclesiastical supremacy, issued the Declaration of Indulgence, which suspended the penal legislation. The parliamentary opposition, grown stronger since 1663, reacted vigorously, engaging in a searching debate on the nature and extent of the king's power to set aside law. In the face of objections that such a power was necessary for the peace and safety of the nation, members of the "country opposition," including men who would serve on the rights committees in 1689,[18] asserted that only subsequent statutes could suspend a statute, and that the Declaration of Indulgence was illegal. Unsatisfied by Charles's response — in which he disclaimed intention of suspending laws where the properties, rights, or liberties of the subjects were concerned and pointed out that never before had a parliament questioned royal power in ecclesiastical matters — the House of Commons passed a resolution which declared that the king was "much misinformed" to think that he had a power to suspend penal laws in ecclesiastical matters.[19] They reinforced the point by refusing to grant supplies for the Dutch War if he persisted, and defeated a bill from the House of Lords to give the king a power to suspend certain statutes for a period of time.[20] Charles withdrew the Declaration of Indulgence and did not again attempt to use that prerogative. Yet, in 1675 in the *Thomas* v. *Sorrel* case, only one judge, John Vaughan, chief justice of the Court of Common Pleas and formerly a member of the House of Commons, where he had argued the same point in 1673, denied that the king had the power to dispense with statutes. Commenting upon Vaughan's decision, a twentieth-century constitutional historian has said that, although learned, it showed that it was "impossible to state the law [on the dispensing power] in a clear . . . form."[21] The historian echoed a seventeenth-century jurist, who at about the time of the Sorrel case wrote of the suspending and dispensing power that nothing was "more loose and disprincipled" in English law.[22]

James II brought the issue to a crisis by also using the dispensing prerogative to give religious toleration to Catholics and Dissenters. The king announced in the November 1685 session of his only parliament his intention to set aside the Test Act and the penal laws so that Catholics might serve as officers in the standing army. His belligerent speech provoked sharp opposition from this most compliant of parliaments. For example, the Tory Seymour charged that to employ Catholics without imposing the Test was "dispensing with all the laws at once." [23] An address prepared by a committee including men who would serve on the rights committees in 1689 asserted that the law which incapacitated Catholics from serving in the army "can no way be taken off but by an act of parliament." [24] James's response was to prorogue the parliament, dismiss several uncooperative judges (as was his prerogative to do), and turn to the law courts to test his authority to dispense with law.[25] *Godden* v. *Hales* (1686) involved Sir Edward Hales, the defendant, who held military office under the crown without satisfying the requirements of the Test Act. An informer, his coachman, Arthur Godden, acting in collusion, sued him in the Court of King's Bench for the award to which informers were entitled under the Test Act. Hales's defense was letters patent under the Great Seal, by which the king granted him dispensation from the Act.[26] Eleven of the twelve justices ruled that the dispensation was good. In handing down the decision, Chief Justice Edward Herbert expressed no opinion on the suspending power but, on the basis of history, law cases (such as the *Case of the Sheriffs* and the *Case of Non Obstante*), and legal commentary, affirmed the validity of the dispensing power. Today, many legal historians dismiss the charge, leveled then and since, that this decision was nothing more than a ruling of "submissive judges," and concur that it accorded with the letter and the spirit of the law.[27]

In the meantime, both before and after this decision, the question of the royal dispensing power was the subject of angry exchanges in the press. Defending the king's authority were such men as Dr. Robert Brady, the Tory historian, who was indebted to Bodin; [28] Roger L'Estrange, who argued that "if the Prince cannot dispense with the law, he cannot govern"; [29] and James Wilson, who maintained that the laws were the king's laws and that the mark of his sovereignty was that he had the power of the sword and the power to dispense with the laws.[30] Such views were disputed by men who would serve on the rights committees in 1689 or in other ways play a revolutionary role. For example, the jurist Sir Robert Atkyns, who was appointed a legal adviser to the House of Lords during the meetings of the Convention, published *An Enquiry into the Power of Dispensing with Penal Statutes,* in which he asserted that the king was just one of three estates in a mixed government, that he was essentially subordinate to the other two estates, and that he had no authority to dispense with the law. This piece had two editions in 1689. Somers, too, thought that the king's setting aside the law was an illegal exercise of royal prerogative.[31] And William Petyt, in *Ancient Right of the Commons of England Asserted,* published in 1680, had argued much the same point.[32] In sum, during the 1680s, contrary opinions about the nature and extent of the dispensing power were voiced, and the issue in law remained unsettled.

According to a recent biographer, James, no lawyer himself (as he was pleased to admit), was sincerely confident, on the grounds of the Hales decision, that he was acting within the law when he used the dispensing power to place Catholics in positions in the government, church, army, and universities, and issued the Declaration of Indulgence in 1687. Although the declaration suspended the penal laws, the authority on which it was based was left vague. James specifically disclaimed a power to suspend laws and, it has been maintained, regarded the declaration as resting on the dispensing power alone.[33] The king exacerbated the situation further in 1688 when he reissued the Declaration of Indulgence with the requirement that the Anglican clergy read it from their pulpits. The clergy regarded this step, rightly, as a threat to the primacy of the Anglican church and to their position within the church. In response, the archbishop of Canterbury and six other bishops presented a petition to the king beseeching him to withdraw his order and impugning the dispensing power. James, trusting that the judges would reaffirm his powers, entered an information against the bishops, charging them with seditious libel.[34] The bishops, whose defense was managed by lawyers who were to serve on the rights committees, were tried in the Court of King's Bench in June 1688, with the prosecution led by a lawyer, Williams, who would also be appointed to the rights committees.[35] Although arguments in the trial did not focus on the dispensing power, this prerogative underlay the proceedings. One jurist expressed the implications of it explicitly: "If [the dispensing power] be once allowed of, there will need no parliament. All the legislature will be in the king."[36] The bishops were acquitted, to the great joy of most Englishmen, but there was no formal ruling on the king's power to suspend or dispense with the law.

William's *Declaration of Reasons* exploited the emotions aroused by the imprisonment and trial of men at the highest reaches of the Anglican church and by the well-founded fear of Anglican Tories that they faced displacement from places of authority in all affairs. The prince's manifesto gave first priority to condemning the dispensing power, which it characterized (quite inaccurately) as "invented and set on foot" by James's evil advisers. Other printed tracts by both Tories and Whigs also stressed the illegality of this prerogative. An account of the trial of the Seven Bishops appeared before January 17, 1689, to refresh further men's memories of that episode.[37] But, as this brief historical overview has shown, the status in law of the suspending power and the dispensing power at the time of the Glorious Revolution was no more settled than it had been at the Restoration. Urged on by members of the "country opposition," among which were men who would become Whigs and serve on the rights committees in 1689, the Commons had twice passed a resolution against it. A minority of judges (until the *Seven Bishops Case*) had ruled against it. None of these steps was definitive. Indeed, as will be seen, some radical Whigs opposed justifying William's invasion by appeal to a right so long exercised by the monarchy. But the rights committees asserted that the illegality of the suspending power was "undoubted" and "ancient," and that the way the dispensing power had been used of late was also an illegal contravention of an "undoubted" and "ancient" right. The Bill of Rights further strengthened the condemnation of the dispensing power and, in effect, outlawed it completely.

Article 3

That the commission for erecting the late Court of Commissioners for Ecclesiastical Causes and all other commissions and courts of like nature are illegal and pernicious.

The Declaration of Rights claimed as the third undoubted right of the nation that James's creation of the so-called "Court" of Ecclesiastical Commissioners and all other like courts and commissions was illegal. Strictly speaking, however, James did not violate the law when he set up the Ecclesiastical Commission.[38] The king's authority to create a commission to act as his surrogate for visiting and disciplining ecclesiastical bodies, including the universities, rested on two statutes. One was article 17 of the Elizabethan Act of Supremacy, which vested in the king visitatorial power over ecclesiastical bodies and persons, including colleges and universities. The article remains in force today. The second was a Restoration law which confirmed the Act of 1641 abolishing the Tudor Court of High Commission and affirmed the king's supremacy over all ecclesiastical affairs and persons.[39] The commission James established explicitly claimed only the powers of ecclesiastical jurisdiction that the two acts of 1641 and 1661 had not declared illegal.

The creation of the commission on July 15, 1686, was one of several steps that marked a change in James's policy. By it he signaled an intention to turn away from Anglican Tories, the traditional supporters of the monarchy, and seek alliance with Whigs and Dissenters to help him achieve toleration.[40] Anglicans suffered. The most important personage to be injured by the commission was Henry Compton, the bishop of London, who was suspended for failing to discipline a rector, John Sharp, for preaching sermons hostile to Catholicism.[41] The most important institution to be hurt by the commission was Magdalen College, Oxford. There, a president of whom the college's fellows disapproved was installed, some Catholics were admitted as fellows, and the college's fellows were severely punished.[42] The potential danger to the Protestant integrity of such institutions and to the domination of Anglican Tories in them was genuine. These dangers — not the legality of the commission — were really the issue.[43]

In contrast to the pre–Civil War Court of High Commission, which did function as a court and did have jurisdiction over laymen as well as clergy, the Ecclesiastical Commission was not a court nor did it call itself one. The commission did not function as a court. It neither fined nor imprisoned individuals, it claimed jurisdiction only over persons in the ecclesiastical hierarchy, and it imposed only the ecclesiastical penalties of suspension and deprivation. Of the seven commissioners only the chairman, Jeffreys (the lord chancellor), and Sir Edward Herbert (the lord chief justice of the Court of King's Bench) were learned in the law. The commission was called a "court" for the first time, not in the Bill of Rights, as Ogg says,[44] but in Prince

William's *Declaration of Reasons*. The word appeared thereafter in proposals submitted to the king in October by the bishops.[45] These two pieces probably influenced the framers of the article, for the question of the Ecclesiastical Commission plays but a minor role in the other pamphlets. But Falkland referred to the creation of an "Ecclesiastical Court" when he initiated the discussion of a declaration of rights, and the rights committee preserved that phraseology.

The condemnation of the commission and the characterization of it as a court were effective propaganda, certain to revive memories of the earlier unpopular Court of High Commission and to appeal to Anglican Tories. In claiming that the king had no power to erect a court of ecclesiastical commissioners, the Declaration of Rights made political capital out of the grievances of a relatively small number of members of the Anglican hierachy, but its claim had no basis in law.

Article 4

That levying of money for or to the use of the crown by pretense of prerogative without grant of Parliament for longer time or in other manner than the same is or shall be granted is illegal.

Article 4 reaffirmed an ancient claim of English subjects that it was their right not to be taxed by the king without the consent of Parliament. The parallel charge (clause 4) in the indictment of James II declared that he had levied money "for other time, and in other manner than the same was granted by Parliament." The claim linked the Declaration of Rights with a long line of previous efforts to the same end. Indisputably the right was ancient. Whether James had violated that right is dubious.

The germ of the right in question lay in Magna Charta; chapter 12 asserted that the king could not levy feudal aids without the assent of his feudal lords.[46] Subsequently, Edward I's well-known statute *De Tallagio non Concedendo* and other early statutes established the principle, commentators agree, that there could be no direct taxation without Parliament's consent.[47] Yet kings, faced with a general rise in prices and a fall in their real income, imposed indirect taxes and justified them by various prerogative rights.[48] By the beginning of the seventeenth century, such steps invariably met with protests. For example, in 1606 a merchant, John Bate, refused to pay the impositions (that is, import duties) which the crown, exercising its rights to impose import duties to regulate trade, had levied. The king brought a test case against Bate and won, the judges reaffirming the power of the king to levy duties on commodities. The issue, exacerbated by an increase in the rate of the impositions and by the fact that crown officials collected it, occupied Parliament in 1610. In lengthy debates, sharpened by the king's order that they desist, which raised the question of freedom of speech and the role of the House of Commons, critics argued the illegality of impositions without

Parliament's consent. The result was a petition of grievances in which impositions were placed first.[49] The question was not resolved, and the king continued to levy impositions in the face of half-hearted objections.[50]

Other forms of extraparliamentary taxation also provoked opposition. For example, Parliament in 1483 outlawed benevolences (a forced "free" gift instituted by the Yorkists), but both Henry VII and Henry VIII levied them. Forced loans secured by promissory notes under the privy seal were also used by Henry VIII, Mary, and Elizabeth I in the sixteenth century. Although forced loans were supposed to be repaid, in some instances they were not.[51] Charles I resorted to forced loans in 1626–27, a step which, with the concomitant ruling that men who were imprisoned for refusing to pay them were not bailable, led directly to the Petition of Right in 1628.[52] The unlawfulness of imposing taxes of any kind without Parliament's approval threaded through the debates. For one example, Sir John Eliot declaimed that "the Ancient law of England, the declaration of Magna Carta and other statutes, say the subject is not to be burdened with loans, tallages, or benevolence. Yet we see them imposed [by the king]. Does this not contradict the law?"[53] The resulting Petition of Right petitioned the king not to levy taxes without Parliament's consent, a principle which Charles acknowledged when he accepted the document in a way satisfactory to the Commons.

Charles nevertheless collected tunnage and poundage (the customs duties on wine and wool granted by Parliament to each of the Tudor kings and to James I for life) without parliamentary approval. The Parliament of 1626 declared that such collections were illegal, but the Privy Council asserted (inaccurately) that tunnage and poundage were independent of parliamentary grant. In 1628, when the passing of the Petition of Right had sharpened tensions between king and parliament, the issue of tunnage and poundage led to a Commons resolution describing the king's "receiving of tunnage and poundage, and other impositions not granted by parliament" as a "breach of the fundamental liberties of the kingdom." Charles, however, continued to collect the duties, and in 1629 another resolution, rammed through the Commons by Eliot and others, who held the Speaker in the chair to prevent an adjournment, denounced the imposing of tunnage and poundage without Parliament's consent.[54]

During the decade when he ruled without Parliament, Charles I resorted to still other taxes, the most notable of which was ship money. Ship money was a further example of the crown's pressing against the limits of the law, for the right of the king to require ships from coastal towns and counties for defense was indisputable. But Charles, having received assurances from the judges that he was acting within the law, applied ship money to inland counties as well, demanding money instead of ships and thereby, in effect, imposing a land tax.[55] This practice was tested in the courts in 1637–38 by John Hampden, whose son Richard and grandson John were on the rights committees in 1689. A majority of the judges ruled for the crown, on the grounds, accepted by both sides, that the king could require his subjects to give aid in ships, arms, or money in the event of an emergency, and on the further grounds, argued by lawyers for the crown, that the king was sole judge of an emergency.[56]

Members of the Short Parliament complained about extraparliamentary taxation, especially impositions and ship money,[57] and the Long Parliament passed acts outlawing ship money and some other forms of indirect taxes.[58] When Cromwell dissolved the Rump Parliament in 1653, anxiety resurfaced that the executive might attempt to levy taxes on its own authority. One observer predicted that if this were done "there will be much ado to get it out of . . . [people's] purses, without force."[59] At the Restoration, one of the first steps taken by the Convention Parliament was to appoint a committee to draft a bill confirming the rights and privileges of Parliament, Magna Charta, the *De Tallagio non Concedendo,* and the Petition of Right.[60] Among the members were men who would serve on the rights committees in 1689: Birch, Lee, and Maynard. Although the bill failed to become a statute because of the dissolution of the Convention, the principle that the king could not levy taxes without Parliament's consent was accepted by all parties.[61] Yet the parliamentary Opposition exercised vigilance against the danger, real and imagined, that the court would tax on its own authority. Thus, in 1673, a bill to prevent the illegal exacting of money was read twice and referred to a committee that included at least nine future members of the rights committees.[62] Nothing came of the bill then, and in 1675 another bill to the same purpose passed a second reading. On this committee, too, were the future members of the rights committees.[63] In 1680, the Commons agreed to bring in still another bill modeled on the two previous ones. Again, they referred it to a committee on which members of the future rights committees served — among them, Birch, Paul Foley, Richard Hampden, and Lee.[64] This bill, too, failed to prosper.

The radical Whigs on the rights committees, then, had had previous experience with this issue, and it was surely they who promoted it as a grievance and a right. Birch and Williams declared in the debate of January 29 that the king had been given the power to levy money without Parliament,[65] and an anonymous member raised the matter again at the committee meeting the next day.[66] The printed pamphlets that called for rights and reform did not include this issue. What, then, was in the minds of the rights committee members?

The circumstances that underlay article 4 and the parallel indictment of the king were that James had collected customs and excise duties without parliamentary approval for three months, from the time he inherited the throne to the meeting of his first parliament. It was normal procedure for a new king to collect customs duties before his first parliament met, but since the excise tax had been granted for the first time to Charles II, there was no precedent for collecting it. Anticipating difficulties, the court sealed a new contract for collecting the excise the day before Charles died, and the judges ruled (8 to 4) that it was valid. Three days after becoming king, James issued a proclamation announcing the ruling and his intention to collect the taxes.[67] Although some objection was expressed — Temple, for example, resigned his post — there was no indignant outrage, and when Parliament met, the collection was retrospectively legalized.[68] The judges' ruling and the actions of Parliament would seem to exonerate the king from the charge of acting illegally, but James had acted unwisely. To smear him with the charge of violating the time-honored and undoubted right that the crown may not impose taxes without Parliament's consent, a right that had been at the center of controversy between king and Parliament for decades, was effective propaganda. It was certain to remind history-conscious contemporaries of those previous controversies and persuade them that James had indeed "endeavored to extirpate the nation's laws."

Article 5

That it is the right of the subjects to petition the king, and all commitments and prosecutions for such petitioning are illegal.

Article 5 claimed the right of the subject to petition the king and asserted the illegality of prosecutions and commitments for petitioning. This article responded indirectly to the issue of the suspending and dispensing powers, and directly to James's prosecution of the Seven Bishops. Clause 2 of the indictment against the king read that he had prosecuted "divers worthy prelates for humbly petitioning to be excused from concurring to the said assumed power," meaning the power to suspend and dispense with law.

The circumstances, already discussed, were that in the spring of 1688 James had issued the Second Declaration of Indulgence and required that it be read in the churches. Alarmed by this step, the archbishop of Canterbury and six bishops urged that the order be ignored. They presented a petition to the king asking him to withdraw it and denying the legality of his power to dispense with the penal laws. James charged the bishops with seditious libel. Defense attorneys (some of whom, it may be reiterated, would serve on the rights committees in 1689) rested their defense in part on the right of the subject to petition the king without fear of reprisals. Thus, one lawyer asserted that it "is the right of the people . . . to approach His Majesty by petition,"[69] and another echoed the point, declaring that "the subjects have a right to petition the king . . ., so say all our books of law."[70] The prosecution's rebuttal that Parliament may petition the king, but that the bishops could not do so out of Parliament, was emphatically rejected by two judges.[71] The trial aroused great public interest, and the verdict of "not guilty" provoked emotional outburst.

Polemical statements endorsing Prince William sought to exploit these feelings on several counts. William's manifesto stressed James's tyranny in charging that the bishops' petition was a seditious libel. It maintained that the petition was "full of respect" and in conformity with the law, and that even

kings with despotic power allowed their subjects the right of petition according to the law. The *Declaration of the Nobility, Gentry and Commonalty at the
Rendezvous at Nottingham, November 22, 1688* cited the denial of the right of
petitioning as a principal reason for opposing James II. Article 5, then,
implicitly vindicated the actions of the Seven Bishops and reiterated the view
expressed in William's manifesto and other printed tracts favoring the prince.

Article 5 was also closely related to an earlier controversy over petitioning.
In the fall of 1679, a flood of petitions demanding the reassembling of Parliament provoked Charles to issue a proclamation against tumultuous
petitions.[72] For several months "petitioners" criticized the proclamation,
while "abhorrers" (persons abhorring the petitioners) upheld it, their activity
marking the origin of what became the Whig and Tory parties. When Parliament finally reassembled in October 1680, members of the Opposition,
including Hampden, Howard, and Sacheverell, continued the campaign
against the proclamation, condemned the judges for allowing it, fervently
asserted the subjects' right to petition the king, and passed a resolution "that it
is (and ever has been) the undoubted right of the subjects of England, to petition the king."[73] They also expelled a member (Sir Francis Wythens) for supporting the king's proclamation[74] and appointed a committee to prepare
heads of an impeachment against Lord Chief Justice Francis North, said to
have authored the offending document.[75] The effect was aborted by the prorogation of Parliament. Such an emotion-laden episode as this, involving
members of the rights committees, was probably also in the minds of committee members when article 5 was included in the list of rights.

Article 5 reaffirmed an indisputable ancient right to petition the king.
Some scholars think Magna Charta, chapter 61, guaranteed such a right.[76]
Petitions, as we have seen, were in early centuries the basis for legislation.
Superseded by bills, they were revived at the time of the Great Rebellion.
The Short Parliament received an extraordinary number of petitions in the
spring of 1640,[77] and the practice grew over the decade. Presbyterians frequently addressed petitions to Parliament to disband the army. Army
agitators petitioned their officers to mediate for them with the Parliament.
The Levellers repeatedly asserted the unqualified right of the subject to present petitions.[78] So numerous and tumultuous did petitions become that after
the Restoration, in 1661, an act against tumultuous petitions was passed.[79]
This statute set out elaborate procedures for petitions on public, as opposed
to private, matters. It required the consent of the authorities (the lord mayor
and Common Council in the case of London) to procure the signatures of
twenty or more persons on a petition. No more than ten persons were to present a petition to the king or to Parliament.

In sum, article 5 was an "undoubted" right of Englishmen which the
parliamentary Opposition had sought to protect for years, especially in
1679–80, and which in 1689 both sides had reason to reaffirm. The article
was also powerful propaganda, designed to appeal to Anglican Tories and to
keep alive the memory of the trial of the Seven Bishops. But it did not strictly

conform to law, for it claimed an *unlimited* right, whereas Restoration law permitted only a bounded right of subjects to petition the king.

Article 6

That the raising or keeping a standing army within the kingdom in time of peace, unless it be with consent of Parliament, is against law.

Article 6 asserted that it was against the law to raise or keep a standing army in the kingdom in time of peace without the consent of Parliament, and the indictment against James charged him with violating the law (clause 5). The indictment also charged the king with quartering soldiers contrary to law, an issue introduced as an amendment by the Lords and ignored in the declaratory section of the document. That omission may well be laid both to haste, for opposition to quartering soldiers was a feature of the anti–standing army attitude, and perhaps to reluctance to blame James for something that could also be charged against William. The claim of right in article 6 was a new law. It reflected the pejorative attitude toward standing armies that had developed over the century, especially since the Restoration. Among the framers of the article were men who had taken the lead in previous parliaments in promoting this attitude. In 1689, they simply declared as law what they wanted to be law, knowing full well that the command of the military forces had been bitterly contested for years.[80]

The standing army — that is, a body of professional, paid soldiers, answerable to the king, and kept standing in time of peace — was unknown in England until the seventeenth century. Until then, the military instruments which the kingdom employed were the feudal array and the local nonprofessional militia, plus soldiers raised for the occasion and disbanded thereafter. Cromwell's New Model Army, raised for the Civil War and kept in arms for the next decade, was the nation's first standing army. It differed from the standing armies of the later Stuarts, the foundations for which were laid at the Restoration. In January 1661, using as an excuse a minor uprising in London, Charles II established without parliamentary approval a small number of permanent guards answerable to and paid by him. The guards formed the nucleus of a standing force which, although miniscule in size when compared to modern and even to seventeenth-century Continental armies, grew over the years. In 1685, using Monmouth's Rebellion as excuse, James II enlarged the army, and in 1688 he escalated the effort in the face of impending invasion, until it stood at about 50,000 men.[81] Moreover, in violation of the Test Act, James gave military commands to Catholics.[82] He announced this move to his parliament in 1685, implemented it by the use of the royal dispensing power, and, having changed the political orientation of the bench, confirmed its legality in 1686 through the case *Godden* v. *Hales*. The number of Catholic officers grew, until in 1688 about 27 percent of the top posts were in their hands, as were key fortresses. Further, although

Charles had "virtually no" Catholic officers in his Irish army, by the end of 1688 there were almost no Protestants left.[83] A standing army in peacetime composed of Protestants was disliked by the parlimantary Opposition for many reasons, but an army filled (as was thought) with Catholics was anathema.

The Stuart kings had the legal right to raise and maintain a peacetime army without the consent of Parliament. Early custom had placed ultimate miliary authority in the king. As feudal lord, the monarch embodied the feudal array. As sovereign, he mustered the local militia. The king's military prerogative was not debated seriously until the Civil War. Then in 1641–42, when the Militia Bill was introduced, men in and out of Parliament argued for transferring command of the militia from king to Parliament. Recognizing that such a transfer would shift sovereignty to Parliament, Charles I rejected the Militia Bill, describing the issue as "the fittest subject for a King's quarrel."[84] The idea that the legislature rather than the executive should have ultimate control over the armed forces of the nation continued to be a central element in future criticism of the military. It was iterated during the Interregnum by a host of critics of the Cromwellian establishment — Presbyterians, Republicans, Levellers, and Fifth Monarchists — but Republicans developed the strongest indictment of the army in both parliamentary debates and the press, and argued that where military power was lodged, there was sovereignty.

At the Restoration, however, this view was swept aside, and for the first time, statutory definition was given the king's military authority. The Militia Act of 1661 unequivocally confirmed the monarch's right to sole command of the military forces of the nation: "the sole supreme government, command and disposition of the militia" as well as, so the act ran, "of all forces by sea and land, . . . is, and by the laws of England ever was, the undoubted right" of the crown. And lest there be any doubt about the role of Parliament, the act specifically stated that "both or either of the Houses of Parliament cannot, nor ought to, pretend to the same [authority]."[85] The right of the king to raise standing forces on his own authority gained reinforcement from the Disbanding Act of 1660, which legislated the disbanding of the Cromwellian army. After declaring that all garrisons were to be reduced to their condition as of 1637 and the soldiers discharged, clause 4 of that act continued: "Except such of them [garrisons and soldiers] or any other His Majesty shall think fit otherwise to dispose and provide for at his own charge."[86] The implication of the words is plain: the king has the right to keep as many soldiers as he wants so long as he pays for them. Subsequent acts — for example, the Act of 1662 to prevent frauds in the customs and the Act of 1670 to suppress conventicles — also gave indirect statutory sanction to the existence of guards raised and paid for by the king.[87] In 1666 Parliament granted £30,000 especially for the use of the guards, thereby giving additional legal support to their existence.[88]

Until 1678 even critics of the standing army acknowledged — as in 1667,

October 1673, and early 1674 — the king's right to raise an army in peacetime so long as he paid for it.[89] But in 1678, as the Popish Plot hysteria engulfed the nation, hostility to the standing army sharpened. M.P.'s recognized that political capital was to be won from dislike of the forces. In January 1678, the parliamentary Opposition implicitly challenged the king's right of military command by claiming that Parliament should nominate the officers of the new regiments.[90] In May, M.P.'s asserted that the only time the king could legitimately raise forces other than the militia was in time of war.[91] At the end of the month, the theme surfaced again. One spokesman asserted that according to English law, "no men can be raised but for foreign service." Williams was even more emphatic: "The king can no more raise men in England, than he can raise money," he said. Friends of the court indignantly replied to this reading of the law. Said Sawyer, "'Tis the first time I ever heard so." The king's right, he declared, "has been constant according to the tenor of the law." Another speaker flatly asserted that "the king may raise, and the king may disband men, by his prerogative." It was even suggested that Williams's remark be written down, but Williams apologized, saying, "I acknowledge my error, and humbly ask your pardon for it."[92] And so, Grey reported, "the thing passed over."

But the issue reappeared six months later, in November 1678, when the parliamentary Opposition bitterly criticized the government for commissioning Catholic officers. One M.P. forthrightly declared: "I am of the opinion that a standing army, in time of peace, whether the officers be Popish or Protestant, is illegal."[93] It was the first time in Parliament that a standing army was explicitly labeled illegal. The following spring, at the end of an angry debate on disbanding the army, the Commons resolved that the continuing of any standing forces other than the militia was "illegal" and a grievance and vexation to the people.[94] The point pertinent to the present argument is that until 1678 no one in Parliament denied the king's right to have a standing army, notwithstanding the increasingly hostile attitude towards that army. Two resolutions — one in 1674 and the other in 1679 condemning the standing army — underline the point: in 1674 the standing army was called a grievance; in 1679 it was called illegal and a grievance. Parliamentary resolutions, of course, do not carry legal authority, but they do show the sentiments of M.P.'s.

Hostility towards the standing forces continued and was expressed in James II's only parliament by men otherwise inclined to favor the king. Seymour, the Tory, was emphatic in his criticism, saying, "I had much rather pay double to these [the militia] from whom I fear nothing, than half so much to those [the army] of whom I must ever be afraid."[95] James's announced policy of using Catholic officers met such resistance that the king prorogued Parliament.

The anti–standing army attitude was complex, containing many ingredients. In the late seventeenth century, critics stressed the political dangers rather than the social and economic costs. It was feared that permanent soldiers would destroy Parliament, law, and liberty; impose absolutism and Catholicism; and disrupt England's mixed and balanced government by force. The army was also feared as an instrument of corruption, by which the executive branch of a bureaucratic state exerted influence over the legislative branch. This point suggests the influence of anti-army ideas developed earlier in the century by James Harrington and others. In modified form these notions had been voiced in parliamentary debates and widely circulated in tracts printed from 1675 to 1681, and were well known to radical Whigs.[96] The new bureaucratic state was identified as a threat to freedom and property. With resources at its command for bribing members of Parliament by the offer of money and/or office so that those members would vote money for a paid, professional standing army, the executive branch of government corrupted the legislative branch. Officers of the standing army sat in Parliament and also contributed to corruption by voting taxes for their own maintenance. A standing army, then, was the means and the end of a process of corruption which left Parliament helpless.

Both Tories and Whigs abhorred a standing army in peacetime, but the radical Whigs, who in previous years had been the most persistent critics and whose intellectual progenitors during the Civil War had laid the ground for the anti-army attitude in England, took the lead in making the issue an article in the Declaration of Rights. They knew full well, as their comments in earlier debates prove, that the king had the legal right to raise and maintain a standing army in peacetime without the consent of Parliament. They claimed new law by declaring that he did not have such a right and in so doing laid the groundwork for removing a long-standing, critically important prerogative of the crown.

Article 7

That the subjects which are Protestants may have arms for their defense suitable to their condition and as allowed by law.

Article 7 claimed as a right of the subject that Protestants may have arms for their defense, suitable to their condition, and as allowed by law. It responded directly to the charge (no. 6) that James had caused Protestants to be disarmed at the same time Catholics were armed and employed contrary to law. The two clauses "suitable to their conditions" and "as allowed by law" were amendments introduced by the House of Lords. Their effect was to limit the right to bear arms to the Protestant upper classes, according to the laws already passed. In the form first proposed to the Lords, the article had claimed that all subjects who were Protestants, regardless of social and economic status, had the right to possess arms. But in its final form, the article confirmed previous laws, except for granting to Protestants the exclusive right to have arms. Two questions surround this article: (1) What explains the terms of the article that was sent to the upper House? and (2) Why did the peers insist upon the amendments?

Article 7 had appeared originally in the Heads of Grievances (clause 7) as a claim that it was necessary for the public safety that Protestant subjects "should provide and keep arms for their common defense, and that arms which have been seized and taken from them [should] be restored." For reasons that have eluded the record, the call to restore arms to Prostestants was deleted in the February 7 draft, leaving the claim that *all* Protestants were guaranteed the right to possess weapons. This claim had several inter-related sources. First, it reflected hostility to the Stuart kings' preference for standing armies, perceived as riddled with Catholics, and their neglect of the militia, comprised of Protestants. In that respect, it was closely related to arti-cle 6, which prohibited a standing army in peacetime without Parliament's consent. The militia, composed ideally of Protestant freeholders and officered by the local aristocracy, was the military force which the parliamentary Opposition said they preferred. The idea that a reformed militia might serve as a counterweight to a professional army first appeared in 1648, when the Militia Ordinance was passed; and it reappeared in 1673, as dislike of Charles II's standing army and his foreign and domestic policies sharpened.[97] Henry Capel said then that the militia "will defend [the nation] and never conquer [it]."[98] In 1674 and again in 1678, the Commons asked Charles to embody the militia and depend upon it rather than upon professional soldiers. The avowed purpose of the Militia Bill of 1678 was to train the militia to be guards to the king, that he "might have no further use of an army."[99] Charles vetoed that bill. The next month the parliamentary Oppo-sition asked for a general arming of the nation against papists, urged the repeal of the nonresisting oath so that Protestant subjects might resist papists who were armed and held a commission from the king, and reinforced its demand by appeal to an act of 1585 which enabled the nobility and gentry to arm against the possibility that Elizabeth I should be murdered by Catholics.[100] After Monmouth's Rebellion in 1685, James planned to discard the militia, describing it as "not sufficient" to protect the nation. He intended to use the militia rates to finance the standing army. Accordingly, he ordered that the weapons of the militia be confiscated in Ireland, Scotland, and, to a lesser extent, in England.[101] During James's only parliament, the Commons' response to this threat was, as already noted, to bring in a bill to make the militia more effective [102] — in order words, to arm Protestants against Catholics.

Although genuine anxiety that a standing army filled with Catholics would overrun the militia composed of Protestants was inherent in these moves, there was also an element of partisan propaganda. Article 7 implicitly underlined the Popish character of the king and his policies and played upon the anxieties of people outside elite political and social categories who, as the mob's attacks against Catholics illustrate, understood national politics at least in part in terms of a papist/antipapist dichotomy.[103] Fear of Catholics, fear of armed Catholics, fear of Catholics in a standing army answerable to a Catholic king, were powerful ingredients in popular political attitudes. In all the steps taken to express disapproval of the standing army and preference for the militia, men who would later serve on the rights committees in 1689 played a leading role.[104]

Second, article 7 was connected with the Commons' objections to the operation of the Restoration Militia Acts, a grievance which appeared as clause 5 of the Heads of Grievances: "The acts concerning the militia are grievous to the subject." The Restoration Militia Acts fixed the sole command of the militia in the king, imposed an oath of nonresistance (i.e., to swear that it was unlawful to take up arms against the king or "those that are commissioned by him"), and empowered the lord lieutenants and their deputy lieutenants to search and seize the weapons of any person deemed a threat to the peace. Charles II had made effective use of these laws to try to snuff out political and religious dissent in the early years of the Restoration. He disarmed Dissenters and the towns they controlled, confiscated their weapons, imprisoned their leaders, and broke up conventicles.[105] By 1668 such steps met with complaints in the House of Commons.[106] But Charles and, later, James II continued to use the militia in these ways, as in the Popish Plot and Exclusion Crisis in 1678–81, the Rye House Plot scare in 1683, and Monmouth's Rebellion in 1685. As members of the rights committees testified in debate, more than one of them had had his arms confiscated and his house searched.[107] Since these steps were being carried out at the same time that the number of Catholics in the army was increasing, there was substance to the charge that the king was taking arms from Protestants and putting them in the hands of Catholics. And it was true that the king was doing this under the authority of the Militia Acts. Clause 5 did not survive in overt form in the Declaration of Rights, but the claim that Protestants had the right to possess arms reflected the idea that the Militia Laws were grievous and tacitly denied the right of the government to confiscate weapons.

Third, the original terms of article 7 reflected neo-Harringtonian ideas. As already discussed, a standing army was perceived as one means for the king, through patronage and influence, to corrupt Parliament. To the extent that subjects, despite their avowed preference for the militia, failed to exercise their right to bear arms (a right which, according to a tradition tracing its way back to Machiavelli and the civic humanists, defined a man's political capacity), they facilitated the corruption of the government.[108] The fact was that the militia had ceased to function as a viable military instrument, and despite repeated calls to reform it, the Commons were not really serious about so doing.[109] To assert, then, that every Protestant had a right to have arms was, in a way, to reaffirm the value of the militia and to imply that legitimate military power resided, not in a standing army, the creature of the executive, but in the independent citizenry, embodied in the militia, the force of the parliamentary gentry. This viewpoint, although it originated with radical critics of the king, was also endorsed by Tories.

The only extended treatment of the idea of arming the nation to have survived occurs in the papers of Thomas Erle, a member of the Convention, but not appointed to the rights committee.[110] Erle argued that every man who had an income of £10 should be provided with a "good musket," which would have required an amendment to the Game Law of 1671 (noted below). Anticipating the objection that such an arrangement would lead to the destruction of game, Erle declared that the gun was not to blame but the person who misused his weapon, and asserted that there were laws to punish a man who destroyed game. There is no evidence that Erle made these points to members of the Convention, but since he took the trouble to write out his thoughts, it is likely that he voiced them. Perhaps he reinforced interest in the issue, but Treby's committee went further than he, asserting the right of all Protestants to possess weapons.

The second question is, Why did the House of Lords amend the language of article 7? First, the idea that *all* Protestants should be permitted to possess a gun surely terrified the upper House. The Lords (as well as others) were appalled at the outrages perpetrated in December by a Protestant mob, which looted Catholic houses and set fire to London. The potential dangers to property and life from permitting all Protestants to have a weapon were self-evident. Second, the right to possess arms had always been closely connected with the subjects' military obligations, which, since the twelfth century, had been equated with subjects' socioeconomic status.[111] Both the citizen militia and the feudal array reflected hierarchical social values and a fear of arming the lower classes. Sixteenth-century militia laws specified the individual's obligation to the militia according to his estate, and the Militia Act of 1662 continued that principle. Theoretically, not every person was supposed to have weapons and serve in the military. Third, for over 150 years, other legislation had restricted the possession of guns and other weapons to well-to-do persons. The purpose was, in part, to protect the peace and assure the safety of subjects. The statute of 1542, for example, complained of "malicious and evil disposed persons" who had violated the peace and committed a multitude of crimes. But the aim was also to keep guns beyond the reach of the lower classes. The qualifications for having a gun had nothing to do with moral character, but rather with economic standing. No one having an income under £100 per year was allowed to keep a gun.[112] During Queen Elizabeth I's reign and beyond, anxiety continued about leaving firearms in the hands of the poor and of disbanded soldiers, because of fear of crime and political insurrection.[113]

Fourth, the peers' amendments almost certainly drew inspiration from the game laws, which, since the fourteenth century, had preserved the hunting privileges of the king and the upper classes by restricting the possession of weapons to the wealthy.[114] Thus, in 1390 a law provided that no layman with an income under forty shillings a year or a cleric with an income under £10 a year might keep a dog, or use nets or any "other engines . . . for to take or destroy . . . gentlemen's game." In 1604 an act complained that game had been destroyed by "men of small worth" and set the qualifications for hunting at £10 per year freehold.[115] Other restrictive acts and practices followed as early Stuart kings sought to protect royal sporting privileges.[116] But after the Restoration, reasons developed for sharing with the aristocracy the power to preserve game. In 1671 the "most stringent and comprehensive" of the game laws limited the right to keep a gun to persons having an estate of £100 a year and gave gentlemen the right to preserve game on their own lands.[117] This act was still in force in 1689. The lords knew intimately well its provisions, for three members of Fauconberg's committee had served on the committee to which the Game Bill was referred in 1671.[118] Members of Treby's committee were also directly familiar with the Game Bill, for four of them had initiated it.[119] Members of both Houses had reasons to preserve their hunting privileges and to fear the threat to property and person from placing arms in the hands of *all* Protestants. That these considerations operated in 1689 is suggested by a Commons debate on a new game bill in 1693. Then, one member proposed an amendment to allow every Protestant to keep a musket. Radical Whigs embraced the proposal, arguing that it promoted the security of the government. But opponents maintained that the measure "savours of the politics to arm the mob, which . . . is not very safe for any government." The amendment was defeated 169 to 65, with Tredenham, a member of the 1689 Commons rights committee, serving as teller for the noes.[120] Probably it was such considerations as these that persuaded men in 1689 to set aside the principle of arming all Protestants.

In its original form as proposed to the Lords by the Commons, article 7 was not an "undoubted" right of the nation, but rather, a declaration of new law contravening established statutes. It drew inspiration from the experience of rights committee members, who had been disarmed under the authority of the Militia Laws. It reflected hostility to the Stuart kings' increasing reliance on a professional standing army made up of Catholics and their neglect of the militia. To a degree, it reflected the anti-Catholic hysteria of the era. Further, it was connected with neo-Harringtonianism, which implied that placing arms in the hands of subjects would help to purify the government of corruption. But in its final form, with the qualifying clauses, the article both reaffirmed ancient laws in giving men the right to possess arms according to their social and economic standing and declared new law in limiting the right to Protestants.

Article 8

That elections of members of Parliament ought to be free.

Article 8 asserted the right of free elections, while a parallel clause in the indictment (no. 7) charged James with violating that right. This article evolved from clause 8 of the Heads of Grievances: "That right and freedom of electing members of the House of Commons, and the rights and privileges of Parliament, and members, as well in the intervals of Parliament as during their sitting, to be preserved." The thirteenth head was also related to the principle of free elections. It read: "Cities, universities, and towns corporate, and boroughs and plantations to be secured against quo warrantos and surrenders and mandates, and restored to their ancient rights." In the February 7 draft, clause 8 was divided into two articles — 8 and 9 — both of which were placed in the category of undoubted rights and also in the category of rights that required new laws. The phraseology — "That election of members of Parliament ought to be free" — survived intact in the Declaration of Rights. But in the February 7 draft the thirteenth head was placed only in the list of rights needing new laws, and it disappeared from the final draft. The issue it addressed — the quo warranto proceedings — was implicit, however, in the assertion of the right of free elections.

The claim of a right to elect freely members of Parliament without interference from the crown was ancient. Two early statutes from the fourteenth century asserted it.[121] Nonetheless, kings from the beginning of parliaments (it has been said) employed various methods to influence the return of members favorable to them.[122] But systematic attention to elections did not begin until the 1530s, when Henry VIII's minister, Thomas Cromwell, exploited the influence of the crown and its councillors upon local powers, capitalized on the feeling of loyalty among the gentry and nobility, and, in at least one instance, ordered on behalf of the king that an election be rescinded.[123] Although some efforts along these lines continued, no subsequent minister in the sixteenth century interested himself in elections to the extent that Cromwell had.[124] James I's efforts to influence who should be returned to his first parliament met with criticism in 1603–4, and a decade later strong protests against the king's "undertakers" — managers of the elections to the Parliament of 1614 — were voiced.[125] Charles I, aided as his father had been by the duke of Buckingham, interfered more blatantly in parliamentary elections than had any previous king. Not only did he use the influence of the crown; he also made critics of the court ineligible for election by picking them for sheriff.[126]

Charles II introduced another method of influencing elections in boroughs: quo warranto proceedings. The commanding presence of Dissenters in cities and towns led as early as 1661 to the proposal that all future corporation charters contain a clause reserving to the king the nomination of town officers.[127] And to achieve immediate results, the court also intermittently used quo warrantos to recall borough charters and reissue new ones securing its influence. Then in 1681, Charles embarked upon a concerted policy to destroy Whig strongholds in the boroughs. Allying himself firmly with the Anglican Tory gentry and aided by "most" of the lord-lieutenants, who exploited the opportunity to create a balance of power between town and country in their favor, Charles procured the forfeiture or voluntary surrender of many borough charters, including that of London.[128] The quo warranto action against London was the subject of a case tried in King's Bench in 1683, with Treby and Pollexfen representing the City. Treby was dismissed as recorder of London. Clearly, the chairman of the first rights committee was intimately aware of the implications of the crown's quo warranto attacks for the independence of boroughs.

James II reaped the advantages of Charles II's remodeling of the corporations and of his own efforts in exercising the crown's influence in the election of a parliament in the spring of 1685. Of 513 men, 400 were new to Westminster, and no more than 40 were thought to be unfriendly to the king.[129] But Seymour, resentful of the impact of remodeling on his own political fortunes and sensitive to the larger implications, charged that quo warrantos imperiled the independence of Parliament. He proposed that a committee examine the returns from all boroughs that had new charters and that supplies be withheld until the committee had finished its investigations.[130] The proposal failed, possibly because of Seymour's poor management, but the reaction to the quo warranto process anticipated that of the Convention four years later. Obviously, Seymour, the most powerful Tory member of the rights committee, was already on record in opposition to that process.

Dissatisfied with the attitude of this parliament towards his announced intention to give army commands to Catholics in violation of the Test Act, James prorogued it in the fall of 1685. He devoted much attention to how he might achieve a more compliant body. His early efforts at closeting (that is, canvassing) prospective candidates aroused resentment.[131] So, in the summer of 1687, he dissolved Parliament and embarked upon a strategy of remodeling the corporations that went beyond what Charles had done. James employed paid agents who were independent of the local scene and placed the administration of the whole on Robert Brent, who reported directly to Sunderland and Jeffreys.[132] (Brent, it should be recalled, was the object of the Convention's wrath in 1689 and Treby's bailing of him a reason for the Commons to criticize the chairman of the first rights committee.[133]) James also reversed the traditional alliance of the crown with the Anglican and Tory gentry, seeking instead alliance with Dissenters and Whigs who had been displaced in Charles's purges, and whom he expected to entice by the prospect of religious toleration and of dominance in the boroughs. James ordered a mass purge of J.P.'s and deputies with the aim of assuring the return of M.P.'s favorable to him.[134] Further, he put three questions to men who were likely candidates for Parliament to test their position on his policy of repealing the Test Act and penal laws.[135] Finally, he used the quo warranto process. Altogether, it has been figured, 200 constituencies, which would have elected 400 out of 513 M.P.'s, received some kind of direct governmental intervention. At least 2,000 individuals, roughly 15 percent of the landed gentry, were asked to answer the three questions.[136] But the gentry, by and large, regarded the three questions as a preengagement which would have undermined the independence of Parliament and as an illegal attempt to destroy the freedom of elections. All these steps, patently in violation of the principle of freedom of parliamentary elections, were, it has been argued, "easily the most important" causes of the revolution, more important even than the attack on the Anglican church.[137]

These tactics of the late Stuart kings were cited as a grievance in William's manifesto, in the *Bishops' Proposals* (discussed in Chapter 5), and in many of the "rights and reform" pamphlets. They were prominently mentioned in the Convention debates. In the seventeenth century, politically conscious persons understood well the connection between such strategies and packing Parliament.[138] James's attempt to recover the good opinion of his subjects by returning the charters in October 1688 met with no success. Why the rights committee decided to omit the clause about quo warranto proceedings has eluded the record, but probably it was because that issue would have involved much time to resolve and the passing of obviously new law. It received attention after the settlement. In February 1689, the Convention simply declared that the right to free parliamentary elections was undoubted. In this claim they did indeed reaffirm an ancient right.

Article 9

That the freedom of speech and debates or proceedings in Parliament ought not to be impeached or questioned in any court or place out of Parliament.

Article 9 also originated in clause 8 of the Heads of Grievances. Clause 8 had referred ambiguously to the "rights and privileges" of Parliament and had called for them to be preserved both in the intervals of Parliament and during its sitting. The Commons rights committeemen selected "freedom of speech and debates or proceedings" from among several recognized "privileges" of Parliament as the ones to be claimed in the Declaration of Rights. They dropped the phrase "as well in the intervals of Parliament as during their sitting," which would have extended the immunity of members of Parliament to the time when Parliament was not in session. In the February 7 draft they placed article 9 in the category of ancient rights and in the category of rights that required new law.

No charge that James had violated the right of freedom of speech in Parliament appears in the indictment against him, although perhaps it was intended to be subsumed in the phrase "divers other arbitrary and illegal courses." William's *Declaration of Reasons* does not mention it, nor do the other printed pieces about rights and reform. During the two brief sessions of James's only parliament there was no episode in which the king could be said to have obstructed members' freedom of speech. Why, then, does the claim appear in the Declaration of Rights?

The right of freedom of speech is, to this day, one of the privileges of Parliament that the Speaker of the House of Commons claims as "ancient and undoubted" at the opening of each parliament, and that the king grants.[139] Without question it is the most important of Parliament's privileges, essential to its functioning as a legislative body. The foundations of the right of freedom of speech in Parliament as a privilege of that body were laid, not in the Middle Ages, but in the reign of Henry VIII. Before the sixteenth century, the Speaker only begged the king for freedom to report the Commons' proceedings and asked forgiveness if he said anything displeasing or infringing upon the royal prerogative. The request implicitly acknowledged that freedom of speech was not a right of Parliament.[140] In 1512 the Act in Strode's Case protected the Commons' proceedings from review by other courts, justifying the step on the grounds that Parliament was the highest court of the land. The act did not affect the power of the crown to punish M.P.'s for words judged offensive to the king spoken in Parliament.[141] A decade later (1523), Sir Thomas More was the first Speaker to petition the king for freedom of speech as a privilege of Parliament. More begged the king to "license and pardon freely" M.P.'s to debate and declare their advice "boldly in every thing incident among [them]." The use of the word "license" indicated that More sought permission for what otherwise would be unlawful and recognized that the permission (or license) was revocable. Moreover, the Speaker limited his request to those matters "incident among [them]," meaning those matters proper for Parliament to consider.[142] Clearly, More regarded the privilege as a limited one. In 1548 Commons itself punished one of its members (John Story) for remarks thought to be offensive to the crown, their act testifying to the absence of freedom of speech and also implying that the Commons possessed concurrent authority with the crown to discipline an erring member. During the reign of Elizabeth I, the Speaker's petition for freedom of speech was regularly entered and granted, but the queen severely limited the topics M.P.'s might discuss, and there occurred several contests over the issue.[143] James I's assertion that the Commons' privileges were granted them by the grace of the king provoked the House to respond, in *The Form of Apology and Satisfaction* (1604), that its privileges were "ancient and undoubted" rights, essential to the conduct of its business, and not to be "withheld, denied, or impaired" by the king.[144] The appeal to history, the claim that its privileges were "ancient," flew in the face of history. The proof the Commons offered was bald assertion. It claimed as historical fact what it wanted to be historical fact. Throughout the seventeenth century, critics of the crown would employ this tactic. In 1604 the issue of freedom of speech as a privilege of Commons was unresolved.

In 1610 the debate on impositions raised again, as we have seen, the question of freedom of speech, and the House of Commons framed a petition reaffirming the claim.[145] In 1621 disputes over foreign policy propelled the right of freedom of speech to the center of controversy. The well-known Protestation presented by the Commons emphatically asserted that the privileges of Parliament were theirs by ancient, undoubted right, and that "every member . . . has and of right ought to have freedom of speech." The Protestation so angered James that he tore it from the journals of the House of Commons,[146] recognizing in the Commons' claim a threat to the sovereignty of the king.

During the reign of Charles I the conflicting views of king and Commons over the right of M.P.'s to freedom of speech further deepened tensions between the two. Faced with increasingly bitter opposition to the collection of tunnage and poundage, Charles I ordered Parliament to adjourn on March 2, 1629. In a famous incident, leaders of the Commons refused to adjourn until they had drawn up a protestation. They held the Speaker in the chair while the protestation was being drafted. Charles called nine members — including Sir John Eliot, Denzil Holles, and Benjamin Vallentine — before the Privy Council. When they refused to answer questions about what they had said and done in Parliament except in Parliament itself, the king, without showing cause, ordered the men arrested. Moreover, the attorney-general and the judges ruled that the Act in Strode's Case, which barred judicial review of words uttered in Parliament, was a private act, a ruling opening the way for the case to come before the courts. The king responded to the defendants' suing for a writ of habeas corpus by filing an information against Eliot *et al.* in the Court of King's Bench. Charles charged the nine members with speaking seditious words during the session of parliament, contempt against the king in resisting adjournment, and conspiracy to keep the Speaker in the chair by force. These charges fell under criminal law, for which there was no immunity. They blurred the issue of the right of freedom of speech in Parliament, for the Court of King's Bench indisputably had jurisdiction over the offenses of conspiracy and sedition if committed in Parliament. The defense demurred, resting its case on the grounds, essentially, of the privileges of Parliament. Eliot *et al.* claimed that only the Commons had the authority to punish them if they had offended, and argued that their acts and words could not be construed as conspiracy and sedition. The judges in 1630 found the defendants guilty as charged and fined them. To protect the privileges of Parliament, Eliot *et al.* refused to pay the fine and were imprisoned indefinitely.[147]

Concern to reaffirm the right of freedom of speech reappeared in the debates of the Short Parliament. M.P.'s described it as the "greatest privilege" and as essential to the operation of Parliament.[148] In 1641 they resolved that the proceedings against Eliot, Holles, and Valentine were a gross breach of that privilege. All these points would have been known to members of the rights committees, for after the Restoration some of them had a part in steps to reaffirm the privileges of Parliament. As noted above with respect to article 4, three members — Birch, Lee, and Maynard — were on the committee appointed in May 1660 to frame a bill for maintaining the rights and privileges of Parliament, which included freedom of speech. The bill passed, but failed to be enacted into a statute before the Convention Parliament was dissolved. The next year, however, the Treason and Treasonable Practices Act[149] reaffirmed Parliament's "just" and "ancient" freedom of speech, four members of the 1689 rights committees serving also on the committee that drew up this statute.[150] Six years later, in 1667, Clarges, Howard, and Lee served on still another committee to consider the matter of privilege and freedom of speech in Parliament, with particular reference to the case of Eliot, Holles, and Valentine.[151] The House agreed with the committee that the Act in Strode's Case of 1512 was a general law, intended to indemnify all members of Parliament for "speaking, reasoning or declaring of any matter . . . concerning Parliament . . . [and that it] is a declaratory law of the ancient and necessary rights and privileges of Parliament."[152] The House concluded that the Court of King's Bench should not have accepted jurisdiction over the case of Eliot *et al.* and resolved that the judgment in that case was illegal and against the privileges of Parliament.[153] The Commons sought the concurrence of the Lords in its resolution. The House of Lords, however, decided to use its judicial capacity as the highest court in the land to act in the matter.[154] In 1668 the peers filed a writ of error in the House of Lords, and upon a motion of Denzil Holles, now Lord Holles of Ifield, they reversed the judgment in the case. At the same time, it should be noted, the Lords upheld the Court of King's Bench's claim of jurisdiction over conspiracy and sedition committed in Parliament. The decision was binding on all lower courts; it ended the possibility of review in the courts of words spoken in Parliament. This decision, however, did not apply to the ancient restraints imposed by the crown on freedom of speech in Parliament.

In the absence of specific evidence about the interest of the rights committee in freedom of speech in 1689, the hypothesis seems irresistable that some among them — perhaps those who had been on the committees in 1660 and 1667, or the lawyers, who certainly knew the history of the issue — seized the opportunity to win freedom of speech in Parliament. First, the committee reaffirmed the principle set out in the Act in Strode's Case and reflected in the reversal in the judgment in the case of Eliot *et al.* by the words that freedom of speech in Parliament should not be "impeached or questioned in any court." Second, it laid the groundwork for abolishing the restraints historically exercised by the crown with the words that freedom of speech in Parliament should not be "impeached or questioned in any . . . place out of Parliament." In doing so, the committee went beyond reaffirming an ancient, indisputable right.

Article 9 also claimed as a right freedom of "proceedings in Parliament." This matter found a parallel in the charge that James had violated the liberties of the nation "by prosecutions in the Court of King's Bench for matters and causes cognizable only in Parliament" (no. 8). This charge appeared as clause 22 in the Heads of Grievances: "Informations in the Court of King's Bench to be taken away." What was an information, and to what circumstances did this clause refer? An information was a legal instrument by which an officer of the crown could bring a person to trial without appearing before a grand jury. The officer "informed" the court that he had enough evidence to warrant a trial before a petit jury, and thus set the law in motion without a presentment and indictment. An information was an ancient procedure — as old as the indictment. Both the king and private subjects used informations for civil and criminal cases, but it was the king's use of an information for political purposes in criminal cases that underlay article 8.[155]

In the sixteenth century, the law indisputedly (according to Holdsworth) gave the king the right to proceed by information for an offense under the degree of felony in the Court of King's Bench, Star Chamber, or Council. The advantages lay with prosecutor: an information saved time and put the accused at a disadvantage, because in the absence of an indictment he did not know the nature of the charges until the information was read at the opening of the trial. But the use of an information was not questioned until the case against Eliot *et al.* in 1630. Holdsworth notes that in Eliot's defense occurred the "first hint of the theory" that an information was an illegitimate procedure in criminal cases. He points out that the argument was based upon rulings that did not apply to informations in criminal cases, and that the argument was ignored in 1641, when the decision in the case was questioned, and in 1667–68, when the decision was overruled. Even the act abolishing the Court of Star Chamber referred to the procedure as legal.[156] Moreover, the legality of informations was asserted during the Commonwealth period, and the procedure was widely used without much complaint during the early years of the Restoration, when, in the absence of the Court of Star Chamber (whose abolition was confirmed), the Court of King's Bench sought to expedite the large number of cases over which it now had jurisdiction. At the end of Charles II's reign and during that of James II, however, informations were used for political purposes against the partisan enemies of the crown. For example, an information was used to bring the Seven Bishops to trial. At those proceedings, Bishop Thomas White of Peterborough objected to the unfairness of having to respond to charges first known to him through the reading of the information.[157] It was used in the cases of Sir Samuel Barnardiston and Sir Thomas Pilkington, which, for other reasons, figured in the Declaration of Rights.[158] It was also used to bring Williams to trial.

It was Williams's case that was in the minds of the authors of article 9. Williams, it will be remembered, was charged in 1684 with licensing, while Speaker of the House in 1680, a pamphlet (Thomas Dangerfield's *Narrative,* reflecting on the duke of York), which the court later declared was a seditious libel. The trial took place in King's Bench in 1686, with Pollexfen serving as defense attorney.[159] Williams's plea was that the court had no jurisdiction over the proceedings of the House of Commons and, therefore, none over his actions as Speaker in licensing the tract. Holdsworth cited this trial as an example of the legally indefensible position of the Commons that their claim of privilege (or jurisdiction) covered a particular act. The Court of King's Bench had jurisdiction over seditious libel. By pleading to the jursidiction of Parliament, Pollexfen prevented the court from inquiring whether the tract was a libel and, then, whether or not the action was privileged. Therefore, according to Holdsworth, the verdict of the court was just and in conformity with law.[160] Neither the House of Commons nor its Speaker acting upon its orders can justify the publication of a libel on the grounds of privilege. Holdsworth's reading of the verdict receives reinforcement from the fact that, although the Commons passed a resolution after the revolution declaring the judgment "illegal," Williams was not able to secure a reversal.[161]

Charles II and James II had, of course, proceeded against Williams for political reasons, and it was this fact and the argument that the privileges of the House had been invaded that aroused sympathy for Williams, the Whig turncoat. By stressing his sufferings at the hands of a king who had brought him to trial on an information and at the hands of a court that had denied his plea of the jurisdiction of Parliament Williams elevated his personal problems to the level of a principle to be defended in the Declaration of Rights.

The first time informations were mentioned as a grievance was at the committee meeting of January 30, when someone (surely Williams?) urged that "all informations in the King's Bench be disallowed" and that "no proceedings shall be for any crime or misdemeanor but by indictment." [162] The Heads of Grievances (clause 22) cited informations as a grievance. This clause provoked acid comments by M.P.'s who argued that not all informations could be construed as grievances and that disallowing the procedure might prove to be "mischievous." [163] But the condemnation of informations was defended, and the rights committee retained the clause in the February 7 draft, placing it in the category of rights that required new law. In this draft, the committee members also made informations a grievance in the indictment of the king, charging him with "causing informations to be brought and prosecuted in the Court of King's Bench" (clause 8). The Lords objected to this charge and asked for clarification. In the responding debate, Treby candidly admitted that the clause was put in "for the sake of . . . Sir William Williams, who was punished out of Parliament for what he had done in Parliament." Another member of the rights committees, Lee, also pointed out that the word "information" was inaccurate if the charge was to be leveled against James II because, although the prosecution of Williams had occurred after he became king, the information was filed during his brother's reign. [164] Determined to assert as a right the privileged character of Parliament's proceedings, the rights committee changed the word "informations" to "prosecutions" and preserved the charge. The committee knew that informations were not illegal. One of its members, Holt, declared after the revolution that while one may complain about the abuse of informations, the procedure itself was legal. [165] Probably the difficulty of demonstrating that either an information or the prosecution against Williams was illegal led the rights committee to avoid an overt parallel claim of rights and to subsume the issue in article 9.

Three articles in the Declaration of Rights deal with procedures in law. Paralleling the charges in clauses 10 through 13 in the indictment of James II, they prohibit excessive bail, excessive fines, and cruel and unusual punishments (article 10), assert that jurors in treason trials must be freeholders (article 11), and prevent the granting or promising of fines before conviction (article 12). This portion of the document sought to restrain the judicial prerogatives of the king. The three articles responded to procedures in law cases tried under James II and Charles II, especially from 1681 to

1685, when the king ruled without Parliament and shifted the scene of conflict with the Whig opposition to the law courts. The articles reflected the parliamentary Opposition's distrust of the judiciary, which began as early as 1667 and became for the Whigs in 1680 an issue second in importance only to Exclusion, and when Exclusion failed, of first importance.[166] The framers of the final version of the declaration sacrificed clauses in the Heads of Grievances that would have changed the tenure of judges and instituted other legal reforms,[167] but the issues they preserved in articles 10, 11, and 12 tacitly condemned the bench. In each instance the judges were responsible for the greivance, whether it was requiring excessive bail, imposing excessive fines, inflicting cruel and unusual punishments, ruling that jurors in treason trials need not be freeholders, or granting and promising fines and forfeitures before conviction. Judges were the object of bitter criticism in the prince's manifesto, other contemporary pamphlets, and the Convention debates. To remind the public of exactly who the judges were in the trials during the reigns of Charles II and James II, a tract with the curious title *The Ashes of the Just Smell Sweet and Blossom in the Dust* listed their names.

There was apparent doubt in the minds of the authors of the declaration that the claims in these three articles were "undoubted" and "indisputed." Each article appeared in both sections of the February 7 draft: in the section of old laws, and in the one of rights that required new laws. These specific issues played no part in William's *Declaration of Reasons* and were of marginal importance in other tracts and pamphlets published at the time of the revolution; they were ignored or barely mentioned in the Convention debates. They were the result of the influence, at the meetings of the rights committee on January 30 and 31, of Whig lawyers who were concerned, out of their own earlier experiences, to protect the needs of defendants.

Article 10

That excessive bail ought not to be required, nor excessive fines imposed, nor cruel and unusual punishments inflicted.

Article 10 drew together three procedures employed by the judiciary in the political trials of the period, the painful effects of which Whig partisans had experienced. Each of them — excessive bail, excessive fines, and cruel and unusual punishments — was declared to be a violation of known law, but at the same time the use of the verb "ought" implied ambivalence about whether these procedures did violate known law. In fact, the status in law of each should be distinguished.

The excessive bail clause in article 10 addressed the problem of judicial abuse in setting the amount of bail. One of the charges against James (no. 10) was that "excessive bail has been required of persons committed in criminal cases to elude the benefit of the laws made for the liberty of the subjects." The excessive bail clause responded to defects in previous laws about bail, especially the Habeas Corpus Act of 1679. In its original form, as clause 19 in the Heads of Grievances, it called for preventing excessive bail in criminal cases, and the indictment of James II retained that phraseology. But article 10 contains no reference to "criminal cases" and, thus, would seem to apply the principle to all cases. The clause implied the *right* of the defendant to bail to avoid pretrial detention, a right which had developed over many centuries. It addressed abuses in administering bail and aimed to deny judges the power to set the amount of bail so high as to avoid the right to bail. Legal historians agree that this clause in article 10 became one of the basic elements in English bail law.[168]

Although a form of bail existed as early as the Anglo-Saxon era, and the Assizes of Clarendon (1166) and Northampton (1176) revealed plainly the connection between arrest and release on bail, the first statutory regulation of bail was the thirteenth-century statute of Westminster I.[169] It provided guidelines for the sheriff and lesser local officers as to bailable offenses but did not bind the king or higher justices. Over the next several centuries the justices of the peace assumed the sheriffs' powers of admitting persons to bail; and in 1554 a statute, aimed at removing certain injustices, spelled out the procedures to be followed in granting bail.[170] These two laws, augmented by other statutes in the seventeenth and eighteenth centuries, formed the basis of English bail law until the nineteenth century. In sum, bail law specified bailable and nonbailable offenses for lesser officers, but gave them considerable discretion in cases that were "dubious." It also gave great power to the Court of King's Bench, or to any judge of that court in time of vacation, to rule on bail.[171]

Closely connected with the right to bail in certain instances was the development of the writ of habeas corpus. Originally a procedural writ to bring the defendant to court, habeas corpus developed into a writ by which an official was required to produce a person in his custody.[172] Rivalry between the Court of Common Pleas and the Court of Chancery account for this development, for the former used the writ of habeas corpus to extend its jurisdiction.[173] In the early seventeenth century, the writ was employed as a way of protecting the liberty of the subject; the common-law courts used it to secure the release of persons committed by the king. Common-law lawyers and parliamentary critics of the king connected habeas corpus with the article in Magna Charta that prohibited imprisonment without due process of law although there was no historical connection between the two. They interpreted "due process of law" to mean due process of the common law, and they argued that Magna Charta made arrests by the king's council or by special writ of the king illegal. They maintained that a person so detained had the right to be delivered by the writ of habeas corpus.

The crown did not accept such views. In 1591 the judges, in an attempt to settle the rules about habeas corpus, specifically recognized the validity of commitments by the council or king.[174] Nonetheless, habeas corpus continued to be regarded as the most effective weapon for protecting the liberty of the subject. English jurists, including Selden in the early part of the century and Hale during the Restoration, agreed that it was the "highest remedy in law for any man that is imprisoned." [175]

Against this general background occurred the steps that led directly to the "excessive bail" clause in 1689: *Darnel's Case* in 1627, the Petition of Right in 1628, the abolition of the prerogative courts at the Civil War, and the habeas corpus act of 1679. *Darnel's Case* concerned five knights who were imprisoned by command of Charles I, without showing cause, for having refused to subscribe to the king's forced loan. They brought an action for a writ of habeas corpus. The principal issue in this case was the power of the crown to imprison a person without showing cause. The defense argued for a writ of habeas corpus, maintained that since the five knights stood accused but not convicted, they should be freed on bail, and declared that their imprisonment violated Magna Charta and other statutes guaranteeing due process in arrest and detention. The court, however, ruled that the king (in the interests of preserving the state) had legal power to commit a person without showing cause. When that happened, the case did not fall under the due process clause, because the cause was unknown. In the absence of cause, the court had no basis for judgment: it could not question the royal right to commit, nor could it grant bail. [176]

The next year the Petition of Right declared this decision to be contrary to law. It claimed that forced loans, contrary to the law, had been levied, and that people who refused to subscribe to them were imprisoned without showing cause and, thus, were denied bail. The petition asked that "no freeman in any such manner as is before mentioned be imprisoned or detained." During the debates on the Petition of Right, members of Parliament had stressed that the decision in *Darnel's Case* undermined laws that guaranteed pretrial release on bail, Sir Edward Coke, for example, declaring that if the cause of imprisonment is not stated, then the right of bail is, in effect, voided. By accepting the Petition of Right by the formula desired by the parliamentary opposition, Charles lost the right to imprison *"per speciale mandatum"*— without showing cause. But as long as Charles had a prerogative court such as the Court of Star Chamber, his power to commit subjects to prison and keep them there without granting habeas corpus or bail was very large. Charles regularly evaded the Petition of Right during the eleven years he ruled without calling a parliament.

At the time of the Civil War, protection of the subject's right to bail was strengthened. The prerogative courts were abolished in 1641 by an act which provided that any subject imprisoned by command of the king or the council should have a writ of habeas corpus from the judges of either the Court of King's Bench or the Court of Common Pleas, that the jailer must report the true cause of imprisonment, and that the court must within three days either bail the prisoner or remand him. [177] Nonetheless, certain defects remained in the law and in legal procedures which Cromwell and then Charles II exploited to detain persons in prison. For example, the act did not cover commitment by the secretary of state. Or, uncertainties surrounded which courts could issue the writ of habeas corpus and whether the writ could be issued during vacation of the court. Moreover, a prisoner could be moved to places like the Channel Islands, where the writ did not apply, or taken out of the jurisdiction of the court.[178]

Beginning in 1668 the House of Commons from time to time tried to deal with such defects by introducing bills for the "better securing of the liberty of the subject."[179] The arrest of a London alderman, Francis Jenkes, for a speech at the Guildhall urging the Common Council to petition the king to call a new parliament reinforced their efforts in 1676. Jenkes was detained for some months on a technicality until one of the judges, his conscience apparently pricked by the clear violation of the law, insisted that he be released.[180] Three years later, in 1679, the Whig party was successful in passing the Habeas Corpus Act, sometimes known as "Shaftesbury's Act," and regarded as the one "solid legislative success" of the Whigs.[181] Promoting it were seventeen men who would serve on the rights committees in 1689.[182] The Habeas Corpus Act set out procedures to prevent abuses in the use of the writ and prohibit detention of the accused in cases which by law permitted bail. That the act was effective in protecting the liberty of the subject and helping assure release on bail is suggested by James II's desire to repeal it and by its suspension in 1689.[183] Nonetheless, the act was limited in that, for example, it did not regulate the amount of bail that might be set.[184] Thus, judges evaded its purpose by setting bail so high that the prisoner was unable to raise the sum, in effect, denying him the right to bail. In December 1680, a committee of the House of Commons appointed to examine the proceedings of the judges in Westminster Hall brought in a report condemning as "illegal and a high breach of the liberty of the subject" the refusing of "sufficient" bail.[185] Seven members of this committee would serve on the rights committees in 1689.[186]

In 1689 the rights committee renewed the effort to protect the liberty of the subject. Although reform tracts ignored the issue of excessive bail, and only a little-known M.P. cried out "extravagant bail" at the very end of the debate on rights,[187] the issue was cited as a grievance at the committee meeting on January 30. Clause 19 of the Heads of Grievances mentioned bail, and clause 25 (which failed to survive) addressed the closely related matter of making provision for the court to investigate the truth of the return of the jailer. Probably mindful that a prohibition against excessive bail was not spelled out in ancient law, the committee put that clause in both categories of the February 7 draft. They preserved it in the final version of the declaration and there asserted that excessive bail "ought" not to be required. In doing so, they went beyond reaffirming old law.

The "excessive fines" clause in article 10 likewise responded to incidents of judicial abuse. The indictment against James II (no. 11) charged that during his reign judges had imposed excessive fines, thereby subverting the laws and liberties of the kingdom. Freedom from excessive fines, indisputably an ancient right of the subject, found its origins in the principles that forbade excessive punishments and required equality between crime and punishment, as in the *lex talionis*. These were old concepts, dating from the Bible, early Greek philosophy, and, in England, the Anglo-Saxon era. After the Norman conquest, a change occurred, and the discretionary amercement, which left the penalty in the hands of the peers of the party amerced, became the rule. Its discretionary character relaxed the old rigid system of punishments, but at the same time provided opportunity for imposing excessive fines. Magna Charta asserted that a free man shall be amerced according to the gravity of the offense, and that the amercement shall not endanger his livelihood — *salvo contenemento,* was the phrase. Following Magna Charta a writ to enforce the concept of *salvo contenemento* developed, fourteenth-century petitions tested it, and other laws confirmed it.[188]

In the early seventeenth century, the levying of fines became entangled in the constitutional and political struggles between the king and his parliamentary critics. The proponents of the common law sought to apply the principle of Magna Charta to fines imposed by the court, Coke, for example, asserting that "an excessive fine is against the law."[189] The Court of Star Chamber, however, imposed heavy fines on the king's enemies, and this, according to a seventeenth-century observer and a twentieth-century historian, led to its downfall.[190] The statute abolishing the Court of Star Chamber in 1641 specifically prohibited any court thereafter from following that court's practices, including the levying of excessive fines. But towards the end of Charles II's reign, the courts imposed ruinous fines on the critics of the crown. In December 1680 the committee of the Commons (already mentioned) which was appointed to investigate the proceedings of the judges examined the transcript of all the fines imposed in King's Bench since 1677 and resolved that in imposing fines the judges had acted "arbitrarily, illegally, and partially," and in favor of Papists.[191] A fortnight later another committee, on which once again members of the future rights committees in 1689 served,[192] prepared a bill for the relief of the subject against arbitrary fines. In debate, Foley complained that "men have been fined, not according to their crimes, but their principles: sometimes because they have been Protestants." Boscawen was especially bitter, calling the judges "great malefactors."[193] The anger about excessive fines also found expression in the impeachment proceedings against one of the judges.[194]

Over the next few years fines became even more excessive and partisan. For example, the Whiggish sheriff of London, Sir Thomas Pilkington, was fined £100,000 in 1682 for words spoken against the duke of York, and in 1683 he and others were tried on a charge of inciting a riot in the election of the London sheriffs and fined, variously, upwards of 1,000 marks.[195] In 1684 Sir Samuel Barnardiston was fined £10,000 for writing letters alleged to be seditious; the sum was so huge that he languished in prison and his estate was ruined.[196] Also in 1684 the judges ruled in John Hampden's case that Magna Charta did not refer to fines for offenses against the king.[197] Members of the 1689 rights committees in both Houses — Williams, John Hampden, and the earl of Devonshire — had suffered heavy fines.[198] Although at the revolution only one tract underlined excessive fines as a grievance of the nation,[199] Temple referred to "strange fines," citing them as a grievance to be redressed,[200] and "excessive fines" were specifically mentioned at the committee meeting on January 30. The rights committee placed the clause in both categories in the February 7 draft and, in the final version of the Declaration of Rights, asserted that excessive fines "ought" not to be imposed. This section of article 10 reaffirmed ancient law.

The "cruel and unusual punishments" clause was still another condemnation of judicial abuse and an indirect criticism of the judiciary. Like the other two clauses in article 10, it formed part of the indictment against James II: the king was accused of allowing judges to inflict "illegal and cruel punishments" (no. 12). The changes in the phraseology of the clause in the successive drafts of the Declaration of Rights are, in the absence of direct evidence, important in understanding the intention of the authors. The words "illegal punishments" occurred first at the January 30 committee meeting, introduced almost certainly by Whig lawyers. The Heads of Grievances (clause 19) preserved the phrase. In the February 7 draft, James II was charged with "illegal and cruel punishments," but the words "cruel and unusual" — not "illegal" — were used in the declaratory section of that draft. The word "unusual," in common use from about 1630, meant "uncommon" or "exceptional." A legal historian has suggested that its use should be laid to "chance and sloppy draftsmanship."[201] While that is not an unreasonable interpretation, the word was appropriate to convey the idea that the punishments were "uncommon" and "exceptional," outside what the law permitted. The word "cruel," while it meant "merciless" in the seventeenth century, also had in common usage a less onerous significance as "severe" or "rigorous."[202] Thus "cruel" and "unusual" may be read as "severe" and "uncommon," which would underscore and add an emotional dimension to the word "illegal," without destroying its meaning. For rhetorical reasons, it may be suggested, "cruel and unusual" replaced "illegal" as adjectives modifying "punishments" in the declaratory portion of the document. The words were, of course, susceptible to other readings. They led the American founding fathers to interpret the clauses as a prohibition against barbarous methods of punishments.[203] But, in fact, the clause addressed the issue of "illegal punishments," meaning punishments that were excessive, disproportionate to the crime, contrary to the law, and outside the authority of the court to impose.

As already noted, the prohibition of excessive punishments and the concern for equating crime and punishment were ancient concerns in English law and custom. In the fourteenth century the principle underlying amercements set out in Magna Charta was extended to physical punishments, and by the opening of the fifteenth century, the idea that the punishment should fit the crime — should not be excessive — was fixed. In 1553 it was reflected in a statute.[204] Although criticism of inhumane and barbarous methods of punishment was voiced in England at the end of the sixteenth century, prohibition of them had not developed by the time of the Revolution of 1688–89.[205] The report of the committee appointed in 1680 to investigate the proceedings of the judges made no reference to the barbarity of the punishments handed out, nor did M.P.'s in the debates in Parliament. The terrible sentence for high treason suffered by the victims of the "Bloody Assizes" in 1685 was nowhere mentioned as requiring change, nor were there protests against the severe whippings used as punishment in the West in 1685 and in London in 1686 and 1687. Yet, as Ogg has pointed out, criticism of the government was construed as seditious libel in 1685, and silence need not be taken as consent.[206] One tract, published in December 1688, referred to the "barbarous, cruel and inhumane whippings of persons through the street" as a reason for the nation's revolt. Referring to the suffering of the Reverend Samuel Johnson, the author blamed Jeffreys for "inventing" this punishment and asserted that the sight of it "stirred the blood of . . . English hearts and occasioned loud complaints." The pamphleteer thought that whippings were inappropriate to a misdemeanor and worried that the "best commoner" in England might therefore "fall under the lash."[207] It seems, then, that people's sensibilities were aroused by the whippings in the West and in London. But they were not warmed to the point of insisting upon the removal of such forms of punishments. Whippings continued to be used in the eighteenth century, and the barbaric punishment for treason was not changed until the nineteenth century.

Recent proceedings in the Court of King's Bench, which had resulted in excessive and therefore illegal punishments, probably prompted members of the rights committees to include the clause. For example, the punishment of Titus Oates, convicted in 1686 on two counts of perjury, was (1) a fine of 2,000 marks, (2) whipping, (3) life imprisonment, (4) pillorying four times a year for the rest of his life, and (5) defrocking.[208] After the revolution, Oates entered a petition for reversal, which was initially denied by the House of Lords. Some lords filed a minority report that explained why they had dissented. First, the court had exceeded its jurisdiction in defrocking Oates. Second, the punishment of life imprisonment and whipping for the crime of perjury was illegal and without precedent. Holt, Pollexfen, and Treby, by then justices, held that the sentence was "contrary to law and ancient practice, and therefore erroneous."[209] Or again, the sentence imposed on the Reverend Samuel Johnson for having published two tracts judged to be seditious libel was (1) a fine of 500 marks and imprisonment until the fine was paid, (2) pillorying, (3) whipping, and (4) defrocking. Johnson also petitioned for reversal, and in June 1689 the House of Commons resolved that the judgment against him was "illegal and cruel."[210] There is no comment on the barbarous nature of punishments so long as they are fixed by law.

What the authors of the clause aimed to condemn was the judges' abuse of their discretionary powers in fixing punishments on the Whig enemies of the king. They wanted to prohibit punishments that were unauthorized by statute, outside the jurisdiction of the sentencing court (as in defrocking), disproportionate in severity to the crime, and therefore, illegal. In sum, the intent of the framers was consistent with ancient custom and law. but the phraseology of the clause had rhetorical overtones which may well have been calculated to make the crimes of James II seem even more heinous.

Article 11

That jurors ought to be duly impaneled and returned, and jurors which pass upon men in trials for high treason ought to be freeholders.

The origin of the claim that jurors in trials for high treason ought to be freeholders and the charge (no. 9) that men who were not freeholders had served as jurors lay in the procedures followed in the treason trials of the early 1680s of men who became Whig martyrs. The article reflected Whig hostility towards the late Stuart judiciary. It also mirrored the struggle between Whigs and Charles and his Tory friends for control of borough corporations, especially the office of sheriff, since the sheriff was responsible for appointing jurors. Thus, the article reflected clause 20 of the Heads of Grievances, which called for reform in "abuses in the appointing of sheriffs."

At the height of the Whigs' power, many boroughs, including London, and many local offices were in Whig hands. Thus, they could impanel men to serve as jurors who would protect them against the judicial measures of the court. This advantage was demonstrated in the Middlesex Grand Jury's return in 1681 of an ignoramus to the indictment of Shaftesbury.[211] Beginning in 1681, however, the court "turned the tables on the Whigs."[212] Exploiting his judicial and administrative prerogatives, Charles instituted quo warranto proceedings against borough corporations; by 1682 London was in his hands.

The quo warranto expedient accomplished two ends: the election to Parliament of men friendly to the court and the impaneling of juries who could be counted on to give verdicts for the crown. It also had the effect of undermining the ruling in Bushell's case (1670) which protected jurors against reprisals for rendering a verdict against the direction of the judge, for if the jurors could be counted on to favor the crown, they would be unlikely to act contrary to the judge's directions. Since the late Stuart kings had appointed judges (as was their right) on a tenure of "at pleasure," they had all along had some control over the bench. The remodeling of the corporations, then, completed an arrangement whereby the court could expect to use the law effectively against its political enemies. Thus, it has been said that the most important constitutional issues in 1681–82 were "the relationship of sheriffs to juries and of juries to common law judges."[213]

The effect of these judicial and administrative procedures was demonstrated by the court's success in bringing Whig critics to trial on charges of treason. Several tracts and pamphlets published in the early 1680s had expressed concern to preserve the independence and integrity of jurors,[214] none more eloquently than Somers's *Security of Englishmens Lives,* already discussed. But the issue that jurors in treason trials must be freeholders was first raised in Lord Russell's trial. Russell entered an exception to a juror on the grounds that he was not a freeholder. Although the principle that jurors must be freeholders (to prevent a poor man from being influenced) was generally accepted,[215] the law on whether a juror must be a freeholder in a treason case tried in a city, especially in London, was unclear. For example, a contemporary tract, written without partisan purpose to set out the custom and the law on juries, stated as fact that the requirement that jurors must be freeholders "did not extend to cities [or] towns corporate."[216] The explanation for this exception was that there were few freeholders in cities (especially London) because estates belonged to the nobility, the gentry, or the corporation.

At Russell's trial, arguments on both sides of the question were aired. Pollexfen and Holt presented the case that jurors in treason trials must be freeholders, but under close questioning, Pollexfen admitted that the laws he was citing did not apply to cases of treason. He was met with the judge's rebuke: "Unless treason, you do not speak *ad idem.*"[217] The prosecution (Sawyer) opposed Pollexfen's claim, citing a lengthy list of laws, custom in cities, and court rulings. All of the judges, whom scholars are now agreed cannot be dismissed as legal incompetents, concurred that the absence of freehold in a juror could not, according to the law, be the cause of a challenge in a treason trial held in London.[218] The requirement that jurors must be freeholders was disallowed in subsequent treason trials, notwithstanding that Whig lawyers continued to press for it.[219]

Russell's trial was in the minds of the authors of article 11. At the meeting of the rights committee on January 31, one of them recounted that when Russell entered an exception, the prospective juror "swore" that "let him except to never so many there would be enough left that he knew would do his work."[220] Committeemen also complained about the way the court had perverted the jury system. "In every county," they said, the freeholders' book either did not contain the names of the "chief gentlemen" or their names were marked with a cross to show that they were "not for the turn of the court." As a consequence, juries were composed of men who were "sure cards" for the crown. Moreover, men were appointed to "labor juries." These irregularities accounted for the "false and corrupt" verdicts that Stuart courts had brought in. Similar concern about the freehold status of jurors and the general threat to the independence of juries appeared in a printed tract, *A Letter to a gentleman at Brussels, containing an account of the causes of the peoples revolt from the crown,* which was dated December 22, 1688, at Windsor. This tract directed the Parliament to take note of certain juries that deserved censure, among them Russell's. Attention was further drawn to Russell's case by a tract written by Henry Booth, Lord Delamere, titled *The late Lord Russell's Case with Observations upon it.*[221]

The rights committeemen were apparently mindful that the law on the freehold status of jurors in treason trials was uncertain, for they placed the claim in both categories in the February 7 draft, designating it as an old right, and acknowledging that it required new law. But they felt strongly enough about the matter to preserve it in the final draft as an undoubted right of the nation, and thereby, they laid the groundwork for new law.

Article 12

That all grants and promises of fines and forfeitures of particular persons before conviction are illegal and void.

Article 12, which declared that all grants and promises of fines and forfeitures of persons before conviction were illegal, was added by the House of Commons to the Heads of Grievances reported by the rights committee. In its original form, as clause 26 in the Heads, the article included a proviso that persons who procured such fines and forfeitures were liable to punishment. James was specifically indicted, in clause 13 of the declaration, for permitting this procedure to occur.

What the article alluded to was a practice that had grown up around the law of treason. The treason law provided that the property of a person convicted of treason was forfeited to the crown. The practice was for courtiers and others to solicit the forfeitures even before a judgment was rendered, thus creating a situation whereby they stood to benefit from a conviction and therefore might be tempted to interfere in the proceedings of the court to encourage conviction. That the king had the right to forfeitures in treason cases and to fines in other cases was not disputed. The question was whether the crown had the right to grant such fines and forfeitures to courtiers and whether courtiers could "beg" them. Ancient laws forbade such tactics,[222] and commentators reinforced the point. For example, Coke asserted that the king could neither grant, promise, nor seize the property of a person indicted for treason before conviction, and explained that otherwise, "undue means and more violent prosecution is *[sic]* used for private lucre."[223] In 1610, Parliament laid plans to cite the begging of fines before conviction as a grievance, but James I intervened, insisting that he detested the practice and promising to grant no more fines to courtiers.[224] In 1628 and 1629 bills were introduced against claiming fines before conviction, but nothing came of them.[225] In 1680, in a debate critical of judicial practices, an M.P. blamed exorbitant fines on the begging of fines by courtiers, who then put pressure on the bench to set the fine at a large figure.[226]

But the procedure had long been practiced, and despite criticism, it continued. For example, at the time of the Northern Rebellion in 1569, Elizabeth I's courtiers competed for the forfeited property of the rebels.[227] During Cromwell's regime, following suppression of threats to his authority, the same thing happened, and under Charles II the procedure was so widespread that the crown's revenue from forfeitures was negligible.[228] But it was during the trials following Monmouth's Rebellion in 1685, Whig propaganda stressed, that the most blatant examples of granting or promising fines and forfeitures before conviction occurred. Undoubtedly these episodes were in the minds of the framers of article 12.

The so-called Bloody Assizes were presided over by Jeffreys, whose name became legend in the West Country because of his alleged unfeeling brutality and vindictiveness during the proceedings.[229] Two to three hundred individuals were tried and convicted as traitors; they suffered the extreme penalty for treason, and their property was forfeited.[230] Moreover, to speed the proceedings, Jeffreys and other judges (including Pollexfen) engaged in massive "plea bargaining"[231] with perhaps as many as 800 more prisoners accused of treason. The jurists encouraged them to plead guilty and suffer transportation, in return for being spared the rigors of the penalty for treason. The profit to be obtained from selling the rebels into penal servitude in the West Indies was considerable, and before the men were tried, courtiers competed to be given consignment of them. In advising the king to avoid assigning the men to "persons that have not suffered" in his service, Jeffreys estimated that each rebel was worth between ten and fifteen pounds.[232] Pardons also were sold. The most famous pardon was that for Edmund Prideaux, a wealthy Whig, whose family paid close to £15,000 directly to Jeffreys.[233] The Bloody Assizes were the most immediate example of an illegal but widespread practice that imperiled the property and rights of the accused, perverted justice, and enriched persons around the court.

The issue received no attention, however, until the debate of February 2. Then two radical Whigs, both members of the rights committee, raised it. Richard Hampden complained that the begging of fines and forfeitures before conviction was "a most mischievous thing" because, he explained, the person granted the fine "turns prosecutor." Boscawen echoed the sentiment and added that anyone who tried to procure such grants should be punished.[234] What moved these men to condemn fines and forfeitures before conviction at this particular time is unclear, but possibly the presentation of a petition, signed by the women of the West, asking that Jeffreys be handed over to them that they might avenge his cruelty to their friends and relations provoked their action.[235] There was a sizable contingent of men from the West (eleven of them) on the rights committee,[236] and their sympathy to the petition may be assumed. Tipping, nephew to Alice Lisle (the seventy-one-year-old woman in whose trial, mentioned above, Jeffreys' severity was notorious), may have promoted interest in the petition and in an issue, condemning fines and forfeitures before conviction, which was related to it. Public outrage at Jeffreys and the proceedings at the Bloody Assizes, suppressed in 1685, overflowed at the time of the revolution.[237] Indignation was expressed in a polemical print (one of few prints designed by Englishmen during the months of revolution) showing the capture of Jeffreys, who was fleeing in disguise.[238] Outrage was expressed also in printed tracts.[239] It is not unreasonable to think that the indignation was reflected in article 12. The rights committee placed the issue in both categories of the February 7 draft, claiming it as an old right and also asking for new law to remedy defects. In the final version of the declaration the committee simply asserted that fines and forfeitures before conviction were illegal. Article 12 also served a propaganda purpose of the radical Whigs in calling to mind the judicial excesses of the detested Jeffreys in the Bloody Assizes just four years before. At the same time the article reaffirmed ancient statutes and legal opinion and sought to correct a long-standing grievance.

Article 13

And that for redress of all grievances, and for the amending, strengthening, and preserving of the laws, parliaments ought to be held frequently.

Article 13 declared that it was an undoubted right of the nation that parliaments should be held frequently to redress grievances and amend the laws. There was no parallel clause in the indictment of the king to charge that he had not summoned parliaments frequently. Although Charles II had violated the Triennial Act at the end of his reign by not summoning a parliament within the prescribed three years, James II had stayed within the terms of that law and had twice, in the fall of 1688, ordered the dispatch of writs calling for an election to Parliament. It was an undoubted ancient prerogative of the king to summon, prorogue, and dissolve Parliament. Possibly the use of the verb "ought" and of the ambiguous adverb "frequently," and the fact that the committee placed the article in both sections of the February 7 draft, thus claiming it as an old right and acknowledging that it required new law, reflected some diffidence in the face of this fact.

Notwithstanding the acknowledged royal prerogative over the calling, proroguing, and dissolving of Parliament, men who wanted to regularize the position of Parliament in England's government had repeatedly claimed that parliaments should be summoned frequently. Such requests, invariably based on two statutes of Edward III (one in 1330 and the other in 1362) which claimed that a parliament should be held once a year, began with the sixteenth century.[240] They continued in the early seventeenth century, as in 1610.[241] In 1621, some members protested that ancient law prevented the king from dissolving Parliament while business pended, but others, Coke among them, reaffirmed the power of the king over Parliament.[242] Following the decade of the 1630s, when Charles I ruled without Parliament, the issue took on urgency. In the Short Parliament of 1640, John Pym characterized the intermission of Parliament as the "one great grievance . . . the fountain of all [grievances]."[243] Other members underlined the need for Parliament to meet every year, and petitions to the Parliament reiterated the point.[244] The next year, the Triennial Act of 1641 nullified the king's authority by providing procedures to assure that no more than three years should elapse between dissolving or proroguing a parliament and summoning another.[245] In subsequent years, Leveller spokesmen laid stress upon the principle that annual or sometimes biennial parliaments were a right of the nation, guaranteed by the aforementioned laws of Edward III.[246]

At the Restoration, however, the Triennial Act was repealed on the grounds that it violated a prerogative of the crown; and the Triennial Act of 1664, while iterating that the laws of Edward III required frequent parliaments and that no more than three years ought to elapse between the dissolution of one parliament and the calling of another, failed to provide enabling mechanism to assure its purpose. Members of the emerging parliamentary Opposition, who would serve on the rights committees in 1689, tried unsuccessfully to strengthen the Triennial Act. Thus, in 1668 Temple introduced a bill which empowered the lord chancellor to issue writs summoning Parliament in the event the king did not order a parliament within three years after dissolving or proroguing a previous one. Although Littleton and Howard supported the effort, other M.P.'s asserted that the bill was "contrary to monarchy" and would "breed jealousy" between king and people.[247] They forced Temple to withdraw it. The attitude of the Commons stiffened, however, at the time of the Popish Plot and Exclusion Crisis. In March 1679 the House drafted a bill to regulate abuses in elections, one of whose provisions was that no future parliament should last for more than two years. Again, in December 1680, the House resolved to bring in a bill for the "more effectual securing of meeting and sitting of Parliament" and appointed a committee to draw it up. Among the members were Birch, Paul Foley, Richard Hampden, Lee, and Powle.[248] The bill, however, was lost by the king's proroguing Parliament.

From then until the revolution, during years virtually free of parliaments, printed tracts written by Whig partisans nourished the idea of frequent parliaments as a principle and as essential to realizing other Whig ideals.[249] For one example, Somers, chairman of one rights committee, argued in *A Just and Modest Vindication* that the statutes of Edward III required that Parliament, the "representative body of the people," should meet annually. He asserted that the king's coronation oath secured that right and maintained that the "constitution" would be imperfect if the prince had the authority to summon and dismiss Parliament at will.[250] Whig tracts stressed a further claim which was necessary to implement frequent parliaments, namely that Parliament should not be dissolved or prorogued until its business was dispatched.

At the time of the revolution, the principle of frequent parliaments had a central place in the rights and reform tract literature and in Temple's programmatic statement about reform. Given the previous parliamentary experience of the rights committee members and their political principles, their interest in the issue was certain. They drafted three clauses specifically about Parliament for the Heads of Grievances: (9) "That Parliament ought to sit frequently, and that their frequent sitting be preserved"; (10) "No interrupting of any session of Parliament, till the affairs that are necessary to be dispatched at that time are determined"; and (11) "That the too long continuance of the same Parliament be prevented." They dropped clauses 10 and 11, but preserved clause 9 in article 13. In the form sent up to the Lords for approval, article 13 retained the phrase "and suffered to sit," which, in effect, would have nullified the king's prerogative to prorogue and dissolve Parliament at his pleasure. The Lords insisted upon deleting the words as contrary to law, which indeed they were. In sum, article 13 was indisputably an ancient claim, repeatedly advanced in the face of the competing prerogative of the crown, but not indisputedly an ancient, "undoubted" right. The Declaration of Rights sought to make it one.

This brief overview of the historical and constitutional background of the rights in the Declaration of Rights shows that the document, with one exception, addressed issues that had been for decades at the center of contention between the king and the parliamentary Opposition. The one exception was article 3, which condemned the "Court" of Commissioners for Ecclesiastical Causes. Notwithstanding the explicit language indicting James II for the grievances of the nation, words that would have specifically excluded Charles II from blame were not included, as some Tories wished. A politically conscious contemporary would have known that the charges could equally well be leveled against Charles II and would have recognized the claim of rights as a resolution of long-term controversies. The declaration asserted that all the grievances were "utterly and directly contrary to the known laws and statutes . . . of this realm" and that all the rights were "ancient" and "undoubted," thereby using time-honored language that had appeared in many earlier statements. But, as we have seen, this statement was not in every case true. Not all the grievances were violations of the known law, and not all the rights were "ancient" and "undoubted." In fact, only six articles did indeed reaffirm old law: articles 4 (regarding taxation without parliamentary consent), 5 (regarding the right of subjects freely to petition the king), 7 (regarding the right of Protestants to keep arms under certain conditions), 8 (respecting the free election of members to Parliament), 10 (the clauses regarding excessive fines and cruel and unusual punishment), and 12 (respecting grants and promises of fines and forfeitures before conviction). And, it should be noted, article 5 asserts an unbounded right of subjects to petition the king, an assertion which ignored the Restoration law that set restrictions on petitioning, while article 7 amends old law by limiting the right to bear arms to Protestants.

On the other hand, eight rights are *not* justly described as "undoubted" and "ancient": articles 1 and 2 (respecting the suspending and dispensing powers), 3 (regarding the "Commission for erecting the late Court of Commissioners for Ecclesiastical Causes"), 6 (respecting raising and keeping a standing army in time of peace without the consent of Parliament), 9 (respecting the right of freedom of speech in Parliament), 10 (the clause regarding the restrictions on excessive bail), 11 (regarding requirements for jurors in treason trials), and 13 (regarding the requirement to hold parliaments "frequently," a challenge to the king's prerogative to call and dismiss parliaments at will).

The committeemen offered retrospective judgments to support their claims, asserting that the law had always been as they now declared it to be. They well knew the instances in which this was not true, for, as this review has shown, thirty-one of the forty-three members had been involved in earlier episodes respecting the issues. They were thus intimately acquainted with the background of the matters they listed in the claim of rights.[251] Although both Tories and Whigs might agree on claiming these rights, by and large the rights were central, not to Tory attitudes, but to Whig ideals which reached back to the Exclusion Crisis and, even further, to earlier libertarian views. The rights committee gave priority to the first three articles and sacrificed clauses in the Heads of Grievances in order to win approval of Tories and the prince, but the Declaration of Rights remains, intrinsically, a document that embodies the principles of Whigs who wanted to change the kingship as well as the king.

II
The Political
and Intellectual Context

5

Prince William and King James
Use the Press

The immediate political and intellectual context within which the Declaration of Rights was drafted during the spring of 1688 through the fall and winter of 1688–89 is central to an understanding of the document. The press was an instrument in the political maneuvering of these months and a vehicle for circulating political ideas and principles, concern for the rights of the nation, and alternative solutions to the crisis. All sides employed printed material, both written and pictorial, in an effort to influence public opinion and reach persons both inside and outside traditionally elite social and political categories. Prince William and his English and Dutch supporters took the lead in this effort, but King James and his friends and critics also used printed tracts and broadsides, as did radical Whigs, who argued for claiming the rights of the nation and reforming the kingship. In these tracts and pamphlets, emanating from several quarters, is to be found a portion of the political and intellectual context of the Declaration of Rights.

The *Declaration of His Highness William Henry, Prince of Orange, of the Reasons Inducing Him to Appear in Armes in the Kingdom of England for Preserving of the Protestant Religion and for Restoring the Lawes and Liberties of England, Scotland, and Ireland* (October 10, 1688), and its postscript, the *Second Declaration of Reasons* (October 20, 1688), was the most important of the pamphlets. It was the first to set out a catalogue of grievances and parallel rights, just as the Declaration of Rights would do. Spread far and wide over England, it brought to every person with the slightest interest in politics the message that a free parliament must be elected, that the parliament should declare the rights of the nation, and that such a step had the approval of the prince. This manifesto became, over the months, a kind of position paper and was used by the prince, his friends, and his foes in discussing solutions to the crisis. James and his friends answered it. Critics of James's policies set out their own list of grievances and rights. Radical Whig pamphleteers enlarged upon and extended it. Members of the Convention repeatedly referred to it, and the rights committees used it to justify what they were doing and even the words they were using. They used it to hold the Dutch prince to an endorsement of the Declaration of Rights.

The idea that the prince should print a tract explaining his invasion came not from William or his close Dutch advisers, but from Englishmen who were deeply involved in the conspiracy to bring him to England. According to Burnet, at least four men — Sir Henry Sidney (younger brother of Algernon Sidney), James Johnstone (Burnet's nephew and son of Archibald Johnstone, the extreme Covenanter), Shrewsbury, and Admiral Edward Russell (cousin of the Whig martyr Lord Russell) — brought to William in August 1688 "advices" and the "heads of a declaration," for which Danby was "chiefly" responsible.[1] Except for Johnstone, these men were the principals of a group of aristocrats who had advised the prince about English affairs for over a year. Everard Weede, heer van Dijkvelt, one of William's confidantes, had contacted them in early 1687. The prince had sent him to England to discover the implications of James's policies for the succession to the English throne, which William's wife, Princess Mary, expected to inherit. Known for his "insinuating smoothness of . . . temper,"[2] Dijkvelt initiated a series of meetings, held at Shrewsbury's London house. The meetings had continued for the express purpose of preparing "such advices and advertisements, as might be fit for the prince to know, that he might govern himself accordingly."[3] Other men present at these meetings included Charles, Viscount Mordaunt, later earl of Peterborough, said to have "set the revolution first on foot";[4] William Cavendish, first duke of Devonshire; Richard Lumley, Baron Lumley; Admiral Arthur Herbert; and Henry Compton, bishop of London. Probably they advised William to oppose repeal of the Test Act, a policy he adopted to the further enlargement of his popularity with Tories as well as Whigs.[5] Burnet asserted that this group "drew [up] the declaration" on which the prince "engaged" in his invasion of England.[6]

These men were to have a part in drafting of the Declaration of Rights. Five (Danby, Devonshire, Lumley, Mordaunt, and Shrewsbury) were on the Lords committee that amended the draft sent up by the House of Commons. Sidney, the most important of them at this time, also made a significant contribution to the document at a critical point in its passage. He had been involved in opposition politics for over a decade. A member of the Parliament of 1679, Sidney became a part of the circle around the earl of Shaftesbury. During the Exclusion Crisis, Shaftesbury sent him to Holland to try to persuade William to come to England. Sidney won William's confidence during this visit and for years remained the Englishman the prince trusted most.[7] At William's express desire, Charles II appointed Sidney commander of the British forces serving in Holland, and the prince himself renewed the appointment in 1685, announcing the step to the new king, James II, in a letter filled with praise for Sidney.[8] Burnet declared that from the autumn of 1687 the "conduct of the whole design was chiefly deposited" in Sidney's hands. With Johnstone's help, Sidney not only managed the correspondence and contacts between William's court and his friends in England, but he also coordinated the signing of the June 30 invitation. Sidney joined William in August 1688 and landed with him in November.[9] A person of great "gentleness and good-nature," an unusually handsome man (as his portrait by Lely at Penshurst reveals), Sidney possessed the gift for reconciling contestants. He used this talent to prevent the loss of the draft Declaration of Rights.

Suggestions from Sidney and Johnstone made over the previous several months had prepared the way for the idea of issuing a manifesto. The two men had stressed that William should use printed tracts in the contest with James II. In a regular, clandestine correspondence with Willem Bentinck, Dijkvelt, and Frederick van Nassau, Count Zuylestein, the prince's major advisers in Holland,[10] Sidney and Johnstone argued that if William wanted to keep the "nation in humour [he] . . . must entertain it by papers." English people were afraid, they said, and "stand in need of a bold triumphing way of writing to keep them in heart." [11] They spelled out a specific press campaign, which the Dutch court followed. For example, they recommended that a history of the prince and his family be written to answer objections about William's character and administration in Holland,[12] and at least five tracts appeared in the fall and winter of 1688–89.[13] They advised William to appeal to both Anglicans and Dissenters and avoid antagonizing either one.[14] Burnet, they said, should write tracts showing that the anger of the Church of England party towards the Dissenters was now much "allayed" [15] and, more, that the church party was not responsible for the persecutions of Dissenters. They maintained that people believed whatever Burnet wrote. His "treasons and libels," as they called them, made everyone, especially the Dissenters, love him. The Dutch court should overlook Burnet's tendencies to meddle and gossip and employ him as a polemicist.[16] In fact, Burnet did serve William as his chief polemicist at this time. Further, Johnstone recommended that William issue a manifesto that would air suspicions about the legitimacy of the baby boy born in June to James II and his Catholic queen, Mary of Modena. Reporting that the rabble did not believe that the baby was genuine, any more than they thought that the duke of Monmouth was dead, he declared that "whoever knows the present disposition of men's spirits in England must know" that it would "do much good" to print the suspicions and supply reasons for them, thus to confirm believers and persuade doubters. Designed to appear to be the "work of a private hand," such a tract should address a free Parliament and ask it to bring to trial the matter of whether James's baby was legitimate. Speed was imperative. Unless William moved within three months, the chances of overturning James's policies would be lost. Johnstone sent a draft of a statement that might be used.[17] In fact, the *Declaration of Reasons* did cast doubt on the legitimacy of James's son and call for a free parliament to investigate the question. For almost a year, then, the prince's trusted English friends had urged the Dutch court to issue printed tracts on specific topics to shape public opinion.

Still further, the famous letter of invitation to the prince dated June 30,

1688, which these same men — Danby, Devonshire, Compton, Lumley, Russell, Shrewsbury, and Sidney — had signed, also hinted at the need for a printed declaration. A hitherto neglected sentence declares that the "false imposing" of James's baby boy was "one of the chief causes upon which the declaration of your entering the kingdom . . . must be founded." [18] The proposal for a manifesto which these men put before William in August 1688, then, was a logical conclusion of recommendations they had already made.

These Englishmen had reason to think that William would approve their suggestion. In 1688 not only was William an experienced publicist, who had already used tracts to promote his political interests in England, [19] but the English themselves had long been accustomed to the public airing of politics in the press. [20] Moreover, the growth of literacy and the increase in the size of the electorate (then between 200,000 and 250,000 voters) reinforced the desirability of using printed material as a means of communication. Potentially, tracts could reach not only the politically and socially elite members of society, but also the nonelite, certainly the middling ranks, and perhaps the marginally literate and illiterate masses as well. [21] In the crisis which English conspirators and Prince William were about to bring to a climax, the support of a broad spectrum of society was highly desirable.

But the prince did not automatically accept the draft sent over to him. He had had much prior experience dealing with disaffected English political leaders and had already demonstrated shrewdness in protecting his own interests. Although the prince had no direct claim to the English throne, he did have a place in the line of succession and legitimate reason for inserting himself in English politics. Born in 1650 to Mary Stuart, the sister of King Charles II and King James II, and posthumously to William II of Orange, this present William was married to another Mary Stuart — the Protestant daughter of James II and his first wife Anne Hyde — and was thus both James's nephew and his son-in-law. A Dutch prince, the stadtholder of the Dutch republic since 1672, and a Calvinist, William, for religious, political, and personal reasons, became the principal opponent on the Continent of the Catholic Sun King, Louis XIV of France. William's marriage to the English princess, which Danby, a Tory, had arranged, was an essential basis for his hopes of winning England's support in his great enterprise against France.

Long before the Revolution of 1688–89, William had been a careful observer of England's internal and foreign policies. While maintaining friendly and correct relations with his royal relatives, he formed close ties with their opposition to bring England into an alliance against France and protect the dynastic interests of his wife and himself. Over the years his personal popularity with the English public grew, as did his political options. All along, he had expectations of one day becoming king of England, and there is no indication, despite charges to the contrary, that he designed a conspiracy to dethrone James during the 1670s and early 1680s. During the Exclusion Crisis of 1678–83, when the "first Whigs" tried to bar James (then duke of York and an avowed Catholic) from the succession to the throne, William wisely resisted the efforts of some politicians to draw him deeply into the controversy and use him to their own advantage.[22] He also made clear at that time that he opposed placing limitations on the prerogatives of the English king.[23]

In 1685 James became king of England and almost immediately alienated a substantial portion of the politically conscious nation, Whigs and Tories alike. Whatever James's ultimate intentions, the steps he took suggested to many people that he aimed to Catholicize the nation, destroy Parliament, violate ancient law and custom, weaken local government, displace the "natural" leaders in shire and borough, and create a centralized government backed by a standing army and allied to Catholic France. Anglican Tories, dismissed from their posts in government and church, Whigs who had opposed James in the Exclusion controversy and whose power had been decisively destroyed by Charles II in the last four years of his reign, and Dissenters who resisted King James's appeal to share in the benefits of his policy of toleration looked to William to assist them in redressing grievances against the king. The failure in 1685 of the invasion of the duke of Monmouth and his subsequent execution removed the prince's only rival to the throne. As early as 1686, Lord Mordaunt urged William to invade England. But it was not until December 1687, when it became known that Mary of Modena, James's second and Catholic wife, was pregnant, that an invasion became a real possibility. And it was not until May 1688 that William agreed with English conspirators that he must come with a force within the year. Otherwise, it was reasoned, the opportunity for him to exercise significant influence on English affairs would be lost. An English republic would be set up and his wife's rightful inheritance would be sacrificed. An English republic, as experience with the governments of the 1650s had shown, might threaten the colonial and commercial enterprises of the Dutch republic.[24] In June, a baby boy was born to James and Mary. Thus, James's son, James Francis, displaced William's wife, Mary, in the line of succession to the English throne and made William's own claim remoter still. Three weeks after the birth, seven major English politicians sent the famous letter of invitation, written at William's insistence, to the Dutch prince. The letter invited William to come to England with a force and promised him support but, significantly, said nothing about the final solution to the crisis nor about William's or James's future role in England's government. That was left quite open. Contacts between William and his English friends quickened as detailed plans were laid during the summer of 1688 for the invasion. In late August Englishmen arrived with their draft for a manifesto.

William, his English and Dutch advisers at The Hague, and some members of the English colony there whose opinion William solicited, all reviewed the draft.[25] Sharp disputes erupted over certain clauses.[26] One dispute concerned the audience to be addressed. On the one hand, men who favored the draft wanted to "draw in the body of the whole nation" and appeal especially to Anglicans and Tories, whose political and religious principles might restrain their enthusiasm for William. They wanted to omit references to the political abuses that had occurred under Charles II because some Tories and Anglicans had been involved then in perpetrating the very crimes from which they themselves had suffered under James II. It was thought that if the manifesto specified earlier grievances, Anglicans and Tories might fear reprisals from William and his friends and seek reconciliation with James.

On the other hand, radical Whig critics of the draft wanted to limit William's appeal to Whigs and Dissenting groups. John Wildman, the former republican and congenital conspirator who had been outlawed since Monmouth's Rebellion, took the lead in persuading several "worthy" Whigs that the draft was unacceptable. Among them were Charles Gerard, the earl of Macclesfield, also an outlaw, said to have suggested during the Exclusion Crisis the murder of the duke of York; [27] Lord Mordaunt; and "many others." Wildman devised a substitute declaration [28] which apparently presented a theory of English government and law and a catalogue of violations from the reigns of Charles II and James II. He wanted William to disavow *all* the violations, implicate the Tories and Anglicans who "had promoted" them, and depend for support on Whigs and Dissenters. The tactical disadvantages to proceeding in this fashion were obvious. Russell pointed out that such an emphasis would alienate many of the nobility and gentry, "almost all the clergy," "all the high church party," and "all the army." Burnet described Wildman as a "constant meddler." He said Wildman's purpose was "deep and spiteful," based on fear that the church party would cooperate with William and that Whigs and Dissenters would suffer as a consequence. Damning Wildman and his friends as atheists, Burnet charged them with aiming to weaken Christianity by promoting divisions between Anglicans and Dissenters. [29] For his part, William, who was no libertarian and had a horror of being thought the captive of any one group, rejected Wildman's draft.

Another dispute arose over the specific grievances to be included and the priority among them. The men who favored the original draft argued that the dispensing power should be the "main ground" for the expedition, because everyone had been alarmed by James's use of it, and therefore, it "would seem very strange" if it were not made the main reason for William's invasion. On the other hand, critics maintained that the dispensing power was a legal power of the crown which had been exercised for ages and that James's stretching of it was not a just basis for an invasion. They charged that political calculation, not sincere abhorrence of the use of the dispensing power, was the real reason for making it the most important grievance of the nation. The aim, they said, was to win over the bishops and high Tories who had suffered the most as a consequence of the king's employing the dispensing power. And, again, their objections were overruled.

Englishmen also argued over the role the trial of the Seven Bishops should play in justifying William's decision "to appear in arms in the kingdom of England." Authors of the original draft maintained that the trial so well reflected both the "ill designs" of the court and the "affections" of the people that a lack of emphasis on it "would be made use of" to persuade people of the "prince's ill will" toward the nation. Critics contended that there was nothing "contrary to law" in the trial. They said that the king had the right to bring any man to trial; that the trial had been fair; that James had lost his case; and that the bishops had been acquitted and discharged. This episode was no grounds for an invasion: it was, rather, another instance of an effort to appeal to conservative groups. Once again, the critics lost their case.

Still other points were contested. First, Burnet was doubtful that the church party genuinely favored reconciliation with Dissenters; given his volubility and the role he played in shaping the declaration for Scotland (discussed below), he surely voiced his concern. But, as he said, assurances to the contrary were so "often repeated from many hands" that William included in his manifesto a promise to try to reconcile all Protestants.[30] Second, at least two men objected to including the clause about James's son. The earl of Shrewsbury did not believe the stories about a supposititious baby prince.[31] And Sir Rowland Gwynne, an ardent Whig and a friend of Lord Mordaunt who earlier had voted for Exclusion and was to land with William in November, was "very much of the opinion" that the legitimacy of the infant prince should not be questioned. He regarded the evidence as inconclusive, and the charge as inappropriate as a justification for invasion. Others, however, "absolutely" insisted upon retaining the clause.[32] As for the prince, it was said that he accepted the legitimacy of the baby, but felt obliged "out of policy . . . to give way to the current of . . . [the] times."[33] Third, a dispute arose over whether to include the claim that people from all walks of life had invited the prince to invade England. That claim iterated the point made in the June 30 letter of invitation, that nineteen-twentieths of the "people" throughout the kingdom favored William, as well as "much the greatest part of the nobility and gentry," "many" of the army officers, "very many" of the common soldiers, and nine out of ten of the seamen. An unidentified adviser credited with promoting the idea in William's declaration later confessed to great uneasiness about having urged it.[34]

The disputes among William's adherents at The Hague led to few changes in the original draft brought from England. The only result, according to Burnet, were some adjustments in a "few expressions" and the omission of "some circumstances."[35] So the prince's manifesto, which was to influence the Declaration of Rights, retained the original draft's emphasis on grievances that would have special appeal for Anglicans and Tories. The disputes about this instrument reflected broad divisions among the forces supporting the prince. They prefigured divisions that would open up in the weeks immediately after William landed, in the Convention debates over the Declaration of Rights in January and February, and in the months after the crisis was settled.

William himself objected to the original draft. His misgivings concerned the sentences in which he promised to call a free parliament and abide by the decisions it made. The sentences read: "We now think fit to declare that this our expedition is intended for no other design but to have a free and lawful parliament assembled as soon as possible." It went on, "And we, for our part, will concur in everything that may procure the peace and happiness of the nation, which a free and lawful Parliament shall determine." The prince wrote to Bentinck: "There is much that needs to be changed. You will see that by the conclusion I am placed entirely at the mercy of Parliament." He continued: "Handing one's fate over to them is not without hazard." As much as he disliked that prospect, William indicated that he did "not think" that it could "be otherwise." [36] William's misgivings apparently continued, for two weeks later, on September 14, he wrote again to Bentinck saying that he wanted to discuss the statement with him in person.[37] But, despite his qualms, the prince obviously decided that more was to be gained than lost in publishing the manifesto.

Three likely considerations explain this decision. First, it was in his interest to deny publicly that he came as a conqueror to unseat his father-in-law. Although William's insistence upon bringing a force which would "be superior" [38] to James's army under any circumstances indicates that he did not entirely dismiss the possibility of a bloody contest, violence against his father-in-law had many disadvantages. The prince preferred the character of Deliverer. Winning the crown of England was probably his purpose all along,[39] but he could hardly avow publicly such an intention. The justification of the invasion offered in the draft served his interests. What he needed was the endorsement of a parliament if he was to achieve a nation united behind him and willing to supply men and money for a Continental war against Louis XIV. The promise to call a free parliament and abide by its decisions was an enormous gamble. What would be his response, James's supporters themselves queried, if the freely elected parliament made decisions inimical to him? But it was not the only gamble the prince took in the revolution.

Second, by accepting the draft of his English friends, William may have thought he was protecting himself against demands for more extreme reforms, such as Wildman and his friends wanted. At this time and for many months thereafter, the prince overestimated the strength of radical groups. It is possible that he believed he was forestalling their importunities by going forward with the proposed text.

Finally, William's decision underlined his awareness of the power of the press and of public opinion. He was willing to subordinate his private views and to "hazard" his fate to Parliament to achieve an appealing public image. The prince's concern that there was danger to him in giving such a large role to Parliament was not misplaced. In some respects, as events were to reveal in the fall and winter of 1688–89, William's political options were limited by his manifesto. But once the decision was made to go forward with the *Declaration of Reasons,* it became, and remained until the crisis was resolved in February 1689, a central ingredient in the prince's campaign.

The style as well as the content of the *Declaration* was the object of careful attention. At William's request, Burnet translated, shortened (although not so much as Burnet wished), and enlivened a draft prepared by Fagel.[40] Burnet's paper, itself interlined and corrected, survives in the Dutch archives.[41] These efforts resulted in one of the most effectively written tracts that appeared in 1688–89. Readable, and for the most part moderate in tone, it argued William's case in a clear and detailed manner, but not at such length as to bore the reader. Even the English ambassador at The Hague, who abhorred the contents of the manifesto, described its style as "civil and smooth" and predicted that it would "gain the people's affections."[42]

After all this attention to substance and style, what was persuasive about the final text[43] of the *Declaration of Reasons?* What was promised that would "gain the people's affections"? What were the grievances that men at The Hague in September 1688 decided would appeal the most to Englishmen? William was depicted as the "Dutch Deliverer," whose aim was to rescue the Protestant religion and the Anglican church and to restore the laws, liberties, and customs of the English nation, all so grievously assaulted. Avoiding a direct attack on James himself, the manifesto blamed his "evil counselors," who "not only by secret and indirect ways, but in an open and undisguised manner" had subjected the nation to "arbitrary government." The violations of these counselors were enumerated, with first priority given to the use of the dispensing power, that "strange and execrable maxim," said (quite erroneously) to have been "invent[ed] and set on foot" by James's advisers. By packing the courts with justices whom they could trust, they had procured a judgment that the dispensing power was a right of the crown. William, however, professed the contrary opinion, arguing that since laws can be made only by king and Parliament, so they can be repealed or suspended only by king and Parliament. Otherwise, the king is "clothed with a despotic and arbitrary power," and the "lives, liberties, honours, and estates of the subjects . . . are entirely subject to him." It could not have been lost on politically knowledgeable people that this assertion aligned the prince with men who had argued along the same lines in the printed controversy on the subject that had occurred less than ten years before.

Almost all the other abuses the manifesto mentioned were connected with James's efforts to Catholicize the nation. The violations included the suspension of the Test Act, the creation of the Court of Ecclesiastical Commission (characterized — again erroneously — as "manifestly illegal"), the suspension of the bishop of London, the removal of the Fellows of Magdalen College, the quo warranto proceedings (by which James aimed to control municipal and county affairs), and the elevation of Papists to high posts in all areas of the government, including the army and the bench. Using an example certain to appeal to Englishmen, the *Declaration* referred to the Irish "massacre" of 1641, and asserted that "the dismal effects of this subversion of the established religion, laws and liberties in England appear more evidently to us by what we see done in Ireland." The situation in Scotland, too, offered examples of what might be expected in England.

Lawful remedies have been to no avail, the manifesto continued. The seven bishops had presented a humble petition in a manner consistent with the law (the *Declaration* was at pains to note) and had been imprisoned and brought to trial as if guilty of "some enormous crime." [44] Even the most "arbitrary and despotic" kings, the *Declaration* averred, permitted their subjects the right of petition within the "limits of the law." The most effective remedy for all the evils was to call a free parliament. But a free and lawful parliament, under the circumstances, was impossible. James's counselors had sought to divide Protestants, sowing dissension between the Church of England and Dissenters. They had sought to preengage electors and candidates to assure that a future parliament would repeal the Test and Papal Laws. And to top all, they had installed Popish magistrates in violation of the Test Act, which fact nullified the magistrates' acts. Hence, "as long as the authority and magistracy is in such hands, it is not possible to have any lawful parliament."

As for himself, William would not sit idly by. The legitimate position of his dear wife Mary and of himself in the succession, the debt Holland owed England for the latter's assistance in the war against France in 1672, the affection shown him and Mary by Englishmen over the years, and the fact that he had been invited — so the *Declaration* said — "by a great many lords, both spiritual and temporal, and by many gentlemen, and other subjects of all ranks" compelled him to come. But he came not as a conqueror. His army was not directed against the English people. Rather, it was a "force sufficient," large enough only to protect William from the "violence" of James's evil advisers. It would be kept under strict control and returned to Holland as soon as possible. Asserting that he had "no other design but to have a free and lawful parliament assembled as soon as possible," William promised that the election would be free and lawful, that the parliament would meet in "full freedom," and that he would "concur" in everything for the "peace and happiness of the nation" that it "shall determine." Elaborating his policy still further, William declared that he intended "nothing" but the "preservation of the Protestant religion, the covering of all men from persecution for their consciences, and the securing to the whole nation the free enjoyment of their laws, rights and liberties, under a just and legal government." Another goal he professed was to reconcile members of the Church of England and all Protestant Dissenters and to assure toleration for any person who would live peaceably, "even Papists themselves not excepted." Still further, the prince resolved, once "quiet" was restored, to call a parliament in Scotland to end the abuses there. For Ireland, he promised no parliament, but rather pledged himself "to study to bring" Ireland to such a condition that "the Protestant and British interest there may be secured," a pledge certain to please men who held property or office in Ireland.

Finally, using the dirty trick recommended by Johnstone and others, William cast doubts on the legitimacy of James's son. "To crown all," the *Declaration* read, "those evil counselors . . . published that the Queen has brought forth a son." But, the manifesto continued, the new parliament should investigate the matter, for "not only we ourselves but all the good subjects of the kingdom do vehemently suspect that the pretended Prince of Wales was not borne by the Queen." It was a daring and outrageous charge. "This is worse," fumed the indignant English ambassador at The Hague, "than the public invasion, and more unpardonable." It would not have been written, he declared, but by "incarnate devils."[45] As events proved, the promise that the new parliament would examine the birth of the baby was disingenuous. In this and other ways, the *Declaration* shaped past events and forecast future steps to serve the stadtholder's interests.

William's court lavished attention on the timing of publication and distribution of the *Declaration of Reasons.* Such attention was essential if the document was to survive the efforts of James's government to suppress it. Steps were taken — not altogether successful — to avoid leaking the contents of the manifesto prior to the prince's landing. William himself signed and sealed the statement on October 1/10.[46] The *Declaration* was everywhere in the fall of 1688. It appeared in four languages — English, Dutch, German, and French[47] — and was printed in Amsterdam, Edinburgh, The Hague, Hamburg, London, Magdeburg, Rotterdam, and York. Copies printed at The Hague bore the official imprimature of the prince: "Printed at The Hague by Arnold Leers by special order of His Highness." Altogether, twenty-one editions in the four languages appeared in 1688, eight of them in English. Intended, clearly, for an international as well as an English audience, the *Declaration* was widely dispersed on the Continent. Copies were handed directly to all ambassadors and ministers at The Hague except the English and French representatives.[48] Through copies in the Dutch language, William justified his undertaking to his Dutch subjects on the same grounds he had employed in asking Their High Mightinesses for support.[49] In like manner, through the German version he informed the German people of his project in the same general terms he had used in soliciting help from the German princes. And the French translation of the manifesto appealed to Huguenots on the Continent as well as to those who had emigrated to England after the revocation of the Edict of Nantes in 1685.[50]

The *Declaration* was distributed from one end of England to the other. "Many thousand copies" were sent across the Channel to be "consigned to some trusty person in London" for distribution. A password — "I come from Exeter" — was devised for the prince's agents and their contacts in England to protect them from "speaking to any wrong person who brings the papers." They were ordered to release the document after the prince had landed and not before.[51] Friends of the prince were given as many as 3,000 copies and asked to distribute them in their counties and among their friends. Bundles of free copies were sent to booksellers, who were invited to sell them at their own profit. Copies were posted through the penny post and sent anonymously to private citizens.[52] Additional copies were turned out by at least one English printer, a John White of Yorkshire. The first, and for a time the only, English printer of the *Declaration,* White was richly rewarded by

William after the prince became king with a monopoly in the city of York and the five northern counties for printing all notices concerning revenue and justice which the government might issue.[53]

Other steps taken to put the tract before the public also reveal its importance to William and his friends. The *Declaration of Reasons* was probably read when William and his party landed at Brixham in Torbay, as a contemporary print by the Dutchman Carolus Allard shows, and as the statue of the prince erected in 1888 on the spot asserts. And when William entered Newton Abbot on his way to Exeter, the *Declaration* was again read, at a spot still marked by a stone.[54] Burnet read the *Declaration* from the pulpit of Exeter Cathedral on the Sunday after the prince's entourage entered the city, and then sent it "in the Prince's name" to all the clergy, "commanding them . . . to read it." Some people in Exeter circulated the *Declaration* and were arrested by the mayor for their trouble.[55] The man employed to carry intelligence between Bristol and Exeter claimed later that he had dispersed the manifesto in Bristol.[56] All around England William's partisans read and posted the *Declaration*. In Cheshire, Henry Booth, Lord Delamere, "himself read . . . the *Declaration* at the Market Cross."[57] At the garrison at Plymouth, the *Declaration* was read to the officers and soldiers, who declared for the prince by "throwing up their hats and huzzas," and then it was posted on the gates of the citadel.[58] It was also read in Falmouth, where it met with "universal acclamations of joy."[59] And it continued to be circulated. In December, the Earl of Bath, at last supplied with a "good quantity" of the *Declaration*, ordered the copies published in all the boroughs and market towns of Cornwall.[60] In one way or another, then, England was saturated with the *Declaration*. As a contemporary wrote, it "passed into the hands of the generality of the nation."[61] The widespread distribution of the *Declaration* signaled the importance of the manifesto to the prince and his friends and also promoted its importance in the mind of the general public.

William's court prepared three other tracts to accompany the *Declaration*. First, the prince himself[62] ordered letters, in the form of printed broadsides, to be addressed to the English army and fleet. These broadsides, dated September 29, were short, simple[63] exhortations in which William urged the men to join him in the defense of the nation's religion, laws, liberties, and properties. He promised them reward if they came in "seasonably," and counseled them not to allow a misplaced sense of loyalty to James to deter them. Directing readers to the *Declaration of Reasons* for a full statement of his intentions, the Dutch prince signed the letters "Your truly well-wishing and affectionate friend." The letters were widely circulated. "Many thousand copies" were printed as broadsides, and the letters also were added to some editions of the *Declaration* in English, Dutch, and German. The *Letter to the Army*, according to an eighteenth-century historian, was "spread underhand over the whole" of England and had "wonderful effect" on the soldiers, in that it persuaded men who did not join William when he landed not to fight for King James until a free parliament was called.[64] Undoubtedly it strengthened William's hand in the contest for the allegiance of the English army.

Second, William's court published a version of the *Declaration of Reasons* specifically for the "ancient kingdom of Scotland." According to Burnet, the Scots at The Hague, among whom was the radical Presbyterian minister Robert Ferguson, an ardent supporter of William at the time, took the initiative in preparing a draft. Their purpose was to suggest publicly that William favored Presbyterianism. Burnet credited himself with alerting the prince to the "consequences" of such a thesis,[65] and, upon William's order, the draft was amended. It was published along with the *Declaration of Reasons* under the same date (October 1/10) in English, Dutch, German, and French. Shorter than the latter, it stressed the violations of law that had occurred in Scotland and called for a "universal concurrence" for the prince, threatening anyone who opposed him. Neither the invitation nor William's army was mentioned, nor was emphasis placed on the dispensing power or the calling of a parliament to redress grievances. The drafting of the *Declaration . . . for . . . Scotland* reveals again the tension between radical and conservative Englishmen at The Hague and the victory for the latter.

Third, Burnet produced a lengthy pamphlet, *An Enquiry into the Measures of Submission to the Supreme Authority; and of the Grounds upon which it may be lawful or necessary for Subjects to defend their Religion, Lives and Liberties,* which was printed in large numbers for distribution at William's landing.[66] The imprimature "By Authority" signaled William's approval and gave it special significance. Expounding ideas that coincided with those expressed by radical Whigs in tracts printed in subsequent weeks and by John Locke in his *Two Treatises of Government,* published after the revolution in the fall of 1689, the piece is of further interest because it raises the question of the relationship of Burnet with Locke and radical Whigs who were in Holland.[67]

It is a moot question whether Burnet drew inspiration from Locke or Locke borrowed from Burnet, but it is clear that *Measures of Submission* presented ideas that were strikingly close to those of Locke. Burnet argues that the law of nature makes all men free, except for wives, who are subject to their husbands, and children, who are subject to their parents. God has authorized no one form of government; civil society is a human creation, originating in a contract among free men to hand over certain of their rights to a governor. Burnet flatly rejects Sir Robert Filmer's argument about the divine right of kings. The two essential parts of government, Burnet contends, are the legislative, the supreme authority, and the executive, a trust which by its nature is accountable to the legislative. In England, the executive authority rests solely in the king, and the legislative is lodged jointly in the king, Lords, and Commons. Laws, oaths, "immemorial prescription," and long possession fix the measures of power and obedience. The English subject is free and enjoys liberties and properties reserved to him by the "constitution," whose "chief design" is to "secure and maintain" those liberties. In all disputes between power and liberty, power must be proved, but "liberty proves itself," for power is founded upon positive law, but liberty rests on the law of nature. The subject has the natural right to preserve his liberties against invasions of the government, but in the current circumstances, he faces certain practical difficulties in exercising that right. Those difficulties are (1) that the law places the militia solely in the king; (2) that an oath, required of all officers in state and church, holds that it is unlawful to take up arms against the king under any pretense; and (3) that a principle imbedded in law and accepted as doctrine by the Church of England declares that the king can do no wrong. How, then, can a subject lawfully resist the king? How can the Church of England resist the king without encountering the charge that it abandoned its principles when it lost favor with the court?

Burnet's answer is complicated. First, he argues that in all obligations there lies a tacit exception. For example, adultery nullifies the bond of marriage. Second, principles may in practice collide, and when they do the lower principle must give way to the higher. For example, an oath may demand nonresistance, but not to the point that society is destroyed; the principle of nonresistance must give way to the principle of self-preservation. Third, if a king undermines the legislative authority (of which he is a part), he annuls his own power and ceases to be king. A king may fall from power by deserting his people, by trying to enslave them, or by being in a state of infancy or insanity. Summing up, Burnet insists that England's government has been threatened by (1) the use of the dispensing and suspending power; (2) the disregard of the Triennial Act and by preengagements (these two points alone prove a "dissolution of the government," a "breaking of the whole constitution"); (3) the creation of the "Court" of High Commission; (4) the packing of the courts, and (5) the expansion of a standing army in time of peace. For all these reasons the contract between the king and people is broken, the government is dissolved, and the people have the right to settle the crown on another person.

The tract was an effective supplement to the *Declaration of Reasons,* and in October William and his friends must have thought that its message would be politically useful. In setting out the contract theory of government, it supplied theoretical foundations not offered by the prince's manifesto. It justified resistance on the grounds that by his acts James had broken the contract and therefore ceased to be king. The acts Burnet cited included maintaining a standing army in peacetime, a grievance ignored by the *Declaration of Reasons. Measures of Submission,* with its appeal to radical Whigs and Dissenters, was the most radical piece Burnet wrote. In December, when he printed another pamphlet, *An Enquiry into the Present State of Affairs,* also by authority, he did not mention the contract theory of government or refer to natural rights and liberties, and when he wrote his *History* he specifically repudiated the theory of dissolution of the government.

Two weeks after the appearance of the *Declaration of Reasons,* a *Second Declaration of Reasons,* a kind of postscript, appeared. A succinct polemic, drafted by Fagel, heavily edited by Burnet,[68] and signed by the prince on October 24, this piece was designed to depreciate the reforms belatedly instituted by James. It made two important points. First, William disparaged the

"malicious insinuations" of persons who suggested that he intended to conquer the nation and become king. The small size of his army and the reputation of the "great" numbers of nobility and gentry accompanying him made
such a charge absurd, he said. Second, he dismissed the king's reforms and
declared — in words that were to become highly significant — that the only
meaningful remedy for the nation's ills was by a "parliament in a declaration
of the rights of the subject that have been invaded, and not by any pretended
acts of grace."

Still further, a third *Declaration of Reasons* appeared, which, although
William repudiated it, was believed to have come from his camp.[69] Dated
November 28, 1688, at Sherburn Castle, this pamphlet was a hysterical
attack on the Papists: it insinuated that they intended to set fire to London
and Westminster and, with the help of French and Irish troops, massacre all
the people there; and it called upon all good Protestants to seize, disarm, and
imprison their Catholic neighbors. Papists, readers were advised, should be
given no quarter, but should be treated as "robbers, freebooters, and banditti." The tract had an "amazing effect," terrifying Londoners, countrymen,
women, children, and Catholics themselves "most wonderfully." Some
thought that the pamphlet was partly responsible for inflaming the London
mob in mid-December.[70] It was also suggested that it played a part in inclin-
ing the English army towards William at a time when its loyalty was fluc-
tuating between king and prince. A contemporary assessment by an observer
hostile to the prince held that it did "more harm to the king's affairs than all
other papers . . . published at that time."[71]

Other printed pieces indisputably from William's court appeared after the
prince landed in England. William had brought a printing press with
him — along with soldiers, horses, and money — as part of his invasion equip-
ment. Within three weeks of his arrival, during the time he was at Exeter, he
was reported to be printing not only "two gazettes a week," but also copies of
letters purported to have been exchanged between England and France,
among other papers.[72] Moreover, William commissioned Burnet to write
pamphlets dealing with the specific questions that were troubling thoughtful
Englishmen. Two pieces — one on the problems that would result from recalling James after his flight, and the other on the reasons for the king's
withdrawing from Rochester — were printed "By Authority."[73] A third, also
by Burnet and issued "By the Prince of Orange's special command," undertook to answer a tract from James II's court that disparaged William's
manifesto.[74] In each case, these "official" pamphlets reinforced the main
themes of the *Declaration of Reasons* and thereby enhanced its significance.

This material had the effect of reinforcing the interpretation already
developed of William, his purposes, and his promises. When the Convention
met at the end of January 1689, neither its members nor persons outside
Westminster with the least interest in politics could have avoided exposure to
the idea that William had invaded England as a selfless Deliverer for the pur-

pose of rescuing the nation's religion, laws, and liberties, and that he had practically invited a free parliament to issue a "declaration of the rights of the nation."

James and his friends did not allow the *Declaration of Reasons* and other tracts in William's propaganda campaign to go unanswered in the press. And critics of James's policies also used the press to put before a broad audience their views on the nation's grievances and rights. As a publicist, James was no match for William, but he was not blind to the power of the printed word. Earlier in his reign, James had rigorously enforced the laws and procedures already established for censoring printed matter. From February 1685 to November 1687, he issued thirty-four warrants to suppress certain pamphlets.[75] In the fall of 1687, during the campaign to remodel local government, the royal court instructed local correspondents to place "books and papers . . . in coffee houses and houses of public entertainment" in an effort to persuade the public of the validity of royal policies.[76] In the spring of 1688, the court inspired rumors, commissioned tracts, and dispersed *gratis* quantities of the king's "papers."[77] At about the same time, James issued a "severe" proclamation restricting printing and offered a reward of £1,000 to discover the author of an offending tract.[78] In April one of William's agents wrote that "neither art, money, nor pains are omitted" in the campaign to influence public opinion.[79] Thus, James's strategy in the autumn was a logical continuation of policies already established.

Even before the king had a copy of William's manifesto in hand, he took steps to counteract it.[80] First, he tried to suppress criticism of his policies by restricting the circulation of news. On October 9 Jeffreys, the lord chancellor, acting on orders from the king, commanded all coffeehouses to keep no written news but the official *London Gazette*, upon pain of forfeiting their licenses.[81] Four days later, a "cart load of seditious books" was burned at Grocer Hall Yard, thereby underlining the seriousness of the government's campaign.[82] At the end of the month (October 26), a royal proclamation complained of "bold and licentious discourses" and of "seditious news" spread in coffeehouses and other public places and forbade the discussion of political affairs by writing, printing, speaking, or listening.[83]

Second, the king held several meetings in October with some bishops and Protestant temporal peers to solicit advice and demand public written denials that they had invited William to England, as the *Declaration* claimed.[84] Whether James would have consulted his Protestant peers at this time of emergency had William's manifesto not identified them as supporting his enterprise is a nice question. In any case, the bishops refused to oblige the king's request for a written denial, but at a meeting on October 3 some of them, at the initiative of William Sancroft, archbishop of Canterbury, put before the king eleven recommendations.

Described as things "absolutely necessary to the settlement of the nation,"[85] the bishops' proposals dealt predominantly with grievances of the

Anglican church. They asked James to dissolve the Ecclesiastical Commission and promise not to erect "any such court" again. They urged the king to prohibit recently appointed bishops (thought to be papist) from exercising authority, fill vacant bishoprics with men qualified by law, suppress Jesuit schools, and restore universities to their "legal state" and the officers of Magdalen College to their "profits" and "properties." Two articles concerned the dispensing power. The bishops begged the king to stop using it, but they stopped short of declaring it illegal, as William's *Declaration* had done. Instead, they recommended that a parliament settle that question. They also asked James to restore municipal charters and call a free parliament to settle affairs and establish a "due liberty of conscience" for all Protestants. In a remark revealing partisan aspirations, they advised the king to restore the nation to the condition he had found it in at his accession and reinstate qualified men in the offices they had then held. The statement ended with a plea to be allowed to try to persuade James to return to the Church of England.

These proposals, bearing the initials "H.N.," were in print by October 9.[86] In view of the fact that they came from the highest reaches of the Anglican hierarchy, from men who only a few months before had defied the king's order to read the Declaration of Indulgence and impugned his right to dispense with the penal laws, who had suffered imprisonment and trial, and whose acquittal had moved the nation to an outpouring of joy, public interest in them was to be expected. "Leaks" as to their content had occurred and occasioned apparent dismay among Nonconformists. The reason "H.N." arranged for their publication was to counter the "ill construction" put on them and to reassure Nonconformists that the bishops would adhere to the position they had occupied when they refused to read the Declaration of Indulgence. The bishops hoped to bring James back to the Anglican church, he explained, and would promote the interests of Dissenters.[87] It was a bold step to publish an account of what had transpired in a private conference between the king and the spiritual leaders of the realm. Alone, the *Bishops' Proposals* suggest the extent to which usual political processes had deteriorated by the beginning of October. They also testify to the fact that persons on all sides of this revolution turned to the press to assist them in achieving political goals.

The *Bishops' Proposals* reveal the reforms in government desired by high Anglican Tories at this time. Their concern focused on issues related to the Anglican church. They demanded an end to quo warranto procedures and a restoration of borough charters, but otherwise ignored matters of interest to Whigs, such as judicial reform or the standing army. If these recommendations had gone into effect (and indeed, James seems to have followed them in instituting his belated reforms the next two weeks), there would have resulted little change in the kingship. The complaint of the radical pamphleteer Rev. Samuel Johnson some years later that the proposals were selfish was justified.[88] These proposals are among the first signs of weakening of ties between Dissenters and Anglicans that had been carefully nurtured over the past eighteen months or so.[89] It is significant that within a fortnight of their appearance, one "H.E." urged that the archbishop of Canterbury himself be apprised of a report that a tract was to be printed charging that the bishops had dispensed with the laws and canons of the church in their own interests as much as the king had done by virtue of his prerogative.[90]

Anglican-Tory partisan considerations underlay the *Bishops' Proposals*. By limiting the complaints to the reign of James II and stressing grievances important to the church, the bishops absolved the Anglican-Tory party of responsibility for the nation's plight. They specifically advocated restoring conditions as they had existed at James's accession, when king, church and Tories were closely allied. They pled to be allowed to meet with the king for the purpose of converting him to Anglicanism. Further, the proposals may have prepared the way for the idea, actively promoted in December and January, that one solution to the crisis was to recall James and limit his authority. After all, the bishops themselves had asked the king to accept certain restrictions. Moreover, it is reasonable to think that the bishops' proposals were taken into account by Tories when the drafts of the Declaration of Rights were under review. Although the declaration is a more reformist document, there are identities between the two.[91] The framers of these proposals wanted to preserve James's rights as much as they wanted to impose restrictions on his authority. Among the authors were men who would work for the king after his flight, promote solutions different from the one finally reached, and attempt to sabotage the draft Declaration of Rights in an effort to ingratiate themselves with William when it was certain that he would become king. Finally, these recommendations provide comparisons with the grievances and rights identified by William's *Declaration of Reasons* and by radical Whigs, who, at about the same time, began to publish their views.

The third thing King James did in countering William's propaganda campaign was to ban absolutely the *Declaration of Reasons* and the broadside letters. In a proclamation issued on November 2, several days before the prince landed, the king dramatically extended the law of treason by declaring it treason for anyone to read, receive, conceal, publish, disperse, repeat, or hand about any of the prince's printed pieces.[92] Moreover, the Privy Council sat the afternoon of the day William landed, drawing up a "counter-declaration" which was rushed to the press the next day. The "counter-declaration" described the prince's army as composed of "foreigners and rebels," the *Declaration of Reasons* as a tissue of specious pretenses, and the invasion as an unchristian and unnatural design upon a father-in-law's crown.[93] In the meantime, on October 29 and November 1, the king ordered two men discovered bringing copies of the *Declaration* into England imprisoned.[94]

Finally, James attempted to influence public opinion to look favorably upon him and his policies. At least three replies to William's manifesto appeared: *Animadversions, Some Reflections,* and *Some Modest Remarks.* If

William is depicted as a Deliverer in his manifestos, in James's replies he is painted as a Conqueror whose motives, reputation, and moral integrity are reprehensible. *Reflections* charged that the prince's aim was to become king of England. As his record of stadtholder of the Netherlands demonstrated, he would be an absolute master.[95] He had so thoroughly "undone" Dutch liberties that the Dutch were glad to be rid of him. It was fatuous to think that William came for the purpose of restoring English liberties. The prince had an army and was unlikely to send it back. With heavy sarcasm the "Reflector" wrote that surely William did not intend to stay in England as a private subject![96] *Animadversions* mused on what might happen if the free parliament William promised should propose a course of action inimical to him.[97]

These tracts linked William with English radicals. They stressed that the prince was a Presbyterian and warned that the Church of England would be destroyed if he succeeded. *Modest Remarks* predicted that church lands would be confiscated and the bishops placed on an annual salary.[98] "Renegadoes," malcontents, radicals like those who had brought Charles I to the block, were the prince's friends. James's penmen enlarged on the dire consequences of the invasion: loss of life, ruin of the countryside, and the horrors of civil war. England's trade would be destroyed, which, it was pointed out, would benefit the Dutch, and explained their concurrence in the prince's undertaking.

Attacking William's integrity in still other ways, these authors charged that the prince spread rumors and "strange stories" and failed to provide evidence of his claims that James was in league with France, that the royal prince was "pretended," or that the spiritual peers had invited him to England. All were lies, they said. If James had sold out to Louis XIV, he should be deposed.[99] Neither William nor Mary could prove their own births so well as James had cleared that of his son. The story about the invitation was a gross appeal to the "mobile."[100] James, they maintained, had never violated law. Indeed, the only laws he had dispensed with were those which had been passed earlier in "the interest of a party," and he had done that for the "ease and peace of his subjects and the benefit of trade." Holland practiced religious toleration to the advantage of her trade. Why should allowing Jesuit chapels be called "prudence" in Holland, but "subverting the government" in England? William had cited the chapels as a grievance, but that charge was inconsistent with his promise to provide liberty of conscience for all, "even Papists not excepting."[101]

Other tracts, written apparently by private individuals, reinforced and expanded these themes. *The Debates in Deposing Kings; and of the Royal Succession of Great Britain* put forward theoretical considerations as to why James should be supported. The anonymous author, borrowing phraseology from the radical Whigs, argued that by the laws of God and nature and the "fundamental constitutions" of the nation, the English monarchy was directly inheritable through a prescribed line of succession, which no crime and no act of Parliament could change. The tract called upon English history to show that since 1066 all parliamentary acts that had violated the principle of direct hereditary succession were null and void. There was no way James could be legally deposed. The piece ended by damning "those cursed Achitopels [sic]" whose aim was to establish "democracy." Another tract, *The Dutch Design Anatomiz'd; or, A Discovery of the wickedness and unjustice of the intended invasion, and a clear proof that it is the interest of all the King's subjects to defend his Majesty and their country against it,* stressed the dangers to England's liberties and trade which William's invasion posed. Comparing William of Orange to William the Conqueror and also to Gustavus Adolphus, king of Sweden — who had been invited to Germany upon the same pretenses as William claimed, and then had devastated the country — the author, a "true member of the Church of England, and a lover of his country," stressed that Dutch commercial interests aimed to ruin England's trade by putting William on the throne, and begged his fellow subjects not to "sell our birthright for a mess of Dutch excised herb-pottage."

Another move James made to deal with William's press campaign provides further evidence of his respect for public opinion. In early December, when it became evident that the proclamation against William's manifesto was ineffectual, James reversed himself and, "to the astonishment of everyone," ordered that the *Declaration* be printed accompanied by *Remarks* and *Animadversions.* [102] This move had the effect, as he may have calculated, of assuring wide circulation of his own tracts. The king reinforced this step by exploiting the *London Gazette,* which printed items "in the most hateful manner" to discredit William. [103] The repeated unsuccessful attempts by the mob on the house of the king's printer, Henry Hills, in mid-November, [104] around the time *Reflections* appeared, and the successful attack on it in mid-December — when the mob not only destroyed the house but also burned forms, letters, and upwards of 300 reams of paper, printed and unprinted — suggest not only that James's past control of the press was bitterly resented, but also that his current tactics in countering William's *Declaration* were having an effect. [105] The effect was strong enough to provoke an anonymous reply [106] and to move William to direct Burnet to write a response, which was printed under the imprimatur "By the Prince of Orange's special command." [107]

Taken as a whole, James's tracts presented a logical and reasonable rebuttal to William's *Declaration of Reasons.* Like the prince's manifesto, they offered practical, pragmatic statements dealing with immediate issues. What theory they provided was simple and uncomplicated. Appealing to a general audience, these pieces may well have stimulated and reinforced the resurgence of public sentiment for the king at the time of his flight. They reveal that a contest of a limited kind took place between king and prince at this time and show that both sides regarded the press as an instrument in the struggle. But as James's government faltered, it was unable to control the press, and the king's flight meant the entire collapse of restrictions. Although tracts sympathetic to James and pointedly hostile to William continued to appear, they did not equal in number the partisan material for the prince that flooded the presses. Later, the king attributed the defections in his army and the nation to this material, which made him, he said, "appear as black as Hell." [108] A pamphleteer also referred to "those little stories" circulated in print which "more than anything else alienated men's affections." [109] The fact was that to the detriment of James's chances, he failed both to control the press and to provide a genuine debate of the issues in the pamphlets. The consequence, pertinent to the story of the Declaration of Rights, was that the press overwhelmingly carried the message that Prince William favored a declaration of the nation's rights and liberties by a freely elected parliament.

6

The Decision to Call a Convention

I n the early morning hours of December 11, his nerves shattered by betrayals, armed uprisings, and the memory of his father's fate, King James II slipped out of London. Before leaving he canceled the writs that he had issued for electing a parliament and burned the ones at hand that had not yet been dispatched. Further to ensure chaos, he also canceled the nominations for new sheriffs, who were needed to carry out the elections, and ordered that the army be disbanded.[1] As his boat slid down the Thames, James dropped the Great Seal, which he had ordered Jeffreys to deliver to him, into the river. The purpose of this act was unmistakable. As James explained in a letter, the "meeting of a parliament cannot be authorized without writs under the great seal. . . . The great seal is missing. . . . All this will create difficulties and incidents which afford me occasion to take suitable measures."[2] Clearly, James's purpose was to throw England into such confusion that he would be recalled and to make it impossible to summon a legal parliament to deal with the crisis. On those grounds he hoped to preserve his own rights and those of his descendants to the crown. His flight was a desperate gamble, and it failed. The king was captured by some fishermen, subjected to indignities, and brought back to London on December 17. William and his friends put specific and not very discreet pressure on him for a second removal from the City. Under Dutch guard, James left London on the eighteenth and took up residence at Rochester, whence, with the connivance of the prince, he escaped to France on December 23.

James's departure created a largely unexpected situation. Political tensions sharpened, sentiment for an aggrieved and abused king grew, and the prince's initial popularity waned. The mob in and out of London (which had engaged in sporadic outbursts for weeks) rioted violently in the City on the nights of December 11, 12, and 13. The threat (real and alleged) to England and the Netherlands from Ireland and France added urgency to the complex domestic politics. All parties jockeyed for personal and partisan advantage as William and English political leaders entered into delicate negotiations. For

126

the first time men discussed openly who should be king. Tracts and pamphlets presented radical ideas for reforming the government and reasserting the nation's rights. Partisan alignments, previously blurred by the near unanimous opposition to James's policies, resurfaced. Not only did a conservative group appear, composed of men who shifted among one or another alternative solutions that did not include giving the crown to the Dutch prince, but also a group of radicals emerged, commonly identified by contemporaries as "commonwealthsmen." As a result of complex and delicate political maneuvering over many weeks, these groups finally agreed that a freely elected parliament in the form of a Convention was essential to solve the crisis. That decision was of critical importance to the history of the Declaration of Rights. If a Convention had not been summoned, if the crisis had been resolved in some other way, it is almost certain that there would have been no Declaration of Rights.

The sentiment that a freely elected parliament must be summoned to resolve the crisis had deepened during the autumn. In November, for example, a contemporary noted that "people are extraordinary for a parliament being called. 'Tis the wish of everybody."[3] This wish had been frustrated over the weeks by James's erratic policy. Earlier James had issued writs for a parliament, but he then canceled them, explaining himself in printed declarations. One such declaration appeared on November 6 and stressed his willingness to summon a parliament as soon as the prince left.[4] In response, some Protestant peers presented the king a written petition on November 16, begging him to call a parliament immediately, and to counter his refusal, they printed the petition as a proclamation of the Lords, a bold and unprecedented step.[5] Tracts, one of them a broadside from the prince's camp at Exeter, reinforced the lords' petition.[6] At about the same time, provincial uprisings occurred, accompanied by manifestoes that demanded a freely elected parliament.[7] Emotionally distracted by news of these uprisings and of the desertion of senior army officers, James again summoned peers who were in London to meet with him and offer him advice. In a stormy session on November 26 the lords once more urged the king to call a parliament, and after a night's reflection James capitulated. On November 30 a proclamation for elections to a parliament to meet on January 15 was issued.

Some parliamentary elections were held on the basis of this proclamation, providing grounds later on for the proposal favored by loyalists. The proclamation also immediately provoked political maneuvering with William, now camped at Hungerford, where a number of Englishmen hastened. The conversations there on December 8 and 9 are pertinent to this study for what they reveal of the continuing role in the political process of the prince's *Declaration of Reasons*. William confirmed his commitment "punctually" to observe the terms of his manifesto. Bentinck dismissed as a "wicked insinuation" the idea that William aspired to the English crown. Clarendon referred to William's manifesto in ways that anticipated a major tactic of the loyalists, namely to try to hold William to strict observance of its terms. He declared that if William adhered to his *Declaration,* which characterized him as interested only in overseeing the election of a free parliament, the crisis could be quickly resolved.[8] The conversations also exposed opposition on the part of some of William's supporters to electing a parliament on James's writs. They feared that because of their absence from England they might fail to be elected and that a parliament loyal to James would be returned. But the prince disagreed.[9] Using James's writs would assure that the parliament would be legal. It would enable him to avoid involvement with Tories who hoped to mediate the crisis to serve their own interests. It reinforced his image as Deliverer. Clarendon was overjoyed at William's position. "God be thanked!" he wrote. "The Parliament is to meet."[10]

What might have happened if James's writs had run and the king had stayed in England are among the fascinating ifs of the Glorious Revolution. On the basis of extensive analysis of James's efforts to pack Parliament, Professor Jones believes that a parliament favorable to James might well have been elected.[11] But James had not negotiated in good faith either with English peers or the Dutch invader. His strategy was to use the negotiations at Hungerford to gain time to send his wife and son to the Continent and to make arrangements for his own flight.[12] What James left behind was the feeling, several times frustrated, that the only solution was to elect a parliament. How this might be done under the circumstances was the central question. It took over two weeks of negotiation to find an answer.

Some peers in London seized the initiative following James's first flight. On December 11, about thirty lords met at the Guildhall to set up a provisional government. They had been summoned by a letter from the archbishop of Canterbury, which Lawrence Hyde, earl of Rochester, and Francis Turner, bishop of Ely, had prepared against the possibility of James's fleeing.[13] Sharp divisions appeared in this and subsequent meetings. On the one hand, over half the peers — including Rochester, Clarendon, Turner, Sancroft, and Thomas White, bishop of Peterborough, all former anti-Exclusionists — formed a band of men loyal to James.[14] Their avowed strategy was to deal with William on the basis of his *Declaration of Reasons.* Their aim was to "make an accord if possible between the king and the prince, to get effectual securities for our religion and laws in a free parliament of His Majesty's calling and to call the king home again with honor and safety." Their underlying purpose — "the only thing designed by many of us," Turner said — was to preserve James's lawful rights.[15] The foundations for a strong Tory presence in the Convention were laid in these meetings in December.

Confronting the loyalists were a number of revolutionaries who aimed to remove James and elevate the prince to the throne. Notable among them were Delamere, Devonshire, and Mordaunt, who had helped arrange William's intervention and would serve on the Lords rights committee. Also important were Ralph, third Baron Montague of Boughton; Thomas, second Baron Culpepper of Thoresway; Francis, Viscount Newport of Bradford;

and Lord Wharton, the latter two of whom would also be on the Lords rights committee. They formed a "violent party," which was "fanatical" in endorsing the prince and his measures.[16]

Although their ultimate goals differed, the peers were united in believing that a parliament must be called. On December 11, they drew up a declaration stressing that point.[17] They thanked William for coming to England for the avowed purpose of "procur[ing] a free Parliament," and promised to assist him to secure the nation's laws, liberties, and properties. Pledging their support of worldwide Protestantism, they referred to the need to provide "due liberty" to Dissenters, but promised support of the "established government in England." The document reflected the equilibrium between the partisan forces at this time; it did not include a clause affirming James's right to the throne (which the loyalists promoted); it did not, as is sometimes said, invite William to London (which the revolutionaries wanted). It was also silent on the matter of a future role for James or William in England's government. On December 13, four lords delivered the declaration to the prince, now at Henley.[18]

On the evening of December 11, the London Common Council also met.[19] They too framed a declaration, reportedly at the urging of Treby.[20] Like the peers' declaration, it stressed the need for a parliament, but the council's paper differed in that it specifically invited William to London and promised that he would be "received with universal joy and satisfaction." Representatives of the City delivered this paper, which was also printed, to William, reaching his camp on December 13, at about the same time the peers did.

The presentation of these two declarations marked the beginning of increasing closeness between William and London. The prince dismissed the Lords' declaration with perfunctory thanks, but accepted the City's paper enthusiastically, announcing that he would come to London "as soon as possible."[21] The invitation, in fact, conformed to the prince's plans, which he had evidently fixed two days before. On the afternoon of the eleventh, about twelve hours after the event, news of James's flight reached William. Burnet reported the pleasure this intelligence gave the prince. The next day, signing himself, "Your most affectionate friend," William wrote a letter to James Butler, duke of Ormonde, saying, "I have thought it absolutely necessary to make all haste I could to London to settle matters there and to prevent the effusion of blood, which for want of my presence might happen, considering the heat people are in."[22] This letter, hitherto unnoticed, repays reflection. It reveals how swift and accurate was the prince's intelligence. It shows that his entry into the city was planned before the City's invitation. It provides further example of William's political adroitness: a foreign prince, he justifies his coming to London to quiet the mob, thereby reinforcing his image as a peaceful Deliverer. It permits speculation that William anticipated the impending mob activity, for it refers to his professed desire "to prevent the effusion of blood" before any such effusion had occurred.

The possible connection between William and the London mob is obscure. On the nights of December 11, 12, and 13, there were violent outrages in London against Catholics, mass houses, and the residences of foreign ambassadors.[23] These disorders were not the first in the revolution. Scattered violence around the country and in London had occurred almost immediately after William landed,[24] whether spontaneously or otherwise, is unknown. But within a week after William's landing, on November 13, it was reported that "great endeavors" were used to excite the London "lads" to create mischief "under the pretense of pulling down the Popish chapels."[25] The situation was serious enough for James to leave eight regiments in the City to control the rabble while he was at Salisbury.[26] The spurious *Third Declaration*, printed on November 28 and circulated in early December, terrified people with its warning of an impending massacre by Irish troops and its counsel to treat Catholics as "banditti," and was thought to have inflamed the mob, as its author intended. The mob, inflated by soldiers from James's disbanded army and by persons suffering economic distress (the immediate consequence of an embargo James placed on all east-coast ports), grew to as many as 20,000 in mid-December.[27] No leader has been identified.[28]

But there may have been connections between the mob and those men who in February 1689 organized the signing and presentation to the Convention of a petition from the citizens of Westminster and London to declare William and Mary king and queen immediately. One of those organizers was John Lovelace, third Baron Lovelace of Hurley, a "violent" Whig suspected of complicity in the Rye House Plot. He had angered James by his remark that subjects were not bound to obey a Roman Catholic justice of the peace and had been summoned before the Privy Council in the spring of 1688. The charge was dropped because of lack of evidence, but William's *Declaration of Reasons* alluded to this episode, thereby inflating Lovelace's status. His fondness for gambling and the fact that he was "constantly tipsy"[29] may have facilitated contacts with the London underground. Another organizer of the petition was a Mr. Luke Robinson of London.[30] The fact that the numerous petitioners — it was said that 15,000 signatures were collected and that 10,000 men would deliver the signed petition to the two Houses[31] — were readily dissuaded from presenting their petition reinforces the hypothesis that the activity of the mob was planned and led. The same point is suggested by a contemporary comment — that the "rabble were masters, if the beasts had known their own strength."[32] That the mob was out of hand only briefly, and did not take over the City, indicates control of some kind. The idea draws further strength from the fact that the mob was dissuaded from ravaging the house of a Catholic when they were told that Delamere would occupy it. Someone had to arrange that announcement in the form of notes affixed to the house.[33] As is well known, political leaders had manipulated the London underground before 1688. Pym had engaged the "lads" for his purposes in the Civil War. Shaftesbury had done the same thing. There was precedent, then, for using the London mob as an instrument for helping to achieve political goals. At the very least, the evidence suggests that William's friends exploited the restlessness of the mob to help the prince's cause and implies that the prince was aware of their activity.

The growing closeness between prince and City received reinforcement. First, the City declined to welcome James officially upon his return after his abortive first flight. Treby, now reinstated as recorder, was responsible for this policy. He persuaded the council that to welcome the king would be dangerous. He argued that although James had the legal authority, William had "the power" — an army — and that the mob, quieted by the City's invitation to William, might be reinflamed and turn their violence against the council. Since James had shown that he really wanted to leave the country, it was an affront, Treby said, to welcome him back to his capital! [34] Second, on December 17 the council, again influenced by Treby, sent William, Morrice declared, an "excellent" letter drafted by the recorder. The excellence of the letter apparently lay in the fact that it promised William that the citizens of the City would expose their "lives and estates" to prevent "all dangers from those restless spirits that have now appeared." According to Morrice, these sentences responded to William's concern, expressed in a letter and voiced by his commissioner, that "tumultuous spirits," meaning not the mob but the loyalists, were trying to "retrieve" what the City had done for him. [35] Treby's letter subtly signaled the City's awareness of the strength of conservative forces and indicated its determination to deal with them. As a result, an unidentified conservative leader, recognizing the power of London to swing the contest to William, transferred his allegiance to the prince. [36] Third, London's official welcome to William testified to its commitment to the prince. Treby again played the central role. Deputizing for a still ailing mayor, he delivered a speech of considerable rhetorical force, in which he labeled James and his ministers the true invaders of the nation, because they had broken the laws and the "constitution of our legislature." Reflecting the phraseology of William's *Declaration,* Treby asserted that William alone would preserve the nation's religion, laws, and liberties. Treby's speech was printed, thus circulating further the position of the City.

And, finally, William's reception in London became the subject of pictures and poems, which recorded the event in flattering terms. A poem congratulating the prince upon his arrival in London assured its readers that William was ambitious for glory, not thrones, and that they need not fear for James's safety. "No Forty-Eights adhorred detest shame. / But a bright Page of pure unsullied Fame" was to be expected. [37] One print, designed by Carolus Allard and issued "with privilege from the great and mighty states of Holland Westfriseland," shows the prince being welcomed with great pageantry, and another by Romeyn de Hooghe also emphasizes the magnificence of the entry. The latter carries a text in both French and Dutch describing the picture. [38] Both pictures are a gloss on the truth. Contemporary observers did report that William was received with enthusiasm, but a devoted partisan of William's lamented the prince's failure to make a splendid entry; and a friend of James's commented that, upon the king's return to the

City from his first flight, James had been received with much greater expressions of affection than William.[39] Nevertheless, the effect of such material was to underscore the friendly relationship between the capital and the prince.

With William in London and James in Rochester, alternative solutions to how to convene Parliament were earnestly explored. One proposal, which gained sufficient currency for the Spanish ambassador to report it,[40] was for William alone (or perhaps William and Mary together) to assume the kingship on the grounds of conquest, as *de facto* monarch(s).[41] As early as December 2 Sir Robert Howard had advised the prince to make this move, arguing that he should build on new foundations, trust no one, and avoid complex negotiations which would dampen people's spirits.[42] On the fifteenth, Pollexfen maintained that James's first flight amounted to a "cession" of his right to the crown, and that William, with his army behind him, should declare himself king.[43] The "greatest lawyers and those that came in with the prince"[44] favored this course for several reasons. First, it would have the effect of legalizing a future parliament. As king *de facto,* William could call a legal parliament which would have the power to "purge all defects" from his title. Second, it would protect Englishmen from the charge of treason, for a statute of Henry VII indemnified anyone who obeyed a king *de facto* during the time a king *de jure* was dispossessed.[45] Third, it was thought that James's friends in Scotland would be unlikely to oppose a *de facto* king, and thus, the step would forestall their uniting with James's supporters in England.[46]

William's inaction for two days suggests that he did not dismiss the idea out of hand. It was compatible with his intention to have the crown, an intention indisputably fixed after James's flight, whatever William's initial purpose in invading England. It was compatible with a step he had taken a week before when he had instructed Admiral Herbert, who held a Dutch commission, to fly the English flag in naval engagements with French ships.[47] It was compatible with his eagerness to send men and supplies to Holland.[48] But, for several reasons, the prince rejected the advice. First, the step was contrary to his avowed policy set out in his widespread *Declaration of Reasons* and iterated and reiterated in other statements printed under his imprimatur to refer the solution to the crisis to a freely elected Parliament. Burnet explained that such a move "would make all that the prince had hitherto done pass for aspiring ambition," would "disgust those who had hitherto been the best affected to his designs," and would make others who were "less concerned in the quarrel" assume he was a conqueror.[49] To a degree, then, William's propaganda limited his political options. Second, the prince was worried that James's soldiers would oppose the idea, and that James's friends would "excite" the army "to a nonconcurrence."[50] Third, Continental nations might object. The Estates-General, whom William had told he had no designs on the English throne, might interpret the step as an indication of the prince's willingness to prefer English trade over Holland's commercial interests.[51] Indeed, the prince was concerned enough about other nations to send an envoy to "Vienna and Madrid . . . to remove the bad impression that they are getting."[52]

For all these reasons, William's decision was politically astute. But, as the prince had said the previous August when considering the draft of the *Declaration of Reasons,* it was not without hazard to entrust his fate to a freely elected parliament. It cost William something in December. The prince wrote impatiently on December 28 to George Frederick, Prince van Waldeck, a Dutch confidante, that if he "were not by nature so scrupulous," he would have been "able to finish the affair soon," and he added, "I have more trouble than you can imagine." Several days later he referred to the patience he needed to handle the situation in England: "If you knew what a life I lead," the prince wrote, "you would certainly pity me."[53] The strain William was under manifested itself in a deepening of his asthmatic cough, repeated colds throughout these weeks, and a weight loss so marked that Mary was seriously concerned when she joined him in February.[54] William's decision not to assume the crown was a turning point in the history of the Declaration of Rights. If he had decided differently, it is almost certain that there would have been no Declaration of Rights.

Once this decision was made, William took the initiative in moving English political leaders towards a resolution of the crisis. On December 20 he summoned the peers to advise him how best to achieve the ends of his *Declaration* in calling a parliament. About seventy lords gathered at St. James's on the twenty-first. The meeting revealed hostility to William.[55] But the reading of the prince's *Declaration of Reasons* and William's assertion that he would "not depart one tittle" from it momentarily removed the dissatisfaction.[56] The peers promised to assist William in calling a free parliament and appointed five lawyers to help them with legal questions. Among the lawyers were Holt, Maynard, and Pollexfen, who would later serve on the rights committee to draft the Declaration of Rights.[57]

But the meeting the next day again produced "divisions" among the peers and quarrels with the prince.[58] The lords who had favored James's interests at the Guildhall meeting continued to work for the king.[59] Described as "considerable,"[60] this faction contained not only "old rotten Tories" (as Morrice characterized them), but the "better sort of the Church of England clergymen," who had refused to read James's Declaration of Indulgence. Their aim remained "to narrow and enervate the prince's designs" and to hold William to the "letter" of his manifesto. They thought that "if they could gain time and perplex things awhile, the nation will be forced to recur to the king."[61] They were heartened by James's return to London, by a meeting at which they and the king agreed to preserve each other, and by James's expressed willingness to make all the concessions required of him, even to being reduced to the condition of a duke of Venice.[62] Thus, these men proposed to make James "all the offers in the world consistent with [the nation's] safety" and to bring him back with his authority specifically limited and with the understanding that he would issue writs for the election of a free parliament.[63] Although this scheme failed of approval, the next day they apparently sent word to James to return to London and drew up propositions to offer him.[64]

Despite the king's successful second flight on the twenty-third, the earl of Nottingham introduced the plan on December 24.[65] He presented a list of restrictions to be placed on James's authority.[66] For example, he called for annual parliaments to sit for at least thirty days, thereby canceling a prerogative of the crown to call, prorogue, and dismiss Parliament at will, and going further than the comparable clause in the Declaration of Rights. He required the king to "hearken to the advice" of Parliament on the questions of religion and the "rights, laws, and liberties of the subject." He called for the prince to be made "guaranty" for James's performance of what the free Parliament demanded. In effect, Nottingham proposed a regency.

Although Whigs such as Delamere opposed the scheme, it is likely that had James not fled, the peers would have agreed to negotiate with him along the lines set out.[67] If that had happened, one may speculate that a document not unlike the final Declaration of Rights would have been imposed on James. Whether he would have observed the restrictions and whether the Tories, who would surely have occupied the principal offices, would have allowed the limitations to erode, as Morrice predicted, are other matters. In any case, Nottingham's proposals may have suggested to the loyalists that limitations should be placed on the prince's power if he became king.

On December 26, the archbishop of Canterbury summoned the bishops to a meeting to decide on "certain limits and restrictions to be laid upon the prince" in the forthcoming Convention. It was said that if William should not concur with their proposals, "they will labor to give him cheque-mate."[68] The idea among Tories of using restrictions on the prince's power as a political weapon apparently first surfaced at this meeting. That the bishops were thinking in these terms in December is important to understanding the passage of the Declaration of Rights in February.

Two other proposals were made. One was to ask the men who had been (or could be) elected on the writs James had issued before his flight to meet and authorize filling the remaining vacancies. In this way the parliament could be regarded as legal. The idea, according to Clarendon, won support, but was "slighted" and failed.[69] The second was that Princess Mary should be declared queen and then she could call a legal parliament. Introduced by William, Lord Paget (Richard Hampden's father-in-law), partly to undermine the strength of the loyalists,[70] this proposal was opposed by James's friends, who were still looking for a way to preserve the king's right to the throne, and by William's supporters.[71]

The expedient finally accepted was that William should issue circular letters calling for the election of a "Convention." To outward appearances a convention would be indistinguishable from a regular parliament. It would be composed of spiritual and temporal peers and of commoners elected by persons who traditionally had the right to vote. Of course, it could not be summoned by writs issued by a lawful king and processed through the Court of Chancery. But the Convention of 1660, judged by the "great lawyers" to be the equivalent of a parliament,[72] provided a precedent. A convention ostensibly placed the resolution of the crisis in the hands of Englishmen and thus restrained the Dutch prince. It left open the solution to the crisis. It provided an opportunity to redress the nation's grievances and declare the rights of Englishmen. Accompanying it was an address to William asking him to assume civil, military, and fiscal authority and to give special attention to Ireland, the latter charge aimed at protecting the interests of Englishmen in that country.[73] It pleased all sides, as the membership of the committee appointed to draw up an address to the prince showed.[74]

Thomas Herbert, eighth earl of Pembroke, was said to have introduced this scheme.[75] Interested in science, especially mathematics, and in the Royal Society, of which he became president in 1689–90, the youthful Pembroke (he was thirty-three years old) was a friend of John Locke, who dedicated his *Essay of Human Understanding* to him. An intellectual who maintained a salon frequented by Isaac Newton, Pembroke was a virtuoso and a collector of coins and statues. He had had little political experience. Thomas succeeded to the family title in 1683, became lord-lieutenant of Wiltshire, and two years later raised the county militia to help repulse Monmouth's Rebellion. But he refused to assist in the quo warranto proceedings in 1687, and James dismissed him from office.[76] In December 1688, he was among those lords who wanted to preserve James's rights. Perhaps his politically experienced and legally knowledgeable father-in-law, Sir Robert Sawyer, instructed him. However that may be, Pembroke did not regard his proposed scheme as precluding the recall of James. On the contrary, at the end of December he was in "good spirits" about the king's prospects and declared that efforts must be made in the upcoming Convention to secure the "King's interests."[77]

Eighty-nine peers subscribed the address and, much to the irritation of former M.P.'s, presented it to William on the twenty-fifth without waiting for their concurrence. But to the astonishment of some "zealous" lords, the prince refused to respond until he had consulted the Commons.[78] In fact, William had already, on December 23, summoned to a meeting on December 26 all men who had served in any of Charles II's parliaments, thus excluding those who had been only in James II's Parliament of 1685. Underlining his close relationship with London, the prince also invited the lord mayor, aldermen, and fifty members of the Common Council of London appointed by them.[79] The invitation was designed to broaden the base of his support, counter the impression that he was indebted alone to peers partisan to him, and dilute the sentiment for James expressed by loyalist lords. William, it was felt, needed to be assured at this time of the concurrence of the Commons.[80] By limiting the invitation to members of Charles II's parliaments, the prince assured a strong Whig presence. The notice was printed by Awnsham Churchill, a radical Whig sympathizer, who, at some personal risk, had printed tracts critical of King James in the spring of 1688 and was then under bail for selling Fagel's *Letter*. After the revolution, Churchill continued to publish Whiggish pieces, among them Locke's *Two Treatises of Government* (1689) and the *Second Letter on Toleration* (1690), and John Selden's *Table Talk*. That Churchill printed William's summons is of interest because it adds further evidence of the support of the prince at this time by radical Whig printers. This notice was among the first printed announcements from William's court to be printed by an English printer.[81]

The meeting on the twenty-sixth at St. James's attracted great interest. It was the first time the prince had appeared before a large body of English commoners. It was the first time a group of M.P.'s had met formally since the fall of 1685. It signaled a sharing of the leadership of the revolution between peers and commoners. Up to December 26, English noblemen had taken the lead in affairs.[82] Thereafter they would continue to play an important role, but one shared with Commons, who, when the Convention met, would seize the initiative.

Addressing the group in brief remarks, William asked how best to pursue the ends of his *Declaration of Reasons* in calling a free parliament to preserve the Protestant religion and restore the nation's rights and liberties — and departed.[83] The immediate response of the two hundred or so men was to adjourn to Westminster, where they would have more room.[84] Whigs dominated the proceedings, prefiguring their role in the Convention. Sir Henry Powle took the chair. A lawyer whose previous parliamentary experience reached back to the Convention Parliament of 1660, Powle had long opposed Stuart policies, especially those respecting the dispensing power and standing armies. He had corresponded with Bentinck and was on intimate enough terms with William to carry the prince's letter of December 16 to the lord mayor and Common Council of London.[85] The Dutch ambassador described him as a "man of excellent understanding and probity."[86] Under his chairmanship the debate was searching. Sir Robert Sawyer spoke for those who wanted "to reform what was amiss and recall James."[87] Others wanted to declare William and Mary king and queen immediately. The "wisest, ablest and honestest . . . men" favored this proposal, Morrice said, but abandoned it because of the strength of the loyalists. They feared a "fatal breach" between the two Houses, with consequent difficulties for the prince. They also feared the hostile reaction of Continental nations.[88] By two o'clock the Commons had accepted the proposal to elect a convention, and a committee, chaired probably by Richard Hampden, drew up an address to William.[89]

The prince appointed Pollexfen to prepare the circular letters calling for an election.[90] Perhaps it was Pollexfen and other lawyers who adjusted the regular election procedures to deal with an emergency situation and protect the interests of the prince and his friends.[91] The letters for the counties were to be addressed to the coroner and, in default, to the clerk of the peace, rather than to the sheriff, the local officer who traditionally served as the returning officer, because it was thought that over half of them were Catholics, a consequence of James's quo warranto proceedings.[92] The letters to the cities, boroughs, and Cinque Ports were to go to an ambiguously named "chief magistrate." The usual forty-day notice for an election was bypassed, and the Convention was scheduled to assemble on January 22, 1689. Moreover, notice of the election need be posted only five days (rather than ten) in counties and only three days in other places. Finally, it was arranged for the letters to be published in all market towns rather than being sent to all parishes and published in all churches immediately after divine service. The details are worth noticing for the care they reveal to preserve legal forms and at the same time protect partisan interests.

The idea that the purpose of the convention was to redress grievances and reaffirm the nation's rights at the same time it solved the crisis threaded through the documents that arranged its meeting. The address to William asking him to call the convention referred to attaining the ends set out in his manifesto. In accepting the request, the prince affirmed that he had come to England for no other purpose than the "preservation of the Protestant religion, and the laws and liberties" of the nation.[93] The circular letters justified all that had been done as a means of attaining the "ends" of William's *Declaration* and affirmed that the prince "desired" the "performance" of what he said in the *Declaration*.[94] Implicit in them, then, was an invitation to the Convention to declare the rights and liberties of the nation. Since the letters were to be posted in every market town, every person with the slightest interest in politics must have been aware of this mandate.

The decision to call a convention to act as surrogate for a free parliament was not predictable nor did it prove easy to attain. Men on all sides agreed to it only after considering several other possible alternatives. It won approval in part because it left open a final decision on who should be king, assured that Englishmen would have a significant say in that decision, and provided an opportunity to declare the grievances and rights of the nation.

7

The Elections to the Convention

The elections to the Convention were carried out during three weeks in January 1689. They were accompanied by lively political maneuvering and speculation. "All men," wrote Burnet, "were forming their schemes, and fortifying their party."[1] Conservative Tories who favored a solution other than giving the English crown to the Dutch prince and revolutionary Whigs who wished to crown William alone or William and Mary jointly contested for votes more vigorously than used to be thought. Both sides employed the press to inform a wide number of people of their position. These weeks of election and preparation for the convening of the Convention are important to understanding the Declaration of Rights for the further light they shed on partisan alignments, strategies, and goals.

The overriding question about the elections is, Were they "free"? A "freely" elected Parliament was what Englishmen on all sides had for months demanded. It was what James had promised as soon as William and his army left England. It was what William had promised in his *Declaration of Reasons*. It was what the prince's circular letters enjoined on properly qualified English subjects — "truly and uprightly, without favour or affection to any person, or indirect practice or proceeding" freely to elect their representatives. Accordingly, it was important to William that the elections should *seem* to be free, whatever the reality. Insofar as there was no direct interference by the central government of a kind practiced by King James, the elections were free. James's elaborate apparatus for packing Parliament had been dismantled. Whatever William may have wanted to do, a restrained role was tactically and practically the only one open to him. Tactically, direct interference would have been impolitic, because it was contrary to his repeatedly avowed policy and the demands of Englishmen. Practically, direct interference was impossible. William's executive authority was specifically limited to January 22, his administration was unsettled, he himself was busy and preoccupied with myriad responsibilities, and the men close to him were still unsure.[2] There was no time, in three weeks, for William to master and use the methods English kings had customarily employed to influence parliamentary elections. The pressures usually exercised by the central government, and even expected in such boroughs as the Cinque Ports and the Isle of Wight, and in seaports such as Portsmouth and Harwich,[3] were not applied. Indeed, there is no reliable evidence that William recommended even one specific person for election.[4] William was at pains to preserve legal procedures. For example, on December 29, as the circular letters were being sealed, he refused, despite the "greatest mediation," to "deliver" them to any "private gentleman's hands."[5] Again, he acted swiftly to bring both the Dutch and the English armies under control for many reasons, among them, to avoid actual and claimed interference in the elections. By proclamations beginning on December 13, the prince regulated the arms, pay, discipline, housing, and regimental assignments of the soldiers, and required an oath from all officers that they would be "true" to him.[6] On January 5, just as the elections were getting underway, William ordered soldiers to vacate boroughs and towns the day before an election was held and not to return until it was over.[7] This step was not disinterested. While it quieted fears that the army would interfere in the elections, it also helped candidates friendly to the prince, for many of James's soldiers resented William.[8] The fact that the Convention's Committee on Elections dealt with only one case involving the intervention of soldiers testifies to the success of William's efforts to maintain traditional procedures.[9] For all these reasons, then, the election was "free," as William and his friends repeatedly declared it was.[10]

But Burnet's observation, that the "prince did in no sort interpose in any recommendation, directly or indirectly,"[11] must be qualified. Indirectly, William and his close Dutch and English adherents took steps to assure that men friendly to him would be elected. As early as December 12, William revealed in a letter to Danby that he was concerned to have men sympathetic to him returned to any parliament that might be called. He recommended that the earl's men disband, return to their counties, and stand for Parliament, "keeping their inclination to me."[12] It is reasonable to think that the prince or his advisers wrote to other English political leaders in the same terms, although in fact no such letters survive. But even if they sent no other letters, William and his friends met with many Englishmen during these weeks. "All the world go to see the Prince at St. Jamess [sic]," reported Evelyn.[13] For example, temporal peers were there on December 18 and 19, and about forty of them dined with William on the twentieth. The prince received spiritual peers on December 19 and 22. Persons of quality and even the "common people" also appeared on the nineteenth, and members of the London corporation on the next day. The gentlemen of the Middle Temple and upwards of sixty Presbyterian ministers were among persons William received on January 1.[14] Conversations at these affairs may have been largely social, but it is unreasonable to think that no political comment was exchanged. In any case, there was political capital to be made from the impression William conveyed by his treating "all persons with great affability and respect,"[15] contrary to his usual coldness and reserve.

Of undoubted significance were the conversations William had with Halifax. The two men may have conferred on the evening of William's arrival in London, when Halifax told William that he might be whatever he pleased, so unsettled were affairs.[16] They certainly had a lengthy conversation on December 30,[17] when the prince talked with unusual candor about matters related tangentially to the election and centrally to the general crisis. William declared that he would not stay in England if James returned, or if he were offered a regency, or if a commonwealth were set up. He also said that "the commonwealth party was the strongest in England," and that at the best, they would make him a "duke of Venice." He asserted that he "did not come over to establish a commonwealth." These remarks are of uncommon importance for understanding William's true attitude towards his avowed purpose, oft-repeated, that he came only to call a free parliament which would reform the government and reassert the nation's rights. In August he had expressed privately to Bentinck his reluctance to commit his fate to a freely elected parliament. Four months later he made it clear to Halifax that he was opposed, even as he had been during the Exclusion Crisis, to any significant limitations on the power of the crown. His emphatic assertions may have been in response to reports that "commonwealthsmen" were saying "very bold things" in London coffee houses. He must have known that they had been identified as one of several parties promoting a solution to the crisis.[18]

Such a frank conversation between William and Halifax on the eve of the election could not have been fortuitous. It seems reasonable to think that William calculated that Halifax would circulate his views to appropriate persons. More, if William confided in Halifax, who had neither been privy to the invasion plans nor trusted by the prince until mid-December, how much more likely is it that he concerted with his close, long-term English friends.[19] In fact, the very day before, William was "shut up a long time with Lord Mordaunt." It cannot be thought that these two men talked anything but politics.[20] It is legitimate to hypothesize that as a consequence of these contacts and of the presence of the prince's friends in the Convention, politically sophisticated M.P.'s had an idea of William's attitude and probable response when the motion to reassert the rights of the nation was introduced. The point illuminates the motive of the Tories, Whigs close to the prince, and men devoted as a matter of principle to the claim of rights.

William's close friends also met with English political leaders during these weeks, not so much to influence the outcome of the elections as the outcome of the Convention. For example, Dijkvelt had two lengthy and warm conversations on January 12 and 14 with Clarendon and tried to see the earl again on the sixteenth. Besides discussing Clarendon's predictions about the proceedings and outcome of the Convention, Dijkvelt also "extremely pressed" the earl to use his influence with the Anglican clergy. He said that William "expected and hoped" that the clergy would "make their applications to him" and complained about the failure of the archbishop of Canterbury to pay his respects.[21] Dijkvelt also said that once affairs were settled, Clarendon could expect reward from the prince in the form of any appointment he should wish. The reward obviously implied that some service would be rendered. If such a *quid pro quo* was offered one potentially powerful Englishman, it is possible that it was offered to others, notice of which has not survived. Bentinck also called on Clarendon to press him for predictions about the outcome of the Convention and assure him of the prince's favor.[22] Again, Burnet engaged in spirited conversations with Clarendon about the posture of affairs, and debated the issues also with "several bishops" in a "long conference" at which "high words" were exchanged.[23] Thus, in the weeks before the Convention William and his little court were not entirely passive. They gained experience in dealing with English political leaders and prepared the way for the same kind of discreet dealing during the Convention.

Some peers and commons exercised their influence in counties and boroughs to elect to the Convention men friendly to William. For example, Danby, in Yorkshire, wrote a letter on December 16 to the mayor of Pontefract in which he criticized men who had failed to serve their county and nation in this time of crisis. Disclaiming interest in a particular candidate, he advised the borough not to "choose any who have only looked on whilst others have ventured their all," [24] plainly meaning not to choose those who favor King James. His point could hardly have been forgotten a month later when elections to the Convention took place. Moreover, Danby urged a man he thought friendly to the king to withdraw his candidacy for the county seat.[25] Again, the bishop of Radnor, a partisan of William, left London on January 1 for Cornwall to be there at the time of election, presumably to use his influence for the prince.[26] Sawyer, James's former attorney-general and a loyalist, complained bitterly of the "ill-usage" he had suffered in his election at Cambridge University, declaring that he had not expected such treatment in the "nursery of ingenuity." [27] Did William's friends devise the skullduggery? In Westmoreland and Cumberland, Sir John Lowther of Lowther went to pains to limit the electioneering efforts of Sir Christopher Musgrave, a Tory loyalist.[28] In the election at New Windsor, Berkshire, peers partisan to William (such as Wharton) may have interfered to assure the election of Henry Powle, as persons unfriendly to the prince charged.[29] Again, William's friends arranged to have elections held first in London, where they were confident of returning men sympathetic to him, as a way of giving direction to smaller boroughs.[30] Finally, the great efforts William's friends made to get themselves elected — one standing for three boroughs, another spending over twelve pounds on the day of the election alone — served the prince's interests as well as their own.[31]

The press also played a role in the election. Tracts written by radical Whigs (discussed in the next chapter) argued for a change in the king and in the kingship and may have influenced the vote of some electors. At least two printed broadsides offered the electorate specific advice on what qualities to consider in casting their votes for members of the Convention. Readers following the advice would have returned candidates favorable to William. *Considerations Proposed to the Electors of the Ensuing Convention,* said to have been "spread by a soldier who came over with the Prince of Orange, who knew nothing of it," offered specific advice. Appearing on January 9, just as the elections were starting, this broadside counseled readers not to choose any candidate who had ridiculed the Popish Plot, submitted to the surrender of charters, or promoted the arbitrary designs of a Popish court, but rather to elect men who had opposed popery and arbitrary power in Charles II's parliaments. The piece ended with the promise that such men as it recommended would expose themselves to the "greatest hazards, to establish your religion, laws and liberties," [32] and thus fulfill the prince's *Declaration.* James's friends took *Considerations* seriously enough to reply directly in a pamphlet charging that it was aimed at undermining the Church of England.[33] A second piece, *A Seasonable Mememto to all the Electors of Knights, Citizens, & Burgesses of England, for the approaching Convention to meet the 22 of this instant January, 1689,*[34] covered the same points as *Considerations,* but added to the list of blackballed persons those who had "played tricks" in the election of 1685.

Men unfriendly to William complained that the prince and his adherents had interfered in the elections. One observer charged them with "very foul play," including "debauching the electors, adjourning the polls, [and the] Lords appearing to influence the elections."[35] Another contemporary claimed that the prince and his friends had employed "all possible industry" to assure the choice of men "ill-affected" to James.[36] A printed tract also asserted that "particular care" was used to elect men certain to oppose the king, such as persons who had been "discountenanced, or browbeaten before, in the way of outlawries," or who themselves or their relations had opposed Charles I.[37] The eighteenth-century historian James Ralph wrote that William and his court had tried to influence the elections and ridiculed Burnet for suggesting otherwise.[38] But Ralph offered no certain proof. It would seem to be a fair conclusion that the political maneuvering of William and his friends during these weeks was discreet. No such tactics as James had employed were used to assure that men favorable to the prince would be returned to the Convention. But William and his court did what they could, and their subtle but real intervention in the electoral proceedings anticipated the subtle but equally real intervention in the deliberations of the Convention.

Conservatives also engaged in partisan maneuvering during the weeks prior to the meeting of the Convention. Macaulay described the Tories as "disunited," "disheartened," and "out of humour with their king."[39] But despite James's absence and untrustworthiness, the political paralysis of the aging archbishop of Canterbury, and divisions within their ranks on the solution to the crisis, the loyalists were active.

The decline in William's popularity, discernible since mid-December, lent hope to the conservatives' measures and attitudes. Friends and foes of the prince acknowledged the change in public attitude from the time the prince landed in England, when his arrival had been anticipated with such general approbation that a contemporary thought it should be called the "merry" invasion.[40] For example, the Dutch ambassador reported in his dispatch of January 1 that "opinions are now different than at the beginning."[41] Partisans of James concurred, one declaring in a printed tract that the "tide has mightily abated since the king's going from Rochester."[42] Events confirmed this judgment. For example, one of William's Dutch guards was found murdered, the prince's life was threatened, and private duels were provoked by political disagreement.[43] William's watch regarded the danger to the prince as serious enough to receive "mostly every night" information "about people who had evil intentions."[44]

A number of factors contributed to this change in popular sentiment. Among them were the indignities James had suffered upon his capture at Faversham, the failure of the prince to make a grand entrance into London ("even this trifle set people's spirits on edge," wrote Burnet[45]), the presence of foreign soldiers at St. James's and the Tower, and the sight of the king leaving the city a second time, in the cold and rain, under Dutch guard. Men especially resented James's second departure, regarding it as a "gross violation" and "utterly against their sense."[46] Burnet wrote ruefully to Herbert on December 25: "We have now turn upon turn. . . . Compassion has begun to work, especially since the Prince sent him [James] word to leave Whitehall. . . . There is discontent enough already."[47] In his private notes he assessed the prince's prospects in even more pessimistic terms, asserting that James's second withdrawal "struck a general damp upon many not only in London but over the whole nation," and opining that if the king had stayed in England the "difficulty in the Convention would have become insuperable" and the outcome "doubtful."[48]

Political principles, partisan advantage, and personal gain united with these sentimental considerations to explain the coolness among some men who had earlier welcomed the Dutch prince. James's flight opened up the question of who should be king of England, which, however naïve hindsight may make it seem, they apparently thought they could avoid. Neither the invitation to William nor his *Declaration of Reasons* referred to a future role for him or James in England's government. If men who promoted the prince's intervention could skirt that issue, how much more so could those who had nothing to do with it. Conservatives, disapproving of James's Catholicizing and centralizing policies because they were injurious to their interests, had hoped to use William as an instrument to change, not the royal person, but the royal policies. Because of its central theme — that he invaded England only for the purpose of calling a free parliament which would restore the nation's religion, rights, and liberties — the prince's *Declaration of Reasons* met with their entire approval. This is what they wanted from him, and that is why they wished to hold him to the letter of his manifesto. Thus, conservatives who were willing to support the prince in the fall were bitterly disappointed when they perceived that, in their view at least, William was not living up to the terms of his *Declaration* and that, on the contrary, he aimed to win the crown. For example, Clarendon wrote in January, "The prince's *Declaration* gained him the hearts of the whole kingdom, but the conscience of many of the best men would not permit them to come into the measures taken since." [49] Seymour said early in January that "all the West went into the Prince of Orange upon his *Declaration,* thinking in a free parliament to redress all that was amiss." But, he continued, now people fear that the prince "aims at something else." [50] Francis Turner, bishop of Ely, among others, concurred, believing that, notwithstanding protestations to the contrary, William was determined to win the crown. [51] Such a prospect moved men like Seymour to reexamine their earlier endorsement.

William's initial popularity also suffered as men considered closely the impact on the government and their personal fortunes of changing the person of the king. Some individuals, such as the earl of Ailesbury and Sir John Reresby, were bound by a sense of honor and their oath of allegiance to remain loyal to James, whatever their disagreement with him. [52] Others, like the earl of Nottingham, believed that unless James's rights were preserved, at least in theory, the monarchy and the Church of England would be irrevocably weakened. [53] Many feared that William, a Calvinist known to have shown marks of favor to Dissenters, would promote Nonconformists before them, and that their dream of reconstructing the relationship enjoyed under Charles II, when king, church, and Tories marched together, would come to naught. [54] The presence of radical Whigs in William's entourage and the activities of commonwealthsmen in London were further reasons for concern. [55] Moreover, conservative aristocrats, accustomed to an intimate relationship with their monarch, resented William's cold reserve, whatever his sometime efforts at affability; even more, the imperious manner of Bentinck, his chief confidante, gave offense. [56] Still another reason for opposing the prince was fear of commercial competition from Holland, whose interests these men expected William to prefer above England's. Seymour dismissed the possibility that England and Holland could ever be happily joined under one ruler on the grounds that both states were pursuing the "same mistress — trade." [57] For such reasons, then, William's standing with the Tories was diminished, and efforts to reach a solution that did not involve elevating William to the throne continued.

The three alternatives brought forward in December by the Tories — to restore James with conditions, to set up a regency, or to make Mary queen in her own right — continued to be pursued during the weeks of the elections to the Convention. The third option, it was said, concerned William and his friends so deeply that they opposed its proponents in the elections and kept Mary in Holland until the crisis was settled. [58] Just which M.P.'s were running on such a "ticket" contemporary sources do not reveal. All that can be said with assurance is that apparently the alternative was discussed; it was not vigorously pushed until after the regency proposal was narrowly defeated in the House of Lords on January 29. The major proponents of the idea of restoring James with conditions have already been identified as that band of about eighteen loyalists who campaigned for James at the meetings of the peers in December and an indeterminate number of men of like mind among the commons, such as Sir Thomas Clarges. Their organizer and most effective spokesman throughout these weeks was Turner, bishop of Ely. By the middle of the month this group, although not abandoning their desire to return James with conditions, apparently accepted regency as a fallback position. They were not altogether inconsistent in doing this, for they envisioned a regency, not for the lifetime of the king, but rather *pro tempore*, until James might be restored. Both plans preserved the king's right to the crown. Thus, the first two schemes — restoring James and setting up a regency — were closer than at first they may seem.

Notwithstanding their lack of success in December, Tory loyalists actively promoted restoring James with restrictions in January. On the very day the circular letters were dispatched, Morrice reported that in "meetings and cabals" the notion was discussed.[59] Two days later, the earl of Pembroke expressed optimism about the outcome of the Convention, saying that all endeavors must be used to protect James's interests.[60] The idea gained public currency. Not only did the Dutch ambassador write about it, but also one of the new newspapers informed its readers that reports were "more and more" that several "great lords" would be sent to James to pray him to return by the time the Convention met.[61] Still further, the archbishop of Canterbury and the bishops reportedly invited members of the clergy in "most" counties to come to London prior to the meeting of the Convention to discuss how strong the interest was in restoring the king.[62] Notice of such a meeting, if it was held, has not survived, but on January 15 John Evelyn dined with a number of spiritual and temporal peers, discussed the state of public opinion, and remarked that one of the four parties in existence — "the Tory part[y]" — advocated "inviting His Majesty again upon conditions."[63] The option remained before the public, for the "common letters" held that "at or before the convention the king will be addressed so to return."[64] Such rumors spread outside London, at least as far as Ludlow, where on January 21, the day before the Convention convened, the report "damped the markets."[65] And after the Convention opened, it was said that "some few were for recalling the king upon conditions, but those very few."[66]

The steps the prince's court took to deal with the loyalists give further proof of the loyalists' importance. For example, William regarded them with sufficient seriousness to state categorically in his conversation with Halifax, mentioned above, that he would not stay in England if James returned.[67] Moreover, within a fortnight of that talk, Burnet called on Clarendon and, in his irrepressible way, blurted out the charge that the earl was in a "cabal to bring back James."[68] Three days later William's close friend and adviser Dijkvelt had another interview with Clarendon, in which he chided him for being less warm for the prince than before. Continuing, Dijkvelt argued that to restore the king with fettered authority was as reprehensible as setting him aside, because to impose limitations on the monarchy was contrary to the doctrine of the church and the oath of allegiance. At about the same time an unidentified person (Burnet?) made the same points in a conference with a number of bishops.[69] Further testifying to the anxiety within the prince's circle was the speed with which the prince's penmen replied to *A Letter to a Member of the Convention,* a pro-James tract. The *Answer,* printed by January 24, accused the author of Catholicism, disparaged the word of James because he was Catholic, declared that limiting the king would set up a commonwealth, and explained that limitations were rejected in the Exclusion Crisis because they would transform the nature of the government.[70] In this way, it should be noted, William's court incidentally but clearly made known its disapproval of the idea of placing conditions upon royal power.

Although not so skilled as William and his friends at molding public opinion, and without the resources their opponents had at hand, the loyalists made an effort to put their ideas before the public. They preached sermons[71] and wrote tracts. For example, *A Letter to a Member of the Convention* (just mentioned), written by Dr. William Sherlocke, strongly urged the Convention to negotiate with James and restore him with such "legal restraints" as would secure the nation's liberties, laws, and religion. Asserting that he could devise conditions that would make it "utterly" impossible for the king to invade England's liberties or religion, Sherlocke argued that any other course would lead to a standing army, high taxes, wars, and domestic dissension, and would weaken monarchy, Anglicanism, and property.[72] Another tract, *A Speech to his Highness the Prince of Orange, by a True Protestant of the Church of England, as established by Law,* called upon William to prevail with James to accept restrictions and then to go home. A broadside, *XII Queries Addressed to M.P.s in the Convention,* declared that unless overtures to the king were made, the Convention would be acting as the Long Parliament had done when it refused to address Charles I.[73] Still other tracts presented general reasons why William should not be placed on the throne. Appealing to law, history, the Bible, common sense, and learned writers such as Grotius, they argued for passive obedience and the inviolability of the oath of allegiance, and stressed that since the king never dies, there can be no vacancy in the English monarchy. Reminding readers that in English law the king can do no wrong, anonymous authors pointed out that James's ministers should be punished, not the king himself. They impugned William's motives, integrity, and policies, disparaged his claim as Deliverer, and said his manifesto was filled with lies and with charges never investigated, much less proved. They argued that the Convention was illegal, that any solution short of restoring James was illegal, and that if the Convention put the crown on the prince's head, the English monarchy would by that act become elective, Anglicanism and property would be threatened, and the mob unleashed.[74]

Perhaps the most effective of all the pamphlets were those by Jeremy Collier, who became a nonjuror and later wrote about the English stage. In the fall and winter of 1688–89, Collier, an Anglican priest and sometime lecturer at Gray's Inn, took an active part in the discussions about the "vacancy" of the crown. He published two tracts at this time, probably in January 1689. One, *The Desertion Discuss'd*, undertook to answer Burnet's pamphlets. It denied that James's flight was an abdication on the grounds that the king had ample reason for fear and that he fled because of the perceived danger to his person. Using an analogy also voiced in the Convention, Collier argued that if a man leaves his burning house, he does not abdicate his right to the house nor leave his authority over it vacant. James, he maintained, did not resign, and the Convention had no power to depose him. The "abdicating doctrine," he asserted, "was perfectly unknown" in English history.[75] The second pamphlet, *Vindiciae Juris Regii; or, Remarques upon a Paper, entituled An Enquiry into the Measures of Submission to the Supream Authority*, also responded to Burnet. In it Collier proposed to show the "false and dangerous reasonings" of Burnet's paper; he denied the right of resistance, the validity of the original contract, and the accountability of kings. English kings, he argued, hold their title by direct hereditary succession and conquest. To depose them is unlawful. Calling upon Grotius for reinforcement, Collier asserted that misrule does not release subjects from the bonds of allegiance. Reversing Burnet's contention, he declared that "power always proves itself," unless special arrangements are made. The liberties of the people are founded, not upon right, but upon royal grace. The laws and the king's hesitation to arouse the people are "sufficient security" against tyranny. The mob is fickle and dangerous; in December it had destroyed more property that "has suffered by stretch of prerogative in one hundred years." Justifying James's policies, Collier blamed the "hellish stories" and "malicious" lies for disturbing the imagination of the nation.[76] Vigorously and clearly written, these two tracts provoked an answer and after the settlement moved the new government to imprison Collier.[77]

In private meetings, the Tories prepared and circulated among each other papers that argued for restoring the king or setting up a regency and against deposing the king. For example, Roger North wrote a lengthy piece titled "The Present State of the English Government," which Archbishop Sancroft (to whom it was transmitted on January 9) valued highly enough to copy out himself. It is possible that the Tory Sir Robert Sawyer read the statement, for his speech in the Commons' debate on January 28, in which he denied that the Convention represented the people, follows North's text very closely.[78] Or again, Turner appealed on January 11 to Sancroft to edit a draft memorandum on deposing and electing kings or breaking the royal succession. He proposed to use the statement in a meeting the next day with other bishops and Dr. Burnet, and then to give it to Bentinck for "quiet delivery" to the prince. The draft was titled "Previous Considerations of what Method is best for the Bishops to use in representing to the Prince of Orange their Sense regarding the King and Kingdom." Turner explained that he intended to approach William, as Sancroft could not do, "purely to serve" James and "preserve the public." His strategy was to promise to help William realize the ends of his *Declaration of Reasons* and to hold the prince to its terms. His draft statement beseeched the prince to "adhere to the rules you have set yourself in [the *Declaration*] to maintain our religion and our laws that we may be able to go along with you without any breach upon our oath of allegiance." Turner felt that the best strategy was to "take occasion from the bold, wild discourses and apparent designs of our Commonwealthsmen at this time," and use them as an excuse for a statement against deposing and electing kings and breaking the succession.[79] The skill with which he represented the case of the House of Lords in the conference debates with the Commons when the Convention met testifies to the care and diligence of his preparations during these weeks.

Another strategy devised by the loyalists was to try to turn the English army against the prince and check William by force, if they failed in the Convention. The idea was not, under the circumstances, unlikely of success. The men and officers of the English army did not automatically transfer their loyalty to the Dutch prince, although many were hostile to James's Catholicism. Friends of William and of James agreed that the basic loyalty of the English army was to James. For example, Burnet cited the "general discontentment, next to mutiny, . . . throughout the whole English army," and confessed that the prince could not trust the English soldiers.[80] Ailesbury wrote that the "common men in the whole army were generally firm" to the king.[81] Buckingham felt that James's fatal error was that he avoided a fight with William. He speculated that "if once blooded, [James's army] would have gone on with him and have beaten the prince of Orange," even as they had defeated the duke of Monmouth. Buckingham based his assessment not just on the soldiers' affection for James, but also on Englishmen's "love of a good fight."[82]

Events confirmed the judgment that the army resented William. As early as December 18, contemporaries noted that English soldiers objected to their removal to distant quarters outside London and their replacement by Dutch soldiers at Whitehall and the Tower.[83] On the nineteenth both men and soldiers "murmured" at the prince's treatment of the king in sending him out of the City.[84] This discontent and the fear that James's friends would exploit it were among the reasons (it will be recalled) why William decided against unilateral assumption of the crown. Loyalists reportedly "practiced" on the men, with a view to inciting them to revolt. For example, rumors flourished in December: it was said that the English soldiers would be sent to foreign battlefields, that their service would be made exceedingly hard, or that they would be disbanded. Unidentified persons reportedly tried to convince the soldiers to disobey orders to embark for Ireland or for Holland. Assessing the situation on December 25, Burnet remarked that "the army seem generally out of humour . . . at what they have done" in deserting their king.[85] Grumblings, desertions, and near mutiny, continuing into the weeks of the Convention meetings, expressed the dissatisfaction of James's former soldiers. Some of them refused to obey orders to march to Holland or to Ireland, to take an oath of allegiance to William, and to drink to the health of the prince.[86]

At the same time, loyalists allegedly tried to weaken the forces on which the prince might expect to depend. That is, they attempted to persuade William to send his army back to Holland, as he had promised in his manifesto that he would do. And they approached Englishmen who had raised men for the prince and argued that they should disband their men.[87] Burnet noted that if William had reduced the number of his Dutch soldiers, it was certain that the English soldiers would have "become more insolent" than they were.[88] Further, loyalists tried to turn English subjects against the prince by aggravating the resentment in some areas of the country against his army because some soldiers had taken free quarter or been guilty of stealing. As already discussed, William was at great pains to counteract these steps and to secure the army in his own interests.

Another strategy of the loyalists, of great interest to this present study, was their plan to disrupt and delay the proceedings of the Convention. On the eve of the Convention, Morrice reported that their plan was to hold themselves in readiness, if William should win the crown, to come forward with a proposal to limit his authority. The diarist explained that "to outward appearances" the loyalists laid aside their scheme of restoring James with conditions because they were not certain they could count on the army to support them. Realizing that they could not approach James without William's knowledge, and fearing that if they failed and William became king their chance of future positions in the prince's government would be ruined, they agreed to accept outwardly the theory of the "demise" of the crown and to disavow a regency. They calculated that the Convention would be divided over who should be king — some wanting Mary, some William, others both. In these circumstances, they intended to revive their plan of restoring James with conditions "under some other colour and surprise the House with it. As it may be under colour of limiting the prince more than any other kings have been if [the Convention] should proclaim him King."[89] This scheme conformed to the one reportedly discussed in late December, when it was suggested that restrictions might be placed upon the prince, which, if he refused, would justify the bishops in giving him "cheque-mate."[90] These two reports of such a strategy reinforce each other and underline the seriousness of the scheme.

Loyalists had good reason to want to reassert certain rights so that conditions like those under which they had suffered could not recur. But the imposition of thorough-going restrictions on the king conflicted with their theory of monarchy, as William's friends pointed out. Morrice (who, of course, was a biased observer) accused the loyalists of disingenuousness. He believed that if James were brought back under restrictions, they would soon be allowed to lapse. Talk of reasserting the nation's rights conformed to the prince's *Declaration of Reasons*, and holding William to its terms was a strategy the conservatives practiced. Still further, they knew as well as any politically conscious person that radical Whigs were promoting rights and reform in the press. To "surprise the House" with a proposal that William's authority should be limited would be irresistible to some members and would almost certainly serve to delay the proceedings while the matter was debated. Also, such a proposal might embarrass the prince's friends, who, whatever their sympathy for the idea, might want to settle the crisis rapidly. In addition, it might discomfit William, who, despite the terms of his *Declaration* and other public statements, had given evidence of not approving restrictions on royal power. The part the Tories played in drafting the Declaration of Rights is illuminated when read in the light of the strategy to limit William's power, proposed two times before the Convention met. Also illuminated is the initial opposition of some Whigs to the idea of drafting a statement about the nation's rights. There can be no doubt that if Morrice reported the strategy, Whig leaders knew about it, for they themselves were a major source of the diarist's information.

In such ways as these, then, the conservatives prepared for the meeting of the Convention. When that body convened, the authority of the prince ceased. Although weakened by division, absence of the king, and other factors, the Tories were not political ciphers. Support for a solution to the crisis other than the one finally agreed to, in fact, claimed a near majority in the House of Lords and a sizable number of members of the House of Commons. If the Whigs were to prevail, it would not be without a struggle. As a contemporary put it on the eve of the Convention, predictions as to the outcome depended on the interests of the observer.[91]

All these activities, arguably, had the effect of raising voter consciousness to the level of national issues. How much local, personal, or national considerations weighed in an elector's decision on how to cast his ballot is impossible to determine. But as a recent study has shown, national considerations played a larger part in early-seventeenth-century voting practices that used to be thought,[92] and for several reasons, it is likely that they were also more important in the elections to the Convention in 1689 than earlier historians believed.[93] Among those reasons are the excitement generated by the extraordinary events of the months leading up to the election; the enormous number of polemical tracts and pamphlets and visual materials which spread news and views to people far outside social and political elites; the growth of literacy; the efforts to influence the choice of members; the later widespread curiosity about the proceedings of the Convention, which encouraged efforts to circumvent laws restricting release of information about its affairs; the sense of the importance of the decisions about to be made; and the growth of the electorate from 200,000 to 250,000, regarded by one historian as the "unique" feature of the period.[94] The evidence for the actual presence of national issues, however, is fragmentary. In a recent study of this election (and that not exhaustive, for done in connection with a larger subject), Professor Henry Horwitz found nine elections in which dynastic and religious questions played a role — but that is eight more cases than once thought.[95] To these may be added five other elections in which voters may have been moved to return a candidate because of his presumed position on national issues. In Southwark, voters elected John Arnold because he "had suffered for the Protestant interest," as well as because he was born there.[96] In Lancaster, Sir Charles Hoghton "was chosen as freely as possible" because the Dissenters in the community supported him,[97] which could only mean that he supported the prince. In a third constituency, the electors of a successful candidate were all "buoyed up with a conceit of his great interest in favor of the prince."[98] Sir John Reresby, who had represented York in the Parliament of 1685, let it be known that he favored King James, and he was defeated.[99] Finally, the corporation of Newcastle refused to accept the prince's circular letters, but two men hostile to William declared themselves elected anyway,[100] surely representing the conservative opinion of that borough. Thus, in fourteen constituencies national issues may have determined the outcome of the vote. Statistically the number is insignificant, but in view of the dearth of material, it may be allowed to carry weight for this seventeenth-century election.

The conduct of the elections was less "smooth" than earlier historians thought. Macaulay maintained that the elections went on "rapidly and smoothly" with "scarcely any contests" because of the general consensus against the king and because of choices already made in the fall when James twice issued writs for a parliament. Professor Horwitz, however, counted sixty contested elections, thus confirming the remark of a contemporary that the elections were "contended fervently in very many places."[101] Apart from contested elections, there is evidence of contention in the elections that indicates less "smoothness" than thought. A contemporary reported "great art and great diligence" used in "caressing the freemen" to develop an interest.[102] At Woebly, a candidate became so enraged at his opponent for allegedly misrepresenting his position on James's proposed repeal of the Test Act and penal laws that he gave him "a hand mark" with his sword.[103] In Westminster, the vote was so close that a "revote" was taken. The Dutch ambassador's explanation that each voter must be heard distinctly and his vote be noted indicates confusion, perhaps deliberately promoted.[104] At Southwark in London, "malapert and disaffected persons" among the electorate apparently disrupted the election.[105]

There is also evidence of interest in widening the franchise. In Buckingham, it was predicted that the "populace" would oppose the return of Sir Richard Temple, not out of aversion to him, but to "get the right of election from the bailiffs and burgesses." Temple's correspondent advised him to think of ways to "quiet the populace" and promised to use his "utmost endeavor to appease them."[106] Again, one of the new newspapers, the *Orange Gazette,* reported "some variety in the suffrages, as they were more or less interested in the affections of the people," thus suggesting that unqualified persons may have voted in the election in London.[107] Moreover, the electorate displayed some self-consciousness in making their choices. Thus, one candidate lost because he did not make a speech, while his opponent did address the electors.[108] The corporation of Harwich defeated a candidate because of his alleged disservice to them.[109] And another hopeful lost at Maidstone because his agent described the freemen as "rabble." [110]

All these considerations indicate that there was not the general unanimity of opinion among the electorate that earlier scholars discovered, and that national issues — who should be king — played a part in the elections. There is no evidence of a debate on the hustings about the nation's rights and liberties and which ones should be reaffirmed. But the press was saturated with material urging the Convention to restore the rights and liberties of the nation; this material included William's *Declaration of Reasons,* the *Bishops' Proposals,* the manifestoes justifying local uprisings, and tracts written by radical Whigs (discussed in the next chapter). The electorate must have felt that the Convention would do something along those lines.

What were the results of the elections? First, contrary to the judgment of earlier historians that the Convention contained a great majority of Whigs, recent scholars have shown that the Commons was not overwhelmingly Whig. Thanks to James's efforts to pack Parliament, the prior decisions made in response to the king's two parliamentary writs in the fall, and the activities of the conservatives in the elections in January, more Tories were elected than has been thought. Whigs enjoyed a marginal superiority of less than 20: there were about 174 Whig members to about 156 Tory M.P.'s. There were thus enough Tories to form a solid opposition in the Convention. Second, 183 "new" members — about 40 more than usual — were elected. In a body of 513 members, "new" members may have held the balance between confirmed Whig and Tory members, and their presence may help explain the "swing to the right" the Convention took.[111] Thus, the House of Commons nearly approximated the political alignment in the House of Lords. There, the proponents of a solution other than the one finally reached were a majority, but for numerous reasons they failed to prevail over the friends of the prince and over the men who were determined to accompany the offer of the crown with a claim of the rights of the nation.

8

"Rights and Reform" Pamphlets

❖

T
he meeting of the Convention, wrote a pamphleteer, provided a "golden opportunity" for the nation to "bring a crown in one hand with the terms or conditions in the other."[1] This sentence encapsulates the message of a quantity of pamphlets herein designated "rights and reform" pamphlets. Written by radical Whigs, these anonymous tracts appeared in the fall and winter of 1688–89 during the weeks encompassing the decision to call a convention, the election to that body, and its meeting. Drawing inspiration from the libertarian tradition of the Civil War, Commonwealth period, and Exclusion Crisis, they advanced no new ideas. But they are not for that reason "uninteresting," as one historian has said.[2] Their radicalism varied, but taken together, these pamphlets offered a programmatic statement about rights and about restrictions on the powers of the king which, had they all been achieved, would have decisively changed the nature of the monarchy. The derivative character of their ideas and the fact that they propounded notions whose importance at the time of the Glorious Revolution has been underestimated make these tracts interesting and important.

We do not know for certain who the authors of these pamphlets were. Probably they were among the men whom contemporaries described as "commonwealthsmen." For example, on December 22, a letter writer identified commonwealthsmen as one of several parties said to be "very busy."[3] It was reported that "bold things" against the Anglican church were discussed in coffee houses and that Robert Ferguson was a leader.[4] In mid-January Evelyn, the diarist, mentioned "republicarians" as a group,[5] and tract writers noted the activity of Dissenters and "commonwealthsmen."[6] On the eve of the Convention, it was reported that some people think that "the first vote will be the exclusion of bishops out of Parliament," and a fortnight later this move was still being rumored.[7] In the Convention, a speaker complained of extravagant schemes discussed in coffee houses.[8] How many supporters of a commonwealth there were is not known; Morrice said that those who hoped that out of the confusion a commonwealth would "come up trumps" were the "least party."[9] That is undoubtedly true, but to be a "commonwealthsman" in

1689 was not, generally speaking, to favor a republic but rather a genuinely limited monarchy. There were more such men as these than historians have granted.

John Wildman, the former republican, was probably the author of *A Memorial from the English Protestants,* said to have been "one of the most influential" pamphlets printed during this time.[10] *A Letter to a Friend, advising him, in this extraordinary Juncture, How to free the Nation from slavery forever* is also assigned to him. It appeared on January 5, 1689, in time to influence the elections and later the debates in the Convention.[11] Wildman was returned to the Convention from Great Bedwin, Wiltshire,[12] and although not a leader of the first rank in the assembly, he was a frequent speaker and, as a member of the rights committee, in a position to influence the drafting of the Declaration of Rights. He was responsible for the proposal, which failed, of bypassing the Lords and going directly to the prince with the declaration. Wildman also assisted in piloting the Bill of Rights through the Convention Parliament.

Wildman was not the only author of the rights and reform tracts to serve in the Convention, but the other two are anonymous. Whoever wrote *A Discourse concerning the Nature, Power, and Proper Effects of the Present Conventions in both kingdoms called by the Prince of Orange* claimed that he was a member of the assembly.[13] And *Some Remarks upon Government, and Particularly upon the Establishment of the English Monarchy Relating to this Present Juncture* included in its title the information that the pamphlet was comprised of *Two Letters, written by and to a Member of the Great Convention, holden at Westminster the 22nd of January, 1688/9.*

John Humfrey, a radical Presbyterian minister who for years had written pamphlets on current topics and handed them directly to members of Parliament, was identified by a contemporary as the author of *Advice Before It Be Too Late.*[14] Robert Ferguson, known as the Plotter, devoted his considerable literary talents to William's cause in *A Brief Justification of the Prince of Orange's Descent into England . . . with a modest disquisition of what may become the wisdom and justice of the ensuing convention, in their disposal of the crown.* Ferguson is also credited with writing *A Representation of the Threatening Dangers, impending over Protestants in Great Britain, Before the Coming of His Highness, the Prince of Orange,* in circulation in Oxford by January 18, 1689,[15] and *A Word to the Wise for Setling the Government,* in print also by January 18.[16] *The Design for Enslaving England Discovered* is perhaps another tract from his pen.[17] A radical Presbyterian minister, Ferguson had participated in earlier controversies and been involved in both the Rye House Plot and the Monmouth uprising, writing, so he claimed, Monmouth's *Declaration.*[18] A self-important man, disappointed that William and his friends welcomed him coolly, Ferguson sought recognition and achieved notoriety when William's entourage was in Exeter by forcing his way into the pulpit of a Presbyterian meetinghouse. Later he created an opportunity to call on a Dutchman in William's entourage to underline his importance by recounting that James had offered him a pardon and "much" money to join him.[19] In part because he felt himself inadequately rewarded by William after the revolution, Ferguson turned against him and became a Jacobite.

Another author was Edmund Hickeringill (1631–1708), an eccentric whose life has been described as a "series of battles in the courts and in the press."[20] After sampling at least three religious persuasions as a youth and following an adventuresome career which took him for a time to Jamaica, he became ordained as an Anglican cleric in 1661. From 1662 to his death he must have enlivened the benefice of All Saints in Colchester by his unorthodox views and behavior. His *A Speech Without-Doors; or, Some Modest Inquiries Humbly Proposed to the Right Honourable the Convention of Estates, Assembled at Westminster, January 22, 1689* was advertised in two issues of the *London Intelligence*. It was the only tract to recommend that the press be freed from restraints.

Edward Stephens (d. 1706), a fifth author, was a practicing lawyer of good repute from Gloucestershire. He took holy orders, although he probably did not hold a benefice. He wrote *Important questions of state, law, justice and prudence, both civil and religious upon the late revolutions and present state of these nations,* which appeared with his *True English Government and Misgovernment of the four last kings, with the ill consequence thereof briefly noted in two little tracts.* By 1690 Stephens had modified his favorable opinion of William.

The known authors of the rights and reform literature, then, were a former republican, two Dissenting ministers, and two Anglican clerics, one an eccentric latitudinarian and the other a man trained also in law.

In addition to the tracts written for the occasion, reprints of earlier pamphlets appeared. Out of at least thirty-four reprints[21] the following were especially pertinent to the question of rights and reform. An account of the debates in the November 1685 session of James II's only parliament was reprinted in *The Faithful Register; or, The Debates of the House of Commons . . . wherein, the points of prerogative, priviledges, Popish designs, standing army, county-militia, supplies . . . are fully discuss'd.* These debates included arguments against a standing army and for reform of the militia, both topics addressed by the Convention. Tracts written by the earl of Shaftesbury's circle, including one on regulating parliamentary elections, appeared in *A Collection of State Tracts . . . Privately Printed in the Reign of Charles II.* Philip Hunton's *Treatise of Monarchy,* originally printed in 1643 and reprinted in 1680, enjoyed two editions in 1689. Among other pieces from the Civil War period was *A Political Catechism; or, Certain Questions concerning the Government, of this Land, Answered in his Majesties own words, taken out of His Answer to the 19 Propositions.* Attributed to Henry Parker, this tract was the major vehicle for transmitting ideas about mixed monarchy, the relationship between the three estates in England's government, and the illegality of the royal dispensing power. It appeared at least four times in 1688 and 1689, once appended to another tract.[22] From the Cromwellian period came *Killing No Murder Briefly Discoursed in Three Questions,* first printed in 1657 in Holland and authored by a Republican. The purpose of the pamphlet was to expound the contract theory of government and justify rebellion against a tyrant, in this case Oliver Cromwell. The implication was, of course, to equate the government of James II with that of Cromwell.[23]

Algernon Sidney's theories reappeared in summary form, the lengthy title announcing the message of the reissue.[24] Several of the earlier pamphlets of the redoubtable radical Whig the Reverend Samuel Johnson also surfaced.[25] Pieces that earlier had been banned or burned reappeared. Thus, *Historical Discourse of the Uniformity of the Government of England,* whose printer Treby had defended in the 1670s, was brought out by the same printer, John Starkey. George Buchanan's *De Jure Regni Apud Scotos,* which had been burned with other books in 1683 by the University of Oxford, was reissued by the printer Richard Baldwin.[26] None of the reissues was perhaps so effective as the anonymous adaptation of Milton's *Tenure of Kings and Magistrates,* under the effective title *Pro Populo Adversus Tyrannos.*[27] In this, Charles I is transformed into James II and the Presbyterians become the Jacobites. In no other tract are the theory of contract, the derivative nature of the power of the king, the ultimate authority of the people, and the right to resist more eloquently expressed. These reprints were surely designed to influence the thinking of the public and the members of the Convention with respect to such specific issues as the dispensing power, standing armies, militia reform, and the role of Parliament. If the reprints are added to the tracts written in 1688–89, a total of fifty-one tracts favoring rights and reform were available to the public.

The rights and reform tracts were only a portion of the large quantity of printed political material that appeared from the fall of 1688 through the spring of 1689. It has not been possible to discover precisely the number of tracts that were printed during these months, but contemporaries noted the profusion of pamphlets, enterprising publishers almost immediately reprinted the "most considerate" of them that they might not "lie buried in a crowd of pamphlets," and contemporary collections testify to both interest and impact.[28] A conservative estimate would put the number of printed pieces in circulation from the fall of 1688 through the end of February 1689 at about three hundred.[29] Thus, about one-sixth (fifty-one) of the total called for asserting the rights of the nation. Some comparative figures underline the importance to contemporaries of claiming the nation's rights: seventy-two tracts were printed in the Engagement controversy of 1649–52, and thirty-seven items in the standing army debate of 1697–99.[30]

It is not possible, either, to say exactly how many copies of a particular pamphlet were printed, but it has been suggested that 1,000 copies would be a usual run. If that is the case, then there were some 50,000 individual pieces to stimulate and confirm interest in rights and reform. This figure could mean that there was one such tract for every ten literate males in the population; one for every four or five men who composed the electorate; and one and a quarter tracts for every one male who had received a higher education.[31] But precisely how many people bought these tracts is not known. Since many of them sold for a penny, they were within the reach of many people.[32] Nor is it known how many people the tracts actually reached through being read aloud in coffee houses, which, with the breakdown of government controls, had resumed their role as scenes of political discussion and dissemination of views, or through being passed from hand to hand, as one broadside specially instructed its readers to do.[33]

Various steps were taken to attract readers of diverse levels of political sophistication. To simplify complex matters and win readers, authors crafted dialogues and devised inviting titles. For example, the anonymous pamphlet *A Political Conference Between Aulicus, a Courtier, Demas, A Countryman, and Civicus, a Citizen: Clearing the Original of Civil Government, the Powers and the Duties of Soveraigns and Subjects. In a Familiar and Plain Way, which may be understood by every Ordinary Capacity* clearly aimed through its title to appeal to readers of "every ordinary capacity." Another inviting title with the same apparent purpose was *A Plain and Familiar Discourse concerning Government, Wherein it is Debated, Whether Monarchy or a Commonwealth be best for the People.* The success of the effort is reflected in the remark of a hostile critic that the issues had been drawn down to every vulgar capacity.[34]

Other efforts were made to promote wide circulation of the tracts. Some pamphlets advertised others. The *London Gazette* and some of the new newspapers carried advertisements: Hickeringill's *Speech Without-Doors* was advertised in two successive issues of the *London Intelligence* as selling for six pennies.[35] Some tracts — perhaps the rights and reform tracts among them, although there is no specific evidence to that point — were hawked about the streets of London. One was dropped, according to personal testimony, at the feet of a customer.[36] One pamphlet, which contained a portion of the Declaration of Rights, was said to have been picked up at a coffee house.[37]

Specific efforts were also made to bring these rights and reform tracts to the attention of members of the Convention who were in a position to act upon their recommendations. Some titles were addressed directly to members of the Convention, as for example *Proposals Humbly offered To the Lords and Commons in the present Convention, for Settling of the Government.* Some writers issued their tracts under two titles, one including a direct address to the members of the Convention, as if to help insure its notice by members of the assembly.[38] Attempts were made to put this material in the hands of M.P.'s. An unsuccessful effort was made to distribute copies of one pamphlet in the antechamber of the House of Commons.[39] Another pamphlet, according to its author, was handed directly to members of the Convention, while still another "was delivered" to the House of Commons just before an important vote on settling the headship of the state to beg members not to forget to enter a claim of rights.[40] Many of the tracts printed before the Convention were reprinted in *Collections* on the eve of the Convention, the timing surely to make them readily available to members. For example, Wildman's *Letter to a Friend* was in print by January 5, 1689, and by January 18 it was reprinted in a *Sixth Collection of Papers.* *A Word to the Wise* could be had in London before

January 18, and it too appeared in a *Sixth Collection*. The *Seventh Collection* was on the streets by January 25, the *Eighth Collection* by January 29, both of them containing other rights and reform pamphlets.[41]

It is certain that members of the rights committee in the House of Commons knew about this material. Wildman was the author of *A Letter to a Friend*. Somers bought many of the tracts. It is likely that the Nonconformists on the committee would have welcomed pamphlets written by Nonconformist ministers. Some of the committee members had a prior and a present personal interest in the press, which permits the inference that they were mindful of material in circulation. Some members had tracts of their own in print. For example, Treby brought out a piece to show the evilness of the French monarchy.[42] Somers's tract, *A Brief History of the Succession,* was reprinted, and was advertised in the January 31–February 4 issue of the *London Gazette*. Wharton's *Letter from Machiavelli to Buondelmontius* also reappeared under a different title.[43] Howard's history of Richard II and other early English kings was available before the Convention opened.[44] Details about the connections between M.P.'s and printers and publishers of the tracts have eluded the record, but Starkey and Treby enjoyed a friendship that reached back a decade. Richard Baldwin printed a piece by Treby in 1681 and brought out a pamphlet by Howard in 1689.[45] Awnsham Churchill must also have been known to many of the committee members. The fact that the successive versions of the Declaration of Rights appeared in print also suggests mutual access between the committee and the press. Moreover, a majority of the committee still retained identification with the political principles of the "first Whigs." It has been shown that earlier they had subscribed to Shaftesburian ideas, articulated them in debates and tracts, and in some cases were involved in or suspected of complicity in radical Whig schemes in the early 1680s. The political principles of many of the committeemen in 1688–89 would have inclined them to a sympathetic reading of these rights and reform tracts.

That so much unlicensed material was in circulation during these months was due to the breakdown of the procedures that had been set up to control the press by the late Stuart kings and testifies to the political trauma the nation was experiencing. Although the Licensing Act was still theoretically in effect, having been reissued by James II's Parliament in 1685,[46] the agencies it had designated for the censoring and licensing of printed matter either were not functioning at all or were severely weakened. From his accession James had, with fair success, enforced the procedures for controlling the press that had been developed under his brother. But after James's flight to France in mid-December, neither the offices of the principal secretaries of state (which were empowered not only to license books on affairs of state, but also to issue warrants of arrest and to make searches), nor the office of the surveyor of the press (which had been created to supervise and control the press under the jurisdiction of the secretary of state), nor the Stationer's Company (whose assistance had been unsatisfactory since 1666), was operating effectively.

Further, the crown and Council, which with the help of compliant judges had also played an important part in Restoration England in controlling the press, were, of course, not functioning either. As a contemporary pamphleteer put it, the "padlock" on printing had been broken; there were so many publications that he predicted that the hawkers would become the next city company.[47] Pertinent to understanding William is the fact that, although his cause was generally well served by an uncensored press, he attempted to control what was printed by trying to reinstitute the Stuart administrative procedures for censoring publications. Early in January he issued an order instructing the master of the Stationers Company and others to search out all "false, scandalous, and seditious books, papers of news, and pamphlets" and to bring the persons responsible for them to justice.[48] Presumably it was on the grounds of this order that the arrest was made of the person trying to distribute the antimonarchical tract in the antechamber of the House of Commons. On the whole, however, it is plain that the order did not deter authors, printers, and publishers from bringing to the public quantities of unlicensed material.

All the rights and reform pamphlets wanted to change the person of the king, but more than that, they wanted to change the kingship. For example, one writer asserted in a tract entitled *A Discourse concerning the Nature, Power, and Proper Effects of the Present Conventions in both Kingdoms called by the Prince of Orange* that "there is far less importance in the Persons that Govern than in the Power of Governing."[49] Another writer warned that if the government were "rebuilt upon its old foundations," it would not last, and in language reminiscent of the language used by preachers addressing the Long Parliament in the Civil War, this author admonished the Convention: "You have a great work to do, . . . 'tis from your councils that after ages must date their happiness or misery."[50] The task proposed for the Convention to undertake was, in the minds of some writers, monumental. It was nothing less, wrote one author, than "the consideration of the *Constitution of the Realm,* and the declaring that Constitution."[51] Another writer felt that the Convention should "confirm the fundamental points of government and mend the rest."[52] And still another pamphleteer admonished the Convention that what they decided "will make numerous posterity happy or miserable," and advised them, as the "most renown'd politician" (Machiavelli) had observed, to bring the nation back to its first principles.[53] Only "unthinking men," iterated another writer, consider the immediate causes of the nation's problems: wiser ones look beyond the last three years to search out fundamental reasons.[54]

The Convention was reassured that it had the power to perform such a task and that it was justified in doing so. To these ends the contract theory of government was set out. The theory was, of course, not new in 1689. With variations, some more radical in implication than others, the theory had been articulated in political treatises during the Middle Ages, the Reformation, the Civil War in England in the 1640s, and the Exclusion Crisis.[55] At the time of the Glorious Revolution, both constitutional contractarianism and philosophical contractarianism appeared side by side; the one linked the idea of contract to positive laws and institutional frameworks, while the other regarded contract as a universal proposition, described in terms of "natural right" or "natural liberty." [56] With respect to the latter, one historian has recently underlined the importance of the work of George Lawson, who emphatically placed ultimate sovereignty in the people, and whose theory Locke adopted and made famous. [57] Historians have discounted the significance of philosophical contractarianism in 1688–89, but it was reflected in the first formulation of the abdication and vacancy resolution, in Convention debates, and in more tracts than have been appreciated: at least twenty-five pamphlets either written for the occasion or reprinted. [58]

The argument of these tracts ran, in brief, as follows: Government was not divine, except in the sense that God ordained that man should have some kind of government; actual political power resided with the people. The people entered into two contracts: the first, or popular, contract engaged all people at the moment they agreed to set up a government and assigned to a king certain specific prerogatives; the second, or "rectoral," contract established laws for the administration of the government. Clearly, the powers of the king were derived from the people. They were limited by the contract; protected by God's law, the law of nature, and the king's oath to uphold the law; and committed to the king only as a trust from the people, who fundamentally held the power. If the king violated the terms of the contract, that act transformed him into a tyrant and released the people from the obligation to obey; the contract was dissolved and the power returned to the people. The people alone have the right to judge when a revolution is needed and when that happens they are free to choose a new government.

This theory, plainly, was full of radical implications. The assertion that the people brought the kingly office into being was an unequivocal rejection of the divine right theory of kingship. If the frame of government was entirely dissolved and the people could set up something new, then the nation's traditional constitutional arrangement of king, Lords, and Commons was threatened, as were the property and status of the upper classes.

The most eloquent expression of the contract theory was *Pro Popolo Adversus Tyrannos,* the reissue of Milton's tract *The Tenure of Kings and Magistrates,* which, as its lengthy title announced, dealt with the *Sovereign Right and Power of the People over Tyrants, Clearly Stated and Plainly Proved. With some Reflections on the late Posture of Affairs.* This piece asserted that "the power of kings is . . . derivative, transferred and committed to them in trust from the people to the common good of them all, in whom the power yet remains fundamentally, and cannot be taken from them without violation of their natural birthright." [59] A tract written for the occasion, Ferguson's *Brief Justification of the Prince of Orange's Descent into England,* iterated these points, adding that when a king violates the contract agreed upon at the institution of government, the people are restored "to their state and condition of primitive freedom." [60]

The people reserved rights to themselves at the institution of their government. In his *Brief Justification* Ferguson declared that of all peoples, Englishmen had been the "most careful," when they first submitted to regal government, to preserve their rights, liberties, and privileges and the "most courageous" in securing them by "new and superadded laws" when they were threatened. The several charters of the people's rights, most particularly Magna Charta, were not grants from the king, but "recognitions" of rights that had been reserved or that "appertained unto us by common law and immemorial custom." Further, there had been no conquest in England's history or discontinuity in her political development; the rights of the people had been confirmed by early kings both before and after the Norman line began. Accordingly, the people have always had the "same title" to their liberties and properties that England's "kings have unto their crowns." A compact or agreement between the people and the ruler was necessary to all legal governments. Governments set up by force had no legal title until, by tacit or explicit consent, the terms of an agreement were laid down.[61] Indeed, Ferguson implied that if something like the Declaration of Rights were not formulated and accepted, the new government, whatever its form, would not be legal.

The argument continued: James II had violated the terms of the original contract. It followed, therefore, that the nation stood as it had in the long-distant past when government was first set up. The difference, in the actual situation of 1689, was that the Convention was a surrogate for all the people. Supreme authority, explained a writer, now rests once more in the community, as represented by the Convention, which has a "higher capacity" than a parliament, a power to make "laws for the Constitution," whereas Parliament could only make laws for the administration of government.[62] Other tracts agreed, among them *A Brief Collection of Some Memorandums,* which described the Convention as "something greater, and of greater power than a Parliament," and *A Letter to a Friend,* which asserted that the Convention "has more power than a Parliament, and is its creator."[63] Thus, the Convention had the authority to declare the constitution and change the kingship as it saw fit.

There were other arguments to justify the plea for a claim of rights. Pamphleteers appealed to the ancient constitution, immemorial custom, old laws, and the practice of forebears. Like tracts printed at the time of the Exclusion Crisis, these tracts of 1688–89 sometimes combined illogically several theories. Thus, following an exposition of the contract theory and the notion of reversion of power to the people when the king violates the contract, based on reason, Ferguson appealed to history to justify resistance and show that Parliament may dispose of the succession to the throne.[64] Moreover, William's *Declaration of Reasons* was often cited to justify a claim of rights. The Convention was assured that for it to reassert the nation's rights was to fulfill the prince's own directive. It was argued that many people had declared for William on the ground of his *Declaration,*[65] and that they looked to the Convention to implement his expressed intentions to redress the grievances of the people and secure their religion, rights, and liberties. Readers were told that the prince had adhered to his word and would continue to do so.[66] Praising the *Declaration* as having a "more free and equal strain than anything" ever to have come from a prince, one writer asserted that William's honor "would be forever blemished if he should counteract" his *Declaration of Reasons.*[67] Another pamphleteer agreed, saying that it was in William's interest to fulfill the promises he had made.[68] Such remarks were surely designed to make it embarrassing for William to object to a statement of restrictions on royal power.

A few of the rights and reform tracts regarded the crisis confronting the nation as symptomatic of profound disorders in the body politic and recommended extreme solutions. An unadorned statement was the broadside *Now Is The Time.* It urged the creation of a council of state made up of forty men from each house of Parliament. The prince of Orange would preside and also serve as general and admiral. Parliament would be elected triennially and meet annually. This arrangement would avoid a standing army — nothing else could, it was asserted — and secure England from popery and arbitrary power. The scheme was to continue during the life of the king and was not to prejudice his Protestant successor. *A Plain and Familiar Discourse concerning Government. Wherein it is Debated, Whether Monarchy or a Commonwealth be best for the People* concluded that a commonwealth was best. "Common liberty," the author declared, "makes all men [in a commonwealth] peers. Like poles in a copse, though some are bigger and higher than others, yet none are over." Arguing that a republican form of government was neither strange nor untested, the author pointed to its use in cities and corporations and declared that on a larger scale it could only be "great and noble." He concluded that "some dare recommend it; it recommends itself." The author of *Advice Before It Be Too Late* danced around the question of a republican solution. He pointed out that the Convention need not choose a king if it did not wish to do so, that the king's refusal to pass good laws led him to think that it might be better not to have a monarch, and that since the king is made for the people, not the people for the king, and the good of the nation comes first, it was surely better that a king should cease than that a whole nation suffer. But the tract ended with the thought that in this "golden opportunity" the nation should bring a "crown in one hand with the terms or conditions" in the other. Two other authors were likewise circumspect. Wildman asserted in his *Letter to a Friend* that "the people may set up what government they please," and while he recommended very substantial change, in terms that made plain his inclination to republicanism, he did not positively argue for a republican solution. Ferguson, although it was said his system was "wholly antimonarchical," specifically rejected a "Democratical Republick" as incompatible with law, history, and custom.[69] Similarly, the author of *Some Remarks upon Government, and Particularly upon the Establishment of the English Monarchy Relating to this Present Juncture* was cautious about recommending the dismantling of the kingship. A member of the Convention, this writer offered an analysis of the distemper in

the body politic in Harringtonian terms. Asserting that England's government was not "so happy nor so well-suited" to the people as most men tried to
represent it, he explained that the reason for this state of affairs was that
political power and property had become separated. Illustrating the point, he
reported that the yearly rents of England (excluding trade, which was in the
hands of the commonalty) were £14 million, of which only £1 million was in
the hands of the king and nobles.[70] To remedy the imbalance in property and
dominion, the tract urged the Convention to give its "most serious thoughts"
to recommendations which included limiting the royal revenue, depriving
the king of absolute power over peace and war, and denying him the right to
call and prorogue Parliament. In an arresting analogy the king was compared to the cat in the manger who cannot eat hay and will not allow the
horse to whom the hay belongs to eat it either. Similarly, the king at present
was obstructing the proper functioning of Parliament by his authority to
refuse to call it and his power to prorogue it before its business was
complete.[71] The author concluded that only if political dominion were placed
in the hands of men who now held the property would the dissensions and
tensions in the nation cease.[72]

But the main thrust of these tracts was to recommend ways in which the
kingship should be restricted, not abolished. Their aim was to shift the
sovereignty to Parliament, to create a system in which Parliament was
supreme. They wanted Parliament to meet annually, or at least frequently,
its meetings assured by a law that would restrict the power of the king to call
and dismiss Parliament at will. Such a recommendation was a clear invasion
of the ancient prerogative of kings. One writer thought that frequent
meetings were a "fence against arbitrary government" and a means of keeping ministers honest,[73] while another maintained that even if there were no
statutes guaranteeing the annual sitting of Parliament, the "fundamental law
of the government, the common law, the law of God and the law of nature"
provided for it.[74] Moreover, authors urged the Convention to "find a solution" to the problem of the king's right to veto legislation passed by both
Houses. The king, furthermore, should be disallowed the power to pardon
persons impeached by Parliament. He should be kept poor, so that he would
always have need of summoning Parliament.[75] His power to decide questions
regarding war and peace should be removed.[76]

The rights and reform tracts also addressed the question of the king's
lawmaking power, a prerogative which was of the essence of sovereignty.
Many tracts argued emphatically that the king's power in the legislative process was coordinate with the Lords and Commons, not above the other two.
Continuing to exploit Charles I's *Answer to the Nineteen Propositions* — which, as
Corinne Weston has shown, critics of the monarchy had done almost from
the moment the statement appeared[77] — these writers asserted that the king
was just one of three estates in a mixed government, that he was essentially
subordinate to the other two estates, and that he had no authority to dispense
with the law. The Convention of 1660, they said, had confirmed the point.

This claim, however, had been the subject of angry denials by Tory spokesmen in 1680. In 1688–89, Ferguson's *Brief Justification of the Prince of Orange's Descent into England* asserted that the "most fundamental and essential, as well as the most advantageous and beneficial" of all restrictions on the king was that the people had a share in making laws and a right of being governed by the laws that were made. Ferguson contended that James's use of the dispensing power had "subverted the very fundamental constitutions of the realm" and argued that the king had assumed a "title to dispense with all . . . laws."[78] Wildman also stressed the illegality of the dispensing power. Amending the views he had held the previous August, when he had urged drafters of William's manifesto not to stress James's use of the dispensing power, Wildman insisted in *A Letter to a Friend* that the government was dissolved by the king's dispensing with the laws.[79]

The most important statement at this time about the dispensing power appeared not in the rights and reform tracts of radical Whigs, but rather in two pamphlets written by Sir Robert Atkyns.[80] To this famous Whig jurist (who had been a justice of the Court of Common Pleas until his removal in 1680, and would become lord chief baron of the Exchequer and Speaker of the House of Lords during the reign of William and Mary), the law was the soul of the body politic, a force underlying the forms of government. Iterating arguments that had been fully aired in the early 1680s, Atkyns maintained that England's king had never possessed the sole power to make law, and that therefore he could not alone dispense with laws. Atkyns explained that laws began in the consent of the community. From time immemorial they were made by public agreement, not imposed by the king. The dispensing power could not be a legal prerogative of the crown, because legal prerogatives were prescriptive, that is, used time out of mind. The dispensing power, on the contrary, was recent and therefore could not be inherent in kingship. The king and the two Houses of Parliament together made the law. He wrote, "The king has not the sole legislature, such as almighty God has over his creatures, but the whole kingdom has a share in that power." This was a feature of a mixed or limited government, such as England's. It followed from these principles, so Atkyns believed, that "none but the lawmaker can dispense with the law"; in other words, the king and the Parliament, not the king alone, had the lawful power to set aside law and only they were the lawful judges of when this discretionary authority should be used. Atkyns granted that the king alone might dispense with laws governing certain things, such as statutes setting the value of land or regulating the shipping of wool. But these were "trifling" matters, and even the power to set aside these laws resulted from parliamentary permission. Atkyns denied that the king possessed such rights with respect to statutes (such as the Test Act) that were of the highest concern to the nation. Ignoring historical evidence of the English king's sole use of the dispensing power, Atkyns presented an interpretation of this power that was compatible with Whiggish political principles.

Thus, although the issue of the royal dispensing power received attention in the rights and reforms tracts, it and the questions closely associated with it — the trial of the Seven Bishops, the proceedings of the Ecclesiastical Commission, and the right of subjects to petition the king [81] — did not play as important a role as they did in William's *Declaration of Reasons,* the *Bishops' Proposals,* and the several drafts of the Declaration of Rights.

Another issue of central importance in the rights and reform tracts was the royal power over the military. It too lay at the heart of sovereignty. This matter had been endlessly debated during the seventeenth century, especially since the Militia Bill/Ordinance controversy in 1641/42, and again in the 1670s. In 1689 *Advice Before It Be Too Late* explicitly asserted that the "power of the sword" should be placed in the hands of Parliament, a step which, plainly, would repeal the Restoration Militia Acts. If that change could be accomplished and the power of appointing judges placed in Parliament, the nation would be, the author thought, "fundamentally delivered from all slavery for ever." [82] This writer believed that the militia should be lodged where legislation is placed, and argued that the division of such "rights of sovereignty" was a "defect" in the government. He described the Restoration Militia Acts as "gross flattery" of the king, and as "void, fundamentally repugnant with the Constitution." Other tracts maintained that there should be no standing army raised or maintained without the consent of Parliament, and one writer declared that if an army were raised without such consent, entering it should be considered an act of treason. (A remarkable extension of the concept of treason, it may be noted!) The number of the king's guards should be limited by law, and the militia should be reformed so that it might serve, recommended this same writer, as the "ordinary guard for the nation." [83] A standing army and martial law were described as entirely "contrary to the Constitution." [84]

Election reform, a corollary of the preeminence given Parliament, was a further concern in these tracts. One author declared that free elections were the most important safeguard for England's freedom. [85] The quo warranto proceedings were decried, and other steps taken by James and his agents to return compliant members to Parliament, denounced. If Parliament was to fulfill its functions, it must be freely elected and M.P.'s must be impervious to corruption through offers of place and pension. Ferguson described the seizure of borough charters and the attempt to influence electors as heinous crimes, for they destroyed the very basis of government. [86] Another author, appalled by the corruption, recommended measures to prohibit the buying of seats, restrict the amount of money spent on campaigns, punish sheriffs for making false returns, and forbid pensions for members once elected. [87] He also proposed restricting the suffrage to the £40 freeholder, on the grounds that he would be less apt to be bribed. [88] Obviously uninterested in democratic equalitarianism, he believed an effort should be undertaken to assure that Parliament truly represented propertied people. Accordingly, he suggested a redistribution of parliamentary seats, pointing out that Old

Sarum consisted of two houses under one landlord in 1688/9 and yet continued to send two members to the House of Commons. Borough constitutions that linked the right of suffrage to certain properties, which could be bought up to guarantee the election of a candidate, should be changed. The present methods of election in boroughs encouraged double elections and false returns. Since the king had the right to nominate the sheriffs, his influence was often pervasive. Under the circumstances, petitioners, who were often the rightfully elected members of Commons, petitioned in vain. So many petitioners crowded into Westminster Hall protesting irregularities in the elections that a wit once remarked, the author recounted, that Parliament was truly meeting in the lobby, not in St. Stephen's Chapel.[89] The secret ballot was another reform which this writer felt deserved the Convention's attention. Iterating this point, a broadside entitled *A Ready way to prevent Bribery* urged the use of the balloting box and a system of colored balls to assure honesty and the election of deserving men. The experience of the East India Company and of other governments — as, for example, that of Venice — were offered as examples. *The Necessity of Parliaments* contained, as its subtitle advertised, "directions for the more regular election of parliament-men." Detailed proposals about the preparation and sealing of the indenture were set out with the avowed purpose of putting the handling of the election returns in the hands of the electors, not the sheriff.[90] Recommendations about regulating elections said to have been found among the earl of Shaftesbury's papers were reprinted "for the consideration of the Convention Parliament." Among the unique suggestions were that each person elected to Parliament take an oath that his vote was not pre-engaged, that no person stand for election in more than one place, and that each candidate be at least twenty-five years old and hold an estate worth £10,000.[91]

Judicial abuse also figured prominently in these pamphlets. For example, *A Brief Collection of Some Memorandums* urged that the tenure of judges be changed from "at pleasure of the king" to "during good behavior," that worthy men be appointed and malefactors punished. The author was confident that such a step would result in a bench that could never be satirized as the present bench had been by a contemporary puppet show, which depicted twelve dancing red robes saying anything they were told.[92] Another thought that the power to appoint judges should lie with Parliament, not with the king.[93] But one pamphlet, *Some Remarks upon Government,* rejected the change in judges' tenure as only palliative, and recommended instead an arrangement of filling judgeships and other offices by a system of election by their professional colleagues: judges by lawyers, privy councillors by the lords, sheriffs by the gentry of the county, and the officers in the state and army by members of Parliament.[94] The proposal was unique to the tract. One author argued that preserving the integrity of jurors was among the most important ways to protect the freedom of subjects. Declaring that jurors may not excuse their illegal verdicts by claiming that judges directed them, he called upon the Convention to take note of four juries that deserved public censure, among them, those that found Russell and Sidney guilty. This author also lamented the "unconsciousable fines" laid on the convicted and regretted the "barbarous, cruel and inhumane whippings of persons" in London and the West at the time of Monmouth's Rebellion. Asserting (inaccurately) that such punishments were "invented" by Jeffreys, this writer insisted that they were inappropriate to a misdemeanor and pointed out that thus many men ran the risk of falling "under the lash." Look, he said, at what happened to a cleric of the church, the Reverend Samuel Johnson.[95] This tract and one other that urged the need to review laws respecting murder and manslaughter were alone in focusing on the details of judicial abuse.[96] But, as already noted, the issue of legal reform was addressed by lawyers on the rights committee.

Tax reform received little attention; *Advice Before It Be Too Late* was alone among the pamphlets in pointing out that the hearth tax should be removed. This was the only tract to underline that the power of taxation rested with Parliament. Likewise, only one tract, *A Speech Without-Doors*, dealt with the question of freedom of the press. Arguing that no books "vend so nimbly" as unlicensed ones, Hickeringill called for a repeal of the Licensing Act, which he said was contrary to the common law (because it obstructed the trade of printing) and to the law of God (because God enjoins men not hide their light under a "napkin"). In his view, the press, the pulpit, and the bench were "golden candlesticks" that illuminated men's understanding.[97] Hickeringill was ahead of his time. The issue was not raised in the Convention (if the surviving accounts are complete), and it was six years (1695) before the Licensing Act was allowed to lapse.

The emphasis in these tracts was upon civil reform, but several urged the Convention to provide for Dissenters to worship freely. A few recommended that the nation's king be prohibited from marrying a Catholic, but only one suggested that Papists be forbidden to live in England and that those there be castrated.[98]

These, then, were the "terms and conditions" which a body of pamphlets urged the Convention to impose on the king. Did these tracts make any difference? Did they have an impact upon the steps taken in the Convention? Although there is only one claim that a specific tract changed votes in the Convention,[99] there is indirect evidence that members were influenced by the pamphlets. Maynard spoke of schemes being concocted in coffeehouses, and Birch, perhaps with such schemes in mind, recommended the drafting of a claim of rights to forestall mob uprisings. Arguments in language very close to that of the tracts appear in debates. For example, Howard's remarks about the people having a divine right to their liberties replicates a passage in Ferguson's *Brief Justification*.[100] Those M.P.'s who advanced the theory of original contract to justify setting aside James may have drawn their views from the tracts or found reinforcement from them. The tracts' demand that the Convention undertake a project to spell out the rights of the nation surely enlarged the general interest in Falkland's proposal. In sum, it may be said that the original abdication and vacancy resolution, as it was drafted on

January 28, and the first draft of the Declaration of Rights, the twenty-eight-point Heads of Grievances, both owed something to this body of rights and reform literature.

But, in the long run the rights committees and the Convention took a "swing to the right" and retreated from many of the ideas in these tracts. Their retreat should not be read as a lack of seriousness about changing the nature of the kingship. What it reflected is the political acuity of the members. These men had had extensive parliamentary experience. Many were professional lawyers. They were certainly able to gauge the strength of Tory forces in both Houses, and they probably had an inkling of the attitude of the prince. Notions about the entire dissolution of the government and the return of power to the people were undoubtedly as uncongenial to some of them as they were to conservative Tories. The men in the Convention were neither social nor political democrats. Moreover, it needs to be remembered that during the weeks of the Convention there was no official Whig (or Tory) party, leaders, doctrine, or scheme. The Whigs had barely escaped complete destruction in the early 1680s. It was a near miracle that they had survived at all, even more that they were as strong as they were in the assembly. They had no overwhelming majority, and if they were to achieve a settlement in which William replaced James and in which at the same time the kingship was changed, they had to be willing to compromise. In the event, they eliminated controversial language about original contract, and they sacrificed many points in the Heads of Grievances which their comments in debate show they would have dearly liked to keep. But they insisted upon retaining the heart of abdication and vacancy and, in subtle ways of organization and language in the document, implied that a contract had been broken. And they insisted upon presenting a claim of rights and in retaining in it issues that lay at the heart of sovereignty — the king's lawmaking and military powers — as well as other issues that restricted monarchy in important ways and underscored the superiority of Parliament. In so doing, members of the Convention drew reinforcement from the rights and reform pamphlets of radical Whigs.

III

The Passage of the
Declaration of Rights

9

The Convention Convenes.
The Debate of January 28, 1689

The Convention convened as scheduled on Tuesday, January 22, but for almost a week neither House took direct action on the crisis. Then, on January 28, the House of Commons engaged in one of the most important debates in English history. From their discussion came the famous resolution that James had "abdicated" the government and that the throne was "vacant." Although members passed this statement with near unanimity, their vote concealed divisions between Whigs and Tories and within party ranks. During the next week the resolution was repeatedly debated in both Houses and in conferences between them in terms so sharp that bloodshed was feared.[1] The abdication and vacancy resolution moved in tandem with the effort to declare the rights of the nation until February 6, when it was accepted by the House of Lords with amendments. The resolution, in justifying elevating Prince William and Princess Mary of Orange to the throne of England, served as the cornerstone of the revolutionary settlement. It was incorporated into the Declaration of Rights.

Certain features of the Convention are important to an understanding of this and other important debates and require brief notice. The assembly was, strictly speaking, an illegal body, but efforts to preserve legal forms were made. In the absence of a lord chancellor, it was necessary to elect a Speaker *pro tempore* of the House of Lords. The victory of Lord Halifax over the earl of Danby was of critical importance in reaching the solution finally agreed to.[2] The absence of a king occasioned several other irregularities. There was no speech from the throne opening the session, and no direction to the House of Commons to proceed to elect a Speaker. Instead, Lord Wiltshire, a firm supporter of the prince, reminded the Commons that their first business was to choose a Speaker. The House elected his candidate, Henry Powle, who had chaired the December meeting of former M.P.'s from Charles II's parliaments.[3] The new Speaker could neither be presented to the king nor ask for

171

confirmation of the ancient privileges of the House of Commons. Moreover, neither Lords nor Commons took the oaths of allegiance and supremacy as usual on opening day.[4] In other respects, such as the place of meeting of both Houses and the appointment of the usual officers and the standing committees of the House of Commons, the Convention did not differ from a regular parliament.

The prince maintained a low profile. Attentive to the comfort of members of the Convention, he had ordered that the rooms for both Houses, which had stood unused for three years, be made ready "with all things necessary as heretofore hath been accustomed" and instructed the Board of Green Cloth to supply food for the peers as "heretofore allowed."[5] William's authority as administrator expired at the convening of the assembly, and to avoid the imputation that he was interfering with the Convention's deliberations, he declined to appear in person. Instead he sent Jephson, his private secretary, with a letter to the Convention, a substitute for the speech from the throne.[6] Contrary to a rumor widely circulated in mid-January that he would spend the period of the sitting of the Convention in Windsor, William stayed at St. James's Palace, and his guards remained in London. Their presence provided grounds for the charge leveled later in tracts that the Dutch army overawed the Convention.[7] There is no such evidence. Data do show, however, that William and his close friends continued, as they had done in preceding weeks, to attempt discreetly to influence the course of events.

Partisan forces were rather evenly matched in the Convention. As already mentioned, about 174 Whig members, about 156 Tories, and 183 men who were serving for the first time in a Parliament constituted the body of 513 men. The average attendance, based on the days when a division was reported in the *Journals,* was 366, the highest average attendance of any parliamentary session in the late seventeenth century. The highest attendance occurred on February 5, when 437 M.P.'s were present.[8] There are only a few details about where members sat: Temple in the "uppermost seat," and Howard and Sawyer next to each other, the latter datum indicating that Whigs and Tories did not rigidly segregate themselves.[9] Some of the leaders suffered poor health during the session: Howard, the octogenarian Maynard, and Pollexfen were "lame." Gout crippled Harbord.[10]

Roughly 8 percent of the members — the forty-three M.P.'s who shaped the abdication and vacancy resolution and the claim of rights and framed the Declaration of Rights — dominated the proceedings.[11] About the same number participated in the major debates. On January 28 forty-one M.P.'s rose sixty-one times to discuss the condition of the nation, while on the twenty-ninth, forty-three members entered debate on the nation's grievances and rights sixty-nine times.[12] The debate on January 28 was filled with excitement and noise. Members interrupted each other, laughed, called out corrections when an M.P. misspoke, prodded speakers to talk louder, and moved about the chamber while a person was addressing the assembly. The long, narrow, high-ceilinged St. Stephen's Chapel was so noisy that a member asked for a recapitulation of the debate, because he "could not hear very well." [13] Anger and "reflections" also characterized this debate. There were bitter exchanges between Tories and Whigs, and hot words also passed among Whigs. The debate the evening of February 7 was disorderly. Members were hungry, satiated, tired, or angry. One M.P. said he had not heard the question, to which another rejoined that he would have heard it if he were not drunk. [14]

The majority of the members of the Convention adhered to a closed doors policy and embraced the principle of confidentiality for their affairs. [15] Despite an effort to the contrary on January 22, they opposed printing their votes and proceedings. They also restricted access to their chambers, passing resolutions to that effect five times in three weeks: on January 28 and 29, and on February 2, 5, and 6. For example, one order commanded the serjeant-at-arms to keep the Speaker's Chamber and the gallery free of unauthorized persons, and another instructed that the key to the back door of the Speaker's Chamber should be laid on the table and not removed without permission. Notwithstanding these efforts, news of the Convention's proceedings circulated. Some of their resolutions were printed on order. "Leaks" occurred. M.P.'s took notes of the debates, wrote to their constituents, and discussed politics in the London coffeehouses. Unauthorized persons eavesdropped. Much to the irritation of some members, a list of M.P.'s who had voted on February 5 against settling the crown on William and Mary appeared in manuscript. [16] Printed material, in the form of new newspapers, broadsides, and tracts, also disseminated information. Printers, publishers, and reporters must have had contacts with M.P.'s, the precise nature of which may never be known. The effect of all this was that the politically conscious public could keep themselves reasonably well informed of the progress of events in Westminster. It was possible to know who had been elected to the Convention, to estimate the partisan alignments in both Houses, to form an idea of the rights and reforms some M.P.'s hoped to achieve, to know something of the ideas expressed in debate, and to suspect the existence of disagreement between men in both Houses and between the two Houses.

From opening day the contest between Tories and Whigs was keen. For example, Whigs successfully elected Powle as Speaker, in the face of the "considerable interest" for the post on the part of Sir Edward Seymour, the Tory leader. He was stunned by his defeat, which was laid to a rumor, circulated the morning of the vote, that he favored the recall of James. [17] Taking advantage of alleged irregularities in Powle's election to the Convention, Seymour's friends entered a motion to void Powle's election to the Speakership. This move failed, but Whigs were evidently sensitive enough to Powle's potential weakness to see advantage in printing a newssheet whose apparent purpose was to confirm the wisdom of the House in their choice of Speaker. [18] Again, the failure of the Convention to proceed immediately to a discussion of the crisis reflected a contest. The prince's *Letter,* read in both Houses on opening day, stressed the dangers to England and Holland from Ireland and France and urged speedy action.[19] Whig partisans tried to persuade the Commons to consider the "state of the nation" the next day.[20] Instead, the debate was delayed almost a week by opposition tactics. Clarges, a Tory, in concert with other Tories in both Houses, insisted that the Commons postpone the debate to allow more members to assemble.[21] The purpose of this move was to give the House of Lords, where the Tories were confident of a majority, the advantage of discussing the crisis first. But the intent of the maneuver was thwarted in the House of Lords by Whig peers, especially Halifax and Devonshire, despite warm support for it.[22] Thus, the first genuine debate on the crisis was held in the House of Commons, thereby underlining that the initiative in affairs had shifted from the Lords to the Commons.

When the Convention reconvened on January 28, the debate on the "state of the nation" in a committee of the whole was long and sharp, the exchange lasting from early morning until three o'clock in the afternoon.[23] At issue were whether James II or another person should be king of England, and whether, in view of James's flight, the throne was vacant or not. The Whigs dominated the proceedings, achieving at the outset a tactical advantage. To the shouts of "No Seymour, No Seymour" from the back benches, they successfully elected Richard Hampden chairman of the Committee of the Whole.[24] In that position Hampden, who was beloved of his colleagues, served Whig partisan interests well. His skill as a parliamentary leader, developed over many years in the House, was evident. He ignored an angry importunity to put the question to a vote before the matter had been thoroughly aired, focused members' attention by reading the question five times, and attempted to quiet hot tempers.[25] Possibly he also used his power as chairman to restrict the Tories' entry in the debate by declining to acknowledge them. (Or it may be that Tory proponents held back, waiting to hear Whig arguments.) Whatever the reason, only fifteen Tories, compared to twenty-six Whigs, participated in the discussion; and half of them did not speak (and then only briefly) until the debate was almost at an end. Under Hampden's chairmanship, members, prodded by Whigs' three times calling for the question, came to a vote on a formulation of the abdication and vacancy resolution pleasing to Whigs, although in the middle of the day it had seemed unlikely that they would ever disentangle themselves from the complexities of their discussion about government.[26]

Whig strategy apparently was to allow the Tories to make the first move in the debate, but evidently Tory forces were not entirely prepared to take the initiative. Once the chairman was chosen, a long pause ensued before Sir Gilbert Dolben, a young man with excellent personal connections, but not among the first rank of the party, opened the discussion.[27] Probably he had failed to coordinate his remarks with senior party leaders, for another long pause followed his "very long and very learned and well delivered" speech.[28] Although the points he made conformed to the Tory position that emerged, no Tory leapt up to support him. Instead, a violent Whig, John Arnold, described as one of the "most noisy, imprudent and ignorant members" of the

party, seconded his motion that the king had voluntarily forsaken the government and that the throne was void.[29] Sir Richard Temple, a former Tory but
zealously for the Whigs in 1689, spoke next. Dolben was left to make his own
defense, and another Tory did not interrupt the march of Whig speakers
until Sawyer rose after eleven entries had been made. The next major Tory
contribution, that of Finch, came after five more Whigs had claimed the
floor.[30]

Other evidence points to some disarray in Tory forces. Of the fourteen
Tories who did speak, only Dolben, Finch, Musgrave, and Sawyer argued at
any length.[31] Of them only Dolben was well received. Finch, Musgrave, and
Sawyer were reduced to explaining themselves.[32] Most of the difficult questions they raised were left unanswered. Sawyer, much to the unconcealed
irritation of some Whigs,[33] focused at length on the absurdity of the idea that
the government had devolved to the people.[34] The imperious Seymour,
whose sense of self-importance was legendary, was laughed at twice by the
House, an unthinkable act in earlier circumstances and indicative of weakness in Tory status and regard at this time. Furthermore, among the major
Tory spokesmen, there was no unanimity on terms and solutions in this
debate, even as there had been no agreement among Tory peers since
December. For example, Dolben, who later revealed himself in favor of
Princess Mary, declined to specify a solution, insisting only upon the fact that
the king's flight was voluntary and amounted to a "demise." Finch hesitated to
make a judgment, but finally announced himself for a regency. Sawyer, after
beclouded remarks, accepted the term "abdication," but, significantly, sought
to inform it with a meaning quite different from that of the Whigs.

Although the Tories seem to have failed to marshall speakers and develop
a common front, they were not entirely lacking in strategy. Seymour was
unaccustomedly silent during the debate and was said to be "very uneasy"
while Dolben addressed the House.[35] A clear explanation for his silence and
discomfort has escaped the record. Was it his intention to let Whigs take the
initiative in the hopes that they would advance a solution in such extreme
terms that the House would be alienated and then Tories could come forward
with a resolution of the crisis either in terms of regency or the elevation of
Mary in her own right? The House suspected he was up to something. The
laughter directed at him occurred when Sawyer (violating parliamentary
rules)[36] mentioned him by name. It signaled the House's belief that the two
men had conspired to "throw in a bone" — that is, to disrupt the
proceedings.[37] The suspicions of the House are of great importance. They
reinforce the evidence (already discussed) of a Tory strategy devised in
December and January to use limitations on royal authority as a means of
delaying a solution. Seymour's later attempt (to be discussed) to sabotage the
Declaration of Rights and poison sentiment against Prince William on the
morning of February 9 may be viewed as compatible with such an intention.
Together these disparate data throw a different light on Seymour's participation the next day in the debate on the nation's rights and grievances.

Another aspect of a Tory strategy appears in the appeal both Clarges and

Sawyer made to William's *Declaration of Reasons*. At Clarges's request, the manifesto was read.[38] Thus, Tories continued the tactic they had employed for months, to try to hold the prince to what he had said. The reading of the manifesto would have reminded the House that William's only avowed purpose was to assure free elections to a parliament, that the prince had blamed James's ministers, not the king himself, and that he had disclaimed personal ambitions. A further tactic was to try to restrict the debate to the state of the nation and avoid consideration of the "remedies" at this time.[39] Such a procedure would have diluted the effect of the lords' refusal to debate the issue first. The aim was to get agreement that the throne was vacant but only "as to the person of the king," by reason of James's voluntary withdrawal and failure to provide for the administration of justice. No Tory in the House of Commons supported — or was willing publicly to support — the return of the king.

The debate turned primarily on the meaning of the words "demise" and "abdicated." Dolben introduced the word "demise," using it in its legal sense, meaning the abandoning of the government by the king through death or action. The term implied the devolution of sovereignty, without an interregnum, and was essential to arguments for elevating Princess Mary alone. Dolben used reason, law, and English history, citing the cases of Edward IV and Richard II, to support the argument that James's flight and suppression of the Great Seal — "whereby the current of justice (which is the soul of government) is wholly stoped"[40] — amounted to a "demise." At no point did Dolben mention the king's alleged violations of the nation's religion, law, or liberties — in other words, his maladministration. Referring to the "learned" Grotius (whose "admirable and perfect book" *De Jure belli and pacis* he approved), François Hotoman, Gabriel Vasquez, "and others," Dolben argued that James had been transformed into a private person, and as England's king, was dead. He moved a resolution that James "having voluntarily . . . abandoned and forsaken the kingdom, it is a voluntary demise" of the government.[41]

Whig partisans objected. Temple insisted that James's maladministration, not just his withdrawal, had caused a vacancy. Reciting James's violations of the nation's religion, laws, and liberties, Temple asserted that when a king tried to "destroy the roots of government" he became a "tyrant." The violations were the "reasons" that will "satisfy the nation that King James has rendered himself inconsistent with government."[42] Thus, the day before there was discussion about grievances and rights, Temple anticipated the connection between them and the "abdication" of the king. The one justified the other. Sir Robert Howard, best known as a dramatist, but also a politician, also objected to "rest[ing] upon a demise when we have suffered so much in our religion, liberties, and properties." He offered the most explicit and eloquent exposition of the idea that maladministration involved "forfeiture" of royal power. That conclusion flowed from the theory of original contract, which Howard expounded to the House. "The Constitution of the government is actually grounded upon pact and covenant with the people," he explained. That contract was made in the long ago past, in time immemorial, when people, living in a state of nature without government, agreed to set up a kingship. It was a bold thing to say in the Commons, as radical pamphleteers were writing in tracts, that the people brought the kingly office into being. It was an unequivocal rejection of the divine right theory of kingship. It was also a denial that the contract between king and people was made at the historical moment when the king takes the coronation oath to abide by the laws of the land. Howard continued to explain to M.P.'s that if the king breaks the contract, he forfeits his right to the crown. The maxim that the "king can do no wrong" has of late been misconstrued, he argued. "Lawyers of old" like Bracton and Fortescue interpreted it to mean that when the king violates the law, he ceases to be a king and becomes a tyrant. When that happens, the power returns to the people. "I have heard of a Jus Divinum," Howard declared, "but I am sure we [the people] have a divine right to our lives, estates, and liberty." Applauding Temple's recital of James's crimes, Howard asserted that the king was worse than all previous monarchs who (like Richard II) had "sucked in the poison of arbitrary power" because he had "left nothing unattempted that might entirely ruin us." The consequence of these actions was more than the word "demise" implied. Howard proposed instead the term "abdicated," which he explicitly defined as meaning that the government "devolved into the people, who are here in civil society and constitution to save . . . [their rights]." "The right is therefore wholly in the people, who are now to new form themselves again, under a governor yet to be chosen." He framed a motion which outlined the final resolution adopted by the Commons. It mentioned James by name, referred to his "Jesuit" advisers, charged him with subverting "all laws," and declared that he is "no longer our king."[43]

Howard's remarks explicitly reflected radical Whig principles. The works of John Milton, an avowed republican, said to be Howard's friend,[44] may have influenced him. So too, perhaps, did the writings of the Reverend Samuel Johnson.[45] Howard's language, moreover, is close to that of the rights and reform tracts. Other M.P.'s made the same points less elegantly. Thus, Maynard thought that all government was based upon a "pact with the people," while another speaker insisted that the origins of kingly power came from the people and not from God.[46] On the twenty-eighth some Whigs were unafraid to proclaim principles which later they soft-pedaled.

Howard's reference to Richard II reflected his knowledge of that king, whose history Howard had written, and published in 1681, as already noted. An expanded version of that work, under a different title, was licensed without his knowledge, Howard claimed, on January 17, 1689, on the eve of the meeting of the Convention, in time to allow M.P.'s to draw comparisons between these earlier monarchs and James II. The identities between Richard II and James II were thought to be particularly apt.[47]

Another Whig, Pollexfen, also objected to the word "demise" and the term "voluntary" in Dolben's formulary. "I would not have gentlemen surprised by the word 'voluntary going away,'" he said. "There is more meant by that than you suppose." [48] If James's flight were voluntary, and a "demise" thereby had occurred, the consequence was that "the Crown is full by succession." If that was the case, "then we have nothing to do here." But, continued Pollexfen, "this was no voluntary departure," any more than it is voluntary when a man hands over his money to highway robbers. Belying his own words, he advised members not to "trouble . . . [their] heads about a demise or differ about words," but rather to recognize pragmatically that the throne was entirely empty. Pollexfen, who had in December urged William to claim the throne by conquest and argued that James's flight meant a "cession" of his authority, was concerned to assure that William's title should be unencumbered. [49]

These points provoked a rejoinder from the Tory Sawyer. In a long repetitive speech, [50] he sought to equate the words "demise" and "abdication" and link them with other terms used in debate: "devolution" and "dereliction." "'Tis all one," he said; they all mean the throne is vacant. At the same time Sawyer denied Howard's definition of "abdication" as meaning a dissolution of the government. Engaging in wordplay and obfuscation, Sawyer used the word "abdication" to describe the effect of James's "voluntary" departure and said that the departure meant that the throne, but not the crown, was void! [51] Thus, Sawyer invested the word with a meaning quite different from that of the radical Whigs. His ploy was successful. When a fellow Tory demanded clarification whether "maladministration or the going away of the King is thought to amount to an abdication," "many of the House" cried out, "Both." [52] Or again, when at the very end of the debate, another Tory, the Honorable Francis Robartes, son of the first earl of Radnor, remarked, "If the question is to have no other consequence than would follow on the king's natural demise will go *nemine contradicente*," [53] no M.P. contradicted his interpretation. Finally, when Sawyer explained the settlement in a letter of February 19, he asserted that few M.P.'s thought that the word "abdication" implied maladministration. [54] The equation of the terms "abdication" and "demise" contributed, arguably, to the near unanimity of the vote on the final resolution. But, however members of the House of Commons viewed it, Tories in the House of Lords bitterly contested the word "abdication," and it became the subject of heated wrangling in and between the two Houses.

A closely related issue on which the debate turned was whether or not — assuming, for the sake of argument, that the government was dissolved and the power returned to the people — the Convention represented the people and could settle the headship. To rebut Howard's argument, Sawyer contended, in terms almost identical to those in a private paper prepared in January by fellow Tory Roger North, that the "people" included "freeholders under 40 shillings a year and all copyholders, and women and children and servants." [55] If one grants that the people possessed such power as the Whigs claimed, the Convention contained no such people nor did it represent them. Not so much as a quarter of the nation is represented in the Convention.

Therefore, all the rest "must be consulted before we can take upon us to dispose of the crown, if the right of disposing it be in the people," for, Sawyer pointed out, "we have no such instructions from those that sent us hither." Further, if the government has devolved to the people, then the lords, who represent "their own estate only," should not be meeting.[56] In any case, Sawyer maintained that the government of England had "always been by 3 estates, Lords Spiritual, Lords Temporal, and Commons," and the monarchy has always been hereditary, and the people have never had the power to dispose of the crown.[57]

Sawyer's remarks about the "people" exposed absurdities in the contract theory of government and in the assumption that the Convention was representative of the "people," and provoked indignant replies from the Whigs. Boscawen, the Presbyterian, whose patience with Sawyer more than once ran thin,[58] declaimed, "I desire to know how the people can be better represented. I think we represent the people fully." Boscawen made it clear that he spoke for the people that have a share in government — "or are fit to have a share in it" — and maintained that the Convention properly represented them.[59] His point was iterated by Treby and Howard.[60]

A further Tory argument of great strength was the charge that the Whigs intended to change the nature of the government. No speaker was more effective in this point than Finch.[61] Reluctant to equate James's flight with an abdication, Finch argued that the English monarchy has always been hereditary and that unless the crown descends, "we, while we complain of the king's violation of our rights, will ourselves violate our very Constitution." If the government is dissolved, he continued, then "we that sit here have no right to our estates." Willing to abandon the maxim "that the king can do no wrong," and insisting that he opposed the return of the king, Finch conceded that James's "zeal to popery" unsuited him to be England's monarch. His solution was a regency. Take the case, he argued, that "the king were a minor or in a frenzy."[62] Under those circumstances he would be unable to rule, and a regent would be appointed. Finch protested that a regency for life would be "no loophole" to restore James, but that it would preserve the traditional nature of the kingship.[63] Finch's idea was absurd in that it plainly controverted the facts of the situation, for James obviously was neither an infant nor "out of his wits," as Treby acidly pointed out.[64] But it could be said that the king was suffering from the moral infirmity of adhering to Catholicism, as some argued in the House of Lords, where regency barely failed. The regency proposal is of further interest as an example of the application of private law to constitutional dilemma.[65] Musgrave reinforced Finch. Denying that the king had subverted the government and doubting the power of the Convention to depose James, this Tory asked for a ruling from the lawyers, whether the assembly could depose the king.[66]

Some Whig lawyers tried to defuse the issue of the right of the Convention to depose the king and to sidestep the theory of original contract. Thus, Maynard asserted that the "question is not whether we can depose the king, but whether the king has not deposed himself." [67] Williams advised dispatch and recognition of the "plain fact" that James had left the kingdom. He refused to "meddle" with whether the flight was voluntary or otherwise. [68] Treby assumed the role of peacemaker. Expressing regret at the "heats," he stated the question "modestly" [69] and tried to steer members away from debating "subtleties and start[ing] at shadows lest there be not a spot of ground in this country on which a Protestant may set his foot." [70] Reinforcing Maynard's point, Treby dismissed the request for a legal ruling on the Convention's power to depose the king, explaining "we have found the throne vacant, . . . we have not made it so." [71] But his position was more forthright and more conformable to that of Whig radicals. However modest his language, Treby asserted that James had abdicated — "renounced his legal government" [72] — that the throne was vacant, and that the Convention must provide for the government. Ridiculing Finch's idea that James might be regarded as a lunatic, Treby pointed out that such an approach preserved the king's right to the crown. Contending that James had gone beyond infringing the liberty and property of private men, beyond the crimes of Richard II, Treby declared the king had invaded the "fundamental laws themselves." "These are violations," declaimed Treby, "which shake off the king." [73] He suggested that the resolution include the words "by advice of Jesuits and other wicked persons, having violated the fundamental laws, etc." [74]

Somers also skirted difficult theoretical issues. If the accounts of his maiden speech are comprehensive, [75] he made no reference to the contract theory of government, nor to the power of the Convention to depose kings, nor to the idea that government had devolved to the people. [76] His earlier tract, *A Brief History of the Succession,* had revealed that Somers did not adhere to the contract theory of government, and the failure to mention it avoided alienating some M.P.'s. But he regarded the crown as a forfeitable trust and believed that Parliament had the power to determine the succession. Maintaining that the Convention's actions would satisfy "the world abroad if it be like other cases," he found a close parallel in the story of Sigismond, king of Sweden, [77] and compared his reign with that of James II. Both kings attempted to Catholicize their respective countries, and failing, both fled. But James's crime was the worse, for he fled to France, England's enemy, which fact confirmed the suspicion of a secret treaty between James and Louis XIV and absolved the people of their allegiance. And more, before James left, he "did utterly incapacitate himself" to be England's king by practicing popery, exchanging emissaries with the Pope, handing over Ireland to the Irish, and attempting to "bring us into popery and slavery." All these acts were "directly against our laws." Although Somers is often credited with fathering the abdication and vacancy resolution, no source shows that it originated with him. On the contrary, the record reveals that several other people — Dolben, Howard, and Treby — offered the motions which were linked together to form the final resolution.

Other Whigs became impatient with the legalistic ambiguities of the lawyers, and "reflections" ensued. The young and irrepressible John Howe, who had early in the proceedings interrupted the distinguished jurist Pollexfen to emphasize his contention that James by his maladministration had "forfeited" the crown, complained that "some of the counsel talk as if they were instructing juries. I wish they would come plainly to the point." He "reflected" so much that the chairman took him down, only to be rebuked himself for doing so by another Whig, Harbord. Apologizing, Hampden remonstrated that the debate should be conducted with moderation and "not with heat and reflections."[78] Boscawen urged members to "choose a king," who will fight the nation's battles, and bypass Princess Mary, who as a woman would be ill-equipped to do that. He cautioned the assembly against fighting with a "bulrush."[79] Sir William Pulteney, M.P. for Westminster who had made a fortune from licensing coaches and coach horses, asserted that James himself must be held responsible for the crisis. "I would fain know," he said, "whom to blame else for all the wrong that has been done us: it has been originally and primarily by no other but the king."[80] In his opinion, an abdication had occurred, the crown was void, and the Convention must exercise its rightful power to settle the succession.

Whig partisans argued their case in speeches reflecting rhetorical talent and previous parliamentary experience. As we have already seen, Treby imitated James by gesture and voice,[81] and Williams injected a humorous note when, in urging the House to recognize the "plain fact" that James had fled to France, England's enemy, and thus the throne was vacant, said in an aside, "We never liked any thing of France but their wine that indeed we like very well."[82] Many of them employed arresting analogies. For example, to illustrate the point that when a king broke the original contract by maladministration the power returned to the people, one speaker compared the monarch to a commander of a fort who turned his guns against the inhabitants of the fort, who had entrusted him with the responsibility to defend them. In that case, the inhabitants could discharge the commander, just as the people may lay aside a king.[83] Another, Sir Henry Capel, appealed to one of Aesop's fables to reinforce his point that a Popish king was unsuited to rule over a Protestant state. "I may say," he declaimed, "that clay and brasse are as consistent together as a Protestant body with a Popish head."[84] His fellow members, educated as they were in the classical tradition, would have recognized Capel's allusion to the fable about the clay pot and the copper kettle. The clay pot, the fable goes, refuses to ford a stream with the copper kettle, because he fears that should they touch he would be smashed. This popular story was invariably used to draw the moral that the poor run the risk of being hurt when they associate with the rich, but in May 1688 the fable had been pressed into political service by an unidentified Whig. As comment on the action of an unknown Whig turncoat (Williams, perhaps?), "The Ballad of the Pott and Pitcher" had circulated in London. The moral, apparent in the following lines, was that Whigs cooperated with James to their peril:

Learn hence ye Wiggs, and act no more like Fools
Nor trust their Friendship, who would make you Tools

Then let not the allyance farther pass,
For know that you are clay, they are brass.[85]

What could more vividly convey the idea that a Protestant state will be smashed by a Popish king than to analogize them to the clay pot and the brass kettle?

Tories resisted the effort of the Whigs to call the question on the resolution, which read: "That King James the Second, having endeavoured to subvert the Constitution of the kingdom, by breaking the original contract between king and people, and, by the advice of Jesuits and other wicked persons, having violated the fundamental laws and having withdrawn himself out of this kingdom, has abdicated the government, and that the throne is thereby become vacant." Several younger men rushed into the debate to try to postpone a vote, but they were overrun by impatient Whigs and the chairman. The resolution contained the major points made by the Whigs, including references to the original contract, Jesuits and other wicked persons, fundamental laws, abdication, and vacancy. It also included a reference to the king's withdrawing himself. Although many members were said to be secretly opposed to the resolution — a vote the next week flushed out 160 of them — only three Tories voted against it on January 28.[86] The explanation for the near unanimity probably lies in the fact that the resolution described the "condition" of the nation but did not explicitly propose a solution. Moreover, the meaning of the key terms "abdication" and "vacancy" was left ambiguous. Spokesmen had defined or discussed them according to their political principles and goals, leaving it to members to choose the meaning that suited them. Thus, "abdication" could mean (as Sawyer and others claimed) that the king had fled and that the throne was vacant only as to his person. The principle of direct hereditary succession meant that in theory the throne was occupied, but by whom was still to be determined. Or "abdication" could mean (as many Whigs said) that by his maladministration James had broken the contract between himself and the nation, the throne was entirely vacant, and the Convention must exercise its rightful authority to fill it. Men on all sides accepted such imprecisely defined words and prepared for further maneuvering. It was in the House of Lords that definitions were debated.

The sense of urgency continued after the resolution passed. Wharton and Colchester, among others, insisted upon an immediate vote in the full House. Ignoring the plea of Tories for an adjournment, impatient M.P.'s dissolved the Committee of the Whole, and the full House passed the resolution with only one negative.[87] Then, with Speaker Powle cautioning members to attend, "for the lords take great notice how votes are attended," Hampden carried the resolution to the Lords that very afternoon.[88] Upon his return, one M.P. further underscored the sense of urgency by asking the

House to return immediately to a committee of the whole "to go on with our business." But upon learning that the Lords "were up," the House of Commons decided to adjourn until 9:00 A.M. the next day. As members apparently lingered in the chamber, Clarges announced himself for "qualifications," perhaps voicing a concern made manifest the next day to identify grievances, reassert rights, and thereby qualify the powers of the king.

10

The Debate of January 29, 1689, on Grievances and Rights

On Tuesday, January 29, 1689, the House of Commons initiated steps that would lead to the Declaration of Rights. The express purpose of the debate that day was to consider the condition of the nation.[1] But in a committee of the whole, chaired by Richard Hampden, some members introduced other matters. Colonel Birch presented a resolution to bar a Popish prince from the throne. The motion read: "It has been found by experience, to be inconsistent with the safety and welfare of the Protestant kingdom, to be governed by a Popish Prince." The words "by experience" met the requirements of lawyers, who wanted to protect laws that had been passed before the Reformation, and of Tories, who had opposed Exclusion a decade before.[2] Once this resolution passed, Wharton moved that the vacancy in the throne be filled by making William and Mary king and queen of England. Neither he nor the seconder, Lord Colchester, referred to a need to specify the rights of the nation.[3] It was a Tory, Anthony Cary, Lord Falkland, who urged the House not to consider filling the throne until they had decided "what powers . . . to give the Crown . . . and what not." He called upon the assembly to review the "foundation" of the nation's government.[4] Two Whigs, Garroway and Williams, endorsed the idea, and a protracted bipartisan debate ensued.

Falkland's proposal could have come as no surprise to any politically conscious person. William's widespread *Declaration of Reasons* had recited James II's violations of the nation's religion, law, and liberties and practically invited a freely elected parliament to declare the rights of the nation. In Tory circles there had been talk since October of restricting the king's power, in order to protect the Protestant religion and prevent arbitrary government. Radical pamphlets and tracts in abundance had recommended that the Convention undertake reforms. The prince's *Letter* calling for elections had identified "restoring the rights and liberties of the kingdom" as the major purpose of the Convention. A broadside said to have been written by Halifax[5] (which attribution would have inflated its importance) had been delivered to the House of Commons the day before, just before the vote on the abdication and vacancy resolution, to urge the House to agree upon the "constitution" before choosing a "governor." Addressed to "all and every" member, the paper counselled M.P.'s to "beware of being so eager on . . . [choosing a king] that . . . [settling the Constitution] be neglected." It begged them to "redeem us from slavery" and warned that "what you omit now is lost forever." On that same day, after the vote on the abdication and vacancy resolution, Clarges had apparently called for "qualifications," possibly indicating a concern to restrict the powers of the king.[6]

Members responded to Falkland's suggestion in the longest and most thoughtful discussion of grievances, rights, and reform that was held during the Convention.[7] Although the majority of speakers were Whigs (27 Whigs to 16 Tories), Tories played a more important part in this debate than they did in any other debate on rights. Seymour, silent the day before, argued the most passionately and eloquently for limiting royal power. Clarges[8] and Musgrave, both proponents at this time of regency, a solution the House of Lords was debating the same day, were among M.P.'s who moved to appoint a committee "to bring in general heads of such things as are absolutely necessary to be considered for the better securing of our religion, and laws, and liberties."[9] Yet behind the general concurrence expressed in this debate lay varying degrees of enthusiasm and diverse motivations, including political principle, partisan strategy, and personal self-interest.

One reason Tories supported Falkland's project was to prevent a recurrence of those royal measures under which they had suffered during the reign of James II. Seymour indignantly asked the House: "Will you let men go on in the same practices they have formerly?"[10] They gave priority to the royal dispensing power, just as William's *Declaration of Reasons* and the *Bishops' Proposals* had done. "I hope we shall never leave that doubtful," said Falkland, and Seymour and Sawyer concurred. They condemned the Ecclesiastical Commission, the quo warranto proceedings, and the "swollen power" of judges, the latter probably with Danby's imprisonment in mind. Although at the end of debate Falkland interjected "exorbitant fines" as a grievance, no Tory systematically addressed the issue of legal reform. As for parliamentary reform, only Sawyer mentioned the need to protect Parliament from arbitrary dismissal. If the surviving accounts are comprehensive, Tories declined Falkland's invitation to "lay the foundation" of England's government and Thomas Christie's[11] call to draft a new Magna Charta. None wished to devise a new kingship. To a man they declared themselves for reaffirming old law and reestablishing the "ancient government." Although none wished to devise a new kingship, the Tories' endorsement of restrictions on the dispensing power, the right to create an Ecclesiastical Commission, and the power to employ the quo warranto process would have modified royal authority.

The second reason Tories endorsed the rights project was that they viewed it as a parliamentary tactic to help them achieve partisan advantage. This interpretation is grounded upon several considerations. First, the circumstances under which Falkland chose to introduce the proposal suggest as much. He interrupted a Whig motion to declare William and Mary king and queen. As a consequence, that motion was postponed and the resolution of the crisis was delayed for two weeks. To delay a decision on the headship of the government was the tactic Tories had used on January 28. There is no reason to think that they had changed their strategy the next day. Second, certain anomalies associated with Falkland himself also suggest that party strategy and personal opportunism underlay his motion. It is unlikely that so young (he was thirty-three years old), inexperienced, and little-known an M.P. as Falkland, who had served previously only in the Parliament of 1685, should have taken the initiative in an assembly of distinguished and seasoned men in bringing forth a proposal of such far-reaching implication without coordinating the step with the Tory leadership. His call to "change things as well as hands," to "lay the foundations" of the government anew, was an intrinsically radical idea.[12] It was an idea incompatible with his previous political activities, all of which had been conservative. For example, as already mentioned, Falkland sponsored a bill in 1685 for indemnifying the Catholic officers, became a deputy-lieutenant of Oxfordshire in February 1688 (the appointment signaling approval of the king), and almost certainly gave favorable answers to the king's three questions in the fall of 1688.[13] Moreover, he retained his post as treasurer of the navy right up to the revolution. Further, if commitment to the principle of limiting the powers of the monarchy was Falkland's only concern — as his remarks on the twenty-ninth suggest — then why, after his urgent and persistent advocacy,[14] did he not speak again in subsequent debates on the topic? Falkland's only other recorded contributions to the passages of the declaration were service on Treby's committee and carrying a message about the document to the House of Lords. Further, although his views on the settlement are clouded, his vote on February 5 against declaring William and Mary king and queen proves that he did not favor that solution, and one remark[15] suggests that he was a "Maryite." It is reasonable to think, therefore, that Falkland's purpose was to forestall the move to elevate William and provide time to maneuver on the question of the headship. Since Seymour's apparent strategy the day before was to delay matters, it is significant that Falkland was on friendly terms with the Tory leader, who, at fifty-six, was so much his senior in years, experience, and status. Cary had bought his post of treasurer of the navy from Seymour in 1681, and in 1690 he was to be indebted to him for his election for Great Bedwin. These data permit the speculation that Falkland coordinated his motion with Seymour, who himself wanted to delay a decision on filling the throne.

Third, Seymour's own role in the passage of the Declaration of Rights reinforces the thesis that tactical considerations played a part. Sir Edward supported Falkland with greater passion than any other M.P., Tory or Whig. He insisted upon proceeding with a definition of grievances at whatever cost in time, danger, and delay, declaiming, "What care I for what is done abroad, if we must be slaves in England, in this or that man's power? If people are drunk and rude below, as was complained of, must that stop proceedings in Parliament?"[16] No one should doubt that he genuinely wanted to limit the crown to avoid a recurrence of James's transgressions. Seymour had opposed the king's Catholicizing and centralizing policies and, in fact, had been largely responsible for bringing over men of substance in the West to William's side. In gratitude, the prince appointed him governor of Exeter, despite some suspicions about his loyalty.[17] Becoming disillusioned by the end of December because he felt, so he said, that William was not adhering to the terms of his *Declaration of Reasons,* Seymour withdrew his support of the prince.[18] Convinced that England and Holland could never be happily united because of their commercial rivalry (each was pursuing the "same mistress — trade," he said), he also came to believe that if William won the crown he would, because of the continued loyalty to James of many English soldiers, need a large and partly Dutch military establishment to maintain himself.[19] Accordingly, Sir Edward worked actively against the prince immediately before the Convention convened.[20] Failing in his bid to be elected Speaker of the Convention on January 22 and chairman of the Committee of the Whole on January 28, he took no part in the critically important debate about abdication and vacancy, but conspired with Sawyer, so M.P.'s thought, to disrupt the proceedings. With only two other members, he voted against the resolution. A rumor circulated that he favored the recall of James; a contemporary thought he favored a regency.[21] The historian of the Tory party has described his moves in the Convention as "obscure."[22] But whether Seymour secretly wanted to restore James or really wanted a regency is immaterial to the point that he could not have desired the success of Wharton's motion to elevate William and Mary to the throne.

Now, a man so politically astute and experienced in parliamentary affairs as he could readily have ascertained (even as observers reported) that the near unanimity of the vote on January 28 concealed profound reservations on the part of many members. Just how many members disliked the resolution could not have been precisely known on the twenty-ninth, but the sharpness and length of the debate revealed that differences existed, and Seymour must have had some inkling of the House's inclinations. (A vote taken a week later, on February 5, it should be remembered, showed that a third of the members were opposed.) Moreover, he could with equal readiness have predicted that the introduction of a motion to specify rights would interrupt the proceedings of the Convention and sidetrack any effort to settle the head-ship question. The political rhetoric outside the Convention was saturated with words about "declaring the rights of the people." Who could oppose such a project? Radical Whigs who favored genuine reform could be expected to endorse it. Whigs in the center who wanted to elevate William first and who could be expected to see disadvantages in delay would be embarrassed, in view of their own principles and William's *Declaration of Reasons, Letters* calling an election, and his *Letter* to the Convention, if they opposed it. It would buy time for political maneuvering by the many M.P.'s who secretly opposed the abdication and vacancy resolution. And if the prince should, in the end, win the throne, Seymour would hardly be averse to restricting *his* prerogatives.

Furthermore, disingenuousness in Seymour's emphatic endorsement of Falkland's proposal is suggested by the fact that at no other time when the Declaration of Rights was discussed in the House did Seymour speak. Although appointed to Treby's committee, he did not serve on Somers's committee, and he is associated with the Declaration of Rights again only in a negative way, in the episode, discussed below, that occurred on February 8–9, when he brought to the House of Commons news of the crisis in which the statement of rights was endangered.

Fourth, close scrutiny of the role of other prominent Tories also invites the suspicion that tactical considerations underlay Falkland's project. Take, for example, Sawyer. Regarded as Seymour's confederate in a scheme to delay the proceedings on the twenty-eighth, Sir Robert was, like Falkland, a Maryite.[23] No more than Seymour could he have favored Wharton's motion. In endorsing Falkland's motion, he made a parenthetical remark pertinent to this argument — namely, that the work of drawing up "heads" would "employ several weeks."[24] The time could be used for promoting the solution he favored. Morrice said of Sawyer that he spoke to the idea of stipulations "only to confound the House."[25]

Or consider the arguments advanced by Christopher Musgrave, a lawyer and an "old Parliament man" said, it should be recalled, to be the "leader of the high Tories and the country gentlemen."[26] He endorsed Falkland's proposal on the grounds that a specification of grievances would explain and justify the abdication and vacancy resolution passed the day before. Arguing that M.P.'s "cannot answer it to the nation or Prince of Orange, till we declare what are the rights invaded," he went on to assert that "when you declare your grievances, every man will take them to be the reason of your vote yesterday."[27] The point could hardly be made more explicit: A declaration of rights and reform should be seen as a justification for the "abdication" and "vacancy" resolution. It would explain to "every man" why members voted for that resolution. It would, to some degree, protect everybody who was involved. As a contemporary observed, if James had not done what he had done, then the actions taken were "treason, rebellion, and utterly unjustifiable."[28]

But was there more to Musgrave's point? Did it also contain a Tory party strategy? One is obliged to ask, Why should Musgrave have been so concerned to *justify* the abdication and vacancy resolution, when on the twenty-eighth he had denied that James had subverted the government, asserted that the terms "demise" and "abdicate" were equivalent, objected to "vacancy" as tantamount to deposition, and doubted the powers of the Convention to depose a king? He was one of the Tories said to have used the "most art" to "divert the House." Musgrave voted for the abdication and vacancy resolution, but not out of conviction. An associate of the earl of Nottingham, he was a proponent of "regency," [29] which on the twenty-ninth remained a possible option and would, of course, have voided abdication and vacancy. In view of his connections, commitments, and prior remarks on the resolution, it is legitimate to argue that Musgrave's purpose was to show the weaknesses of the abdication and vacancy theory. In other words, Musgrave may have felt that if grievances were collected for all to see, it would be possible to demonstrate that they were insufficient to warrant "abdication" on the grounds of maladministration, as some Whigs had claimed. Thus, a statement of grievances and rights could confirm doubts about the resolution in the minds of members who already harbored misgivings and raise questions in the minds of others. In consequence, delays might be achieved and the arguments advanced by Musgrave and others the day before further explored, the arguments, that is, that James's voluntary flight created a "demise," and that "regency" or the crowning of Princess Mary were the appropriate and legitimate answers to the crisis. Moreover, like Seymour and Falkland, neither Sawyer nor Musgrave had a word to say in subsequent debates on the Declaration of Rights. Silence and absence of participation are neutral considerations, but when linked with these other data they strengthen the argument that tactical considerations figured in these Tories' endorsement.

Fifth, the fact that only two Tories spoke out against the project reinforces the same point. Dolben and Sir John Knight, a man known for harsh persecution of Catholics, [30] mentioned only the dangers to Protestants in Ireland and the threat of a countercoup by Catholics in England if time were taken to discuss grievances and rights. [31] Not one Tory suggested that the project violated his political principles, and not one objected to any of the measures in the long list of rights and reforms put forward by the Whigs. Now, a Tory might agree as readily as any Whig that the monarchy should be limited in certain ways and the king required to adhere to the law, but as has been said, Falkland's project to decide what powers to give the king and what not was intrinsically radical, and the specific suggestions proposed by some radical Whigs were far-reaching. It is incredible that no Tory should have felt that the proposal was theoretically repugnant or that some of the proposed restrictions were unacceptable. Is it possible that the backbenchers were brought into line by the Tory leadership? If that did not happen, then one must grant unanimity of opinion between Tories and radical Whigs on limiting the English crown. That kind of unanimity is not credible.

Sixth, further comments by Whigs in and out of Parliament provide support for the idea that Falkland's motion concealed an ulterior purpose. For example, Maynard counseled members not to delay settling the government "under whatever *fair pretence*," arguing that his knowledge and experience of past times made him fear that the time taken in debating restrictions on the crown would "give occasion to moles, who work under ground, to destroy the foundations [i.e., the abdication and vacancy resolution] you laid yesterday." [32] Referring to the public debate, Maynard declaimed, "Many speak in coffeehouses and better places, of fine things for you to do, that you may do nothing but spend your health, and be in confusion." [33] Pollexfen, too, stressed the point that the proposition would consume time and promote confusion, asserting that "the greatest enemy you have cannot advise better." [34] And again, while commending the proposition as excellent in itself, Pollexfen stated, "If it have the effect to confound us, [it is] a dreadful proposition." [35]

A Whig outside of Parliament, Roger Morrice, was certain that a Tory strategy played a part in Falkland's proposal. He asserted flatly that "Intreaguers" of "great ability and craft" were involved in a "specious" effort to "make stipulations and limit the monarchy." He described their insistence upon drawing up "antecedent stipulations," as insincere and "disingenuous." [36] As already noted, he charged that Sawyer spoke to the motion "only to confound the House." Morrice's suspicions doubtless stemmed from his understanding that Tories had earlier wanted to restore James with conditions, and his belief that if the Tories were successful, the conditions would be allowed to dissolve. It should be recalled that Morrice reported that the plan had been laid aside, but not abandoned, because of doubts about the loyalty of the English army. It should be remembered also that on January 26, just three days before Falkland's speech, Morrice predicted that the Tories would "revive" their scheme and "surprise the House with it," perhaps "under colour of limiting the prince more than any other kings have been if they should proclaim him king." [37] Burnet held a similar view of the Tory interest in identifying the rights of the nation. Pointing out that the idea of restricting the monarch was inconsistent with the doctrine of unconditional allegiance, he declared that it was advanced "in compliance with the humour of the nation," [38] not because it reflected Tory political convictions.

Finally, a pamphlet sympathetic to the Whigs leveled the charge that James's friends "will use all their art . . . to embroil the Convention in schemes of reform so as to distract the nation and recall the king in the turmoil." [39] If politically astute Whigs could predict that confusion and division would be likely consequences of Falkland's project, equally politically astute and experienced Tory members were surely aware of such a possibility.

As for the Whigs, their motivations in promoting a claim of rights were also manifold. They regarded a declaration of rights as a means of forestalling a mob uprising. Colonel Birch predicted that "discontents will rise much higher" if nothing is done but fill the throne. [40] They also saw tactical advantages to the project. Like the Tories, they must have known that the near unanimity on the abdication and vacancy resolution concealed profound reservations. It will be recalled that in the debate Temple had suggested the need to give reasons in support of the thesis that James had abdicated by his maladministration. Then he had said, "When you come to give reasons, you will satisfy the nation that King James has rendered himself inconsistent with government."[41] John Hampden spoke to the same point when he endorsed Falkland's project, saying, "[The nation] will ask why the king has abdicated the government."[42] Identifying grievances and rights could be regarded as a way of strengthening the abdication and vacancy resolution. The grievances of the nation were the proof of "abdication" and "vacancy." Moreover, in the process of identifying the nation's grievances, the Whigs would have an opportunity to name and punish their political enemies, who, during the reign of Charles II, had shared responsibility for the violations they complained about under James. Sacheverell, if not the author at least a proponent of the so-called "Sacheverell clause" introduced a year later with the intent of depriving Tories of place and office for seven years, urged the Convention to look backwards a long way, at least twenty years, to the reign of Charles II, when Tories dominated the administration, to discover grievances.[43] He charged that members of the Cavalier Parliament had received pensions, bribes, and offices in return for supplying the crown with ample revenue. Serjeant Maynard also stressed that members of former parliaments were corrupt, saying pointedly that he "could name them."[44] In like manner, Harbord thought that the "principal thing is to make examples" of men who had violated the laws.[45] Temple also believed that such persons should be called to account,[46] while Boscawen declaimed that "arbitrary power is ill in a prince, but abominable to one another."[47] One of William's Dutch associates reported that Sir Rowland Gwynne, a former Exclusionist who had returned from exile in Holland, was ready "to go for many people in Parliament."[48] Vengeance against the king's ministers and parliamentary pensioners was one reason for opening an inquiry into the nation's grievances. Scholars are mistaken, in my view, to declare that James's government was not ministerial and that dismay at corruption played no role in the indictment against him.[49]

In still another way, political strategy figured in both Tory and Whig endorsement of Falkland's proposal. Both sides regarded the setting out of grievances and rights as a protection against the Dutch prince, who, it was certain, would have a role — still undefined — in England's government. This consideration was not directly voiced in debate — political self-interest dictated otherwise — but it was present. For example, it was inherent in the eagerness with which members denied that they distrusted the prince. On the Whig side Garroway expressed confidence that William would not "take it ill" if conditions were set forth to secure the nation in the future.[50] Birch thought that a declaration would enhance the "strength and credit" of the assembly.[51] Capel declared that far from being a "prejudice to the crown," a statement of grievances was a "security to it"; indeed, he said, the crown was indebted to the day's proceedings.[52] For the Tories, Falkland protested that he had no doubts at all about William and Mary, and that what was done before the crown was even offered "will be no argument of distrust."[53] Contemporary observers also implied that fear of the Dutch "deliverer" was present in the action the Convention had undertaken. Morrice explained that "Boscawen and some men of his principles" (i.e., Whig principles) favored Falkland's proposal "only to avoid the imputation of betraying the nation, in case the succeeding king should strain the prerogative beyond the law."[54] Edward Harley, a supporter of William's, reported that the step was taken because "for general satisfaction it was judged most prudent" to secure the nation's rights before the king was declared.[55] Redressing grievances before declaring the king, then, was a kind of insurance against the prince, whose attitudes and future policies were on January 29 still to some degree unfathomed. Despite efforts to create a favorable image, William himself was not well-known outside a small circle, and his reign as Stadtholder of the Netherlands gave no proof of an abiding concern for the liberties and rights of the Estates-General, the cities, or the "people," a point which his foes had stressed in tracts and pamphlets. Moreover, England and Holland were commercial rivals, and while the relationship between the two countries had been cordial for over a decade, men with long memories — and there were many of those in the Convention — could recall when the two states were at war and Dutch prints had attacked England viciously.[56] Besides, William was a foreigner, however close his connection to the Stuarts. Tested only indirectly in English politics, William must have seemed to many M.P.'s a force which prudence dictated should be subject to some restraint. It will be remembered that the English authors of the prince's *Declaration of Reasons* stressed that same point.

But the most important reason for Whigs to support Falkland's proposal was the opportunity it offered to reform the government in ways they and their progenitors had been discussing for decades. Echoing the title of the tract *Now is the Time,* John Hampden maintained that "now is the time" to act when the nation is "still free and not tied by oaths" to a king, while another speaker thought that "all the world will laugh at us, if we make a half-settlement."[57] Some Whigs called for reform in extravagant terms. One (Sacheverell) asked for a general overhaul of all the legislation since the Restoration, declaring that he could not find "three laws, from twenty years upwards, that deserve to be continued."[58] Another (Williams) recommended searching beyond the Conquest for guidance; there is, he said, "original contract in your votes."[59] And a third, John Hampden, asserted, "'Tis necessary to declare the Constitution and rule of government," with a view to establishing that the king was one of three estates and therefore subordinate to the other two, lords and commons.[60] Whig spokesmen went beyond generalities. Early in the debate, Temple presented a lengthy programmatic statement that set out the specifics of the Whig position.[61] His proposals, reduced to "three heads essentially necessary," coincided with those drafted in preparation for the Convention by a less active member, Thomas Erle, whose manuscript provides additional proof of how widespread was the interest in changing the government.[62]

The first "head" that Temple presented in debate concerned Parliament. Of utmost importance was the assurance that Parliament should be called regularly and at frequent intervals and allowed to sit until it accomplished its business. Echoed by others, Temple lamented the weaknesses of the Triennial Act,[63] but Sacheverell explicitly criticized the royal prerogative to call and dismiss parliaments at pleasure, and pointed to "an old law" that prohibited the proroguing of Parliament until grievances had been redressed, which, he maintained, was still in force, and complained of its repeated violation.[64] Temple, drawing upon his lengthy experience in parliamentary elections, called for electoral reform, not in terms of the franchise or the secret ballot or redistribution of seats (as a pamphlet recommended), but to prevent regulation of borough corporations and coercion of electors by the king and his ministers through quo warranto proceedings. Temple regretted that corporations were "made tools to nominate whom they [crown and ministers] please." Other Whigs charged that James's ministers had corrupted the electoral system by removing the "most deserving and loyal people" if they opposed the designs of the ministry.[65] Extending the concern about elections, Sacheverell recommended that stiffer penalties be handed out for making false returns, a point which the large number of contested elections to the Convention may have underlined.[66] Temple sought to enlarge Parliament's power further by denying the power of the throne to pardon persons impeached by Parliament.[67] In effect, he and Boscawen were calling for making ministers accountable to Parliament.

The second head "essentially necessary" was to locate military power in time of peace in Parliament. Supported by Boscawen, Lee, Maynard, and Williams, men who had repeatedly protested Charles II's military policies in the 1670s and objected to James II's standing army in 1685, Temple argued that it was essential to "provide against a standing army without consent of Parliament" in peacetime. He asserted that until the reign of James II, an army was no part of the government.[68] Elaborating the point, Lee declared that "there was an opinion, formerly, of the Long Robe that must be exploded, 'That the king may raise what army he pleases, if he pay them.'" Charging that the minister who first advocated the doctrine was richly rewarded, Lee asserted that to allow the king such a right was tantamount to supporting slavery.[69] Reflecting a parliamentarian tradition that reached back at least to the Militia Bill/Ordinance Controversy of 1641/42, the proposal called for the removal of a royal prerogative which the king had always exercised and, in effect, for the repeal of a section of the Disbanding Act of 1660.[70]

Temple and others were also concerned about the inherent arbitrariness of the Restoration Militia Acts, which, Temple said, were used to "disarm all England."[71] Maynard also strongly criticized the Militia Bill, declaring that it had an abominable purpose — to disarm the nation so as to justify a standing army.[72] Williams, too, recommended that the Convention review the Restoration Militia Acts and, as he put it, "he in whose hands you will put command [power over it] should be our head."[73] He was asking for a review of the crown's prerogative power over the militia and intimating that that power should be placed in Parliament, just as radical pamphleteers had urged in tracts addressed directly to the Convention, and as the parliamentary opposition had promoted for decades. This recommendation cannot possibly be regarded as a declaration of old law, which Williams must have known. Accordingly, his advice, offered in the same speech, to "enact no new constitution, but . . . pursue the old" can only be seen as duplicitous.[74]

The third major issue in Temple's list was legal reform. He was especially concerned that the caliber of men appointed as judges be improved. Williams, in a scathing denunciation of the bench, iterated the point. "Weak judges will do weak things," he said; "their master commands them; they read no books, and know nothing to the contrary."[75] In a direct attack upon a prerogative of the king to appoint judges at pleasure, Temple urged that the tenure of judges be for life and that they have salaries, not fees. In a further attempt to reaffirm the primary role of Parliament, he also argued that, as in the past, great law cases should be sent to Parliament for decision, not to judges. Judges should have authority only to state the meaning of the law, not to make it. In blunt terms, Temple declared that he wanted Westminster Hall to have as little power as possible. Finally, he recommended that steps be taken to prevent sheriffs from making unjust returns of juries and to protect the individual against "strange fines."[76]

As the debate proceeded, members all around the assembly shouted out their suggestions for further legal and administrative reforms. Two M.P.'s recommended that the Act of Treason be reformed to require two witnesses to one fact in a charge of treason and to provide counsel in cases of treason and felony.[77] "Extravagant bail" and "Lord Lieutenants," cried one M.P., while another called out, "King's Bench," referring probably to the abuses associated with informations in that court.[78] Some members touched upon the need for reform of the revenue. They opposed taxation without parliamentary approval and condemned former parliaments for granting the king exorbitant sums, thereby making him independent.[79] Boscawen objected to a clause in the Militia Act for "trophy money" — that is, a tax on estates of a certain size — and charged that the methods of collection violated the law.[80] Colonel Birch urged that the hearth tax be abolished. Describing it as a "badge of slavery," Birch declared that taking it away would bring William "more strength than twenty armies."[81]

Personal suffering underlay some of the grievances. For example, Boscawen illustrated the arbitrariness of the Militia Acts by confiding that he himself had been unjustly disarmed and imprisoned.[82] Sacheverell, in an apparent reference to the quo warranto proceedings, complained that he was "informed against and fined for standing to my oath of the Corporation."[83] The article about informations in King's Bench, it was later admitted, was included "for the sake of" Williams.[84] Finally, Tipping, who wanted to assure that counsel be provided in cases of treason and felony, had himself been denied counsel in a felony case and suffered as a consequence. It is absolutely certain that many other M.P.'s had, over the last ten years or so, experienced some personal indignity attributable to the arbitrariness of the crown and that, accordingly, they looked upon Falkland's proposal as a chance to vindicate their own suffering and to seek personal reparation.[85]

The recommendations for reform suggested by Whig M.P.'s went far beyond those advocated by Tory members. Their proposals reflected long-standing issues, some of them repeatedly raised over the past forty years by men (these Whigs among them) who were appalled at the increasing centralization, bureaucratization, and absolutism of the Stuart government. Whig proposals included the reform of Parliament, the principle of "no standing armies in time of peace without the consent of Parliament," militia reform, the accountability of ministers, the tenure of judges, many details of legal reform, and certain aspects of local administration. Many of their suggestions were not old, established law, as they must have known, but a particular interpretation of the law or a political principle to which they adhered. If implemented, the changes would have caused a decisive shift of prerogative powers from the king to Parliament and the creation of a very different kind of kingship from that of the Stuarts. It is true that Tories and Whigs expressed identical views on several points, including the need to protect Parliament from arbitrary dismissal, the evilness of quo warranto, and the desirability of legal reform, but Whigs omitted reference to the dispensing power, the issue of greatest importance to Tories, and Tories, judging from their remarks, had no urgent convictions about the many issues Whigs recommended for reform. Yet, in the event, there was sufficient agreement between the two sides for Falkland's motion to succeed.

Some Whigs, however, were reluctant to proceed with the project, skeptical about its effect, and suspicious of its purpose. "Divers of the lawyers, . . . most signally Pollexfen, Maynard, Treby and Somers," Morrice reported, expressed misgivings.[86] How is it to be explained that the leaders of the rights committees were initially unenthusiastic about the proposal? Their reluctance did not proceed from theoretical repugnance, as they themselves protested.[87] Rather, it reflected legal and tactical considerations, a reading of national and international politics, and an understanding of Prince William. Suspicion that Falkland's proposal concealed a partisan tactic aimed at advancing the interests of the Tories was one reason for the reluctance of the lawyers. These Whig lawyers wanted to fill the throne immediately. Upbraiding the Convention in what must have been sneering tones, Pollexfen said, "To stand talking and making laws, and in the meantime have no government at all." He instructed members in English constitutional law, insisted upon the limits of the power of the Convention, and declared that law cannot be made without a king. Ridiculing the notion of fashioning a new Magna Charta, he dismissed the idea that all laws passed during the reign of James II should be annulled.[88] Maynard, too, heaped scorn on the idea of composing a new Magna Charta and of searching the records for an ancient constitution. "It has been said, we must go beyond the conquest. Puzzled to find what was law in Saxon times; [it is a] tedious and fruitless search."[89] So much for ancient precedents in the mind of this practical man of affairs! Naming a king was to him the essential step; without a king the nation was "without power, without justice, without mercy."[90]

Other reasons were adduced to justify setting aside the project until after the government was settled. There was no time, at this juncture of affairs, to identify grievances and reassert rights. Such a project would take five years, declared Maynard, with rhetorical extravagance.[91] In the meantime, Ireland might be destroyed (a consideration that would have weighed heavily with members whose estates there were threatened) and Holland "hazarded."[92] An unfavorable international reaction was certain. "If but a noise of this goes beyond sea, that you are making laws to bind your prince, it will tend to confusion," warned Pollexfen.[93] Predicting deeper divisions in a nation already divided, Pollexfen asserted that a likely consequence of the project would be the return of King James.[94] Anticipating a negative reaction, he pointed out that a statement of rights would require agreement from the upper House, and that the process of reconciling differences would be time-consuming.[95] Furthermore, the attitude of the clergy would compound the confusion. "Some of [them] are for one thing, some for another; I think," said Pollexfen, "they scarce know what they would have."[96] In the meantime, the nation stood exposed to an army still harboring men loyal to King James and in danger of mutiny and to mobs in London and elsewhere bent on mischief.[97] Pollexfen urged the Convention to learn from the experience of the Exclusion Crisis, when, he said, men "talked so long" that they "were sent away without doing anything."[98]

The irascible William Harbord joined the lawyers in opposing Falkland. But whereas they temporized their objections, he seemed willing to reject the project outright. If the army revolts, he pointed out, laws and declarations will offer no protection. The things needed to preserve England's liberties were a settled government and the sword of a king. The punishment of individuals who had broken the constitution would provide a more effective bulwark than "papers." All that was desired, he contended, could be achieved at another, more appropriate time, by withholding supply.[99] Morrice elaborated this point, saying that "we have our purses entirely in our own hands, and if [William] should prove unwilling might . . . deny him any revenue." Since no part of the revenue would continue, the prince would have to come to Parliament. For these reasons, Morrice thought that Falkland's proposal was "altogether unnecessary."[100] Withholding supply to achieve redress of grievances was, of course, a time-honored parliamentary tactic. After the Convention was transformed into a parliament, members who had promoted the Declaration of Rights became proponents of limiting William's revenue in ways Harbord and Morrice had mentioned.[101]

Further arguments against the project concerned William. Pollexfen suggested that the prince might object. "Your terms may be such at last," he said, "that when you come to offer the crown with new limitations, not known before, it may be rejected."[102] In view of William's repeated assertion that he came only to rescue the nation's rights and liberties, and his invitation to the Convention to declare those rights, it seems improbable that Pollexfen would have conveyed the threat of a rejection without William's approval or, at least, without knowledge of William's views. There is, however, no direct evidence that he held talks with the prince or his court about his response to a claim of rights. The lawyers also made the point that whatever the prince signed or swore to before he became king would not in strict law oblige him afterwards.[103] Accordingly, there was no point in presenting a statement of rights before settling the headship. Still further, it was argued that William would regard a claim of rights as a sign of ingratitude. This argument insinuated that support of the project might be a political liability in the future. Finally, the lawyers reassured the House that there was nothing to fear from William, and that there was no need of protective devices. Pollexfen pointed out that the prince "might have taken the crown [by force] instead of leaving us in debate." [104] Morrice indignantly defended William's integrity, asserting that the nation had William's word (in his manifesto) that he would pass any bill offered him.[105]

Proponents of the measure countered each of these objections. Colonel Birch declared that it would take no more than a day to mention the "heads" of the grievances and rights of the nation.[106] He and others reassured the assembly, on the grounds of William's manifesto, that the project would not displease the prince, indeed that it was necessary to fulfill William's purposes.[107] The prince's *Declaration of Reasons* and the coronation oath which he would take as king secured his future observance of a claim of rights, the assembly was told. One Whig went further, recommending that when the heads were presented to William, an oath should be administered.[108]

The lawyers' opposition melted away, and they themselves offered advice on how to handle to project. Maynard warned members to stick to the "obvious and apparent" and avoid too many particulars. "Don't overload your horse," he said.[109] Pollexfen presented a paper of eight heads which he had "collected" during the debate, including "Parliaments, the Revenue, . . . the Militia," and no pardons to a parliamentary impeachment.[110]

This long debate resulted in a motion to appoint a committee to bring in general heads of things that were absolutely necessary for securing the laws and liberties of the nation. Observers outside the House reported that the Commons intended that the rights should limit the powers of the future king. The Tory Reresby wrote that the reason for appointing a committee to bring in heads was that "before any person was named to fill the throne they would frame conditions upon which he should be accepted as king, and tie him up more strictly to the observance of them than other princes had been before." [111] The implication was that William would have to accept the claim of rights in order to receive the crown. The Presbyterian Morrice referred to the House's "debate of stipulations antecedent to the proclaiming king or queen" and explained that members "opened the nature of our government and Constitution, and what of right belongs to the crown, and what to the subject that both might know their due." He went on to say that the rights were to be "sworn to by the king and queen antecedent to their coronation." [112] Two other contemporaries also remarked that the stipulations were to be "subscribed to by that P and Prncss. that should ascend the throne." [113] Either by oath or signature, then, the new king and queen would oblige themselves to observe the claimed rights, whose effect was to limit royal power.

Thus, at the end of the two days' debate on January 28 and 29, the cornerstone of the revolutionary settlement had been laid. The abdication and vacancy resolution provided the justification for setting aside the king. The motion to appoint a committee to identify grievances and rights prepared the way for a claim of rights which would change the kingship. On both matters, despite concealed objections and different motivations, Tories and Whigs expressed general agreement. Although Tories took the initiative on both matters and evidence suggests that they favored restrictions on royal power to avoid a recurrence of conditions under James, their principal reason for promoting rights was to delay a decision on the headship of the government. It was Whigs who dominated the discussion both days.

11

January 30–February 2, 1689

The task of bringing in general heads of "such things as are absolutely necessary for securing the laws and liberties of the nation" was given to a committee of thirty-nine members, each one of whom was asked by the chairman to stand up as his name was called.[1] Notwithstanding objections because the day was the anniversary of the execution of King Charles I, the House instructed the committee to meet in the Speaker's Chamber at 8:00 A.M. on January 30 and to report "with all convenient speed," some members expressing the hope that the committee might be ready when the House reconvened that very afternoon.[2]

The inner dynamics of this committee are clouded, but not entirely hidden. In the absence of attendance lists, it is impossible to say with certainty which or even how many of the members attended the meetings. At least three members were required to be present, for Speaker Powle instructed "all or any three" of the committee to prepare the report.[3] That all thirty-nine men attended any meeting is unlikely, but that more than three appeared is reasonable in view of the excitement generated by the initiating debate, the importance of the issue, the interest promoted by the press, the close professional and familial connections among the members, and the high average attendance during the Convention. More, the presence of so many men in the House surely encouraged attendance at meetings of a committee responsible for such an important issue.[4]

Who, then, was likely to be present? First, it is virtually certain that Treby, whom the committee appointed chairman, was there. It was general practice in parliamentary procedure for the committee to choose the man who best understood the issue at hand to serve as chairman,[5] and since Treby presented the committee's report to the full House, his presence at meetings would be essential. Second, it is reasonable to think that John Somers, who was to be selected later as the chairman of the committee of twenty-one to prepare a response to the Lords' vote settling the crisis and who took the initiative in preserving the House's claim of rights, was also present. Third, it seems likely that the four men who performed specific tasks for Treby's and

Somers's committees over the next two weeks were there, for their selection by fellow members would indicate an above-average interest in the work of the committee. These four men were Wharton, who was sent to the House of Lords to request a conference meeting to reconcile differences between the two Houses on the draft declaration; Williams and Richard Hampden, both of whom reported to the full House what had transpired at conference meetings with the Lords; and Lord Falkland, who carried up to the peers the commons' response to their proposed amendments.[6] Williams's interest in banning informations,[7] first cited as a grievance at the committee meeting, lends further support to the hypothesis of his presence. Richard Hampden (if the record is complete) spoke more than any other member in the debates in the full House on the Declaration of Rights,[8] which reinforces the likelihood that he attended the committee's meetings. Fourth, it is possible that the other members who took an active part in subsequent debates on rights in the House also helped prepare the first draft. The most important of these men were Birch, Boscawen, Paul Foley, Howard, Lee, Temple, and Wildman.[9] That the hearth tax was much discussed in the committee meeting strongly suggests the presence of Birch, who alone had argued for dropping that tax on January 29. Temple's preparation of a speech organizing the rights into three manageable categories implies an interest sufficient to suggest that he attended the committee meeting. Fifth, it is arguable that Pollexfen, who had also prepared a paper of eight heads to guide the committee, appeared at the meeting. Morrice reported that the paper had been referred to the committee.[10] The emphasis on legal issues suggests that lawyers were present. Of those already arguably in attendance, Treby, Somers, Williams, and Pollexfen were lawyers. But in the debate on January 29 it was a nonlawyer, Thomas Tipping, who had suggested that the question of allowing counsel in cases of treason and felony should be a head, and since that issue was raised at the meeting, it is possible that Tipping was there. If the above reasoning is acceptable, at least fifteen men [11] attended the meetings of the committee. Of these fifteen, only two were Tories in 1688–89 — Falkland and Williams — and Williams, as explained, was a turncoat Whig who worked with Whigs on the claim of rights. Of the Whigs, all but three — Pollexfen, Temple, and Tipping — were radical Whigs.

The committee met on January 29 and 30 and compiled a lengthy list of twenty-three grievances and rights, including the points raised in debate and in printed tracts and also issues which had either been ignored or barely mentioned earlier.[12] Measures to protect the integrity of Parliament claimed first priority: that is, annual elections, prohibition against dissolving Parliament until it finished its business, protection against too lengthy parliaments, preservation of parliamentary privileges both during and in the intervals of their sitting, and prohibition of pardons of parliamentary impeachments. Members also stressed opposition to armies kept standing in peacetime without the approval of Parliament and declared the Militia Acts a grievance. They identified nonparliamentary taxes as a grievance and called for a new law to confirm Parliament's ancient right of taxation. They also urged reform of two taxes — the hearth tax and the excise — but decided to leave those matters to the full House. Furthermore, the committee recommended that future monarchs be required to take an oath to preserve the Protestant religion and the nation's law and liberties at the time of assuming the "administration of government." The coronation oath, they said, required change to remove references to the "holy church," references which Catholics maintained obliged the king to restore Popery.

Finally, the lawyers (almost certainly) focused on legal procedures in trials and aspects of judicial abuse. Thus, excessive bail, excessive fines, and "illegal punishments by whipping" were identified as grievances, the latter for the first time. The committee also demanded changes in the proceedings in treason trials. Members claimed that there should be two witnesses to the same fact and that the accused should be given a copy of the indictment, allowed counsel, and given time to prepare himself for trial. Much was also said about juries. One person charged that in every county the freeholders' books either did not contain the names of the "chief gentlemen," or "by private orders" they showed "crosses set against" the names of those who were "not for the turn of the court." Thus did the court assure, it was said, that no person of importance opposed to it would be named to a jury. The result was many grievous and illegal verdicts. The committee heard stories of men appointed to "labour juries," the trial of Lord Russell being stressed to illustrate the point. Members also called for many changes in the bench. Judges' tenure should be changed to good behavior, their salaries established and paid out of the public revenue, and their fees abolished. One member demanded that informations be disallowed in the Court of King's Bench — indeed, that proceedings in all crimes be by indictment. This issue, raised for the first time, reflected the special pleading of Williams,[13] and was to cause problems in both Houses later. Members complained about abuses in the appointment of sheriffs and called for measures that would assure that only the proper authorities (judges in Exchequer) would appoint sheriffs.

These private discussions of the rights committee are of uncommon importance, for they reveal what radical Whigs hoped to achieve. Their priorities were to protect the integrity of Parliament and strengthen the rights of individuals against judicial abuse. By contrast, Tories placed emphasis upon condemning the suspending and dispensing powers and the creation of the Commission on Ecclesiastical Affairs. Whigs also found these grievances offensive, but they did not rank them of first importance, as was shown earlier in their discussions of grievances in William's *Declaration of Reasons,* in rights and reform tracts, and in Convention debates. This fact makes significant their willingness to place first the suspending and dispensing powers and the creation of the Ecclesiastical Commission in the claim of rights, surely in order to appeal to Tories and win general approval of the document. Moreover, in these private discussions members condemned judicial abuse in specific terms — excessive bail, excessive fines, cruel and unusual punishments, informations, and the qualifications of jurors in treason trials. Almost certainly, it was the lawyers who promoted interest in these legal technicalities. Lawyers are commonly said to have played a prominent role in seventeenth-century parliaments generally and in the Revolution of 1688–89, but it has not previously been possible to show their contribution to specific articles in the Declaration of Rights.

Members concluded the meetings with a discussion of what should be the "proper work" of the committee and decided that it was to identify the grievances that had endangered the nation's "Constitution," declare the laws that were threatened, and then (significantly enough) declare "what further was necessary" to secure the Constitution. Accordingly, they ignored the earlier advice of lawyers to mention only a few rights and simply reaffirm the old constitution. On the contrary, their report, called the Heads of Grievances,[14] contained many clauses which were new law and claimed new rights. For example, it was new law to assert that the suspending and dispensing powers of the crown were illegal (clause 1). To deny the king authority to raise whatever troops he pleased during peacetime so long as he paid them was new law (clause 6). To say that Parliament should sit until its business was dispatched but not sit too long was to remove the royal prerogative to call and prorogue Parliament (clauses 10 and 11). To disallow pardons to be pleadable to an impeachment in Parliament was new law (clause 12). To change the tenure of judges to good behavior (rather than at the pleasure of the king) and to fix their salaries and pay them out of the public revenue were new laws (clause 18). To call for religious toleration for Protestants and for uniting all Protestants in public worship "as far as may be possible" was to ask for very new law indeed (clause 16). Other new rights and laws were the articles on jurors in treason trials (clause 21), on informations in the Court of King's Bench (clause 22), and on reforming treason laws and trial proceedings (clause 17).

There is no evidence that at this meeting members were troubled by the fact that the Heads of Grievances was, in seventeenth-century constitutional and political terms, a radical document whose claims (if implemented) would have decisively restricted the powers of the king and dramatically changed the nature of the government. They were, at this point, apparently eager to seize the opportunity to forward their political and legal principles. The lawyers and other experienced parliamentarians on the committee knew, of course, the instances in which they were claiming as law what they wanted to be law rather than what in fact was law. It was a time-honored tactic in seventeenth-century England for parliament men to win new rights by claiming to recover old law. Historians seem to have forgotten that fact in their ready acceptance of the assertion appearing in the final version of the Declaration of Rights, that the document was nothing more than a reaffirmation of ancient law.

There was danger, as M.P.'s in subsequent debates insisted, in presenting so many claims. So why did this committee of experienced parliamentarians

and lawyers take the risk? Haste alone is not the answer. For reasons discussed below, the report was not presented until February 2, so the committee had three days to refine it if they had wanted to do so. Rather, tactical
considerations, arguably, explain the large number of articles in the Heads of
Grievances. "Uncertain" how many of the heads the full House would agree
to, the committee included all the recommendations mentioned in debate to
ensure the widest possible support in the full House. Moreover, members
surely regarded this first draft as a trial balloon to test the reaction of Tories
in both Houses and the prince to see how much reform would be tolerated.

The committee timed the presentation of the report to the full House with
tactical considerations in mind. According to Morrice, the committee
brought the report to the House at 6:00 P.M. on January 30, and was told to
present it Friday morning, February 1. But Treby did not reach the House
on the appointed day until after the House had risen. Morrice explained his
tardiness by the fact that not only did he have a very bad cold, but that the
"wise men of the House" thought it prudent not to present the report until
"after one night's consideration because of the great disagreement that was
like to be between the two Houses upon the vote of the Lords not to agree
with the Commons that the throne was vacant."[15] Clearly, they did not want
to imperil the statement of rights by having it caught in the cross fire between
the two Houses over the amendments the lords wanted to make to the
January 28 resolution. Those amendments also reached the House of Commons on February 1 after it had risen.[16] Thus, the lower House was ready on
Saturday, February 2, for two momentous issues: the Lords' response to the
abdication and vacancy resolution, and the report of "things essential to be
redressed" to preserve the nation.

In the meantime, during the past four days, the House of Lords had been
debating at great length and with increasing warmth alternative ways to settle
the crisis. Before considering the peers' response to the Commons' resolution,
a brief statement about certain aspects of the House of Lords in the Convention is necessary.[17] As already noted, the Lords appointed Halifax Speaker
pro tempore, a step required by the absence of the lord chancellor. Halifax was
at this time a partisan of the prince, and his appointment, which was contested by Danby, gave some advantage to William's friends. These
friends — among whom were notably Delamere, Devonshire, Mordaunt,
Newport, and Wharton — numbered about fifty.[18] The other partisan group-
ings, already prefigured in the December meetings, comprised the peers who
favored a regency (loyalists) and those who wished to elevate Mary in her
own right (Maryites). Among the former were Turner, all the bishops except
London and Bristol, Clarendon, and Ailesbury; these men initially regarded
regency as a temporary expedient which would lead ultimately to James's
return. Also favoring regency were Nottingham, Pembroke, and Rochester,
who sincerely promoted it as a solution which would preserve the hereditary
monarchy. Their chief concern was for the kingship rather than for the

king.[19] Nottingham told both Burnet and Dijkvelt that he would be willing to make William regent for James's life, but that he could never agree that the crown was vacant.[20] Altogether, the lords favoring regency totalled about fifty-two and, it is now known, were able by their own strength to control the upper House from January 31 to February 6.[21] The third group, the Maryites, was led by Danby and included the bishop of London and Lord Fauconberg. Danby's squadron, as it was called, numbered only three to four lords, not six to eight, as previously thought; and their role in the several votes on the transfer of the crown was not of crucial importance. They did join with the revolutionary peers to defeat regency on January 29, but both Danby and Fauconberg voted on January 31 to offer the crown to William and Mary. By this vote they revealed their willingness to compromise their commitment to Mary as queen in her own right earlier than has been assumed.[22] Danby was elected chairman of the committee of the whole on the three successive days — January 29, 30, and 31 — that the peers debated the Commons' abdication and vacancy resolution. Fauconberg would serve as chairman of the Lords' rights committee, of which Danby was a member.

The high average attendance of the lords during the Convention testified to the importance attached to the proceedings. Out of an estimated total of 153 peers,[23] the average number present was 95 — 81 temporal peers and 14 spiritual lords.[24] During the critically important debates from January 29 through February 6, the average attendance increased to 103, with temporal peers averaging 88 and spiritual lords 15. Despite the absence of the archbishop of Canterbury, their titular leader, the bishops took an active part in the proceedings, one of their number, Turner, distinguishing himself for eloquent, well-prepared statements against the settlement favored by the Commons. It has been calculated that 116 individual peers attended the debates on the crown.[25]

The presence of so many peers also reflected the efforts of partisan forces. For example, by letter dated January 27, Halifax urged absent lords to hasten to London.[26] Nottingham importuned a lord to be present on January 29, the day appointed for the "great debate" on the nation.[27] Peers who supported William persuaded fellow lords who seldom if ever attended the meetings of the House to appear to vote for the abdication and vacancy resolution. Thus, the earl of Lincoln, who was thought to be half-mad and never attended the House, appeared on February 6, saying that he came to do whatever Lord Shrewsbury and Lord Mordaunt would have him do.[28]

William and his friends took other steps to win over a majority of the peers. When it became clear that the French ambassador was actively promoting divisions among the lords, William ordered him to leave England within twenty-four hours.[29] The prince, contemporaries reported,[30] repeatedly urged speedy resolution of the crisis, citing the dangers from Ireland, where many lords held property, and implying an intention to settle affairs there in the interests of Protestants. When London crowds insulted Tory peers as they entered Westminster, William put a stop to such activities.[31] The prince used his close Dutch advisers Bentinck and Dijkvelt to maintain contact with strategically placed lords. Thus, following a "secret" conversation with William, Dijkvelt had a long talk with Nottingham.[32] In the opinion of a Dutch observer, William's "friends" were working on his behalf.[33] It was thought by another Dutchman that the Lords' meeting of January 28 (when the Commons were debating the state of the nation) was held expressly to give opportunity to William's friends to plan in advance and to "prevail upon" peers who were thought unfriendly to the prince.[34] Burnet credited himself with having had a "great share . . . in the private managing" of the debates in the House of Lords, "particularly with many of the clergy, and with men of the most scrupulous and tender consciences." [35] Without offering specific proof, lords hostile to the prince accused him in print of using threats and promises to achieve the passage of the abdication and vacancy resolution.[36]

William himself summoned a group of peers to meet with him, probably on February 3, to tell them plainly what his requirements for the settlement were — namely, the crown of England, which he would be willing to share jointly with Mary, but with the administrative authority vested in himself alone.[37] This firm announcement was one of the factors that moved the lords finally to accept the abdication and vacancy formula. William was aware of the differences among the lords and sensitive enough to those differences to ask a Dutch emissary in London not to report them in his letters to Holland.[38] Finally, pressure on the lords to adopt a certain course of action was applied without much subtlety during the crisis of February 8–9, to be discussed.

The House of Lords, like the Commons, adhered to a policy of confidentiality for its proceedings, and like the debates of the Commons, news of the peers' discussions reached the public.[39] For example, the diarist John Evelyn surreptitiously eavesdropped on the debate of January 29 by positioning himself "by the prince's lodgings at the door of the lobby to the House." [40] Or again, the names of the peers who opposed the abdication and vacancy resolution in the vote of February 6 appeared in a broadside titled *The Names of the Lords Spiritual and Temporal, who deserted against the word Abducted* [sic], *and the Throne Vacant.*[41]

The debates on the crown were long and arduous, with the peers sitting till late at night and arguing at times so fiercely and passionately on all sides that, as mentioned before, bloodshed was feared.[42] The reports of bitterness and acrimony themselves suggest that the issues were thoroughly examined, and in the case of at least one debate — that of January 29 — a contemporary specifically reported that the chairman managed it "fairly and equally." [43]

On January 29, the Lords received the abdication and vacancy resolution. A number of Tory peers — principally Clarendon, Nottingham, Rochester, and Turner — seized the initiative in the debate, rejected the Commons' resolution, and proposed instead a regency.[44] For our purposes the main interest of this discussion lies in the peers' general assault on the abdication and vacancy vote. Clarendon maintained that the concept of "abdication" violated the legal maxim that the king never dies and the oath of allegiance. Arguing that it would please neither the "world abroad nor [the] major part" of the nation, the earl appealed to William's *Declaration of Reasons,* a portion of which he read, to support his argument. Bishop Turner dismissed the resolution in an acid remark calculated surely to remind members of the trial of the earl of Strafford during the Civil War. He said the Commons' vote was like accumulative treason, no particular of which amounted to a forfeiture. Pembroke questioned not only whether a king could abdicate, but whether James really had done so. He used the analogies of a seaman throwing his goods overboard in a storm to save his life and of a man running from his house when it was on fire. In neither case did a man renounce his goods or house. Nottingham argued that a king cannot forfeit his crown, nor a parliament "take a forfeiture," and maintained that if James has forfeited the right of his heirs, then "the whole constitution is dissolved and every man has equal right and equal power." Nottingham pointed out that in any case James had not abdicated the crown of Scotland and that if Scotland dissented from steps the Convention took, it would be a genuine danger to the settlement. Dismissing the "pretence of the late times" that the king was a coordinate body with the Lords and Commons, he denied that a king may be called to account as a trustee of certain powers.[45] Notwithstanding the eloquence and cogency of the regencyites' argument and the support of all the bishops except Compton, the regency proposal lost by a narrow margin of two or three votes,[46] thereby preserving the abdication and vacancy resolution for further consideration.

On January 30, the Lords began a systematic review of the Commons' resolution paragraph by paragraph. The words "breaking the original contract between king and people" provoked, according to Burnet, "great disputes." Some lords denied absolutely that any such thing existed. Where was it kept? they inquired. How could it be found? If it existed and was so valuable, how could it have been lost?[47] The peers' legal counsel were consulted on "what the original contract is, and whether there be any such or not."[48] The lords had appointed nine lawyers to "advise them on legal matters," choosing men known to adhere to Whig political principles.[49] Among them was Sir John Holt, who would serve on the rights committee in the House of Commons, and Sir Robert Atkyns, who had published tracts against the royal dispensing power. All nine lawyers responded in favor of the concept of "original contract."[50] Freely admitting that they could find no such word in "books or cases; not anything that touches on it," they agreed that nonetheless there must be an original contract. They appealed for support to early English laws, legal and constitutional authorities (such as Fortescue, Hooker, Coke, Selden, and Grotius), and James I's comment in 1609 about the existence of a paction between king and people. As noted above, Atkyns came closer than did the other counsel to suggesting that the original contract "must refer to the first original of government," implying thereby that it was agreed to in the mist of time, not at some specific point, as

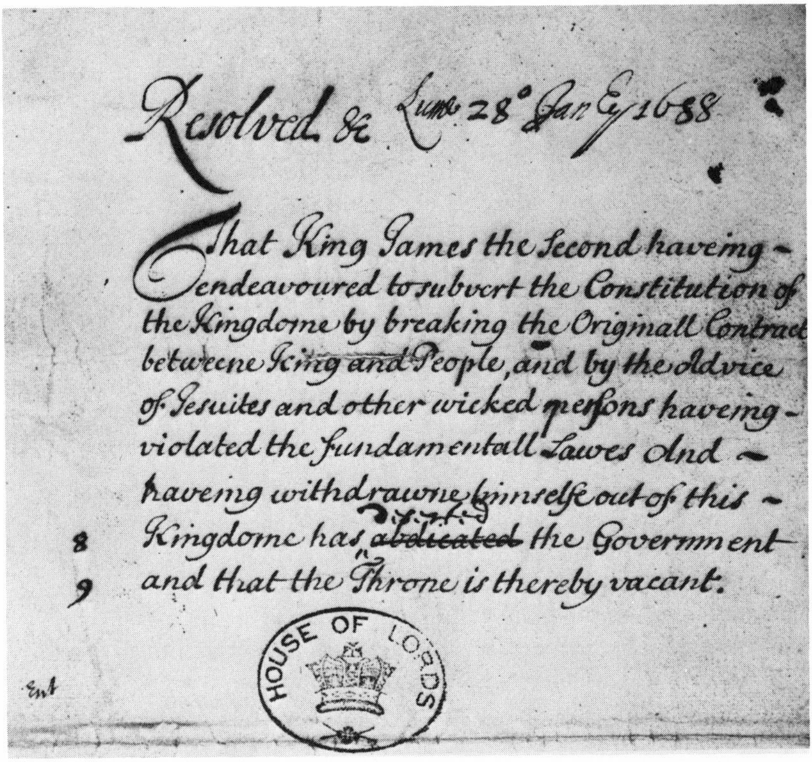
Resolved &c Lunae 28° Jan: 1688

That King James the Second haveing
endeavoured to subvert the Constitution of
the Kingdome by breaking the Originall Contract
betweene King and People, and by the Advice
of Jesuites and other wicked persons haveing
violated the fundamentall Lawes And
haveing withdrawne himselfe out of this
8 Kingdome has abdicated the Government
9 and that the Throne is thereby vacant.

Figure 2. "Abdication" and "vacancy" resolution, showing proposed amendments by Lords. The abdication and vacancy resolution, passed by the House of Commons on January 28, 1689, was a cornerstone in the revolutionary settlement. It provoked intense debate for three days in the House of Lords. As shown, the lords tried to amend the language by changing "abdicate" to "desert" and by deleting "vacancy" altogether. They finally accepted the Commons' language late on the evening of February 6, 1689, in a compromise that removed entirely other controversial clauses. (Courtesy of the House of Lords Record Office.)

for example when the Germans settled England or when the king takes an oath at his coronation, the argument laid out most fully by William Petyt. Atkyns did not imply that he adhered to the view expressed in the House of Commons that when the contract was broken, power reverted to the people. In fact, no counsel addressed that question directly, an omission which could not have pleased Their Lordships.

Although a contemporary reported that the lawyers' explanation of "original contract" satisfied everyone, the peers in fact sat until 10:00 P.M. and had a "very warm" debate.[51] The words that the king had "subverted the government" were also closely scrutinized.[52] In the end, the lords voted 54 to 43[53] to agree to the first clause, but two days later the Dutch ambassador reported that an effort was underway to substitute "breaking the coronation oath" for the words "breaking the original contract."[54]

The lords turned next to the second clause of the Commons' resolution, which read: "by the advice of Jesuits and other wicked persons having violated the fundamental laws." Although a contemporary intimated that there were objections to the words "having violated the fundamental laws," the clause was "carried . . . by eleven" votes.[55] But these words did not appear in the February 7 draft prepared by Treby's committee, probably because the Whig leadership had got wind of the objection and wanted to propitiate the Tory peers. The peers also accepted clause 3 — "having withdrawn himself out of the kingdom."

The fourth clause of the resolution contained one of the key terms. It read: "has abdicated the government." After listening to a reading of William's letter to James in which he advised the king to remove himself from London and go to Ham House, the lords voted to substitute the word "deserted" for "abdicated."[56] At this time they did not prepare a statement of reasons for the proposed amendment, which removed a central term of the Commons' resolution.

The final clause of the Commons' motion — "that the throne is thereby vacant" — was held over for debate to the next day. On January 31, the peers again engaged in a furious discussion lasting until "near twelve." First, they defeated a motion to declare William and Mary king and queen. The vote was 47 for and 52 against the motion, with the majority of Danby's group — Danby himself, Bishop Compton, and Fauconberg — voting to declare William and Mary king and queen.[57] Second, the Lords took up the question of the vacancy of the throne. They appealed in vain to their legal assistants for advice about the implications of a vacancy. Every one of the lawyers declined to comment, on the grounds that it was a matter for the lords to decide. Said Holt, "It is the main question which your Lordships are to determine." Another lawyer ventured the less than helpful observation that there was a possibility of a vacancy if the entire royal family became extinct.[58] All the bishops, even Compton, opposed the idea of "vacancy," provoking the charge that they were to blame for the nation's miseries during the past sixty years and the intimation that they should be driven from the kingdom. They rejoined that their opponents were "rebels and traitors."[59] After further "peevish and angry" remarks from radical Whig peers (Delamere declared that he would fight "with his sword in his hand" if James returned), regency-ites and Maryites, stressing that a "vacancy" transformed the hereditary monarchy into an elective one and that there were dangers from Scotland and Republicans in such a step, combined to defeat "vacancy" by 55 to 41.[60] The Lords thus proposed to amend the Commons' formula by deleting altogether the second key term. With these critically important amendments, the peers returned the resolution to the lower House.

On Saturday, February 2, then, the Lords' amendments to the abdication and vacancy resolution and the report from Treby's committee awaited debate. Tension and excitement marked the scene at Westminister. One man was arrested in the Painted Chamber for dispersing papers recommending a commonwealth; another man, for threatening to kill the prince. So great was public interest in the Commons' debate that the Speaker's Chamber and the Gallery had to be cleared of persons who were not members of the House.[61] Speaker Powle introduced Treby's report first, thus giving members the opportunity to debate it before becoming embroiled in the contentious questions surrounding the abdication and vacancy resolution. In contrast to the passionate discussion on January 29, the discussion was brief and low-keyed. Tories took no part. If Falkland and Seymour were pleased by the form which the committee gave the recommendations they had expressed so forcefully the preceding Tuesday, they did not reveal it. If Musgrave felt that the report vindicated the abdication and vacancy resolution, on which grounds he had endorsed the project four days earlier, he did not comment. Their silence reinforces the theory that their original emphatic support of the project contained a partisan ingredient. No one mentioned the political principles underlying the call to determine what powers to give to the king. Members ignored the implications of the articles for the nation's constitution and operation of government. The fact that many clauses were patently not a reaffirmation of old law at all, but rather the assertion of new law, was overlooked. Rather the discussion[62] concerned head 22, which read: "Informations in the Court of King's Bench to be taken away." As explained above,[63] an information was a legal instrument by which an officer of the crown could bring a person to trial without appearing before a grand jury and presenting an indictment. Members of the rights committee objected to the article as drawn. The main criticism was that the language was too general. Advised Maynard, "Say what informations are a grievance, and what not." Pollexfen and Hampden felt that taking away all informations in King's Bench might be "mischievous." Finch wanted to apply the prohibition to other courts. In what must have been exasperated tones, Birch exclaimed, "If this takes so much time here, what will it do in the House of Lords? Therefore pen it clearly." Placed on the defensive, Treby sought to justify the clause, saying that he could make "a long discourse" on the evilness of informations and that the abuse was not confined to the Court of King's Bench. He explained that the committee deliberately chose to avoid particulars, counting on a future law to handle the matter. But he did not agree to modify the article, and head 22 remained unchanged in the second draft of the committee's report.

Five other clauses were added. One, introduced by Edward Bigland, a well-known lawyer from the Midlands and a friend of Sacheverell,[64] prohibited the buying and selling of judicial offices, including the office of sheriff. Other M.P.'s, including Treby, extended the point to all offices. Although Speaker Powle was moved to point out that "some offices are as lawful to sell as a man's private inheritance," the general prohibition appeared in the committee's second draft, thereby testifying again to the presence of a concern to combat corruption. Two more technical legal matters were introduced, one regarding the writs of habeas corpus and mandamus, the other voiding the granting or promising of fines and forfeitures before conviction and providing penalties for persons who procured them. Hampden bitterly criticized fines "as a most mischievous thing." Boscawen agreed, saying that the practice "encourages perjury" and insisting upon a penalty for "whoever begs . . . a grant." Williams wanted to void all grants of fines for a misdemeanor. At this, the Speaker once more intervened to caution the House against extending the list: "Many of these things are against the law," he said, "but in these heads you only renew your claim." Nonetheless, the clause was added. Finally, two heads calling for redress of abuses connected with levying and collecting the hearth tax and the excise won approval of the House.

Although Grey described the report as "Heads of the Articles of Government," no such claim was made by M.P.'s at this time. Pollexfen asserted that the articles under discussion were "but heads, and no law," reflecting his belief that the Convention did not possess the power to make law and his certain knowledge that many clauses did indeed go beyond a reaffirmation of old law (no lawyer so skilled as he could have been unaware of that). Others echoed that idea, implying that a regular bill would be introduced later. Sacheverell, for example, described the report as "in the nature of a declaratory petition of right," and as things "laid down as heads only." The reason for Sacheverell's unaccustomed moderation — in sharp contrast to his call on the twenty-ninth for a repeal of all laws since the Restoration — is not clear. It is possible, however, that he was sending William and his friends the message that other radical Whigs would also disingenuously convey, namely, that the claim of rights contained nothing but old law.

The draft was received, according to Morrice, "with much unanimity," more than was expected. The *London Intelligence,* reporting in general terms on parliamentary events, optimistically predicted a settlement in "a few days." [65] In fact, no decision was made on the disposition of the report. The general concurrence — or absence of contention — may have testified to a general enthusiasm for the report, but it seems more likely that it reflected the fact that no difficult questions were raised in the debate. Tories who had expressed their views on reform and limitations of the king so forcefully on the twenty-ninth and who might have been expected to enliven the discussion had nothing to say. The limited character of the discussion is further explained by the fact that members were more deeply interested in the discussion of the lords' amendments to the abdication and vacancy resolution, in other words, in what was for many the more pressing issue of settling the headship.

Indeed, so fragile was the commitment of some Whigs to the idea of drawing up a statement of rights that in the middle of the discussion, a mob organized by Lord Lovelace and other enthusiastic partisans of the prince [66] presented a petition from the citizens of London and Westminster to declare Prince William and Princess Mary king and queen immediately. [67] Neither this petition nor any other presented to the Convention called for setting out the grievances and rights of the nation. The "true" purpose of the petition, Morrice explained, was to persuade the lords to agree to the Commons' abdication and vacancy resolution, for unless they did, civil war was feared.[68] The opposition of the bishops had given "great offence," and their vote on regency was interpreted as a desire to restore James.[69] The "people of London" threatened to "make shortskirts" out of the "longskirts [the bishops]," who, they said, were playing "the devil."[70]

For reasons explained by a contemporary, the petition was not signed,[71] but was carried to both houses in the rain by a "great" number of persons who acted in a "tumultuous manner."[72] Both the House of Lords and the House of Commons refused to hear the petition on the grounds that it was unsubscribed and also for the reason that to accept such a petition would compromise the freedom of parliamentary debate and subject the deliberations of the Convention to pressure from the mob.[73] In the face of this rebuff, an effort was made to get the petition signed. Copies of the petition were printed and circulated in London coffeehouses on Saturday evening and at other places the next day. It was said that 15,000 signatures were collected and that 10,000 men would deliver the signed petition on Monday, February 4.[74] Hearing of this and fearing that some peers would be influenced to concur with the Commons, unidentified conservative lords, according to Morrice, urged William to order that the petition be suppressed, promising repeatedly that they would concur with the Commons. William agreed, lest his foes should excite the mob, claim that they "were driven away from Parliament," as they said James was forced out of England, or charge that the Convention was unable to act freely. At the request of the prince, who told Lovelace not to proceed further with the petition, the mayor of London issued a printed order on February 4 that the petition, on pain of arrest, should be suppressed.[75] The episode is of interest on three counts. It showed willingness on the part of William's English adherents to enlist the support of persons outside socially and politically elite groups and to bring pressure to bear on M.P.'s who were making the critical decisions. It revealed that some radical Whigs in both Houses were willing to go forward with resolving the issue of the headship without presenting the claim of rights. And it demonstrated still again the political acuteness of the prince.

William and his close advisers, however, apparently reconsidered their handling of this episode. An unsigned letter, drafted for the prince's signature and addressed to the London corporation, called for a meeting of the "great body of Commons" at the Guildhall to "remove all misunderstandings" about the order to suppress the petition. The letter explained that the prince's request to the mayor implied no disrespect to the citizens of London nor intention of preventing them from presenting their grievances by petition or otherwise "as the law does allow," but was meant only to stop "tumultuous assemblies with petitions that might seem to disturb the Conventions." It praised Londoners for their "zeal for Protestantism," thanked them for their loan, promised to repay it "with interest," and vowed to undertake to advance their trade and the flourishing state and condition of the city and nation alike.[76] Whether this letter was actually sent or not is immaterial to the point that William's court was concerned enough that the suppression of the petition might have antagonized the citizens of London to draft it. Such concern was compatible with the efforts of the prince and his friends to bring his case directly to the people.

In contrast to the debate on Treby's report, the discussion of the lords' amendments to the abdication and vacancy resolution was lengthy and strenuous.[77] On the one hand, Tories who had argued against the resolution on January 28, urged agreement with the lords. They insisted that (1) "union" between the two Houses was essential under the circumstances and that the Commons would be blamed for a breach; (2) "desertion" was indeed the more proper word to describe what had happened; and (3) there was no difference in the meaning of the two terms. Sawyer, as he had done earlier, disingenuously equated them, declaring, "All that the Lords mean by 'Abdication,' you mean by 'Desertion.'"[78] Finch concurred with this reading of the terms.

On the other hand, Whig spokesmen insisted upon keeping the term "abdicate." Repeating arguments and learned references made in previous debates, they maintained that that word properly expressed all the premises of the resolution — namely, that "King James had subverted the fundamental laws, violated the original contract, and withdrawn himself," which, they were at pains to point out, the lords had accepted. They stressed that although James had signed no paper, his violations of the law were an "abdication" of the government. This point, it must be underlined, was the link between the Heads of Grievances and the Commons' resolution. Although Treby's draft was not mentioned (at least in the surviving accounts), it is impossible that members were unaware that the draft just discussed set out the specific violations to which the resolution referred. Whigs rejected the word "deserted" because it meant that the throne was still full and it left open the possibilities of a return of the king or the elevation of Mary alone. Complaining that the lords refused to identify who was sitting on the throne, at least two Whig members of Treby's committee were willing to fill the vacancy immediately without presenting a statement of rights. Said one, "The best way is to go on and fill it up, and put all out of doubt."[79]

Fortunately for the fate of the claim of rights, the House took no such step. Instead, members rejected the Lords' amendments and, upon Temple's motion, appointed a committee to meet at five o'clock that afternoon to draft reasons for the rejection.[80] Of the twenty-seven members appointed to that committee, twenty-one were also on Treby's committee. The other six included William Palmes, who was to play a part on February 7 in the passage of the Declaration of Rights, and Sir John Holt. The partisan character of this committee (there were only four Tories),[81] the strong effort of the Tory M.P.'s in the debate of February 2, and the intransigence of the House of Lords at this time are important to the subsequent shaping and movement of the Heads of Grievances.

12
February 2–6, 1689

❖

For the next four days — February 2 through February 6 — the Heads
of Grievances and the abdication and vacancy resolution moved in
tandem, the former awaiting decision on the latter. Until late in the
evening of February 6 the two Houses were deadlocked over the resolution.
In the meantime, on February 4, the lower House initiated a step to amend
significantly the first draft of the claim of rights. These debates help to
explain the wording and form of the final version of the Declaration of
Rights.

On February 4, the House of Lords received the Commons' reasons for
adhering to the terms "abdicated" and "throne vacant" and turned once more
to their learned counsel for a ruling on the word "abdicated." [1] The Whig
lawyers were as unhelpful on this term as they had been earlier on the word
"vacant." Declaring that "abdicated" was unknown to English law but that it
signified "somewhat more than 'desert,'" they offered the duplicitous interpretation that it applied only to the king himself and did not extend to his
heirs. Thus, they adopted the meaning that Sawyer had sought to give the
term, not the one employed by its original proponents in the lower House.
Notwithstanding the lawyers' interpretation of the word, the regencyites and
Maryites combined again to reject "abdication" and to delete "vacancy." [2]
Explaining themselves in a written statement prepared by a committee
chaired by Nottingham, the peers vowed willingness to "secure the nation
against the return of James," but rejected "vacancy" on the grounds that it
made the crown elective. Maintaining that a king has no power to bar the
right of his heirs to the throne, they argued that allegiance was due to the next
heir, which, setting aside James's son, was Princess Mary. The peers also
insisted that "deserted" should replace the word "abdicated," and returned the
resolution to the lower House with the proposed amendments intact. Nottingham's paper testified to the newly found strength of the Maryites at this
time. [3]

Still another long debate, notable for revealing the strength of William's foes and the willingness of his friends to retreat from positions occupied the previous week, took place on February 5 in a crowded House of Commons. The Maryite M.P.'s[4] came out in force to support the lords' amendments to the resolution. Agreeing that the abdication and vacancy formula transformed the monarchy into an elective kingship and thus destroyed England's ancient constitution, they argued that to uphold it invited war with Scotland and enmity from "all the crowns in Christendom." As a consequence, Protestants the world over would suffer. At home the "mob may . . . overrun the property and standing of their betters." Asserting that the workable and legal solution to the crisis was to make Mary queen in her own right, they dilated on the advantages of so doing and also stressed that since William, upon his own admission in his manifesto, had not come for the crown, he could not object. To elevate him to the throne in the place of his wife was to "sully" his glory.[5]

On the other hand, radical Whigs argued for adhering to the resolution. Colonel Birch delivered the most impassioned and extreme rebuttal. Declaring that a statute of Queen Elizabeth and other laws had given Parliament the right to dispose of the crown, he implored the House to "say but where your power is, and the debate is at an end. Take it into your hands, where God, in his Providence has given it you. . . . The power of disposing of the crown is in the Lords and Commons; and by virtue of that power fill the vacancy." He reminded the House that there were heirs to the throne "all up and down" Europe, and "poor England, for want of speaking one plain word, will be ruined." Reassuring members, he employed an idea that earlier Civil War tracts had used, namely that by divine right Parliament cannot do an unjust thing.[6] Wharton concurred with these radical sentiments, expostulating that he owned driving James out and would do it again.[7] But other supporters of the formula were at pains to blunt the implications of Birch's remarks. For example, Temple and Pollexfen protested that "no man goes about to change the monarchy." "No man ever dreamed of [making it elective]."[8] Radical Whigs also disclaimed the idea that the crown was elective. Boscawen said as much, but admitted that in an "intricate" case, Parliament had the power to fill the crown. Even Howard, who on January 28 had talked of the "divine right of the people," on February 5, counseled members to let their own interests predominate. Noticing that the lords were themselves guilty of electing a king if they chose Mary over the baby, he queried, "Is it not elective, to take one and leave another?" With Pollexfen, Howard interjected a practical note, surely reflecting what he knew of William's views, namely that the prince was unlikely to accept a role subordinate to his wife.[9]

The vote on adhering to the word "abdicated" passed without a division. Why the Tories in the lower House were willing, after their enthusiastic endorsement of the Lords' report, to accept the term is not clear, but it may well have reflected the fact that "abdicated" could be variously interpreted, as Sawyer had all along maintained and as the peers' legal advisers intimated. On the motion to adhere to the word "vacant," the Tories, their confidence inflated by the volume of the noes in a voice vote — a volume designedly augmented by the Whigs — were willing to divide. Unfortunately for them, the vote was 282 to 151, and the effect was, of course, to reveal who was opposed. The appearance, in defiance of the rules of the House, of a manuscript list of the names of M.P.'s who had voted against "vacancy" sharpened their irritation and chagrin. In this instance, the Whigs had the better of their opponents. By encouraging a division and circulating a list, they aimed, clearly, to compromise the political futures of the Tories.[10]

On February 6, the disagreement between Whigs and Tories in both Houses and between the two Houses over the abdication and vacancy resolution reached a climax in the famous conference committee meeting in the Painted Chamber. The meeting attracted so much interest that the managers were unable to make their way through the crowd of "strangers" and M.P.'s, who defied all orders to leave until the clerk of the House of Commons appeared with the serjeant-at-arms.[11] In conformity with the rules of both Houses, the debate, which lasted between three and four hours,[12] was closed; but one Mr. Blaney, who was in a "private place to take down all that was said," produced a very full account.[13] Macaulay described the conference as a "mere form" and the arguments as "verbal and technical."[14] Later historians have generally accepted Macaulay's judgment.[15] In fact, a close examination of the terms to be used in a statement of such great importance was to be expected. The participants did not think they were engaged in verbal quibbling. Said Nottingham, "It is not a question barely about words, but things, which are now disputing."[16] The underlying political principles were plain to them and to any careful reader of the debate. Although the discussion contained no new points, it admirably summed up the arguments that had been made in both Houses since the Convention opened. The managers chosen for the conference represented the majority opinion in each House. Among the twenty-two M.P.'s, nineteen of whom were on the rights committee, were Birch, Boscawen, Richard Hampden, Howard, Maynard, Pollexfen, Somers, Treby, and Wildman. Only one Tory, Falkland, was appointed.[17] The lords named sixteen peers, all but one of whom favored regency.[18] Neither Danby nor Halifax was among them. Clarendon, Nottingham, Pembroke, Rochester, and Turner were the only peers, if the record is complete, who spoke.

The rhetorical talents of lords and M.P.'s were evenly matched. If Treby spoke well, avoiding excessive legal references, using effective analogies, and making a prosopopeia of James II, as he had done in the debate of January 28, Nottingham "well answered" him.[19] Somers, who stood next to Treby, was also singled out for speaking "very learnedly," but four different peers challenged the point the young lawyer made, and both Treby and Maynard rescued him from embarrassment.[20] The aged Maynard, who entered the debate more than anyone else, was said to have tried to be witty, but "came off very bungling."[21] Most of the spokesmen for the Commons were lawyers, but the lords, although not professionally trained in the law, effectively disputed their legal interpretations. For example, Nottingham, while professing admiration for Pollexfen's legal knowledge, suggested that a point he had made was not pertinent to the issue, differed with Holt on the law about trusts, and countered Maynard's contention that the legal maxim *Nemo est haeres viventis* (there is no heir to the living) prevented a regular succession to the throne with the argument with the king may be dead civilly and that there was no distinction in law between a civil and natural death with respect to successors.[22]

The debate is important to the drafting of the Declaration of Rights because of remarks about the terms of the abdication and vacancy resolution, which, it will be recalled, disappeared from the final version of the document. Clarendon firmly opposed the phrase "breaking the original contract." It was a "language," he said, "that has not been long used in this place; nor known in any of our law books, or public records: It is sprung up, but as taken from some later authors, and these none of the best received."[23] Disputing the interpretation of the Lords' legal counsel, the earl denied, on the grounds that the heir succeeds at the moment of the death of a king, that the coronation oath was part of an original contract. Admitting the existence of an original contract at the time government was first instituted, Turner insisted that a fundamental feature of that contract was that "king, lords, and commons in parliament assembled" had the authority to make or alter laws. Neither the Lords nor the Commons alone had the power to make law, nor could the two Houses together without the king. Arguing that not every breach of the original contract voids it nor gives the people the power to change the succession, Turner maintained that laws made subsequently to the original contract were "as much a part" of it "as the observing old" laws. Thus, the statutes establishing the oath of allegiance to the king were laws which the nation was obliged to obey. Equally, the nation was obliged to obey the laws, made at the time of the original contract, which established the English monarchy as a hereditary kingship.[24]

These remarks went to the heart of the Commons' argument. All along, Whig M.P.'s had insisted that "abdicated" expressed the premises of the resolution, several times emphasizing those premises by reading them. If "breaking the original contract" were removed and with it, by implication, the closely related "violating the fundamental laws," then only "withdrawing from the kingdom" was left, and that phrase implied that the throne was full and preserved the concept of hereditary monarchy. In rebuttal, Treby sought to reinforce the concept of original contract. Calling for support from Hooker, whom he described as "one of the best men, the best church men, and the most learned of our nation," and as an adherent of the theory of original contract, and from Charles I, the darling of the Tories, whom he said endorsed Hooker, Treby also reminded the peers that they had already voted to accept the clause containing the words "original contract." They must be held to that vote, he implied. Treby also maintained that, whatever the laws enacted subsequently to the original contract, the original contract reserved a superior power to the legislature to use in times of emergency, "such as ours now." [25]

The lords raised objections to the word "abdicated." It was "too large a term," Turner said. It was not found in English common law, declared Nottingham, and meant in civil law a voluntary and express renouncing, which did not accord with the facts.[26] But they made it plain that they could accept "abdication," and that the "hinge" of their disagreement swung on the words "the throne is vacant." If the words meant that the throne was vacant with respect to James and his heirs, then, the peers declared, the kingship was elective, the constitution broken, and the government of Lords and Commons dissolved. The "election" of a king, even on a one-time-only basis, would provide precedent for other elections and was entirely unacceptable.[27]

In response, the Commons' spokesmen tried to make their position seem conservative. As they had done in debates in the lower House, they insisted that the Commons did not want to change the kingship. Thus, Maynard reassuringly declared that "the word *Elective* is none of the Commons word; neither is the making the kingdom elective the thing they had in their thoughts or intention; all they mean . . . is to provide a supply for this defect in the government brought upon it by the late king's maladministration." [28] Others elaborated these points. Sidestepping the question whether the Lords and Commons had the power to depose a king for maladministration, they maintained that James's acts, as the "premises" of the resolution said, amounted to an abdication. Said Treby, "What occasion was there for such a declaration as this, if nothing were concluded from it? That were only to give the kingdom a compendious history of those miseries they have too well learnt by feeling them." [29] This point was implicitly connected to the claim of rights the Commons had compiled. Although the claim of rights was not mentioned directly, Treby, as chairman of that committee, of course knew that the committee's report contained the evidence for his argument. The consequences of abdication, the argument continued, were inescapably that the crown was vacant. The vacancy was no fault of the Commons. "It is not we that have brought ourselves into this state of nature," Treby declaimed. Yet, that fact notwithstanding, Maynard maintained that the "Constitution is the same; the laws . . . are the same." [30]

Reinforcing their image as the conservators of the ancient constitution, the Commons' managers characterized the Lords' proposals as revolutionary. A regency is a "strange and impracticable thing," said Pollexfen, which would "introduce a new principle of government, a commonwealth." [31] Further, Treby sought to establish that the Commons were doing "no more than our ancestors did before us," [32] a phrase which appeared in the final version of the Declaration of Rights. They maintained that necessity compelled them to fill the throne this one time. Sympathizing with all the difficulties, Howard offered entirely pragmatic advice: "Use what words you will, fill up, or nominate, or elect, it is the thing we are to take care of, and it is high time it were done." [33]

Yet, however eager the Commons' managers were to blunt them, radical political ideas underlay these views. To declare the throne vacant was, as the Tories charged, to make the kingship elective, even if just for one time. The Lords and Commons were said to be exercising a power to supply the vacancy in a time of emergency, but when else did it really matter? To appeal, as Maynard did, to the "law of nature (that is above all human laws)" to justify filling the throne had radical overtones. To say, as Howard did, that the Lords and Commons had sufficient legal power to supply a vacancy and that everything the Convention had done was legal was to express left-wing Whig theories. A like significance also attended Holt's remark that government and magistracy were but a trust which ceased when the king violated the terms of the trust.[34] There was justice in Nottingham's charge of double-talk. In a telling remark, he said, "You understand your own words to signify less than they do really impart." [35]

Although the conference ended inconclusively, the matter was resolved later that same evening. Following a heated and protracted debate in their own chamber, the lords voted by a margin of up to twenty votes to accept the abdication and vacancy resolution.[36] Clarendon felt that the lords who opposed the resolution "had by far the better of the argument, both upon the point of reason, and according as the law now stands." [37]

But they capitulated for several reasons. Arguments by Halifax that the necessity of the situation demanded accepting the Commons' formula carried much weight, however unsatisfactory and flimsy those arguments seemed to Clarendon.[38] The agreement, reached after a bitter exchange between Danby and Halifax, to omit from the old oath of allegiance the words *de jure* eased consciences.[39] Halifax's suggestion to modify the new title of the king and queen to read "with all the appurtenances thereunto belonging," without mentioning Scotland, blunted the argument that Scotland might not agree with the steps being taken.[40] Further, Burnet credited himself with using his good offices with the peers to persuade them to agree. He also claimed that "the dubious sense" of the word "abdicated" contributed to the agreement.[41] Still further, some peers were moved by fear of civil war, mob uprising, and economic depression, and the sense that a government in the hands of the prince was better than no government at all.[42]

But what really persuaded the lords was the sense that there was no other viable answer. As noted above, William had, at a meeting on February 3 with Halifax, Danby, and other lords, confirmed earlier hints that he would return to Holland rather than accept a regency or a position subordinate to his wife. Perhaps the lords took into account that William, whose health was particularly delicate at this time, would likely predecease Mary.[43] Moreover, Mary herself destroyed the option her supporters had promoted. Having at some earlier, undisclosed time through the good offices of Burnet (if his own account is to be credited) renounced to William any interest in ruling in her own right, the princess had more recently rebuked Danby in a sharp letter, a copy of which she sent to the prince, for suggesting that she might be elevated to the throne as queen and that William might serve as her consort.[44] Further, the arrival, in the "midst of the arguments," of the earl of Dorset and Lord Churchill with a message from Princess Anne urging the lords to concur with the resolution of the House of Commons removed another difficulty. The message, it was said, "hastened the conclusion."[45] As the debate drew to a close, there was so much confusion and noise that nothing could be heard. The question was called and carried.[46] Loyalists, who had maintained an overall majority up to February 6, were able to muster no more than 46 votes. Absenteeism and defection among their own number, the arrival of peers ready to vote for William, the support of Danby and his group, and the votes of revolutionary peers brought the majority vote to 64.[47] Thereupon it was moved — contemporaries have assigned the honor variously to Halifax, Danby, and Winchester[48] — to declare the prince and princess of Orange king and queen of England.

The news of the vote was greeted with great joy by people around Parliament. Although it was late, there were bonfires and ringing of bells in London. The next morning, the bells continued to peal out all over the city and in nearby villages.[49]

In the meantime, in the House of Commons, Colonel Birch had reminded members on February 4 that they had made no arrangements respecting Treby's report. "We have been scrambling a long time for our religion and properties," he declared. "Shall these things lie there, and no more?" One reason apparently for Birch's concern at the lack of action on the report was his fear of what might happen should the Heads become public. In fact, they appeared in print on either February 4 or 5. His advice was to "put some title to them, and send them to the Lords immediately."[50] Other Whigs, however, urged that a major change be made before the report was sent to the Lords. They wanted to separate the clauses concerning allegedly ancient rights from those requiring new law. Wildman appealed to the procedure followed in the case of the Petition of Right. Proponents of the Petition of Right had "refused to have new law," claiming that their demands were "aborigine," Wildman pointed out. Lee agreed, explaining that only "ancient rights," those "things laid asleep, or ill exercised by the late government," should be claimed. Capel also concurred. Observing that the House had been branded often with "alteration of the government," he declared that "'tis our right to assert our freedom" and maintained that "we only assert our rights and liberties pursuant to the prince's *Declaration.*"[51]

Why radical Whigs should have endorsed this step requires explanation. First, the proposal was a tactical move to avoid imperiling the validity of acknowledged ancient rights by mixing them together with claims that obviously required new laws.[52] It reflected the legal and parliamentary experience of many members of the rights committee. Second, the step may have been a response to objections raised by the prince. The presence on Treby's committee of Jephson, William's personal secretary, and of other friends guarantees that the prince's court knew about the project to spell out the powers of the king. Capel's remark that the House had often been accused of changing the government and his defense that not only was it their right to proclaim their liberties, but that all they were doing was "pursuant" to William's manifesto, reinforce the suggestion. Three days earlier, on February 1, the Spanish ambassador, Don Pedro Ronquillo, reported that William opposed placing any restrictions on the rights of the crown or encumbering the offer of it with conditions.[53] He declared that the Heads of Grievances were a "disputed matter" between the prince and the House of Commons. The Florentine ambassador, Terriesi, formed the same impression.[54] Also on February 1, one of the Dutchmen in London noted that William had instructed Dijkvelt to speak to members of the Convention about an undisclosed matter (having to do with the Heads of Grievances?).[55] Moreover, the eighteenth-century historian Echard charged, on the basis of information from "a private hand," that the "management of the prince" caused the proponents of the Declaration of Rights to "shorten" it.[56]

There is a third possible explanation for the step. The call to model the claim of rights on the Petition of Right may have been designed to prepare the way to win the same form of assent from whomever was king as the Commons had won from Charles I in 1628. Charles's reply had made the Petition of Right theoretically binding in law, a fact certainly known to seventeenth-century parliamentarians. Temple's remarks inspire this interpretation. Declaring that the document about rights must go "with your instrument of government," he went on to say that "the throne must be actually filled before you deliver that petition."[57] The comment suggests that he had in mind first settling the crown and then presenting a "petition of right." If the king employed the proper response, that would invest the petition with legal force, just as had been done sixty years earlier. If that were indeed the intention, then there was no place for claims that obviously required new legislation.

Finally, it is possible that the proposal reflected anxiety over the response the House of Lords would make to a claim of rights. On February 2, the peers had shown themselves firmly against the Commons' resolution; such hostility might well extend to the statement of rights. Perhaps Wildman, who several days later would urge the House to bypass the peers and go directly to the prince with grievances, had taken to heart Pollexfen's earlier warning that the peers might object and concluded that the lords would be more likely to accept a statement of allegedly established rights than a long list of issues many of which unquestionably required new law. (Wildman's misgivings about the attitude of the peers towards rights were confirmed several days later.)

In any case, the House instructed Treby's committee, to which Holt was now added, to meet at 3:00 P.M. in the Speaker's Chambers to reorder their original report so as to distinguish the clauses that reaffirmed old rights from those that required new law, and to decide upon an appropriate title for it.[58] These same men had been engaged in drawing up reasons against the Lords' amendments to the abdication and vacancy resolution, and were called upon repeatedly during the next two days to debate that issue in the Commons and in the conference meeting with the Lords. In view of these distractions, it is doubtful that Treby's committee was able to give much time in fulfilling the House's instructions about reordering the clauses in the Heads of Grievances.

Yet, an effort was made by an unknown person or persons to preserve the claim of rights and to assure that changes would be made in the nation's kingship. In defiance of the ruling of the House on January 22 not to permit the printing of its votes, and in the face of complaints that the debates of the House had been noticed outside Westminster,[59] a broadside titled *The Publick Grievances of the Nation adjudged necessary by the honorable House of Commons to be redressed* was published. Listing the twenty-eight articles that the committee and the House had compiled, it appeared possibly as early as February 4, certainly no later than February 5,[60] surely with the purpose of enlisting public support for all the heads. There is no hint who was responsible for the appearance of the committee's report, but it almost certainly was a Whig who saw advantage in informing the public. Moreover, one of the new London newspapers, The *London Mercury; or, Moderate Intelligencer,* apprised its readers on February 5 that the House of Commons had prepared a statement of grievances. The paper reported that the lower House had drawn up "such grievances to be redress'd that nothing but malice or envy, or our intestine divisions" can make the nation unhappy.[61] The appearance in print of the first draft was to be followed (as already noted) by the publication of subsequent drafts.

Written accounts also spread news of the Commons' project. Two subscription newsletters — the Bulstrode Newsletters and the Newdigate Newsletters — reported the work on claiming the rights of the nation.[62] So, too, did private correspondents,[63] some of whom copied out the successive drafts, and at least one of whom, as we have seen, sent his friend an account of the discussions in Treby's committee.

Moreover, accounts of the project were surely discussed by some M.P.'s or their associates in London coffeehouses. Despite James II's efforts in October to suppress the coffeehouses, they continued to serve as places of political discussion and dissemination of news.[64] Printed material about Convention affairs could be found there. Among that material was a portion of the draft Declaration of Rights under the title "A Form of Settling the Crown . . . Communicated to the House of Lords for their Concurrence." It was specifically mentioned as having been picked up in a coffeehouse.[65]

How successful the effort was to reach the public with information about the claim of rights will never be known. But it may be asserted that politically conscious Englishmen in London and the counties could have known something of the steps the Convention was taking with respect to grievances and rights. But on February 4 or February 5, when the first draft of the Heads of Grievances appeared, the question that absorbed everyone's attention was the abdication and vacancy resolution. Not until that was settled between the two Houses late in the evening of February 6 did the focus shift once more to the question of the rights of the nation.

13

February 7–8, 1689

❧

The next day, February 7, the sense of relief over the concurrence of the lords and the feeling of urgency to settle the government were so great that the Heads of Grievances were very nearly lost in the House of Commons. Even before receiving the official message from the lords that they had agreed to the January 28 resolution, Lord Wiltshire and Wildman moved a well-attended House to proceed forthwith to "nominate" William and Mary king and queen.[1] Neither referred to the claim of rights. An effort to preserve the claim came not, as might be expected, from a leading proponent of the project, but from William Palmes, who was not on the rights committee but had helped draft the House's reasons for rejecting the lords' amendments to the abdication and vacancy resolution and through that effort had been brought into close working relationship with committee members. Disclaiming intention of opposing the motion to fill the throne, Palmes declared he wanted to "hear what the committee will report of the preliminary heads," which, he said, "will be ready . . . presently."[2]

It will be remembered that three days before, the House had asked the committee to separate the lengthy list of heads into two categories, one of allegedly ancient rights, the other of issues which required new law. But a "long debate"[3] followed Palmes's remarks, suggesting absence of enthusiasm in some quarters for proceeding with the report. No Tory reiterated the arguments made by fellow Tories on January 29, their silence again reenforcing the hypothesis that partisan considerations figured in their earlier extravagant statements. But radical Whigs Boscawen, Hampden, and Wharton counseled the House "not to lose all these heads the gentlemen are doing, but act as a wise assembly."[4] Finally, the House decided to postpone until the next day consideration of the lords' vote and ordered Treby's committee to be "revived."[5] This decision was an important victory for the men in the House who wished to change the kingship as well as the king.

Instructed to report "with all convenient speed," Treby presented the second draft of the claim of rights that afternoon. His remarks to the House suggested an absence of harmony within the committee. Declaring that the committee had gone as far as it could go, Treby confessed that there was no title as yet and said that until the House decided "what use to make of them,"[6] it was not possible to decide whether to record the heads in the Court of Chancery. He admitted that the committee disagreed about "the manner of presenting"[7] the statement and, further, that it could not decide "to whom to address the grievances."[8] His report marked a retreat from the arguments advanced by radical Whigs the week before, in the debates of January 28 and 29. It reflected the impact of Tory objections to the abdication and vacancy resolution and to theories about original contract, the dissolution of the government, and the sovereignty of the people.

It was at this stage in the drafting process that decisions were made that set the outline for the final version of the Declaration of Rights. Those decisions may be briefly summarized, for they have already been noticed in the discussion of the shape of the final document in Chapter 1. First, the committee supplied an introduction which, in words that recalled William's *Declaration of Reasons,* asserted that James II, with the assistance of evil counselors, had "endeavoured" to subvert the nation's religion, laws, and liberties. Whereas William's *Declaration* had avoided blaming James directly for the nation's plight, this draft specifically named the king. The legal maxim "the king can do no wrong" had to be set aside if James's removal were to be justified.[9] Although the manifesto had specifically claimed that the king's evil ministers had "overturned the religion, laws and liberties" of the realm, the draft temporized, using the word "endeavoured." This word implied that a dissolution of the government had *not* occurred, and that the nation had *not* been returned to a state of nature.

Second, the committee prepared an indictment of the king in thirteen particulars drawn from the Heads of Grievances.[10] The heads selected and the priority assigned them suggest the committee's concern to placate Tories in both houses. The first charge against James was his use of the dispensing and suspending powers, which Tory Anglicans had emphasized. The second charge was the king's "committing and prosecuting divers worthy prelates" who had petitioned against the dispensing power, in other words the trial of the seven Anglican bishops. The third charge also set out a grievance which Tories especially had emphasized — namely, the erection of a "Court" of Ecclesiastical Commissioners. Tory spokesmen on January 29 had stressed these matters. Then followed five charges which Whigs had stressed in the initiating debate on grievances: levying taxes by pretense or prerogative (clause 4); raising and keeping a standing army in time of peace without the consent of Parliament (5); disarming Protestant subjects (6); violating the freedom of parliamentary elections (7); and causing informations to be brought in the Court of King's Bench for matters properly cognizable only in Parliament, and by "divers other arbitrary and illegal courses" (8). Five alleged violations in legal proceedings completed the indictment. Unqualified and corrupt men have served on juries (9); and excessive bail (10), excessive fines (11), and cruel and illegal punishments (12) have been used. Also condemned were grants and promises made of fines and forfeitures before the conviction of the party (13). All these things, Treby's report asserted, without providing references to the laws in question, were "utterly and directly contrary to the known laws, and statutes, and freedom, of this realm."

Third, the committee incorporated the key terms of the Commons' abdication and vacancy resolution in its report, declaring that "the said late King James the Second" had "abdicated" the government, and thereby, "the throne [was] vacant." But it deleted the "premises" of that resolution: the words "breaking the original contract," "having violated the fundamental laws," and "withdrawn himself out of the kingdom." Just the day before, Clarendon and other peers had either rejected outright or redefined "original contract" to suit their political principles, while Treby and others had insisted that the term was a prerequisite to the words "abdicated" and "the throne vacant." The omission abandoned the position of the radical Whigs, so eloquently presented by Howard on January 28, that the original contract was broken, the government dissolved, and the power returned to the people. Thus, the committee avoided offending Tories and moderate Whigs in both Houses. The words "violated the fundamental laws" were closely related to the concept of original contract. Since the time of the Civil War, the words had appeared in debates and printed statements critical of the king. The terms had occasioned lengthy debate among the peers, and their absence in Treby's draft was a further signal of willingness not to insist upon controversial language. James's "withdrawing from the kingdom" was the meaning that Tories had given to the word "abdicated." Whigs had rejected that interpretation because it implied that the throne remained filled. The absence of the phrase was a Whig preference. One may surmise that Tory and Whig leaders reached an agreement that these provocative premises to the Commons' resolution would be omitted, but that the critically important conclusion — that the king "has abdicated the government; and that the throne is thereby vacant" — would be included. Neither "abdication" nor "vacancy" had been precisely defined in debates, and they were no more closely defined in the draft. But their placement in the document intimates a meaning. That they come directly after the indictment implied that it was James's *acts* which constituted the "abdication," behind which idea lay the notions of original contract and violation of the fundamental laws. In this subtle way the Whigs preserved their interpretation. The final version of the Declaration of Rights retained this arrangement of the text.

Fourth, Treby's report supplied material explaining events. It recounted that William of Orange — the "glorious instrument of delivering this kingdom from Popery and arbitrary power" — upon the request of the lords spiritual and temporal and "divers principal persons of the commons" had caused letters to be sent to the Protestant peers and to the counties, cities, and other places, for electing such persons "as were of right to be sent to Parliament." It characterized the assembly which convened on January 22 as a "full and free representative of this nation" and asserted that its purpose was to establish the kingdom's "religion, laws, and liberties," that they "might not again be in danger of being subverted." It explained that to attain those ends, the Commons, "as their ancestors in like case, have usually done," "unanimously declare" certain rights. The committee, clearly, was attempting to link its claim of rights to earlier claims of rights, to call to mind the Petition of Right and other remonstrances and addresses with which men of political experience, legal training, and historical bent were well acquainted. In this way, it underscored the traditional nature of its actions and claims. The use of the word "unanimously" was to prove optimistic.

Fifth, the report listed twelve alleged ancient rights, drawing them from the Heads of Grievances and matching them generally (although not precisely, as already noticed) with points in the indictment of the king. With a few changes in the language, the committee preserved original heads 1-4, 6-10, 19, 21, and 26. It divided head 8 into two articles, one claiming that the election of members of Parliament ought to be free, and the other specifying that freedom of speech, and debates or proceedings in Parliament ought not to be impeached or questioned outside of Parliament. The words "freedom of speech" were new, introduced for the first time in this second draft. The committee moved to the category of issues that required new law the claim that parliamentary privileges were a right which should be preserved in the *intervals* of Parliament as well as during its sitting. The substance of heads 9 and 10 were combined into a new article, that for "redress of all grievances, and for the amending, strengthening, and preserving of the laws, parliaments ought to be held frequently, and suffered to sit." The report described the articles in this section as the nation's "ancient" and "undoubted" rights and liberties, although, as already shown, not all of the articles were, in fact, ancient and undoubted.

Sixth, the committee prepared a category of rights that required new law, introducing it with the statement that in the interests of "making a more firm and perfect settlement of the said religion, laws, and liberties," it was "proposed and advised" that Parliament pass appropriate new legislation. Thereupon followed twenty clauses from the Heads of Grievances: heads 5, 8, 9, 11, 13-28. Notable among the clauses laid aside for "future parliaments" to deal with were militia reform (head 5); reform in the tenure and pay of judges (18); tax reform, with respect to the hearth tax and excise (27 and 28); reform of the treason law (17); protection of corporate bodies against quo warrantos (13); prohibition against a member of the royal family's marrying a Papist (14); and provisions allowing Protestants liberty to exercise their religion.

Five clauses appeared in both categories of issues. That heads 8, 9, 19, 21, and 26 were in both categories suggests uncertainty whether they were indeed old rights, as claimed. But whatever ambiguity these points suggested in the minds of the committee, this section ended with the unambiguous statement that the Commons do "claim, demand, and insist upon" all the rights "as their undoubted rights and liberties."

Seventh, the committee omitted from either section the twelfth head, which disallowed royal pardons of an impeachment in Parliament. Treby said that the committee had eliminated it for "divers weighty reasons," which he failed to specify. But one may surmise that the committee had decided to remove the claim for three compelling reasons; one, to avoid offending Danby, who, with others, had slipped through the hands of the parliamentary Opposition during the reign of Charles II because of the royal right of pardon; [11] two, to avoid offending those persons, including the prince and his close friends, who felt that the clause too severely diminished the powers of the king; and three, to avoid introducing a claim to a right which obviously could not be characterized as an ancient law.

It was also at this stage in the drafting process that a decision was made on the form of the verb to be employed in the articles. As indicated in Chapter 1, the declaratory form of the verb was employed in six articles (1–5 and 11). It conveyed an unequivocable assertion of rights. The committee seems to be saying that on these points there was no legal question and to be signaling their intention to insist upon them. But, as we have seen, these issues remained open to interpretation. Notwithstanding the flat assertion that these were the ancient rights of the nation, the committee, in effect, was proclaiming as law what they wanted to be law.

On the other hand, the subjunctive form of the word appears in the other six clauses (6–10 and 12). Clearly the language is not obligatory. These articles set out what is desirable, what "ought" to happen, not what is law. It is reasonable to suggest that the qualifying language reflected the work of the lawyers on the committee, who knew well the state of the law on the claims.

Although it is impossible to know for certain which members of the committee were responsible for this draft, it is likely that the chairman, Treby, took a prominent part and that other lawyers did too. The language and the logical organization of the document suggest as much. So, too, does the fact that the articles on bail, fines, punishments, jurors, and forfeitures — in other words, the issues raised almost certainly by the lawyers in the meetings of the committee — appeared in the category of old, established rights. It is reasonable that lawyers should have put in that category the clauses that addressed matters relating to their own profession. Further, the fact that so many heads were placed in the category of rights requiring new law reinforces the hypothesis that lawyers prevailed in the writing of this draft. Only lawyers, so far as the record shows, had expressed concern over claiming rights which were not grounded in law. In doing so they contradicted their own willingness to do just that in certain cases. If lawyers had not been so prominent on the committee, perhaps more clauses in the Heads of Grievances would have been placed in the category of old rights. The category of alleged old rights, however, did contain claims not grounded in law. For example, the articles about the royal suspending and dispensing powers, standing armies, and freedom of speech in Parliament represented new law on matters of critical importance to achieving parliamentary sovereignty. It is reasonable to suggest that radical Whigs, such as Boscawen, Hampden, and Wharton (who urged the House to receive the committee's report) had insisted upon including these articles in the category of old law.

The debate on Treby's report was lengthy and, to Morrice's dismay, evidently unedifying. Sitting late into the evening, members were variously so hungry, tired, or satiated with food and drink that the debate was "tumultuous," with men exchanging threats and insults.[12] There is no suggestion in Grey's account, certainly incomplete, that the full House disputed the committee's decisions on which rights to claim as ancient law and which to leave for a future parliament to secure.[13] No Tory expressed himself on whether the report satisfied the reforms fellow partisans had so eloquently demanded on January 29. No objections were, apparently, raised against the elimination of the twelfth head. Members did not assist the committee on the matter of a title.

But the full House took three steps that influenced the final version of the declaration. One concerned the succession to the crown after William and Mary, a matter which the lords had not mentioned. M.P.'s moved to bar a Papist from the throne and to preserve the rights of Princess Anne.[14] The matter of succession was to become an issue contended by Tories and Whigs in both Houses and by the two Houses during the months when the Declaration of Rights was being transformed into a statute. Second, the House raised the question of how affairs of government would be handled in a jointly held monarchy. And, third, they argued for the first time that the statement of rights should be linked to the resolution about offering the crown to William and Mary. Said Lee, "A declaration of the rights of the subject [should] go along with the declaration of filling up the throne."[15] Observers interpreted members as intending to lay their "new articles of government . . . before the new king, that he might know upon what terms he was to have the crown."[16] Significantly, the report was in print that very evening, surely for the purpose of arousing public support for it and assuring that it would not be lost.[17]

On February 8 another determined effort was made to preserve the claim of rights. The House had before it the Lords' resolution to declare William and Mary king and queen and, after debate, agreed to place the "sole administration of the government" in the prince of Orange alone and to specify the succession of the crown after William and Mary to four removes. A committee of twenty-one members was then appointed to amend accordingly the Lords' resolution, declaring the prince and princess king and queen.[18] Eighteen members of this committee were also on Treby's committee,[19] guaranteeing familiarity with the claim of rights. The Speaker instructed all "or any three" of the members to withdraw "immediately" to the Speaker's chamber.[20] It will never be known for sure who among the twenty-one men attended this other committee meeting except for Somers, who emerged as chairman, and Richard Hampden, who performed a task for the committee: reporting from a conference with the lords. Treby, the chairman of the committee of thirty-nine, was probably also present. But, even more so than in the case of Treby's committee, the attendance was probably high, for this committee was charged with amending the resolution that would settle the revolution. It is therefore of paramount importance that the committee was overwhelmingly Whig. Only four members (Falkland, Finch, Sawyer, and Wogan) were long-term Tories. Seymour, the greatest Tory of all, was not appointed. Gregory, who voted with the Tories on the settlement of the crown, was an old Whig. Williams, the turncoat Whig, was added to the committee on February 12. Williams, it will be recalled, favored the claim of rights, but voted with the Tories on the settlement of the crown.

Why Somers should have been chosen chairman over the more senior and experienced Treby has already been considered.[21] Whatever the explanation, it was Somers who returned to the House to report that in the course of their deliberations, the committee had encountered a "difficulty."[22] Clearly, someone (Somers?) had perceived that an opportunity was at hand to advance the claim of rights by connecting it to the amendments to the vote of the Lords. Somers asked the direction of the House. In response, there ensued a debate which revealed three things pertinent to understanding the declaration.[23] First, not one Tory, if Grey's account is complete, commented on a question of transcendent importance to the fate of the document. Their silence suggests, at the least, indifference, perhaps hostility. When added to the other data, it enhances the hypothesis that the Tories initiated the project to declare the rights of the nation largely for tactical reasons. If the preservation of the statement of rights had depended on Tories in the House of Commons, the document would have been lost. Second, the debate exposed disagreement among Whigs over how to handle Treby's report. On the one hand, Wildman urged the Commons to bypass the Lords and send the statement directly to the prince. Naïvely assuming William's approval, Wildman declared that such a procedure guaranteed every *"punctum"* of their claim. He feared that the Lords would disagree with the articles. Further — possibly because he had heard that the peers' committee on privileges had been meeting — he also feared that the Lords would insist that their own rights be included. Hampden emphatically disagreed. "I remember," he said, "upon all occasions, when your rights have been asserted, that you have gone to the Lords." His remark suggests his awareness that in the early part of the century men had come to believe that the king could not deny a petition from *both* Houses. The prince would find it more difficult to dismiss the statement of rights if both Houses presented it. Hampden quoted exactly the key sentence from William's *Second Declaration* — "No remedy but a full declaration of our grievances in Parliament" — to underline that the participation of both Houses of Parliament was needed.

Third, members insisted that the claim of rights be presented at the same time the crown was offered. Hampden admonished the Convention, saying, "As you desire the reputation of a grave and wise council, let the committee connect the Heads of the Articles and represent them all together." Temple shared Hampden's viewpoint, arguing strenuously against filling the throne and "nothing with it." Another member, Eyre, pressed the same point, arguing that if they waited until the crown was settled, the Lords might reject the Commons' claim of rights on the grounds that the rights were the "ancient flowers of the crown, and cannot be parted with." Continuing in picturesque language, he said, "I would not have our purchase, like the Indians, to give gold [i.e., the crown] for rattles." The House agreed to this procedure, giving another victory to those Whigs who wanted to change the kingship as well as the king. It specifically instructed the committee to connect the Commons' amendments respecting the administration of the government and the succession to the vote of the Lords declaring William and Mary king and queen, join these with the heads that were "declaratory of ancient rights, leaving out the heads introductory of new law," and link the whole with the new oaths drafted by the Lords.[24] Accordingly, the committee "tackt" together all the resolutions the Convention had passed. Somers presented the report, and the House approved it that same day.[25]

Three aspects of this report require comment. First, it followed to the letter the first section of Treby's report, which alone explains the speed with which the work was accomplished. That fact raises the question whether Treby should not share with Somers the credit for the Declaration of Rights.[26] Second, it introduced an explicit reference to — indeed, it borrowed the very words of — William's *Second Declaration of Reasons*. To connect the claim of rights and the offer of the crown, Somers's committee fashioned a paragraph which said that the Convention was "particularly invited" to make "demand of their rights" by the prince's manifesto, which had said (citing the key terms exactly, as Hampden had done) that "the only means for obtaining a full redress and remedy" of grievances was by a "Parliament in a Declaration of Rights of the subject." Later on February 12, in arguing against one of the Lords' proposed amendments to the draft, Somers again referred to the prince's *Declaration*. He said it confirmed the opinion of the committee and declared candidly that the committee had "followed" the words of the manifesto.[27] To place an appeal to the prince's manifesto in the document itself as the justification for their claim of rights was to put great pressure on William to accept that claim. Should he be inclined to reject it, he would be faced with the embarrassment of publicly disavowing his own well-known statement. Clearly, members of this committee in the House of Commons were playing political hardball.

Third, the report followed the organization of Treby's draft. It began with a list of ways James and his evil advisers had endeavored to subvert the nation's religion, law, and liberties. Next came the abdication and vacancy statement, implying by that sequence that the king's acts constituted his abdication, and that the consequence was a vacancy in the throne. Also following Treby's report, Somers's committee stripped the January 28 resolution of all its premises — about "breaking the original contract," violating the "fundamental laws," and "withdrawing from the kingdom." That this step was taken twice underscores that it was deliberate. By omitting the controversial phrases, the committee aimed to offend as few people as possible. But by keeping the heart of the resolution and placing it where they did in the text, the committee members retained the intrinsic meaning of the resolution for politically sophisticated readers to understand. The committee then declared the kingdom's alleged "ancient rights," justifying their claim by William's own *Declaration of Reasons* and using such words as "vindicating," "asserting," "declaring," "claiming," "demanding," and "insisting upon" with respect to the statement of rights. Then they connected the statement of rights and the offer of the crown by the word "accordingly." That word meant, and was so used in the seventeenth century, "in accordance with the sequence of ideas; agreeably or conformably to what might be expected; in natural sequence, in due course; so." The text reads that the Lords Spiritual and Temporal and the Commons "do pray the said prince and princess of Orange to accept [the crown] accordingly." The organization of the document clearly implies that the offer of the crown was conditional upon William's accepting the itemized rights. There was nothing inevitable about how the parts of the document should be arranged. A different sequence from the one chosen was certainly possible. For example, the crown could have been offered first, the offer justified by the misdeeds of James II, and then the nation's rights asserted. Such an arrangement would not have implied that the crown was conditional upon the prince's accepting the statement of rights. Further, the language states that the itemized rights are ancient and are now being "asserted" and "declared," — that is, set out, made clear. The implication is that they have the force of law and hence limit the powers of the monarchy. There was no doubt in the minds of observers that such was the nature of Somers's draft. Two among several commentators described it as a "new instrument of government," which, as a third observer put it, the Convention "intended to lay before the prince and to desire remedy in at the same time that they offered him the crown of England."[28]

Agreeing that a conference with the Lords was necessary, the House deputized Wharton to request one. And upon his return with the announcement that the Lords would foregather in the Painted Chamber for a conference, the Commons resolved that Somers's committee should deliver the "paper of heads, amendments, and other particulars" to the Lords and manage the conference. At this conference meeting on February 8, the upper House received their first official notice of the Commons' claim of rights.[29]

14

The House of Lords
and the Declaration of Rights

ate on the afternoon of Friday, February 8, Charles Powlett, marquis
of Winchester, a Whig of advanced years who had feigned madness
during the reign of James II, and whose continuing bizarre behavior
caused comment among members of the prince's court,[1] returned to the
House of Lords from the meeting in the Painted Chamber with a copy of
Somers's draft.[2] He reported that although the Commons agreed generally
with the Lords' vote to declare William and Mary king and queen and with
the peers' draft of new oaths, they had prepared certain amendments for the
Lords' concurrence. The paper was read and ordered to be considered first
thing the next morning.[3]

Somers's report precipitated a sharp if short-lived crisis during the evening
of February 8 and the next day, which threatened the Declaration of Rights
and laid bare William's views on the matter. Bentinck told a member of the
House of Commons that the prince did not like the "restrictions and limitations" that were being placed upon the crown.[4] Rumors circulated that
William was "very angry with those that had made mention of them," and
that men close to him shared the view that he should not accept any "stipulations."[5] According to an eighteenth-century historian, the prince sent his
friend Lord Wharton to "several lords" to express his determination to return
to Holland if he were offered a crown upon conditions.[6] Jacobite tracts written in the early 1690s also reported that William threatened to leave England
if the Convention insisted on limiting the royal prerogative.[7] Such an attitude
was consistent with that predicted earlier in tracts hostile to William and in
the Convention by M.P.'s who knew the prince's mind.[8]

Hoping to win partisan advantage, a number of unidentified bishops and
temporal peers attempted to exploit this situation.[9] In a private meeting with
the prince that evening, they told him that the stipulations were indeed
restrictions upon the crown. The claims, they said, "stripped him of all
power" and reflected "great disingenuity and distrust." Using "great art,"

these men tried to "prejudice" William against the individuals who were promoting the statement of rights, describing them as "factious and seditious people — enemies of monarchy." They said that if the prince would depend on them, they could make him king without any restrictions. They assured William that the House of Lords would "never agree with the Commons." William's response is not reported, but clearly, the prince did not reject this proposition out of hand that evening, for the crisis deepened the next morning when the news of his disapproval circulated in Westminster. The rumor was spread "universally" and "extremely endeavoured and skillfully insinuated." Seymour, who on January 29 had insisted upon claiming rights, aggravated the situation by saying he would lay any wager that the proclamation of the new monarchs would be delayed. In the House of Lords, unidentified peers "laboured with all their might" for two hours to "exalt the dispensing power," with the aim of sabotaging the statement of rights and achieving "a fatal breach between the two houses." The result was that, for a time, "the whole body" of peers, all the Tories in the House of Commons, and "most of those that came over with the prince" (because they thought William favored the proposal) "seemed to fall in" with the scheme. It looked as if the stipulations would "very likely" be given up.

Men who favored the claim of rights were filled "with consternation and dispair." If they abandoned the claim of rights they would lose their reputation as champions of the nation's laws and liberties. But if they persisted, they ran the risk of causing a break with the lords, losing credit with the prince, and sacrificing future political preferments. They rushed about to try to save the situation.

An important spokesman for rights (Temple) importuned one of William's advisers, explaining that the conditions had been reduced by one third and arguing disingenuously that they now contained nothing but an explication of the old laws.[10] An unidentified person asked a member of William's Dutch entourage to intervene with William. That Dutchman refused, fearing the prince's temper, but reported that Dijkvelt urged William to accept the declaration of rights.[11] A group of men, among them Sir Henry Sidney (at this time, it should be recalled, William's closest English confidant), hastened directly to the prince.

Unfortunately, this interview with William is imperfectly reported, but apparently, Sidney argued that the proponents of rights were the prince's "most faithful servants." They intended "no snare to him" in their declaration. Using a threat, he pointed out that for William to oppose the statement would have "dangerous consequences." It would "leave the steady, sober part of the nation very uneasy," and provoke a "fatal division" between the two Houses. He also asserted persuasively but duplicitously that the terms "contained nothing . . . but the known laws." One may speculate that in return for William's consent that the statement be read at the time the crown was offered, it was agreed that the prince would not be asked to sign or take a formal oath to uphold it, as earlier reports had indicated. For his part, William denied that he had ever "expressed his sense one way or another," disavowed any person who had suggested the contrary as one who "had done him a very great injury," and declared that he was "satisfied with whatever they did for their own security." [12] William's answer defused the situation. The House of Commons adjourned early, and the peers who had instigated the episode "veered about and let all their heats and exorbitances vanish." They agreed that they would suggest no changes to the draft that they felt would be unacceptable to the lower House. [13]

The resolution of this crisis marked a turning point in the efforts of men who wanted to present a claim of rights and to change the kingship as well as the king. If they had failed to win agreement, then clearly the claim of rights would have had no part in the proclaiming of William and Mary king and queen. Testifying to how serious a crisis might have developed, one person described William's capitulation as a "special instance of divine providence." [14] From February 9, it was certain that the statement of rights would be presented at the same time as the offer of the crown. The Convention, therefore, would have to devise a special ceremony; William and Mary could not be simply proclaimed. It was equally certain that, although differences were papered over, profound disagreement with the statement of rights lay just beneath the surface.

This brief episode is important to an understanding of the Declaration of Rights. First, it makes almost incontrovertible the hypothesis that the Tories' enthusiastic initiation of the project to "resolve what powers to give to the king and what not" concealed partisan tactical considerations. Falkland, who had introduced that proposal on January 29, evidently did nothing at the moment of crisis on February 9 to rescue the statement. Seymour only aggravated the situation. His behavior was incompatible with his statement a fortnight before when he urged the Convention at whatever cost in time and energy to declare the nation's rights. The reported willingness of the Tories in the House of Commons to give up the stipulations further argues the case. So too does Burnet's comment that "some" men who had "*pretended* much zeal for [rights] pressed, even a little indecently, that it might not be done." [15] The crisis confirms, as Morrice suspected, that the Tories were insincere in endorsing a claim of rights. It also prefigures the interparty rivalry and jealousy that was to characterize politics after the revolution.

Second, the episode clarifies whether contemporaries regarded the statement of rights as a condition on the powers of the monarchy. The Tories who made the proposition to William must have thought so. The heart of their argument was that the stipulations restricted the authority of the king and reduced William to a cipher. If they had regarded the statement as entirely *pro forma,* without legal significance, what would have been the point in approaching the prince? Likewise, if William and his court had believed that the claim was simply an exercise in rhetoric, why should they have been agitated one way or the other? Somers's draft linked together the major resolutions of the Convention. If it were agreed that the sections on rights were not binding, then it could be argued that another section — the offer the crown — was not binding. This was the very point made a year later by William in a conversation with Halifax, when he queried, "What if a new Parliament should question the validity of all done in this [the Convention], and consequently the kingship?" [16] For their part, Whig proponents wanted the claim of rights to carry legal weight. Why else did they go to the trouble to promote and preserve it? It was more than a rhetorical statement with them. The language they used, regarded by one scholar (probably correctly from a strictly legal point of view) as precatory, rather than obligatory,[17] was as strong as they dared make it. But it is not inexplicit; as already noted, the word "accordingly," for example, appropriately conveyed the meaning intended. No public act at this time was, strictly speaking, legal, but the document setting out the resolution of the crisis had to be seen as tantamount to law if it were to have significance. It may be recalled that in the conference debate of February 6, Treby queried, "What occasion was there for such a Declaration as this, if nothing were concluded from it? That were only to give the kingdom a compendious history of those miseries they have too well learnt by feeling them." Only some lawyers argued otherwise, contending that the Convention could not, in the absence of a king, make a law. They and others in the course of the debates indicated an intention after the government was settled to follow the claim of rights with a statute. In the suc-ceeding months, that is what happened: the Declaration of Rights was transformed into a regular statute, the Bill of Rights, so that there could be no question of its legality, even as the Convention, by its own act, was transformed into a regular parliament, so that there could be no doubt of the legality of its acts. These considerations offer an answer to the controverted question whether the Declaration of Rights was thought to restrict the powers of the monarchy. In sum, many contemporaries wanted it to and thought it did; some lawyers argued that in strict law it did not; and to make certain that it did, Parliament passed a regular statute within ten months.

Third, the crisis also illuminates the question of whether the claim of rights was a condition of the offer of the crown. There is no evidence that anyone suggested that the offer of the crown to William should be withdrawn if he did not accept the claim of rights. The political maneuvering was subtle, and as already pointed out, there were several arguments against the Whigs' taking such a step. But a threat was entered, namely, that should William refuse the claim, his most devoted supporters (the "steady, sober part of the nation") would be left "very uneasy" and a "fatal division" would occur between the two Houses. These points apparently followed word from the prince that he would return to Holland if the Convention persisted in linking the offer of the crown and the claim of rights. No evidence survives about what words passed between William and Convention leaders. One can only hypothesize that William agreed to the linkage and to being presented the document in return for Convention leaders' agreeing not to require of him an oath or a signature. At least one contemporary regretted that William had been proclaimed king without first taking an oath and queried whether allegiance was due him.[18] But on balance, Englishmen arguably gained more from the compromise than did William, for they won from him a public commitment that was politically difficult to repudiate.

William's disavowal of Bentinck must be regarded as disingenuous. As Dutch stadtholder, William had been no libertarian, a fact which his supporters disclaimed and his detractors exploited. In December, the prince had candidly said to Halifax that he had not come to establish a commonwealth. In early February, two foreign ambassadors had reported his irritation over the Commons' project. It is possible that pressure from his court caused the Commons to prune the Heads of Grievances. The linking of the claim of rights to the offer of the crown in such a way as to intimate that the former was a condition on the latter and that it limited the powers of the kingship provoked the prince to outrage on February 8. His irritation was keen enough that he did not disavow the Tories' proposition until his closest English adviser, using reassurance and threat, persuaded him to do so. After the settlement, when steps were under way to make the declaration a statute, he confessed that he objected to transforming all of the provisions into law, but that the "condition of his affairs overruled his inclinations."[19]

If William really did not want the statement of rights, why did he capitulate? Why did he not flatly refuse to accept the claim and then agree to the Tories' proposition? Three major considerations may be suggested. First, the prince preferred the role of "trimmer." He had said as much to Halifax in their interview in December, and he amply demonstrated that principle in his political appointments after becoming king. He did not want to oblige himself to the Tories, nor weaken the support of the Whigs, nor cause a division between the two Houses, nor delay the settlement. What he wanted above all was to unite the nation behind him and persuade the Parliament to finance his campaign against Louis XIV. William, as already mentioned, was fully aware of the differences of opinion among Englishmen and sensitive enough to ask a Dutch emissary in London not to report them in his letters to Holland. A dispute over the nation's rights, whatever the outcome, could only heighten divisions. It was wiser politically to avoid a confrontation. William wanted the English crown badly enough to accept a statement which he disliked.

Second, William may have overestimated the number, significance, and degree of radicalism of the proponents of the claim of rights. He had consistently inflated the importance of republicans in England. After the settlement he identified the men who favored a repeal of the hearth tax and a modest financial settlement as "commonwealthsmen." They were the same men who promoted rights. He may have felt that by accepting the statement, he was forestalling more radical demands. The duplicitous assurances of Englishmen that the claim of rights contained no new rights, but simply affirmed old, existing law, probably also influenced his decision.

A final consideration was surely a concern that if he opposed the claim of rights, he would shatter the public image of himself, his intentions, and his policies which his own propaganda and the writings of others had created. His early misgivings about the draft manifesto ghostwritten by his English friends proved to be well-founded. He had accepted the manifesto's major themes. They had been spread far and wide in print. Anyone in England with the slightest interest in politics had been bombarded with declarations that insisted he was a Deliverer who had come only to rescue the nation's religion, laws, and liberties. Selfless and disinterested, he had promised to call a "free parliament" and leave it to the parliament to settle the crisis. More, he had practically instructed that free parliament to declare the rights of the nation and to take steps to assure that they would never be invaded again. Politically conscious people outside Westminster knew about the efforts to draft a Declaration of Rights. Despite procedural orders to the contrary, news of what was happening in the Convention spread in London and to the counties. Newspapers and newsletters reported, however briefly, that M.P.'s were engaged in drawing up a claim of rights. Private correspondents sent news of the project and wrote out the list of heads. It was not a matter of dealing privately with just the members of the Convention.

The proponents of the declaration exploited this situation. They called upon the prince's own manifesto to justify what they were doing, and they incorporated into their document the very words William had used. This made it exceedingly awkward for him to reject the statement and thereby disavow his own words. The situation testifies to the important role of printed propaganda in the revolution. Winning agreement from the prince was perhaps the only time in the complicated political maneuvering of the Glorious Revolution that English political leaders had the better of William.

Once the crisis was resolved, the House of Lords considered Somers's report and amended it from February 9 through February 12. Although the peers declared that "withal . . . they did in substance agree" with the draft, it took lengthy, well-attended debates in the upper House, the deliberations of a specially appointed committee, and several conference committee meetings with the Commons to reconcile their amendments.[20] An unidentified person, in an apparent effort to inhibit further change, printed the penultimate draft of the document under the title *The agreement of the House of Lords, during this session, with the concurrence of the House of Commons, to this present eleventh of February, in the great affairs of these nations.*[21] Despite the title, the lords both in the whole House and in committee amended this draft.

The lords appointed a committee of thirteen peers to prepare reasons in support of their amendments.[22] Heavily weighted in favor of the prince, the committee contained neither dukes nor bishops. Two members (Nottingham and Pembroke) had favored regency. Two (Danby and Fauconberg) had been Maryites, although both voted on January 31, 1689, to offer the crown to William and Mary, that vote showing that they moderated their enthusiasm for Mary as queen in her own right earlier than used to be thought.[23]

The other nine (Winchester, Bath, Devonshire, Shrewsbury, Mordaunt, Newport, Delamere, Lumley, and Wharton) were adherents of William. Eleven of the thirteen were on one or more lists compiled before the revolution identifying them as opposed to King James and/or opposed to the repeal of the Test Act and penal laws.[24] Several members had been active in arranging the prince's intervention. Four had signed the June 30 invitation . Five had participated in the drafting of William's *Declaration of Reasons*.[25] Delamere, Devonshire, Danby, and Lumley had been involved in the uprising in the North. In varying degrees, these Williamite peers subscribed to political principles characteristic of the radical Whigs.

Like the rights committee members in the Commons, these committeemen had had much previous parliamentary experience. Danby, of course, had organized the Tory party in the late 1670s. He, Nottingham, Devonshire, and Delamere had served in the House of Commons. Also like their opposites in the lower House, these peers were of advanced years: eight of the thirteen were over forty-five years old. They ranged in age from 76 (Wharton) to 29 (Shrewsbury). As with the Commons, the number of members attending committee meetings and conferences with the lower House is unknown, but Fauconberg managed meetings on February 11 and 12, and Winchester and Delamere reported to the House of Lords what had transpired at meetings on the twelfth.[26]

Little evidence has survived about the views of these committee members towards the nation's rights. Probably the Whig members were among the lords reported on February 1 to be in favor of drawing up a statement of grievances and rights. Van Citters, citing the authority of the "best informed people," declared that unidentified peers wanted to link the presentation of the crown with a statement on the reasons why James was "deposed" and on the rights of the nation. They had deliberately decided not to take the initiative in doing so because they knew that the Commons had appointed a committee to that end, and they wished to avoid threatening the enterprise by "provoking" the lower House, described as always jealous of its privileges.[27] Lord Mordaunt was surely enthusiastic about the project. Undoubtedly his wife reflected his views when she wrote that the Convention provided "an occasion not of amending the government, but of melting it down and making all new." Lady Mordaunt turned to Locke for a "right scheme of government" because he had been "infected by that great man, Lord Shaftesbury."[28] Lord Wharton surely endorsed the Commons' project. In a paper written probably during the winter of 1688/89, in preparation for the Convention, he had set out a proposal for remodeling the government.[29] Briefly, in his scheme the two Houses of Parliament would have authority to approve the appointment of royal ministers, members of the Privy Council, and judges. The king's authority over the House of Lords would be restricted by requiring both Houses to approve the elevation of men to the peerage and by barring the king from attending the debates of the upper House. Moreover, Parliament would have authority to create new boroughs and change the representation of present ones. Wharton also proposed changes in the militia. Only freeholders who had an annual income of at least £20 or held a copyhold for life of £30 were to serve in the militia. Such freeholders would be given the power to "nominate" the militia officers. This idea was similar to that put forward in 1685 in the duke of Monmouth's *Declaration,* and it also had affinities with still earlier recommendations offered by the Levellers.[30] The purpose was to bring control of the militia closer to people in the local counties and to dilute the authority of the central government. Furthermore, Wharton advocated that only such freeholders should be chosen to serve as jurors. Clearly, the effect of his proposal was to reduce the power of the king while increasing that of Parliament and the propertied freeholder. His biographer has concluded that Wharton regarded the revolution as an "opportunity . . . to effect a drastic alteration in the constitution."[31] Certainly his ideas were compatible with those discussed by the rights committees in the House of Commons. It is reasonable to think that he promoted Somers's draft in the House of Lords.

Delamere and Devonshire may also be presumed to have taken an active part in championing the claim of rights in the committee and the full House. Both had had much previous experience in and out of Parliament in oppositional politics. Delamere, the son of Sir George Booth, who had organized the 1659 "plot" for the restoration of Charles II, came from a family of strong parliamentarian and Protestant sympathies.[32] In the House of Commons he had opposed Charles's efforts to strengthen royal prerogatives, denounced M.P.'s who accepted bribes from the crown, criticized judicial abuse and the corruption of the bench, and promoted Exclusion. Shaftesbury rated him "worthy" on his 1679 list. Imprisoned several times on suspicion of involvement in the Rye House Plot and in Monmouth's Rebellion, Delamere secured release each time. Personally sympathetic to Dissenters, his religious views tinged with puritanism, Delamere fulfills the criteria established in this study to qualify him as a radical Whig.

Devonshire may also be classed a radical Whig. A member of the House of Commons before inheriting the earldom in 1684, as Cavendish he was active in efforts whose underlying principles were later reflected in the Declaration of Rights. For example, in 1676 he moved that the act of Edward III for annual parliaments be laid on the table and argued that the fifteen-month prorogation of the Cavalier Parliament was tantamount to a dissolution, a point reflected in article 13. He joined forces with M.P.'s who opposed the standing army, defended the privileges of the Commons, promoted the passage of the Habeas Corpus Act, and, with Delamere, condemned the judges, carrying up to the Lords the articles of impeachment against one of them. Cavendish favored the exclusion of James, and was also marked "worthy" by Shaftesbury in his 1679 list. He appeared as a witness for the defense at Russell's trial, but had no connection with the Rye House Plot nor with Monmouth's enterprise.

A man of quick temper, Cavendish, after becoming earl of Devonshire, was involved in an altercation in which he caned a man for impugning his loyalty to James after the duke became king. The upshot was that an information was filed in King's Bench charging him with a misdemeanor for striking a person in the king's palace. The case is significant for this study because it was cited in connection with the clauses about the judiciary in the Declaration of Rights. Devonshire paid £30,000 in bail to remain free pending trial. He rested his case on his privilege as a peer and his right not to be tried for a misdemeanor "during" the sitting of Parliament. But the court found him guilty and fined him £30,000. Devonshire's friend, Delamere, wrote about these proceedings in a piece which excoriated the judges for levying excessive bail and fine, and charged that partisan politics inspired the case.[33]

Devonshire was involved in the conspiracy to bring over William of Orange and was one of the "Immortal Seven" who signed the invitation to the prince. With Delamere and others he organized a rising in the North, the first of the provincial uprisings that so demoralized King James. Delamere rallied his tenants in a speech (later printed) which, in effect, was a call to arms to root out popery and slavery. He recommended the prince's *Declaration of Reasons* to his listeners. The strategy for the rising called for Delamere and Devonshire to meet at Nottingham. There, on November 24, 1688, they jointly proclaimed in the marketplace the *Declaration of the Nobility Gentry and Commonalty at the Rendezvous at Nottingham, November 22, 1688.*[34] This printed piece identified the grievances and rights of the nation in ways that reflected William's *Declaration of Reasons* and prefigured the Declaration of Rights. It asserts that the subscribers have gathered to defend the nation's laws, religion, and properties, which have "descended" to them as the "undoubted birthright" of Englishmen. It sets out "grounds" for endorsing William, blaming the "late Jesuitical Privy Council," not the king directly. In a form anticipating the Declaration of Rights, a catalogue of grievances follows. As in William's *Declaration* and the *Bishops' Proposals,* the dispensing power wins first place in the list. Next come condemnations of placing unqualified Catholics in positions of power and of using the quo warranto procedure. But unlike the *Bishops' Proposals,* this statement indicts the government for packing the bench and forbidding subjects to petition the king, characterizing the latter offense in picturesque terms as "rendering the laws a nose of wax." No mention is made of the Ecclesiastical Commission. Unlike both William's *Declaration* and the bishops' statement, this manifesto identifies the standing army as a grievance. Concern for the Nonconformist conscience is implied. This manifesto, published just two and a half months before the Lords addressed the Commons' draft claim of rights, clearly suggests that Devonshire and Delamere would have been among those peers who favored the claim.

A piece that Delamere wrote after the Revolution reinforces the presumption of his commitment to the Declaration of Rights. The earl declared that setting aside James and "electing" William was the first step towards repairing the government. He went on to assert that the crown was offered to William "not so much because he was the chief instrument of our deliverance, although we owe him much for that, but rather in hopes of having the effect of his Declaration," in other words, of winning the reforms enumerated in the manifesto. Delamere explained that it was in William's interests to do what he had promised, and that the nation was therefore "most likely" to get grievances redressed by the prince than by any other person. William, Delamere thought, "could not but be sensible of the reproach and hazard he ran . . . [if] having found fault with King James's administration . . ., he did not amend whatever was amiss."[35] Delamere favored taking away the dispensing power because it "swallows up" the law and "puts every man's right at an uncertainty."[36] He regretted the defeat of the effort to change the tenure of judges from "at the pleasure of the king" to "during good behaviour."[37] He was appalled at the corruption practiced by the Stuarts. Charles II taught James II, he said, how to corrupt Parliament by influencing elections, by using the offer of places, pensions, and other bribes, and by "closeting." The result was that members had become "men of dependence."[38] He was also horrified by the practice of putting unqualified men into places of authority. He called such men "through-stick men," persons, that is, who would stick at nothing to please the king.[39] He regarded the creation of the Ecclesiastical Commission as a violation of law.[40] He deplored the court's denying subjects the right of petitioning, arguing that such a restraint put men under the necessity of using the sword.[41] Finally, Delamere was convinced that any standing military force, including the king's guards, was illegal and a grievance. "It will be easier to find a world in the moon, than that the law has made the guards a lawful force, or that any statute has established any force," he wrote.[42] Given these views, it is altogether likely that Delamere would have bent every effort to forward and strengthen the draft statement of rights.

Thomas Belasyse, second Viscount Fauconberg (1627–1700), was chosen chairman of the committee.[43] Sixty-two years old, Fauconberg had had considerable political experience as a servant of both Oliver Cromwell and Charles II. A member of a prominent family from northern England, he had, in opposition to his father and grandfather (whom he succeeded to the viscounty of Fauconberg in 1652), supported Parliament's side in the Civil War and become a strong adherent of Cromwell. The two men were close enough that in 1657 Cromwell negotiated a marriage between Fauconberg, a firm Anglican, and Mary, his third daughter. An able person of great personal charm, Fauconberg conducted a goodwill mission to France for his father-in-law and became a member of Oliver Cromwell's "Other House." After the Restoration, Charles II appointed him ambassador to Venice in 1669 and in 1679 made him a privy councillor. Through his family, Fauconberg had connections with the Catholic community. His uncle was John Belasyse, Baron Belasyse, one of the five Catholic lords impeached of high treason on the testimony of Titus Oates.

Viscount Fauconberg declined to support James's Catholicizing policies. His name appears on lists of peers who opposed the king and the repeal of the

Thomas Belasyse, second Viscount Fauconberg (1627–1700)

Married to Oliver Cromwell's daughter and experienced as diplomat and servant of Charles II, Fauconberg chaired the committee in the House of Lords that amended the Commons' draft Declaration of Rights. (Courtesy of the National Portrait Gallery, London.)

Test Act. He was relieved of his post as lord-lieutenant of North Riding in 1687, ending expectation for preferment from James. Fauconberg was marginally involved in the rising at York, sending £500 to Danby, his distant relation, to defray some of the expenses.[44] In the Convention, he served on the committee to examine the circumstances of the death of the earl of Essex and on the committee to draw up reasons for the lords' amendments to the abdication and vacancy resolution. He also chaired the Committee on Privileges that met on January 28 to consider the special privileges of the lords.[45] Possibly his work on that committee, which was much concerned to assert the right of lords to be tried only in Parliament, and not by a jury of men who were not their peers, sharpened his interest in the claim of rights sent up by the lower House.[46] As already mentioned, although Fauconberg was a Maryite, he voted with Danby on January 31, 1689, to offer the throne to William and Mary, indicating thereby willingness to compromise his political preferences. Yet he could not bring himself on February 4 to vote to agree with the Commons on the word "abdicated," and may have "retired between the hanging and the door next to the Bishops' room" to avoid the vote. On February 6, however, he did vote to accept the word "abdicated." In each of these votes, Fauconberg followed the lead of Danby, one of only two or three others in the House to do so.[47] Furthermore, he was appointed to the committee to manage the conference with the Commons on February 8, when the Declaration of Rights was received, and he also managed two more conferences with the lower House the next week.[48] Although not of the first rank in political importance, Fauconberg was a knowledgeable, competent man with experience in negotiating delicate political matters. After the revolution, William elevated him to an earldom.

As instructed, the committee met at 8:00 A.M. on Monday, February 11, in the prince's lodgings. A fragment of the minutes of the committee, preserved in the House of Lords Record Office, fails to disclose who or how many lords attended the meeting but does show that the committee proposed some amendments of its own as well as supplying reasons to support the changes the full House wanted.

The amendments the lords proposed varied in importance.[49] Some were minor adjustments in language, to assure conformity with pertinent laws.[50] Some testified to the peers' sensitivity to their special status.[51] Some reflected the sensitivity of men whose views had not prevailed. For example, the lords objected to the idea that the reaffirmation of rights was "unanimous." They insisted that William's *Declaration of Reasons* had "encouraged" — not "invited" — the Convention to demand their rights. They declined to characterize the demand of rights as the "only means for obtaining a full redress and remedy therein," a deletion which the Commons, in turn, rejected, calling upon William's *Declaration,* whose words they admitted they had followed to confirm their opinion. The lords withdrew the change.

Other amendments drew inspiration from partisan considerations. One adjustment would have specifically limited the indictment of grievances to the reign of James II, thereby protecting Tories who had been involved in the court's excesses during the reign of Charles II.[52] To the phrase that William would secure the nation from future threats to its religion, laws, and liberties, the Lords' committee added the words "as they were established by the laws and statutes of this realm, at the time of the accession of the late King James the Second to the crown." But the Commons objected because the words implied a willingness to "countenance" the "attempts" on the nation's rights and liberties "in the former reign."[53] Those Whig members of the Commons who had wanted to condemn the proceedings of the past thirty years, not just of the past three years, prevailed in this instance.

Still another proposed change concerned the charge that James had caused informations to be brought and prosecuted in King's Bench.[54] It will be remembered that lawyers in the Commons had objected to the clause in the Heads of Grievances about informations. That clause had been dropped as a matter which required new law. But Treby had insisted upon the evilness of informations, and reference to them had been preserved in the indictment of James. The lords, however, maintained that they did not fully understand what was meant by the charge, nor what instances there had been of it, and asked the Commons to explain themselves, if they insisted upon keeping the article.[55] The debate in the Commons in response to the lords' comments[56] suggests that the lawyers had been inattentive when the article was first framed and shows that the personal grievance of one member determined the inclusion of the article. Pollexfen asserted that the word "information" should have been "prosecution," Lee admitted that the clause did "arise from a mistake," Holt complained about the grammar, and Eyre recommended that the House agree with the lords in the matter as a way of healing divisions. Once more, perhaps with some sense of embarrassment that a point which he had defended before was again in contention, Treby rose to explain that the article was put in the draft "for the sake of . . . Sir William Williams, who was punished out of Parliament for what he had done in Parliament." Treby felt that the clause might be explained, but urged that it not be omitted. Williams reinforced his plea, maintaining that Lord Lovelace and Lord Devonshire, as well as he himself, had suffered the ill effects of informations. He pointed out that although these episodes had begun earlier, the actual prosecution had taken place during James's reign. Such reasoning won the assent of the Commons. When Somers's committee reported the next day, they insisted upon retaining the article, declaring that it was a "very high grievance that causes cognizable only in Parliament" should be drawn into lower courts. But they amended the clause to read "By prosecutions in the Court of King's Bench for matters and causes cognizable only in Parliament, and by divers others arbitrary and illegal courses,"[57] which proved to be satisfactory to the lords.

Other adjustments were of constitutional and political importance. The Commons had said that the "administration of government" should be placed in William's hands, words some people thought had "republican" overtones. The Lords proposed, and the Commons accepted, that the "sole and full exercise of regal power" shall be in William's hands, words thought to underscore the monarchical character of the government. A contemporary regarded the amendment as important enough to warrant special mention,[58] and a twentieth-century historian has described it as "crucial."[59] An equally significant adjustment agreed to by the lower House was the removal of the words "and suffered to sit," which had been placed at the end of the clause that declared "Parliament ought to be held frequently." The Lords justified the deletion on the grounds that "the assembling and holding of Parliament"[60] is all the statutes permit. The removal of those words reaffirmed the prerogative of the king to dismiss Parliament at his pleasure and testified to a retreat on the part of the "worthy" Whigs who in debate had clamored for restriction on that power.

Amendments proposed to the clauses about military authority resulted in substantial change to the draft document. On February 9, an unidentified lord moved to add the words "and quartering soldiers, contrary to law" to the article which indicted James for raising and keeping a standing army within the kingdom in time of peace without the consent of Parliament. He argued that free quarter had aggravated the grievance of a standing army and was a patent violation of the Petition of Right.[61] Curiously, this proposal, which might be expected to have won immediate assent, provoked such sharp disagreement that a division was taken. Forty-four peers voted yes (with Nottingham, no adherent of William at this time, serving as teller), while thirty-three lords voted no (with Devonshire, an admirer of the prince and a radical Whig, serving as teller).[62] The minority asked leave to enter their dissents. In the manuscript journals preserved in the House of Lords Record Office appears an entry not recorded in the printed journals, which reads: "And accordingly these Lords following do enter dissents by subscribing their names." The sentence, now only faintly discernible, has been erased, and no names are visible.[63] Did some lords subscribe their names and then change their minds? Why should Devonshire, who ten years earlier as a member of the House of Commons had been a strong anti–standing army man, vote against the amendment condemning free quarter? The probable reason is that he and others hesitated to indict James for an act they knew could also be charged against William, whose army, the good intentions of the prince notwithstanding, was guilty of taking free quarter. Perhaps their political principles then moved them to reverse their inclination to enter dissents. If this is an accurate explanation, the episode reveals the tension between the prince's interests and the principles of his most ardent adherents.

Other abortive actions of the Lords further reveal this tension. For example, the peers proposed deleting the words "in time of peace" from the clause "there shall be no standing army in time of peace without the consent of parliament," which would have extended parliamentary control of the armed forces to times of war as well as peace. Surely it was William's friends that perceived the implications of the proposal and argued successfully for a reversal.[64] Or again, Fauconberg's committee considered recommending that the entire article about standing armies be deleted, which would have preserved royal authority over the armed forces in peacetime.[65] Almost certainly, the prince's friends were behind this suggestion. But the anti–standing army tradition was too strong, and nothing came of the idea. Moreover, Fauconberg's committee persuaded the Lords to pass an order, separate from the Declaration of Rights, as a "provision against the keeping of a standing army." The order concerned the forces "now in being" or to be raised later for reducing Ireland or helping the nation's allies according to treaties. It declared that such forces might be continued until "otherwise ordered in Parliament."[66] The intention almost certainly was to legalize the existing army under William's command and to assure that it not escape control of Parliament. For unspecified reasons, the House of Commons took no action on the order.[67]

The Lords insisted upon amending the article about the right of subjects to bear arms. Somers's draft read: "That the subjects which are Protestants may provide and keep arms for their common defence." According to this phraseology, every Protestant was given the right to keep arms. The lords, however, proposed that for "provide and keep" the word "have" be substituted; that the word "common" be deleted; and that the following words be added: "suitable to their condition, and as allowed by law." These proposed adjustments, as already discussed,[68] reflected the peers's sensitivity to their social status and privileges, to the dangers of arming *all* Protestants, and to early laws that had restricted the possession of weapons to persons of certain economic degree. The Commons accepted the changes without comment.

Finally, the Lords recommended adjustments to the clauses on the king's power over law, which, although rejected by the Commons in the form proposed, led to significant changes in Somers's draft. The peers wanted to limit the Commons' prohibition of the king's right to dispense with laws, unless with the consent of Parliament, by adding the words "as by consequence would subject all the laws to his will and pleasure." In considering the issue, they sought advice from their legal advisers.[69] Atkyns maintained that the king had no authority to dispense with the law, but the other lawyers disagreed. Montague said such authority was allowed "by law books."[70] Dolben asserted that the judges had repeatedly reaffirmed the right and that English kings, in fact, had dispensed with laws for over two hundred years. The Pope had brought in the power. Levinz concurred, but declared that the right to dispense did not extend to the issues addressed in James's Declaration of Indulgence. Reassured, the House of Lords decided to add the words. They further amended the clause in the declaratory section of Somers's draft by adding the phrase "and the power of dispensing with laws, as it was exercised and extended in the reign of the late King James the Second." They explained that the Commons' general condemnation of the dispensing power would harm individuals because it would bring into question the validity of a great number of patents and grants from the crown.[71] They did not explain that the amending language also would limit the indictment of the dispensing power to the reign of James II, thereby protecting the Tories, who, under Charles II, had been party to the exercise of that power.

The debate in the House of Commons revealed sympathy for these proposed changes. Although one spokesman asserted that James's use of the dispensing power was "the greatest and crying grievance of the nation" and that it had "no solid foundation in law," others pointed out that the prohibition of all power of dispensing will "undo many persons." [72] The House referred the matter to Somers's committee. There, the views of radical Whigs prevailed. The committee rejected the Lords' amendments to the indictment of James on the grounds that the proposed language "affirmed" the dispensing power as it had been exercised in the "former reign." [73] Thus, they refused to exempt specifically from criticism the policies perpetrated during the reign of Charles II. They proposed to make two articles of the one clause about law, one condemning outright the suspending power and the other indicting the dispensing power "as it has been assumed and exercised of late." By substituting the words "of late" for the words "the reign of the late King James the Second," Somers's committee subtly extended criticism to the earlier period. The peers accepted this formula, but in the months to come, when the declaration was being shaped into the Bill of Rights, they revived their effort to limit the clauses about the dispensing power.

In such ways, then, did the House of Lords respond to the claim of rights. Tories in the upper House provoked a crisis which could have resulted in sabotaging the claim. Although they came around to approving the statement, it was radical Whigs among the peers, just as among the M.P.'s, who championed the draft.

By the end of the afternoon of February 12, the two Houses had reached agreement on the text. Matters were expedited by the Lords' arranging that the amendments proposed by the Commons be regarded as amendments of their own, thus avoiding further conference meetings. [74] The title "Declaration" was decided upon, [75] and, at the initiative of the Commons, it was arranged that the document should be engrossed in parchment to remain among the records in Parliament, and also that it be enrolled in the Court of Chancery, to remain in perpetuity. [76] Thus, the problems that had remained unsolved when Treby reported to the House on February 7 were settled under Somers's direction.

Contemporary observers continued to describe the claim of rights as limitations on royal power. Clarendon referred on February 11 to the "new frame of government" that was being drafted. [77] Reresby reported the expressed confidence that the "invasions . . . on the liberties of the people by the former king [were] now expected to be redressed." [78] Morrice wrote that the Declaration of Rights contained the "state of the government." [79] One of the new London newspapers referred to the document as the "preliminaries" that "are necessary to be presented with the Crown." [80] Such was the prevailing view of the document on the eve of the presentation ceremony and the proclamation of the new king and queen.

15
February 13, 1689:
Ceremonies and Processions

On February 13, 1689, in a symbolic ceremony at about 10:30 A.M. in the Banqueting Hall of Whitehall Palace, the Declaration of Rights was read to William and Mary and then the crown of England offered to them. Their acknowledgment of the claim of rights and their acceptance of the crown in a speech by the prince on behalf of himself and his wife marked the end of the most critical phase of the Glorious Revolution. Immediately thereafter William and Mary were proclaimed king and queen in London, the event marked by staged processions and contrived verbal exchanges, sanctified by sermon and prayer in the afternoon, and celebrated by bonfires and merrymaking in the evening.

The events of this day were informed with political meaning. They are properly to be seen as a continuation of the political maneuvering that characterized the weeks preceding and during the Convention. They offer clues that deepen understanding of the political process underlying the Revolution and clarify aspects of the Declaration of Rights. Analysis shows that the principals in the Glorious Revolution engineered the processions and ceremonies to create public images and impressions and organized the ceremony in the Banqueting Hall to win from William an implicit political commitment that could not be obtained directly — a commitment that assured that this revolution would change not only the English king, but also the kingship.

A decade ago, it might have been necessary to justify use of ceremonies and processions as evidence for understanding the political process. Today, thanks to pioneering work by historians and anthropologists,[1] ceremonies and processions are recognized as legitimate parts of the historical record, properly regarded as cultural artifacts capable of being "read," just as conventional documentary evidence is read. They were important aspects of political life in early modern Europe. As the literacy rate was low[2] and the means of communication limited, political leaders communicated with the

248

public by means of symbols and symbolic ceremonies, which conveyed political ideas and comment. Although the events of February 13 are often mentioned in studies of the Glorious Revolution, the entire record — written, pictorial, and architectural [3] — has not been closely studied. Direct evidence is, admittedly, a bit thin in some places. Information on the kind of wine William and Mary preferred for washing their feet is easier to find than data on what they wore at the presentation ceremony, what was served at the gala that evening, how much the ceremony cost, and who paid for it.[4] The absence or thinness of some material can probably be explained by the haste with which the proceedings were devised, the breakdown of the administrative machinery during this "interregnum," and the reluctance of some men to preserve the evidence of their intimate involvement in elevating the new monarchs. There are, however, sufficient direct data and circumstantial evidence to permit legitimate inferences.

The ceremonies of February 13 came, as has been seen, at the end of a period of sharp negotiating and deepening political tension. During these days, some men at the center of events expressed a pessimistic view of affairs. For example, the prince himself, who was reported to look worried, remarked that now it was "hosanna," but soon he could expect to be "crucified."[5] Lord Halifax, the Speaker of the House of Lords, confessed that he had "no great hopes of a lasting peace" and that Scotland, Ireland, and England were all still unsettled.[6] Indeed, J. P. Kenyon has estimated that less than five percent of the governing class would have agreed to the settlement if they had realized clearly what they were doing.[7] Perceptive observers from all walks of life could have known about the difficulties. Despite the "closed doors" policy of both Houses and their efforts to preserve the confidentiality of their affairs, it has been shown that oral, written, and printed sources circulated news of what was happening in Westminster. The arrangements for the ceremony and proclamation, then, were made against a background of tension about the terms of the settlement and of relief that bloodshed had been avoided.

The proceedings, moreover, were contrived in great haste, in tandem with the larger political decisions of the Convention. Arrangements were not completed until the early morning of the thirteenth.[8] Swiftness of action, however, need not imply absence of calculated purpose or prior consideration. Prince William and his allies had already used deliberately and skillfully every available device, including printed tracts, broadsides, pictures, and commemorative medals, to mold the opinion of a broad spectrum of society. Their intense interest in this first major public event may be assumed. The surviving record does not specify a "committee on arrangements," but indirect evidence suggests that the men in the House of Commons who were responsible for drafting the Declaration of Rights helped to design the ceremony and, as will be shown, that they were deeply concerned about what should be presented. The fact that politically conscious people looked for certain specific things in the ceremony — some, for instance, hoped that Mary, if not William, would apologize for displacing James — strengthens the conclusion that the proceedings were of more than casual interest to persons in and out of the Convention.[9] Moreover, the absence of any report of a misstep, a misspoken word, a hesitation, or an embarrassment of any kind in these stylized events reinforces the idea that those involved practiced what one writer calls "impression management."[10]

The major function of the proceedings was, of course, to proclaim the prince and princess of Orange king and queen of England. A closely related aim was to demonstrate to people in England and abroad the joyous unanimity of a united nation at this resolution of the crisis. The day's events were also designed as a spectacle to entertain participants and spectators and express relief that the upheaval was over. Both William and the Convention had an interest in seeing that these purposes were well fulfilled.

There was apparent concern to perform the proclamation ceremonies in the traditional way and uncertainty how in the existing circumstances, when the requisite administrative structures had collapsed, this could be achieved. One M.P. pointed out that the usual procedures for proclaiming a new king called for the Privy Council to meet, name the heir, confer with the lord mayor of London, and order the proclamation. But there was no privy council in being to do that. Drawing an analogy from the law of property, this member compared English subjects to a tenant who might "attorn" to a new lord.[11] The point of interest is not the analogy, which was far-fetched and not repeated, but rather the confusion it suggests about how the Convention might proceed. The Dutch ambassador reported that, since February 8, the Convention had been "continually occupied in planning in what manner" the prince and princess would be proclaimed.[12] In the event, the House of Lords, at the very last moment, ordered the proclamation to be performed "in the usual manner and at the usual places accustomed on like occasions." They specifically declared that their order was a sufficient warrant.[13] The generality of the language and the specific assertion that the order was a sufficient warrant would seem to reflect their anxiety about the matter. Concern was also expressed over which local officer in the counties should receive the proclamation. Sheriffs would customarily be addressed, but since so many of them were Catholic, left over from James II's remodeling of local government, it was decided to direct the document to the coroner![14] Moreover, members labored over drafting the official proclamation. The text they finally agreed upon is significantly different from that of the documents proclaiming earlier Stuart kings. The Privy Council is not named, but the House of Commons and "others of the commons of the realm" are specifically mentioned along with the lords spiritual and temporal and the lord mayor and citizens of London as the persons proclaiming the new monarchs.[15] Clearly, the drafters broadened the base of persons responsible for the proclamation and, by so doing, implied wide support for the step.

During the time that the political and constitutional aspects of the proclamation were troubling people, the duke of Norfolk, who simply continued to function as the earl marshall, took steps, apparently without any warrant from the Convention, to ensure that the public ceremonies traditionally associated with proclaiming a new monarch would be carried out. Beginning on February 7 and in a rising flurry on February 12, written and verbal orders went out, calling upon the heralds "to be ready (when commanded) to proclaim" the new monarchs, instructing the Jewell House to recall all maces, ordering the repair and assignment of maces, and alerting the high constable of Westminster and the keeper of the Tower as to their responsibilities for the proclamation.[16] There must have been many such orders and perhaps many meetings, notice of which is lost, to arrange the logistics of the proclamation ceremony. One should not underestimate the attention to details which the smooth carrying out of the proclamation reveals nor the interest in fulfilling prescribed formulae it suggests.

In fact, the proclamation was very grand, on the whole traditional and evocative of the past. An ancient officer of the crown, Knight Garter, Principal King of Arms, carried the document in a splendid procession from Westminster to the Banqueting Hall. Following the ceremony there, the assembled company of peers and M.P.'s joined the heralds, serjeants-at-arms, trumpeters, and others at Whitehall Gate. The trumpets sounded three times and at the last blast were answered by a "great shout" from the crowd. Whereupon Knight Garter read the official document "in short periods or sentences," the people replying with "several repeated shouts." Then, moving in another brilliant procession, with kettledrums, bugles, and trumpets, he proclaimed it four more times in London in the presence of the lord mayor, other city officials, and "vast multitudes." The streets of London were lined on both sides by members of the Orange, Green, Blue, and White regiments of the city militia.[17]

An untraditional and polemical note was injected into the ceremonies by a curious exchange at Temple Bar. Upon the knock at the gate, an officer therein inquired, "Where is King James II?" Someone responded, "He is dead. He is dead. He is dead." Others heard, "He has abdicated the government."[18] These statements clearly aimed to justify the elevation of the new monarchs. Sensitive observers would have noticed that the latter comment supported the abdication and vacancy formula, which had caused such bitter fights in and between the two Houses of the Convention just the week before. Surely that comment was uttered by a partisan of the formula in order to underline it in public.

In addition to announcing that England had a new king and queen, these proceedings also expressed joy, unanimity, and relief. The procession, the banners, the stirring sounds of trumpets, bugles, and kettledrums, the presence of ancient officers of the crown in gorgeous regalia, and so on, must have been splendid and inspiriting. All contemporary reporters testify that masses of people turned out, lining the streets, standing on balconies, and leaning from windows.[19] A large number of persons took part in the official proceedings; upwards of fifty persons are specifically mentioned, and many others are implied by the official account preserved in the *Journals of the House of Commons*.[20] A broadside, *The Manner of the Proclaiming of King William, and Queen Mary, at White-Hall and in the City of London, Feb. 13, 1688/89*, insisted that the crowds "filled the air" with "such shouts as were scarcely ever heard." The people, it was said, were transported with delight, "each striving to exceed" the other in "public demonstration thereof."

The reputedly large and enthusiastic crowd invites comment. It is possible that the official accounts exaggerated the numbers and zeal of people to magnify the occasion. But the confirmation of these points by private reports makes that unlikely. Granting, then, a huge crowd, a question is, Were people "encouraged" to appear? There is no direct evidence that they were, and the turnout may have been spontaneous. But it should be recalled that William and his English and Dutch friends had made the most concentrated effort in England's history to shape the opinion of a broad spectrum of society in favor of the prince. Printed and visual materials were aimed at people far outside elite categories. If the people appeared spontaneously, some credit must go to this unprecedented propaganda campaign. Moreover, it is not unreasonable to think that an immediate effort was made to bring out a substantial number of people and to instruct them in their response. The success achieved just ten days earlier in obtaining signatures to a petition to the Convention — it was said some 15,000 names were subscribed in two days and 10,000 men were ready to deliver the petition[21] — supports the hypothesis. That the shouts of the crowd were orchestrated with the steps in the proclamation adds strength to the idea. The weather was cold and "tempestuous," and had been for days.[22] This might have discouraged the appearance of some people if an effort had not been made to bring them out. One may suggest further that men hoped the large number of people and the excitement of the processions would make less noticeable the absence of a great many peers. Despite an effort to ensure a good turnout, only 35 to 41 out of a possible 153 lords attended, and of them, only 3 bishops appeared in the procession.[23] The archbishop of Canterbury was absent, and Henry Compton, the bishop of London, was called on to preach a sermon that afternoon. A fortnight later, a member of the House of Commons excoriated the spiritual peers for absenting themselves at the proclamation.[24] Moreover, the comment of a Tory observer that although there were many expressions of joy, "a great many [people] looked very sadly upon it,"[25] reinforces the thought that the hearty shouts and the competition among individuals to excel each other in the "public demonstration" of their approbation may have been to some degree contrived. Finally, if anyone was inclined to a contrary expression — as by the end of the month the street songs clearly showed that some were[26] — the presence of members of the Orange, Green, Blue, and White regiments of the city militia along both sides of the streets of London would have discouraged that expression.

In the evening, as at earlier critical moments in the revolution,[27] bonfires burned all over the city. They were visible symbols of approval of the settlement, and appeared at "particular persons' doors" to signify that approval. Some of the bonfires were ingeniously devised to convey political messages. One of "extraordinary great height," placed in St. James's Square, depicted the Pope and the Devil. Before them, an effigy of Jeffreys, manipulated by an "engine," pleaded his "great service." Then all the figures were cast into the fire and burned.[28] The most elaborate and costly of all the bonfires was four stories high; at its summit was an effigy of Father Edward Petre, James's detested Jesuit adviser and confessor. As the bonfire was consumed, Father Petre was blown up, "even as he would have done the nation," explained one admiring account. Placed outside Watts Coffee House in German Street, the scene of earlier political discussions and of previous bonfires, this bonfire, designed by a Captain Silver, was "contributed to" by peers and members of the Convention Parliament.[29] Such complicated creations cost money, required gunpowder, and must have taken time to design and construct. How much money was expended on the displays is not known, but the fireworks celebrating the Treaty of Ryswick eight years later reportedly cost £10,000.[30] It is a tantalizing thought that some of the bonfires may have been partly fueled with papers that one looks for in vain in the Public Record Office! In addition to the bonfires, rockets and fireworks timed to go off at intervals illuminated the city throughout the evening.

Written, printed, iconographic, and oral accounts carried news of the proclamation all over England and abroad. The official proclamation, upon the order of the Convention,[31] appeared in print immediately. It went through five editions in February. A lengthy account of the proclamation was entered in the *Journals of the House of Commons*, the only time such a step was taken in the seventeenth century. Entering the record of the proclamation invested it with legality and regularity. *The Manner of the Proclaiming*, just mentioned, was on the streets of London by February 13.[32] It identified persons, described their regalia, and provided a detailed account of the processions and ceremonies. Pictures also appeared. An anonymous Dutch print, reproduced here as Figure 3, was published in Amsterdam within the year, clearly conveying to viewers the idea of the joyous unanimity of the nation in elevating William and Mary to the throne. It shows a grand procession of peers, members of the Convention Parliament, pursuivants, Knight Garter, Principal King of Arms carrying the proclamation of the new monarchs, trumpeters, and others, dressed resplendently (we know from written accounts) in blue and scarlet, bearing large maces,[33] on foot, on horseback, and in coaches. The procession makes it way with banners held aloft and flags flying from Westminster to the Banqueting House at Whitehall. The print depicts a confident English establishment on its way to a settlement of the political crisis while a crowd of people applauds the event.

Appealing to a different public taste, a song, *The Subject's Satisfaction: Being a new song of the proclaiming of King William and Queen Mary the 13th of February*, was printed beneath a picture of William and Mary sitting under two angels holding one crown.[34] One verse stressed the joy with which the ceremony was

Figure 3. Grand procession on February 13, 1689. Lords, Commons, and traditional officers of the crown make their way on February 13, 1689, from Westminster to the Banqueting Hall for the presentation ceremony. Crowds of people line the streets and lean from balconies showing their approval by gestures and expression. (Courtesy of the Guildhall Library. The print also appeared in an anonymous work, *Engeland Beroerd onder de Regeering van Koning Jacobus de II* [Amsterdam 1689].)

received, and another discounted as a "Popish rumor" that the House of Lords and the House of Commons had ever been "at variance." The *London Gazette*, formerly the official newspaper of Charles II and James II, broke its self-imposed silence and printed a full account of the proclamation. Several of the new newspapers, which had all along been sympathetic to William, ran detailed and enthusiastic stories. In all, observers described the proclamation as having been done in "the accustomed manner" and thought it "as splendidly performed as ever any was before."[35] Such was the impression conveyed by the Dutch ambassador and by the prince himself, who wrote immediately to persons on the Continent disclaiming any ambition to be king.[36] The carrying out of the proclamation in the traditional way, with the officers of the crown, the members of the Convention, and the officers of the city of London participating, with the bugles and trumpets blaring, and the crowds shouting, concealed the significant change in the royal succession that had occurred. These things helped to legitimize the revolution and create the impression that the ancient constitution had not been breached.

Another function of the proceedings was to present publicly a statement of the rights of the nation and to link that statement to the offer of the crown. In the Banqueting Hall about 10:30 in the morning of that Ash Wednesday, a carefully contrived ceremony was held (Frontispiece). It was witnessed only by members of the Convention[37] and close friends of the prince. Preceded by the Gentleman Usher of the Black Rod, the Speakers of both Houses led the peers and commons across the length of the great hall lined with yeomen of the guard, made at intervals three deep obeisances and approached Prince William and Princess Mary as they sat hand-in-hand under a canopy of state. Lord Halifax requested permission to present a declaration agreed upon by both Houses. Permission being granted, the deputy-clerk of Parliament read the Declaration of Rights from a parchment copy, and then the crown of England was offered to William and Mary. Rising to respond for them both, while the princess signified her assent by "her looks and a little curtsy,"[38] Prince William accepted the crown and acknowledged the Declaration of Rights in brief remarks. His acceptance speech (Fig. 4) was greeted inside with a great shout and masses of people outside echoed the cry.[39] William and Mary then left the hall.

This ceremony was the unique aspect of the day's events. Many times before (especially in the seventeenth century), Parliament had presented to a reigning king instruments, in the form of petition, remonstrance, advice, and address, which set forth the grievances and the rights of the subject. Six times before 1689, the English had removed their king, each time justifying the step in apologias that defined the authority of the monarchy.[40] But never before had an instrument, in any form, been presented to a person *before* he was king and *at the time* he was offered the crown. Nor before had such an instrument been shaped to suggest that acceptance of it was the condition for the offer of the crown and that its terms restricted the prerogatives of the crown. The reading of the Declaration of Rights before the crown was offered reflected a political victory of men who favored changing the kingship as well as the king over those who wanted only to change the king. Clearly, if the latter had had their way, a ceremony simply proclaiming the new monarchs would have been all that was necessary. Nevertheless, there was more symbolism and image-making than legal substance in this unique ceremony.

The actions of members of the Convention in making preparations for the presentation ceremony reveal a concern to underscore in subtle ways the importance of the claim of rights. First, the document was titled "Declaration," a stronger term than "Address" or "Petition," as has been discussed. The phrase "Declaration of Rights of the subject" had appeared in William's manifesto, so the choice of words may be seen as another public link to the prince's manifesto as well as an effort to convey the idea that the Convention was stating already established and accepted rights.[41] Second, in requesting an interview with the prince to settle the details of the time and place of the ceremony, the lords specifically stated that the purpose of the ceremony was "to wait on [the prince] with their Declaration." No mention was made of the crown.[42] Third, at the initiative of the Commons, both Houses, surely in an effort to give the document as much status and legal force as possible, ordered that the declaration should be engrossed in parchment, enrolled in the rolls of Parliament, and entered in the Court of Chancery "to remain in perpetuity."[43] Although the declaration was not a bill, they treated it as if it had properties of a bill. A pamphlet printed shortly after the ceremony argued that since the Declaration of Rights was engrossed and enrolled, it was "conclusive and binding."[44] Fourth, the presentation copy of the Declaration of Rights — the one the clerk read in the Banqueting Hall — was given marks of importance. As already noted, the parchment was two and one half inches wider than that normally used for bills, and it was decorated with two red lines on either side of the text. Fifth, the House of Lords agreed to meet at 8:00 A.M. the morning of February 13 in their chamber and "go in a body" with the declaration to the Banqueting Hall. Further, they suggested that the members of the House of Commons do likewise, recommending that the M.P.'s "go along" with them.[45] Such an arrangement for peers and commoners to meet first at Westminster, rather than at any other place, and to arrive at the Banqueting Hall as a body, rather than individually, may be seen as an effort to give public testimony to the corporate nature of Parliament and its importance in the proceedings to follow. Most important of all, the language (by and large) and the arrangement of the material in the Commons' draft of the Declaration of Rights were retained. As has been shown, the document was crafted in such a way as to convey certain political impressions. In sum, all these details suggest that, whatever the actual legal force of the declaration, the Convention did many different subtle things to underline the importance of the document and to create the belief that it was a precondition for receiving the English crown and that it limited the royal prerogative.

Although the initiative in arranging the events of February 13 remained with the Convention, William and his close friends played a role in the preparations. It fell to William to choose the time and place of the presentation ceremony.[46] He chose the Banqueting Hall. There were other possible sites: for example, Westminster Hall or Westminster Abbey (the likely choice if an emphasis upon Anglicanism were desired), or the House of Lords chamber (where the Petition of Right had been presented).[47] There is no "minute" that reveals why the prince selected the Banqueting Hall, but it had been the center of the Stuart court's activities and used for manifold purposes. A good-sized hall, measuring 110 feet long by 55 feet wide and high, its ceiling gorgeously decorated by Rubens, the Banqueting Hall was ideally suited for public ceremonies. Here Stuart kings had received members of Parliament, and ambassadors presented their credentials.[48] Here Charles II was joyfully received on May 29, 1660, upon his return to the throne. Interestingly enough, lords and members of Parliament had approached and addressed him in a manner very like that used in 1689.[49] Finally, it could hardly have been lost on any sensitive observer — especially since the specter of civil war had influenced the debates — that just forty years before, on January 30, 1649, Charles I had walked through this same hall on his way to the scaffold outside the window. This revolution, the choice of the Banqueting Hall seemed to say, has brought no such bloodshed and divisions as occurred in 1649, but rather has brought a reconciliation as in 1660.

It was also William's decision to hold the ceremony on Ash Wednesday, a day more important in the religious calendar of the Anglican Church than for the Calvinist faith in which William had been raised. It is a nice question whether Mary, whose boat was already on the Thames when the decision was made, would have urged her husband, had she been present, to postpone the ceremony until Thursday in deference to the sensibilities of devout Anglicans. The argument in favor of holding the ceremony on Ash Wednesday, according to Burnet, was that it "had a particular decency in it, that princes immediately when they were set on the throne should come and humble themselves in dust and ashes before God."[50] Did William choose the day to signal his religious inclinations and indicate his sympathy with Dissenters? The point is moot. But one may speculate that the choice of day implied just that. And the idea is reinforced by the service of thanksgiving held later in the afternoon in the Chapel Royal. The service, conducted (as already noted) by Compton, attracted a "very great audience," which delighted, reported one newspaper, "to see a King and Queen of England together worshipping God in the Reformed Religion."[51]

In addition to deciding the day and place of the ceremony, William surely thought about how to present himself. For the first time he would appear before the members of the Convention. What was he to wear? How was he to act? Less than four months before, William had made a dazzling entry into Exeter mounted on a "milk white palfrey armed cap a pied, a plume of white feathers on his head."[52] He could not appear in that outfit! Indeed, military dress of any kind would not conform to the image that he had taken pains to project; interestingly enough, none of the prints of the occasion show him wearing so much as a sword.[53] Iconographic material portrayed him as an Orange Tree, a lion, and a Roman senator, none of which was appropriate to the occasion. For the ceremony, William probably wore a simple cinnamon-colored suit, interlined with flannel to protect his chest, racked by a deepening of his asthmatic cough, against the cold.[54] Probably his waistcoat was a rich gold and silver brocade with gold buttons, also interlined with flannel. William West, his embroiderer, very likely embroidered on his coat the star seen in the print.[55] Sitting under the canopy, a symbol of nobility, which, of course, he claimed in his own right, William presented a rather modest, certainly civilian, surely benign picture. As the ceremony unfolds, he plays a passive role. The Speakers of the two Houses approach him. They begin the exchange. He signifies assent to their request to present their declaration. The deputy-clerk of the Parliament reads the declaration. William responds. That is all. William was content that he and Mary should leave the hall immediately after the speeches were concluded. They make no further public appearances until late in the afternoon at Compton's sermon and in the evening at a party at Whitehall. All of this is entirely consistent with the image of a selfless deliverer who came only with a "force sufficient" — as his *Declaration of Reasons* insisted — in response to the call of the nation to restore England's laws, religion, and liberties.

In addition, William must have instructed Mary how she should present herself during the ceremony — even as he had told her what attitude to assume when she reached England.[56] Her actions in the Banqueting Hall were too stylized to be spontaneous. William and Mary entered hand-in-hand and sat holding hands. This posture was probably designed to placate the Maryites and to underscore the dual nature of the monarchy, notwithstanding the fact that William had insisted that the administrative powers be vested in himself alone. Mary said nothing during the ceremony. Indeed, anything she might have said would have been liable to misinterpretation, and there is no evidence at all that the hopes of some Englishmen that she would apologize for what was happening were ever discussed with her or William. "Her looks and a little curtsy," her acknowledged beauty,[57] above all her presence by her husband's side, were her contributions to the ceremony. If she had any feeling about the ceremony, she failed to note it in her memoirs.[58]

Another major contribution William made to the ceremony was to respond for himself and Mary to the reading of the Declaration of Rights and the offer of the crown. The speech prompted shouts of joy and repays study. William reversed the order of things as they had been presented in the declaration. Two could play this game! He accepted the crown *first* and then referred to the statement of rights. Moreover, William's oral remarks about Parliament were, apparently, different from the official version. Observers reported that the prince declared not only that he would preserve the nation's rights and maintain the Protestant religion, but also that he would place no

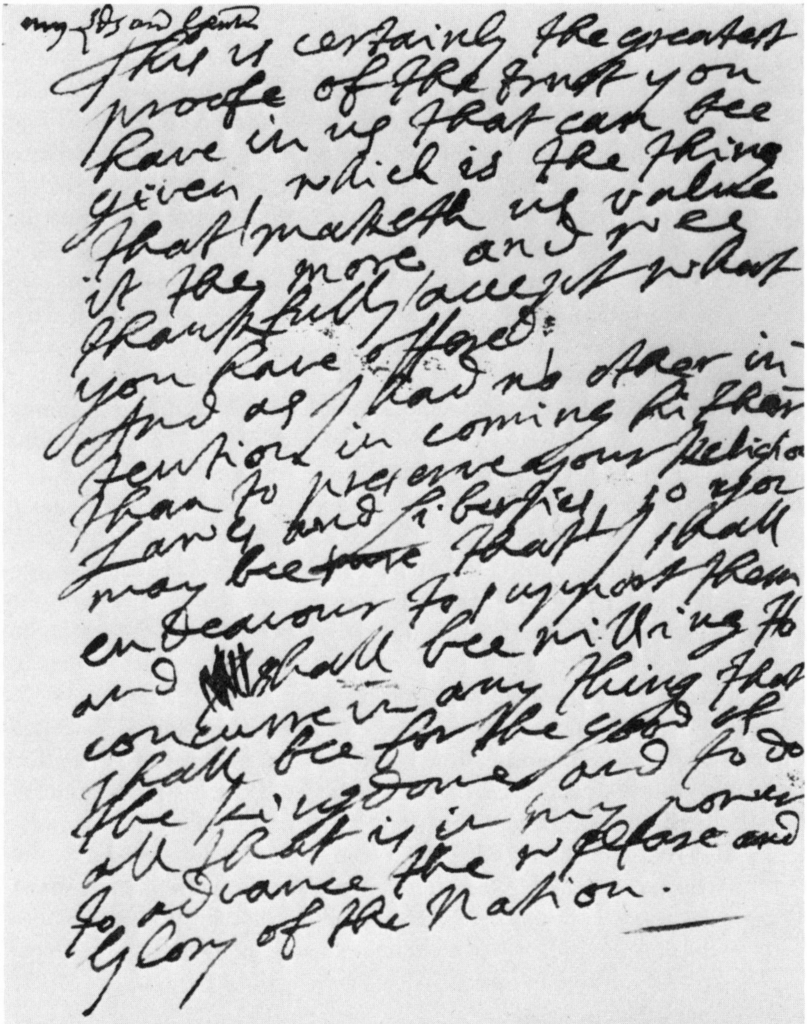

my Lds and Gentm
This is certainly the greatest
proofe of the trust you
have in us that can bee
given which is the thing
that maketh us value
it the more and wee
thankfully accept what
you have offred.
And as I had no other in-
tention in coming hither
than to preserve your Religion
Lawes and liberties so you
may bee sure that I shall
endeavour to support them
and shall bee willing to
concurre in any thing that
shall bee for the good of
the kingdome and to do
all that is in my power
to advance the welfare and
glory of the Nation.

Ent.

Figure 4. William of Orange's acceptance speech. Prince William delivered a speech acknowledging the claim of rights and accepting the crown of England at the ceremony in the Banqueting Hall on February 13, 1689. (Courtesy of the House of Lords Records Office.)

obstacle in the way of Parliament's privileges, prefer their advice to his own views, and consult them often.[59] The official version of the speech, a holograph copy of which is preserved in the House of Lords Record Office, is more restrained. In it William is reported to have said only that he would "endeavor to support" the nation's religion, laws, and liberties, and would concur in "anything" that shall be for the "good" of the kingdom.[60] Both accounts agree that the prince took no solemn oath, made no binding pledge, signed no paper.[61] But both accounts show that William did not ignore the statement of rights. However his remarks are reported, he said more probably than he really wanted to. In a high and serious moment, the prince made a public commitment to "endeavor to support" — at the least — the nation's religion, laws, and liberties. And he did this before a body whose authority was confirmed within a fortnight by a statute transforming it into a regular parliament. As the next nine months showed, despite continuing reluctance, William felt himself obliged, because of the circumstances of his affairs, to go forward with transforming the declaration into the Bill of Rights. Surely one of those circumstances which obliged him was his public commitment to the declaration (see Fig. 4).

The Convention's immediate handling of William's acceptance speech suggests their concern to hold him to his commitment. On February 14, the Speaker of the House of Commons requested a written copy of the speech "to prevent any mistake," and the next day introduced the official version, which, of course, was entered in the record of the House. On February 15, the House of Lords, upon receiving the official version, ordered William's response to be printed and published with the Declaration of Rights. And more, they ordered it to be added to the engrossed declaration in parchment and enrolled in Parliament and Chancery.[62] Interestingly enough, a contemporary observer complained about the date — the fifteenth — under which William's answer appeared in the printed document. Describing it as a "great mistake," he pointed out that a reader might think that the answer had been made on the fifteenth rather than the thirteenth, and implied that a precedent had been set for the king to exercise royal power without the restraints of the Declaration of Rights.[63]

Other printed pieces carried news of the ceremony and the Declaration of Rights. The official proclamation referred to the declaration. *The Manner of the Proclaiming of King William and Queen Mary* specifically noted that the prince and princess had accepted the crown "pursuant" to the declaration and that the document had been presented "in writing." The entire text of the declaration also appeared in the body of a pamphlet which was printed and reprinted in the spring.[64] The *London Gazette* and the new newspapers reported the ceremony, one declaring that the "Grand Convention" had presented their declaration in writing and that William had "promised to perform to the utmost" all it required.[65]

At least one medal commemorating the ceremony of February 13 was cast (Fig. 5). Measuring two and one half inches across, this large coin (one of

Figure 5. Medal commemorating the Declaration of Rights. This large medal, designed by Anton Meybusch, a medallist active on the Continent, commemorated the ceremony of February 13, 1689. On one side is a bust of William only, the omission of Mary suggesting unfamiliarity with the terms of the settlement. On the obverse, William, dressed as a Roman with spear in hand, proffers a cap of liberty to three figures, representing England, Scotland, and Ireland. Broken yokes, symbolizing Catholicism and tyranny, strew the ground, while rays from the Eye of Providence bathe the scene. The legend reads: "Veni, Vici, Libertatem redidi," "I came, I conquered, I restored liberty." (Courtesy of the Department of Medals, British Museum.)

261

which survives in the collection of the British Museum) was designed by Anton Meybusch, a medalist of German origin active in Stockholm, Paris, and Copenhagen.[66] It is not known whether or not the medal was commissioned, but it seems likely that neither the new king nor his friends had anything to do with it. Meybusch probably made the medal in Stockholm for the collectors' market. Thus, it is of interest for what it shows about a Continental medalist's understanding of events in England. That understanding was clouded. First, only William is depicted; no reference is made to Mary. On one side is only a bust of William, a patent insult to English Maryites and a clear misrepresentation of the settlement. There is no proof of a polemical intent in the omission of Mary, and it may be simply that Meybusch thought of William as the major figure in the revolution and so represented him alone. Second, the obverse of the medal shows William dressed as a Roman, standing with a spear in one hand. He proffers a cap of liberty to three kneeling female figures, who symbolize England, Scotland, and Ireland. The cap of liberty was a well-established device, used by the Dutch for over a hundred years as a symbol of their fight for liberty from Spanish overlords in the sixteenth century. The cap had appeared on many other medals in 1688/89 to indicate that William had come to restore England's laws, liberties, and religion.[67] On this particular medal, broken yokes symbolizing Catholicism and tyranny strew the ground, while rays from the Eye of Providence bathe the scene. The overall message reiterates the major theme in William's propaganda, namely, that he had come to restore the nation's rights. The medal also implies that the nation is suppliant to the prince and that their rights derive from him. The use of the word "Vici" in the legend heavily reinforces this impression. The legend reads, "Veni, Vici, Libertatem redidi" – "I came, I conquered, I restored liberty." Probably Meybusch was not aware of the delicacy surrounding the point of whether or not William was a conqueror. Although both William's friends and foes used various versions of conquest theory to justify the revolution,[68] the prince himself had gone to lengths about this time to avoid the image of conqueror, denying such an idea in his manifesto, refusing to claim the crown on those grounds, and ordering any soldier who intimated as much to be punished. The suggestion on the medal that William gave rights rather than responded to the nation's demand for them would have suited the prince's view of the Declaration of Rights, but it is doubtful that this medal could have pleased the new king.

Oral, written, printed, and visual material carried news of the ceremony, proclamation, and Declaration of Rights throughout England and to Europe. This material conveyed the impression that the corporate body of Parliament had made a settlement with which William passively concurred. It underlined the dual nature of the monarchy, thereby reinforcing the legitimacy of the settlement and placating those who favored Mary. Change was portrayed in traditional forms and thus minimized. Such an impression suited English political leaders and William too, who wrote immediately to his friends and Catholic allies on the Continent, disclaiming ambition to be king of England.

The heart of the proceedings on February 13 — the presentation ceremony in the Banqueting Hall, that ceremony unique in England's history — reflected the determination and skill of a small number of men in the House of Commons. It represented a political victory over other English political leaders who wanted simply to change the king and also over William, perhaps the only time in these months that Englishmen got the better of the shrewd Dutch prince. The ceremony implied, in terms of seventeenth-century political notions, a libertarian idea: the preeminance of Parliament in England's mixed government. Leaders of an irregular assembly — the Convention — presented to the Dutch prince and princess a written declaration in which they claimed specific rights of the subject, several of which, as has been shown, were new law, and *then* offered the nation's crown. The public reading of the document in a highly structured ceremony invested it with importance. The choice of words, the arrangement of the parts of the document, the unfolding of the ceremony, created the impression that the document was a condition, both for the offer of the crown and on its powers. The men who sponsored the Declaration of Rights wanted to achieve a new kingship, and in the ceremony of February 13 they did so symbolically. These symbols were politically powerful. Despite his reluctance, William found it simply too awkward not to go forward with the Bill of Rights, the document that indeed set forth legally the principles of a genuine constitutional monarchy.

IV
The Epitome of
the Glorious Revolution

16

The Bill of Rights

✦

The most important consequence of the Declaration of Rights was the passage of a statute known to this day as the Bill of Rights and properly regarded as the epitome of the Glorious Revolution. The Bill of Rights replicated the Declaration of Rights, save for a few amendments, but the two documents should be distinguished. The Bill of Rights gave undoubted legal authority to all the provisions in the declaration, thereby fulfilling the aspirations of the declaration's principal proponents, who wanted the revolutionary settlement and the claim of rights to be regarded as tantamount to law and had gone to great lengths to achieve that impression. Lawyers, however, had all along maintained that the Convention did not have the power, from a strictly legal point of view, to make law, and had indicated the intention, once the crisis was settled, of transforming the Declaration of Rights into a statute. That process took ten months and was carried out under political circumstances obviously different from those underlying the passage of the Declaration of Rights.[1]

The campaign to make the Declaration of Rights into a law began on March 5, 1689, when it was resolved in the House of Commons that a bill should be prepared to enact the declaration and prevent a Papist from succeeding to the throne.[2] By then, the authority of the assembly to make law had been assured, for a fortnight earlier, on February 23, the Convention had regularized its status by declaring itself a legal parliament in a bill signed by William. This step marked a victory for Whigs, among whom Birch, Lee, Maynard, Temple, and Treby took the lead in arguing that the Convention had always been equivalent to a parliament, and that to suggest otherwise was to imperil the settlement of the crown and the "instrument of government" — the claim of rights. On the contrary side, Tories such as Clarges, Sawyer, and Seymour maintained that according to law, the Convention was not a legal body, and that a regularly elected parliament was essential. It was a "constitutional outrage," thought a Tory peer, to continue the Convention as the Convention Parliament. These arguments, aired in tracts as well as debates in Westminster, magnified the differences in partisan opinion as to whether the Convention and the steps it had taken were indeed legal, and also concealed the expectation on both sides that fresh elections would favor the return of Tories. The success of the Whigs in this effort meant that the two ingredients required for making undoubted law — an undoubtedly legal parliament and an acknowledged (if not yet coronated) king — were in place.

On March 5 a committee of eleven M.P.'s — eight of whom, including Somers and Treby, had served on the earlier rights committees, and six of whom were Whigs — was elected to prepare a bill to make a law of the Declaration of Rights.[3] Managed by Treby, newly appointed to the post of attorney-general, the bill moved slowly but without encountering opposition through its first and second readings on April 4 and 21. Although there is no evidence that the king took steps to sidetrack the proposal, he was not enthusiastic about it. It was during this time that William confided to Halifax his disinclination to confirm all the articles in the Declaration of Rights, but admitted that the condition of his affairs "overruled his inclination."[4]

On May 1 a committee of the whole, chaired by Treby, amended the draft in details that have failed to survive and ordered it engrossed.[5] Perhaps it was at this time that a preamble and new material connecting the parts of the document were added. The effect of this new material, whenever it was added, was, as already noted,[6] twofold. First, it reinforced the claim that the rights were undoubted. The new words in the Bill of Rights described the rights as "true, ancient, and indubitable," and asserted that they shall be "esteemed, allowed, adjudged, deemed, and taken to be." The ambiguities suggested by the form of the verbs in the several clauses of the Declaration of Rights were thereby removed, and all the rights emphatically asserted. Second, the preamble stated that "the Lords Spiritual and Temporal and Commons assembled at Westminster" do "lawfully, fully, and freely" represent "all the estates of the people of this realm." This language affirmed the legality of the Convention and also suggested that the two Houses, without a king, were sufficient to represent the "estates of the people of this realm." It implied that at the moment when the revolutionary settlement was being proclaimed, the sovereign power rested with the Convention. The political theory inherent in such a proposition is that of the radical Whigs. The language must be taken seriously, for it was deliberately added to the Declaration of Rights by the framers of the Bill of Rights. Who added the new material is not known, but probably it was Treby or Somers.

A week later, on May 8, at its third reading, the draft Bill of Rights ran into serious difficulties. Two issues were raised that entangled the document in partisan politics and impeded its passage for months. The issues revealed the continuing fragility of some Tories' commitment to the settlement and the determination of some Whigs further to restrict royal power over the law. The first issue concerned the succession to the throne. Charles Godolphin, a Tory and a brother of Sidney Godolphin, the Treasury commissioner,[7] wanted to amend the succession clause in the Declaration of Rights by adding words that would prevent the Bill of Rights from being used to "prejudice the right of any Protestant prince or princess in their hereditary succession" to the crown.[8] Ostensibly this language simply reaffirmed the hereditary character of the crown, within a Protestant line, should William, Mary, and Anne die without issue. That hereditary character had, clearly enough, been violated by the revolution and by the very specification to four removes of the succession in the Declaration of Rights. The amendment reflected concern over what might happen should the persons named die. Would chaos ensue while a solution was sought? Would the nation be weakened and thus imperiled in its relations with foreign countries? Would advocates of limited monarchy exploit the situation to win further concessions from the crown? Would the throne become elective? Such considerations might recommend the amendment to a large number of people.

But, apparently, the measure really concealed bitter partisanship. High Anglican Tories, it was said, had designed it, after lengthy consideration, to "overthrow all the former proceedings."[9] Such an extreme purpose is doubtful. But it is certain that the proviso and the arguments for it impeached the revolution settlement, the Declaration of Rights, and, by implication, the Whig leadership. For example, one speaker supported it because it would "disappoint" men who advocated a commonwealth. Another thought it would prevent the government from reverting to the people in the event William, Mary, and Anne died, this M.P. understanding "abdication" and "vacancy" in the throne to mean the dissolution of the government.

The proviso provoked a sharp response from Whigs. They charged that the motion was designed to bring in the Baby Prince of Wales, who might be raised a Protestant or say that he was one. They suggested that their Tory colleagues had concocted the idea in league with the French or some other foreign minister. Hampden, sputtering with indignation, declared that no gentleman could support the measure. He declaimed, "To bring in this, to put a doubt upon all you have done already! — I am against it." Capel bitterly objected to the reference to commonwealthsmen. Treby and Somers, calling upon history and law, argued that common-law principles would achieve the same end, and counseled rejecting the amendment.[10] But Whig objections themselves were not without a double significance. Whigs wanted no further specification of the succession, in part because thereby they gave up a possible future opportunity to wrest further concessions from the monarchy should the royal line fail. In rebuttal, Tories sought to soften these Whig arguments by adding words that would have barred the Baby Prince of Wales from the throne, but this proposed change was defeated 179–125, and with it the proviso itself was lost.[11]

The second issue raised on May 8 was the royal dispensing power. Without recorded debate, the Commons added a rider whose purpose was to deny the king the right of *non obstante* "of or to any statute, or any part thereof," unless specifically allowed in the statute itself. The rider contained, however, a grandfather clause that exempted all charters, grants or pardons issued before June 1, 1689.[12] It is not known who was responsible for this amendment, but indirect evidence suggests that Treby, Howard, Capel, and Williams took an active part in the process. It was Treby who was designated to carry the bill to the lords. And a week later in a debate on another matter (the indemnity issue), these four Whigs trumpeted against the dispensing power. Then, one charged that the dispensing power made men slaves, "no freer than in Turkey," while another described it as a "bloody sacrifice to the Prince's pleasure." [13] There is also no certain evidence as to why this amendment was brought forward at the third reading, rather than earlier. Maybe it was in retaliation for the proposed amendment about the succession. Up to May 8, Whigs had refrained from reopening the issue of the dispensing power, an issue on which they had compromised in the Convention. Perhaps Tory criticism provoked them to try to achieve what the first draft of the Declaration of Rights shows they wanted, namely to outlaw the royal dispensing power as well as the suspending power. Some Tories had earlier favored such a step. In the event, the rider was accepted.

With these two recommended adjustments, the draft bill was sent up to the House of Lords. The bill bore for the first time a title which included the word "rights." It read, "An Act declaring the Rights and Liberties of the Subject, and the settling of the Succession of the Crown." [14] Their lordships showed keen interest in it, debating it in an ad hoc committee and in a committee of the whole. Predictably enough, in view of the Lords' attitude in January and February, the peers responded negatively to the proposed rider on the dispensing power. On May 24, the upper House asked their legal counsel for an opinion. Responding was Holt, now chief justice of the Court of Common Pleas and also a member of the Commons' committee to draft the Bill of Rights. In February he had been a member of the rights committee in the Commons and then had argued against the royal dispensing power. Now, however, Holt reversed himself, describing the Commons amendment as a step that would repeal the "practice of hundreds of years." Distinguishing laws the king may and may not dispense, he sought to preserve to the king some power to dispense with law. Pollexfen was also hostile to the rider, but his words are reported in such elliptical terms that his meaning is opaque. [15] In any case, the upper House rejected the Commons' proposed rider respecting the dispensing power. At the same time they ordered the judges to prepare a separate act for regulating *non obstantes*.

Further, the Lords took steps to assure that the crown would always be worn by a Protestant. They prepared two amendments, one forbidding the monarch to marry a Catholic, and the other requiring the heir to the throne to take an oath, as provided in the Test Act, before his proclamation. Thus, the religion of the heir (as proved by the taking of an oath), and not the principle of direct hereditary succession, was to be the condition for ascending the throne. Privy councillors were to administer the oath should the heir be out of the country. Inherent in these requirements was a fundamental change that set England apart from continental countries. [16] That is, the requirements reversed the European principle that the religion of the ruler determined that of his subjects. In England, the Bill of Rights required the monarch to be of the same religion as most Englishmen — Protestant. The consequence was to exclude by law the descendants of the Stuarts in the Orleans line and the Palatine line, except for one branch. Moreover, the effect was to narrow the range of eligible marriage partners for English royalty. This clause, reinforced eventually in the Act of Settlement by the specification of the House of Hanover in the line of succession, was to assure that England's kings and queens would marry within Protestant royal families.

Finally, the peers reopened the matter of the succession to the throne. The Lords avoided the general statement suggested earlier by Godolphin which had caused an uproar in the House of Commons. Instead, on May 22, with Fauconberg chairing a committee of the whole, Burnet, recently appointed bishop of Salisbury and thus a member of the upper House, proposed limiting the succession by specifically naming Sophia, duchess of Hanover, and her issue.[17] Sophia, the granddaughter of James I through her mother Elizabeth, was the closest of the most certainly Protestant individuals in the line of succession. To name the duchess was to set aside, in a legal document, the claims of many persons in the legitimate line and to violate still further the principle of direct hereditary succession. The motives for this step were different from those underlying the earlier effort in the House of Commons. This time the initiative came from the king himself. William was conscious of his delicate health [18] and of the peril to his European policy should the succession to the throne be doubtful. Moreover, he regarded the amendment as useful to his immediate diplomatic purposes, namely, to secure close ties between England and Hanover and reinforce the break between Hanover and France. An undated, unsigned paper in the Portland Manuscripts of "reflexions" on the most proper method of regulating the succession of the crown and avoiding a Catholic king shows how earnestly William's court hoped that Sophia would be named. She and her progeny of seven children would cut off the hopes of all Popish aspirants.[19] Accordingly, the king asked Burnet to introduce the limitation. The peers accepted the amendment without recorded objection.[20] With these four amendments, the draft Bill of Rights was returned to the House of Commons on May 25.

It was not until mid-June — on the nineteenth and twentieth — that the Commons considered the peers' amendments to the draft Bill of Rights. On the proposal to prohibit a monarch's marrying a Papist, they concurred. On requiring the heir to the throne to take the oath in the Test Act before being proclaimed, they agreed, but objected to giving authority to the Privy Council to administer the oath to an heir who was out of the country and to incapacitate him should he refuse. The exchange on this point provides additional evidence of the concern of Whigs to place power in the hands of Parliament, that is, the Commons. One spokesman wanted the House of Commons summoned, another commended William for calling together the Commons as well as the peers the previous December, and a third thought the lord mayor of London and "nobility of the town" should share authority with the councillors. Sacheverell was concerned lest the requirement to take the sacrament according to the rites of the Church of England eliminate a Lutheran or Calvinist, and provoked great offense by criticizing the Church of England.[21] Playing the peacemaker, Richard Hampden urged members to commit the clause, pointing out that in differing from the lords, they ran the risk of weakening the settlement. As might be expected, the twenty-two-man committee appointed to consider the clause included eleven members of the earlier rights committee.[22]

On the Lords' rejection of the Commons' rider respecting the dispensing power, the debate was ambivalent. Lawyers generally favored preserving the king some power to dispense with the law, their remarks proving that they knew all along that the Declaration of Rights stripped the king of a power over the law that he had formerly possessed. Treby admitted that "many" kings had employed the dispensing power "without reproof of Parliament" and in conformity with statute law. Williams thought that if the king did not enjoy the power to dispense, subjects would suffer. The royal dispensing power is, he said, as "necessary for the people as eating and drinking." Other members protested, Sacheverell cautioning the House that if they agreed with the lords, the "dispensing power is confirmed for the future." In the end, this matter was also sent to committee.[23]

The Lords' proposal to specify the duchess of Hanover in the limitation of the succession the Commons rejected *nemine contradicente*.[24] How is this hostility to the House of Hanover to be explained? Macaulay thought that the attitude reflected the Commons' anger with the Lords over the latter's refusal to reverse the judgment against Titus Oates, a martyr still to many Whigs.[25] This view has gone unchallenged, but, in fact, multiple reasons, of which Oates's case was only one, explain the opposition to naming Sophia. First, partisan views on amending the succession clause had already been developed in the debate the previous month on Godolphin's rider. Whig hostility in June to the Lords' specification was consistent with the earlier position that group had held. Burnet thought that the left wing of the Whig party did not want to throw away a possible opportunity to win additional concessions from the king should William, Mary, and Anne die; the bishop blamed Wildman and "all the republican party" for the defeat of the amendment.[26] Second, there are intimations that some men felt that a kind of sanctity inhered in the Declaration of Rights. One speaker advised against doing anything contrary to that document.[27] Third, there was hesitancy to solidify a connection with a foreign house, especially one so recently friendly to France, and an inclination to replicate Queen Elizabeth's practice of not showing her hand. Observed a hostile M.P., "There may be revolutions and changes; this Princess of Hanover may turn Catholic." He praised Queen Elizabeth for not determining the succession.[28] Fourth, the fact of Anne's pregnancy (she was delivered of a son the next month) induced the hope that further limitations were unnecessary and might prove to be embarrassing. Fifth, high Anglican Tories (an eighteenth-century historian singled out Musgrave and Seymour) joined Whigs in opposition because the naming of Sophia offended their legitimist principles.[29] Sixth, friends of Danby, now duke of Carmarthen, enlarged the number of men opposed to the measure for partisan and personal reasons. Although Carmarthen had, in the House of Lords, supported Burnet's rider to name Hanover, his friends in the Commons opposed it to reinforce friendly connections between the duke and the Whigs. Aware that earlier Whig hostility to Carmarthen was likely to resurface, they used opposition to naming Sophia to ingratiate themselves with the Whigs and thus protect Carmarthen. Already in early June the House of Commons had resolved that the king could not pardon a person whom Parliament had impeached. Moreover, several Whigs had endorsed the motion that William be asked to dismiss any minister who had been impeached by Parliament; Carmarthen was such a minister.[30] It had taken intervention by the king, Dijkvelt, and others to persuade the proponents to drop this motion.[31] Carmarthen apparently felt threatened enough to agree that his friends in the lower House should follow a policy different from the one he had embraced in the Lords. The *quid pro quo* for helping to defeat the Lords' amendment would be assistance in defeating a possible move to remove him as a minister who had been impeached by Parliament.

Finally, hostility between Lords and Commons over the issue of reversing Oates's sentence, was, indeed, one reason the Commons were unsympathetic to the Lords' amendments to the Bill of Rights. The anger of the Commons at the Lords' position on Oates's case reflected more than the belief that Oates should be vindicated because he had suffered such grievous punishment in the previous reign. As the debates of June 4 and 11 show, the Commons were also concerned that failure to reverse the sentence would impugn the claim set out in article 10 of the Bill of Rights. That article, it will be recalled, declared that there shall be no "cruel and unusual punishments," that is, punishments that exceeded the law and the authority of the bench, as was the case with the punishment inflicted on Titus Oates. Howard and Howe, for example, made clear that they favored trying Oates for perjury, but that they also wanted to discredit the proceedings of Court of King's Bench, which could be accomplished by reversing the sentence.[32] This same interest in discrediting King's Bench and in applying the principle of article 10 to redress wrongs suffered by Whig martyrs appeared again four days later in the move to reverse the sentence imposed on the Reverend Samuel Johnson.[33]

Yet, in June there was no certain indication that the Bill of Rights would not prosper nor the two Houses remain hostile. Admitting the presence of a "difference," a correspondent blamed the "enemies" of the new regime for inflating that difference and predicted that the upper House would come around to accepting the Commons' bill to reverse the judgment in Oates's case.[34] Similarly, a Dutchman close to William noted the Commons' irritation over the Lords' treatment of Oates, and their desire to attack Carmarthen and perhaps Halifax in retaliation, but concluded that the "great heat had somewhat subsided."[35] Thus, for all these reasons, the Commons sent to committee three of the Lords' proposed amendments to the Bill of Rights: (1) to name Sophia in the succession, (2) to refuse the Commons' rider about the dispensing power, and (3) to arrange that the Privy Council should tender the oath abjuring transubstantiation to the heir to the throne before he or she should be proclaimed. A Whig (Lee) expressed dismay over the delays.[36]

The two Houses remained at an impasse over the Bill of Rights and absorbed in other matters — the funding of the war, the settling of the militia, and the fixing of the revenue. Disillusionment on the part of the new king with his ministers' failure to press earnestly and effectively for adequate supply, and disillusionment on the part of many politicians with the new king's handling of the war and his continued preference for Dutch advisers, complicated affairs.[37] But on July 8, the members of the House of Commons considered what bills before them they should "proceed upon" and assigned third priority to the Bill of Rights.[38] Conference meetings between the Lords and Commons were arranged, progress was achieved, and further advances anticipated. Having asked all the judges in town to assist them, the peers agreed on July 15 to the Commons' rider respecting the dispensing power,[39] an agreement whose fragility was to be revealed in the fall, when again the upper House reopened the issue of the dispensing power with a view to preserving the king some authority to dispense with the laws. On July 20, the Commons were hopeful that the Lords would drop their insistence that the duchess of Hanover be named in the succession.[40] There was sufficient likelihood of this happening for Evelyn to be alarmed and to point to "Republicans and Dissenters" as the ones who favored it.[41] He need not have worried, for several things occurred during these days to stiffen the resolve of the peers to adhere to their amendment. William was personally active. The king told Halifax on July 28 that he "would speak to the Lords to stick on the clause of Hanover." Although he did not take this step,[42] he did raise the subject at a council meeting. There, he declared that Mary and the prince and princess of Denmark wanted Sophia to be named.[43] Perhaps Burnet, who had earlier introduced Sophia's name, continued to argue for the limitation. Halifax "strongly" advocated the restriction.[44] Moreover, during these days the Commons' bitter response to the Lords' refusal to reverse the judgment against Oates poisoned relations between the two Houses. The Commons' indictment of the peers was so sharply critical that it almost certainly stiffened the determination of the upper House to name Hanover.[45] At a conference meeting, the Lords heard the Commons justify their opposition to naming Sophia on two grounds: one, that the limitation was not mentioned in the Declaration of Rights, a reason underlining the importance of the document; and two, that naming Hanover might be "dangerous" and harmful to England.[46] To these points, the lords countered that in a law that "settles forever the liberties of the subject," it was appropriate to carry the limitations further than had been done in the declaration of those rights. They argued that one of the many papists in the Stuart line of succession might pretend to be converted to Protestantism to win the throne, and that no danger was so great as to have a disguised papist wear the crown. They argued, too, that since the limitation had been proposed, to disappoint Hanover might provoke that duchy to steps inimical to England.[47] But a division in their own house showed 38 to 29 lords voting to adhere to naming Sophia.[48] On the thirty-first, at another conference meeting with the Commons, Burnet, the Lords' "chief manager," reported this position.[49] Significantly, Wildman, the principle manager for the Commons, made an effort to keep the debate on the Bill of Rights alive. But the Lords' representatives maintained that they had no authority to continue the discussion.[50] Somers complained a fortnight later at the refusal of the lords to continue the debate and accused them of interrupting the "good correspondence" between the two Houses.[51] But the possibility of reestablishing a "good correspondence" was lost by the king's adjournment of this parliament on August 20.[52]

By the time Parliament reassembled in October, circumstances were more propitious for the passage of the Bill of Rights. From a negative point of view, it was by now abundantly clear that the new regime rested on no firm foundation of support. In May and June, Dijkvelt had expressed concern that affection for William had not grown. For example, in late June, continued loyalty to James among the soldiers had caused a small revolt in two garrisons. Five soldiers had been hanged.[53] In July there were rumors that William was to be killed, the queen seized, and London fired. In response, the watch in the City had been doubled and guns placed around Whitehall.[54] In October warrants were issued for the arrest of persons who had spoken scandalous words.[55] In November someone expressed his dissatisfaction by cutting the crown and scepter from the picture of the king that hung in the Guildhall.[56] Perhaps the evident weakness of the regime promoted the idea on all sides that the document containing the settlement of the revolution should be passed.

Furthermore, at about this time in mid-November, printed tracts appeared that may have helped energize M.P.'s to pass the bill that set out the nation's rights. Although no pamphlet directly addressed the issue, the *History of the late Revolution in England* recounted recent events in ways flattering to the "Glorious Deliverer" King William, who, it was said, had rescued the nation from an "abyss of slavery"; and the *Proceedings of the Tryal of the Seven Bishops* jogged men's memories about that traumatic trial fifteen months earlier and the issues in it (the dispensing power and the right to petition) that enjoyed high priority in the list of rights. Both were available at The Angel in Westminster Hall.[57] Also sold at The Angel in mid-November was *The Two Treatises of Government,* not known then to be by John Locke. It justified in theoretical terms the steps taken the previous spring, not only in establishing the throne of King William, but also in claiming the nation's rights. Locke looked upon his *Two Treatises,* in part, as a justification of the Declaration of Rights, and it is possible that he chose this particular time to publish it (the book received a license on August 23) to help revive interest in the passage of the Bill of Rights.[58]

In like manner, discussion at this time on the pros and cons of continuing the Convention Parliament brought forward the thought that a newly elected parliament would almost certainly "take into consideration the Abdicating Act and all other acts," and advanced the feeling that it would not be "fit for those acts to come into question much less be rejected." Such discussions may also have persuaded political leaders of the urgency of confirming the Declaration of Rights by making it a statute.[59]

William, too, facilitated the passage of the document. The king had decided upon a conciliatory policy. Frustrated at the failure of the Money Bill and the indemnity measure, acutely conscious that he would have to deal with Parliament to get funds, and irritated by Parliament's attempts to restrict his powers through the Militia Bill, William confided to Halifax that he intended to steer a middle course between the two parties and to try to win over Anglican Tories while not losing Whig Dissenters, whom he increasingly regarded as supporting a commonwealth.[60] In preparing to meet Parliament in the fall, the king, with unusual civility, invited criticism of his draft speech for opening Parliament, and accepted changes, largely suggested by Hampden, that had the effect of making his remarks "more parliamentary."[61] Moreover, William concurred in a plan, already concerted by Lee and others, to prorogue Parliament briefly upon its reassembly. This step was regarded as the most expeditious way to develop legislative momentum, for the effect would be to wipe the slate clean of pending bills and permit a fresh start.

At risk was the Bill of Rights, but on October 24, the House of Commons took the initiative and appointed a committee of twenty M.P.'s to bring in a bill for establishing the rights of the subject. On the committee were Treby, Howard, Paul Foley, and Williams, among others who had championed the Declaration of Rights.[62] There is no explanation why Somers failed to be elected to this committee, nor why it was Paul Foley who emerged as the member who reported from the committee at the bill's first reading.[63] But Somers's absence from the committee should not be read as disenchantment with the statement of rights. During these weeks there is no certain evidence about any of his activities respecting the passage of the Bill of Rights, including the claim that he sought John Locke's advice.[64] But the next year, as will be seen, Somers rushed into print with the most powerful defense to appear of the Declaration of Rights and the Bill of Rights.

Within two weeks, on November 6, the bill was ready for a third reading. In this debate, anxiety once more surfaced that the removal of the royal suspending and dispensing power might be harmful to the subject. Seymour, ever obstructive, recommended holding the Money Bill hostage to the Bill of Rights, by laying the former on the table until the latter was perfected and passed. But Morrice reported that the bill passed with "less opposition" than had been expected and praised Sacheverell for doing all "he could" to achieve that end.[65] The document was approved *nemine contradicente*,[66] and Paul Foley carried it to the Lords that same day.

From November 6 to 23 the peers debated *de novo* the draft Bill of Rights.[67] For reasons imperfectly explained, the peers did not raise the succession question nor press to specify Sophia in the line of inheritance to the throne. Perhaps William retreated in the face of earlier Whig opposition and in hopes of encouraging passage of a satisfactory revenue bill. Perhaps the fact that Anne's baby, although desperately ill in September,[68] was still alive suggested that no further limitation was needed. Perhaps Whig peers used their influence to persuade fellow peers that making law of the whole Declaration of Rights was more important that amending the succession clause. Whatever the reason, the issue was laid to one side; not until the Settlement Act of 1701 was further specification given the succession.

The peers reintroduced clauses to guarantee that no papist should become sovereign in England. The clauses provided that a king or queen might not marry a Catholic and that the heir to the crown must take the Test Oath before he could exercise authority. Testifying to the new spirit of cooperation between the two Houses on the Bill of Rights, the peers did not require that members of the council administer the oath to the king, a proposition the Commons had disliked earlier. Rather, it was agreed that the monarch take the Test Oath either upon the day of his coronation or before the Lords and Commons in Parliament. A further amendment, moreover, provided that should the heir refuse to take the oath, subjects were absolved from allegiance. This extraordinary amendment, proposed by Burnet and seconded by Shrewsbury, passed, to Burnet's amazement, "without any opposition or debate."[69] In fact, the point did provoke discussion about what might happen if an heir not only refused the Test Oath but also refused to call Parliament. The duke of Bolten observed that the Triennial Act was the solution to that problem and that the names and memory of those men who had framed it should be held in as great respect as the authors of Magna Charta. Other lords, especially spiritual peers, objected to Bolten's remarks, saying that the Triennial Bill had been passed in a time of sedition and that it had so fettered the king he could not be a "free monarch." Bolten and his friends did not attempt to amend the Bill of Rights, but rather proposed that a bill be brought in repealing the act made in Charles II's time that had repealed the Triennial Act.[70] Nothing more was heard of that bill this session, but the exchange reveals the continuing concern of Whigs to restrict royal authority.

The issue that caused the greatest difficulty was the dispensing power. Once more, the upper House attempted to preserve some authority to the king to dispense with the laws, arguing that the abolition of this prerogative might be "prejudicial to the subject."[71] On November 14 the lords again turned to the judges for assistance on the question, ordering them to "prepare a bill for regulating Non Obstantes, with all convenient speed."[72] On the twenty-first, the judges reported that they had found the problem of "marvellous [the word "infinite" was crossed through] difficulty," and that they thought they would need a "very long time" to draw up a bill.[73] Underlining the seriousness of their intention, the peers decided to adjourn the debate until the next day, ordering all the judges to attend, and all the lords in and about the town to be summoned to attend.[74] In what must have been a lengthy exchange on the twenty-second, the peers and their legal advisers examined whether the removal of a royal dispensing power would harm subjects.[75] The lawyers procrastinated, Holt and Pollexfen pointing to the "very great difficulty" of the question and the need for "considerable time" after "term was out" to reflect upon it. In response to specific questions — what cases the king must be allowed the power to dispense, in what cases he might be allowed such an authority, and whether he can dispense in no cases — the lawyers were unclear. They cited precedents rather than answering the questions directly. Dolben finally said, "I can say no more than yesterday. It will be very difficult."[76] It was left to a Whig peer, the duke of Bolten, to introduce a motion that moved the proceedings along. He proposed that for the future the king might dispense with no laws, unless the law itself gave him that power, and that Parliament should this session pass an act that would enumerate all the laws the king should have the power to dispense. His proposal was "vehemently opposed" by peers who had formerly favored a regency as the solution to the crisis, and by such spiritual peers as the bishop of London. But they did not press the matter, according to Morrice, because of fear of losing the vote.[77] The upshot was that the Lords accepted the Commons' proviso with two amendments: (1) *non obstantes* were to be "void and no effect" except "in such cases as shall be specifically provided for by one or more bill or bills to be passed during this present session of Parliament," and (2) *non obstantes* issued before October 23, 1689, were to be regarded as in effect. At the same time the peers ordered the judges to draw up a bill declaring statutes that may and may not be dispensed. The judges presented such a bill on December 5, but it was dropped in the Committee of the Whole.[78]

The only effort to amend the draft Bill of Rights (as distinguished from ordering the preparation of a separate bill) occurred on November 23. Then, in a thinly attended House, the duke of Bolten and the duke of Devonshire introduced a rider barring a royal pardon to a parliamentary impeachment without the consent of both Houses.[79] Such a clause, it will be remembered, had appeared in the Heads of Grievances of January 28, but had been removed for "divers weighty reasons" and was omitted from the final version of the Declaration of Rights. Although Whigs in the House of Commons had clamored in June against the king's power to pardon an impeachment, no such provision was in the draft Bill of Rights. In November partisan considerations as well as political principle underlay Bolten's proposal. The target of the amendment was Carmarthen. The opinion of the judges was asked, but they again declined to answer directly. Holt protested that the peers themselves were the proper judges and twice asked to be excused from offering an opinion. Pollexfen and Eyre spoke to the same end, Eyre pointing out that "our books are wholly silent in this matter."[80] Nottingham delayed the proceedings still further with a long speech until the chamber began to fill. A voice vote proved inconclusive, but a division showed that the rider failed 50 to 17, with Delamere acting as the teller for the minority. Twelve lords, including radical Whigs Delamere and Lovelace, entered their dissents and reasons for dissent. Among the reasons was that the right to pardon persons impeached by Parliament put the king's prerogative above the government, "which is inconsistent with the reason and nature of this constitution." [81] Dissenting lords further argued that it was inconsistent to vote against the power to dispense but allow the king the power to pardon, for the two powers were of equal evil. The protests notwithstanding, no further attempt was made to remove the royal power to pardon. It was not a matter of softened conviction, but rather of political considerations. The majority of Whigs did not want to harm or insult Carmarthen, who had advanced the cause of the revolution, and they did not want to give an advantage to Carmarthen's rival, Halifax, who was still unrepentant regarding his role at the time of the Exclusion Crisis. [82] Not until the Act of Settlement was the king's power to bar a parliamentary impeachment removed.

No further changes to the draft Bill of Rights were put forward, and on November 23 the bill was returned to the House of Commons. Desultory attempts to deny the king the power to pardon parliamentary impeachments and to secure still further the king's religion by requiring certification that he had taken the sacrament according to the rites of the Church of England met with no success. On December 10, the Bill of Rights was approved. On December 16, William signed it into law. [83]

The signing of the Bill of Rights into law was accompanied by no fanfare and occasioned no commentary (that has survived) on the part of anyone. But two days later, December 18, the first anniversary of William's arrival in London, a great bonfire was arranged in Fleet Street, at Temple Gate. Hearing of it, the London "mob" came in "three pageants" carrying effigies of Jeffreys, the judges associated with the dispensing power, and the three foremen of the three juries in the cases of Russell, Sidney, and Cornish. The mob held a mock trial of these offenders of the nation's laws and liberties and found all of them guilty of high treason. As the guilty made confession and dying speeches, they were hanged on the gibbet as traitors and then burnt in the bonfire. As the effigies were consumed in the fire, the mob cried out, "Long live King William and Queen Mary and confound all their enemies." [84] It is possible that some of the mob or some observers perceived this street theater as a tribute to the Bill of Rights.

The passage of the Bill of Rights did not follow a smooth and rapid course. In the absence of compelling urgency to settle the crisis (the circumstances within which the Declaration of Rights was drafted) and in the face of many pressing foreign and domestic problems competing for attention, the task did not enjoy top priority. Partisan rivalry between Tories and Whigs was sharper than before, and jealousy between the two Houses was keen. The king was resigned, if not actively hostile. It took persistence and parliamentary skill on the part of radical Whigs in the House of Commons (such as

Treby, Richard Hampden, Paul Foley, Sacheverell, and Wildman) and in the House of Lords (such as Bolten and Devonshire) to advance the Bill of Rights. Inexplicably, Somers was not prominently involved in the passage of the bill, a fact which should not be taken to indicate a change of mind, for later he wrote emphatically in defense of it. Concern to secure the nation against a Catholic king by adjustments to the Bill of Rights overwhelmed at times concern for rights. Yet language was introduced to remove ambiguities in the Declaration of Rights and reinforce the claim that the rights were indisputed and undoubted. And a rider eventually passed that, in effect, outlawed the royal dispensing power, thus strengthening article 2 of the Declaration of Rights, which, in declaring the dispensing power illegal, had included the phrase "as it has been assumed and exercised of late." But the effort to introduce a clause barring a royal pardon to a parliamentary impeachment failed, as did the passing interest in revising the Triennial Act. Willingness on all sides to compromise and recognition by both partisan groups of the value of translating into undoubted law the Declaration of Rights assisted the passage of the Bill of Rights, but as in the case of the declaration, it was radical Whigs who dominated the debates and held the majority on the committees. To them as a group, rather than to any one person, is due credit for the act that was said to "settle forever the rights of the subject."

Conclusion: A New View
of the Declaration of Rights
and the Bill of Rights

his study suggests the need to amend aspects of traditional and
current scholarly views of the Declaration of Rights and the Bill of
Rights. Previous historians have failed to examine closely and
critically either the text or the political and intellectual context within which
the documents were drafted and passed. They have tended to accept uncriti-
cally the language and shape of the Declaration of Rights and the Bill of
Rights, and have characterized both as nothing more than reaffirmations of
undoubted and ancient laws and rights. Moreover, they have relied, by and
large, upon *ex post facto* judgments of the documents, judgments themselves
reflecting partisan political assumptions and needs and not based on rigorous
investigation. But when the Declaration of Rights and the Bill of Rights and
the rights they claim are approached historically, and the process of drafting
and passing them is traced chronologically, when the political and intellectual
context is analyzed and the major proponents scrutinized as a group and as
individuals, then a different picture of the nature and significance of the
documents emerges.

The Declaration of Rights did not achieve all its supporters hoped for, but
it did achieve more than is sometimes appreciated. Before the financial settlement was negotiated, before the wars on the Continent were fought, before
the crown of England was settled, radical Whigs in the Convention developed a blueprint of what they wanted the powers of the monarchy to be,
how they envisioned the relationship between king and Parliament, and what
rights they desired for the individual. In the face of opposition from Tories in
both Houses, especially the House of Lords, and from the prince, they
insisted upon linking a claim of rights to the offer of the throne and presenting the document in a specially contrived ceremony. If they had failed to
achieve this linkage, then William and Mary would simply have been proclaimed king and queen of England, as some people wanted. Whether or not
proponents of a claim of rights would have been successful in entering their

claim after the proclamation of the new monarchs is problematical at best. Their success in achieving the linkage of the settlement of the crown and the statement of rights was neither inevitable nor predictable; it is properly regarded as a significant political victory. The Declaration of Rights laid the foundations for genuine political and constitutional changes whose promise was fulfilled in the statutory formulation, the Bill of Rights. These two documents, then, undermine the notion that the Revolution of 1688–89 was nothing more than a palace coup.

The claim of rights was presented in a formal written document which was given marks of importance and treated as if it were a statute, thereby enhancing its significance. Moreover, the authors used language and organized the parts of the final version of the Declaration of Rights in such a way as to convey certain political impressions. The most important of those impressions were that the claim of rights was a condition which William had to accept to win the crown, that it legally restricted the prerogatives of the monarchy, and that it only restored the "ancient" and "undoubted" rights of the nation. The presentation ceremony reinforced these points. For many reasons, among them his own propaganda effort, William concurred in these arrangements, and although he signed no document and took no formal oath to uphold the rights, he did deliver an acceptance speech, which was later appended to the Declaration of Rights, in which he avowed willingness to abide by them. Subsequently, the prince as king admitted that although he had no desire to see the Declaration of Rights transformed into a regular statute, circumstances were such that he had no choice in the matter. Among those circumstances was that the claim of rights and the other terms of the settlement of the crisis of 1688–89 were linked in the same document presented to and accepted by him in a public ceremony. Six times before 1689 the English had removed their king and each time had justified the step in written apologias that defined the authority of the monarchy, but never before had they presented such an instrument, in any form, to a person *before* he was proclaimed king. The importance of the claim of rights is more readily grasped if one considers what it would have meant had its principals failed to link it with the offer of the throne, include it in a formal, written statement, and present it to the new king and queen before their proclamation.

The words and organization of the parts of the Declaration of Rights were the deliberate choice of men who were skilled and experienced parliamentarians and lawyers. The form was not prescribed. A different arrangement would have conveyed a different political impression. The success of the authors in influencing understanding of the document may be seen in the fact that it has taken almost three hundred years to set the record straight. First, the Declaration of Rights was not a condition which William had to accept to win the throne. There is no evidence that at any time was William presented an ultimatum that if he refused the claim of rights, he would be denied the offer of the crown. There is evidence that not-so-subtle pressures were put upon him to indicate the political disadvantages should he persist in opposing the claim. It is almost certain that a compromise between the document's proponents and the prince was worked out, which explains in part the truncated nature of the final version. Second, the Declaration of Rights was not, legally speaking, a restriction on the powers of the monarchy until it was transformed into a statute. From a strictly legal point of view, the Declaration of Rights could not carry the force of law; in the revolutionary circumstances of the winter of 1688–89, no step could have such weight. All along, lawyers and Tories insisted that the Convention could not make law, but others maintained that the assembly had a higher authority than a regularly summoned parliament, and that the claim of rights was tantamount to law. Many persons outside of Westminster thought that it was. To make certain that its status was unassailable, the proponents of the Declaration of Rights mounted a successful effort to transform it into an undeniable law, the Bill of Rights.

The authors of the Declaration of Rights asserted that they, like their ancestors before them, were doing nothing more than restoring old, acknowledged rights of Englishmen which had been grievously violated. There is nothing surprising about such an assertion; throughout the seventeenth century, constitutional change was regularly clothed in conservative dress. What is surprising is the willingness of historians to accept this claim at face value. If one approaches each of the rights in the document from a historical perspective, it becomes readily apparent that not all the claims were the undoubted ancient rights of the realm nor were all the grievances charged against King James II violations of the known laws and statutes of England. Eight rights were not "undisputed" and "ancient": articles 1, 2, 3, 6, 9, 10 (excessive bail clause), 11 and 13. On the other hand, articles 4, 5, 7, 8, 10 (excessive fines and cruel and unusual punishment clauses), and 12 did indeed reaffirm old law. Yet, articles 5 and 7 amended old law in certain particulars. The Bill of Rights strengthened the language of the declaration and gave *all* the rights the undoubted force of law. Both the Declaration of Rights and the Bill of Rights are properly regarded as radical reforming documents, in the sense that they resolved long-standing disputes in ways favorable to Parliament and the individual, and according to libertarian political principles that had been articulated earlier. They dealt with royal prerogatives that lie at the very heart of sovereignty: royal power respecting law, military authority, and taxation. They sought also to strengthen the role of Parliament, by claiming the rights of free election, free speech, free debate, free proceedings, and frequent meetings. And they guaranteed rights to the individual — to petition the king without fear of reprisal, to bear arms (under certain restrictions), to be protected against certain judicial procedures (excessive bail, excessive fines, cruel and unusual punishments, and the granting and promising of fines and forfeitures before conviction). In short, historians who regard the revolutionary settlement as nothing more than a restatement of acknowledged rights have misread, or not read at all, the legal and constitutional background of the thirteen rights claimed in the Declaration of Rights and the Bill of Rights.

The process of passing the Declaration of Rights through the Convention was more complicated than has been appreciated. Proponents of the document employed sophisticated political judgment and skill to facilitate its passage. For example, Treby delayed presenting the first report to avoid entangling it in the debate on the headship, and Powle then gave the advantage to that report by placing it first on the agenda. Jealousy between the two Houses, a proposal to bypass the upper House, opposition from the prince, and a crisis provoked by some lords were features of the political maneuvering. The Declaration of Rights moved through the assembly in tandem with the abdication and vacancy resolution and, at the instigation of men who were responsible for both, was finally linked together with it. The principal supporters of the Declaration of Rights were not Tories, as is sometimes said, but radical Whigs, among whom were former "first Whigs" who had been close to Shaftesbury less than ten years before, Dissenters, and men sympathetic of Nonconformity. The principals in the passage of the Bill of Rights were these same men. In both cases, men acted from complex motives, including political principle, personal advantage, partisanship, and power politics. The passage of the Bill of Rights was likewise neither smooth nor certain. In the absence of compelling urgency to pass the bill, and in the face of many competing domestic and foreign issues, the Bill of Rights languished. As in the case of the Declaration of Rights, jealousy between the two Houses, rivalry between Tories and Whigs, and the disinclination of King William complicated the process. Concern to secure the nation against a Catholic king overwhelmed at times concern for rights. It took ten months of persistence and parliamentary skill on the part of its supporters before the Bill of Rights was signed into law.

The final version of the Declaration of Rights was a much-watered-down version of the Heads of Grievances, the first draft. Historians who have been aware of this fact have offered reasons to account for it. The pressing need to settle affairs rapidly in the face of dangers, real and alleged, from France, Ireland, the London mob, and the English army — the explanation given by Macaulay — remains valid. Anxiety over possible disagreement with Scotland reinforced the sense of urgency. The twenty-eight-point Heads of Grievances contained issues that required more time to consider than prudence would permit. But the disapproval of the prince, suggested by Pinkham and then documented by others, was also a powerful consideration. William's role in the work of the settlement was not a passive one, as early historians maintained. He and his close associates influenced the decisions made by the Convention. Almost certainly William was responsible, in part, for reducing the number of claimed rights. In addition, the profile of the drafting committee holds clues to still further reasons. Among the leading figures were lawyers in whose attitude may be perceived tension between advocating restrictions on royal authority and protecting a strict interpretation of the law. It is they who argued that the Convention had no power to make law and that what William signed as prince could not bind him as king. Although they were willing to include in the final document rights that were not ancient or indisputed, it is almost certainly they who promoted the ideas of dividing the original heads into two parts, one of rights that were old law and the second of claims that required new law, and then of dropping the second part. The lawyers' concern to adhere to the old law, then, provides a further explanation for the pruning of the first draft. Moreover, there was need to placate Tories, especially those in the House of Lords, to win their endorsement for the claim. Furthermore, the major proponents of the claim of rights, although legitimately described as radical or "worthy" Whigs, were not extremists. None was an avowed republican in 1689; none, certainly, was a social or economic revolutionary. Although some were bitterly critical of the Anglican Church, none advocated disestablishment or complete religious toleration. These men were also experienced politicians and parliamentarians; as such, they were willing to compromise, to take what they felt certain of achieving, and to make the most of that achievement. Finally, they were all men of substance who were wary of the possibility of another violent Civil War like the one forty years before, with its concomitant threat to property, life, and social status. In sum, a number of reasons explain why the original reformist goals of the major proponents failed to be reached.

The manipulation of public opinion through the use of printed pamphlets, visual materials, and ceremonies was more important than has been understood to the process of passing the Declaration of Rights and to the revolution in general. An effort was made to win the approval of a broad spectrum of society, including Englishmen outside socially and politically elite categories. The printing of the several drafts of the Declaration of Rights informed the public, sought to enlist their assistance, tried to hold the House of Lords to agreement, and put pressure on William to accept a statement of which he disapproved. As a result, in part, of the effort in the press, a broad consensus of approval for the settlement was achieved when it was most needed — during the deliberations of the Convention. Although the revolution was initiated by a small number of nobles, its resolution and the drafting of the claim of rights was largely engineered by a small group of gentry and representatives of boroughs in the House of Commons, who appealed to persons outside the Convention, thus testifying to a recognition at that moment of the potential power of the lower classes. Scholars who regard the revolution as a coup d'etat limited to a small number of people at the highest reaches of society have not understood the nature of the political process that was followed from the fall through the spring of 1689. Further, the use of propaganda helps to explain how it happened that the solution to the crisis — with which, it has been claimed, less than 5 percent of the governing class would have agreed if they had realized clearly what they were doing at the time — was in fact accepted.[1]

The major proponents of the Declaration of Rights and the Bill of Rights were radical Whigs in the House of Commons and the House of Lords. As a group, they were seasoned men, experienced in politics and in Parliament, their views on the issues that appeared in the Declaration of Rights and the Bill of Rights already announced. Some of them had held high office; many of them were trained in law or practicing lawyers. Outstanding among them in the House of Commons were Birch, Richard Hampden, John Hampden, the Foley brothers, Somers, Treby and Wharton; in the House of Lords, Delamere, Devonshire, Mordaunt, and Wharton. Bishop Burnet also facilitated passage of the Bill of Rights.[2] Less than a decade before, the principals of a claim of rights had tried to change the succession to the throne by passing a law and had argued in tracts and pamphlets for limitations on royal authority. Less than a decade before, they had been almost destroyed as a party, their leaders executed or exiled, their adherents dispersed and silenced. Their survival was the real miracle of the Glorious Revolution. In 1689 they had neither shed nor repudiated the libertarian themes in a political philosophy which some of them had earlier helped to promulgate. In 1689 they dominated the committees in the Convention that drafted the settlement of the crown and the claim of rights. They also dominated the debates on both. The original terms of the abdication and vacancy resolution with the reference to original contract and the first draft of the Declaration of Rights — the Heads of Grievances in twenty-eight points — explicitly stated their political views and goals.

The final version of the Declaration of Rights, however, was a compromise that reflected the highly complicated political situation in January and February 1689 and the political shrewdness and willingness to compromise of the principals. The document's major proponents accepted the changes they thought essential and possible to achieve. The priority they assigned the claims was designed, in part, to appeal to Tories and win support from them. But the political and constitutional principles that underlay the Declaration of Rights remained those that informed the Heads of Grievances and the original version of the abdication and vacancy resolution. Those principles were part of a libertarian reforming tradition about the kingship and the rights of English subjects that reached back through the Exclusion Crisis to the Civil War and Commonwealth period. This tradition was not radical in the sense of positing genuine social and economic change in society. But these ideas were radical in the sense that they were on the left hand side of the essential issue of the seventeenth century — whether king or Parliament should exercise sovereignty. Although some early spokesmen were avowed republicans, most argued for keeping a limited monarchy and locating ultimate authority in the House of Commons of a parliament composed of king, lords, and commons. In the 1670s this tradition resurfaced in tempered form and was adopted by the country opposition. At the time of the Exclusion Crisis in 1679–81 the first Whigs rearticulated these notions, some of which were accepted also by the first Tories. Bitterly contested in the 1680s by royalist spokesmen, these same ideas were expressed in 1689 in a quantity of pamphlets and in the debates in the Convention. They are the ideas that underlie the Declaration of Rights and the Bill of Rights. Thus in 1688–89 there was a larger role for contract theory, the right to resist, and the role of the people than has been recognized. In its essence, then, the Declaration of Rights was a statement, which, however inexplicit its language, reflected radical Whig principles that had originated in the Civil War experience and were aimed at changing fundamentally the Stuart monarchy. After the revolution the attitude of some of the proponents of the document changed when they occupied high positions in government. Their *ex post facto* explanations and comments are unreliable and unacceptable guides to their views at the time of the revolution.

The role of the Tories in the passage of the Declaration of Rights and of the Bill of Rights has been misunderstood. To them does not belong, as has been claimed, the "chief merit" of the Declaration of Rights.[3] The Tories used the widespread interest in drafting a claim of rights to delay and confuse the proceedings. Then when it became clear that the prince did not favor a claim of rights which restricted his power, a group of Tories in the House of Lords attempted to negotiate a deal with him, whereby they assured William that he would be made king without acknowledging the claim of rights if he agreed to depend upon Tories and appoint them to positions of power. This proposal was rejected and a crisis averted because of personal appeals by Whigs to the prince, William's political astuteness, and the influence of his propaganda, which had depicted him as a Deliverer who had come only to rescue and restore the nation's liberties. In the case of the Bill of Rights, again it was radical Whigs who managed the passage and did what they could to quiet conflict between Whigs and Tories in and between both Houses. There were many articles in the Declaration of Rights and the Bill of Rights to which Tories subscribed, and Tories did vote for passage of both documents. Nonetheless, the philosophy underlying the documents originated with men on the left, and it was they who most vigorously promoted the passage of both the Declaration of Rights and the Bill of Rights.

Credit for authoring the Declaration of Rights is usually assigned to John Somers. The evidence is inconclusive, but what there is indicates that Pollexfen, Sacheverell, Temple, and Treby were the ones who contributed most significantly to the text. There is no surviving evidence to indicate that Somers said anything in the Convention about the substance of the document, but one may presume from his writings before and immediately after the revolution that he heartily approved of the several rights. Moreover, Richard Hampden, Treby, Wharton, and Williams deserve credit for assisting in the passage of the declaration through the House of Commons. And Paul Foley, Sacheverell, and Treby — not Somers — seem to have played the major role in the passage of the Bill of Rights. The thought is unescapable that had the then-young Somers failed of election to the Convention, the first time he was returned to Parliament, a claim of rights would have been advanced and perhaps prospered without him.

Yet, there are three reasons that justify assigning Somers a major responsibility for the Declaration of Rights: (1) he was chairman of the second rights committee, a position testifying both to his understanding of and support for the document and to the regard of his fellow committeemen; (2) he initiated the step that led to the Convention's agreeing that the claim of rights should be joined with the offer of the crown and other resolutions passed by the body; and (3) he wrote an eloquent and powerful defense of the Declaration of Rights to counter criticism of the document. In *Vindication of the Proceedings of the late Parliament of England, An. Dom., 1689,* which appeared in print in early 1690, Somers argued that if the Convention had done nothing else but enact the rights and liberties of the subject and settle the succession of the crown, all Englishmen were indebted to it. Complimenting King William for "prudently" complying with the Convention's "just desires" to claim the nation's rights, Somers underlined four articles which, he said, secured England from "oppression, tyranny, and arbitrary power." Those articles concerned (1) suspending and dispensing powers; (2) taxation only with the consent of Parliament; (3) the keeping of a standing army in time of peace only with the consent of Parliament; and (4) the settlement of the royal succession. He maintained that the Declaration of Rights secured freedom and liberty for England because the nation's kings, although they possessed real power, must act according to law. "Our happiness, then, consists in this," wrote Somers, "that our princes are tied up to the law as well as we. . . . Our government not being arbitrary, but legal, not absolute, but political, our princes can never become arbitrary, absolute or tyrants." Acknowledging that the Convention omitted two important points — the settlement of the militia and the indemnity question — Somers noted that anything the assembly had left undone might be accomplished by a succeeding parliament. He concluded that the "late happy revolution was a real one, how odd soever, and unlooked for." [4]

Somers was responding to an unidentified "seditious" pamphlet critical of the settlement. In general, the public and private response over the next decade to the Declaration of Rights ranged from disappointment to professed outrage that the document had not accomplished more. For example, a radical-thinking friend of Locke lamented the failure of the Declaration of Rights to provide religious toleration, a view with which Locke surely concurred. [5] The commonwealthman Walter Moyle while acknowledging the contribution of the Revolution of 1688–89 to protecting England from tyranny regretted that "the boundaries and limits of prerogative" were not "so well stated" as was desirable. [6] Tories were bitterly critical. One regretted that the opportunity was lost in 1689 to resettle the constitution on foundations that would effectively bound the king's prerogatives and protect the nation's liberties, and blamed the Whigs, who, he said, abandoned the effort in favor of self-interest.[7] The *English Man's-Complaint* was especially irate that the command of the militia was left in the hands of the king. In 1692 another tract writer set out reasons justifying a new Bill of Rights, arguing that although there were "useful and good" provisions in the present Bill of Rights, they were "too generally expressed"; he itemized particulars he wanted addressed.[8] Finally, sometime between 1690 and 1695 Halifax, perhaps in a speech, revealed that at the time the Bill of Rights was under consideration "some" men wanted the right of the king to make war without consent of Parliament to be restricted and implied that the question should again be addressed.[9]

The professed disappointment notwithstanding, it is legitimate to ask if it made any practical difference that the Bill of Rights was passed and signed by King William. Some scholars argue that the financial settlement and/or the succeeding wars were the real factors that changed the English monarchy and the relationship between king and Parliament.[10] While the impact of war and finance was, of course, enormous, the Bill of Rights deserves credit, too. It stated principles against which actions were tested. Thus, the article denying the king the right to have a standing army in peacetime without the consent of Parliament served as a weapon in the standing army controversy ten years later in 1697–99, when the successors of the radical Whigs argued for the disbandment of William's victorious army. The king was obliged, in conformity with that article, to win the consent of Parliament to maintain a peacetime establishment. Or again, the restrictions that the Bill of Rights placed upon the royal dispensing power created a different legal situation. That situation was dealt with by statutes passed in 1694 and 1696. And in 1766 when the issue of the royal dispensing power was raised again by a proclamation of King George III which contravened a law, the Bill of Rights and the arguments used in 1689 were cited by opponents of the action.[11] Further, no king after 1689 dared on his own to tax English subjects either directly or indirectly. The right to speak freely in Parliament without risk of judicial review or restraint from the crown has prevailed.[12] Moreover, in fulfillment of the avowed intent of some members of the Convention expressed during the passage of the Declaration of Rights, many of the reforms which had been mentioned in debates and pamphlets and in the first draft were, in fact, translated into statutes during the next eleven years: for example, the Triennial Act (1694), the Treason Trials Act (1696), and the Act of Settlement (1701), which included a provision changing the tenure of judges.

The document also exerted influence on England's colonies in America. The colonists in 1689 greeted the news of the revolution and the passage of the Declaration of Rights and the Bill of Rights with enthusiasm. For them the Bill of Rights solved problems that they shared with English subjects.[13] In 1776 they again turned to the principles and substance of the Bill of Rights to justify independence. It is not difficult, whatever the contrary suggestion,[14] to substantiate the claim that the Revolution of 1689 and the Bill of Rights had a direct influence on the American Revolution. As one example, the eighth article of the Bill of Rights of the United States — "Excessive bail shall not be required, nor excessive fines imposed, nor cruel and unusual punishments inflicted" — was drawn directly from the tenth article in the 1689 Bill of Rights.

Over the next one hundred years politicians and theorists interpreted the meaning of the revolution and commented on the Bill of Rights according to their partisan allegiance and needs. This is one reason why the true nature of the Bill of Rights has not been properly understood. It is an error to think that no deeply held political principles motivated politicians in 1689. If Whigs had adhered to their programmatic ideal, they might well have precipitated a civil war, or provoked the prince sufficiently to abandon England (as his spokesman threatened), or sacrificed entirely their personal political futures. But as it was, the ambiguities in the statement about James's leaving the throne and the compromises in the claim of rights provided material for diverse inferences to be drawn about the revolution, the aims of the revolutionaries, and the nature of the claim. Professor Kenyon has shown that the revolution was an "embarrassment" to both Whigs and Tories during the "rage of party" that followed.[15] The Whigs, a minority in the country at large, split in the 1690s. Court Whigs, among whom Somers is counted, became increasingly conservative. They resisted the effort of Tories to link them with republican notions, deism, and popular rights and to tar them with the charge of "deposing" James II. They dissociated themselves from Old, or Country, Whigs, among whom they might have been classified had they adhered to views expressed in 1688–89. Old Whigs joined with Country Tories to form a "New Country Party," which generally reiterated the arguments of the right of resistance, the contractual basis of government, and the sovereignty of the people (however "people" was defined) that had appeared in debates and tracts at the time of the revolution. Many of the men who had promoted the Declaration of Rights and the Bill of Rights died in the nineties. Of the forty-three committeemen in the House of Commons, twenty-one — including Birch, Boscawen, the Foley brothers, the Hampdens, Howard, Pollexfen, Sacheverell, and Treby — were dead by 1701. Of the thirteen peers who had served on the rights committee in the Lords, seven — including Devonshire, Delamere, Fauconberg, and Wharton — were dead by 1708. In the trial of Dr. Henry Sacheverell in 1710 and the decision of 1711 to sacrifice the Dissenters in exchange for help from the Tories in defeating the proposed peace treaty, the bankruptcy of Court Whiggism was laid bare. Debate on "revolution principles" was no longer the focus. Passive obedience to Parliament and parliamentary sovereignty became official Whig doctrine with the success of the Septennial Act of 1716 and the ascendancy of Sir Robert Walpole. For their part Country Whigs and Country Tories denounced "corruption" and oligarchy, as Professor Pocock has explicated.[16] In very different circumstances at the end of the eighteenth century, the Revolution of 1688–89 and the Bill of Rights again became a theme of partisan polemics. On the one hand, Edmund Burke, for example, interpreted the revolution as entirely conservative, reading into what was said and done his own conservative ideas. On the other hand, radicals, like John Wilkes and Catherine Macaulay, for example, blamed the revolutionaries for not going further in the Bill of Rights, but also praised them for what they had accomplished. Whig and Tory philosophies on the revolution in the eighteenth century are very complex, overlapping in ways that historians now recognize, thanks to the work of H. T. Dickinson, Julian Franklin, and Margaret Jacob,[17] as well as that of Kenyon and Pocock. But no eighteenth-century Tory or Whig studied carefully the episode about which they were commenting, and while much may be learned about eighteenth-century thought from their statements, very little can be learned about the aims and aspirations of men who shaped the revolution settlement and drafted the Declaration of Rights and the Bill of Rights.

This book maintains that only when the text and context of the Declaration of Rights and the Bill of Rights are examined is a sure understanding of the nature of the documents and the intention of their authors possible. The Declaration of Rights was informed by a long-term libertarian political philosophy. The passage of the Declaration of Rights and of the Bill of Rights and the final versions of both were significantly influenced by a highly complicated political situation. In fact, the elevation of William and Mary to the throne of England and the presentation of a claim of the nation's rights were the results of subtle political maneuvering at a time of crisis that was real and threatening to participants, notwithstanding that little bloodshed occurred. A real contest occurred between those men who wanted simply to change the king and those who wanted also to change the kingship. The latter won, although compromise of their goals was necessary for that victory. If they had failed and the Revolution of 1688–89 had been accomplished without a claim of the nation's rights joined to the offer of the throne, then the Glorious Revolution would have been simply a coup d'etat. But with the Declaration of Rights and the Bill of Rights at the center of the constitutional and legal settlement, the Revolution of 1688–89 is properly viewed as a real revolution that restored certain rights that had been assaulted by the Stuarts and, in resolving certain long-term controversies, created a new kingship. The events of the revolution and the terms of the Bill of Rights destroyed the essential ingredients of the ancient regime: the theory of divine-right monarchy, the idea of direct hereditary succession, the prerogatives of the king over law, the military, taxation, and judicial procedures that were to the detriment of the individual. Seen in broad perspective, then, the Revolution of 1688–89 and the Bill of Rights mark a watershed in the political and constitutional history of England and West Europe. It is the greatest, in the sense of being the most effective, of the revolutions that occurred in early modern European history. And its legacy was ongoing in the revolution (and the documents accompanying it) that occurred at the end of the eighteenth century in the American colonies.

Appendixes

Appendix 1

THE DECLARATION OF RIGHTS

Die Martis 12 February 1688/9.

THE DECLARATION OF THE LORDS SPIRITUAL AND TEMPORAL, AND COMMONS, ASSEMBLED AT WESTMINSTER

[This document was read to Prince William and Princess Mary in the Banqueting Hall on February 13, 1689. The Prince accepted it. The text is that of the "presentation copy" held by the House of Lords Record Office.]

Whereas the late King James the second, by the Assistance of divers Evil Counsellors, Judges, and Ministers, imployed by him did endeavour to Subvert and extirpate the Protestant Religion, and the Lawes and Liberties of this Kingdome.

[1.] By assuming and exercising a Power of dispensing with and Suspending of Lawes, and the Execution of Lawes without Consent of Parliament.

[2.] By committing and prosecuting diverse worthy Prelates for humbly petitioning to be excused from concurring to the said assumed Power.

[3.] By issuing and causing to be Executed a Commission, under the Great Seale, for erecting a Court called the Courte of Commissioners for Ecclesiasticall Causes.

[4.] By levying Money for and to the use of the Crown by pretence of Prerogative for other Time and in other manner than the same was granted by Parliament.

[5.] By raiseing and keeping a standing army within this Kingdom in time of Peace without Consent of Parliament and quartering of Souldiers contrary to Law.

[6.] By causing several good Subjects being Protestants to be disarmed at the same time when Papists were both armed and Employed contrary to Law.

[7.] By violating the freedome of Election of Members to serve in Parliament.

[8.] By prosecutions in the Courte of King's Bench for matters and Causes Cognizable only in Parliament And by divers other Arbitrary and illegal Courses.

[9.] And whereas of late Years partial corrupt and unqualified persons have been returned and served on Juryes in tryalls and, particularly divers Jurors in Tryalls for high Treason which were not freeholders.

[10.] And excessive Bayle hath been required of persons Committed in Criminal Cases to elude the benefitt of the Lawes made for the liberty of the Subjects.

[11.] And excessive fynes have been imposed.

[12.] And illegal and cruell punishments inflicted.

[13.] And several Grants and promises made of fynes and forfeitures before any Conviction or Judgment against the persons upon whom the same were to be levied.

All which are utterly and directly contrary to the knowne Lawes and Statutes and freedome of this Realme.

And whereas the said late King James the second having abdicated the Government and the throne being thereby vacant.

His Highnesse the Prince of Orange (whom it hath pleased Almighty God to make the glorious Instrument of delivering this Kingdom from Popery and Arbitrary Power) Did (by the advice of the Lords Spirituall and Temporall and divers principall persons of the Commons) Cause Letters to be written to the Lords Spirituall and Temporall being Protestants and other Letters to the several Countyes Citties Universities Burroughs and Cinqe Ports for the chuseing of such persons to represent them as were of right to be sent to Parliament to meet and sitt at Westminster upon the two and twentieth day of January in this Year 1688 in order to such an establishment as that their Religion Lawes and Libertyes might not againe be in danger of being subverted.

Upon which Letters Elections haveing been accordingly made.

And thereupon the said Lords Spirituall and Temporall and Commons pursuant to their respective letters and Elections being now assembled in a full and free representative of this nation taking into their most serious consideration the best meanes for atteyneing the ends aforesaid Doe in the first place (as their Ancestors in like Case have usually done) for the vindicating and asserting their antient rights and Liberties, Declare.

[1.] That the pretended power of suspending of Lawes or the execution of Lawes by Regall Authority without Consent of Parliament is illegall.

[2.] That the pretended power of dispensing with lawes or the Execution of lawes by regall authority as it has been assumed and exercised of late is illegall.

[3.] That the Commission for erecting the late Courte of Commissioners for Ecclesiasticall Causes and all other Commissions and Courts of like nature are illegall and pernicious.

[4.] That levying of money for or to the use of the Crowne by pretence of Prerogative without Grant of Parliament for longer time or in other manner, than the same is or shall be granted is illegall.

[5.] That it is the right of the Subjects to petition the King and all Committments and prosecutions for such petitioning are illegall.

[6.] That the raiseing or keeping a Standing Army within the Kingdom in time of Peace unlesse it be with consent of Parliament is against Law.

[7.] That the Subjects which are Protestants may have Armes for their defence Suitable to their Condition and as allowed by Law.

[8.] That Elections of Members of Parliament ought to be free:

[9.] That the freedome of Speech and debates or proceedings in Parliament ought not to be impeached or questioned in any Courte or place out of Parliament.

[10.] That excessive Bayle ought not to be required nor excessive fynes imposed nor cruel and unusuall Punishments inflicted.

[11.] That Jurors ought to be duely impannelled and returned and Jurors which passe upon men in tryalls for high Treason ought to be freeholders.

[12.] That all Grants and promises of fynes and forfeitures of particular persons before conviction are illegall and void.

[13.] And that for redress of all greivances and for the amending, strengthening and preserving of the Lawes, Parliaments ought to be held frequently.

And they do claime demand and insist upon all and singular the premises as their undoubted Rights and Liberties and that noe Declarations Judgements Doeings or proceedings to the prejudice of the People in any of the said premisses ought in any wise to bee drawne hereafter into Consequence or Example.

To which demand of their rights they are particularly Encouraged by the declaration of his Highness the Prince of Orange as being the only Meanes for obteyning a full redress and remedy therein.

Haveing therefore an intire Confidence that his said Highness the Prince of Orange will perfect the deliverance soe farr advanced by him and will still preserve them from the violation of their rights which they have here asserted and from all other attempts upon their Religion Rights and Liberties.

The said Lords Spirituall and Temporall and Commons Assembled at Westminster doe Resolve,

That William and Mary Prince and Princesse of Orange bee and bee declared, King and Queen of England France and Ireland and the Dominions thereunto belonging to hold the Crowne and Royall Dignity of the said Kingdom's and Dominions to them the said Prince and Princess during their lives and the life of the Survivor of them and that the Sole and full exercise of the Regall Power be only in and executed by the said Prince of Orange in the Names of the said Prince and Princesse during their Joynt lives And after their deceases the said Crowne and Royall Dignity of the said Kingdoms and Dominions to be to the heires of the body of the said Princesse: And for default of such Issue to the Princesse Anne of Denmarke and the heires of her body. And for default of such Issue to the heires of the body of the said Prince of Orange.

And the said Lords Spirituall and Temporall and Commons doe pray the said Prince and Princesse of Orange to accept the same accordingly.

And that the Oathes hereafter mentioned bee taken by all persons of whom the Oaths of Allegiance and Supremacy might be required by Law instead of them. And that the said Oathes of Allegiance and Supremacy bee abrogated.

I A. B. doe sincerely promise and sweare That I will bee faithfull and beare true Allegiance to their Majesties King William and Queen Mary. Soe help mee God.

I. A. B. doe sweare That I doe from my heart Abhoure, Detest, and Abjure as Impious and Hereticall this Damnable Doctrine and Position That Princes Excommunicated or Deprived by the Pope or any Authority of the see of Rome may be deposed or Murdered by their Subjects or any other whatsoever And I doe Declare That noe foreign Prince Person Prelate State or Potentate hath or ought to have any Jurisdiction Power Superiority Preeminence or Authority Ecclesiasticall or Spirituall within this Realme. Soe help mee God.

It is Ordered By the Lords Spirituall and Temporall and Commons now assembled at Westminster That this Declaration be ingrossed in Parliament and inrolled amongst the Rolls of Parliament and Recorded in Chancery.

[no date]   Signed: Jo. Browne, Cleris
                               Parliamentere.

Die Lundris 15 February 1688
His Majesties Gratious Answer to the Declaration of Both Houses.

My Lords and Gentlemen:

This is certainly the greatest proofe of the Trust you have in us that can be given which is the thing that maketh us value it the more and Wee thankfully Accept what you have offered. And as I had no other Intention in coming hither than to preserve your Religion Laws and Liberties so you may be sure That I shall endeavour to support them and shall be willing to concur in anything that shall be for the Good of the Kingdome and to doe all that is in My Power to advance the Welfare and Glory of the Nation.

Ordered by the Lords Spirituall and Temporall Assembled at Westminster That his Majesties Gratious Answer to the Declaration of both Houses and the Declaration be forthwith Printed and Published And that his Majesties Gratious Answer this day be added to the Engrossed Declaration in Parliament to be Enrolled in Parliament and Chancery.

Appendix 2

THE HEADS OF GRIEVANCES

[The Heads of Grievances was the first draft of the Declaration of Rights. It contained twenty-eight articles, twenty-three presented by a committee of the House of Commons, five more added by members in debate on February 2. The articles and the portions of articles that survived in the Declaration of Rights and/or the Bill of Rights are italicized.]

1. *The pretended power of dispensing or suspending laws, or the execution of laws by royal prerogative, without consent of Parliament, is illegal.*

2. *The commission for erecting the late court of commissioners for ecclesiastical causes and all other commissions and courts of like nature are illegal and pernicious.*

3. *Levying money for or to the use of the crown by pretence of prerogative, without grant of Parliament for longer time, or in other manner than the same shall be so granted, is illegal.*

4. *It is the right of the subjects to petition the king; and all commitments and prosecutions for such petitioning are illegal.*

5. The acts concerning the militia are grievous to the subject.

6. *The raising or keeping a standing army within this kingdom in time of peace, unless it be with the consent of Parliament, is against the law.*

7. *It is necessary for the public safety, that the subjects, which are Protestants, should provide and keep arms for their common defense,* and that arms which have been seized and taken from them be restored.

8. *The right and freedom of electing members of the House of Commons,* and *the rights and privileges of Parliament,* and members, as well in the intervals of Parliament as during their sitting, to be preserved.

9. *That Parliament ought to sit frequently,* and that their frequent sitting be preserved.

10. No interrupting of any session of Parliament, till the affairs that are necessary to be dispatched at that time are determined.

11. That the too long continuance of the same Parliament be prevented.

12. No pardon to be pleadable to an impeachment in Parliament.

13. Cities, universities, and towns corporate, and boroughs and plantations to be secured against *Quo Warrantos* and surrenders and mandates, and restored to their ancient rights.

14. *None of the royal family to marry a Papist.* [In Bill of Rights only.]

15. *Every king and queen of this realm, at the time of their entering into the exercise of their royal authority, to take an oath for maintaining the Protestant religion, and the laws and liberties of the nation,* and that the coronation oath be reviewed. [In Bill of Rights only.]

16. Effectual provision to be made for the liberty of Protestants in the exercise of

299

their religion and for uniting all Protestants in the matter of public worship as far as may be possible.

17. Constructions upon the statutes of treason, and trials and proceedings and writs of error, in cases of treason, to be regulated.

18. Judges commissions to be made *quam diu se bene gesserint;* and their salaries to be ascertained and established, to be paid out of the public revenue only, and not to be removed nor suspended from the execution of their office, but by due course of law.

19. *The requiring excessive bail* of persons committed in criminal cases, *and imposing excessive fines and illegal punishments to be prevented.*

20. Abuses in the appointing of sheriffs, and in the execution of their office, to be reformed.

21. *Jurors to be duly impannelled and returned,* and corrupt and false verdicts prevented.

22. *Informations in the Court of King's Bench to be taken away.* [Implicit in article 8 of the indictment against James and in article 9 of the declaratory section of the Declaration of Rights.]

23. The Chancery and other courts of justice, and the fees of office, to be regulated.

24. That the buying and selling of offices may be effectually provided against.

25. That upon return of *habeas corpus* and *mandamus,* the subject may have liberty to traverse such return.

26. *That all grants of fines and forfeitures are illegal and void;* and that all such persons as procure them be liable to punishment.

27. That the abuses and oppressions in levying and collecting the hearth money be effectually redressed.

28. That the abuses and oppressions in levying and collecting the excise be effectually redressed.

Note to Appendixes 3 and 4

The following two charts on the rights committees in the House of Commons and the House of Lords provide selected political data about the committeemen. Appendix 3 documents some of the characteristics of the committeemen in the House of Commons that are discussed in Chapters 2 and 3. It shows that as a group these men were experienced in parliamentary affairs, seasoned in age, sympathetic to Nonconformity, and radical Whig in politics. Appendix 4 documents material discussed in Chapter 14 about the peers appointed to the rights committee in the House of Lords. That committee was heavily weighted by men who favored Prince William and subscribed to the political principles of the radical Whigs.

Information about such social characteristics as position in family, marital status, number of children, education, offices held prior to the Revolution, income, appearance, and personality was available for some but not all of the individuals, and so is not included here.

Much of the material in the two appendixes is from the unpublished files of the History of Parliament Trust.

Appendix 3

THE RIGHTS COMMITTEES IN THE HOUSE OF COMMONS

Name	Dates	Age	Prior Parliaments[1]	Constituency, 1689
1. Birch, Col. John	1616–1691	73	PR, C, Ex	Weobley, Hereford
2. Boscawen, Hugh	1625–1701	64	PR, C, Ex	Cornwall
3. Capel, Sir Henry	1638–1696	51	C, Ex	Cockermouth, Cumberland
4. Christie, Thomas	1622–1697	67	Ja	Bedford Boro.
5. Clarges, Sir Thomas	c. 1618–1695	71	PR, C, Ex, Ja	Oxford University
6. Colchester, Lord (Styled): Richard Savage	c. 1654–1712	35	Ex	Liverpool, Lanc.
7. Cotton, Sir Robert III	1644–1717	45	Ex, Ja	Cambridgeshire
8. Ellys, Sir William	1654–1727	35	Ex	Grantham, Lincoln
9. Etterick, William	1651–1716	38	Ja	Christchurch, Southampton
10. Eyre, Giles	1635–1695	54	C	Salisbury, Wilts
11. Falkland, Lord (Styled): Anthony Cary	1656–1694	33	Ja	Great Marlow, Bucks
12. Finch, The Hon. Heneage	c. 1649–1719	40	Ex, Ja	Oxford University
13. Foley, Paul	1645?–1699	44	Ex	Hereford City
14. Foley, Thomas	c. 1641–1701	48	Ex	Worcestershire
15. Garroway, William	1616–1701	73	C, Ex, Ja	Arundel, Sussex
16. Gregory, William	1624–1696	65	Ex	Hereford Boro., Herefs.
17. Hampden, John	1656?–1696	33	Ex	Wendover, Bucks
18. Hampden, Richard	1631–1695	58	PR, C, Ex	Wendover, Bucks
19. Harbord, William	1635–1692	54	Ex	Launceton (alias Dunhever) Cornwall

1. PR – elected to pre-Restoration parliament(s); C – elected to Cavalier Parliament; Ex – elected one or more Exclusion Parliaments; Ja – elected to James II's Parliament (1685).

2. T – Tory; W – Whig. The identification is based on lists reprinted in Browning, *Danby,* 3:164– and in Eveline Cruickshanks, John Ferris, and David Hayton, "The House of Commons Vote on Transfer of the Crown, 5 February 1689," *BIHR* 52 (May 1979): 37–47; NL-T or NL-W indicates t the name is not in the lists (NL) and that the partisan designation is, therefore, provisional, although many instances it is unquestionably accurate.

3. See Chapter 2 above. W – Worthy; H – Honest; B – Bad; V – Vile.

olitics, 689²	Order of Appointment to Treby's Committee	Order of Appointment to Somers's Committee	No. of Committee Assignments	Nonconformist Sympathizer	Close to William of Orange	Shaftesbury's Rating³	Exclusion
W	1		7	Yes	No	W	Pro
W	3	12	8	Yes	No	W	Pro
W	22	17	7	No	No	W	Pro
NL-T	35		1	No	No		Anti
T	29		6	No	No	W	Anti
W	19		2	No	Yes		?
T	18		1	No	No		Anti
W	39		2	Yes	No	H	Pro
T	15		2	No	No		?
NL-W	28	3	3	Yes	No		?
NL-T	16	8	6	No	No		?
T	11	16	4	No	No	B	?
W	38	21	5	Yes	Yes	H	Pro
W	14		3	Yes	Yes	H	Pro
W	13	20	7	No	No	W	Pro
T		13	3	No	No	W	?
W	31		2	Yes	Yes		Pro
W	25	15	8	Yes	Yes	W	Pro
W	6		5	No	Yes		?

Appendix 3 — *Continued*

Name	Dates	Age	Prior Parliaments[1]	Constituency, 1689
20. Hobart, Sir Henry	c. 1658–1698	31	Ex	Norfolk
21. Holt, Sir John	1642–1710	47		Bere Alston, Devon
22. Howard, Sir Robert	1626–1698	63	C, Ex	Castle Rising, Norfolk
23. Jephson, William	c. 1647–1691	42	Ex	Chipping Wycombe, Buck
24. Lee, Sir Thomas	1635–1691	54	C, Ex, Ja	Buckinghamshire
25. Littleton, Sir Thomas	1647–1710	42		New Woodstock, Oxford
26. Maynard, Sir John	1602–1690	87	PR, C, Ex, Ja	Plymouth, Devon
27. Musgrave, Sir Christopher	c. 1631–1704	58	C, Ex, Ja	Carlisle, Cumberland
28. Pollexfen, Henry	c. 1632–1691	57		Exeter, Devon
29. Sacheverell, William	1638–1691	51	C, Ex	Heytesbury, Wilts
30. Sawyer, Sir Robert	1633–1692	56	C, Ex	Cambridge University
31. Seymour, Sir Edward	1633–1708	56	C, Ex, Ja	Exeter, Devon
32. Somers, John	1651–1716	38		Worcester City, Worcester
33. Temple, Sir Richard	1634–1697	55	PR, C, Ex, Ja	Buckingham Boro., Bucks
34. Tipping, Thomas	1653–1718	36	Ja	Wallingford, Berks
35. Treby, Sir George	1634–1700	46	C, Ex	Plympton Earl, Devon
36. Tredenham, Sir Joseph	d. c. 1707	48?	C, Ex, Ja	St. Mawes, Cornwall
37. Waller, Edmund II	1652–1700	37		Amersham, Bucks
38. Wharton, The Hon. Thomas	1648–1715	41	C, Ex, Ja	Buckinghamshire
39. Wildman, John	1621–1693	68	PR, Ex	Great Bedwin, Wilts
40. Williams, Sir William	1634–1700	55	C, Ex	Beaumaris, Anglesey, Wale
41. Wiltshire, Lord (Styled): The Hon. Charles Powlett	1661–1772	28	Ex, Ja	Southampton
42. Wogan, William	1638–1708	51	Ex, Ja	Haverfordwest, Pembroke Wales
43. Wrey, Sir Bourchier	c. 1653–1696	36	Ex, Ja	Liskeard Boro., Cornwall

1. PR — elected to pre-Restoration parliament(s); C — elected to Cavalier Parliament; Ex — elected one or more Exclusion Parliaments; Ja — elected to James II's Parliament (1685).

2. T — Tory; W — Whig. The identification is based on lists reprinted in Browning, *Danby*, 3:164–7 and in Eveline Cruickshanks, John Ferris, and David Hayton, "The House of Commons Vote on t Transfer of the Crown, 5 February 1689," *BIHR* 52 (May 1979): 37–47; NL-T or NL-W indicates th the name is not in the lists (NL) and that the partisan designation is, therefore, provisional, although many instances it is unquestionably accurate.

3. See Chapter 2 above. W — Worthy; H — Honest; B — Bad; V — Vile.

litics, 689[2]	Order of Appointment to Treby's Committee	Order of Appointment to Somers's Committee	No. of Committee Assignments	Nonconformist Sympathizer	Close to William of Orange	Shaftesbury's Rating[3]	Exclusion
W	21		1	Yes	No		?
L-W	Added Feb. 4	1	4	No	No		?
W	20	19	4	Yes	Yes	V	Pro
W	5		4	Yes	Yes		?
W	4	18	8	Yes	No	W	Pro
W	23	11	5	No	No		?
L-W		2	3	Yes	No	W	?
T	33		4	No	No	V	Anti
L-W	7	6	6	Yes	Yes		?
L-W	2	4	6	Yes	No	W	Pro
T	24	10	4	No	No	V	Pro
T	9		3	No	No	V	Anti
W	27	9	5	Yes	No		Pro
L-W	26	7	8	No	No	V	Pro
W	34		2	No	Yes		Pro
W	8	5	5	Yes	Yes	W	Pro
T	30		3	No	No		Anti
L-W	36		3	Yes	No		Pro
W	32		2	Yes	Yes	W	Pro
W	10		4	Yes	Yes		?
T	17	Added Feb. 12	5	Yes	No	W	Pro
L-W	12		4	No	Yes		Pro
T		14	2	No	No	H	?
T	37		1	No	No		?

Appendix 4

THE RIGHTS COMMITTEE IN THE HOUSE OF LORDS

Name	Dates	Age	Politics, 1689[1]
1. Charles Powlett, 6th marquess of Winchester	1625?-1699	64	W
2. John Grenville, 1st earl of Bath	1628-1701	61	W
3. Thomas Osborne, 1st earl of Danby	1631-1712	58	M
4. William Cavendish, 4th earl of Devonshire	1640-1707	49	W
5. Daniel Finch, 2nd earl of Nottingham	1647-1730	42	R
6. Thomas Herbert, 8th earl of Pembroke	1656-1733	33	R
7. Charles Talbot, 12th earl of Shrewsbury	1660-1718	29	W
8. Thomas Belasyse, 2nd Viscount Fauconberg	1627-1700	62	M
9. Charles Mordaunt, Viscount Mordaunt	1658-1735	31	W
10. Francis Newport, 1st Viscount Newport	1619-1708	70	W
11. Henry Booth, 2nd Baron Delamere	1652-1694	37	W
12. Richard Lumley, 1st Baron Lumley	d. 1721	c. 47	W
13. Philip Wharton, 4th Baron Wharton	1613-1696	76	W

1. W — Williamite; M — Maryite; R — Regencyite.
2. See David H. Hosford, "The Peerage and the Test Act: A List, c. November 1687," *BIHR* (1969): 116-20.
3. See Browning, *Danby*, 3:153-163 (a list of peers opposed to James II).
4. See Eveline Cruickshanks, David Hayton, and Clyve Jones, "Divisions in the House of Lords the Transfer of the Crown and Other Issues, 1689-94: Ten New Lists," *BIHR* 53 (May 1980): 56-£
5. To offer crown to William and Mary.
6. To agree with the Commons in the word "abdicated."
7. To agree with the Commons in the word "abdicated."

Opposed to James in 1687		Votes on the Transfer of the Crown, 1689[4]		
Bonrepaux's List[2]	Danby's List[3]	January 31[5]	February 4[6]	February 6[7]
undeclared	unlisted	Yes	Yes	Yes
undeclared	unlisted	—	Yes	Yes
X	X	Yes	—	Yes
undeclared	X	Yes	Yes	Yes
X	X	No	No	No
X	unlisted	No	No	No
X	X	Yes	Yes	Yes
X	X	Yes	—	Yes
X	X	Yes	Yes	Yes
X	X	Yes	Yes	Yes
X	X	Yes	Yes	Yes
X	X	Yes	Yes	Yes
X	X	Yes	Yes	Yes

Abbreviations
and Short Titles

AHR	*American Historical Review*
ARA	Algemeen Rijksarchief, The Hague
Add. Mss.	Additional Manuscripts, British Library
Ailesbury, *Memoirs*	*Memoirs of Thomas, 2nd earl of Ailesbury,* ed. W. E. Buckley, 2 vols. (London, 1890).
BIHR	*Bulletin of the Institute of Historical Research*
BL	British Library, London
Bodl.	Bodleian Library, Oxford University
Burnet, *HOT*	Gilbert Burnet, *Bishop Burnet's History of His Own Time,* 6 vols. (Oxford, 1833).
Burnet, *Supplement*	H. C. Foxcroft, ed., *A Supplement to Burnet's History of My Own Time* (Oxford, 1902).
CHPL	The Carl H. Pforzheimer Library, New York
CJ	*Journals of the House of Commons*
CSPD	*Calendar of State Papers,* Domestic Series, 1660–1702
Clar. Corr.	*Correspondence of Henry Hyde, Earl of Clarendon, and of his brother Laurence Hyde, Earl of Rochester,* ed. S. W. Singer, 2 vols. (London, 1828).
Clarendon State Papers	F. J. Routledge, ed., *Calendar of the Clarendon State Papers Preserved in the Bodleian Library, 1660–1726,* 5 vols. (Oxford, 1970).
DNB	*Dictionary of National Biography*
Dalrymple	Sir John Dalrymple, *Memoirs of Great Britain and Ireland* [1681–92], 2 vols. (London and Edinburgh, 1771–73).
de Beer, *Evelyn's Diary*	E. S. de Beer, ed., *The Diary of John Evelyn,* 6 vols. (London, 1955).
Delamere, *Works*	Henry Booth, second Baron Delamere, first Earl of Warrington, *Works* (London, 1694).

309

EHR	*English Historical Review*
Ellis Corr.	G. J. W. Agar-Ellis, Lord Dover, ed., *The Ellis Correspondence: Letters Written during the Years 1686, 1687, 1688, and Addressed to John Ellis,* 2 vols. (London, 1831).
FSL	Folger Shakespeare Library, Washington, D.C.
Grey	Anchitell Grey, *Debates of the House of Commons, from the year 1667 to the year 1694,* 10 vols. (1763).
HJ	*Historical Journal*
HL	Henry E. Huntington Library, San Marino, Calif.
HLRO	House of Lords Record Office, London
HMC	Historical Manuscript Commission, London
HPT	History of Parliament Trust, London
Hatton Corr.	E. M. Thompson, ed., *Correspondence of the Family of Hatton, being chiefly letters addressed to Christopher, First Viscount Hatton, 1601–1704,* 2 vols., printed for the Camden Society, n.s., vol. 23 (1878).
Holdsworth, *HEL*	Sir William S. Holdsworth, *A History of English Law,* 13 vols. (London, 1922–52).
Huygens, "Journaal"	"Journaal van Constantyn Huygens, den zoon, van 21 October 1688 tot 2 September 1696," *Werken Uitgegeven door het Historisch Genootschaap,* n.s. 23 (Utrecht, 1876–78): 53–219.
JBS	*Journal of British Studies*
KUL, Bonnet's dispatches	University of Kansas Library. Microfilm of Acta betr. des Residenten Bonnet relat: aus England 1689 January–June, Repertorium XI. 73 (original in Deutsches Zentralarchiv, Merseburg, German Democratic Republic).
LQR	*Law Quarterly Review*
LJ	*Journals of the House of Lords*
Lords Mss.	HMC, *Manuscripts of the House of Lords. 1678–93,* 4 vols. (London, 1887–94, vol. 2 (covering 1688–89).
Luttrell, *Brief Historical Relation*	Narcissus Luttrell, *A Brief Historical Relation of State Affairs from September 1678 to April 1714,* 6 vols. (Oxford, 1857).
Morrice	Roger Morrice, "Entr'ing Book, Being an Historical Register of Occurrences from

	April, Anno, 1677 to April 1691," 4 vols. (original in the Dr. Williams's Library, London; photocopy in author's possession).
NLW	National Library of Wales, Aberystwyth
NUL	Nottingham University Library
OED	*Oxford English Dictionary*
PRO	Public Record Office, London
Parlia. Hist.	William Cobbett, ed., *The Parliamentary History of England, From the Norman Conquest, in 1066, to the Year 1803,* 36 vols. (London, 1806–20).
Reresby, *Memoirs*	Sir John Reresby, *Memoirs of Sir John Reresby,* ed. Andrew Browning (London, 1936).
Sachse, *Lord Somers*	William L. Sachse, *John, Lord Somers: A Political Portrait* (Manchester, 1975).
Schwoerer, "A Jornall of the Convention"	Lois G. Schwoerer, "A Jornall of the Convention at Westminster begun the 22 of January 1688/9," *BIHR* 49 (1976): 242–63.
Schwoerer, *NSA*	Lois G. Schwoerer, *"No Standing Armies!" The Antiarmy Ideology in Seventeenth-Century England* (Baltimore, 1974).
Simpson, "Notes of a Noble Lord"	Alan Simpson, "Notes of a Noble Lord, 22 January to 12 February 1688/9," *EHR* 52 (1937): 87–98.
Somers, *HSP*	John Somers, "Notes of Debate, January 28, January 29," in *Miscellaneous State Papers, from 1501 to 1726,* ed. Philip Yorke, Earl of Hardwicke, 2 (London, 1778): 401–25.
Somers's Tracts	*A Collection of Scarce and Valuable Tracts . . . Selected from Public as well as Private Libraries, Particularly That of the Late Lord Somers,* ed. Sir Walter Scott, 13 vols. (London, 1809–15).
SR	*Statutes of the Realm,* ed. Alexander Luders et al., 11 vols. (London, 1810–28).
St. Tr.	Thomas B. Howell, ed., *Cobbett's Complete Collection of State Trials and Proceedings for High Treason,* 34 vols. (London, 1809–28).
Steele, *Proclamations*	Robert Steele, ed., *A Bibliography of Royal Proclamations of the Tudor and Stuart Sovereigns and of Others Published under Authority, 1485–1714,* 2 vols. (Oxford, 1910).

van Terveen, "Verbaal . . . Witsen"   J. G. van Terveen, ed., "Uittreksels uit het Bijzonder Verbaal Nopens de Deputatie en Ambassade Daarop Gevolgd in Engeland, 1689, Gehouden Door Mr. Nicolass Witsen, Burgemeester te Amsterdam," in *Geschieden Letterkundig Mengelwerk van Mr. Jacobus Scheltema*, 3, pt. 2 (Utrecht, 1823): 137–71.

Notes

Preface

1. For example, Schwoerer, "A Jornall of the Convention," pp. 242–63. Also, BL, Add. Mss. 51, 950, fols. 12–13.

2. Schwoerer, *NSA,* p. 147, n. 47.

3. John Carswell, *The Descent on England: A Study of the English Revolution of 1688 and Its European Background* (London, 1969), preface, refers to a contemporary notice of the burning of political papers. I have no proof that the papers of leading figures associated with the Declaration of Rights met the same fate, but it is surely possible.

4. There are three major sources: Anchitell Grey, *Debates in the House of Commons, from the year 1667 to the year 1694* (London, 1769); John Somers, "Notes of Debate, January 28, January 29," in *Miscellaneous State Papers, from 1501 to 1726,* ed. Philip Yorke, Earl of Hardwicke (London, 1778); and Schwoerer, "A Jornall of the Convention."

The Declaration of Rights and the Bill of Rights:
The Historians' View

1. Bodl., Rawlinson Mss. D 1079, fol. 14v; the same remark appears in FSL, "Newdigate Newsletters," L.c. 1944.

2. David Ogg, *England in the Reigns of James II and William III* (Oxford, 1955), p. 242.

3. Robert Frankle, "The Formulation of the Declaration of Rights," *HJ* 17, no. 2 (1974): 265–79. Henry Horwitz, "Parliament and the Glorious Revolution," *BIHR* 47 (1974): 47–49, treats an episode in the passage of the declaration.

4. See Thomas Babington Macaulay, Lord Macaulay, *History of England from the Accession of James II,* ed. C. H. Firth, 6 vols. (London, 1913–15), 4:1663–64, for a brief account with which A. S. Turberville agreed (see *The House of Lords in the Reign of William III,* Oxford Historical and Literary Studies [Oxford, 1913], pp. 160–61). A fuller analysis is in Alan Simpson, "The Convention Parliament of 1688–89," (D. Phil., Oxford University, 1939), pp. 174–90.

5. For example, Edmund Bohun, *History of the Desertion; or, An Account of all the publick affairs in England, from the beginning of September 1688 to February 12 following,* licensed on April 10, 1689, and the anonymous *History of the Late Revolution in England, with the causes and means by which it was accomplish'd. Together with the Settlement thereof,* available in print in the middle of November 1689 (the date of publication appears in the *London Gazette,* November 14–18, 1689). Abel Boyer, *History of King William III,* 3 vols. (London, 1702–3), offered a similar view.

6. For example, Burnet, *HOT* (1st ed. 1724–34); Thomas Somerville, *History of Political Transactions and of Parties from the Restoration of King Charles the Second to the Death of King William* (London, 1792); and Edmund Burke. Other writers intimated but failed to develop a different

interpretation: for example, Laurence Echard, *History of England From the First Entrance of Julius Ceasar and the Romans, To the Conclusion of the Reign of King James the Second, and the Establishment of King William and Queen Mary Upon the Throne, in the Year 1688,* 3 vols. (London, 1707-18); James Ralph, *The History of England during the reigns of King William, Queen Anne and King George I, with an introductory review of the reigns of the royal brothers, Charles and James; in which are to be found the seeds of the Revolution,* 2 vols. (1744-46); Sir John Dalrymple, *Memoirs of Great Britain and Ireland from the Dissolution of the last Parliament of Charles II until the Sea-Battle off La Hogue,* 2 vols. (London and Edinburgh, 1771-73); and James MacPherson, *History of Great Britain from the Restoration to the Accession of the House of Hannover,* 2 vols. (London, 1776).

7. In this instance Macaulay did not follow the lead of Sir James Mackintosh, whose *History of the Revolution in England in 1688* (London, 1834) he used. See ibid., pp. 623, 636, 641-42, and 644, for Mackintosh's view.

8. Macaulay, *History of England,* 3: 1297, 1306-11. The contradictions are probably due to Macaulay's failure to reconcile the evidentiary inferences (of which he was surely aware) and his political ideals.

9. See Joseph M. Hernon, Jr., "The Last Whig Historian and Consensus History: George Macaulay Trevelyan, 1876-1962," *AHR* 81 (1976): 66-97.

10. George Macaulay Trevelyan, *The English Revolution, 1688-89* (London, 1938), pp. 161-63.

11. Mark Thomson, *The Constitutional History of England* (London, 1938), 4:175.

12. Lucile Pinkham, *William III and the Respectable Revolution: The Part Played by William of Orange in the Revolution of 1688* (Cambridge, Mass., 1954), pp. 234-35.

13. Frankle, "The Formulation of the Declaration of Rights," pp. 275-79.

14. Horwitz, "Parliament and the Glorious Revolution," pp. 47-49.

15. Horwitz (ibid.) and Jennifer Carter, "The Revolution and the Constitution," in *Britain after the Glorious Revolution,* ed. Geoffrey Holmes (London, 1969), pp. 39-58.

16. Frankle, "The Formulation of the Declaration of Rights," and Howard Nenner, "Constitutional Uncertainty and the Declaration of Rights," in *After the Reformation: Essays in Honor of J. H. Hexter,* ed. Barbara Malament (Philadelphia, 1980), pp. 291-308. Professor Nenner kindly allowed me to read his article in typescript.

17. Nenner, "Constitutional Uncertainty and the Declaration of Rights," pp. 304, 305.

18. J. R. Jones, *The Revolution of 1688 in England* (London, 1972), p. 327.

19. Lawrence Stone, "The Results of the English Revolutions of the Seventeenth Century," in *Three British Revolutions,* ed. J. G. A. Pocock (Princeton, 1980), p. 64.

20. Edmund Burke, *Reflections on the Revolution in France,* ed. Thomas H. D. Mahoney (New York, 1955), esp. pp. 17, 18, 24-25, 30, 32, 35, 37.

21. The two latest general studies are Jones, *The Revolution of 1688 in England,* and Stuart Prall, *The Bloodless Revolution: England, 1688* (New York, 1972). Two new books written for a popular audience are John Miller, *The Life and Times of William and Mary,* with an introduction by Antonia Fraser (London, 1974), and Henri and Barbara van der Zee, *William and Mary* (London, 1973).

22. The following books deal with the Convention debates, but not for the purpose of explaining the Declaration of Rights: Julian Franklin, *John Locke and the Theory of Sovereignty: Mixed Monarchy and the Right of Resistance in the Political Thought of the English Revolution* (Cambridge, 1978); J. P. Kenyon, *Revolution Principles: The Politics of Party* (Cambridge, 1977); and Howard Nenner, *By Colour of Law: Legal Culture and Constitutional Politics in England, 1660-1689* (Chicago, 1977).

Chapter 1

1. London Meteorological Office, Rawlinson Mss. Weather Diary, January-February 1689. I am indebted to Mrs. J. M. Cowland, library information officer, for locating the diary and sending me a photocopy of the appropriate page.

2. John Walker was cousin and deputy to John Browne, clerk of Parliament, who was absent presumably because of illness and old age. See HLRO, Mss. Minutes, February 13, 1688/89.

3. FSL, "A Short Account of the Revolution in England in the year 1688," bound in Sir Robert Southwell's Collection of Mss. Material on the Glorious Revolution, V.b. 150, fol. 16. Also, FSL, Newdigate Newsletters, L.c. 1976.

4. FSL, "A Short Account of the Revolution in England," fol. 15.

5. It is filed with the Original Acts of William and Mary and tagged no. 1, although it is not strictly speaking a statute. The parchment roll is made up of three membranes of approximately thirty inches, twenty-seven inches, and six inches long, respectively. The parchment has a suedelike finish. Two red lines were customarily placed on either side of the text of documents in the Garter Rolls at the time (H. S. Cobb, deputy-clerk, HLRO, to author, March 26, 1975).

6. For example, the Petition of Right, 1628; the Grand Remonstrance, 1640; the Nineteen Propositions, 1642; and the Humble Petition and Advice, 1657, are unsigned.

7. Gary Wills, *Inventing America: Jefferson's Declaration of Independence* (New York, 1978), pp. 340-48. The document was signed over many days, not in a fixed ceremony, as famous paintings depict.

8. Morrice, 2:445, 447, 448; BL, Add. Mss. 51, 950, fols. 16v–17; Bodl., Rawlinson Mss. D 1079, fol. 3v; HMC, *Portland Mss.,* 3:425.

9. Morrice, 2:447.

10. Charles's second answer, finally wrested from him, invested the Petition of Right, some scholars now believe, with statutory authority: see David Berkowitz, "Reason of State in England and the Petition of Right, 1603-1629," in *Straaträson Studien zur Geschichte eines politischen Begriffs,* ed. Roman Schnur (Berlin, 1975), pp. 209-10; Elizabeth R. Foster, "Petitions and the Petition of Right," *JBS* 14 (November 1974): 24-25, 43-44.

11. A holograph copy of the official version of his speech, which differs somewhat from private contemporary accounts and from the version an early-nineteenth-century historian reported as entered in *CJ,* survives in HLRO. See Figure 4. *CJ,* 10:30; *LJ,* 14:128; KUL, Bonnet's dispatches, February 15/25, 1688/89; ARA, Collectie van Citters, no. 25, February 15/25, 1688/89; HMC, *Portland Mss.,* 3:428; Sir James Mackintosh, *History of the Revolution in England in 1688* (London, 1835), p. 646. Presumably the version entered in *CJ* was lost in the fire in 1834.

12. *CJ,* 10:26; *LJ,* 14:126; Grey, 9:72; HMC, *House of Lords Mss., 1689-90,* p. 30. HLRO, Main Papers, contain the original draft of the order.

13. *LJ,* 14:128. The copy of the Declaration of Rights entered in Chancery is at PRO, C 212/18/1. The copy of the Bill of Rights, a regular statute, is at HLRO.

14. HLRO, Braye Mss. 43; Mss. Minutes, February 8, 1688/9.

15. See Figure 1. The document is held by HLRO.

16. *CJ,* 10:19, 20, 21; Grey, 9:51.

17. Grey, 9:42, 51, 52; Somers, *HSP,* 2:422; Bodl., Rawlinson Mss. D 1079, fol. 16; HLRO, Braye Mss. 43, fol. 30v; Morrice, 2:466; *CJ,* 10:25. The words "remonstrance," "protestation," and "apology" were also used interchangeably.

18. Foster, "Petitions and the Petition of Right," pp. 21-45; Foster to author, September 8, 1978.

19. "Address," it was explained, signifies a written application made by the House to the king or queen, and the idea is conveyed by the words "message," "petition," "supplication," "declaration," and "remonstrance."

20. Berkowitz, "Reason of State," p. 202. For private petitions of right, parliamentary petitions of right, and petitions as part of the legislative process, see ibid., pp. 201-4; Foster, "Petitions and the Petition of Right," esp. pp. 27-30, 32-33, 35-39; and Holdsworth, *HEL,* 9:7-45.

21. Foster, "Petitions and the Petition of Right," pp. 37-39, 43.

22. Ibid., pp. 24-25.

23. Ibid., pp. 44-45, quoting Basil Duke Henning, ed., *The Parliamentary Diary of Sir Edward Dering* (New Haven, 1940), pp. 116-17,

24. Cf. J. H. Plumb, *The Growth of Political Stability in England, 1675-1725* (London, 1967), p. 22.

25. *OED;* also see Elisha Coles, *An English Dictionary: Explaining the difficult Termes that are used in Divinity, Husbandry, Physick, Phylosophy, Law, Navigation, Mathematicks and other Arts and Sciences* (London, 1676). Other contemporary dictionaries give essentially the same definition.

26. John Cowell, *The Interpreter; or, Booke containing the signification of words, wherein is set forth the true meaning of all . . . such words and termes as are mentioned in the law writers or statutes of this . . . kingdome,* which went through four editions before 1689 and one in 1701.

27. Esther S. Cope, "The King's Declaration Concerning the Dissolution of the Short Parliament of 1640: An Unsuccessful Attempt at Public Relations," *Huntington Library Quarterly* 11 (August 1977): 325.

28. For example, in January 1642, Parliament issued two instruments titled "declaration," while in July 1642 ten "declarations" appeared, followed by seven in August 1642. See Edward Husbands, *An Exact Collection of all remonstrances, declarations and votes* (London, 1642).

29. William H. Dunham, Jr., and Charles T. Wood, "The Right to Rule in England: Depositions and the Kingdom's Authority, 1327-1485," *AHR* 81 (October 1976): 738-61, deals with the first five incidents.

30. Grey, 9:8, 14, 19, 23.

31. See H. J. Oliver, *Sir Robert Howard (1626-98): A Critical Biography* (Durham, N.C., 1963), pp. 242-46. Howard's *History of the Reign of Edward and Richard II* appeared in 1690. A recent study is A. Tuck, *Richard II and the English Nobility* (London, 1973).

32. See Chapter 2 for definition of word "radical."

33. *CJ,* 10:22.

34. See Lois G. Schwoerer, "Press and Parliament in the Revolution of 1689," *HJ* 20 (September 1977): 545-67, for the general question of how the public learned of what was happening at Westminster.

35. The title of the broadside was *The Names of the Lords Spiritual and Temporal, Who Deserted [not Protested] against the Vote in the House of Peers, the Sixth Instant, against the Word Abducated* (sic) *and the Throne Vacant,* printed for J. Newton. The sheet appeared between February 7 and 11; on February 11 the Lords made an effort to find out who was responsible for it. See HMC, *House of Lords, 1688-89,* p. 18, and HLRO, Mss. Minutes, February 11, 1689.

36. HLRO, Willcocks Coll., VI, 20. The copy of the Heads of Grievances mentioned in HMC, *12th Report,* app., pt. VII, LeFleming Mss. p. 235, under date of February 7 is the February 2 report. It is not at the Bodleian as stated, but at the Cumbria Record Office. That copy is in manuscript not printed form.

37. A broadside, printed on both sides, n.p., n.d. Copies at HL, 276772, and Bodl., Carte Mss. 180, fol. 542.

38. *LJ,* 14:128.

39. Gillyflower was said to be one of the most important of the Westminster Hall booksellers. See Henry R. Plomer, *A Dictionary of the Printers and Booksellers who were at work in England, Scotland, and Ireland from 1668 to 1725* (Oxford, 1922), pp. 128, 153, 232.

40. Copies at HL, 134874, and FSL, 181542.

41. J. R. Jones, *Country and Court: England, 1658-1714* (London, 1978), p. 254.

42. Documents in Andrew Browning, ed., *English Historical Documents, 1660-1714* (London, 1966), vol. 8 of *English Historical Documents,* ed. David C. Douglas, pp. 127, 131, 133, 135, show the limitations on the succession imposed by the Bill of Rights and the Act of Succession, 1701.

43. Jones, *Country and Court,* p. 253.

44. Paul Birdsall, " 'Non Obstante': A Study in the Dispensing Power of English Kings," in *Essays in History and Political Theory in Honor of Charles Howard McIlwain* (Cambridge, Mass., 1936), pp. 75-76.

45. Corinne C. Weston, *English Constitutional Theory and the House of Lords, 1556-1832* (London, 1965), p. 115, n. 51.

46. Christopher Hill, *The Century of Revolution, 1603-1714* (Edinburgh, 1961), p. 276.

Chapter 2

1. The rights committee in the House of Lords and its leading members are discussed in Chapter 14 and Appendix 4. See Appendix 3 for the Commons committeemen.

2. A prosopographic study of the members of the Convention is needed. Material for such a project will soon be available with the publication of the work of the History of Parliament Trust in London. George L. Cherry's *The Convention Parliament, 1689: A Biographical Study of Its Members* (New York, 1966), must be used with caution. The problem of how many and which members attended the meetings of the committees is discussed in Chapter 11.

3. Appendix 3 indicates the previous parliamentary experience of each of the committeemen. Maurice Ashley, *John Wildman, Plotter and Postmaster: A Study of the English Republican Movement in the Seventeenth Century* (London, 1947), pp. 84-85, states that Wildman, one of the seven "old parliament" men, was excluded before the House met, but there is no known evidence for this conclusion: see Barbara Taft, "The Humble Petition of Several Colonels of the Army: Causes, Character, and Results of Military Opposition to Cromwell's Protectorate," *Huntington Library Quarterly* 42 (November 1978): 20, n. 10. A total of eighty former members of the Cavalier Parliament were in the House: see J. H. Plumb, "The Elections to the Convention Parliament of 1689," *Cambridge Historical Journal* 5 (1937): 244. In the last group — former members of Exclusion Parliaments — it is impossible to distinguish Sir Robert Cotton, first Bart. (c. 1635-1712), from Sir Robert Cotton II (1644-1717). I have followed the HPT in identifying the latter as the Cotton appointed to the Committee of Thirty-Nine. Plumb's figures for members of the Convention who were in the Exclusion Parliaments are 164 in 1678-79, 187 in 1679, and 192 in 1680-81 (ibid., p. 244).

4. See Appendix 3. Williams was returned but not seated. The three new men were Thomas Christie, William Etterick, and Thomas Cary, Lord Falkland. Plumb calculates that a total of 196 members of the Parliament of 1685, 99 of whom also sat in the Parliaments of 1678-79 and 1680-81, were in the Convention ("Elections to the Convention Parliament," p. 244). Henry Horwitz finds 193 members from the Parliament of 1685 (*Parliament, Policy, and Politics in the Reign of William III* [Manchester, 1977], p. 9).

5. Plumb, "Elections to the Convention Parliament," pp. 244, 245.

6. This point is developed in Chapter 4 below.

7. *CJ*, 9:640; Grey, 7:369-70; Schwoerer, *NSA*, pp. 96-98.

8. They were Birch, Boscawen, Clarges, Paul Foley, Garroway, Richard Hampden, Lee, Littleton, and Maynard. See *CJ*, 9:324, 683.

9. Grey, 9:35.

10. The average age of the fourteen Tory members was 50.8 years. The youngest and the oldest were among the twenty-nine Whigs, whose average age was 50.2 years.

11. See Appendix 3.

12. Plumb, "Elections to the Convention Parliament," pp. 241, 244. There were roughly 160 Tories and 175 Whigs. Plumb's figures are based largely on two division lists which are reprinted with annotations in A. Browning, *Thomas Osborne, Earl of Danby and Duke of Leeds, 1632-1712*, 3 vols. (Glasgow, 1944-51), 3:164-72. See also H. Horwitz, "The General Election of 1690," *JBS* 11 (November 1971): 82-83, 87, and n. 3.

13. *CJ*, 10:15, 22. The clerk took down the names of M.P.'s in the order that they were appointed to the committees. There is, of course, the chance that he got the names out of order. Parliamentary rules permitted each member to name one person only to a committee (George Petyt, *Lex Parliamentaria; or, A Treatise of the Law and Custom of the Parliaments of England* [London, licensed December 6, 1689], p. 207).

14. J. R. Jones, *The First Whigs: The Politics of the Exclusion Crisis, 1678-1683* (London, 1961), chaps. 7 and 8.

15. Ibid., p. 6.

16. For example, Christopher Hill, *The World Turned Upside Down* (New York, 1972); Bernard S. Capp, *The Fifth Monarchy Men: A Study in Seventeenth-Century Millenarianism* (London, 1972).

17. Grey, 9:57.

18. Ibid., pp. 237, 488.

19. *OED.*

20. See J. R. Jones, "Shaftesbury's 'Worthy Men': A Whig View of the Parliament of 1679," *BIHR* 30 (1957): 232-41, where the designations are explained.

21. See Appendix 3. Clarges, Gregory, and Wogan were *W* or *H* on Shaftesbury's list, but in 1689 they were allies of the Tories. Williams was also *W* on Shaftesbury's list; in 1689, however, he supported the Tories on "abdication," and the Whigs on the claim of rights.

22. See Appendix 3.

23. In regard to the Rye House Plot, on Boscawen and Hampden see HPT; on Wildman, see Ashley, *John Wildman,* pp. 238-48; on Wharton, see John Carswell, *The Old Cause: Three Biographical Studies in Whiggism* (London, 1954), pp. 60-61. Jephson, Littleton, Waller, and Wharton's names appear on a list of members of the Green Ribbon Club reproduced in Sir George Sitwell, *The First Whig: An Account of the Parliamentary Career of William Sacheverell* (Scarborough, 1894), app., pp. 197-203. I am grateful to Dr. Barbara Taft for lending me photocopies of the relevant pages from this privately printed book. Treby's name is on another list of members in The Pepys' Library, Magdalene College, Cambridge, Miscellanies, vii, fols. 489-91. Professor James Jacob kindly sent me a photocopy of his notes of the list. See also J. R. Jones, "The Green Ribbon Club," *Durham University Journal,* n.s. 18 (1956): 17-20.

24. Douglas R. Lacey figured that thirty Presbyterians or Congregationalists were elected to the Convention in January and three more were returned by June 20. (See *Dissent and Parliamentary Politics in England, 1661-1689* [New Brunswick, N.J., 1969], p. 224 and n. 57. Lacey's Appendix 3 shows a total of thirty-five Presbyterians or Congregationalists, with a note explaining that no more than thirty-three sat at any one time.) Lacey counted eight Dissenters on Treby's committee (pp. 229-30 and n. 73), but according to his own chart there were nine. Edmund Waller II, not Sir William Waller, was on the committee. According to Lacey, the following members were, in varying degrees, Presbyterian or Congregationalist in 1689: Boscawen, Ellys, Paul Foley, Thomas Foley, John Hampden, Richard Hampden, Hobart, Maynard, and Edmund Waller. Nine others evidently had sympathetic ties with the Dissenters. In addition to the ones named in my text, they were Birch, Eyre, Jephson (his father was a Presbyterian), Lee, and Wildman. See Lacey, pp. 379-80 (Birch) and 418-19 (Lee); HPT biographies (Eyre, Jephson); and FSL, Newdigate Newsletters, L.c. 1956 (Wildman).

25. Sachse, *Lord Somers,* pp. 3-4, 221; Michael Landon, *The Triumph of the Lawyers* (Tuscaloosa, Ala., 1970), pp. 53, 54, for Treby and Pollexfen. Wharton was the son of the prominent Presbyterian peer Phillip, fourth Lord Wharton. Landon (p. 195) notes also that Williams was connected with a Dissenting congregation.

26. HPT.

27. Lacey, *Dissent and Parliamentary Politics,* p. 165.

28. Ibid., pp. 382-83 (Boscawen); p. 412 (Hobart); pp. 422-23 (Maynard).

29. Jephson and Littleton were members of the Green Ribbon Club.

30. Morrice, 2:445.

31. See Appendix 3 for the fourteen Tories. Temple sided with the Whigs in 1689. For Musgrave, see *DNB.*

32. *DNB;* Keith Feiling, *History of the Tory Party, 1640-1714* (Oxford, 1924), pp. 142, 143, 253, 261-62.

33. The lawyers and their parties were Christie (T), Etterick (T), Eyre (W), Finch (T),

Gregory (T), Holt (W), Jephson (W), Littleton (W), Maynard (W), Musgrave (T), Pollexfen (W), Sacheverell (W), Sawyer (T), Somers (W), Treby (W), Waller (W), Wildman (W), Williams (T), and Wogan (T). Wildman is included on the authority of Ashley, *John Wildman,* pp. 13–14. Christie was apparently learned in the law (see HPT draft biography), but his name does not appear in the admissions records of the Inns of Court.

34. Finch was solicitor-general in 1677–86; Williams, in 1687–88; Sawyer served as attorney-general from 1681; Gregory, Holt, and Maynard were serjeants-at-law.

35. Gregory was recorder for Gloucester, Holt for Reading and Abingdon, Maynard for Plymouth, Somers for Worcester, Treby for Plympton, and Williams for Chester.

36. The recorder served as the principal legal adviser and leading judicial functionary of the borough, presiding over the Borough Court of Quarter Sessions, and performing other legal duties, such as administering the oath of office to the mayor. The term was ancient, dating back to the fourteenth century in some boroughs, such as Bristol. The post, which gradually was differentiated from that of steward, required a man "learned in the laws of England and of the degree of the utter barristers." The right of appointment varied. In some cases it was held by the borough corporation alone, in some by the corporation subject to approval of the crown, and in others by the crown alone. The recorder of London was always chosen by the lord mayor and aldermen. In establishing the order of precedence among members of the legal profession, Sir William Blackstone ranked the recorder of London ninth, just after serjeants-at-law. See Sidney and Beatrice Webb, *English Local Government: The Parish and the Country,* introd. B. Keith-Lucas (London, 1963), 2:322–23, 309 n. 1, 357; Holdsworth, *HEL,* 12:4.

37. See David Ogg, *England in the Reign of Charles II,* 3rd ed., 2 vols. (London, 1961), 2:617, 624–26; *St. Tr.,* 8:223–446.

38. Members of the defense team on the committee were Finch, Pollexfen, Sawyer, Somers, and Treby. (The other two defense lawyers were Sir Francis Pemberton and Sir Cresswell Levinz.) Williams, who had momentarily abandoned his former Whig connections and accepted the post of solicitor-general, argued the case for the crown.

39. Sachse, *Lord Somers,* p. 21.

40. HPT.

41. The others were Eyre, Finch, Gregory, Holt, Littleton, Maynard, Musgrave, and Waller.

42. Sawyer and possibly Wildman. Of committee members who were not trained in law, only Howard attended university, and about his presence at Oxford there is doubt (Oliver, *Sir Robert Howard,* p. 6).

43. From Middle Temple came Etterick, Jephson, Maynard, Somers, Treby, and Waller. Etterick and Somers were admitted the same year, 1669 (Sachse, *Lord Somers,* p. 10). Gregory, Holt, Musgrave, Sacheverell, Williams, and Wogan were educated at Gray's Inn; Finch, Littleton, Pollexfen, and Sawyer at Inner Temple; and Eyre at Lincoln's Inn. Wildman was apparently privately instructed (Ashley, *John Wildman,* p. 13). Christie's name does not appear in the admissions records of any of the Inns of Court; he, too, must have been privately instructed in the law.

44. The recovery of an account of the debates in Treby's committee documents this assertion. See below, Chapter 11.

45. Schwoerer, "A Jornall of the Convention," p. 260. Also *The Debate At Large, Between The Lords and Commons, at the Free Conference Held in the Painted Chamber, in the Session of the Convention, Anno 1688. Relating to the Word, Abdicated, and the Vacancy of the Throne In the Commons Vote,* 2nd ed. (London, 1710), pp. 23–24.

46. Schwoerer, "A Jornall of the Convention," p. 256.

47. Grey, 9:12.

48. Nenner, *By Colour of Law,* p. 3 and chap. 1.

49. J. G. A. Pocock, *The Ancient Constitution and the Feudal Law: A Study of English Historical Thought in the Seventeenth Century* (Cambridge, 1957), is the classic study.

50. Grey, 2:17 (a Col. Strangeways) and 19 (Sir Thomas Lee); 9:99 (Eyre).

51. Barbara J. Shapiro, "The Codification of the Laws in Seventeenth-Century England," *Wisconsin Law Review* (1974), pp. 428-65.

52. Nenner, *By Colour of Law,* pp. 16, 19, 22-23.

53. Barbara J. Shapiro, "Law and Science in Seventeenth-Century England," *Stanford Law Review* 21 (April 1969): 727-66; Nenner, *By Colour of Law,* pp. 5-7.

54. See n. 33, above.

55. See maps in Browning, *English Historical Documents, 1660-1714,* pp. 255, 257, 425.

56. Professor Jones has pleaded for "municipalizing" research in the revolution (*The Revolution of 1688,* p. 11), and a study of each man's role in local politics — beyond the scope of this book — might prove to be illuminating.

57. *Observations upon the late Revolution in England,* in *Somers's Tracts,* 10:338.

58. Other men who bore personal grievances were Boscawen, Capel, Gregory, John Hampden, Harbord, Howard, Temple, Tipping, and Wildman.

59. They were Lord Colchester, Paul Foley, Thomas Foley, John Hampden, Richard Hampden, Harbord, Howard, Jephson, Pollexfen, Tipping, Treby, Wharton, Wildman, and Lord Wiltshire.

60. HPT.

61. Ibid.

62. Huygens "Journaal," p. 72.

63. See Jones, *The Revolution of 1688,* p. 313.

64. They were Capel, Savage (Lord Colchester), Finch, Wharton, and Powlett (Lord Wiltshire).

65. The knights were Capel, Clarges, Cotton, Gregory, Hobart, Holt, Howard, Maynard, Sawyer, Temple, Treby, Tredenham, Williams, and Wrey. The baronets were Ellys, Hobart, Littleton, Seymour, Temple, Williams, and Wrey. Pollexfen, Somers, and Wildman were knighted after the revolution.

66. Plumb, *The Growth of Political Stability,* p. 62.

67. Boscawen, Richard Hampden, Lee, and Temple were on eight committees; Garroway and Birch (who was chairman of the Committee on Elections and Privileges), on seven; and Clarges, Falkland, Pollexfen, and Sacheverell, on six.

68. Pinkham, *The Respectable Revolution,* p. 234.

69. For these points, see Chapter 3.

70. *DNB.*

71. The table of contents of *State Tracts,* vol. 1, attributes to "Mr. Eyres" authorship of *Reflections upon the late great Revolution; written by a Lay-Hand in the Country for the satisfaction of some Neighbours.*

72. Morrice, 2:437.

73. HPT.

74. Ibid.

75. See below, Chapter 5.

76. Lacey, *Dissent and Parliamentary Politics,* p. 453; HPT.

77. Luttrell, *Brief Historical Relation,* 4:313.

Chapter 3

1. There is no biography of Treby, but see HPT and *DNB.* Landon, *The Triumph of the Lawyers,* studies Treby, Pollexfen, and Williams, among other Whig lawyers.

2. HMC, *13th Report,* app., pt. 6, pp. 21-23.

3. See Chapter 2, n. 23, above.

4. Landon, *The Triumph of the Lawyers,* p. 54.

5. *CSPD, 1677-78,* pp. 446, 449. Professor David Berkowitz, whose study of John Selden is forthcoming, confirms that Selden was the primary author.

6. HMC, *13th Report,* app., pt. 6, p. 24. For Starkey, see Henry R. Plomer, *A Dictionary of*

the *Printers and Booksellers who were at work in England, Scotland, and Ireland from 1641 to 1667* (Oxford, 1968). Starkey also printed in 1675 Henry Neville's translation *The Works of the famous Nicholas Machiavel.* Thus, he may have had contact with Thomas Wharton, who wrote a "Letter" (discussed below) that was appended to it.

7. The title was *A Collection of Letters and other Writings relating to the horrid Popish Plot printed from the Originals in the Hands of George Treby, Esq.* In two parts. (FSL, T2102, T2104.)

8. HMC, *7th Report,* app., p. 473.

9. Landon, *The Triumph of the Lawyers,* pp. 101-2.

10. The title was *Truth Vindicated; or, A Detection of the Aspersions and Scandals cast upon Sir Robert Clayton and Sir George Treby, Justices, and Slingsby Bethell and Henry Cornish, Sheriffs, of the City of London, in a Paper published in the name of Dr. Francis Hawkins, Minister of the Tower, intituled, The Confession of Edward Fitz-Harris, Esq.*

11. See account in *St. Tr.,* 8:667.

12. Morrice, 2:388. 390.

13. See K. H. D. Haley, *The First Earl of Shaftesbury* (Oxford, 1968), pp. 699-700, for a brief account.

14. *DNB.* Treby had matriculated from Exeter College in 1660.

15. Landon, *The Triumph of the Lawyers,* p. 202.

16. Morrice, 2:365, and see below, p. 131.

17. Speech in the Guildhall Library; also in FSL, Newdigate Newsletters, L.c. 1977.

18. Morrice, 2:419.

19. Grey, 9:65-70; Jones, *The Revolution of 1688,* p. 159. Danby and Devonshire also recommended bailing Brent.

20. I am indebted to J. P. Ferris for this contemporary description of Treby.

21. See below, Chapters 9 and 12.

22. From a poem, quoted in the *DNB,* by Nahum Tate, who had profitted from Treby's bounty.

23. Maurice Cranston, *John Locke: A Biography* (London, 1957), p. 325, n. 1. Sachse, Somers's recent biographer, does not comment upon his appearance or voice.

24. Sachse, *Lord Somers,* p. 9, 19, 189-90, 194, 198; Christopher Hill, *Milton and the English Revolution* (New York, 1977), pp. 230, 295 n. 1, 321.

25. Sachse, *Lord Somers,* pp. 3-4, 203, 221.

26. Ibid., pp. 10, 15. Haley, *The First Earl of Shaftesbury,* does not mention Somers.

27. See my "John Locke and the Revolution Whigs" (Paper delivered at the conference "John Locke and the Political thought of the 1680's," Washington, D.C., March 1980).

28. See Sachse, *Lord Somers,* p. 15, for authorship.

29. *A Just and Modest Vindication of the Proceedings of the Last Two Parliaments,* pp. 1-2, 37, 45, 47.

30. Ibid., pp. 22, 16, 32, 28.

31. *The Security of Englishmen's Lives; or, The Trust, Power, and Duty of the Grand Jurys of England,* p. 8.

32. Ibid., p. 12.

33. Ibid., p. 19.

34. Ibid., pp. 17, 85, 88.

35. Sachse, *Lord Somers,* pp. 20-25.

36. Weston, *English Constitutional Theory and the House of Lords,* p. 120.

37. Sir George Duckett, ed., *Penal Laws and Test Act: Questions Touching Their Repeal Propounded in 1687-88 by James II* (London, 1882), pp. 328, 336, 336n, 339.

38. HPT.

39. HPT.

40. See Godfrey Davies, "The Political Career of Sir Richard Temple (1634-1697) and Buckingham Politics," *Huntington Library Quarterly* 4, no. 1 (1940): 47-83; Clayton Roberts, "Sir Richard Temple: The Picktank Undertaker," ibid. 41 (February 1978): 137-55.

41. *DNB.*

42. Schwoerer, "A Jornall of the Convention," p. 250.

43. HL, Temple Papers, fols. 228-29.

44. Huygens, "Journaal," p. 84. Temple had talked with Huygens at least once before: see ibid., p. 69.

45. A brief statement of Temple's political views, including his conviction that the condition of England was not compatible with that of a democratic commonwealth, is in HL, Stowe Mss., fols. 1-28.

46. Margaret Verney, ed., *Memoirs of the Verney Family,* 4 vols. (London, 1892-99), 4:448.

47. See Horwitz, *Parliament, Policy, and Politics,* p. 133; also pp. 70, 72, 75, 107, 108, 110, 127, 129, 213.

48. *DNB.*

49. He sat for Wendover, Bucks, in 1660, 1661, 1679, and 1689; for Buckinghamshire in 1681.

50. Lacey, *Dissent and Parliamentary Politics,* pp. 59, 69, 145 (for dissent); 74, 85 (for foreign policy).

51. *DNB.*

52. *CJ,* 10:11, 13-15, 18, 19.

53. Grey, 9:419.

54. H. C. Foxcroft, *Life and Letters of Sir George Savile, First Marquis of Halifax,* 2 vols. (London, 1898), 2:248.

55. *DNB.*

56. Williams's vote is revealed in Eveline Cruickshanks, John Ferris, and David Hayton, "The House of Commons Vote on the Transfer of the Crown, 5 February 1689," *BIHR* 52 (May 1979): 47. This list corrects the one printed in Browning, *Danby,* 3:164-72.

57. Landon, *The Triumph of the Lawyers,* p. 54.

58. Ibid., pp. 55-56, 68-71, 156-57.

59. HPT.

60. Other cases were Edmund Fitzharris in 1681, Thomas Papillon in 1684, and Richard Baxter in 1685.

61. Landon, *The Triumph of the Lawyers,* pp. 188-89.

62. Grey, 9:146.

63. See *St. Tr.,* 7:183-523, for the trial.

64. Burnet, *HOT,* 3:234, 2:443 and *n; DNB.*

65. Morrice, 2:373.

66. Ibid., p. 437.

67. See Chapter 10 for Pollexfen's role.

68. Landon, *The Triumph of the Lawyers,* pp. 45, 53.

69. *DNB.*

70. NUL, Portland Mss., PwA 2161, 2175; Ailesbury, *Memoirs,* 1:122.

71. Burnet, *HOT,* 2:209. Burnet does not explain why he used the adjective "perplexed," a strong word in the late seventeenth century, indicating bewilderment and disorientation (*OED*).

72. Devon County Record Office, Mss. of Drake family of Buckland Abbey, 346 M/F 889-890.

73. See above, p. 45.

74. Carswell, *The Old Cause,* p. 43.

75. *DNB.*

76. HPT.

77. Robert A. Beddard, "'The Violent Party': The Guildhall Revolutionaries and the Growth of Opposition to James II," *Guildhall Miscellany* 3 (April 1970): 130.

78. Carswell, *The Old Cause,* p. 45.

79. HPT.

80. Carswell, *The Old Cause,* p. 68n.

81. *DNB.*

82. BL, Add. Mss. 38, 495, fols. 140, 142. Godwin was released after two weeks.

83. Beddard, "'The Violent Party,'" p. 132.

84. Grey, 9:11, 64.

85. Carswell, *The Old Cause,* p. 41.

86. For the authorship of the letter, see Caroline Robbins, ed., *Two English Republican Tracts* (Cambridge, 1969), pp. 15, 20, and references therein.

87. *DNB;* C. M. Simpson, *The British Broadside Ballad and Its Music* (New Brunswick, N.J., 1966), pp. 449-55.

88. *DNB.*

Chapter 4

1. The original article treating the suspending power and the dispensing power together was divided into two, thereby making thirteen articles. See Appendices 1 and 2 for the Declaration of Rights and the Heads of Grievances.

2. W. R. Anson, *The Law and Custom of the Constitution* (Oxford, 1922) 1:350-351.

3. Holdsworth, *HEL,* 6:217; Carolyn A. Edie, "Revolution and the Rule of Law: The End of the Dispensing Power, 1689," *Eighteenth-Century Studies,* 10, no. 4 (1977): 435.

4. Holdsworth, *HEL,* 6:218-29; Edie, "Revolution and the Rule of Law," p. 435; E. F. Churchill, "The Dispensing Power of the Crown in Ecclesiastical Affairs," *LQR* 38 (1922): 297-316, 420-34.

5. The phrase usually employed in granting a dispensation; it acquired a quasi-technical sense; see Holdsworth, *HEL,* 6:221, n. 2.

6. Edie, "Revolution and the Rule of Law," p. 436, n. 5.

7. G. R. Elton, ed., *The Tudor Constitution* (Cambridge, 1960), pp. 19-20, 21, 25-26.

8. Ibid., p. 225.

9. Elizabeth R. Foster, ed., *Proceedings in Parliament, 1610,* 2 vols. (New Haven, 1966), 2:38, 184, 190, 218, 228, 241-45, 275.

10. For the idea that Glanville intended restrictions, see Janelle R. Greenberg, "Tudor and Stuart Theories of Kingship: The Dispensing Power and the Royal Discretionary Authority in Sixteenth and Seventeenth Century England" (Ph.D., diss., University of Michigan, 1970), pp. 164-67.

11. For what follows, see Weston, *English Constitutional Theory and the House of Lords,* esp. pp. 23-25, 29-31, 34-43; "The Theory of Mixed Monarchy under Charles I and After," *EHR* 75 (1960): 426-43; and "Concepts of Estates in Stuart Political Thought," in *Representative Institutions in Theory and Practice* (Brussels, 1970), pp. 87-130.

12. Ogg, *England in the Reign of Charles II,* 1:354.

13. Nenner, *By Colour of Law.*

14. J. P. Kenyon, *The Stuart Constitution, 1603-1688* (Cambridge, 1966), p. 405; for Kenyon's comments see pp. 401-2.

15. *Parlia. Hist.,* 4:262; *CJ,* 8:440, 442.

16. Kenyon, *The Stuart Constitution,* p. 402; E. F. Churchill, "The Dispensing Power and the Defense of the Realm," *LQR* 37 (1921): 412-41.

17. Carolyn A. Edie, *The Irish Cattle Bills: A Study in Restoration Politics* (Philadelphia, 1970).

18. Future members of the rights committees were Birch, Garroway, Howard, Lee, Littleton, Maynard, Meres, and Sacheverell.

19. Charles's response is printed in Kenyon, *The Stuart Constitution,* pp. 408-9. On the House of Commons' resolution, see Grey, 2:12-26, 55, 56, 58, 59; *CJ,* 9:25-52, 256.

20. Edie, "Revolution and the Rule of Law," p. 438; Holdsworth, *HEL,* 6:222.

21. Anson, *Law and Custom of the Constitution,* 1:349.

22. Francis North, Lord Guilford, quoted in Ogg, *England in the Reign of Charles II,* 1:353.

23. Grey, 8:358; for the debates of November 12-16, see pp. 354-63.

24. Ibid., p. 362. The committeemen were Clarges, Falkland, Hampden, Maynard, Meres, Musgrave, and Seymour.

25. See Alfred F. Havighurst, "James II and the Twelve Men in Scarlet," *LQR* 64 (1953): 522–46.

26. *St. Tr.*, 11:1166–1316.

27. Birdsall, "'Non Obstante': A Study in the Dispensing Power of English Kings," esp. pp. 70–76; Holdsworth, *HEL*, 6:225; Nenner, *By Colour of Law*, pp. 100–101; Churchill, "The Dispensing Power of the Crown in Ecclesiastical Affairs," p. 420–34.

28. Corinne C. Weston, "Legal Sovereignty in the Brady Controversy," *HJ* 15 (1972): 409–31, a recent article revealing the strength of the Tory side.

29. Roger L'Estrange, *Two Cases Submitted to Consideration* (London, 1687), p. 5.

30. James Wilson, *Jus Regium Coronae; or, The King's Supreme Power in Dispensing with Statutes* (London, 1688), pp. 7, 10, 21.

31. John Somers, *A Just and Modest Vindication* (London, 1689), p. 22.

32. Weston, "Legal Sovereignty in the Brady Controversy," pp. 425–27.

33. John Miller, *James II: A Study in Kingship* (London, 1978), pp. 157, 165. Kenyon, *The Stuart Constitution*, p. 403, also regards James's Declaration of Indulgence as "less sweeping" than that of 1672. The text is in Kenyon at pp. 410–13.

34. See Ogg, *England in the Reigns of James II and William III*, pp. 198–200, for a brief account. For definition of an information, see below, p. 000. At one point, the rights committee cited the use of informations as a grievance.

35. *St. Tr.*, 12:183–524.

36. Quoted in Anson, *The Law and Custom of the Constitution*, 1:353.

37. De Beer, *Evelyn's Diary*, 4:615.

38. See Ogg, *England in the Reigns of James II and William III*, pp. 175–79.

39. 13 Car. II, c. 12, *SR*, 5:315–16.

40. Miller, *James II*, pp. 155, 152.

41. *St. Tr.*, 11:1123–65.

42. Miller, *James II*, pp. 170–71.

43. Ibid., p. 155.

44. Ogg, *England in the Reigns of James II and William III*, p. 176.

45. See below, Chapter 5.

46. William S. McKechnie, *Magna Carta: A Commentary on the Great Charter of King John* (Glasgow, 1914), pp. 231–40.

47. Ibid., p. 238. For a recent view, see Elton, *The Tudor Constitution*, p. 42.

48. Kenyon, *The Stuart Constitution*, pp. 53–62.

49. Foster, *Proceedings in Parliament, 1610*, esp. 1: xv–xvi, 88, 132–33, 254; 2: 152, 170–97, 221–23, 225–49, 267, 396, 410–11.

50. Kenyon, *The Stuart Constitution*, p. 56.

51. Elton, *The Tudor Constitution*, pp. 43–44.

52. Kenyon, *The Stuart Constitution*, pp. 59–60.

53. Robert C. Johnson et al., eds., *Commons Debates, 1628* (New Haven, 1977), 2:57, 67, 72; also speeches by Sir Edward Coke (ibid., pp. 64, 69. 74) and Sir Thomas Wentworth (ibid., pp. 71, 68, 72).

54. Kenyon, *The Stuart Constitution*, pp. 60–62.

55. Ibid., pp. 88–89, 104.

56. For a discussion of the legal issues tending to vindicate the majority decision, see D. L. Keir, "The Case of Ship Money," *LQR* 52 (1936): 546–74.

57. E. S. Cope and W. H. Coates, eds., *Proceedings of the Short Parliament of 1640*, Camden Fourth Series, vol. 19 (London, 1977), pp. 73, 113, 143, 148, 152–53, 156–57, 160, 162, 172–74, 178, 182, 215, 218, 219, 228, 245, 247, 256–57, 275–76, 278, 322.

58. Kenyon, *The Stuart Constitution*, p. 192.

59. FSL, Add. Mss. 662. I owe this reference to Barbara Taft.

60. *CJ*, 8:42, 49, 57, 71, 86.

61. Browning, *English Historical Documents, 1660–1714,* p. 147.

62. They were Birch, Boscawen, Capel, Hampden, Howard, Littleton, Meres, Sacheverell, and Temple. *CJ,* 9:304, 305.

63. Birch, Boscawen, Clarges, Lee, Littleton, and Maynard. *CJ,* 9:324.

64. *CJ,* 9:683.

65. Somers, *HSP,* 2:413, 415.

66. BL, Add. Mss. 51,950, fol. 12.

67. Miller, *James II,* p. 135, n. 1; Havighurst, "James II and the Twelve Men in Scarlet," p. 526.

68. Jones, *Country and Court,* p. 227; Jones, *The Revolution of 1688,* pp. 59–60.

69. *St. Tr.,* 12:369–70 (Finch).

70. Ibid., pp. 392–93 (Levinz); cf. p. 371 (Pollexfen).

71. Ibid., pp. 402n, 403–6, 407.

72. Steele, *Proclamations,* 1:3703, dated December 12, 1679.

73. Grey, 7:369–70; *CJ,* 9:640.

74. Grey, 7:371-72.

75. Grey, 8:52–53, 61–67, 71.

76. E. Porritt, *The Unreformed House of Commons: Parliamentary Representation before 1832* (Cambridge, 1903), pp. 258, 528. McKechnie, *Magna Carta,* pp. 465-77, discusses the article in broader terms.

77. Cope and Coates, *Proceedings of the Short Parliament,* pp. 47–48, 275–89.

78. For petitioning campaigns to achieve various goals, see David Underdown, *Pride's Purge: Politics in the Puritan Revolution* (Oxford, 1971), pp. 78–79, 93–95, 97–99, 107–10, 116–19, 131–32, 178–81, 352; and H. N. Brailsford, *The Levellers and the English Revolution,* ed. Christopher Hill (Stanford, 1961), pp. 189–90. Examples of Leveller tracts are Richard Overton, *An Appeale from the degenerate Representative Body the Commons of England Assembled at Westminster: To the Body Represented, The free people in Generall of the severall Counties, Cities, Townes, Burroughes and Places within this Kingdom of England, and Dominion of Wales* (London, 1647), in *Leveller Manifestoes of the Puritan Revolution,* ed. Don M. Wolfe (London, 1944), p. 195; and Richard Overton, *The Hunting of the Foxes from New-Market to Triploe Heath to Whitehall, By five small Beagles (late of the Armie); or, The Grandie-Deceivers Unmasked (that you may know them)* (London, 1649), in ibid., pp. 356, 362, 373, 381.

79. 13 Car. II, c. 5, *SR,* 5:308. The Act of 1648 in *Acts and Ordinances,* 1:1139, anticipated it: see Holdsworth, *HEL,* 6:426.

80. For what follows, see Schwoerer, *NSA.*

81. John Miller, "Catholic Officers in the Later Stuart Army," *EHR* 88 (1973): 45–46. Miller notes the difficulties in arriving at precise figures. He calculates that in 1688 James's army was 40,117, but does not notice a list in PRO, SP 8/2, pt. 2, fols. 99–100, which gives the total as 53, 716 officers and men.

82. Officers had to take the Test three months after being commissioned, so the Catholic commissions were legal for that period (Miller, *James II,* p. 143).

83. Miller, "Catholic Officers," pp. 39, 43, 45, 47–50.

84. Lois G. Schwoerer, "Fittest Subject for a King's Quarrel," *JBS* 11 (1971): 45–76.

85. *SR,* 5:308-9.

86. *SR,* 5:238.

87. *SR,* 5:250, 650; Thomson, *A Constitutional History,* 4:155.

88. Ogg, *History of England in the Reign of Charles II,* 2:444.

89. Schwoerer, *NSA,* pp. 91, 102, 104-7.

90. Ibid., p. 120.

91. Grey, 5:325, 326 (the second set of pages so numbered), 331, 332.

92. Grey, 6:42, 44, 43, 47.

93. Grey, 6:218.

94. Grey, 7:67-73.

95. Grey, 8:357.

96. See J. G. A. Pocock, ed., *The Political Works of James Harrington* (Cambridge, 1977), introd., pp. 128-52, for the most coherent statement of a thesis started in other articles and books by the author. The tracts were *A Letter from a Person of Quality to his Friend in the Country,* printed in 1675 and written by someone in Shaftesbury's circle; and Andrew Marvell's *The Growth of Popery and Arbitrary Government,* printed in two editions in 1681. Pocock labels these ideas "neo-Harringtonian," but in fact their sources included works by other men as well.

97. Schwoerer, *NSA,* pp. 56-58, 70.

98. Grey, 2:218.

99. Grey, 6:214.

100. J. R. Western, *The English Militia in the Eighteenth Century: The Story of a Political Issue, 1660-1802* (London, 1965), pp. 82-83.

101. Miller, *James II,* pp. 211-12. Also, John Miller, "The Militia and the Army in the Reign of James II," *HJ* 16 (1973): 659-79.

102. *CJ,* 9:75-76. For the Commons' attitude towards the militia, see Western, *The English Militia,* pp. 6-7, 11-16, 77-85; and Schwoerer, *NSA,* pp. 56, 70, 103, 105, 127-28, 142-43.

103. See Robin Clifton, "The Popular Fear of Catholics during the English Revolution," *Past and Present* 52 (August 1971): 23-55, for a study of the scope and origins of the fear of Catholics in the Civil War. William L. Sachse, "The Mob and the Revolution of 1688," *JBS* 4 (November 1964): 23-40, studies the activities of the mob in the Revolution of 1688-89.

104. Notably Birch, Clarges, Garroway, Lee, Littleton, Sacheverell, and Williams.

105. Western, *The English Militia,* pp. 30-40.

106. Ibid., p. 48.

107. Grey, 9:31, 32; Somers, *HSP,* 2:416, 417. Boscawen, Maynard, and Temple complained about the disarming of the nation. Sir Robert Atkyns, the jurist, also expressed indignation that the sword with which Charles II had knighted him at the Restoration had been confiscated during the Rye House Plot scare; and peers such as Delamere, Stamford, and Macclesfield complained that their houses had been searched for weapons (Western, *The English Militia,* p. 69).

108. Pocock, *Works of James Harrington,* p. 136.

109. Schwoerer, *NSA,* pp. 131-32, and Western, *The English Militia,* pp. 48-53, 77-85.

110. Cambridge University, Churchill College Archives, Erle Mss. 4/4, pp. 18-22. In preparation for the meeting of the Convention, Erle wrote down his thoughts on how to settle the kingdom. I am indebted to J. P. Ferris for calling this source to my attention.

111. Schwoerer, *NSA,* pp. 12-15.

112. *SR,* 3:457-59, 832-34.

113. C. G. Cruickshank, *Elizabeth's Army* (Oxford, 1966), p. 8.

114. Sporting rights were a prerogative of English kings from at least the time of William the Conqueror and were granted to certain subjects. See Chester Kirby and Ethyn Kirby, "The Stuart Game Prerogative," *EHR* 46 (1931): 239-54, and Chester Kirby, "The English Game Law System," *AHR* 38 (1933): 240-62.

115. *SR,* 2:65; 4, pt. 2:1055.

116. Kirby and Kirby, "The Stuart Game Prerogative," pp. 240-49.

117. *SR,* 5:745; Kenyon, *The Stuart Constitution,* p. 494.

118. Delamere, Fauconberg, and Newport: see *LJ,* 12:481.

119. The members were Howard, Lee, Maynard, and Seymour. See *CJ,* 9:219.

120. Henry Horwitz, ed., *The Parliamentary Diary of Narcissus Luttrell, 1691-1693* (Oxford, 1972), p. 444. I am grateful to Professor Horwitz for calling this debate to my attention.

121. 3 Edw. I, c. 5, *SR,* 1:28; and 7 Hen. IV, c. 15, *SR,* 2:156.

122. Porritt, *Unreformed House of Commons,* pp. 367-78.

123. Elton, *The Tudor Constitution,* pp. 283-84.

124. Ibid., p. 285; J. E. Neale, *The Elizabethan House of Commons* (London, 1949), chap. 14.

125. Porritt, *Unreformed House of Commons,* p. 382.

126. Ibid., pp. 383-84, 391.

127. Ibid., p. 393.

128. Ogg, *England in the Reign of Charles II,* 2:634-39.

129. R. H. George, "Parliamentary Elections and Electioneering in 1685," *Transactions of the Royal Historical Society,* 4th ser. 19 (1936): 167-95; Ogg, *England in the Reigns of James II and William III,* p. 143.

130. Jones, *The Revolution of 1688,* pp. 60-61, 161-62, 163.

131. Ibid., pp. 65-66.

132. Ibid., pp. 138-45.

133. See above, Chapter 3.

134. Jones, *The Revolution of 1688,* pp. 135, 138-40, 155.

135. The questions are listed in Ogg, *England in the Reigns of James II and William III,* p. 188. The secret instructions and the answers are reprinted in Sir George Duckett, ed., *Penal Laws and Test Act: Questions Touching Their Repeal Propounded in 1687-88 by James II* (London, 1882).

136. R. H. George, "The Charters Granted to English Parliamentary Corporations in 1688," *EHR* 55 (1940): 47-56.

137. Jones, *The Revolution of 1688,* pp. 129-30, 166-67, 174.

138. R. H. George, "A Note on the Bill of Rights: Municipal Liberties and Freedom of Parliamentary Elections," *AHR* 42 (1937): 670-79.

139. Anson, *The Law and Custom of the Constitution,* 1:162, 166-68.

140. See J. E. Neale, "The Commons' Privilege of Free Speech in Parliament," in *Tudor Studies,* ed. R. W. Seton-Watson (London, 1970 [reissue]), pp. 259-65. David S. Berkowitz shows in a forthcoming paper that medieval precedents for the right of freedom of speech in Parliament were "few" and "uncertain." See "Freedom of Speech and Parliamentary Sovereignty, 1254-1688" (unpublished paper), pp. 19, 24. I am grateful to Professor Berkowitz for allowing me to read and quote from his paper.

141. Berkowitz, "Freedom of Speech and Parliamentary Sovereignty, 1254-1688," pp. 27-32, 50.

142. Ibid., pp. 33-34. See also Neale, "The Commons' Privilege of Free Speech in Parliament," pp. 267-68.

143. Berkowitz, "Freedom of Speech and Parliamentary Sovereignty, 1254-1688," pp. 36-37, 50 (for Story's case), 38-51 (for Elizabeth I's reign).

144. Ibid., pp. 54-59. See also Holdsworth, *HEL,* 6:93, n. 2.

145. Foster, *Proceedings in Parliament, 1610,* esp. 2:92-93, 96, 110-13, 224-25, 371-73.

146. Wallace Notestein et al., eds., *Commons Debates, 1621,* 7 vols. (New Haven, 1935), esp. 2:502-7, 521-28, 536-42.

147. Holdsworth, *HEL,* 6:97; Kenyon, *The Stuart Constitution,* pp. 31-32.

148. Cope and Coates, *Proceedings of the Short Parliament,* p. 141; see also pp. 56, 140, 144, 149, 159, 189.

149. 13 Car. II. 1. c. par. 6, *SR,* 5:306.

150. *CJ,* 8:249. The four were Boscawen, Lee, Maynard, and Meres.

151. *CJ,* 9:3.

152. *CJ,* 9:19; Grey, 1:37-38, 47.

153. *CJ,* 9:25.

154. Berkowitz, "Freedom of Speech and Parliamentary Sovereignty, 1254-1688," pp. 112-15; also Kenyon, *The Stuart Constitution,* p. 32; Holdsworth, *HEL,* 6:269 and n. 4.

155. Holdsworth, *HEL,* 9:236-45; Elton, *The Tudor Constitution,* pp. 167, 456.

156. Holdsworth, *HEL,* 9:241-42.

157. Ogg, *England in the Reigns of James II and William III,* p. 199.

158. See below, p. 91. Other cases in which informations were used included those of Rev. Samuel Johnson, Lord Russell, and the earl of Devonshire.

159. *St. Tr.,* 13:1370-1442.

160. Holdsworth, *HEL,* 6:260-70.

161. Ibid., p. 270; *St. Tr.,* 13:1442.

162. BL, Add. Mss. 51,950, fol. 12.

163. Grey, 9:42-43.

164. Grey, 9:81 for Treby and Lee.

165. Quoted in Holdsworth, *HEL*, 9:244.

166. A. F. Havighurst, "The Judiciary and Politics in the Reign of Charles II," *LQR* 66 (1950): 231, 238.

167. They were clause 17 (Constructions upon the statutes of treason, and trials and proceedings and writs of error, in cases of treason, to be regulated); clause 18 (Judges' commissions to be made *quam diu se bene gesserint;* and their salaries to be ascertained and established, to be paid out of the public revenue only, and not to be removed nor suspended from the execution of their office, but by due course of law); clause 23 (The Chancery and other courts of justice, and the fees of office, to be regulated); and clause 25 (That upon return of *habeas corpus* and *mandamus,* the subject may have liberty to traverse such return).

168. See Caleb Foote, "The Coming Constitutional Crisis in Bail," *University of Pennsylvania Law Review* 113 (1965): 959-99; 1125-85; Hermine H. Meyer, "Constitutionality of Pretrial Detention," *Georgetown Law Journal* 60 (1972): 1139-94; and Holdsworth, *HEL*, 9:112-19, 6:34-39, 213-14.

169. 3 Edw. I, c. 15, *SR*, 1:30. The date was 1275.

170. 1 & 2 Phil. & M., c. 13.

171. E. DeHaas, *Antiquities of Bail* (London, 1940), referenced in Meyer, "Constitutionality of Pretrial Detention," pp. 1146, 1151, 1154, 1156.

172. Meyer, "Constitutionality of Pretrial Detention," p. 1185.

173. Holdsworth, *HEL*, 9:109-11.

174. Ibid., p. 114.

175. Ibid.

176. Ibid.; Meyer, "Constitutionality of Pretrial Detention," pp. 1180-84.

177. Holdsworth, *HEL*, 9:115.

178. Ibid., pp. 115-16; Kenyon, *The Stuart Constitution,* p. 425.

179. Holdsworth, *HEL*, 9:117. The House of Commons introduced such bills in 1668, 1669, 1674, 1675, and 1677, but none passed.

180. Ogg, *England in the Reign of Charles II,* 2:510.

181. Helen Nutting, "The Most Wholsome Law: The Habeas Corpus Act of 1679 in the House of Lords," *AHR* 65 (1960): 527-40; Haley, *Shaftesbury,* pp. 510, 526-28, 535.

182. They were Birch, Boscawen, Capel, Clarges, Garroway, Holt, Howard, Lee, Littleton, Maynard, Meres, Musgrave, Sacheverell, Sawyer, Seymour, Temple, and Williams; see *CJ,* 9:87-88, 129, 298, 326, 376, 391, 582.

183. Kenyon, *The Stuart Constitution,* p. 425.

184. Ogg, *England in the Reign of Charles II,* 2:512, specifies the limitations.

185. *CJ,* 9:692.

186. *CJ,* 9:661. They were Birch, Capel, Foley, Hampden, Lee, Meres, and Sacheverell.

187. The M.P. was Hobart: Somers, *HSP,* 2:422.

188. See Anthony F. Granucci, "'Nor Cruel and Unusual Punishments Inflicted': The Original Meaning," *California Law Review* 57 (1969): 844-47.

189. Quoted in *St. Tr.,* 1:xxxv.

190. Ibid., 11:1362; J. H. Baker, "Criminal Courts and Procedure at Common Law, 1550-1800," in *Crime in England, 1500-1800,* ed. J. S. Cockburn (London, 1977), p. 44.

191. *CJ,* 9:689, 692.

192. *CJ,* 9:696. They were Boscawen, Clarges, Paul Foley, Thomas Foley, Hampden, Maynard, Musgrave, and Treby.

193. Grey, 8:227-28. Grey does not indicate whether Paul or Thomas Foley spoke.

194. *St. Tr.,* 8:163-216. Sir William Scroggs was saved by prorogation of the parliament, but he was subsequently removed as chief justice.

195. *St. Tr.,* 9:187-298. A mark, valued at 160 pennies or two-thirds a pound sterling, was often used in stating the amount of a fine (*OED*).

196. *St. Tr.,* 9:1334-72.

197. *St. Tr.,* 9:1125.

198. Williams was fined £10,000; Hampden, £40,000; and Devonshire, £30,000 (*St. Tr.,* 13:1370-1442, 9:1054-1126, 11:1354-72).

199. *A Letter to a Gentleman at Brussels, giving an account of the people's revolt* (Windsor, December 2, 1688), p. 9.

200. Somers, *HSP,* 2:416.

201. Granucci, "'Nor Cruel and Unusual Punishments,'" p. 855.

202. *OED.*

203. Granucci, "'Nor Cruel and Unusual Punishments,'" pp. 839, 860-65.

204. Ibid., p. 847.

205. Ibid., pp. 848-52.

206. Ogg, *England in the Reigns of James II and William III,* pp. 152-53.

207. *A Letter to a Gentleman at Brussels,* p. 7.

208. *St. Tr.,* 10:1316-17.

209. *St. Tr.,* 10:1325. The debate reinforces the view that these were the proceedings the rights committee had in mind. See Grey, 9:287.

210. *St. Tr.,* 11:1350-54.

211. See Holdsworth, *HEL,* 6:213, n. 8, for a contemporary account of jury selection.

212. Ogg, *England in the Reign of Charles II,* 2:520.

213. Havighurst, "The Judiciary and Politics in the Reign of Charles II," p. 242.

214. See, for example, Sir John Hawles, *The Englishman's Right: a dialogue between a Barrister-at-Law and a Jury-Man, setting forth the Antiquity, the excellent designed use, the Office and the Priviledges of Juries, by the Law of England* (London, 1680), and Hawles, *The Grand Jury Man's Oath and Office Explained and the Rights of English men asserted. A Dialogue between a Barrister-at-Law, and a Grand Jury Man* (1680).

215. Ogg, *England in the Reign of Charles II,* 2:519.

216. Giles Duncombe, *Trials per Pais; or, The Law Concerning Juries by Nisi-Prius* (London, 1665), p. 72. Reprinted in 1666, 1682, 1685, 1700, and 1766.

217. *St. Tr.,* 9:591.

218. *St. Tr.,* 9:592-94.

219. See Williams's instructions to Algernon Sidney; two times he noted that "want of a freehold" is a "good cause" for excepting a juror (*St. Tr.,* 8:826).

220. BL, Add. Mss. 51,950, fol. 12v.

221. Found in PRO, SP 32/16, fols. 14-23.

222. 8 Hen. VI, c. 16 and 18; Hen. VI, c. 6.

223. Quoted in Henry Maddock, *An Account of the Life and Writings of Lord Chancellor Somers* (London, 1812), p. 334.

224. Foster, *Proceedings in Parliament, 1610,* 1:12, 2:359-60, 368, 382-83.

225. *CJ,* 1:874, 897, 920, 921-22.

226. Grey, 8:228.

227. Miller, *James II,* p. 142.

228. Ibid.; Ogg, *England in the Reign of Charles II,* 2:431.

229. Two revisionist studies of Jeffreys are H. Montgomery Hyde, *Judge Jeffreys* (London, 1940), pp. 223-28, and G. W. Keeton, *Lord Chancellor Jeffreys and the Stuart Cause* (London, 1965), chap. 11.

230. Hyde, *Judge Jeffreys,* p. 223, places the figure at fewer than 200. Macaulay, *History of England,* 1:642, vividly describes the rigorous collection.

231. Granucci, "'Nor Cruel and Unusual Punishments,'" p. 854, uses the term.

232. Keeton, *Lord Chancellor Jeffreys,* pp. 321, 325.

233. Ibid., p. 326.

234. Grey, 9:44.

235. The petition was printed as a broadside: *The Humble Petition of the Widdows and Fatherless Children in the West of England [for the punishment of Lord Chancellor Jeffreys]. Presented to this pres-*

ent Convention (London, 1689). William recounted that when he landed, more than fifty women kissed his feet and begged him to put Jeffreys in their hands because he had hanged their husbands (van Terveen, "Verbaal . . . Witsen," p. 136).

236. They were Boscawen, Harbord, Holt, Maynard, Pollexfen, Seymour, Treby, Tredenham, Williams, Wogan, and Wrey. See Appendix 3 for their constituencies.

237. Ogg, *England in the Reigns of James II and William III*, p. 153.

238. Schwoerer, "Propaganda in the Revolution of 1688-89," *AHR* 82 (1977): 862.

239. *The Bloody Assizes; or, A compleat history of the life of George Lord Jefferies, from his birth to this present time* (1689); *The Chancellor's Address and Confession to Both Houses of Parliament. Whereby His Black Crimes, Illegal Actings, Damnable Designs, and Wicked Intentions are laid bare and open, to satisfie the Nation* (1689); *The Dying Speeches, Letters Prayer, &c of those eminent Protestants who suffered in the West of England under the cruel sentence of the late Lord Chancellor* (1689).

240. Betty Kemp, *King and Commons, 1660-1832* (London, 1959), p. 16.

241. Foster, *Proceedings in Parliament, 1610*, 2:71, 382.

242. Notestein, *Commons Debates, 1621*, 3:337, 340, 352; 4:133, 434; 6:222; 7:634.

243. Cope and Coates, *Proceedings of the Short Parliament*, p. 258.

244. Ibid., pp. 113, 155, 175, 218, 224, 275-76, 278.

245. Kemp, *King and Commons*, pp. 16-17; Kemp points out that the authors of the act did not regard annual meetings as desirable.

246. Wolfe, *Leveller Manifestoes*, pp. 10, 27, 29, 46, 80, 287, 332, 403, 404, 495.

247. Grey, 1:82-84; *CJ*, 9:52. Temple's speech is at Bodl., Mss. Eng. hist. c. 201, fols. 92-95.

248. Ogg, *England in the Reign of Charles II*, 2:481-82; *CJ*, 9:683. Grey does not report a debate on the matter.

249. B. Behrens, "The Whig Theory of the Constitution in the Reign of Charles II," *Cambridge Historical Journal* 7 (1941): 60-61.

250. Somers, *A Just and Modest Vindication*, pp. 1-2, 10, 11, 17, 37, 45, 47.

251. Indeed, twelve committee members took part in earlier episodes involving at least six of the issues in the Declaration of Rights: they were Birch, Boscawen, Clarges, Garroway, Richard Hampden, Howard, Lee, Littleton, Maynard, Sacheverell, Seymour, and Williams.

Chapter 5

1. Burnet, *HOT*, 3:283-84, 300; N. Japikse, ed., *Correspondentie van Willem III en van Hans Willem Bentinck, eersten graaf van Portland*, 5 vols. (The Hague, 1927-37), 1:49. Danby's role in drafting the *Declaration of Reasons* rests on Burnet's account alone. His biographer notes that Danby's activities during August and September 1688 are unknown: see Browning, *Danby*, 1:388-89.

2. Burnet, *HOT*, 1:601; Burnet, *Supplement*, p. 197.

3. Burnet, *HOT*, 3:180. See Jones, *The Revolution of 1688 in England*, pp. 218-21, 238.

4. Burnet, *HOT*, 4:348.

5. David Hosford, *Nottingham, Nobles and the North: Aspects of the Revolution of 1688*, Studies in British History and Culture, vol. 4 (Hamden, Conn., 1976), pp. 16-19. Also see Henry Horwitz, *Revolution Politicks: The Career of Daniel Finch, Second Earl of Nottingham, 1647-1730* (London, 1968), pp. 51-53; Foxcroft, *Life and Letters of Sir George Savile*, 1:494-98.

6. Burnet, *HOT*, 3:181. Despite a suggestion to the contrary by Nicholas Tindal, there is no evidence that John Somers participated in drafting William's manifesto. See Sachse, *Lord Somers*, pp. 10, 24, and p. 27 nn. 68-70. Nicholas Tindal, who translated and continued Rapin de Thoyras's *History of England*, 2:770, asserted that the *Declaration of Reasons* had Somers's "previous approbation," but offered no evidence.

7. Burnet, *HOT*, 3:277; Burnet, *Supplement*, pp. 284, 294.

8. R. W. Blencowe, ed., *Diary of the Times of Charles the Second by The Honourable Henry Sidney (Afterwards Earl of Romney) Including His Correspondence with The Countess of Sunderland . . . To*

Which Are Added, Letters Illustrative of the Times of James II and William III, 2 vols. (London, 1843), 2:251-52 (hereafter *Diary and Correspondence of Sidney*).

9. Burnet, *HOT,* 3:277; Burnet, *Supplement,* p. 370; Blencowe, *Diary and Correspondence of Sidney,* 2:270-71. The mutual high regard between Sidney and William later cooled. For example, see BL, Add. Mss. 51,511, fols. 43v, 47.

10. See Jones, *The Revolution of 1688,* chap. 8, "William's English Connection," esp. pp. 222-34; Burnet, *Supplement,* pp. 284, 370, 494; Blencowe, *Diary and Correspondence of Sidney,* 2:251-52, 270-71.

11. NUL, Portland Mss., PwA 2124e; also see ibid., 2099-2100, 2110-2111, 2112-2113, 2118-2119, 2120-2122, 2126, 2141-2142, 2143-2144, 2159.

12. Ibid., PwA 2097c. The concern was not new. Earlier, according to Burnet, Dijkvelt had been instructed "to remove the ill impressions . . . of the prince." The Anglicans thought that William was a Presbyterian; the Dissenters, that he was "arbitrary and imperious"; others that he was a "papist" (Burnet, *HOT,* 3:174).

13. They were *Character,* a broadside printed at The Hague on October 12, 1688; *The Character of His Royal Highness William Henry Prince of Orange,* printed "with Allowance" sometime during the meeting of the Convention (p. 7); *A Dialogue between Dick and Tom; concerning the present posture of affairs in England,* licensed January 18, 1689; *The History of the most Illustrious William, Prince of Orange: Deduc'd from the First Founder of the Antient House of Nassau, Together with the most Considerable Actions of this Present London,* advertised as appearing "tomorrow" in the December 12-14, 1688, issue of the *English Currant* and noticed in the four succeeding issues; and *Popish Treatises Not to be Rely'd Upon: In a Letter from a Gentleman at York, to his Friends in the Prince of Orange's Camp. Addressed to all Members of the next Parliament,* whose title places its appearance in late December or January 1688-89. An earlier account of the prince appeared in Sir William Temple, *Observations Upon the United Provinces of the Netherlands,* which went through six editions in English between 1673 and 1693. Temple's account of William was used verbatim in the last two tracts just mentioned.

14. NUL, Portland Mss., PwA 2126f verso, 2139-2140, 2145, 2161-2162; PwV 61.

15. Burnet, *Supplement,* p. 494.

16. NUL, Portland Mss., PwA 2120-2121, 2122-2123, 2124-2125, 2126a, b, e, 2129a verso. Sidney and Johnstone were certain that Burnet's life was in danger (PwA 2133-2134, 2141-2142, 2137-2138, 2143-2144, 2175-2176). See H. C. Foxcroft and T. E. S. Clarke, *A Life of Gilbert Burnet, Bishop of Salisbury* (London, 1907), app. 2, p. 535, for tracts Burnet wrote from 1687 to early 1688. For an enthusiastic evaluation of one tract, see FSL, Letters of James Frazer to Sir Robert Southwell, V.b. 287, p. 47.

17. NUL, Portland Mss., PwA 2159, 2171, 2173-2174, 2165-2166, 2167f. The original draft, with a note in Bentinck's hand that Johnstone was the author, is at PwA 2086. It is reprinted in Japikse, *Correspondentie,* 2:603: Doubts about the birth surfaced almost immediately, as did vicious satirical verse; for the verse, see George de F. Lord, ed., *Poems on Affairs of State,* vol. 4, *1685-1688,* ed. Galbraith N. Grump (New Haven, Conn., 1968), pp. 235-72.

18. Dalrymple, app. 1, pp. 228-31. A convenient copy of the letter is in Browning, *English Historical Documents, 1660-1714,* p. 121. Wharton was said to have drafted the invitation (Carswell, *The Old Cause,* p. 68n). There is no certain evidence that he did.

19. On William as a publicist, see K. H. D. Haley, *William of Orange and the English Opposition, 1672-1674* (Oxford, 1953), pp. 52-53, 97-98, 105-7, 111, 222. As an example of a tract, see Peter du Moulin, *England's Appeal from the Private Cabal at Whitehall to the Great Council of the nation, the Lords and Commons in Parliament assembled* (1673), reprinted in 1689.

20. See G. R. Elton, *Policy and Police: The Enforcement of the Reformation in the Age of Thomas Cromwell* (Cambridge, 1972), chap. 4; Cromwell's campaign was the first time any government in Europe had employed *printed* propaganda (pp. 206-7). Also see Jennifer Loach, "Pamphlets and Politics, 1553-8," *BIHR,* 48 (1975): 31-44; and William Haller, *Tracts on Liberty in the Puritan Revolution, 1638-1647* (New York, 1934). For some later examples, see Carolyn A. Edie, "The Popular Idea of Monarchy on the Eve of the Stuart Restoration," *Huntington Library Quarterly* 29 (1976): 343-73; O. W. Furley, "The Whig Exclusionists: Pam-

phlet Literature in the Exclusion Campaign, 1679-81," *Cambridge Historical Journal* 13 (1957): 19-36; Haley, *William of Orange and the English Opposition;* H. Rusche, "Merlini Anglici: Astrology and Propaganda from 1644 to 1651," *EHR* 80 (1965): 322-23, and "Prophecies and Propaganda, 1641 to 1651," *EHR* 84 (1969): 752-70; Lois G. Schwoerer, "'The Fittest Subject for the King's Quarrel': An Essay on the Militia Bill Controversy, 1641-1642," *JBS* 11 (1971): 45-76, and *NSA,* chap. 8; and W. A. Speck, "Political Propaganda in Augustan England," *Transactions of the Royal Historical Society,* 5th ser. 22 (1972): 17-32.

21. Lawrence Stone, "Literacy and Education in England, 1640-1900," *Past and Present,* 42 (1969), pp. 109, 112, 125, 128. For comments about the diffusion of ideas from literate to illiterate or marginally literate groups, see R. S. Schofield, "The Measurement of Literacy in Pre-Industrial England," in *Literacy in Traditional Societies,* ed. Jack Goody (Cambridge, 1968), pp. 312-13 and n. 1, and Natalie Z. Davis, *Society and Culture in Early Modern France* (Stanford, Calif., 1975), pp. 72-73, 189-226, 241.

22. See Stephen Baxter, *William III* (London, 1966), pp. 160-77, and Jones, *The First Whigs,* pp. 83, 85, 90, 128-30, 136, 140, 151, 194-96, for William's role.

23. Blencowe, *Diary and Correspondence of Sidney,* 2:138-39.

24. Baxter, *William III,* pp. 223-34, gives the most coherent and persuasive analysis of these months. Also see Jones, *Revolution of 1688,* chap. 8 and pp. 250-53, 280-81, 285-86.

25. The original draft has not survived.

26. Burnet noted "great exceptions" to the draft and reported that the differences were reconciled "not without some difficulty!" (*HOT,* 3:308, 210; also Burnet, *Supplement,* p. 495). The English ambassador to The Hague, Ignatius White, Marquis d'Alberville, also reported "great disagreements" (BL, Add. Mss. 41,816, fol. 251).

27. Burnet, *HOT,* 3:56n.

28. Wildman's draft has not survived.

29. Burnet, *HOT,* 3:308-10, and Burnet, *Supplement,* pp. 331-32, 494-96, for the disputes that follow, unless otherwise noted.

30. Burnet, *Supplement,* p. 495.

31. D. H. Somerville, *The King of Hearts: Charles Talbot, Duke of Shrewsbury* (London, 1962), pp. 44-45.

32. Huygens, "Journaal," 23:67. Gwynne was exempted from the general pardon James issued on October 2, 1688.

33. Ailesbury, *Memoirs,* 1:186.

34. Morrice, 2:383.

35. Burnet, *HOT,* 3:310.

36. Japikse, *Correspondentie,* 1:49.

37. NUL, Portland Mss., PwA 1659.

38. Burnet, *HOT,* 3:303.

39. Baxter, *William III,* p. 233.

40. Burnet, HOT, 3:300; Burnet, *Supplement,* p. 522.

41. Koninklijk Huisarchief, Manifest van den Koning Willem III aan de Engelsche Natie, 1688, Oct. 10 (N.S.), Minuut van Gilbert Burnet, IX, a. 15 (old number 2638).

42. BL, Add. Mss. 41,816, fol. 249. This was one of several perceptive observations about affairs during this time by a man whose political acuity and personal integrity have been controverted. See E. S. de Beer, "The Marquis of Albeville and His Brothers," *EHR* 45 (1930): 397-408. Cf. Jones, *Revolution of 1688,* pp. 217, 257-58, 261; and J. P. Kenyon, *Robert Spencer, Earl of Sunderland, 1641-1702* (London, 1958), p. 136n.

43. *CJ,* 10:1-5.

44. That the bishops' petition was consistent with the law was a central point in their defense.

45. BL, Add. Mss. 41, 816, fols. 249-249v.

46. Burnet, *HOT,* 3:301; Burnet, *Supplement,* p. 285. The steps frustrated efforts of the English ambassador to secure a copy, but James was well informed of the contents and perhaps already had a copy shortly after September 14/24: see BL, Add. Mss. 41,816, fols.

189v-190 (Sept. 14/24), referring to an "enclosed paper" which "about Monday next will be published as a manifest." (The paper is not in the collection.) Also, ibid., fol. 181v (Sept. 7/17) mentions "the manifest . . . which is to be made public both here and in England as soon as the fleet is at sea." On September 28, James, at the first of several interviews with some bishops showed them, it was reported, "at least part of the Prince's *Declaration*" (FSL, "A Short Account of the Revolution," fol. 4v). On that same day he issued a proclamation in which he referred to William's "publishing perhaps some plausible reasons of . . . [his] coming hither." See *Ellis Corr.*, 2:223; *Clar. Corr.*, 2:190, 192.

47. That the *Declaration* was not printed in Latin underlines the broad general audience its authors intended to reach.

48. BL, Add. Mss. 34,487, fol. 35.

49. See the report of William's appeal to the States-General in a secret session of October 4, 1688, in BL, Add. Mss. 34,512, fols. 6v-15. It was reported that William met separately with members and argued his case only on the grounds of his wife's rights (F. C. Turner, *James II* [New York, 1948], p. 415 and n. 1). A paper to be used by foreign ministers in justifying Holland's support of the expedition largely reiterated the *Declaration of Reasons:* see BL, Add. Mss. 41,821, fols. 271-72.

50. A study of the role of the Huguenots in the revolution is needed. Articles scattered through the *Proceedings of the Huguenot Society of London* deal with Huguenots during the period from different points of view. Also see Roy A. Sundstrom, "Some Original Sources Relating to Huguenot Refugees in England, 1680-1727," *Albion* 6 (1976): 3-9; and Robin D. Gwynn, "James II in the Light of His Treatment of Huguenot Refugees in England, 1685-86," *EHR* 92 (1977): 820-33, demonstrating James's hostile policies.

51. Burnet, *HOT*, 3:301; Japikse, *Correspondentie*, 2:618-19; BL, Add. Mss. 41,816, fol. 261.

52. BL, Add. Mss., 41, 816, fols. 263-263v; John Carswell, *From Revolution to Revolution: England, 1688-1776* (London, 1973), p. 29; *Clar. Corr.*, 2:494; Reresby, *Memoirs,* p. 524.

53. *CSPD, 1689-90,* p. 122. Also C. H. Temperley, *A Dictionary of Printers and Printing* (London, 1839), p. 572.

54. Macaulay saw the stone in the nineteenth century (*History of England*, 2:244). It remains in place today.

55. *Ellis Corr.*, 2:296-97; CHPL, Bulstrode Mss., vol. 12, Newsletters, November 9, 1688, 2nd letter.

56. *Calendar of Treasury Books, 1689-92,* 9, pt. 1: 280. He used this service to reinforce his request for a place as the king's waiter.

57. *Ellis Corr.*, 2:308.

58. HL, Hastings Mss., HA 6074, 6075. Almost all of this material has been reprinted in HMC, *Report on the Manuscripts of the Late Reginald Rawdon Hastings,* 4 vols. (London, 1928-47), 2:197-99.

59. *English Currant*, no. 3, December 14-19, 1688. For other examples, see CSPD, *James II,* 3: nos. 2005, 2044; Morrice, p. 369; John Banks, *The History of the Life and Reign of William III* (London, 1744), p. 224.

60. *CSPD, James II,* 3: no. 2044; also in Japikse, *Correspondentie*, 3:71.

61. *Quadriennium Jacobi; or, The History of the reign of James II from his first coming to the crown to his desertion* (London, 1689), p. 223. The tract was licensed and entered according to order.

62. Burnet, *HOT,* 3:301.

63. The draft and fair copy of the *Letter to Seamen* (NUL, Portland Mss., PwA 1663, 1664) illustrate the editing necessary to achieve brevity and correct English syntax and spelling.

64. Banks, *History of the Life and Reign of William III,* p. 207.

65. Burnet, *HOT,* 3:302. Arnout van Citters reported in mid-October 1688 that, according to a rumor circulating at James's Court, letters had been received in Scotland from Ferguson saying that William would establish Presbyterianism (BL, Add. Mss. 34,512, fol. 113). James Ferguson, *Robert Ferguson the Plotter; or, The Secret of the Rye-House conspiracy and the story of a strange career* (Edinburgh, 1887), does not mention the matter.

66. Burnet, HOT, 3:301. Burnet had drafted this paper earlier for Princess Mary (Foxcroft and Clarke, *Life of Gilbert Burnet,* p. 244). It was printed in Holland in October (Burnet, *Supplement,* p. 286), and was circulating in Oxford in mid-December (Bodl., Mss. Wood D).

67. See my "John Locke and the Revolution Whigs," an unpublished paper delivered at a symposium entitled "John Locke and the Political Thought of the 1680's," sponsored by the Conference for the Study of Political Thought and the Folger Institute of Renaissance and Eighteenth Century Studies, Washington, D.C., 1980. Also, Julian H. Franklin, *John Locke and the Theory of Sovereignty: Mixed Monarchy and the Right of Resistance in the Political Thought of the English Revolution* (Cambridge, 1978), app. 2.

68. Japikse, *Correspondentie,* 2:620-21 and n. 3. The final text is reprinted in *CJ,* 10:5.

69. The *London Courant,* no. 2, December 12-15, 1688, carried an emphatic denial of William's responsibility for the tract. Anthony Wood noted the denial (Bodl., Mss. Wood, D 29). The authorship has been attributed to Hugh Speke and the Reverend Samuel Johnson, the political pamphleteer. For the former, the *DNB* contains useful data; the latter is not noticed. Speke, who "controlled" or perhaps owned a press, claimed authorship, but the claim has been discounted on the ground that it was entered as a means of currying favor.

70. Burnet, *HOT,* 3:338-39 and n.; FSL, "Newdigate Newsletters," L.c. 1938; *A Dialogue between Dick and Tom,* p. 4; de Beer, *Evelyn's Diary,* 4:609, n. 3; Bodl., Ballard Mss. 45, fol. 55; HMC, *Portland Mss.,* 6 vols. (London, 1899-1931), 3:420.

71. *Reflections upon our late and present Proceedings in England* (London, 1688/9 [before February 13, 1689]), p. 13; reprinted in Edinburgh, 1689.

72. FSL, "Newdigate Newsletters," L.c. 1938; *Ellis Corr.,* 2:313. CHPL, Bulstrode Mss., vol. 12, Newsletters, December 7, 1688, refers to pieces that are not now possible to identify. *A Modest Vindication of the Petition of the Lords Spiritual and Temporal for the Calling of a Free Parliament* was specifically dated November 21, 1688, at Exeter.

73. The titles are *An Enquiry into the Present State of Affairs; and, in particular, Whether We Owe Allegiance to the King in these Circumstances? And whether we are bound to treat with him, and call him back, or Not?* and *Reflections on a Paper intituled His Majesty's Reasons for withdrawing himself from Rochester.* For attribution to Burnet, see Foxcroft and Clarke, *Life of Gilbert Burnet,* p. 244 and app. 2, p. 539.

74. *A Review of the Reflections on the Prince of Orange's Declaration.* See Foxcroft and Clarke, *Life of Gilbert Burnet,* app. 2, p. 538.

75. See *CSPD, James II,* vols. 1-3 passim. Also Frederick S. Siebert, *Freedom of the Press in England, 1476-1776: The Rise and Decline of Government Controls* (Urbana, 1952).

76. Duckett, *Penal Laws and Test Act,* p. 196; also pp. 195, 222-23.

77. NUL, Portland Mss., PwA 2141, 2143, 2145, 2147, 2161, 2167. Among the rumors were that the Princess Mary had converted to Catholicism and that William had been assassinated, the latter described as a self-fulfilling prophecy modeled on the history of the French king, Henry IV. See also FSL, "Letter of James Frazer to Sir Robert Southwell," V.b. 287, pp. 57-60. The most important of the king's "papers" were [John Northleigh?], *Parliamentum-Pacificum; or, The Happy Union of King and People in an Healing Parliament: Heartily Wish't for, and Humbly Recommended, By a True Protestant, and no Dissenter* (licensed February 15, 1688) and the *Answer to Fagel's Letter.*

78. See NUL, Portland Mss., PwA 2143, for notice of the reward. See Steele, *Proclamations,* no. 3859, for the suppressing and preventing of seditious and unlicensed books and pamphlets. The proclamation limited the buying and selling of books and specifically prohibited peddlers from selling any book. The next day a warrant empowered the master and wardens (and their messenger) of the Company of Stationers to search for unlicensed books and bring them and offenders to the authorities: see *CSPD, James II,* vol. 3, no. 760.

79. NUL, Portland Mss., PwA 2159.

80. James received information about the declaration in mid-September (BL, Add. Mss. 41,816, fols. 181v-190; BL, Add. Mss. 36,707, fol. 42; FSL, "A Short Account of the Revolution," V.b. 150, fol. 3v; *Clar. Corr.,* 2:494).

81. *Ellis Corr.,* 2:243. The day before, the lord chancellor had sent for the justices of

Westminster and Middlesex and told them the order must be rigorously enforced (BL, Add. Mss. 38,495, fols. 140v–141).

82. HMC, *LeFleming Mss.*, p. 215.

83. Printed in the *London Gazette*, no. 2394. A second edition appeared in London in 1688. *A Dialogue between Dick and Tom*, p. 4, described it as a "padlock" on the news. Original copies of all the proclamations James issued in the fall of 1688 are conveniently bound in FSL, Sir Robert Southwell's Collection of Mss. Material on the Glorious Revolution.

84. James met with spiritual and temporal peers on September 28 and October 3, 8, 10, and 11. He met alone with the archbishop of Canterbury on September 30. Sancroft and the bishops conferred at Lambeth Palace on October 1. See de Beer, *Evelyn's Diary*, 4:600 and n. 4; *An Account of the Late Proposals of the Archbishop of Canterbury, with some other Bishops to His Majesty. In a Letter to M.B., esq.*, signed N.N. (this is the full title of the *Bishops' Proposals*).

85. The phrase was echoed in the Convention debates on the Declaration of Rights.

86. De Beer, *Evelyn's Diary*, 4:601 and n. 1.

87. "H.N." explained that the printed proposals were not a copy of the paper presented to the king, for the bishops refused to release one. But he assured readers that the tract conveyed accurate information "obtained by another method, which in prudence" he dared not disclose.

88. Samuel Johnson, *An Argument Proving that the Abrogation of King James . . . was according to the Constitution of the English Government* (London, 1692), p. 25; cf. p. 23.

89. See Lacey, *Dissent and Parliamentary Politics.*

90. Bodl., Tanner Mss. 28, fol. 213.

91. A contemporary noticed the similarities: *Quadriennium Jacobi*, p. 257. So too did Ogg, *England in the Reigns of James II and William III*, p. 210.

92. Printed in *London Gazette*, no. 2396, and mentioned in *Ellis Corr.*, 2:272–73. James so nearly fulfilled the terms of his November 2 proclamation that it was extremely difficult for anyone about the court to get his hands on a copy of the *Declaration of Reasons*. At one of the meetings with the bishops in November, selected portions of the manifesto were read aloud, but the king refused to allow anyone present actually to peruse his copy. But one day, he took Clarendon into his "closet" to let him look at William's manifesto. Finally, Clarendon persuaded Princess Anne to lend him her copy. She agreed on the condition that he would return it promptly, for Anne had induced James to lend her his only copy and she had to return it to him the next day (*Clar. Corr.*, 2:199, 200, 494, 503).

93. CHPL, Bulstrode Mss., vol. 12, Newsletters, November 5, 1688, 2nd letter; *Ellis Corr.*, 2:279. The "counter-declaration," dated November 6, 1688, went through four editions and was reprinted in the *London Gazette* on November 8. At least one contemporary felt that the statement was effective (FSL, William Westby, "A Continuation of my memoires or memoranda book, January 1687/8–January 1689," V.a. 350, p. 44v).

94. BL, Add. Mss., 34,510, 4:255–26, 228, 241; BL, Add. Mss. 36,707, fol. 45; *Ellis Corr.*, 2:272–73; de Beer, *Evelyn's Diary*, 4:603–4, and n. 1. Humphrey Lanham, a captain in one of the English regiments in Holland, described as "very bold and confident," was examined before the king at a meeting of the Privy Council and sent to Newgate. On November 17, a grand jury refused to find a bill against him (CHPL, Bulstrode Mss., vol. 12, Newsletters, November 17, 1688).

95. *Some Reflections Upon his Highness the Prince of Oranges Declaration*, pp. 1–2. *Reflections* was in print as early as November 13 (BL, Add. Mss. 34,510, 4:246).

96. *Reflections*, pp. 1, 6, 11, 12.

97. *Animadversions upon the Declaration of His Highness the Prince of Orange*, pp. 54–57 (bound in a collection of tracts; hence the pagination).

98. See also *Animadversions*, p. 61.

99. It was grounds for deposition in current political theory if a king sold out his kingdom to another: see Franklin, *John Locke and the Theory of Sovereignty*, p. 98.

100. *Some Modest Remarks upon the Declaration of His Highness the Prince of Orange; Animadversions*, pp. 60, 62; *Reflections*, pp. 1, 10.

101. The point that liberty of conscience was the cause of Holland's "trade riches and

power" also appeared in 1687 instructions to the court's agents (Duckett, *Penal Laws and Test Act*, p. 198).

102. BL, Add. Mss. 34,510, 4:265-66.

103. Ibid., p. 267.

104. On November 13, over 1,000 persons attacked the printer's house, the third time the mob had done so (*CSPD, James II*, vol. 3, no. 1915).

105. The *English Currant*, no. 2, December 12-14, 1688. See Sachse, "The Mob and the Revolution of 1688," pp. 23-40.

106. *An Answer to a Paper, Intituled, Reflection on the Prince of Orange's Declaration* (n.p., n.d.).

107. *A Review of Reflections on the Prince of Orange's Declaration* was printed for Awnsham Churchill. The tract was in Anthony Wood's hands "in the beginning of December" (Bodl., Mss. Wood D 529).

108. J. S. Clarke, *The Life of James the Second, King of England, etc., Collected out of Memoirs Writ of his own Hand, Published from the Original Stuart Manuscripts in Carlton-House*, 2 vols., (London, 1816), 2:274. *His Majesties Most Gratious Declaration to all His Loving Subjects*, issued at St. Germain on April 17, 1693, iterated the point.

109. *A Speech of a Commoner to a Fellow Commoner*, in *Somers's Tracts*, 9:305. Like criticism of the prince's methods in the press was voiced by *The State-Prodigal his Return: Containing a true State of the Nation. In a Letter to a Friend* (London, 1689), pp. 1, 2.

Chapter 6

1. Leopold van Ranke, *History of England, principally in the Seventeenth Century*, 6 vols. (London, 1875), 4:463-64.

2. *Clar. Corr.*, 2:223n; Dalrymple, 2:341; BL, Add. Mss. 34,510, 4:293. For the fate of James's Great Seal, showing that it was reincised and used by William and Mary, see Hilary Jenkinson, "What Happened to the Great Seal of James II," *Antiquaries Journal* 23 (January–April 1943): 1-13.

3. FSL, Westby, "Memoires," p. 50; also BL, Add. Mss. 45,731, fol. 71; de Beer, *Evelyn's Diary*, 4:606; and HMC, *LeFleming Mss.*, pp. 213, 225.

4. See Henry Horwitz, "Parliament and the Glorious Revolution," *BIHR* 47 (1974): 36, for dates of issuing and withdrawing the writs. James's printed declarations may be found in FSL, Sir Robert Southwell's Collection of Mss. Material on the Glorious Revolution, V.b. 150.

5. For an account of the petition, see Horwitz, *Revolution Politicks*, pp. 56-58.

6. *A Modest Vindication of the Lords Spiritual and Temporal for the Calling of a Free Parliament*. See also *The Common Interest of King and Kingdom In This Confus'd Conjuncture Truly Stated. And to consist in the speedy calling of a free Parliament*.

7. The most important was *The Declaration of the Nobility, Gentry, and Commonality at the Rendezvous at Nottingham, November 22, 1688*, discussed in Chapter 14, below. Others were *The General Association, Of the Gentlemen of Devon, to his Highness the Prince of Orange, November 19, 1688* (Exxon); and *An Engagement of the Noble-Men, Knights, and Gentlemen at Exeter, to Assist the Prince of Orange, in the Defence of the Protestant Religion, Laws, and Liberties of England, Scotland, and Ireland*.

8. *Clar. Corr.*, 2:214-15.

9. Ibid., pp. 219, 221-22.

10. Ibid., p. 223.

11. Jones, *The Revolution of 1688*, pp. 165-75.

12. So the French ambassador reported (*Clar. Corr.*, 2:212n, 223n).

13. See Robert R. Beddard, "The Guildhall Declaration of 11 December 1688 and the Counter Revolution of the Loyalists," *HJ* 11 (1968): 403-20.

14. There were about eighteen of them (ibid., pp. 404, 411).

15. Robert A. Beddard, "The Loyalist Opposition in the Interregnum: A Letter of Dr. Francis Turner, Bishop of Ely, on the Revolution of 1688," *BIHR* 40 (1967): 102, 106.

16. Beddard, "'The Violent Party,'" contains brief biographical sketches of Montague, Culpepper, Newport, and Wharton.

17. Beddard, "The Guildhall Declaration of 11 December 1688," p. 408.

18. *Clar. Corr.*, 2:224. The four lords were the earl of Pembroke, the bishop of Ely, Lord Weymouth, and Lord Culpepper. The bishop of St. Asaph came, too, in an unofficial capacity. The declaration, printed in three editions and in the *London Gazette*, no. 2409, lists the names of the twenty-nine peers who agreed to it on December 11 and the names of the seventeen lords who ordered it printed. Original copies are at BL, Stowe Mss. 370, fol. 5v, and FSL, Sir Robert Southwell's Collection of Mss. Material on the Glorious Revolution, V.b. 150.

19. Morrice, 2:347; FSL, "Newdigate Newsletters," L.c. 1946. It is not clear, as is sometimes said, that Rochester and Turner summoned them: see Beddard, "The Guildhall Declaration of 11 December 1688," p. 418.

20. Morrice, 2:385. A copy is at FSL, 202797.

21. *Clar. Corr.*, 2:224; Morrice, 2:360; and Beddard, "The Guildhall Declaration of 11 December 1688," pp. 419-20.

22. Bodl., Carte Mss. 40, fol. 502.

23. Sachse, "The Mob and the Revolution of 1688," pp. 23-40.

24. BL, Add. Mss. 29,594, fol. 131, Add. Mss. 34,487, fol. 35, and Add. Mss. 34,510, 4:241-42; FSL, Westby, "Memoires," pp. 45, 47, and "Newdigate Newsletters," L.c. 1934, 1944; *Ellis Corr.*, 2:290-93. And see Sachse, "The Mob and the Revolution of 1688," pp. 23-40. There were also some disorders in the north (Margaret Child, "Prelude to Revolution: The Structure of Politics in County Durham, 1678-88," [Ph.D. diss., University of Maryland, 1972], pp. 403-4).

25. *Ellis Corr.*, 2:291; FSL, Westby, "Memoires," pp. 43, 44, 47.

26. Bodl., Carte Mss. 139, fol. 303.

27. HMC, *Dartmouth Mss.*, 3 vols. (London, 1887-96), 2:233; FSL, "Newdigate Newsletters," L.c. 1946; Jones, *The Revolution of 1688*, p. 306.

28. Earlier, under-officers in the City's government, such as Richard Nelthorp and Richard Goodenough, had served as Whig party organizers: see Jones, *The Revolution of 1688*, p. 307, n. 35.

29. *DNB.*

30. Morrice, 2:453-55. Gary S. DeKrey, whose Ph.D. dissertation (Princeton, 1978) deals with London in the reign of William III, thinks that Robinson may be Leonard Robinson, later Sir Leonard and chamberlain of the Corporation, a leading City Dissenter (DeKrey to Schwoerer, May 12, 1978).

31. Huygens, "Journaal," pp. 80-81; FSL, "Newdigate Newsletters," L.c. 1969.

32. John Sheffield, Duke of Buckingham, *Works*, 2 vols. (The Hague, 1726), 2:74; cf. Turner's letter *BIHR* (Beddard, "The Loyalist Opposition in the Interregnum," p. 106).

33. *London Courant*, no. 2, December 12-15, 1688.

34. Morrice, 2:365, 385.

35. Morrice, 2:388, 374, 378. The City's letter is reprinted in Japikse, *Correspondentie*, 3:87-88. The letter from William dated December 16 was brought to London by Sir Robert Howard and Henry Powle.

36. Morrice, 2:378-79.

37. The poem, titled *A Congratulatory Poem to His Highness, the Prince of Orange upon His Arrival at London*, was a broadsheet dated London, 1688. Poems and odes in abundance memorialized almost every event of the revolution. Some of these verses are printed in Lord, *Poems on Affairs of State*. There is a large collection of manuscript poems and odes at the Huntington Library and the Nottingham University Library. C. V. Wedgwood, *Poetry and Politics under the Stuarts* (Cambridge, 1960), pp. 186-90, mentions the poems written in 1688-89, but neither they nor the street songs have been systematically treated. As already noted, Thomas Wharton, the author of "Lilliburlero," claimed that he had sung King James II out of three kingdoms. The attribution of the "Rock-a-Bye Baby" nursery rhyme to the events of 1688-89,

put forward by Katherine E. Thomas, *The Real Personages of Mother Goose* (New York, 1930), pp. 288-90, is regarded as "purely speculative" by Peter Opie, ed., *The Oxford Dictionary of Nursery Rhymes* (Oxford, 1951); Opie to Schwoerer, August 13, 1974. Nevertheless, the "Rock-a-Bye Baby" tune is a variation of the one to which "Lilliburlero" is sung.

38. Guildhall Library, Print Room, Pageant L 22.2.

39. FSL, "Newdigate Newsletters," L.c. 1950; *London Courant*, no. 4, December 18-22, 1688; *English Currant*, no. 3, December 14-19, 1688; Morrice, 2:404; Burnet, *HOT*, 3:358; and remarks quoted in Beddard, "The Loyalist Opposition in the Interregnum," p. 107.

40. Quoted in van Ranke, *History of England*, 4:483.

41. Burnet, *HOT*, 3:361-62, mentions William alone; Morrice, 2:378, refers to William and Mary.

42. Dalrymple, 2:337-39. For the dating and authorship of the letter, see Foxcroft, *Halifax*, 2:20, n. 3.

43. *Clar. Corr.*, 2:225-26, also 213, 217, 218, and 228; BL, Add. Mss., 29,594, fol. 139.

44. Morrice, 2:378.

45. Burnet, *HOT*, 3:361-62.

46. Morrice, 2:378.

47. Jones underscores the significance of this little-noticed order (*The Revolution of 1688*, p. 310). It may be seen in Japikse, *Correspondentie*, 3:78-79.

48. P. L. Müller, ed., *Willem von Oranien und Georg Friederich von Waldeck*, 2 vols., (The Hague, 1873-80), 2:114 ff. Waldeck was William's general in the Netherlands.

49. Burnet, *HOT*, 3:361-62.

50. Morrice, 2:383.

51. Morrice, 2:382.

52. Müller, *Willem und Waldeck*, 2:126.

53. Ibid., pp. 122, 128.

54. D. Doebner, ed., *Memoirs of Mary, Queen of England (1689-1693), Together with Her Letters* (London and Leipzig, 1886), p. 11; Morrice, 2:425; Huygens, "Journaal," pp. 68, 71, 85.

55. Foxcroft, *Halifax*, 2:59.

56. Bodl., Ballard Mss. 22, p. 56; BL, Stowe Mss. 370, fol. 47; Morrice, 2:384, 392; *Clar. Corr.*, 2:233.

57. Treby was also nominated, but a quarrel with the Bedford family prevented his appointment: Morrice, 2:383. See above, Chapter 3.

58. Bodl., Ballard Mss. 45, fol. 22; cf. BL, Add. Mss., 38,495, fols. 2-3, where the Dutch ambassador reported "great difficulties."

59. In addition to those already mentioned, this group included all the bishops (except the bishops of London, St. Asaph, and Bristol), Robert Bruce, the first earl of Ailesbury; Daniel Finch, second earl of Nottingham; and Thomas Herbert, eighth earl of Pembroke.

60. Bodl., Ballard Mss. 45, fol. 22.

61. Morrice, 2:379, 381-82, 383.

62. Ibid., p. 381; Dalrymple, 2:336-37, 252-54; *CSPD, 1687-89*, no. 2099, p. 381; Horwitz "Parliament and the Glorious Revolution," p. 37. This willingness, it was said, conformed to William's *Declaration of Reasons*.

63. Bodl., Ballard Mss. 45, fol. 22; Burnet, *HOT*, 3:362.

64. Morrice, 2:397, 401, 406, 409, also 379, 380, 383; BL, Add. Mss. 38,496, fol. 7v.

65. E. M. Thompson, ed., "Correspondence of Admiral Herbert during the Revolution," *EHR* 1 (1886): 535. The peers sat from morning until past five in the afternoon (*Clar. Corr.*, 2:234). "Very few or no bishops" were present (Morrice, 2:392.).

66. See Horwitz, *Revolution Politicks*, pp. 68-69, for Nottingham's list of restrictions.

67. HMC, *Dartmouth Mss.*, 3:141.

68. Morrice, 2:400, 401.

69. Burnet, *HOT*, 3:362; *Clar. Corr.*, 2:235. Out of 513 writs, 184 had gone out. See Horwitz, *Parliament, Policy, and Politics*, p. 7.

70. Morrice, 2:395. Paget sympathized with Presbyterians: see Lacey, *Dissent and Parliamentary Politics*, p. 353, n. 13, and pp. 469-70.

71. Dalrymple, 1:186; *Clar. Corr.*, 2:235; Bodl., Ballard Mss. 45, fol. 22; Morrice, 2:381, 395.

72. Morrice, 2:436.

73. Foxcroft, *Halifax*, 2:44-45 and n. 5.

74. Loyalists Nottingham and Ely, Maryite bishop of London, and Williamites Delamere and Wharton were on the committee (Foxcroft, *Halifax*, 2:59).

75. Horwitz, *Parliament, Policy, and Politics*, p. 8, n. 24, quoting Althorp Savile Mss., box 4, Halifax's notes of the debate of December 24.

76. Maurice Cranston, *John Locke: A Biography* (London, 1957), pp. 166, 259, 287, 289-93, 295; *DNB* entry for Pembroke.

77. *Clar. Corr.*, 2:235, 238, 256n, and 224. The Lords had gone so far on December 15 as to examine Jeffreys (arrested in the act of flight on the thirteenth) to determine whether arrangements had been made so that Parliament might meet on James's writs (Foxcroft, *Halifax*, 2:36).

78. FSL, "Newdigate Newsletters," L.c. 1953; *Clar. Corr.*, 2:236. The Dutch ambassador thought this a very wise move (ARA, Collectie van Citters, no. 25, December 26/January 5 1688/9).

79. *CJ*, 10:5; William was said to look upon these persons as what "might pass for . . . the People" (BL, Stowe Mss. 354, fols. 150-150v).

80. *The History and Proceedings of the House of Commons from the Restoration to the Present Time* (London: printed for Richard Chandler, 1742), 2:196.

81. NUL, Portland Mss., PwA 2159, 2161; FSL, "Newdigate Newsletters," L.c. 1952. For Churchill see Henry R. Plomer, *A Dictionary of the Printers and Booksellers Who Were at Work in England, Scotland, and Ireland from 1668 to 1725* (Oxford, 1922), pp. 69-70. A copy of the summons is at Cumbria Record Office, Lonsdale Papers, item 68.

82. This point, argued by J. P. Kenyon, *The Nobility in the Revolution of 1688* (Hull, 1963), and Hosford, *Nottingham, Nobles, and the North*, is less true after December 26.

83. *CJ*, 10:5.

84. Upwards of 400 people crowded into Westminster (*Parlia. Hist.*, 5:23; Morrice, 2:397; Reresby, *Memoirs*, p. 543).

85. This is the letter referred to in n. 35 above.

86. ARA, Collectie van Citters, no. 25, December 29/January 7, 1688/9.

87. Bodl., Rawlinson Mss. D 1079, fols. 2v, 3.

88. Morrice, 2:396-97.

89. *CJ*, 10:6; Morrice, 2:409; Grey, 9:1-2. It is not certain which Hampden chaired the committee of thirteen, which included seven future members of the rights committee, among them Treby and Wildman.

90. Huygens, "Journaal," p. 75.

91. See *Parlia. Hist.*, 5:23, and *CJ*, 10:6-7.

92. FSL, "A Short Account of the Revolution," V.b. 150, fol. 13. On the eve of his first flight, James had canceled the nominations for new sheriffs; thus, few had taken up their commissions.

93. *CJ*, 10:7.

94. *CJ*, 10:7-8.

Chapter 7

1. Burnet, *HOT*, 3:373.

2. Plumb, "Elections to the Convention Parliament," p. 240.

3. Ibid., pp. 245-48.

4. Ibid., p. 245, n. 46.

5. Morrice, 2:408.

6. Steele, *Proclamations*, vol. 2, nos. 3923, 2929, 2946, 3951, 3952; BL, Add. Mss. 38,496, fol. 7; Morrice, 2:412, 426, 427, 435, 443; *London Gazette*, nos. 2418, 2419, 2421.

7. Steele, *Proclamations,* vol. 2, no. 3945; Luttrell, *Brief Historical Relation,* 1:494; Morrice, 2:417–18. The order appeared in the *Universall Intelligence,* no. 10, January 5–8, 1688/9.

8. Plumb, "Elections to the Convention Parliament," p. 235, n. 1.

9. *CJ,* 10:31; at Wallingford, Berkshire, soldiers returned to the city in violation of the order and threatened the mayor if he did not certify the return of a particular candidate.

10. Burnet, *HOT,* 3:373; Grey, 9:4, 104.

11. Burnet, *HOT,* 3:373.

12. J. H. Plumb and Alan Simpson, "A Letter of William Prince of Orange to Danby on the Flight of James II," *Cambridge Historical Journal* 5 (1935): 107–8.

13. De Beer, *Evelyn's Diary,* 4:611.

14. Morrice, 2:364, 366–67, 417; FSL, "Newdigate Newsletters," L.c. 1951; *English Currant,* no. 8, January 2–4, 1688/89; Luttrell, *Brief Historical Relation,* 1:493. On January 17, William dined with Isaac Newton, among others (Morrice, 2:429).

15. Morrice, 2:364.

16. Foxcroft, *Halifax,* 2:44–45.

17. Ibid., pp. 203–4 (from "The Spencer House Journals"). Burnet had "a deep conference" with Halifax a fortnight earlier (HMC, *14th Report,* app., pt. 9, p. 456).

18. Bodl., Ballard Mss. 45, fol. 22; Morrice, 2:396; BL, Add. Mss. 36,707, fol. 52.

19. Simpson, "The Convention Parliament," p. 120, makes this point.

20. *Clar. Corr.,* 2:237. Mordaunt had reached London by December 13 (de Beer, *Evelyn's Diary,* 4:612, n. 1).

21. *Clar. Corr.,* 2:244, 246.

22. Ibid., p. 252.

23. Ibid., p. 244; FSL, "Newdigate Newsletters," L.c. 1957; Morrice, 2:429, 430; Bodl., Ballard Mss. 45, fol. 24. Other members of William's entourage reported conversations with English politicians (Huygens, "Journaal," pp. 66, 67).

24. HMC, *14th Report,* app., pt. 9, p. 454.

25. Plumb, "Elections to the Convention Parliament," pp. 248–49.

26. *The Portledge Papers: Being Extracts from the Letters of Richard Lapthorne, Gent. of Hatton Garden, London, to Richard Coffin, Esq., of Portledge, Bideford, Devon,* ed. Russell J. Kerr and Ida Coffin Duncan (London, 1928), p. 56.

27. Bodl., Mss. Tanner, 28/2, fol. 316 (new numbering).

28. Plumb, "Elections to the Convention Parliament," pp. 249–50.

29. See BL, Add. Mss. 27, 382, fol. 86v; *A Short History of the Convention; or, New Christen'd Parliament* (London, by April 29, 1689); *A Letter from an absent Lord to one of his friends in the Convention* (London, April 20, 1689); *Some Remarks Upon Our Affairs* (n.p., n.d.).

30. Leopold von Ranke, *History of England, principally in the Seventeenth Century,* 6 vols. (London, 1875), 4:490.

31. William Harbord was elected for Launceston, Thetford, and Scarborough (Plumb, "Elections to the Convention," p. 250, n. 73). Sir Richard Temple spent £12.12s.8d. on the day of the election (HL, Stowe Mss., Temple Papers, Box 48, fldr. 1688/89).

32. Copy in the Cambridge University Library, Selden Mss., 3,235, is dated by E. Bohun. I thank the librarian for supplying a photocopy.

33. *A Dialogue between Dick and Tom* (licensed January 18, 1688/89).

34. A copy is in BL, Narcissus Luttrell collection, C, 122, 1.5.

35. BL, Add. Mss. 27,382, fol. 86v, "Humanum est errare" (printed in 1689). The *DNB* identifies John Sheffield, third duke of Buckingham, as the author, but the piece is not included in his published works.

36. Buckingham, *Works,* 2:83, 84.

37. *Observations upon the late Revolution in England,* in *Somers's Tracts,* 10:338.

38. James Ralph, *The History of England during the reigns of King William, Queen Anne and King George I, with an introductory review of the reigns of the royal brothers, Charles and James; in which are to be found the Seeds of the Revolution,* 2 vols. (London, 1744–46), 42–44. See Carswell, *The Old Cause,* pp. 202–4, for biographical details about Ralph.

39. Macaulay, *History of England*, 2:334.

40. FSL, Westby, "Memoires," p. 40.

41. BL, Add. Mss. 38,496, fol. 7; also Burnet, *HOT*, 3:371.

42. *A Speech of a Fellow-Commoner of England, to his Fellow Commoner of the Convention* (January 1689), in *Somers's Tracts*, 9:304; this tract went through two editions in 1689. Also [Dr. William Sherlocke], *A Letter to a Member of the Convention* (before January 24, 1689), p. 2; also two editions in 1689.

43. *Ellis Corr.*, 2:374; Morrice, 2:399; *London Courant*, no. 4, December 18-22, 1688; *London Mercury*, no. 2, December 13-18, 1688.

44. Huygens, "Journaal," p. 58.

45. Burnet, *HOT*, 3:358.

46. Morrice, 2:379.

47. Thompson, "Correspondence of Admiral Herbert during the Revolution," p. 535.

48. Burnet, *Supplement*, pp. 495-96.

49. *Clarendon State Papers*, p. 687.

50. *Clar. Corr.*, 2:252.

51. Bodl., Tanner Mss. 28/2, fol. 320; also Ailesbury, *Memoirs*, 1:230; de Beer, *Evelyn's Diary*, 4:611-12.

52. Ailesbury, *Memoirs*, 1:196; Reresby, *Memoirs*, pp. 544-45.

53. Horwitz, *Revolution Politicks*, p. 72.

54. Reresby, *Memoirs*, p. 541; BL, Add. Mss. 38,496, fol. 7.

55. *Clar. Corr.*, 2:238.

56. Burnet, *Supplement*, p. 495.

57. Reresby, *Memoirs*, p. 547; Morrice, 2:383.

58. De Beer, *Evelyn's Diary*, 4:614; Luttrell, *Brief Historical Relation*, 1:497; Buckingham, *Works*, 2:97-98.

59. Morrice, 2:393-94.

60. *Clar. Corr.*, 2:238.

61. *London Mercury; or, The Orange Intelligence*, no. 7, December 31-January 3, 1688/89; BL, Add. Mss. 38,496, fol. 7v.

62. Morrice, 2:420.

63. De Beer, *Evelyn's Diary*, 4:614; Bodl., Ballard Mss. 45, fol. 24.

64. Morrice, 2:427; Bodl., Ballard Mss. 45, fol. 24; KUL, Bonnet, fol. 39v; FSL, "Newdigate Newsletters," L.c. 1964.

65. HMC, *Portland Mss.*, 3:421.

66. Reresby, *Memoirs*, p. 546.

67. Foxcroft, *Halifax*, 2:203.

68. *Clar. Corr.*, 2:244.

69. Ibid., p. 246; Morrice, 2:431.

70. *An Answer to the Author of the Letter to a Member of the Convention.*

71. See collection of sermons at FSL, "A Collection of Sermons in the Revolution time, and the first year of King William and Queen Mary, 1688, 1689." Also see Morrice, 2:382.

72. See Charles F. Mullett, "A Case of Allegiance: William Sherlocke and the Revolution of 1688," *Huntington Library Quarterly* 10 (1946-47): 83-103, for Sherlocke's role in the revolution.

73. This broadsheet is at Bodl., Tanner Mss. 459, fols. 13-14. See also, for example, *Honesty is the Best Policy.*

74. See, for example, *Avis donne a son altesse Royale Monseigneur le prince d'Orange. Par un de ses plus fideles serviteurs* (The Hague, January 29, 1689); *An Honest Man's Wish for the Prince of Orange* (n.p., 1688); *Remonstrance and Protestation of all good Protestants of this Kingdom, against deposing their Lawful Sovereign Kg. James the Second* (London, 1689); and *Seasonable and Honest Advice to the Nobility, Clergy, Gentry, Souldiery and other the King's Subjects, upon the Invasion of His Highness the Prince of Orange. Reflections upon our Late and Present Proceedings in England* (before February 13, 1689; rpt. Edinburgh, 1689).

75. *The Desertion Discuss'd. In a Letter to a Country Gentleman,* pp. 1, 2, 4, 6, 8. For Collier, see *DNB.*

76. *Vindiciae Juris Regii,* pp. 1, 5, 8-14, 16-17, 21, 25, 26, 29-31, 34-35, 41, 42, 47.

77. See Mark Goldie, "Edmund Bohun and *Jus Gentium* in the Revolution Debate, 1689-1693," *HJ* 20 (1977): 569-86, for a discussion of conquest theory in Tory thought after the settlement.

78. Grey, 9:22; Schwoerer, "A Jornall of the Convention," pp. 252-53. The manuscript is in BL, Add. Mss. 32,520, while Sancroft's copy may be found in Bodl., Tanner Mss. 459. Simpson, "The Convention Parliament," pp. 67-72, identifies Roger North as the author. North, the biographer, historian, and Tory lawyer, was brother to Francis North, Lord Guilford, the lord chancellor.

79. Bodl., Tanner Mss. 28/2, fols. 318-321v.

80. Burnet, *HOT,* 3:370.

81. Ailesbury, *Memoirs,* 2:213.

82. Buckingham, *Works,* 2:65.

83. De Beer, *Evelyn's Diary,* 4:612 and n. 2.

84. *Clar. Corr.,* 2:231 and 234.

85. Foxcroft and Clarke, *Gilbert Burnet,* p. 259.

86. Morrice, 2:391, 407, 427, 432, 433-34, 435, 449, 455; Luttrell, *Brief Historical Relation,* 1:494-96.

87. Morrice, 2:381, 397.

88. Burnet, *HOT,* 3:370.

89. Morrice, 2:433-34.

90. See above, p. 134.

91. NLW, Ottley papers, 469 (1). Dr. Clyve Jones called my attention to this manuscript.

92. Derek Hirst, *Votes and Voters: The Representative of the People?* (London, 1976), studies the early seventeenth century.

93. Forty years ago, Trevelyan, *The English Revolution, 1688-89,* pp. 147-48, concurred with conclusions set out in Plumb's pioneering article on the elections that the dynastic question was remarkably unimportant in the elections. Although acknowledging that the "wider religious question was occasionally of some force," Plumb concluded that local and personal issues and the conviction that "James II could not be recalled" decided the contests ("Elections to the Convention Parliament," pp. 252, 253-54).

94. Plumb, *The Growth of Political Stability,* pp. 27-29, 35. The increase in inflation (thus raising the number of 40-s. freeholders), in population, and in size of towns explains the growth of the electorate. A systematic study of votes and voters for 1660-1715 is needed.

95. Horwitz, "Parliament and the Glorious Revolution," pp. 40-41. Plumb found only one election in which the national political issue was directly mentioned ("Elections to the Convention Parliament," p. 252).

96. *Orange Gazette,* no. 6, January 17-21, 1688/89.

97. Lacey, *Dissent and Parliamentary Politics,* p. 224.

98. HMC, *Portland Mss.,* 3:422.

99. Simpson, "The Convention Parliament," p. 28.

100. Ibid., n. 2. See ARA, Collectie van Citters, no. 25, January 15/25, 1688/89; HMC, *12th Report,* pt. 7, pp. 233-34.

101. Horwitz, "Parliament and the Glorious Revolution," pp. 40-42; Morrice, 2:436.

102. Sir John Bramston, *Autobiography* (London, 1845), pp. 345-46.

103. Bodl., Carte Mss. 130/239 (old numbering).

104. ARA, Collectie van Citters, no. 25, January 11/21, 1688/89.

105. *Orange Gazette,* no. 6, January 17-21, 1688/89.

106. HL, Stowe Mss., Temple Papers.

107. *Orange Gazette,* no. 4, January 7-10, 1688/89.

108. HMC, *Portland Mss.,* 3:422.

109. Simpson, "The Convention Parliament," p. 21.

110. Plumb, "Elections to the Convention Parliament," p. 252.
111. Ibid., pp. 244, 245, 241.

Chapter 8

1. John Humfrey, *Advice Before It Be Too Late; or, A Breviate for the Convention* (London, 1689), p. 4 (unpaginated).
2. Jones, *The Revolution of 1688,* p. 317.
3. BL, Add. Mss. 36,707, fol. 52.
4. Bodl., Ballard Mss. 45, fol. 22.
5. De Beer, *Evelyn's Diary,* 4:614. See also Bodl., Mss. Tanner 496, fol. 6v; *Clar. Corr.,* 2:238, 248-50; *Clarendon State Papers,* 5:686. For other notices, see FSL, "Newdigate Newsletters," L.c. 1964; BL, Add. Mss. 36,707, fol. 56.
6. *A Dialogue between Dick and Tom* (licensed January 18, 1688/89), p. 14; Sherlocke, *A Letter to a Member of the Convention,* in *Somers's Tracts,* 10:186.
7. NLW, Ottley Papers, 469 (1); de Beer, *Evelyn's Diary,* 4:620.
8. Grey, 9:32.
9. Morrice, 2:396.
10. The full title read *A Memorial from English Protestants to their Highnesses the Prince and Princess of Orange, concerning their Grievances, and the Birth of the Pretended Prince of Wales* (November 1688). It also appeared under the title *An Account of the Reasons of the Nobility and Gentry's Invitation of His Highness the Prince of Orange into England, Being a Memorial from the English Protestants concerning their Grievances* (1688). This was licensed and entered according to order (Maurice Ashley, *John Wildman, Plotter and Postmaster* [London, 1947], p. 273). See Ashley, p. 300, for a list of all of Wildman's pamphlets, including several whose attribution to Wildman is doubtful.
11. The date, taken from *Bibliotheca Lindesiana: Catalogue of English Broadsides, 1505-1897* (Aberdeen, 1848), is confirmed by the fact that the *Letter* was reprinted in *A Sixth Collection of Papers Relating to the Great Revolutions in England and Scotland,* which was advertised in the *London Intelligence,* no. 3, January 19-22, 1688/89.
12. His son, also John, was returned to the Convention from Wootton Bassett. Plumb confuses the two John Wildmans in "Elections to the Convention Parliament," p. 251, n. 74.
13. He announced himself as "being upon the place [i.e., the Convention]."
14. Lacey, *Dissent and Parliamentary Politics,* pp. 226-27; cf. pp. 56, 65, 68, 69. Lacey's authority is Edmund Calamy, *An Abridgement of Mr. Baxter's History of His Times,* 2 vols., 2nd ed. (London, 1713). For assignment of the tract to Wildman, see *DNB* and Ashley, *John Wildman,* p. 300.
15. For the date, see Bodl., Mss. Wood D 29, p. 529.
16. For attribution, *Somers's Tracts,* 10:198; for date, BL, Add. Mss. 25,377, fol. 282.
17. The Bodleian catalogue assigns it to Ferguson. Algernon Sidney has also been credited with it.
18. For biographical details see *DNB* and James Ferguson, *Robert Ferguson, The Plotter; or, The Secret of the Rye-House Conspiracy and the Story of a Strange Career* (Edinburgh, 1887).
19. Van Terveen, "Verbaal . . . Witsen," p. 141.
20. *DNB; London Intelligence,* nos. 7 and 8, February 2-5 and 5-9, 1688/89. A collection of Hickeringill's miscellaneous tracts and essays, in prose and verse, was printed in 1707.
21. The number in my file.
22. Weston, *English Constitutional Theory and the House of Lords,* pp. 37-40, 113-114, n. 49, and app. 2.
23. The author was Edward Sexby. "William Allen," the name appearing on the 1689 edition of *Killing No Murder,* was a pseudonym for Sexby. See C. H. Firth, "Killing No Murder," *EHR* 17 (1902): 308-11.
24. *Sidney Redivivus; or, The opinion of the late honourable Collonel Sidney, as to civil government.*

Wherein is Asserted and Clearly Proved That the Power of Kings is Founded in the Consent of the People; who have a Right to call them to an Account for Male-Administration, and to Restore themselves to their Native Liberty. By which the late Proceedings of the Nation against James II are Justified (London, 1689).

25. Dr. Samuel Johnson, *The Opinion is This: that resistance may be used, in case our religion and rights should be invaded* (first printed in 1683); *A Second Five Year's Struggle against Popery and Tyranny: Being a Collection of Papers Published by Samuel Johnson During his last Imprisonment of five Years and ten Days* (London, 1689); and *Several Reasons for the Establishment of a Standing Army and the Dissolving the Militia,* a heavily sarcastic piece against James II's standing army first printed in 1685.

26. Mark Goldie, "The Revolution of 1689 and the Structure of Political Argument," forthcoming paper, table 6. I thank Dr. Goldie for allowing me to read this paper in typescript. Quentin Skinner, *The Foundations of Modern Political Thought,* 2 vols. (Cambridge, 1978), 2:339-43, underlines the radical features of Buchanan's thought.

27. G. A. Sensabaugh, *That Great Whig Milton* (Stanford, 1952), p. 133.

28. *A Compleat Collection of Papers, in Twelve Parts: Relating to the Great Revolutions in England and Scotland. From the Time of the Seven Bishops Petitioning K. James II, against the Dispensing Power, June 8, 1688, to the Coronation of King William and Queen Mary, April 11, 1689* (London: Richard Janeway, 1689), "To the Reader." Richard Baldwin brought out a rival collection. The tracts were reprinted in successive collections — *A First Collection, A Second Collection,* and so on — until they were all reprinted again in *A Compleat Collection.* There were several private collections: for example, the collection of Narcissus Luttrell (BL, C, 122, 1.5), that of Anthony Wood (Bodl., Mss. Wood D 29), and that of John Somers. Somers's collection was reprinted in *A Collection of Scarce and Valuable Tracts . . . Selected from . . . Public as well as Private Libraries, Particularly That of the Late Lord Somers,* 16 vols. (London, 1748-51), later edited by Sir Walter Scott in 13 vols. (London, 1809-15). I am indebted to David Hosford for calling my attention to Wood's collection. In the early eighteenth century, Humphrey Bartholomew (b. 1702), University College, Oxford, collected some 50,000 pamphlets, including many from 1688-89; the Bartholomew collection can be found at the Bodleian. For contemporary comments about the profusion of tracts, see Luttrell, *Brief Historical Relation,* 1:497; Grey 9:63; and Hickeringill, *A Speech Without-Doors,* p. 32.

29. My file contains about that number. Over a hundred tracts were reprinted in *A Compleat Collection.* The chronological file at the Folger Library for 1688 and 1689 contains approximately 700 and 830 entries, respectively. Goldie, "The Revolution of 1689 and the Structure of Political Argument," pp. 5, 6, and 8, calculates that 2,000 titles appeared in 1689, and shows that the only other years in the seventeenth century when so many tracts were printed were 1642, 1648, and 1660. It is, of course, impossible to date precisely most of the tracts. But dates (and price) are noted often by Luttrell and Wood, and sometimes in correspondence and newspapers. Some eighteenth-century catalogues, such as *Bibliotheca Lindesiana: Catalogue of English Broadsides, 1505-1897,* also give the date of publication. Original copies of many tracts are in BL, Bodl., FSL, HL, and in a few cases, PRO. For a guide to the tracts in the Dutch archives, many of which were translated into Dutch and reprinted in Holland, see W.P.C. Knuttel, comp., *Catalogus van de Pamfletten-Versameling Berustende in de koninklijke bibliotheek,* 11 vols. (The Hague, 1895-1916) vol. 2, pt. 2 (1668-88), and vol. 3 (1689-1713). A study of the tract literature from the fall of 1688 through the spring of 1689, such as that by Mark Goldie, would surely yield interesting information.

30. Goldie, "The Revolution of 1689 and the Structure of Political Argument," pp. 5, 6.

31. For this calculation, I have followed the model set out in ibid., p. 8, n. 26. I have estimated literacy as about 40 percent of Gregory King's figure of 1,300,000 adult males (Stone, "Literary and Education in England, 1640-1900," pp. 109, 112, 125, 128), the electorate as between 200,000 and 250,000, and those having a higher education as roughly 40,000 adults in 1689 (based on table in Lawrence Stone, "The Educational Revolution in England, 1560-1640," *Past and Present* 28 [1964]: 64).

32. For price, see note 29.

33. Bodl., Rawlinson Mss. D 1079, fol. 4v.

34. Jeremy Collier, *Vindiciae Juris Regii; or, Remarques upon a Paper, entituled An Enquiry into the Measures of Submission to the Supream Authority* (London, 1689), p. 29.

35. *London Intelligence*, nos. 7 and 8, February 2-5 and 5-9, 1688/89.

36. *A Dialogue between Dick and Tom*, p. 10. The tract was *Considerations Proposed to the Electors of the Ensuing Convention*.

37. HLRO, Braye Mss. 43, fol. 29v, February 11, 1688/89; HLRO, Mss. Minutes, February 11, 1688/89.

38. *Now is the Time: A Scheme for a Commonwealth* appeared also as *A Modest Proposal to the Present Convention*. The titles of at least twenty tracts contain a reference to the Convention.

39. Morrice, 2:449.

40. Humfrey, *Advice Before It Be Too Late;* Bodl., Rawlinson Mss. D 1079, fol 4v.

41. The date of Wildman's tract appears in *Bibliotheca Lindesiana*. The dates of the appearance of the collections are in Bodl., Mss. Wood D 29. Further examples may be adduced by examining the table of contents of the several collections.

42. *The Intrigues of the French king, and others, for extirpating the Protestant religion, by them called the Northern heresie and establishing Popery* (1689).

43. Caroline Robbins, *Two English Republican Tracts* (Cambridge, 1969), p. 20. The new title was *Machiavel's Vindication of himself*, printed again in 1691.

44. See above, Chapter 1.

45. Baldwin printed Treby's *Truth Vindicated; or, A Detection of the Aspersions* (1681) and Howard's *A true relation of the manner of the deposing of King Edward II . . . And also, An Exact account of the proceedings and articles against King Richard II* (1689).

46. The Licensing Act was first issued on June 10, 1662, and renewed periodically until 1679, when it was allowed to lapse. James II's parliament revived it in June 1685, specifying that it was to remain in force for seven years and from then to the end of the next session of Parliament. See Siebert, *Freedom of the Press in England*, pp. 238 and n. 4, 249-60, and chap. 13. Between 1660 and the fall of 1688 Charles II and James II issued ten proclamations against unlicensed printed matter.

47. *A Dialogue between Dick and Tom*, p. 4.

48. The order was printed in the *London Gazette*, January 7-10, 1688/89, and noticed by Morrice, 2:427.

49. *A Discourse concerning the Nature, Power, and Proper Effects of the Present Conventions* (London, 1689), pp. 8-9.

50. *Some Remarks upon Government, and Particularly upon the Establishment of the English Monarchy Relating to this Present Juncture. In Two Letters written by and to a Member of the Great Convention, holden at Westminster the 22nd of January, 1688/9* (London, 1688), pp. 18, 28.

51. Humfrey, *Advice Before It Be Too Late*, p. 1 (unpaginated). Italics in original.

52. *Proposals to this present Convention, for the perpetual security of the Protestant Religion, and the liberty of the subjects of England* (London, 1689), broadside.

53. *Some Short Considerations relating to the Settling of the Government; humbly offer'd to the Lords and Commons of England, now Assembled at Westminster* (London, 1689), pp. 1, 4.

54. *A Letter to a Gentleman at Brussels, containing an account of the causes of the people's revolt from the crown* (Windsor, December 22, 1688), p. 1.

55. See Skinner, *The Foundations of Modern Political Thought*.

56. See Harro Höpfel and Martyn P. Thompson, "The History of Contract as a Motif in Political Thought," *AHR* 84 (1979): 940-43.

57. Franklin, *John Locke and the Theory of Sovereignty*. The title of Lawson's tract is *Politica sacra & civilis; or, A model of civil and ecclesiastical government Wherein . . . are debated the principal controversies of the times concerning the constitution of the State and the Church of England*. First printed in 1660, although written earlier still, this piece was reprinted in 1689 in two editions.

58. Franklin, *John Locke and the Theory of Sovereignty*, pp. 100, 108, 119-20, and 122, n. 79, noted only three such tracts; while Goldie, "The Revolution of 1689 and the Structure of Political Argument," pp. 17-18 and 11, n. 5, found only six between February 6, 1689, and the end of 1694.

59. *Pro Popolo Tyrannos; or, The Sovereign Right and Power of the People over Tyrants, Clearly*

Stated and Plainly Proved. With some Reflections on the Posture of Affairs (London, 1689), pp. 8, 10.

60. Ferguson, *A Brief Justification of the Prince of Orange's Descent into England,* in *A Collection of State Tracts Publish'd . . . in 1688 and during the Reign of King William III,* 3 vols. (London, 1705-7), 1:136.

61. Ibid., pp. 136-38. The same point about consensual government appeared in *Some Short Considerations Relating to Settling of the Government Humbly Offered to the Lords and Commons now assembled* (London, 1689), p. 2.

62. Humfrey, *Advice Before It Be Too Late,* pp. 2-3 (unpaginated).

63. *A Brief Collection of some Memorandums, humbly offered to the consideration of the Great Convention and of the succeeding Parliament* (London, 1689), p. 7; *A Letter to a Friend,* in *Somers's Tracts,* 10:195-96. Cf. *A Discourse concerning the Nature,* pp. 16-17; *Four Questions Debated* (London, 1689), p. 9; and *A Word to the Wise for Settling the Government* (London, 1689).

64. Ferguson, *A Brief Justification,* in *State Tracts,* 1:139-44.

65. *A Discourse Concerning the Nature,* p. 7.

66. *Some Remarks upon Government,* p. 5; Ferguson, *A Brief Justification,* in *State Tracts,* 1:146.

67. *A Political Conference between Aulicus, a Courtier; Demas, a Countryman; and Civicus, a Citizen: Clearing the Original of Civil Government, the Powers and the Duties of Soveraigns and Subjects, In a Familiar and Plain Way, which may be understood by every Ordinary Capacity* (London, 1689), pp. 1-2, 45.

68. *A Free Conference concerning the Present Revolution of Affairs in England* (London, 1689), pp. 28-29.

69. NLW, Ottley Papers, 468 (11); Ferguson, *A Brief Justification,* in *State Tracts,* 1:141.

70. *Some Remarks upon Government,* p. 17. One other tract saw the problem in Harringtonian terms (*A Letter to a Gentleman at Brussels,* pp. 5-6), but it offered no extended analysis.

71. *Some Remarks upon Government,* p. 20. Why the author should have substituted the word "cat" for "dog" in the ancient proverb is unclear. See Morris P. Tilley, *A Dictonary of Proverbs in England in the Sixteenth and Seventeenth Centuries* (Ann Arbor, 1950), and *OED.*

72. *Some Remarks upon Government,* pp. 5, 12, 17, 18, 27.

73. *A Brief Collection of Some Memorandums,* p. 9.

74. *The Necessity of Parliaments: with seasonable directions for the more regular election of parliament-men* (London, 1689), pp. 5, 6, 7.

75. *A Brief Collection of Some Memorandums,* pp. 9-11; Humfrey, *Advice Before It Be Too Late,* pp. 4-5 (unpaginated); Ferguson, *A Brief Justification,* in *State Tracts,* 1:138; *A Discourse Concerning the Nature,* p. 9.

76. Humfrey, *Advice Before It Be Too Late,* pp. 4-5 (unpaginated); *Some Remarks upon Government,* p. 23.

77. See note 22.

78. Ferguson, *A Brief Justification,* in *State Tracts,* 1:138, 140.

79. Wildman, *A Letter to a Friend,* p. 15.

80. For what follows see Atkyns, *An Enquiry into the Power of Dispensing with Penal Statutes* (London, 1689), pp. 6, 7, 16, 18, 20, 21, 27, 28, 31, 50-53. This tract had two editions in 1689. Atkyns also dealt with the dispensing power in *The Power, Jurisdiction and Priviledge of Parliament and the Antiquity of the House of Commons Asserted* (London, 1689). Corinne Weston and Janelle Greenberg stress Atkyns's contribution in these terms in their forthcoming book, to be titled "Subjects and Sovereigns: The Grand Controversy over Legal Sovereignty in Stuart England." See also *Some Short Considerations relating to the Settling of the Government; Humbly offer'd to the Lords and Commons of England, Now Assembled at Westminster* (London, 1689), p. 3; *A Friendly Debate between Dr. Kingsman, a Dissatisfied Clergy-man, and Gratianus Trimmer* (London, 1689), p. 50.

81. *A Brief Collection of Some Memorandums,* p. 12, is the only tract to claim the right of the subject to petition the king.

82. Humfrey, *Advice Before It Be Too Late,* p. 3 (unpaginated).

83. *A Brief Collection of Some Memorandums,* pp. 11-12.

84. *A Discourse concerning the Nature,* p. 9.

85. *A Letter to a Gentleman at Brussels*, p. 6.

86. Ferguson, *A Brief Justification*, in *State Tracts*, 1:140.

87. *A Brief Collection of Some Memorandums*, pp. 9-11.

88. Ibid., p. 24. The author calculated that by 1689 £40 was the equivalent of the fifteenth-century suffrage requirement of 40s. for county electors.

89. Ibid., p. 25.

90. *The Necessity of Parliaments*, pp. 18-21.

91. *Some Observations concerning the regulating of Elections for Parliament, found among the Earl of Shaftesbury's Papers after his Death, and now recommended to the Consideration of this present Parliament*, in *Somers's Tracts*, 8:396-403. Haley, *Shaftesbury*, pp. 739-40, n. 2, doubts the earl's authorship.

92. *A Brief Collection of Some Memorandums*, p. 10.

93. Humfrey, *Advice Before It Be Too Late*, p. 3 (unpaginated).

94. *Some Remarks upon Government*, pp. 21, 22, 23, 26.

95. *A Letter to a Gentleman at Brussels*, pp. 6, 7, 9, 11, 12.

96. *A Brief Collection of Some Memorandums*, p. 14.

97. Hickeringill, *A Speech Without-Doors*, pp. 32, 34.

98. *A Brief Collection of Some Memorandums*, p. 2, and also pp. 9, 14; *A Discourse Concerning the Nature*, p. 16; Hickeringill, *A Speech Without-Doors*, pp. 9, 11, 12.

99. *A Short History of the Convention; or, New Christ'ned Parliament* (London, by April 29, 1689), a broadside, claimed that Ferguson's *Brief Justification* had changed votes.

100. Ferguson, *A Brief Justification*, in *State Tracts*, 1:137.

Chapter 9

1. Morrice, 2:454; BL, Add. Mss. 40,621, fol. 12, 14v; Burnet, *HOT*, 3:398n, 405n.

2. Grey, 9:2n; LJ, 14:101; Foxcroft, *Halifax*, 2:46 and n. 4, citing A. Boyer, *The History of King William the Third*, 3 vols. (London, 1702-3), 1, pt. 2:319, which reports a contest between Halifax and Danby.

3. *CJ*, 10:9.

4. For the customary procedures, followed at the opening of the previous parliament in 1685, see *CJ*, 9:713; *LJ*, 14:4, 8.

5. PRO, LC 5/148, p. 334.

6. *CJ*, 10:9.

7. FSL, "Newdigate Newsletters," L.c. 1959; Huygens, "Journaal," p. 69; Bodl., Ballard Mss. 45, fol. 27; *London Intelligence*, no. 3, January 19-22, 1688/89; Reresby, *Memoirs*, p. 545. Such a tract was *The Loyal Martyr Vindicated* (1691).

8. *CJ*, 10:16, 20, 21, 24, showing totals of 376, 437, 366, and 283, respectively, including two tellers on each side. Browning, *English Historical Documents, 1660-1714*, pp. 956-57, gives attendance figures for each parliament from 1660 to 1714. His figures for the Convention are inaccurate.

9. Schwoerer, "A Jornall of the Convention," pp. 250, 260. For seating in the Commons in the eighteenth century, see Peter D. G. Thomas, *The House of Commons in the Eighteenth Century* (London, 1971), pp. 127-37.

10. *CJ*, 10:20; HPT for Harbord's gout.

11. See above, Chapter 2.

12. These figures are based upon the printed accounts of the debates (noticed in note 23, below), the manuscript of Somers's account at the New York Public Library, Hardwicke Mss. XXXIII, fols. 4-28b (which shows six more entries in the debate of January 29 than does the printed version); and Morrice, 2:445, the only source to mention that Somers and Treby entered the debate of January 29.

13. Schwoerer, "A Jornall of the Convention," pp. 251, 253, 255, 256, 258, 262. St. Stephen's Chapel measures 90 by 30 feet. The ceiling was lowered in 1691-92. See Orlo

Cyprian Williams, *The Topography of the Old House of Commons* (London, 1953), pp. 2-3. This is a limited edition work, a copy of which is at HLRO.

14. Morrice, 2:461-62. FSL, "Newdigate Newsletters," L.c. 1972, reported that the "debates ran high."

15. For a larger discussion of what follows, see Schwoerer, "Press and Parliament in the Revolution of 1689," esp. pp. 545-56.

16. Ibid., n. 56.

17. Huygens, "Journaal," p. 72; Morrice, 2:436; BL, Add. Mss. 40,621, fol. 5; ARA, Collectie van Citters, no. 25, January 22/February 1, 1688/89. Citters said Seymour, confident of success the night before, was defeated "beyond his belief."

18. Schwoerer, "Press and Parliament in the Revolution of 1689," pp. 559-62.

19. *LJ,* 14:101; *CJ,* 10:9, 12.

20. Grey, 9:4-5; Morrice, 2:437.

21. Grey, 9:5; *CJ,* 10:11; Morrice, 2:441. Attendance was not taken on the twenty-second, but on the twenty-sixth, over 400 M.P.'s were present (Morrice, 2:442; *London Intelligence,* no. 5, January 24-29, 1688/89; Kerr and Duncan, *The Portledge Papers,* p. 58).

22. *Clar. Corr.,* 2:253-54; Simpson, "Notes of a Noble Lord," pp. 87-98; FSL, "A Short Account of the Revolution," V.b. 150, fol. 13v. Nottingham had gone hunting on the twenty-fourth and missed opportunities to respond to Clarges's urgent request that he persuade the Lords to debate the question immediately.

23. Morrice, 2:444. This debate is more fully reported than any other one during the Convention. See Grey, 9:6-25; Somers, *HSP,* 2:401-12; Schwoerer, "A Jornall of the Convention," pp. 242-63, and Morrice, 2:445.

24. Grey, 9:6-7; Schwoerer, "A Jornall of the Convention," p. 249; Morrice, 2:444; Horwitz, *Parliament, Policy, and Politics,* p. 9. See above, Chapter 3 for biographical details about Hampden.

25. Schwoerer, "A Jornall of the Convention," pp. 251, 256, 258, 259, 260.

26. Ibid., pp. 251, 259, 260; Morrice, 2:444.

27. He was the son of John Dolben, the late archbishop of York, and nephew of Sir William Dolben, a prominent Whig lawyer appointed counsel to the House of Lords who may have suggested that he prepare the speech (HPT; *LJ,* 14:102). Dolben was thirty years old. His youth was remarked (Morrice, 2:444).

28. Schwoerer, "A Jornall of the Convention," p. 249.

29. It is probable that Arnold did not understand the implications of Dolben's motion. He was also known as "cut-throat Arnold" for his part with Shaftesbury in reviving in 1681 the nation's flagging interest in the Popish Plot (HPT).

30. Schwoerer, "A Jornall of the Convention," pp. 252-57.

31. According to Morrice, 2:444, Finch and Musgrave "did with most art labour to divert the House."

32. Schwoerer, "A Jornall of the Convention," pp. 258, 260.

33. Ibid., pp. 254-55, 259, 260.

34. Ibid., pp. 252-53.

35. Ibid., p. 253. Neither Grey, Somers, nor the compiler of "A Jornall" reports Seymour as speaking. FSL, "Newdigate Newsletters," L.c. 1965, specifically says he did not speak. Only Richard Chandler, *The History and Proceedings of the House of Commons from the Restoration to the Present Time,* 14 vols. (London, 1742-44), p. 203, credits Seymour with a speech of "great warmth," but he gives no reference.

36. George Petyt, *Lex Parliamentaria* (London, 1689), p. 169.

37. Schwoerer, "A Jornall of the Convention," p. 253. To "throw in a bone" is an allusion to the difficulty a bone causes when it is tossed between dogs.

38. Ibid., pp. 253, 256; Grey, 9:15.

39. Grey, 9:7, hints at such a tactic, but the draft of Dolben's speech makes it explicit: see BL, Stowe Mss. 840, fols. 1-9.

40. BL, Stowe Mss. 840, fol. 2.

41. Grey, 9:9.

42. Ibid., pp. 9-10.

43. Ibid., pp. 19-20; Schwoerer, "A Jornall of the Convention," pp. 250-51.

44. Hill, *Milton and the English Revolution,* p. 214. Oliver, *Sir Robert Howard,* p. 115, qualifies the idea of "friendship" between the two men.

45. Oliver, *Sir Robert Howard,* p. 272.

46. Schwoerer, "A Jornall of the Convention," pp. 250, 251, 255, 258; NLW, Ottley Papers, 1469. Capel, Howe, Pulteney, and Temple reportedly argued for a "devolution" of the government. There may have been others whose speeches were unrecorded; the vehemence of Sawyer's rejoinder about the "people" suggests as much.

47. As noted in Chapter 1, four other speakers (Dolben, Pulteney, Sawyer, and Treby) mentioned Richard II in the January 28 debate: see Grey, 9:8, 14, 19, 23; Somers, *HSP,* 2:401, 404, 409; Schwoerer, "A Jornall of the Convention," pp. 250, 255, 260. Shakespeare's *Richard II* and tracts had spread knowledge of Richard's deposition. James II was sensitive to the comparison. In November 1688, Clarendon recorded that the king, remarking that he would not see himself deposed, said "that he had read the story of King Richard II" (*Clar. Corr.,* 2:211). It may be recalled that at Nottingham in August 1387 Richard II launched a policy of revenge against his enemies, summoning the sheriffs of the English counties and Londoners to get a commitment of military and political support in part to pack Parliament and putting questions to judges to show that the king was above the law.

48. Grey, 9:20-21; Schwoerer, "A Jornall of the Convention," p. 251.

49. HPT.

50. Grey, 9:21; Somers, *HSP,* 2:403-4; Schwoerer, "A Jornall of the Convention," pp. 252-54.

51. Schwoerer, "A Jornall of the Convention," p. 260.

52. Ibid.

53. Somers, *HSP,* 2:411.

54. Bodl., Rawlinson Mss. D 1232, fols. 7-8.

55. Schwoerer, "A Jornall of the Convention," pp. 252-53, where it is shown that Sawyer was not, as sometimes suggested, championing the rights of the people. For North's paper, see above, Chapter 7.

56. Grey, 9:22.

57. Schwoerer, "A Jornall of the Convention," p. 252.

58. Grey, 9:216. On April 19, Boscawen said, "I am suspecting my own understanding in law, when Sawyer asserts a thing."

59. Schwoerer, "A Jornall of the Convention," pp. 254-55.

60. Ibid., pp. 259, 260; Grey, 9:13.

61. Schwoerer, "A Jornall of the Convention," p. 258; Grey, 9:17-19; Somers, *HSP,* 2:410-11.

62. Temple also suggested this interpretation of the king's condition, but for the purpose of justifying the power of the Convention to settle the succession (Grey, 9:10).

63. Grey, 9:24.

64. Schwoerer, "A Jornall of the Convention," p. 259.

65. Nenner, *By Colour of Law,* pp. 181-83.

66. Schwoerer, "A Jornall of the Convention," p. 258.

67. Somers, *HSP,* 2:407; Grey, 9:11-12; Schwoerer, "A Jornall of the Convention," pp. 258-59.

68. Schwoerer, "A Jornall of the Convention," p. 256; Grey, 9:15.

69. Schwoerer, "A Jornall of the Convention," p. 259.

70. Somers, *HSP,* 2:409.

71. Grey, 9:13.

72. Somers, *HSP,* 2:409.

73. Ibid.; Schwoerer, "A Jornall of the Convention," pp. 259-60.

74. Somers, *HSP,* 2:410.

75. The sources are Grey, 9:16–17, and Schwoerer, "A Jornall of the Convention," pp. 256–57. Somers did not include his own speech in his notes on the debate. He did, however, make private notes about alternative solutions to the crisis, which confirm his disinterest at this time in the theory of original contract. The notes are in New York Public Library, Hardwicke Mss. XXXIII, fols. 172–79. Alan Simpson reproduced some of them ("The Convention Parliament," app. B).

76. Kenyon, *Revolution Principles: The Politics of Party*, p. 7 is mistaken in identifying Somers as speaking on January 28 for original contract.

77. Sigismond (1566–1632) was king of Poland from 1587 to 1632 and of Sweden from 1592 to 1599. Aiming, it was believed, to strengthen the monarchy and reinstate Catholicism in Sweden, Sigismond clashed with his uncle Charles. Defeated in battle, Sigismond fled ,and was deposed by the Swedish Parliament, which, in 1604, proclaimed Charles king of Sweden. Several accounts of these events were available to members of the Convention: A. Nixon, *The Warres of Swethland. With the Ground and Originall of the said Warres . . . betwixt Sigismund, King of Poland, and Duke Charles his Unkle, lately Crowned King of Swethland* (1609); J. Fowler, *History of the troubles of Suethland and Poland which occasioned the Expulsion of Sigismundus the Third, King of those Kingdomes, and his Heires forever from the Suethish Crown,* 2 editions (1656); *The Causes and Manner of Deposing a Popish King in Swedelend, Truely Described* (1688). Also, S. von Pufendorf's history of Sweden was printed in Stockholm in 1688 and translated into English in 1702. A modern account is C. Hallendorff and A. Schuck, *History of Sweden* (New York, 1970), pp. 188–208.

78. Schwoerer, "A Jornall of the Convention," pp. 251, 259; Grey, 9:12. Howe was thirty-two years old. Morrice, 2:444, remarked upon his youth.

79. Grey, 9:23; Schwoerer, "A Jornall of the Convention," p. 255. The speech was well received, according to Morrice, 2:444.

80. Schwoerer, "A Jornall of the Convention," p. 255.

81. The compiler of "A Jornall of the Convention," p. 260 noted that Treby made "a prosopopeia in the name of King James 2nd." Treby imitated James again in the debate in the Painted Chamber with representatives of the Lords: see below, Chapter 12.

82. Schwoerer, "A Jornall of the Convention," p. 256.

83. Ibid., p. 255. This analogy was repeatedly used in tracts connected with the Militia Bill/Ordinance controversy of 1641–42. For one example, see H. Parker, *Observations upon some of his Majesties late Answers and Expresses* (July 2, 1642), p. 3.

84. Schwoerer, "A Jornall of the Convention," p. 252.

85. Bodl., Ballard Mss. 22, fol. 47. I am grateful to Professor G. H. Jones for suggesting that "clay and brass" might refer to Aesop's fable. The fable appeared fifteen times (eight in English, seven in Latin) between 1484, when John Caxton first printed it in English in a collection of Aesop's fables, and 1689.

86. Schwoerer, "A Jornall of the Convention," p. 260; FSL, "A Short Account of the Revolution," V.b. 150, fol. 13v; BL, Add. Mss. 40,621, fol. 7. The three opponents of the resolution were Seymour; Charles, Viscount Fanshawe; and Edward Hyde, Viscount Cornbury, Clarendon's son.

87. Cast by Fanshawe (Morrice, 2:444; Somers, *HSP,* 2:412).

88. For what follows, see Schwoerer, "A Jornall of the Convention," pp. 262–63.

Chapter 10

1. *CJ,* 10:15.

2. Grey, 9:26–29; Leopold von Ranke, *History of England principally in the Seventeenth Century,* 6 vols. (London, 1875), 4:500.

3. Grey, 9:29; Somers, *HSP,* 2:414. Sir Duncombe Colchester's name appears in Somers's notes of the debate, but it is more likely that Wharton's friend Lord Colchester seconded the motion.

4. Grey, 9:30.

5. Bodl., Rawlinson Mss. D 1079, fol. 4v. The attribution is doubtful. Foxcroft does not mention the broadside.

6. Schwoerer, "A Jornall of the Convention," p. 263.

7. There are two accounts of the debate: Grey, 9:26–37 and Somers, *HSP,* 2:413–25.

8. Browning, *Danby,* 1:428.

9. Somers, *HSP,* 2:424. Cf. Grey, 9:37; *CJ,* 10:15.

10. Grey, 9:35. For the points that follow, see Grey, 9:30; Somers, *HSP,* 2:415, 419, 420, 421, 422, 423, 424.

11. Christie, a little-known M.P. from Bedford Borough, had been an anti-Exclusionist and in the Parliament of 1685 a defender of the king. Probably trained in the law, Christie, sixty-seven years old in 1689, was a long-term friend of two lawyers, Roger North and William Wogan. He temporized in answering James's three questions, but through the influence of Lord Ailesbury remained on the commission of the peace. In the Convention, Christie served on Treby's committee, but not Somers's. Although active in subsequent months in the Convention Parliament, he displayed political indifference: see HPT.

12. Grey, 9:32; Somers, *HSP,* 2:414, 417.

13. See above, Chapter 3.

14. He addressed the House more than any other speaker and attempted to rebut even the venerable Maynard.

15. Somers, *HSP,* 2:414. Horwitz, "Parliament and the Glorious Revolution," p. 47, identified Falkland as a Maryite.

16. Grey, 9:35; Somers, *HSP,* 2:419.

17. BL, Add. Mss. 51,511, fol. 70. Halifax reported that William assigned someone to watch Seymour at Exeter. One of William's English agents wrote in December 1687 that Seymour would probably favor but not always agree with the prince (NUL, PwA 21106).

18. *Clar. Corr.,* 2:224, 246.

19. Reresby, *Memoirs,* p. 547.

20. Huygens, "Journaal," p. 70.

21. Reresby, *Memoirs,* p. 547.

22. Feiling, *History of Tory Party,* p. 253, n. 1.

23. Grey, 9:73; Feiling, *History of the Tory Party,* p. 252, n. 2, characterized Sawyer's role in the Convention as "somewhat obscure."

24. Somers, *HSP,* 2:421.

25. Morrice, 2:447.

26. *DNB.*

27. Somers, *HSP,* 2:422; Grey, 9:36.

28. Morrice, 2:381.

29. Feiling, *History of the Tory Party,* pp. 249, 252, 253, 265.

30. HPT.

31. Somers, *HSP,* 2:416 (Knight) and 421 (Dolben).

32. Ibid., p. 417; Grey, 9:32. Italics supplied.

33. Grey, 9:32.

34. Grey, 9:34.

35. Somers, *HSP,* 2:418.

36. Morrice, 2:445, 447.

37. Ibid., pp. 433–34.

38. Burnet, *HOT,* 3:373–74.

39. *A Free Conference concerning the present revolution of affairs in England* (London, 1689), p. 14.

40. Somers, *HSP,* 2:420; Grey, 9:35.

41. Grey, 9:10.

42. Somers, *HSP,* 2:420–21.

43. Grey, 9:33.

44. Somers, *HSP,* 2:417.

45. Ibid., p. 421.

46. Grey, 9:31.

47. Grey, 9:32.

48. Huygens, "Journaal," p. 71.

49. J. G. A. Pocock, *The Machiavellian Moment* (Princeton, 1974), p. 423.

50. Grey, 9:30.

51. Somers, *HSP,* 2:420.

52. Ibid., p. 422.

53. Ibid., p. 419.

54. Morrice, 2:447.

55. BL, Add. Mss. 40,621, fol. 7.

56. See M. Dorothy George, *English Political Caricature to 1792,* 1 (Oxford, 1959): 48–50.

57. Somers, *HSP,* 2:415; Grey, 9:33, 36.

58. Grey, 9:33.

59. Somers, *HSP,* 2:415.

60. Grey, 9:36.

61. Somers, *HSP,* 2:415-16; Grey, 9:31. Original notes for the speech are in HL, Temple Papers, fols. 228-229. Temple spoke fourth after Falkland. Von Ranke, *History of England,* 4:503, described Temple's remarks as holding a "very remarkable place in the history of the English constitution."

62. Churchill College, Erle Mss. 4/4. I am grateful to J. P. Ferris of the History of Parliament Trust for calling my attention to this manuscript. Erle voted against "abdication" and "vacancy" (see Cruickshanks, Ferris, and Hayton, "The House of Commons Vote on the Transfer of the Crown," p. 43), but advocated extensive changes in the powers of the king.

63. Grey, 9:31; Somers, *HSP,* 2:416.

64. Grey, 9:33; Somers, *HSP,* 2:418. The "old law" Sacheverell referred to was an alleged statute of Richard II which was said to have prohibited dissolution of Parliament before redress of grievances. Whigs regularly appealed to such a statute to buttress their point, some of them candidly admitting that they could not verify its existence. See Behrens, "The Whig Theory of the Constitution," pp. 60–61 and n. 53.

65. Grey, 9:31, 32, 33; Somers, *HSP,* 2:418.

66. Somers, *HSP,* 2:418.

67. Ibid., p. 415.

68. Ibid., p. 416; Grey, 9:31.

69. Grey, 9:35; Somers, *HSP,* 2:420 The reference is to Sunderland.

70. See above, Chapter 4.

71. Grey, 9:31; Somers, *HSP,* 2:416.

72. Grey, 9:32; Somers, *HSP,* 2:417.

73. Grey, 9:30; Somers, *HSP,* 2:415 ("whether the power over it [the militia] in the crown or people?").

74. Grey, 9:30; Somers, *HSP,* 2:415.

75. Grey, 9:30; Somers, *HSP,* 2:415.

76. Grey, 9:31; Somers, *HSP,* 2:416.

77. Somers, *HSP,* 2:422 (Capel) and 423 (Tipping).

78. Ibid., pp. 422 (Hobart) and 423 (Temple).

79. Ibid., pp. 415, 418 (Williams and Sacheverell).

80. Grey, 9:32; Somers, *HSP,* 2:416.

81. Somers, *HSP,* 2:420; Grey, 9:36.

82. Grey, 9:32; Somers, *HSP,* 2:416.

83. The remark, omitted in the printed notes, appears in Somers's manuscript notes at New York Public Library, Hardwicke Mss. XXXIII, fol. 9v.

84. Grey, 9:81. And see above, Chapter 4.

85. A study of the entire membership would answer the question of how many M.P.'s were personally aggrieved.

86. Morrice, 2:447. Morrice's account alone mentions speeches by Somers and Treby.

87. Grey, 9:32, 33; Somers, *HSP,* 2:417, 418.

88. Grey, 9:34.

89. Grey, 9:32; Somers, *HSP,* 2:417.

90. Somers, *HSP,* 2:417.

91. Grey, 9:32.

92. Grey, 9:36; Morrice, 2:447.

93. Grey, 9:33-34. Jephson, William's private secretary, concurred (Somers, *HSP,* 2:423).

94. Somers, *HSP,* 2:418.

95. Grey, 9:33; Somers, *HSP,* 2:418.

96. Grey, 9:34.

97. Somers, *HSP,* 2:418; Grey, 9:36.

98. Somers, *HSP,* 2:419.

99. Grey, 9:36; Somers, *HSP,* 2:421.

100. Morrice, 2:447.

101. Clayton Roberts, "The Constitutional Significance of the Financial Settlement of 1690," *HJ* 20 (1977): 59-76.

102. Somers, *HSP,* 2:419; Grey, 9:34.

103. Grey, 9:34; Morrice, 2:447.

104. Somers, *HSP,* 2:419; Grey, 9:34.

105. Morrice, 2:447.

106. Somers, *HSP,* 2:420, 422; Grey, 9:34, 35.

107. Somers, *HSP,* 2:415, 416, 420, 422; Grey, 9:30, 31.

108. Grey, 9:35, also 31; Somers, *HSP,* 2:415.

109. Grey, 9:32.

110. Somers, *HSP,* 2:422; FSL, "Newdigate Newsletters," L.c. 1965; Morrice, 2:445, 448; HMC, *Portland Mss.,* 3:425. Pollexfen's paper has not been found.

111. Reresby, *Memoirs,* p. 564.

112. Morrice, 2:447, 448.

113. Bodl., Rawlinson D 1079, fol. 3v; HMC, *Portland Mss.,* 3:425.

Chapter 11

1. Grey, 9:37.

2. Somers, *HSP,* 2:425; *CJ,* 10:15. FSL, "Newdigate Newsletters," L.c. 1965 noted that the committee was to "make report tomorrow."

3. *CJ,* 10:15; Somers, *HSP,* 2:425; FSL, "Newdigate Newsletters," L.c. 1965. It was common practice for the Speaker to specify a quorum for committee meetings, as *CJ* shows.

4. For attendance in the House, see above, Chapter 9.

5. George Petyt, *Lex Parliamentaria* (London, 1689), p. 211. Since 1621, it had been customary for the committee and not the House to appoint committee chairmen: see *Orders, Essential, Fundamental and Standing Orders, Reports, Declarations, Memorandums, Rules, Agreements and Resolutions of the House of Commons relating to their Forms of Proceeding, Privileges, etc., Collected out of the Journals* (London, 1756), p. 74.

6. For these four men, see *CJ,* 10:24, 27.

7. See above, Chapter 4.

8. Grey, 9:42, 43, 44, 71, 75, 80.

9. Ibid., pp. 43, 74 (Birch); 44, 71 (Boscawen); 44, 74 (Foley); 79 (Howard); 51, 75 (Lee); 52, 74, 79 (Temple); 51, 71, 79 (Wildman).

10. Morrice, 2:445.

11. In summary, they were Birch, Boscawen, Falkland, Paul Foley, Richard Hampden, Howard, Lee, Pollexfen, Somers, Temple, Tipping, Treby, Wharton, Wildman, and Williams.

12. What follows is taken from the only account of the committee debates to have survived, BL, Add. Mss. 51,950, fols. 12-13. Stanley West, the correspondent, avowedly got his information from an unidentified "parliament man" (fols. 10v, 14).

13. See above, Chapter 4.

14. See Appendix 2.

15. Morrice, 2:453.

16. *Clar. Corr.*, 2:257; *LJ*, 14:113.

17. A modern study of the House of Lords in the Convention and during the reign of William is needed. A. S. Turberville's *The House of Lords in the Reign of William III*, Oxford Historical and Literary Studies, vol. 3 (Oxford), was printed in 1913. Horwitz, *Parliament, Policy and Politics*, which contains an appendix on the lords' votes in the period 1689-1702, gives some attention to the upper House.

18. Horwitz, "Parliament and the Glorious Revolution," p. 44, n. 5. A new list identifies 46 to 63 Williamites: see Eveline Cruickshanks, David Hayton, and Clyve Jones, "Divisions in the House of Lords on the Transfer of the Crown and Other Issues, 1689-94: Ten New Lists," *BIHR* 53 (May 1980): 65.

19. Horwitz, *Revolution Politicks*, p. 77.

20. Burnet, *HOT*, 3:378; Huygens, "Journaal," p. 80.

21. The names of the forty-nine peers who voted for regency on January 29 are in *Clar. Corr.*, 2:256n. Horwitz has identified three more peers who wanted a regency: the earl of Burlington, Viscount Hatton, and the bishop of St. Asaph. All the bishops but London voted for regency. See Horwitz, "Parliament and the Glorious Revolution," p. 44, n. 3, and p. 45, nn. 2, 3.

22. Cruickshanks, Hayton, and Jones, "Divisions in the House of Lords on the Transfer of the Crown and Other Issues," pp. 60, 65. Horwitz set the number of Danby's group at six to eight (Horwitz, "Parliament and the Glorious Revolution," p. 44, n. 3, and p. 45, nn. 2 and 3).

23. Turberville, *The House of Lords in the Reign of William III*, p. 2.

24. Browning, *English Historical Documents, 1660-1714*, p. 956.

25. Horwitz, *Parliament, Policy, and Politics*, p. 95.

26. Foxcroft, *Halifax*, 2:48. Letters of excuse, in response, are printed in HMC, *Lords Mss.*, pp. 13-14. A list of absent lords with the reason indicated by each name is in HLRO, Mss. Minutes, January 25, 1688/89.

27. BL, Add. Mss. 29,594, fol. 141.

28. *Clar. Corr.*, 2:261; cf. Alan Simpson, "Notes of a Noble Lord," p. 95; also Hosford, *Nottingham, Nobles, and the North*, pp. 66-67.

29. Burnet, *HOT*, 3:288n.

30. Reresby, *Memoirs*, p. 546; HMC, *Portland Mss.*, 3:423.

31. Turberville, *The House of Lords in the Reign of William III*, p. 143.

32. Huygens, "Journaal," p. 80.

33. Van Terveen, "Verbaal . . . Witsen," p. 139; Leopold von Ranke, *History of England, principally in the Seventeenth Century*, 6 vols. (London, 1875), 4:509.

34. ARA, Collectie van Citters, no. 25 January 29/February 8, 1688/89.

35. Burnet, *HOT*, 3:397.

36. *A Letter from an Absent Lord to one of his Friends in the Convention* (April 20, 1689); *A Short History of the Convention; or, New Christened Parliament* (in circulation by April 29, 1689).

37. Burnet, *HOT*, 3:395-96; *Clar. Corr.*, 2:246-47; Foxcroft, *Halifax*, 2:203; Huygens, "Journaal," p. 81. Halifax and Danby were among the lords present.

38. Van Teerven, "Verbaal . . . Witsen," p. 139.

39. Schwoerer, "Press and Parliament in the Revolution of 1689," p. 549.

40. De Beer, *Evelyn's Diary*, 4:619.

41. Schwoerer, "Press and Parliament in the Revolution of 1689," p. 555, n. 56, pp. 564-65.

42. For examples of fierce exchanges, see Morrice, 2:446, 450; Bodl., Ballard Mss. 45, fol. 25; de Beer, *Evelyn's Diary*, 4:626.

43. Morrice, 2:447.

44. *LJ*, 14:110. For the debate, see Danby's notes in BL, Egerton Mss. 3345, bundle 3, reprinted in Horwitz, "Parliament and the Glorious Revolution," pp. 50-52; HMC, *Lords Mss.*, pp. 14-15.

45. For Nottingham's speech, see also Horwitz, *Revolution Politicks*, pp. 75-76.

46. *LJ*, 14:110; HMC, *Lords Mss.*, pp. 14-15. The sources vary as to the exact vote. For bishops, see Morrice, 2:447; Bodl., Rawlinson Mss. D 1079, fol. 4.

47. Burnet, *HOT*, 3:384-85.

48. HMC, *Lords Mss.*, p. 15.

49. *LJ*, 14:102; Simpson, "Notes of a Noble Lord," p. 91; *Clar. Corr.*, 2:252.

50. Notes on their remarks are in HMC, *Lords Mss.*, pp. 15-16.

51. Bodl., Ballard Mss. 45, fol. 25; Morrice, 2:445.

52. BL, Add. Mss. 40,621, fol. 10.

53. HMC, *Lords Mss.*, p. 16. Unofficial sources reported the vote differently, as 54 to 44 (CHPL, Bulstrode Mss., vol. 12, February 1, 1688/89) and as 56 to 48 (Morrice, 2:445).

54. ARA, Collectie van Citters, no. 25, February 1/11, 1688/89.

55. Morrice, 2:445; BL, Add. Mss. 40,621, fol. 10.

56. HMC, *Lords Mss.*, pp. 16, 18.

57. *LJ*, 14:112; FSL, "Newdigate Newsletters," L.c. 1967. New lists show that Danby and his followers voted for the motion. See Cruickshanks, Hayton, and Jones, "Divisions in the House of Lords on the Transfer of the Crown and Other Issues," p. 60.

58. HMC, *Lords Mss.*, pp. 16-17.

59. Morrice, 2:452. De Beer, *Evelyn's Diary*, 4:620, and NLW, Ottley Papers, 1469, also report threats against the bishops.

60. *Clar. Corr.*, 2:257; HMC, *Lords Mss.*, p. 17. Cruickshanks, Hayton, and Jones, "Divisions in the House of Lords on the Transfer of the Crown and Other Issues," p. 60, show that Danby's group probably voted against vacancy. ARA, Collectie van Citters, no. 25, February 1/11, 1688/89, stressed members' anxiety over Scotland's possible negative reaction.

61. Morrice, 2:449; *CJ*, 10:18.

62. Grey, 9:42-43.

63. See Chapter 4.

64. Bigland (c. 1620-1704), M.P. for Nottingham, had supported Sacheverell in the charter controversy (HPT).

65. Morrice, 2:453; *London Intelligence*, no. 6, January 29/February 2, 1688/89.

66. John Lovelace, third Baron Lovelace of Hurley, offered the petition in the House of Lords, while Anthony Rower, M.P. for Penryn Borough, Cornwall, attempted to have it read in the House of Commons. Luke Robinson was identified as a proponent of the petition from London. See Morrice, 2:453-54; Grey, 9:45; *Clar. Corr.*, 2:258; FSL, "Newdigate Newsletters," L.c. 1967; KUL, Bonnet's dispatches, January–June 1689, fols. 41v-42. The prince and his closest friends were suspected of complicity, but, as Reresby said (*Memoirs*, p. 310), there was no proof that this was the case.

67. Grey, 9:45; *Clar. Corr.*, 2:258; FSL, "Newdigate Newsletters," L.c. 1967. This petition, as Professor Jones notes, only superficially resembles those organized in the previous decade by Shaftesbury, for the latter were aimed at persuading the king, the former at moving Parliament (*The Revolution of 1688*, pp. 315-16). A manuscript copy of the petition, without signatures (the only one, apparently, to have survived), is at the Hertfordshire County Record Office, D/EP F26. The petition was printed in its entirety in the *London Intelligence*, no. 7, February 2-5, 1688/89.

68. Morrice, 2:454, 446, 453; BL, Add. Mss. 40,621, fol. 12.

69. BL, Add. Mss. 40,621, fol. 14v.

70. Huygens, "Journaal," p. 80.

71. The petition was unsubscribed to avoid the "noise" and "great concourse" of people that would have accompanied an effort to collect signatures (Morrice, 2:454). The Tumultuous Petitioning Act, Car. II, sess. 1, c. 5 (1661) required the consent of the authorities (the lord mayor and common council in the case of London) to procure the

signatures of twenty or more persons on a petition. No more than ten persons at a time were permitted to present a petition to the king or Parliament, upon pain of fine and imprisonment (*SR,* 5:308). For a brief statement of how petitions were handled by Parliament, see Maurice Bond, *A Guide to the Records of Parliament* (London, 1971), pp. 172-73, 210, 240-41.

72. Reresby, *Memoirs,* pp. 548-49; Huygens, "Journaal," p. 80; Bodl., Rawlinson Mss. D 1079, fol. 7; but see Morrice, 2:453-54, who puts the number of persons variously at about twenty and at between twenty and forty. In all events, the petitioners were in violation of the law.

73. Grey, 9:45; *Clar. Corr.,* 2:258.

74. Huygens, "Journaal," p. 80; FSL, "Newdigate Newsletters," L.c. 1969.

75. Morrice, 2:454; Luttrell, *Brief Historical Relation,* 1:499-500; KUL, Bonnet's dispatches, February 5/15, 1688/89, fol. 42; ARA, Collectie van Citters, no. 25, February 5/15, 1688/89.

76. NUL, Portland Mss., PwA 2305, fol. 47b.

77. Grey, 9:46-49. Although the account in Grey is short, a "long debate" was reported: see Bodl., Rawlinson Mss. D 1079, fol. 6v.

78. Grey, 9:47.

79. Grey, 9:49. Littleton and Tipping were the speakers.

80. *CJ,* 10:18.

81. Clarges, Dolben, Falkland, and Williams.

Chapter 12

1. *LJ,* 14:115; HMC, *Lords Mss.,* p. 17.

2. HMC, *Lords Mss.,* p. 17, gives the vote against "abdication" as 51 to 55, the one against "vacancy" as 53 to 54. Morrice's figures are 54 to 49 and 55 to 54, respectively (2:456). Thirty-nine peers, five of whom — Delamere, Devonshire, Lumley, Mordaunt, and Shrewsbury — would serve later on the Lords' rights committee, entered their dissents. Danby and Fauconberg are not recorded as voting: see Cruickshanks, Hayton, and Jones, "Divisions in the House of Lords on the Transfer of the Crown and Other Issues," p. 61. See Appendix 4 above.

3. Reresby, *Memoirs,* p. 551; *LJ,* 14:117. Three of Mary's supporters — Danby, Compton, and Fauconberg — were on the committee.

4. Clarges, Etterick, Finch, Sawyer, and Tredenham.

5. Grey, 9:54-56, 57-58, 60-61.

6. Grey, 9:59-60. The Elizabethan statute of 1571 protected Parliament from a charge of treason by declaring it treason for anyone to deny Parliament's power to settle the succession. Maynard also referred to this law (p. 58).

7. Grey, 9:64.

8. Grey, 9:63.

9. Grey, 9:62-64. Neither Treby nor Somers, if the record in Grey is complete, took part in these exchanges.

10. Bodl., Rawlinson Mss. D 1079, fols. 11v-12; Morrice, 2:459; Grey, 9:90. This is the list which historians use to help identify party loyalties in 1688-89. See Appendix 3.

11. *CJ,* 10:20; *LJ,* 14:118-19; Bodl., Rawlinson Mss. D 1079, fol. 12v.

12. Morrice, 2:459.

13. Laurence Echard, *The History of England, From the First Entrance of Julius Ceasar and the Romans, to the Conclusion of the Reign of King James the Second, And the Establishment of King William and Queen Mary upon the Throne, in the Year 1688* (London, 1720), p. 1143. Mr. Blaney, otherwise unidentified, also made a shorthand report of the trial of the seven bishops. For that and a fair copy thereof, he was paid £43. See de Beer, *Evelyn's Diary,* 4:615, n. 2, with reference to John Gutch, *Collectanea Curiosa; or, Miscellaneous Tracts, relating to the History and Antiquities of England and Ireland,* 2 vols. (Oxford, 1781), 2:378. It is reasonable to assume that Mr. Blaney

made a fair copy of his shorthand notes of the February 6 debate. If that is so, it would account for the large number of manuscript accounts of this debate surviving in the Bodleian Library and the British Library Manuscript Room. The first printed account appeared in 1695 under the title *The Debate At Large, Between The Lords and Commons, at the Free Conference Held in the Painted Chamber, in the Session of the Convention, Anno 1688. Relating to the Word, Abdicated, and the Vacancy of the Throne in the Commons Vote* (2nd ed., 1710; 3rd ed., 1714, with different title). A facsimile printing appeared in 1972. References are to the 1710 edition.

14. Macaulay, *History of England,* 3:1296.

15. Turberville, *The House of Lords in the Reign of William III,* p. 145, described the arguments as "very puerile."

16. *Debate at Large,* p. 19.

17. *CJ,* 10:20.

18. *LJ,* 14:118. The earl of Oxford was the only appointee not in Clarendon's list of regency lords: see *Clar. Corr.,* 2:256.

19. Bodl., Ballard Mss. 45, fol. 27v; *Debate at Large,* pp. 23-24, 49.

20. Bodl., Ballard Mss. 45, fol. 27v; *Debate at Large,* pp. 14, 18, 20, 40, 41, 58. The peers were Clarendon, Nottingham, Rochester, and Turner.

21. Bodl., Ballard Mss. 45, fol. 27v.

22. *Debate at Large,* pp. 20, 37.

23. Ibid., p. 18.

24. Ibid., pp. 17, 51.

25. Ibid., pp. 21, 22, 47.

26. Ibid., pp. 15, 20.

27. Ibid., pp. 19, 33, 34, 36, 37, 45, 54.

28. Ibid., p. 33.

29. Ibid., p. 58. Also see speeches by Pollexfen (p. 32), Sacheverell (p. 30), and Paul Foley (p. 57).

30. Ibid., p. 13.

31. Ibid., p. 32; cf. Sacheverell (p. 30).

32. Ibid., p. 58.

33. Ibid., p. 44.

34. Ibid., pp. 12, 43, 52.

35. Ibid., p. 56; also p. 53.

36. *LJ,* 14:118-19. FSL, "Newdigate Newsletters," L.c. 1973, and Bodl., Rawlinson Mss. D 1079, fol. 13, give different figures for the division.

37. *Clar. Corr.,* 2:260; Simpson, "Notes of a Noble Lord," pp. 95-96. The reasons were not entered in the Lords' *Journal:* see *LJ,* 14:119.

38. Simpson, "Notes of a Noble Lord," p. 94.

39. Bodl., Ballard Mss. 45, fol. 27; Foxcroft, *Halifax,* 2:55; Ailesbury, *Memoirs,* p. 234.

40. Morrice, 2:460.

41. Burnet, *HOT,* 3:386, 397-98.

42. Simpson, "Notes of a Noble Lord," pp. 94-95; *Clar. Corr.,* 2:261-62; Morrice, 2:460; Burnet, *HOT,* 3:398n, 405n.

43. Feiling, *History of the Tory Party,* p. 254. Morrice, 2:425, reported on January 12 that William's chronic cough had worsened, but was now improved. Mary described William, on February 12, as in "very ill condition as to his health," with a violent cough and very thin (Doebner, *Memoirs of Mary,* p. 10).

44. Burnet, *HOT,* 3:395-97. C. H. Firth, *A Commentary on Macaulay's History* (London, 1938), pp. 316-17, doubts Burnet's story.

45. FSL, "Newdigate Newsletters," L.c. 1972; Bodl., Rawlinson Mss. D 1079, fol. 13.

46. Simpson, "Notes of a Noble Lord," pp. 94-96; *Clar. Corr.,* 2:261.

47. Cruickshanks, Hayton, and Jones, "Divisions in the house of Lords on the Transfer of the Crown and Other Issues," pp. 61-65 and 65, n. 60.

48. Browning, *Danby,* 1:431; Foxcroft, *Halifax,* 2:55; Morrice, 2:459-60.

49. Morrice, 2:459, 462; Bodl., Rawlinson Mss. D 1079, fol. 13.

50. Grey, 9:51.

51. Grey, 9:51-52.

52. Frankle, "The Formulation of the Declaration of Rights," pp. 268-69 and n. 25, which notes that this same sensitivity emerged in 1690.

53. Ibid., p. 276.

54. Ibid.

55. Van Teerveen, "Verbaal . . . Witsen," p. 139.

56. Laurence Echard, *The History of the Revolution and the Establishment of England in the Year 1688* (London, 1725), p. 261, quoted in Frankle, "The Formulation of the Declaration of Rights," p. 275.

57. Grey, 9:52.

58. *CJ*, 10:19.

59. On January 30. See Grey, 9:38 and cf. ibid., pp. 90 and 144.

60. The February 4 date is suggested by Birch's warning that day of adverse effects if the articles were made public. On February 5, Edward Harley noted in a letter to Robert Harley that he was enclosing a copy of the Heads (Grey, 9:51; BL, Add. Mss. 40,621, fol. 16).

61. Other newspapers, such as the *London Gazette* or the *Orange Gazette*, did not refer to the Heads of Grievances.

62. CHPL, Bulstrode Mss., vol. 12, February 1 and 8; FSL, "Newdigate Newsletters," L.c. 1967, 1970, 1974, 1975.

63. For example, Kerr and Duncan, *The Portledge Papers*, p. 59, February 9, 1688/89; ARA, Collectie van Citters, no. 25, February 8/18, 1688/89; West Sussex Record Office, Winterton Mss., no. 482, Robert Chaplin to Sir Edward Turnour, February 9, 1688/89; Bodl., Mss. Don. C. 39, fol. 107; BL, Add. Mss. 40,621, fol. 16.

64. P. Fraser, *The Intelligence of the Secretaries of State and Their Monopoly of Licensed News, 1660-1688* (Cambridge, 1956), pp. 131-32. See pp. 114-31 for a brief account of the development of coffeehouses.

65. HLRO, Mss. Minutes, February 11, 1688/89. It was appended to the end of *The Names of the Lords Spiritual and Temporal, Who Deserted [not Protested] against the Vote in the House of Peers, the Sixth Instant.*

Chapter 13

1. *CJ*, 10:20, 21. The word "nominate" had offended members when used on January 29, but it passed unnoticed in this debate.

2. Grey, 9:70. Palmes (b. 1638), M.P. for Malton, Yorkshire, and a member of the Country party in the Cavalier Parliament, was rated "doubly worthy" by Shaftesbury in 1678 (HPT).

3. Grey, 9:71.

4. Ibid.

5. *CJ*, 10:20; FSL, "Newdigate Newsletters," L.c. 1970, reported that the committee was "reactivated."

6. *CJ*, 10:21-22; Grey, 9:72.

7. Frankle, "The Formulation of the Declaration of Rights," p. 270, quoting two contemporary sources.

8. HLRO, Willcocks Coll., Hist. Coll., VI, 20, Lord Yester to Lord Tweeddale, February 7, 1688/89.

9. See Clayton Roberts, *The Growth of Responsible Government in Stuart England* (Cambridge, 1966).

10. See Appendix 2.

11. Ogg, *England in the Reign of Charles II*, 2:453, 485, 588, 654.

12. Morrice, 2:461-62.

13. Grey, 9:72-75.

14. *CJ*, 10:22; Grey, 9:73.

15. Grey, 9:74-75.

16. *Clar. Corr.*, 2:262; Bodl., Rawlinson Mss. D 1079, fol. 14; Morrice, 2:461; Huygens, "Journaal," p. 83.

17. HLRO, Willcocks Coll., Hist. Coll., VI, 20, Lord Yester to Lord Tweeddale, February 7, 1688/89, specifically refers to this draft as being in print, but no copy seems to have survived.

18. *CJ*, 10:22; Grey, 9:75-79.

19. The three members not on Treby's committee were William Gregory, Maynard, and William Wogan. Gregory (1625-96), M.P. for Hereford Borough, was a former Speaker of the House of Commons (in 1679), a baron of the Court of Exchequer, and an old Whig, rated "worthy and doubly worthy" in Shaftesbury's list. Critical of Catholic officers in James's army, Gregory had further alienated the king in 1685 by giving a judgment against the dispensing power (HPT). Gregory, however, voted with the Tories on the settlement of the crown (Cruickshanks, Ferris, and Hayton, "The House of Commons Vote on the Transfer of the Crown, 5 February 1689," *BIHR* 52 (May 1979): 43). Wogan (1635-1708), M.P. for Haverford West, was a moderate Tory who voted against offering the crown to William and Mary. A lawyer, Wogan was made serjeant-at-law in October 1689.

20. *CJ*, 10:22.

21. See above, Chapter 3.

22. *CJ*, 10:23.

23. Grey, 9:79-81. In my view, Dr. Frankle ("The Formulation of the Declaration of Rights," p. 269) has misread this debate. He misses the fact that Somers had asked the House for instructions on how to handle the several resolutions. This debate responds, I believe, to that request. See remarks by Howard, Temple, and Hampden. Eyre refers to the crown, not to the other grievances. Note his use of the word "papers," which surely refers to the Lords' vote offering the crown to William and Mary, and the Commons' claim of rights for the nation.

24. *CJ*, 10:23.

25. Ibid.

26. Landon, *Triumph of the Lawyers*, p. 238, argues that Treby rather than Somers was the "chief member" of the committee appointed to draft the Declaration of Rights, pointing out that Treby was the chairman. But Dr. Landon does not take into account that Somers was the chairman of the committee that linked the several resolutions of the Convention into one document.

27. *CJ*, 10:26.

28. *Clar. Corr.*, 2:262; HLRO, Willcocks Coll., Hist. Coll., VI, 21; Reresby, *Memoirs*, p. 552. See also Morrice, 2:463; FSL, "The Newdigate Newsletters," L.c. 1974; Bodl., Rawlinson Mss. D 1079, fol. 14v.

29. *CJ*, 10:24.

Chapter 14

1. See *DNB;* Huygens, "Journaal," p. 85. The earl wore two wigs, one on top of the other, and always covered his face with a white cloth when he went outside. He was sixty-four years old.

2. This is the paper mentioned above in Chapter 1.

3. HLRO, Mss. Minutes, February 8, 1688/89; ibid., Braye Mss. 43, draft journal; *LJ*, 14:121.

4. HLRO, Willcocks Coll., Hist. Coll., VI, 21.

5. Morrice, 2:463, 464.

6. Laurence Echard, *History of England*, 3 vols. (London, 1707-18), 3:1148.

7. [Nathaniel Johnston], *The Dear Bargain; or, A True Representation of the State of the English Nation under the Dutch, In a Letter to a Friend* (1690), in *Somers's Tracts,* 10:369-70; and [Sir James Montgomery], *Great Britain's just Complaint for her late Measures, present Sufferings, and the future Miseries she is exposed to* (1692), in ibid., p. 440.

8. See above, Chapters 5 and 10.

9. For what follows, see Morrice, 2:463-65; BL, Add. Mss. 40,621, fol. 20; HLRO, Willcocks Coll., Hist. Coll., VI, 21. A contemporary thought all the bishops were opposed to the claim of rights (BL, Add. Mss. 40,621, fol. 22).

10. Huygens, "Journaal," p. 84.

11. Van Terveen, "Verbaal . . . Witsen," p. 141.

12. Morrice, 2:465.

13. Ibid.

14. BL, Add. Mss. 40,621, fol. 20.

15. Burnet, *Supplement,* p. 310; italics supplied.

16. Foxcroft, *Halifax,* 2:246 (the Spencer House Journals).

17. Howard Nenner, "The Convention of 1689: A Triumph of Constitutional Form," *American Journal of Legal History,* October 1966, p. 295.

18. BL, Add. Mss. 27,382, fol. 87v.

19. Foxcroft, *Halifax,* 2:217 (the Spencer House Journals).

20. *CJ,* 10:25. Eighty-nine lords were present on February 9, ninety-five on the eleventh, and ninety-seven on the twelfth (*LJ,* 14:122, 123, 124). On February 9, for example, the House sat until 5:00 P.M. (*Clar. Corr.,* 2:262). A lord explained that many peers continued to attend the meetings of the House, not because they approved of the proceedings, but because they feared "great severities from the new government" if they did not (Simpson, "Notes of a Noble Lord," pp. 97-98).

21. A broadside, printed on both sides. No place, no date. Copies at HL, 276772, and Bodl., Carte Mss. 180, fol. 542.

22. *LJ,* 14:122. See Appendix 4.

23. Cruickshanks, Hayton, and Jones, "Divisions in the House of Lords on the Transfer of the Crown and Other Issues," pp. 60, 83. See Appendix 4.

24. Browning, *Danby,* 3:152-58; David H. Hosford, "The Peerage and the Test Act: A List, c. November 1687," *BIHR* 43 (May 1969): 116-20.

25. Danby, Devonshire, Lumley, and Shrewsbury had signed the June 30 invitation and with Mordaunt had helped write the prince's manifesto.

26. *CJ,* 10:25, 27; *LJ,* 14:124.

27. ARA, Collectie van Citters, no. 25, February 1/11, 1688/89.

28. Quoted in Maurice Cranston, *John Locke: A Biography* (London, 1957), p. 308. Text in E. S. de Beer, ed., *The Correspondence of John Locke,* 5 vols. (Oxford, 1976-79), 3:527-29.

29. Bodl., Carte Mss. 81, fol. 766. The paper is undated. See C. F. Trevallyn Jones, *Saw-Pit Wharton: The Political Career from 1640 to 1691 of Philip, fourth Lord Wharton* (Sydney, 1967), pp. 260-62; Lacey, *Dissent and Parliamentary Politics,* pp. 226, 232-33. Horwitz, *Parliament Policy and Politics,* p. 100, n. 5, incorrectly assigns this proposal to Thomas Wharton.

30. Schwoerer, *NSA,* p. 149; also pp. 138, 54.

31. Jones, *Saw-Pit Wharton,* p. 262.

32. Unless otherwise noted, biographical details are from the *DNB.*

33. *St. Tr.,* 11:1354-66.

34. Hosford, *Nottingham, Nobles, and the North,* pp. 84, 91-93. Dr. Hosford maintains that notwithstanding the November 22 date on the broadside, it was proclaimed on the twenty-fourth.

35. *The Works of Henry Booth, Lord Delamere, 1st Earl of Warrington, 1652-94* (London, 1694), pp. 367-69, 375.

36. Ibid., p. 356.

37. Ibid., p. 357.

38. Ibid., pp. 361, 365.

39. Ibid., p. 358.

40. Ibid., p. 359.

41. Ibid., p. 364.

42. Henry Booth, Lord Delamere, *The Late Lord Russell's Case, with Observations upon it* (London, 1689), pp. 14, 12, 15.

43. See *DNB;* Antonia Fraser, *Cromwell, The Lord Protector* (London, 1974) pp. 600-601, 642, 644, 656-57.

44. Margaret Child, "Prelude to Revolution: The Structure of Politics in County Durham, 1678-88" (Ph.D. diss., University of Maryland, 1972), pp. 406, 408, 420.

45. HLRO, Minutes of Committee on Privileges, January 28, 1688/89; *LJ,* 14:114, 116.

46. The Lords' Committee on Privileges met January 28 and February 4 (perhaps), 8, 11, and 12. It was said that a peer "has not so fair a trial as a commoner" because the king selected the jurors as he wished (HLRO, Minutes of the Committee on Privileges January 28, 1688/89; HMC, *Lords Mss.,* p. 87). On February 11, the committee ordered Petyt to search the records about the privileges of the peers in their trials, and following his report, it successfully moved that the House of Lords order a search of the records of the crown office on the subject (*LJ,* 14:124). After the settlement, the peers pursued the question further. The Committee on Privileges was also preoccupied, interestingly enough, with such privileges as the right, when Parliament was sitting, to take a deer upon the sounding of a horn and keep the venison, the right of lords to wear their coronets when the king came to the House wearing his crown, and the reciprocity of New Year's gifts between king and peers.

47. For the votes, in sequence, see Cruickshanks, Hayton, and Jones, "Divisions in the House of Lords on the Transfer of the Crown and Other Issues," pp. 60, 61 and n. 26, 64, 65. See Appendix 4.

48. *LJ,* 14:121; *CJ,* 10:25, 27.

49. The original draft of the amendment is in HLRO, Main Papers, 8, fols. 81-81v.

50. For example, the word "cities" was placed before the word "universities" in the paragraph about elections to the Convention.

51. For example, the lords insisted that the language be adjusted to show that they were *not* elected.

52. HLRO, Minutes of the Committees, p. 23.

53. *CJ,* 10:25, 26.

54. *CJ,* 10:23; HLRO, Minutes of the Committees, p. 23.

55. *CJ,* 10:25.

56. Grey, 9:81-82.

57. *CJ,* 10:26.

58. Bodl., Ballard Mss. 45, fol. 28.

59. Beddard, "'The Violent Party': The Guildhall Revolutionaries and the Growth of Opposition to James II," p. 132.

60. *CJ,* 10:25.

61. *LJ,* 14:122; *CJ,* 10:25.

62. HMC, *Lords Mss.,* p. 29.

63. HLRO, Mss. Journals, vol. 61, p. 64; ibid., Braye Mss. 43, fol. 27.

64. HMC, *Lords Mss.,* p. 29, HLRO, Mss. Minutes, February 9, 1688/89.

65. HLRO, Minutes of the Committees, p. 23.

66. HLRO, Mss. Journals, vol. 61, p. 67; *CJ,* 10:25.

67. J. R. Western, *Monarchy and Revolution* (London, 1972), p. 339, n. 2.

68. See above, Chapter 4.

69. HMC, *Lords Mss.,* p. 29.

70. HLRO, Mss. Minutes, February 9, 1688/89.

71. HLRO, Minutes of the Committees, p. 23; *CJ,* 10:25.

72. Grey, 9:82-83.

73. *CJ,* 10:26.

74. *CJ,* 10:27.

75. Morrice, 2:466; Bodl., Rawlinson Mss. D 1079, fol. 16.

76. *CJ*, 10:27.

77. *Clar. Corr.*, 2:262.

78. Reresby, *Memoirs*, p. 554.

79. Morrice, 2:467.

80. *London Intelligence*, no. 9, February 9-12, 1689; FSL, "Newdigate Newsletters," L.c. 1973, 1974, 1975.

Chapter 15

1. See the provocative studies by Victor Turner, *The Ritual Process: Structure and Anti-Structure* (Chicago, 1968), and Erving Goffman, *Interaction Ritual: Essays in Face-to-Face Behaviour* (London, 1972), and *The Presentation of Self in Everyday Life* (London, 1959). Also see Sidney Anglo, *Spectacle, Pageantry, and Early Tudor Policy* (Oxford, 1969); Natalie Z. Davis, *Society and Culture in Early Modern France: Eight Essays* (Stanford, Calif., 1975); Gerard Reedy, "Mystical Politics: The Imagery of Charles II's Coronation," in *Studies in Change and Revolution: Aspects of English Intellectual History, 1640-1800*, ed. Paul J. Korshin (New York, 1972), pp. 19-42; and Roy Strong, *Splendour at Court: Renaissance Spectacle and Illusion* (London, 1973).

2. See above, Chapter 5.

3. The Banqueting House was refurbished in 1973. See the useful pamphlet John Charlton, *The Banqueting House, Whitehall*, published by the Department of the Environment, Ancient Monuments and Historic Buildings (Edinburgh, n.d.).

4. The records of the lord chamberlain, the lord steward, and the master of the robes at the Public Record Office are full of gaps for the months January and February 1689. Mary preferred Palme wine and William champagne (LS 1/32). The absence of an accounting of the expenses for the proceedings suggests that William bore the cost.

5. Huygens, "Journaal," p. 85; van Terveen, "Verbaal . . . Witsen," p. 134. Also see Müller, *Willem und Waldeck*, 2:137.

6. Reresby, *Memoirs*, p. 553.

7. J. P. Kenyon, *The Stuart Constitution, 1603-1688* (Cambridge, 1966), p. 1.

8. HLRO, Braye Mss. 43, fol. 31v. The excitement of the moment is shown in the "scribble" books of the clerk. Words are repeated or omitted, the handwriting is hasty, and two black slashes run across the page.

9. De Beer, *Evelyn's Diary*, 4:624.

10. Goffman, *Presentation of Self in Everyday Life*, p. 11.

11. Schwoerer, "A Jornall of the Convention," pp. 253-54. No such exact formula for proclaiming a king existed before the seventeenth century. The speaker was Sir Robert Sawyer.

12. BL, Add. Mss. 38,496, fol. 19.

13. *LJ*, 14:127.

14. BL, Add. Mss. 40,621, fols. 18, 24; BL, Add. Mss. 34,515, p. 2. Also, see an oblique reference, perhaps to this point, in HLRO, Willcocks Coll., VI, 20. Letters for electing members of the Convention, it will be recalled, had also been directed to the coroner.

15. Steele, *Proclamations*, pp. 476-77; cf. pp. 107, 166, 343, 384, 437, and 512 for proclamations of other Stuart kings. In the proclamation of Charles II, dated May 8, 1660, the Commons are also mentioned. The question of which persons should have the authority to proclaim a king surfaced again in June in debates on the Act of Succession (Grey, 9:345-46, 351-52).

16. PRO, L/C 9, fols. 43, 73, 73v; Bodl., Rawlinson Mss. D 1079, fol. 14v; Bodl., Ballard Mss. 45, fol. 28; *Universal Intelligence*, no. 12, February 13, 1688/89; *Orange Gazette*, no. 12, February 12-15, 1688/89.

17. The official proclamation was printed under date of February 13. *The Manner of the Proclaiming of King William, and Queen Mary, at White-Hall in the City of London, Feb. 13, 1688/9*, a broadside, supplies many details. Also, Luttrell, *Brief Historical Relation*, 1:501; Bodl., Rawlinson Mss. D 1079, fol. 17; *Orange Gazette*, no. 12, February 12-15, 1688/89. The lord

mayor, Sir John Chapman, was ill and confined to his coach, a circumstance doubtless explaining his passive role.

18. Morrice, 2:467.

19. A member of William's Dutch entourage specifically noted that he saw the proceedings from his window: see Huygens, "Journaal," p. 86.

20. *CJ*, 10:29.

21. See above, Chapter 11.

22. London Meteorological Office, Rawlinson Mss. Weather Diary, January–February 1689.

23. Reports of the number of peers attending the ceremony vary: see *LJ*, 14:127; HLRO, Braye Mss., fols. 31v, 32; HLRO, Mss. Minutes, February 13, 1688/89. A notice to attend the House on February 13 was sent to all absent lords.

24. Grey, 9:112. A poem, *Upon the Sicknesse of the Archbishop of Canterbury*, dated February 14, 1689, bitterly criticized Sancroft for his absence.

25. Reresby, *Memoirs*, p. 554.

26. Van Terveen, "Verbaal . . . Witsen," p. 142; on February 25, Witsen noted that "taunting songs are sung in the street; the Butterboxes [i.e., the Dutch] have given us a King." The term "Butterboxes" was pejorative; it had been used in the 1650s in vicious pictorial satire against the Dutch. See George, *English Political Caricature to 1792*, 1:42, 50. By the end of February, desertion in the army had decimated the ranks (Luttrell, *Brief Historical Relation*, 1:505; Reresby, *Memoirs*, pp. 557–58; Morrice, 2:474).

27. A bonfire celebrating William's acceptance in late December of the administration of the government was also placed outside Watts Coffee House and was contributed to by persons who were elected to the Convention. See *Orange Gazette*, no. 1, December 31, 1688, and the *London Courant*, no. 6, December 25–29, 1688. The news that the House of Lords had accepted the abdication and vacancy resolution was greeted with bonfires the night of February 6. See Morrice, 2:459, 462; Bodl., Rawlinson Mss. D 1079, fol. 13. The night of Mary's arrival, bonfires were so numerous that people thought the city was on fire. See *London Mercury*, no. 12, February 12, 1688/89; ARA, Collectie van Citters, no. 25, February 12/22, 1688/89.

28. Morrice, 2:467; *London Mercury; or, Moderate Intelligencer*, no. 12, February 11–14, 1688/89.

29. *Orange Gazette*, no. 12, February 12–15, 1688/89. Earlier cartoons and medals had featured Jeffreys and Petre in the most unflattering terms. See Schwoerer, "Propaganda in the Revolution of 1688–89," pp. 861–65.

30. The figure is reported in John Eliot Hodgkin, *Rariora: Being Notes of some of the Printed Books, Manuscripts, Historical Documents, Medals, Engravings, Pottery, Etc., Etc.* (London, 1902), 3:vi (second page so numbered). This volume contains engravings of firework displays and a list of books on fireworks.

31. The Lords made specific arrangements about the printing of the proclamation both before and after the prince was proclaimed (HLRO, Mss. Minutes, February 12, 1688/89).

32. The date is written on the copy of the broadside in BL.

33. For maces, see PRO, L/C 9, fols. 43, 72v, 73, where their value is given as over £300.

34. The tune for the song was used two months later for a coronation song, *The Protestants Joy; An Excellent New Song on the Glorious Coronation of King William and Queen Mary, which in much Triumph was Celebrated at Westminster on the 11th, instant April*, Licensed according to Order.

35. *London Mercury; or, Moderate Intelligencer*, no. 12, February 11–14, 1688/89; Reresby, *Memoirs*, p. 554; *CSPD, William and Mary*, 1:1; BL, Add. Mss., 38,496, fols. 19v, 23, 23v. But one disgruntled onlooker thought he had never seen a "worse sight" (BL, Add. Mss. 36,707, fol. 57).

36. ARA, Collectie van Citters, no. 25, February 15/25, 1688/89; BL, Add. Mss. 38,496, fols. 21, 21v; Müller, *Willem und Waldeck*, 2:137, 139.

37. The two doorkeepers of the House of Commons were ordered to allow none but members of the Convention to enter the Hall (*CJ*, 10:28). See Fig. 1.

38. FSL, "A Short Account of the Revolution," fol. 15; FSL, "Newdigate Newsletters," L.c. 1976; *CJ*, 10:29.

39. FSL, "Newdigate Newsletters," L.c. 1976; KUL, Bonnet's dispatches, February 15/25, 1688/89, fol. 60.

40. See William Huse Dunham, Jr., and Charles T. Wood, "The Right to Rule in England: Depositions and the Kingdom's Authority, 1327-1485," *AHR* 81 (October 1976): 738-61. The dates were 1327, 1399, 1460, 1483, 1485, and 1649.

41. Morrice, 2:466; Bodl., Rawlinson Mss. D 1079, fol. 16; HLRO, Braye Mss. 43, fol. 30v; FSL, "A Short Account of the Revolution," fol. 15.

42. *LJ*, 14:126-27; HLRO, Mss. Journals, 61:78.

43. *CJ*, 10:26; *LJ*, 14:126; HMC, *Lords Mss.*, p. 30.

44. *The Present Convention a Parliament* (London, 1688 [before March 25, 1689]), p. 18. A second edition appeared in 1689.

45. *LJ*, 14:127; *CJ*, 10:28; HLRO, Braye Mss. 43, fol. 31v; HLRO, Mss. Journals, 61:81.

46. *CJ*, 10:28; *LJ*, 14:126-27.

47. Elizabeth R. Foster, "Petitions and the Petition of Right," *JBS*, 14 (November 1974): 2.

48. See Charlton, *The Banqueting House*, where the uses are detailed. The sovereign received members of Parliament here in the early part of the century. Also Esther Cope to Schwoerer, January 13, 1977.

49. *CJ*, 8:49; *LJ*, 11:46.

50. Burnet, *Supplement*, p. 311. The decision on whether the proclamation should follow immediately after the presentation ceremony was left to the Convention (BL, Add. Mss. 38,496, fols. 19v, 21v; ARA, Collectie van Citters, no. 25, February 15/25, 1688/89).

51. *Universal Intelligence*, no. 12, February 13, 1688/89. Compton's text was taken from Galatians 6:15: "For in Christ Jesus neither Circumcision availeth any thing, nor Uncircumcision, but a new creature." The sermon was not printed, and apparently no written copy has survived. Edward Carpenter, *The Protestant Bishop: Being the Life of Henry Compton, 1632-1713, Bishop of London* (London, 1956), does not comment on it.

52. BL, Add. Mss. 34,487, fol. 42. Two printed accounts are *A true and exact relation of the Prince of Orange his publick entrance into Exeter* (London, 1688); and *The Expedition of His Highness the Prince of Orange for England, Giving an Account of the most remarkable Passages thereof, from the Day of his setting sail from Holland to the first Day of this instant December, 1688* (London, 1688).

53. The prince's *Declaration of Reasons*, it will be remembered, disclaimed the idea of conquest. William issued an order on January 2, 1688/89, that any of his soldiers who suggested that he had conquered England be punished; see the *Orange Gazette*, no. 4, January 7-10, 1688/89.

54. William had a heavy cough in mid-January and a bad cold ten days later. Mary described him on February 12 as in "very ill condition" and very thin. See Morrice, 2:425; Huygens, "Journaal," pp. 68-71; Doebner, *Memoirs of Mary*, p. 10.

55. PRO, L/C 9/386, pp. 47, 57, 66, 68. Natalie Rothstein kindly allowed me to go through her photocopies of this collection. The identification of the cinnamon-colored suit, the first one ordered in the period beginning February 13, 1689, as the one William actually wore at the ceremony is reasonable, but not certain. The print shows William dressed in a suit such as that described in the Lord Chamberlain's accounts. (See Frontispiece.)

56. See de Beer, *Evelyn's Diary*, 4:624-25, n. 3.

57. At the coronation two months later, it was remarked that there had never been a more ugly king or a more beautiful queen (Huygens, "Journaal," p. 112; F. J. L. Krämer, ed., "Mémoires de Monsieur de B . . . ou Anecdotes, Tant de la cour du Prince d'Orange Guillaume III, que des principaux seigneurs de la republique de ce temps," *Bijdragen en Mededeelingen van het Historisch Genootschap* 19 [Utrecht, 1898]: 82).

58. There is no mention of the ceremony either in Doebner, *Memoirs of Mary*, of in Mechtild, Comtesse Bentinck, ed. *Lettres et Mémoires de Marie Reine D'Angleterre* (The Hague, 1880).

59. KUL, Bonnet's dispatches, February 15/25, 1688/89; ARA, Collectie van Citters, no. 25, February 15/25, 1688/89. Cf. HMC, *Portland Mss.*, 3:428.

60. The official version of the speech was not very different from the speech of December 28, 1688, when William agreed to take on the administration of affairs until a Convention was elected (*CJ*, 10:7). See above, Chapter 1, and Fig. 4.

61. At least one contemporary complained that William had been proclaimed king without taking an oath and questioned whether, therefore, any allegiance was due him (BL, Add. Mss. 27,382, fol. 87v, "Humanum est errare").

62. *CJ*, 10:30; *LJ*, 14:128.

63. FSL, "A Short Account of the Revolution," fol. 17.

64. *An Account of what was done between the time the Prince of Orange came to London, till the Proclaiming him King of England*, reprinted in *A Compleat Collection of Papers, in Twelve Parts.*

65. *London Gazette*, February 11-14, 1688/89; *London Mercury; or, Moderate Intelligencer*, no. 12, February 11-14, 1688/89; *Universal Intelligence*, no. 12, February 13, 1688/89.

66. I am grateful to Dr. G. van der Meer, Koninklijk Kabinet, The Hague, for supplying information about Meybusch. The best biography is in Georg Galster, *Danske og Norske Medailler og Jetons ca. 1533-ca. 1688* (Copenhagen, 1936), pp. 103-234.

67. At least ten medals bearing the device appeared at this time. See Nicholas Tindal, *The Mettalick History of the Reigns of King William III and Queen Mary, Queen Anne, and King George I*, 4 vols. (London, 1747), vol. 3, plates 1-3. Attached to his edition and translation from the French of Paul Rapin de Thoyras, *The History of England*, 28 vols. (London, 1726-47). See also Schwoerer, "Propaganda in the Revolution of 1688/89," p. 865 and n. 79.

68. See Goldie, "Edmund Bohun and *Jus Gentium* in the Revolution Debate, 1689-1693."

Chapter 16

1. Although source material for the passage of the statute is thin, old and new evidence together permit a fuller account than that written over one hundred years ago by Macaulay, the only account in print. See Macaulay, *History of England*, 4:1663-64. Turberville, *House of Lords in the Reign of William III*, pp. 160-61, adds nothing to Macaulay. A fuller statement is in Alan Simpson, "The Convention Parliament of 1688-89" (D. Phil., Oxford University, 1939), pp. 174-90.

2. Grey, 9:92-106; Bodl., Mss. Eng. hist. c. 201, fols. 65v-66; Morrice, 2:470; de Beer, *Evelyn's Diary*, 4:627; Feiling, *History of the Tory Party*, p. 263.

3. *CJ*, 10:42.

4. Foxcroft, *Halifax*, 2:216, n. 7, 217.

5. *CJ*, 10:96, 101, 117.

6. See above, p. 28.

7. William's advisers did not trust Godolphin: see Huygens, "Journaal," p. 121.

8. *CJ*, 10:126.

9. BL, Loan 29/164, bundle 2, quoted in Horwitz, *Parliament, Policy, and Politics*, p. 28.

10. Grey, 9:237-42.

11. *CJ*, 10:126; Morrice, 2:552.

12. *CJ*, 10:126.

13. Grey, 9:256-58. Edie, "Revolution and the Rule of Law," pp. 442-44, confuses the chronology of the debates respecting the dispensing power.

14. *CJ*, 10:126.

15. HMC, *Lords Mss.*, pp. 346-47.

16. See above, p. 28.

17. *LJ*, 14:208.

18. The king continued to suffer from a deep cough and was repeatedly described as ill-looking, pale, or faint (Huygens, "Journaal," pp. 97, 98, 102, 105, 107, 111, 112, 116, 157, 165).

19. NUL, Portland Mss., PwA 2303.

20. Burnet, *HOT,* 4:28; Doebner, *Memoirs of Mary,* pp. 72-76; HMC, *Lords Mss.,* pp. 345-46; *LJ,* 14:215, 217.

21. Morrice, 2:577-78.

22. Grey, 9:345-46, 351-52; *CJ,* 10:187, 190. The debate on this amendment is ignored by Macaulay. The eleven members included Capel, Hampden (whether father or son is unknown), Sacheverell, Seymour, Wildman, and Williams.

23. Grey, 9:353-55.

24. *CJ,* 10:187.

25. Macaulay, *History of England,* 4:1664, followed by Turberville, *The House of Lords in the Reign of William III,* p. 160. Simpson, "The Convention Parliament," pp. 180-83, varies from Macaulay.

26. Burnet, *HOT,* 4:28.

27. Grey, 9:345.

28. Ibid.

29. John Oldmixon, *The History of England during the Reigns of King William and Queen Mary, Queen Anne and King George I* (London 1735), p. 11.

30. Grey, 9:282-86; *CJ,* 10:165; Morrice, 2:569.

31. Browning, *Danby,* 1:450-55.

32. Grey, 9:286-94.

33. *CJ,* 10:193-94.

34. Bodl., Carte Mss. 228, fol. 186, Jephson to Wharton, June 4, 1689.

35. Huygens, "Journaal," p. 140 (June 13, 1689).

36. Grey, 9:346.

37. Horwitz, *Parliament, Policy, and Politics,* pp. 32-33.

38. *CJ,* 10:211.

39. *LJ,* 14:279, 281.

40. *CJ,* 10:230.

41. De Beer, *Evelyn's Diary,* 4:645.

42. Foxcroft, *Halifax,* 2:227.

43. Oldmixon, *History of England,* p. 11.

44. Foxcroft, *Halifax,* 2:71, 117-18.

45. Huygens, "Journaal," p. 162.

46. *CJ,* 10:213-14.

47. *LJ,* 14:281.

48. *LJ,* 14:298. HLRO, Mss. Min., July 29, 1689, shows that the peers ordered that further debate on the Bill of Rights be the "first business for July 30" and that all members be notified to attend.

49. *CJ,* 10:246.

50. Ibid.

51. *CJ,* 10:264; Simpson, "The Convention Parliament," pp. 187-88.

52. *CJ,* 10:271.

53. Huygens, "Journaal," p. 145; cf. pp. 132, 143, 147, 212.

54. FSL, "Newdigate Newsletters," L.c. 2044.

55. *CSPD, William and Mary,* 1:308.

56. Morrice, 3:13. The lord mayor and aldermen offered an award of £500 to discover who did this (*London Gazette,* November 21-25, 1689).

57. *London Gazette,* November 14-18, 1689.

58. See my unpublished paper, "John Locke and the Revolution Whigs," delivered at the symposium "John Locke and the Political Thought of the 1680's," Folger Library, March 1980.

59. Morrice, 2:607.

60. Foxcroft, *Halifax,* 2:224-33, 242.

61. Morrice, 2:617.

62. The others were Capel, Garroway, and Falkland. See *CJ,* 10:273.

63. *CJ*, 10:276-77.

64. See Maurice Cranston, *John Locke: A Biography* (London, 1957), p. 325.

65. Morrice, 2:653.

66. Grey, 9:396-97; *CJ*, 10:280.

67. *LJ*, 14:344-51.

68. Huygens, "Journaal," pp. 176, 177.

69. HMC, *Lords Mss.*, pp. 347n (quoting Burnet), 348; *LJ*, 14:344-46. Another amendment, hitherto unnoticed, requiring the monarch to produce a certificate attested by six peers (three spiritual and three temporal) that within three months of taking the Test Oath he had received the sacrament according to the Church of England was rejected by the House of Commons, a rejection reflecting surely the concern articulated earlier by Sacheverell that Lutherans or Calvinists not be debarred.

70. Morrice, 2:672, 3:1.

71. HMC, *Lords Mss.*, p. 348.

72. *LJ*, 14:332.

73. HMC, *Lords Mss.*, p. 348; *LJ*, 14:348.

74. HLRO, Mss. Minutes, November 21, 1689.

75. Ibid., November 22, 1689.

76. HMC, *Lords Mss.*, p. 348-49.

77. Morrice, 3:4.

78. HMC, *Lords Mss.*, p. 349, 361; *LJ*, 14:362, 418.

79. Huygens, "Journaal," p. 210; *LJ*, 14:351.

80. HMC, *Lords Mss.*, p. 345.

81. *LJ*, 14:351.

82. See Browning, *Danby*, 1:453; Clayton Roberts, *The Growth of Responsible Government in Stuart England* (Cambridge, 1966), pp. 250-52.

83. *CJ*, 10:293-94, 305, 310.

84. Morrice, 3:53-54.

A New View of the Declaration of Rights and the Bill of Rights

1. J. P. Kenyon, *The Stuart Constitution, 1603-1688* (Cambridge, 1966), p. 1.

2. Burnet's descendants have installed a tablet in Salisbury Cathedral whose inscription includes testimonial to the bishop's contribution to the passage of the Bill of Rights.

3. James Mackintosh, *History of the Revolution in England in 1688* (London, 1834), p. 598.

4. John Somers, *Vindication of the Proceedings of the late Parliament of England, An. Dom., 1689,* in *Somers's Tracts,* 10:257-58, 261, 263, 266, 267, 268. For attribution to Somers, see Sachse, *John Somers,* p. 36, n. 41.

5. E. S. de Beer, ed., *The Correspondence of John Locke,* 5 vols. (Oxford, 1976-79), 3:571, 597, 698-99.

6. Caroline Robbins, ed., *Two English Republican Tracts* (Cambridge, 1969), p. 33.

7. John Sheffield, Duke of Buckinham, *Works,* 2 vols. (London, 1726), 2:81, 86. This account is the same as that in Bishop John Warner's papers at Bodl., Mss. Eng. hist. b. 205, fols. 92-108.

8. Sir Bartholomew Shower, *Reasons for a New Bill of Rights: humbly submitted to the Consideration of the Ensuing Session of Parliament* (London, 1692), pp. 1-3, 9, 10-12, 30.

9. Foxcroft, *Halifax,* 2:138.

10. Clayton Roberts, "The Constitutional Significance of the Financial Settlement of 1690," pp. 59-76.

11. Janelle Greenberg, "Tudor and Stuart Theories of Kingship: The Dispensing Power and the Royal Discretionary Authority in Sixteenth- and Seventeenth-Century England" (Ph.D. diss., University of Maryland, 1970), pp. 523-35.

12. For an account of cases involving article 9 between 1688 and 1972, see David R. Mummery, "The Privilege of Freedom of Speech in Parliament," *LQR* 94 (April 1978): 276-90.

13. See David S. Lovejoy, *The Glorious Revolution in America* (New York, 1972).

14. See Jones, *The Revolution of 1688,* p. 330.

15. Kenyon, *Revolution Principles.*

16. J. G. A. Pocock, *The Machiavellian Moment,* and "Burke and the Ancient Constitution: A Problem in the History of Ideas," *HJ* 3 (1960): 125-43.

17. H. T. Dickinson, *Liberty and Property: Political Ideology in Eighteenth-Century Britain* (New York, 1977); Franklin, *John Locke and the Theory of Sovereignty;* and Margaret Jacob, *The Newtonians and the English Revolution, 1689-1720* (Ithaca, N.Y., 1976).

Selected Bibliography

Primary Sources

MANUSCRIPT MATERIAL [With some exceptions, only the number of the collection is given.]

Algemeen Rijksarchief (The Hague): Collectie van Citters, No. 25.

Bodleian Library: Ballard Mss. 22; Ballard Mss. 45; Carte Mss. 40, 139, 228; Mss. Eng. hist. b.205; Mss. Eng. hist. c.201; Mss. Eng. hist. d.307; Rawlinson Mss. D 1079; Rawlinson Mss. D 1232; Mss. Tanner 28; Mss. Tanner 459; Mss. Tanner 496.

British Library: Add. Mss. 5947; 9363; 22,183; 22,910; 25,377; 27,382; 29,564; 29,578; 29,594; 32,095; 32,520; 32,681; 33,923; 34,502; 34,504; 34,510; 34,512; 34,514; 34,515; 34,516; 36,707; 38,175; 38,495; 38,496; 40,621; 41,816; 41,821; 41,823; 45,731; 51,950; Egerton Mss. 2621; Egerton Mss. 3346; Harleian Mss. 1243.393; Lansdowne Mss. 255; Loan 29/140; Loan 29/164; Stowe Mss. 304; Stowe Mss. 354; Stowe Mss. 370; Stowe Mss. 840.1-9.

Cambridge University, Churchill College Archives: Erle Mss. 4/4.

Folger Shakespeare Library: James Frazer's Letters (August 1685-88): V.b. 287; "The Newdigate Newsletters, Addressed to Sir Richard Newdigate, 1st Bart., and to 2nd Bart., 1673/74-1715": L.c. 1-3950; Sir Robert Southwell's Collection of Mss. Material on the Glorious Revolution, containing, *inter alia,* "A Short Account of the Revolution in England in the year 1688," possibly by Southwell, V.b. 150; other Southwell papers: V.b. 294; V.b. 305; William Westby, "A Continuation of my memoires or memoranda book, January 1688-January 1689": V.a. 350.

Guildhall Library: Mss. 12,158; Chamber Accounts 40/35.

Hertfordshire County Record Office: D/EP F 26.

House of Lords Record Office: The Book of Orders for the Convention (January 22-January 25, 1689-90); Braye Mss. 43; Hist. Coll., Mss. 33; Hist. Coll. 155, H.C., 1973; Main Papers, 5-19; Mss. Minutes; Mss. Journal, vol. 61; Minutes of Committee on Privileges; Minutes of the Committees; votes of the House of Commons; Willcocks Coll., Hist. Coll.; original draft and final copy of the Declaration of Rights; original engrossed copy of the Bill of Rights; various other original papers connected with the passage of the declaration.

Henry E. Huntington Library: Hastings Mss. 13889 LcBl; Stowe Mss.: Temple Papers (uncatalogued).

National Library of Wales: Ottley Papers.

New York Public Library: Hardwicke Mss. XXXIII.

Nottingham University Library: Portland Mss.: PwA 1590–1841, 2087–2310.

The Carl H. Pforzheimer Library: Bulstrode Mss., vol. 12, Newsletters.

Public Record Office: P.B., Misc. Rolls 18; SP 31/4; 31/5; C 57/7; and the records of the Lord Chamberlain, the Lord Steward, and the Master of the Robes.

University of Kansas Library: Microfilm of Acta betr. des Residenten Bonnet relat: aus England 1689 January–June 1689, Repertorium XI. 73. The original is in Deutsches Zentralarchiv, Merseburg, German Democratic Republic.

West Sussex Record Office: Winterton Mss. 482.

Dr. Williams's Library: Roger Morrice, "Entr'ing Book, Being an Historical Register of Occurrences from April, Anno, 1677 to April 1691," 4 vols. I have used a photocopy (now in my possession) of the original from the library of the late Douglas R. Lacey.

PRINTED LETTERS AND DIARIES   [The place of publication is London unless otherwise indicated.]

Ailesbury, Thomas Bruce, second Earl of. *Memoirs.* Ed. W. E. Buckley. 2 vols. 1890.

Beddard, Robert. "The Loyalist Opposition in the Interregnum: A Letter of Dr. Francis Turner, Bishop of Ely, on the Revolution of 1688." *BIHR* 40 (May 1967): 101–9.

Blencowe, R. W., ed. *Diary of the Times of Charles the Second by The Honourable Henry Sidney (Afterwards Earl of Romney) Including His Correspondence with the Countess of Sunderland . . . To Which Are Added, Letters Illustrative of the Times of James II and William III.* 2 vols. 1843.

Bramston, Sir John. *Autobiography.* Ed. Lord Braybrooke. 1845.

Browning, Andrew, ed. *Memoirs of Sir John Reresby.* Glasgow, 1936.

Buckingham, John Sheffield, third Duke of. *Works of John Sheffield, Earl of Mulgrave, Marquis of Normanby, and third Duke of Buckingham.* 2 vols. The Hague, 1726.

Burnet, Bishop Gilbert. *History of His Own Time: with Notes by the Earls of Dartmouth and Hardwicke, Speaker Onslow, and Dean Swift.* 6 vols. Oxford, 1833.

Clarke, J. S., ed. *The Life of James II Collected Out of Memoirs Writ of His Own Hand.* 2 vols. 1816.

Cosnac, G. J., and E. Pontal, eds. *Mémoires du Marquis de Sources sur le Règne de Louis XIV.* 13 vols. Paris, 1883–93.

Dalrymple, John. *Memoirs of Great Britain and Ireland From The Dissolution of the last Parliament of Charles II until the Sea-Battle off La Hogue.* 2 vols. London and Edinburgh, 1771–73.

de Beer, E. S., ed. *The Diary of John Evelyn.* 6 vols. 1955.

Doebner, R., ed. *Memoirs of Mary, Queen of England (1689–1693) Together with Her Letters.* London and Leipzig, 1886.

Dover, George James Welbore Agar-Ellis, first Baron, ed. *The Ellis Correspondence: Letters Written during the Years 1686, 1687, 1688, and Addressed to John Ellis, esq. Secretary to the Commissioners of His Majesty's revenue in Ireland*. 2 vols. 1831.

Ellis, Sir Henry, ed. *Original Letters, Illustrative of English History*. 3rd series. 4 vols. 1827.

Foxcroft, H. C., ed. *Life and Letters of Sir George Savile, First Marquis of Halifax*. 2 vols. 1898.

—————. *A Supplement to Burnet's History of My Own Time*. Oxford, 1902.

Horwitz, Henry, ed. *The Parliamentary Diary of Narcissus Luttrell, 1691-1693*. Oxford, 1972.

Japikse, N., ed. *Correspondentie van Willem III en van Hans Willem Bentinck, eersten graaf van Portland*. 5 vols. The Hague, 1927-37.

Josten, C. H., ed. *Elias Ashmole (1617—1692): His Autobiographical and Historical Notes, His Correspondence, and Other Contemporary Sources Relating to His Life and Work*. 5 vols. Oxford, 1966.

"Journaal van Constantyn Huygens, den zoon, van 21 October 1688 tot 2 September 1696." *Werken Uitgegeven door het Historisch Genootschap*, n.s. 23 (Utrecht, 1876-78): 53-219.

Kenyon, J. P. "Charles II and William of Orange in 1680." *BIHR* 30 (1957): 95-101.

Kerr, R. J., and I. C. Duncan, eds. *The Portledge Papers: Being Extracts From The Letters of Richard Lapthorne, Gent. of Hatton Garden, London, to Richard Coffin, esq., of Portledge, Bideford, Devon*. 1928.

Krämer, F. J. L. *Archives ou correspondance inédite de la maison d'Orange-Nassau*, 3rd ser.: *1689-1702*. 3 vols. Leiden, 1907-9.

—————, ed. "Mémoires de Monsieur de B . . . ou Anecdotes, Tant de la cour du Prince d'Orange Guillaume III, que des principaux seigneurs de la république de ce temps." *Bijdragen en Mededeelingen van het Historisch Genootschap* 19 (Utrecht, 1898): 62-124.

Luttrell, Narcissus. *A Brief Historical Relation of State Affairs from September 1678 to April 1714*. 6 vols. Oxford, 1857.

Mechtild, Contesse Bentinck, ed. *Lettres et Mémoires de Marie Reine d'Angleterre*. The Hague, 1880.

Müller, P. L., ed. *Willem III von Oranien und Georg Friedrich von Waldeck*. 2 vols. The Hague, 1873-80.

Plumb, J. H., and Alan Simpson. "A Letter of William Prince of Orange to Danby on the Flight of James II." *Cambridge Historical Journal* 5 (1935): 107-8.

Serrurier, C., ed. *Uit de Correspondentie van Prins Willem III*. Amsterdam, 1938.

Singer, S. W., ed. *Correspondence of Henry Hyde, Earl of Clarendon, and of his brother Laurence Hyde, Earl of Rochester*. 2 vols. 1828.

Thompson, E. M. "Correspondence of Admiral Herbert during the Revolution." *EHR* 1 (1886): 522-36.

—————, ed. *Correspondence of the Family of Hatton, being chiefly letters addressed to Christopher, First Viscount Hatton, 1601-1704*. 2 vols. Printed for the Camden Society, n.s., vol. 23. 1878.

Van Terveen, J. G., ed. "Uittreksels uit het Bijzonder Verbaal Nopens de Deputatie en Ambassade Daarop Gevolgd in Engeland, 1689, Gehouden Door Mr. Nicolass Witsen, Burgemeester te Amsterdam." In *Geschieden Letterkundig Mengelwerk van Mr. Jacobus Scheltema*, 3, pt. 2 (Utrecht, 1823): 131–71.

Verney, Margaret, ed. *Memoirs of the Verney Family*. 4 vols. 1892–99.

Warrington, Henry Booth, second Baron Delamere, first Earl of. *Works*. 1694.

PARLIAMENTARY MATERIAL [The place of publication is London unless otherwise indicated.]

An Account of the Proceedings of the Lords and Commons, In the Parliament House, upon their first Convention; With the several Debates and Speeches relating thereunto. Printed for W. D. 1688.

Calendar of State Papers, Domestic Series, 1660–1702.

Calendar of Treasury Books, 1660–1718. Ed. W. A. Shaw, et al. 32 vols. 1904–62.

Cobbett, William, ed. *The Parliamentary History of England. From the Norman Conquest, in 1066, to the Year 1803*. 36 vols. 1806–20.

Cope, E. S., and W. H. Coates, eds. *Proceedings of the Short Parliament of 1640*. Camden Fourth Series, vol. 19. 1977.

Cruickshanks, Eveline; John Ferris; and David Hayton. "The House of Commons Vote on the Transfer of the Crown, 5 February 1689." *BIHR* 52 (May 1979): 37–47.

Cruickshanks, Eveline; David Hayton; and Clyve Jones. "Divisions in the House of Lords on the Transfer of the Crown and Other Issues, 1689–94: Ten New Lists." *BIHR* 53 (May 1980): 56–87.

The debate At Large, Between The Lords and Commons, at the Free Conference Held in the Painted Chamber, in the Session of the Convention, Anno 1688. Relating to the Word, Abdicated, and the Vacancy of the Throne In the Commons Vote. 2nd ed. Printed for J. Wickins. 1710.

de Beer, E. S. "Members of the Court Party in the House of Commons, 1670–1678." *BIHR* 11 (1933): 1–23.

Foster, Elizabeth R., ed. *Proceedings in Parliament, 1610*. 2 vols. New Haven, 1966.

Great Britain, Parliament. *Journals of the House of Commons*.

———. *Journals of the House of Lords*.

———. *Return of the names of Every Member . . . in each Parliament*. 2 vols. 1878.

Grey, Anchitell. *Debates of the House of Commons, from the year 1667 to the year 1694*. 10 vols. 1763.

Haley, K. H. D. "A List of the English Peers, c. May 1687." *EHR* 64 (1954): 302–6.

Historical Manuscript Commission. *Manuscripts of the House of Lords. 1678–93*. 4 vols. 1887–94. Vol. 2 (1688–89).

Hosford, David H. "The Peerage and the Test Act: A List, c. November 1687." *BIHR* 42 (May 1969): 116–20.

Howell, Thomas B., ed. *Cobbett's Complete Collection of State Trials and Proceedings for High Treason*. 34 vols. 1809–28.

Johnson, Robert C., et al., eds. *Commons Debates, 1628*. 4 vols. New Haven, 1977.

Jones, J. R. "Shaftesbury's 'Worthy Men': A Whig View of the Parliament of 1679." *BIHR* 30 (1957): 232–41.

List of the Knights, Citizens and Burgesses, Summoned by the Letter of His Highness the Prince of Orange to Meet at Westminster the 22th of January, 1688/9 as they have been returned to the Office of the Clerk of the Crown in Chancery. Printed for John Starkey and A. and W. Churchill. 1689.

Routledge, F. J., ed. *Calendar of the Clarendon State Papers Preserved in the Bodleian Library, 1660–1726.* 5 vols. Oxford, 1970.

Schwoerer, Lois G. "A Jornall of the Convention at Westminster begun the 22 of January 1688/9." *BIHR* 49 (1976): 242–63.

Simpson, Alan. "Notes of a Noble Lord, 22 January to 12 February, 1688/89." *EHR* 52 (1937): 87–98.

Somers, John. "Notes of Debate, January 28, January 29." In *Miscellaneous State Papers, from 1501 to 1726,* ed. Philip Yorke, second Earl of Hardwicke, 2 vols., 2:401–25. 1778.

Steele, Robert, ed. *A Bibliography of Royal Proclamations of the Tudor and Stuart Sovereigns and of Others Published under Authority, 1485–1714.* 2 vols. Oxford, 1910.

Statutes of the Realm. Ed. Alexander Luders et al. 11 vols. 1810–28.

Timberland, Ebenezer, publ. *The history and proceedings of the House of Lords, from the Restoration to the present time.* 8 vols. 1742–43.

NEWSPAPERS, POEMS, ICONOGRAPHIC MATERIAL

English Currant, nos. 1–9, December 12, 1688–January 4/9, 1689.

Harllum Currant, no. 1, February 14, 1689; no. 2 (as *Harlem Currant*), February 19, 1689.

London Courant, nos. 1–9, December 12, 1688–January 5/8, 1689.

London Gazette, winter-spring 1688–89.

The London Intelligence, nos. 1–10, January 15, 1689–February 12/16, 1689.

The London Mercury; or, Moderate Intelligencer, no. 1, December 15, 1688. Continued as *The London Mercury; or, The Orange Intelligence,* nos. 7–9, December 31–January 3, 1689. Continued as *The London Mercury; or, Moderate Intelligencer,* nos. 10–13, January 10, 1689–February 18, 1689.

The Observator, no. 1, December 24, 1688.

Orange Gazette, nos. 1–18, December 31, 1688–March 9, 1689.

Roman Post-Boy; or, Weekly Account from Rome, nos. 1–4, March 16–April 6, 1689.

Universal Intelligence, nos. 1–14, December 11, 1688–February 18, 1688/89.

Poems on Affairs of State: Augustan Satirical Verse, 1660–1714. Ed. George de F. Lord. 7 vols. New Haven, 1963–75.

British Museum, Department of Coins and Medals. *Medallic Illustrations of the History of Great Britain and Ireland to the Death of George II.* Comp. Edward Hawkins; ed. Augustus W. Franks and Herbert A. Grueber. London, 1969.

Hodgkin, John Eliot, ed. *Rariora: Being Notes of Some of the Printed Books, Manuscripts, Historical Documents, Medals, Engravings, Pottery, etc.* London, 1902.

Kunzle, David. *The Early Comic Strip: Narrative Strips and Picture Stories in the European Broadsheet from c. 1450 to 1825.* Berkley and Los Angeles, 1973.

Loon, Gerard van. *Histoire Méttalique des XVII provinces des Pays-Bas, depuis l'abdication de Charles-Quint, jusqu'à la paix de Bade en MDCCXVI.* 5 vols. La Haye, 1732-37.

O'Donoghue, Freeman M., comp. *Catalogue of the Collection of Playing Cards Bequeathed to the Trustees of the British Museum by the Late Lady Charlotte Schreiber.* London, 1901.

Stephens, F. G., comp. *Catalogue of Prints and Drawings in the British Museum: Political and Personal Satires.* London, 1870.

Willshire, William Hughes. *A Descriptive Catalogue of Playing and Other Cards in the British Museum Accompanied by a Concise General History of the Subject.* . . . London, 1876.

COLLECTIONS OF PRINTED TRACTS AND PAMPHLETS [Unique single tracts exist in the Bodleian Library, the British Library, the Folger Shakespeare Library, the Henry E. Huntington Library, and Dutch repositories.]

A Collection of State Tracts Publish'd on the occasion of the late revolution in 1688 and during the Reign of King William III. 3 vols. London, 1705-7.

A Compleat Collection of Papers, In Twelve Parts: Relating to the Great Revolutions in England and Scotland, From the Time of the Seven Bishops Petitioning K. James II. against the Dispensing Power, June 8, 1688, to the Coronation of King William and Queen Mary, April 11. 1689. London, 1689.

Gutch, John. *Collectanea Curiosa; or, Miscellaneous Tracts, relating to the History and Antiquities of England and Ireland, the Universities of Oxford and Cambridge, and a variety of other subjects. Chiefly collected, and now first published, from the Manuscripts of Archbishop Sancroft.* 2 vols. Oxford, 1781.

Harleian Miscellany. Ed. J. Malham. 12 vols. London, 1808-10.

Luttrell, Narcissus. Collection of tracts at BL, C, 122, 1.5.

Scott, Sir Walter, ed. *A Collection of Scarce and Valuable Tracts . . . Selected from . . . Public as well as Private Libraries, Particularly That of the Late Lord Somers.* 13 vols. London, 1809-15.

State Tracts: in two parts. The first being a collection of several treatises relating to the government, privately printed in the reign of King Charles II; the second part consisting of a further collection . . . 1660 to 1689. 2 pts. London, 1692-83. Pt. 1 was published separately in 1689.

Secondary Works

Ashley, Maurice. *The Glorious Revolution of 1688.* New York, 1966.

Baxter, Stephen B. *William III.* London, 1966.

Beddard, Robert A. "The Guildhall Declaration of 11 December 1688 and the Counter-Revolution of the Loyalists." *HJ* 11 (1968): 403-20.

———. "'The Violent Party': The Guildhall Revolutionaries and the Growth of Opposition to James II." *Guildhall Miscellany* 3 (April 1970): 120-36.

Behrens, B. "The Whig Theory of the Constitution in the Reign of Charles II." *Cambridge Historical Journal* 7 (1941): 42-71.

Birdsall, Paul. "'Non Obstante': A Study in the Dispensing Power of English Kings." In *Essays in History and Political Theory in Honor of Charles Howard McIlwain*, pp. 37-76. Cambridge, Mass., 1936.

Blackstone, Sir William. *Commentaries on the Laws of England in Four Books.* Philadelphia, 1893.

Browning, A. *Thomas Osborne, Earl of Danby and Duke of Leeds (1632-1712).* 3 vols. Glasgow, 1944-51.

Burton, L. F., et al. "Political Parties in the Reigns of William III and Anne: The Evidence of Division Lists." *BIHR*, special supplement no. 7. (November 1968).

Carswell, John. *The Descent on England: A Study of the English Revolution of 1688 and Its European Background.* London, 1969.

———. *The Old Cause: Three Biographical Studies in Whiggism.* London, 1954.

Carter, Jennifer. "The Revolution and the Constitution." In *Britain after the Glorious Revolution, 1689-1714*, ed. Geoffrey Holmes, pp. 39-58. London, 1969.

Cherry, George L. "The Legal and Philosophical Position of the Jacobites, 1688-1689," *Journal of Modern History* 22 (1950): 309-21.

———. "The Role of the Convention Parliament in Parliamentary Supremacy." *Journal of the History of Ideas* 17 (1956): 390-406.

Churchill, E. F. "The Dispensing Power and the Defence of the Realm." *LQR* 37 (1921): 412-41.

Davies, Godfrey. "The Political Career of Sir Richard Temple (1634-1697) and Buckingham Politics." *Huntington Library Quarterly* 4 (1940): 47-83.

Dickinson, H. T. "The Eighteenth-Century Debate on the Sovereignty of Parliament." *Transactions of the Royal Historical Society,* 26 5th ser. (1976): 189-210.

———. *Liberty and Property: Political Ideology in Eighteenth-Century Britain.* New York, 1977.

Duckett, Sir George, ed. *Penal Laws and Test Act: Questions Touching Their Repeal Propounded in 1687-88 by James II.* London, 1882.

Dunn, John. *The Political Thought of John Locke: An Historical Account of the Argument of the "Two Treatises of Government."* Cambridge, 1969.

Edie, Carolyn. *The Irish Cattle Bills: A Study in Restoration Politics.* Philadelphia, 1970.

———. "Revolution and the Rule of Law: The End of the Dispensing Power, 1689." *Eighteenth-Century Studies* 10 (Summer 1977): 434-50.

Feiling, Sir Keith. *A History of the Tory Party, 1640-1714.* Oxford, 1924.

Ferguson, James. *Robert Ferguson the Plotter; or, The secret of the Rye-House Conspiracy and the Story of a Strange Career.* Edinburgh, 1887.

Fink, Zera S. *The Classical Republicans: An Essay in the Recovery of a Pattern of Thought in Seventeenth-Century England.* Evanston, 1945.

Foote, Caleb. "The Coming Constitutional Crisis in Bail." *University of Pennsylvania Law Review* 113 (1965): 959-99, 1125-85.

Foxcroft, H. C., and T. E. S. Clarke. *A Life of Gilbert Burnet, Bishop of Salisbury.* London, 1907.

Frankle, Robert J. "The Formulation of the Declaration of Rights." *HJ* 17 (1974): 265–79.

Franklin, Julian H. *John Locke and the Theory of Sovereignty: Mixed Monarchy and the Right of Resistance in the Political Thought of the English Revolution.* Cambridge, 1978.

Fraser, P. *The Intelligence of the Secretaries of State and Their Monopoly of Licensed News, 1660–1688.* Cambridge, 1956.

Furley, O. W. "The Whig Exclusionists: Pamphlet Literature in the Exclusion Campaign, 1679–81." *Cambridge Historical Journal* 13 (1957): 19–36.

George, M. Dorothy. *English Political Caricature to 1792: A Study of Opinion and Propaganda.* Vol. 1. Oxford, 1959.

George, R. H. "The Charters Granted to English Parliamentary Corporations in 1688." *EHR* 55 (1940): 47–56.

———. "A Note on the Bill of Rights: Municipal Liberties and the Freedom of Parliamentary Elections." *AHR* 42 (1937): 670–79.

Goldie, Mark. "Edmund Bohun and *Jus Gentium* in the Revolution Debate, 1689–1693." *HJ* 20 (1977): 569–86.

Granucci, Anthony F. "'Nor Cruel and Unusual Punishments Inflicted': The Original Meaning." *California Law Review* 57 (1969): 839–65.

Haar, C. van de. "Romeyn de Hooghe en de Pamflettenstrijd van Jaren 1689 en 1690." *Tijdschrift voor Geschiedenis* 64 (1956): 155–77.

Haley, K. H. D. *The First Earl of Shaftesbury.* Oxford, 1968.

———. "The Judiciary and Politics in the Reign of Charles II." *LQR* 66 (1950): 62–78, 229–52.

———. *William of Orange and the English Opposition, 1672–74.* Oxford, 1953.

Hill, Christopher. *Milton and the English Revolution.* New York, 1977.

Holdsworth, Sir William Searle. *A History of English Law.* 13 vols. London, 1922–52.

Holmes, Geoffrey. *The Trial of Doctor Sacheverell.* London, 1973.

———, ed. *Britain after the Glorious Revolution, 1689–1714.* London, 1969.

Horwitz, Henry. "The General Election of 1690." *JBS* 11 (1971): 77–92.

———. "Parliament and the Glorious Revolution." *BIHR* 47 (1974): 36–52.

———. *Parliament, Policy, and Politics in the Reign of William III.* Manchester, 1977.

———. *Revolution Politicks: The Career of Daniel Finch, Second Earl of Nottingham, 1647–1730.* London, 1968.

Hosford, David. *Nottingham, Nobles, and the North: Aspects of the Revolution of 1688.* Studies in British History and Culture, vol. 4. Hamden, Conn., 1976.

Hyde, Harford M. *Judge Jeffreys.* London, 1940.

Jones, G. F. Trevallyn. *Saw-Pit Wharton: The Political Career from 1640 to 1691 of Philip, fourth Lord Wharton.* Sydney, 1967.

Jones, J. R. *Country and Court: England, 1658–1714.* London, 1978.

———. *The First Whigs: The Politics of the Exclusion Crisis, 1678–1683.* London, 1961.

———. *The Revolution of 1688 in England.* London, 1972.

Kemp, Betty. *King and Commons, 1660–1832.* London, 1959.

Kenyon, J. P. "The Revolution of 1688: Resistance and Contract." In *Historical Perspectives Studies in English Thought and Society in Honour of J. H. Plumb,* ed. Neil McKendrick, pp. 43–70. London, 1974.

————. *Revolution Principles: The Politics of Party.* Cambridge, 1977.

————. *Robert Spencer, Earl of Sunderland, 1641–1702.* London, 1958.

Kirby, C. "The English Game Law System." *AHR* 38 (1932–33): 240–62.

Kirby, C., and E. Kirby. "The Stuart Game Prerogative." *EHR* 46 (1931): 239–54.

Lacey, Douglas R. *Dissent and Parliamentary Politics in England, 1661–1689: A Study in the Perpetuation and Tempering of Parliamentarianism.* New Brunswick, N.J., 1969.

Landon, Michael. *The Triumph of the Lawyers: Their Role in English politics, 1678–89.* Tuscaloosa, Ala., 1970.

Laslett, Peter, ed. *John Locke: Two Treatises of Government.* Cambridge, 1960.

Macaulay, Thomas Babington, Lord. *History of England from the Accession of James II.* Ed. C. H. Firth. 6 vols. London, 1913–15.

McLean, A. J. "George Lawson and John Locke." *Cambridge Historical Journal* 9 (1947): 69–77.

Meyer, Hermine H. "Constitutionality of Pretrial Detention." *Georgetown Law Journal* 60 (1972): 1139–94.

Miller, John. "Catholic Officers in the Later Stuart Army," *EHR* 88 (1973): 35–53.

————. *James II: A Study in Kingship.* London, 1978.

————. "The Militia and the Army in the Reign of James II." *HJ* 16 (1973): 659–79.

Mullett, Charles F. "A Case of Allegiance: William Sherlocke and the Revolution of 1688." *Huntington Library Quarterly* 10 (1946–47): 83–103.

————. "Religion, Politics, and Oaths in the Glorious Revolution." *Review of Politics* 10 (October 1948): 462–74.

Nenner, Howard. *By Colour of Law: Legal Culture and Constitutional Politics in England, 1660–1689.* Chicago, 1977.

————. "Constitutional Uncertainty and the Declaration of Rights." In *After the Reformation: Essays in Honor of J. H. Hexter,* ed. Barbara Malament, pp. 291–308. Philadelphia, 1980.

————. "The Convention of 1689: A Triumph of Constitutional Form." *American Journal of Legal History,* October 1966, pp. 282–96.

Nutting, Helen. "The Most Wholesome Law: The Habeas Corpus Act of 1679 in the House of Lords." *AHR* 65 (1960): 527–40.

Ogg, David. *England in the Reign of Charles II.* 3rd ed. 2 vols. London, 1961.

————. *England in the Reigns of James II and William III.* Oxford, 1955.

Oliver, H. J. *Sir Robert Howard (1626–1698): A Critical Biography.* Durham, N.C., 1963.

Pinkham, Lucile. *William III and the Respectable Revolution: The Part Played by William of Orange in the Revolution of 1688.* Cambridge, Mass., 1954.

Plumb, John H. "The Elections to the Convention Parliament of 1689." *Cambridge Historical Journal* 5 (1937): 235–55.

————. *The Growth of Political Stability in England, 1675–1725.* London, 1967.

———. "The Growth of the Electorate in England from 1600 to 1715." *Past and Present* 45 (1969): 90–116.

Pocock, J. G. A. *The Ancient Constitution and the Feudal Law: A Study of English Historical Thought in the Seventeenth Century.* Cambridge, 1957.

———. "Burke and the Ancient Constitution: A Problem in the History of Ideas." *HJ* 3 (1960): 125–43.

———. "James Harrington and the Good Old Cause: A Study of the Ideological Context of His Writings," *JBS* 10 (1970): 30–48.

———. *The Machiavellian Moment.* Princeton, 1974.

———. "Machiavelli, Harrington, and English Political Ideologies in the 18th Century." *William and Mary Quarterly* 22 (1965): 549–83.

———. "Robert Brady, 1627–1700: A Cambridge Historian of the Restoration." *Cambridge Historical Journal* 10 (1951): 186–204.

Prall, Stuart E. *The Bloodless Revolution: England, 1688.* New York, 1972.

Robb, Nesca A. *William of Orange: A Personal Portrait.* 2 vols. London, 1962–66.

Roberts, Clayton. "The Constitutional Significance of the Financial Settlement of 1690." *HJ* 20 (1977): 59–76.

Rostenberg, Leona. "Richard and Anne Baldwin, Whig Patriot Publishers." *Papers of the Bibliographical Society of America* 47 (New York, 1953): 1–42.

Sachse, William L. *John, Lord Somers: A Political Portrait.* Manchester, 1975.

———. "The Mob and the Revolution of 1688." *JBS* 4 (November 1964): 23–40.

Schwoerer, Lois G. *"No Standing Armies!" The Antiarmy Ideology in Seventeenth-Century England.* Baltimore, 1974.

———. "Press and Parliament in the Revolution of 1689." *HJ* 20 (1977): 545–67.

———. "Propaganda in the Revolution of 1688–89." *AHR* 82 (1977): 843–74.

Shapiro, Barbara. "Codification of the Laws in Seventeenth-Century England." *Wisconsin Law Review* (1974), pp. 428–65.

———. "Law and Science in Seventeenth-Century England." *Stanford Law Review* 21 (1969): 727–66.

Siebert, Frederick S. *Freedom of the Press in England, 1476–1776: The Rise and Decline of Government Controls.* Urbana, 1952.

Simpson, Alan. "The Convention Parliament of 1688–89." D.Phil. thesis, Oxford University, 1939.

Skinner, Quentin. *The Foundations of Modern Political Thought.* 2 vols. Cambridge, 1978.

———. "The Ideological Context of Hobbes's Political Thought." *HJ* 9 (1966): 286–317.

Stone, Lawrence. "Literacy and Education in England, 1640–1900." *Past and Present* 42 (February 1969): 69–139.

Straka, Gerald M. *Anglican Reaction to the Revolution of 1688.* Madison, Wis., 1962.

———. *The Revolution of 1688 and the Birth of the English Political Nation.* 2nd ed. Lexington, Mass., 1973.

Thompson, Martyn P. "The Reception of Locke's Two Treatises of Government, 1690–1705." *Political Studies* 24 (1976): 184–91.

Thomson, Mark. *Constitutional History of England,* vol. 4: *1642 to 1801.* London, 1938.

Turberville, Arthur Stanley. *The House of Lords in the Reign of William III.* Oxford Historical and Literary Studies, vol. 3. Oxford, 1913.

Walker, R. B. "The Newspaper Press in the Reign of William III." *HJ* 17 (1974): 691–709.

Western, J. R. *Monarchy and Revolution: The English State in the 1680s.* London, 1972.

Weston, C. C. "Concept of Estates in Stuart Political Thought." In *Representative Institutions in Theory and Practice,* pp. 87–130. Brussels, 1970.

_____. *English Constitutional Theory and the House of Lords, 1556–1832.* London, 1965.

_____. "Legal Sovereignty in the Brady Controversy." *HJ* 15 (1972): 409–31.

Index

The Johns Hopkins University Press

This book was composed in Baskerville text
and display type by Capitol Communication Systems.
It was printed on 50-lb. Eggshell Offset Cream paper
and bound in Holliston Roxite cloth by the
Maple Press Company.